APULEIUS MADAURENSIS

GRONINGEN COMMENTARIES ON APULEIUS

APULEIUS MADAURENSIS
METAMORPHOSES

Books VI 25-32 and VII
Text, Introduction and Commentary

B. L. HIJMANS Jr. – R. Th. VAN DER PAARDT
V. SCHMIDT – R. E. H. WESTENDORP BOERMA
A. G. WESTERBRINK

GRONINGEN
BOUMA'S BOEKHUIS bv. PUBLISHERS
1981

ISBN 90 6088 079 X

©1981 by Bouma's Boekhuis bv., Groningen

No parts of this book may be reproduced in any form, by print, photoprint, microfilm or any other means without written permission from the publisher

The publication of this book was made possible through a grant from the Netherlands Organisation for the Advancement of Pure Research (Z.W.O.)

CONTENTS

Preface	VII
Abbreviations	IX
Bibliography	XIII
Introduction	1
Note to the Text	7
Text – *Met.* 6,25–7,28	9
Chapter 6,25	24
Chapter 6,26	31
Chapter 6,27	41
Chapter 6,28	47
Chapter 6,29	55
Chapter 6,30	62
Chapter 6,31	68
Chapter 6,32	76
Chapter 7,1	80
Chapter 7,2	86
Chapter 7,3	95
Chapter 7,4	101
Chapter 7,5	108
Chapter 7,6	117
Chapter 7,7	126
Chapter 7,8	133
Chapter 7,9	138
Chapter 7,10	145
Chapter 7,11	157
Chapter 7,12	159
Chapter 7,13	164
Chapter 7,14	169
Chapter 7,15	176
Chapter 7,16	183
Chapter 7,17	192
Chapter 7,18	199
Chapter 7,19	205
Chapter 7,20	210
Chapter 7,21	216

Chapter 7,22	224
Chapter 7,23	230
Chapter 7,24	238
Chapter 7,25	246
Chapter 7,26	255
Chapter 7,27	260
Chapter 7,28	269
Appendix I	275
Appendix II	279
General Index	281

PREFACE

It pleases us that reasonably soon after the appearance of our commentary on book IV 1-27 (*GCA* 1977) we have been able to complete a second volume, comprising books VI 25-32 and VII. From the many favourable reactions, both personal and in print, we draw the conclusion that our method meets with approval; the critical remarks, which we were equally pleased to receive, will, we hope, result in improvements in the present and subsequent volumes.

As in the previous volume, our main aim is interpretation of the text, taking into account recent scholarship. Partly because of consideration of space, but especially in order to take advantage of the work of expert scholars abroad whose contributions were valuable to our own work, certain more general aspects were reserved for another publication: *Aspects of Apuleius' Golden Ass (AAGA)*, Groningen 1978, edited by two members of our team, Dr. B. L. Hijmans Jr. and Dr. R. Th. van der Paardt. Several specialists both from the Netherlands and from abroad contributed to that volume.

A change took place in our team: Mr. E. R. Smits' time is taken by different work; Dr. V. Schmidt, also a member of the Classical Institute at the Rijksuniversiteit Groningen, has joined the group in his place. The monthly sessions of the group were regularly attended by Dr. Corrie W. Ooms and occasionally by Prof. Dr. P. H. Schrijvers: we thank both of them for their contributions. Dr. Ooms moreover translated by far the larger part of the volume into English (the remainder was looked after by Dr. Hijmans).

We are fortunate once again to have found Prof. Philippa Goold prepared – a move to the USA and a busy schedule notwithstanding – to read and correct the entire manuscript; as in the previous volume her attention was not confined to the English: her critical remarks have resulted in a whole series of improvements in the commentary. Thanks are due also to Drs. H. H. Woldring, of Apeldoorn, who kindly placed his candidate's thesis on *Met.* 7,1-8 (unpublished) at our disposal.

Some small changes of format are introduced in the present volume: e.g. books and articles are listed in two bibliographies and cited in the commentary only by author and year. The bibliographies have been brought up to date as far as possible; a few titles that escaped us earlier have been added now. The indexes have been simplified, but will, we hope, be found adequate.

Thanks are due again to the "Netherlands Organisation for the Advancement of Pure Research" for financial help with the publication, to the staff of the University Library at Groningen, of the Buma Bibliotheek at Leeuwarden and of the *Thesaurus Linguae Latinae* at Munich for their kind assistance and indispensable support.

It was a joy to visit the Thesaurus Institute in June 1977 with a group of advanced students from Groningen University, who were introduced to the collection by the Staff of *ThLL* and who studied several words relevant to our commentary in the unpublished material. Their results have been duly incorporated. During other visits members of our group have encountered the same cooperative spirit shown on that occasion.

Groningen, september 1980   R. E. H. Westendorp Boerma

ABBREVIATIONS

Henceforth we shall refer to *all* publications by author, year and page. For that reason we here list the publications mentioned for the first time in the present volume. For items not mentioned here we refer to R. T. van der Paardt 1971 IX–XIII, *GCA* 1977, IX–XVI and to the Bibliography in the present volume, below p. XIII.

M. von Albrecht, *Die Parenthese in Ovids Metamorphosen und ihre dichterische Funktion*, Hildesheim 1964.

T. Anbeek, *De schrijver tussen de coulissen*, Utrecht 1978.

G. Anderson, *Lucian, Theme and Variation in the second Sophistic*, Leiden 1976.

J. André, *L'alimentation et la cuisine à Rome*, Paris, 1961.

L. Arbuson, *Colores Rhetorici*, Göttingen² 1963.

B. Axelson, *Unpoetische Wörter*, Lund 1945.

M. Bernhard, *Gnomon* 6 (1930), 305–311.

Th. Birt, *Sprach man avrum oder aurum? RhM* (1897), NF 52 Ergänzungsheft.

H. Blümmer, *Zu Apuleius Met., Hermes*, 29 (1894), 294–312.

H. Blümmer, *Textkritisches zu Apuleius' Metamorphosen, Mélanges Nicole*, Genève 1905, 22–38.

P. Boyancé, *Platon et le vin, Lettres d'Humanité* 10 (1951), 3–19.

S. Brandt, *Infinitivus futuri passivi auf -uiri, ALL* 2 (1885), 349–354.

B. Brotherton, *The Introduction of Characters by Name in the Metamorphoses of Apuleius, CPh* 29 (1934), 36–52.

F. Bücheler, *Altes Latein, RhM*. 39 (1884), 408–427.

E. Burck, *Römische Wertbegriffe*, Darmstadt 1967.

D. Burr Thompson, *An Ancient Shopping Center. The Athenian Agora*, Princeton 1971.

J. B. Carter, *Epitheta deorum quae apud poetas Latinos leguntur*, Leipzig 1902.

L. Casson, *Travel in the Ancient World*, London 1974.

J.-P. Chausserie-Laprée, *L'expression narrative chez les historiens latins. Histoire d'un style*, Paris 1969.

P. H. Damsté, *Spicilegium criticum ad Apulei Metamorphoseon Libros, Mnemosyne* NS. 56 (1928), 1–28.

G. Devoto, *Storia della lingua di Roma*, Bologna ²1944.

G. Devoto, *Geschichte der Sprache Roms*, Heidelberg 1968.

S. Dresden, *Rabelais-Nuchtere dronkenschap*, Amsterdam 1972.

G. E. Duckworth, *The Nature of Roman Comedy, A Study in Popular Entertainment*. Princeton 1952.

R. Duncan-Jones, *The Economy of the Roman Empire*, Cambridge 1974.

P. Flobert, *Les verbes déponents Latins des origines à Charlemagne*, Paris 1975.

H. Foerster, *Abriss der lateinischen Paläographie*, Stuttgart² 1963.

C. A Forbes, *Charite and Dido. CW* 37 (1943/4), 39.

E. Fraenkel, *Horace*, Oxford 1957.

E. Fraenkel, *Non satis lectus*, *MH* 23 (1966), 114–117.

H. Fraenkel, *Griechische Wörter*, *Glotta* 14 (1925) 1–13.

P. Frassinetti, *Cruces Apuleiane*, *Athenaeum* 38 (1960), 128.

K. Freeman, *Vincent or the Donkey*, *G & R* 14 (1945), 33–41.

J. Gagé, *Les classes sociales dans l'empire romain*, Paris 1964.

P. Garnsey, *Social Status and Legal Privilege in the Roman Empire*, Oxford 1970.

J. v. Geisau, *De Apulei syntaxi poetica et graecanica*, Münster 1912.

A. Gerlo, *Q.S.Fl. Tertullianus de Pallio*, Welteren 1940.

G. P. Goold, *Manilius Astronomica*, London 1977.

H. van Gorp, *Inleiding tot de picareske verhaalkunst*, Groningen 1978

R. Grassberger, *Die Unzucht mit Tieren*, Vienna 1968.

J. G. Griffith, *Apuleius, Metamorphoses VI, 29, 3*, *Hermes* 96, (1968/69), 762.

T. Hägg, *Narrative Technique in Ancient Greek Romances, Studies of Chariton, Xenophon Ephesius and Achilles Tatius*, Stockholm 1971.

L. Havet, *Multo tanta plus, bis tanta plus*, *ALL* 11 (1900), 579.

R. Helm, *PhW* 50 (1930), 501–514.

W. Heraeus, *PhW* 52 (1932), 80.

L. Herrmann, *L'âne d'or et le christianisme*, *Latomus* 12 (1953), 188–191.

G. Highet, *The Speeches in Vergil's Aeneid*, Princeton N.J., 1972.

O. Hirschfeld, *Die kaiserlichen Verwaltungsbeamten, bis auf Diocletian*, Berlin 1905.

R. P. Hoogma, *Der Einfluss Vergils auf die Carmina Epigraphica*, Nijmegen 1959.

W. Iser, *Der implizite Leser*, München 1972.

A. H. M. Jones, *The Roman Economy*, Oxford 1974.

C. P. Jones, *Parody in Catullus 44*, *Hermes* 96 (1968), 379–383.

H. Kenner, *Weinen und Lachen in der griechischen Kunst*, Wien 1960.

H. Kleinknecht, *Die Gebetsparodie in der Antike*, Stuttgart 1937; repr. Hildesheim 1967.

A. Kambylis, *Die Dichterweihe und ihre Symbolik, Untersuchungen zu Hesiodos, Kallimachos, Properz und Ennius*, Heidelberg 1965.

A. Kronenberg, *Ad Apuleium*, *Mnemosyne* 66 (1928), 29–54.

E. Lämmert, *Bauformen des Erzählens*, Stuttgart ⁵1972.

G. Landgraf, *Glossographie und Wörterbuch*, *ALL* 9 (1896), 355–446.

O. Lau, *Schuster und Schusterhandwerk in der griechisch-römischen Literatur und Kunst*, Bonn 1967.

H. Lausberg, *Handbuch der literarischen Rhetorik, Eine Grundlegung der Literaturwissenschaft*, München 1960.

H. Lausberg, *Romanische Sprachwissenschaft*, Berlin 1962–1969.

H. Lauter-Bufe, *Zur Stilgeschichte der figürlichen pompejanischen Fresken*, Erlangen 1967.

F. Leo, *Lexikalische Bemerkungen zu Apuleius*, *ALL* 12 (1902), 95–101.

F. Leo, *Der Monolog im Drama, Ein Beitrag zur griechisch-römischen Poetik*. Abh. der königlichen Gesellschaft der Wissenschaften zu Göttingen, philologisch-historische Klasse, Neue Folge Band X Nro 5. Berlin, 1908.

A. Lesky, *Gesammelte Schriften, Aufsätze und Reden zu antiker und deutscher Dichtung und Kultur*, Bern 1966.

H. Lewy, *Sobria Ebrietas, Unters. zur Geschichte der Antiken Mystik*, Giessen 1929.

J. Liegle, *Pietas*, in H. Oppermann, *Römische Wertbegriffe*, Darmstadt 1967, 229–273.

E. Lindholm, *Stilistische Studien*, Lund 1931.

E. Löfstedt, *Beiträge zur Kenntnis der späteren Latinität*, Stockholm 1907.

G. Luck, *Über einige Interjektionen der lateinischen Umgangssprache*, Heidelberg 1964.

G. Luck, *The Latin Love Elegy*, London 1969.

P. A. MacKay, *The Tradition of the Tales of Banditry in Apuleius*, G & R. 10 (1963), 147–152.

R. MacMullen, *Ennemies of the Roman Order, Treason, Unrest, and Alienation in the Empire*, Cambridge, Mass. 1966.

J. Marouzeau, *Quelques aspects de la formation du Latin littéraire*, Paris 1949.

L. B. van der Meer, *Etruscan Urns from Volterra, Studies on Mythological Representations I–II*, Meppel, 1978.

F. Millar, *The Emperor in the Roman World*, London 1977.

K. von Nägelsbach, *Lateinische Stilistik*, Nürnberg ^{9}1905 (repr. Darmstadt 1963).

Ch. Moussy, *Gratia et sa famille*, Paris 1966.

E. Norden, *Ennius und Vergilius*, Berlin 1915 (repr. Stuttgart 1966).

E. Norden, *Agnostos Theos*, Leipzig-Berlin 1913 (repr. Darmstadt 1956).

M. B. Ogle, *The House-door in Greek and Roman Religion and Folklore*, AJPh 32 (1911), 251–271.

Olck, *Esel (PW 6, 1)*, 626–676.

H. Oppermann, *Römische Wertbegriffe, Hrsg. von Hans Oppermann*, Darmstadt 1967.

M. E. Paoli, *Vita Romana*, Firenze ^{5}1948.

F. H. Parigger, *Aanschouwelijkheidsdrang als factor bij de beteekenis-ontwikkeling der latijnsche praepositie*, Utrecht 1941.

M. Petschenig, Studien zu den Metamorphosen des Apuleius, WS 4 (1881), 136–163.

H. G. Pflaum, *Les carrières procuratoriennes équestres sous le haut empire romain I–IV*, Paris 1960–1961.

L. C. Purser, *The Story of Cupid and Psyche as related by Apuleius*, London 1910.

L. C. Purser, *Notes on Apuleius' Metamorphoses*, Hermathena 32 (1906) 45.

R. Pfister, *Vulgärlatein und Vulgärgriechisch*, RhM 67 (1912), 195–208.

F. Quadlbauer, *Properz 3,1*, Philologus 112 (1968), 83–118.

K. Quinn, *Virgil's Aeneid: A Critical Description*, London 1968.

E. Rohde, *Psyche*, Tübingen ^{4}1907.

E. Rohde, *Der griechische Roman und seine Vorläufer*, Leipzig ^{3}1914.

E. Rohde, *Zu Apuleius*, RhM 40 (1885), 66–113.

B. Romberg, *Studies in the Narrative Technique of the First-person Novel*, Stockholm 1962.

N. Rudd, *Colonia and her Bridge*, TAPhA 90 (1959), 238–242.

W. Schadewaldt, *Monolog und Selbstgespräch, Untersuchungen zur Formgeschichte der griechischen Tragödie*, Berlin 1926.

M. Schamberger, *De P. Papinio Statio verborum novatore*, Diss. Phil. Halenses (1907), vol XVII 2–4.

M. Schanz-C. Hosius, *Geschichte der römischen Literatur*, München ^{4}1935.

O. Schlutter, *Zur lateinischen Glossographie II*, ALL 10 (1898), 187–208.

O. Schönwerth, C. Weyman, *Ueber die lateinischen Adjektiva auf -osus*, ALL 5 (1888), 192–222.

P. H. Schrijvers, *Het wonderlijke van het alledaagse*, Hermeneus 45 (1973/74), 15–22.

G. Serbat, *Les structures du Latin. Le système de la langue classique; son évolution jusqu'aux langues romanes*, Paris 1975.

W. Sidney Allen, *Vox Latina. A Guide to the Pronunciation of Classical Latin*, London 1965.

K. Stanzel, *Typische Formen des Romans*, Göttingen ⁸1976.

E. Stemplinger, *Antiker Aberglaube in modernen Ausstrahlungen*, Leipzig 1922.

E. Stemplinger, *Antiker Volksglaube*, Stuttgart 1948.

J. M. C. Toynbee, *Death and Burial in the Roman World*, Ithaca (NY) 1971.

H. Tränkle, *Die Sprachkunst des Properz und die Tradition der lateinischen Dichtersprache*, Wiesbaden 1960.

A. Vanisek, *Etymologisches Wörterbuch der lateinischen Sprache*, Leipzig ²1881.

R. Verdière, *Paideia* 18 (1963), p. 187.

E. Vermeule, *Aspects of Death in early Greek Art and Poetry*, Berkeley (Calif.) 1979.

J. van der Vliet, *Compilare, Concipulare*, ALL 9 (1896), 461–2.

J. ter Vrugt-Lentz, *Mors immatura*, Leiden 1960.

H. Wagenvoort, *Pietas*, Groningen 1924.

O. Weinreich, *Studien zu Martial*, Stuttgart 1928.

O. Weinreich, *Fabel, Aretalogie, Novelle*, München 1931.

K. D. White, *Farm Equipment of the Roman World*, Cambridge 1975.

P. Willems, *Le droit romain public depuis la fondation de Rome*, Louvain ⁷1910.

W. Wimmel, *Kallimachos in Rom. Die Nachfolge seines apologetischen Dichtens in der Augusteerzeit*, Wiesbaden 1960.

BIBLIOGRAPHY

We continue here the bibliography given in *GCA* 1977, XIII ff. Reviews: G. Ballairo, *GIF* N.S. 9 (1978), 125–126; L. Callebat, *Latomus* 38 (1979), 703–706; K. Dowden, *CR* 29 (1979), 68–71; J. C. Fredouille, *REL* 56 (1978), 497–498; Christine Harrauer, *Anzeiger f.d. Altertumsw.* 32 (1979), 182–184; D. Knecht, *AC* 48 (1979), 697–698; H. J. Mason, *Phoenix* 35 (1981), 184–186.

Text with translation

El asino de oro. Introducción, traducción y notas de L. Rubio Fernandez. Revision de M. C. Diaz y Diaz. Madrid 1978.

Apuleius, *Das Märchen von Amor und Psyche*. Lateinisch/Deutsch, übersetzt und herausgegeben on Kurt Steinmann, Stuttgart 1978.

Commentary

A. Massili, *Apuleio, Metamorfosi XI*, Pisa 1964.

Studies

AAGA 1978, see B. L. Hijmans Jr. – R. Th. van der Paardt.
F. R. Abate, *Diminutives in Apuleian Latinity*, The Ohio State University Ph. D. 1978.
G. Anderson, *Studies in Lucian's comic fiction*, Leiden 1976, 34–67.
G. Augello, *Tre note critico-testuali alle Metamorfosi di Apuleio*, *Sileno* 1 (1975), 177–186.
G. Augello, *Studi Apuleiani*, Palermo 1977.
C. Billotta, *Note sulle Met. di Apuleio*, in: E. Bonanno, V. Milazzo, C. Billotta, *Note linguistiche su Catone, Catullo ed Apuleio*, Catania 1975, 41–68.
R. R. Brown, *The Tales in the Met. of Apuleius. A study in religious consciousness*, Florida State Univ. Tallahassee Ph. D. 1977.
E. J. Brzenk, *Apuleius, Pater and the Bildungsroman*, in: *AAGA* 1978, 231–237.
L. Callebat, *La prose des Métamorphoses: génèse et spécifité*, in: *AAGA* 1978, 167–187.
U. Carratello, *Noterelle filologiche su Valerio, Marziale ed Apuleio*, *GIF* 27 (1975) 218–226.
E. Cavallini, *Motivi saffici in Apuleio*, *GFF* 1 (1978), 91–93.
C. Cherpack, *Ideas and prose fiction in antiquity*, *CLS* 11 (1974), 185–203.
E. Cizek, *Le roman 'moderne' et les structures du roman antique*, *BAGB* IV 33 (1974), 421–444.
E. Cizek, *Les structures du roman antique*, in: *Erot. Ant.*, 106–128.
K. Dowden, *The White Horse in Apuleius*, in: *Erot. Ant.*, 142–143.
K. Dowden, *Eleven notes on the text of Apuleius' Metamorphoses*, *CQ* N.S. 30 (1980). 218–226.
Gertr. C. Drake, *The Ghost Story in the Golden Ass by Apuleius*, *PLL* 13 (1977), 3–15.
B. Effe, *Der missglückte Selbstmord des Aristomenes*, *Hermes* 104 (1976), 362–375.
M. H. Eliassen-de Kat, *Gorters Mei en de mythe van Amor en Psyche*, *Spiegel der Letteren* 14 (1972), 1–16.
Erot. Ant., see B. O. Reardon.
D. Fehling, *Amor und Psyche: Die Schöpfung des Apuleius und ihre Einwirkung auf das Märchen. Eine Kritik der romantischen Märchentheorie*, Mainz-Wiesbaden 1977.

G. Gagliardi, *Spirito e forma nel romanzo di Apuleio*, La parola e le idee 6 (1964), 229–238 (also in: *Da Petronio a Reposiano*, Napoli 1967, 60–83).
G. N. Ginsburg, *Rhetoric and Representation in the Metamorphoses of Apuleius*, Arethusa 10 (1977), 49–61.
P. Grimal, *La fête du rire dans les Métamorphoses d'Apulée*, Studi classici in onore di Quintino Cataudella, Catania 1972, vol. III, 457–465.
J. Gwyn Griffiths, *Isis in the Metamorphoses of Apuleius*, in: *AAGA 1978*, 141–166.
R. Heine, *Picaresque Novel versus Allegory*, in: *AAGA 1978*, 25–42.
F. E. Hoevels, *Märchen und Magie in den Metamorphosen des Apuleius von Madaura*. Amsterdam 1979.
B. L. Hijmans Jr. – R. Th. van der Paardt Edd., *Aspects of Apuleius' Golden Ass*. Groningen 1978 = *AAGA 1978*.
B. L. Hijmans Jr., *Significant names and their function in Apuleius' Metamorphoses*, in: *AAGA 1978*, 107–122 (cf. *Erot. Ant.*, 144–145).
B. L. Hijmans Jr., *Asinus Numerosus*, in: *AAGA 1978*, 189–209.
B. L. Hijmans Jr., *Apuleiana Groningana V: Haemus, Met. 7,5*, Mnemosyne IV 31 (1978), 407–414.
S. Journoud, *Apulée conteur: Quelques réflexions sur l'épisode de l'Ane et de la Corinthienne (Métam., X 19, 3–22,5)*, Acta Classica Univ. Scient. Debrecen. 1 (1965), 33–37.
V. Longo, *Forme aretalogiche nella novella di Aristomene in Apuleio (Met. 1,5–20)*, Stud. Cat. Vol. III, 467–474.
C. V. Lopez, *Tratamiento del mito en las novelle de las Metamorfosis de Apuleyo*, CFC 10 (1976), 309–373.
M. C. De Luca, *De Apuleio Madaurensi et de Africa*, in: *Africa et Roma* (Acta omnium gentium...), Roma 1979, 365–371.
C. Marangoni, *Il nome Asinio Marcello e i misteri di Osiride (Apul. Metam. XI,27)*, A A Pat 87 (1974/75), Parte III, 333–337.
C. Marangoni, *Per un' interpretazione delle 'Metamorfosi' di Apuleio: L'episodio degli Otri (II32) e la* ἔκφρασις *dell' atrio di Birrena* (II4), Atti e Mem. dell' Accad. Patavina di Scienze, Lettere ed Arti 89 (1976/77), III, 97–104.
C. Marangoni, *Corinto simbolo Isiaco nelle 'Metamorfosi' di Apuleio*, Atti dell' Istituto Veneto di Scienze, Lettere ed Arti 136 (1977/78), 221–226.
H. J. Mason, *Apuleius' Metamorphoses and Lucius sive Asinus since Rohde*, in: *Erot. Ant.*, 146–148.
H. J. Mason, *Fabula Graecanica: Apuleius and his Greek sources*, in: *AAGA 1978*, 1–15.
I. Massey, *The gaping Pig: Literature and Metamorphosis*, Cambridge 1976, 34–58.
M. Mayrhofer, *On two stories in Apuleius*, Antichthon 9 (1975), 68–80.
G. Megas, *Das Märchen von Amor und Psyche in der griechischen Volksüberlieferung*. Athens 1971.
N. Moine, *Augustin et Apulée sur la magie des femmes d'auberges*, Latomus 34 (1975), 350–361.
C. Moreschini, *Apuleio e il platonismo*, Firenze 1978, 19–50.
F. Opeku, *Physiognomy in Apuleius*, in: C. Deroux Ed., *Studies in Latin Literature and Roman History* I, Bruxelles 1979, 467–474.
R. Th. van der Paardt, *Verteltechniek in Apuleius' Metamorphosen*, in: *Handelingen van het vierendertigste Nederlands Filologencongres*, Amsterdam 1976, 37–42 (cf. *Erot. Ant.*, 27–28).
R. Th. van der Paardt, *Various aspects of narrative technique in Apuleius' Metamorphoses*, in: *AAGA 1978*, 75–94.
R. Th. van der Paardt, *Met Thomas Mann van Apuleius naar Cervantes*, Hermeneus 50 (1978), 32–35.
P. Parroni, *Apuleius, Met. 4,31*, Res Publica Litterarum I (1978), 233–239.
F. Pejenaute, *Situaciones ambiguas en el Asinus Aureus de Apuleyo*, Durius 3 (1975), 27–52.
A. Pennacini, P. L. Donini, T. Alimonti, Anna Monteduro Roccavini, *Apuleio letterato, filosofo, mago*, Bologna 1979.
G. Pennisi, *Apuleio e l'additamentum a Met. X,21*, Messina 1970.

J. L. Penwill, *Slavish Pleasures and profitless Curiosity: Fall and Redemption in Apuleius' Metamorphoses*, Ramus 4 (1975), 49–82.
A. Portulano, *Cristianesimo e religioni misteriche in Apuleio*, Napoli 1972.
F. Portalupi, *Frontone, Gellio, Apuleio: Ricerca stilistica*, I, Torino 1974.
D. B. Pottle, *The Platonic elements in the Met. of Apuleius*, Tufts Univ. Mass. Ph. D. 1978.
B. R. Reardon Ed., *Erotica Antiqua: Acta of the International Conference on the Ancient Novel* (July 1976), Bangor 1977 (= *Erot. Ant.*)
S. Rocca, *Il motivo dell' innamoramento a prima vista nell' Apuleiana Amore e Psiche ed il romanzo greco*, MCSN 1 (1976), 33–47.
G. N. Sandy, *Apuleius' Metamorphoses: 1876–1976*, in: *Erot. Ant.*, 8–12.
G. N. Sandy, *Book 11: Ballast or Anchor?* in: *AAGA 1978*, 123–140.
T. Sarafof, *L'influence d'Ovide sur la langue et le style d'Apulée dans les Métamorphoses*, in: *Ovidianum, (Acta conv.)* Bucarest 1976, 537–540.
C. C. Schlam, *Cupid and Psyche: Apuleius and the Monuments*, University Park, Pennsylvania 1976.
C. C. Schlam, *Sex and Sanctity; the relationship of male and female in the Metamorphoses*, in: *AAGA* 1978, 95–105.
V. Schmidt, *Der viator in Apuleius' Metamorphosen (Apuleiana Groningana VI)*, Mnemosyne IV 32 (1979), 173–176.
A. Scobie, *Ass-Men in Middle, Central and Far Eastern Folktales*, Fabula 16 (1975), 317–323 (cf. *Erot. Ant.*, 149–150).
A. Scobie, *El curioso impertinente and Apuleius*, Rom. Forsch. 88 (1976), 75–76.
A. Scobie, *A Chilean Ass-Tale*, Fabula 17 (1976), 275–277.
A. Scobie, *An Ancient Greek Drakos-Tale in Apuleius' Metamorphoses VIII, 19–21*, Journal of American Folklore 90 (1977), 339–343.
A. Scobie, *The influence of Apuleius' Metamorphoses on some French Authors, 1518–1843*, Arcadia 12 (1977), 156–165.
A. Scobie, *The Structure of Apuleius' Metamorphoses* in: *AAGA* 1978, 43–61.
A. Scobie, *The Influence of Apuleius' Metamorphoses in Renaissance Italy and Spain*, in: *AAGA* 1978, 211–230.
G. Schwarz, *Apulei Metamorphoses 1,2: desultoriae scientiae*, in: C. Deroux Ed., *Studies in Latin Literature and Roman History* I, Bruxelles 1979, 462–466.
N. E. Singleton, *Venus in the Met. of Apuleius*, The Ohio State Univ., Ph. D. 1977.
James Tatum, *Apuleius and The Golden Ass*, Ithaca & London 1979.
J. H. Tatum, *The Two lives of the Sophist Apuleius*, in: *Erot. Ant.*, 140–141.
J. H. Tatum, *The Latin Novels*, in: *Erot. Ant.*, 153–164.
H. van Thiel, *Abenteuer eines Esels oder die Verwandlungen des Lukios*, München 1972.
J. J. M. Tobin, *On the Asininity of Dogberry*, English Studies 59 (1978), 199–201.
Luisa Vertova, *The Tale of Cupid and Psyche in Renaissance Painting before Raphael*, JWJ 42 (1979), 104–121.
Elizabeth Visser, *Louis Couperus and Apuleius*, in: *AAGA* 1978, 239–245.
P. G. Walsh, *Spes romana, spes christiana*, Prudentia 6 (1974), 33–40.
P. G. Walsh, *Petronius and Apuleius*, in: *AAGA* 1978, 17–24 (cf. *Erot. Ant.*, 13).
R. E. H. Westendorp Boerma, *Apuleiana Groningana IV*, Mnemosyne IV 30 (1977), 431–433.
A. G. Westerbrink, *Some Parodies in Apuleius' Metamorphoses*, in: *AAGA* 1978, 63–73.

INTRODUCTION

a. *The structure of 6, 25–7, 28.*

Towards the end of *Met.* 3, 27 the reader was introduced to a band of robbers, whose adventures take up the better part of Book 4. Their housekeeper attempted to divert a captive young lady (whose name is not mentioned till 7, 12: 163, 10) *narrationibus lepidis anilibusque fabulis* (4, 27: 96, 14; cf. *GCA* 1977, 207 *ad loc.*). Actually the girl is not subjected to a medley of stories but treated to the single major tale of Amor and Psyche, which takes up all of 4, 28–6, 24. The present volume of our commentary starts with the sentence that closes the frame of that story (6, 25: 147, 3-6)[1]. This starting-point is the logical consequence of our earlier choice to end the commentary on Book 4 at 4, 27 (96, 15)[2]. Here, too, the incision (between 6, 24 and 25) is a much deeper one than the formal break between two books (the one between 6 and 7 is marked, like the one between 3 and 4, by an indication of time)[3].

The main events of the present section are the following:

6, 25-32	the ass attempts to escape with the girl; they are recaptured[4].
7, 1-3	the ass hears that Lucius has been accused of robbing Milo's house.
7, 4-13	Tlepolemus rescues Charite; the band of robbers is disposed of. 7, 5-8: the tale of Haemus (= Tlepolemus in disguise).
7, 14-16	the ass's reward turns sour; he is harnessed to a mill, attacked by stallions, and
7, 17-28	maltreated by a nasty *puer*, who also accuses him of unacceptable sexual behaviour; finally he is punished for not saving the *puer* from death.

A very much larger proportion of this section of the *Metamorphoses* is devoted to the ass's own experiences than to others' experiences witnessed by him. Only the Haemus tale belongs in the latter category, though it is a special case in so far as the observing witness soon after (163, 5 f.), and the observant reader even sooner, notices that the entire tale is not an exaggerated report of 'real' events, as were the robber tales of Book 4, but a fabrication supporting a disguise. One might include in the same category the report of the robber-spy who reports the

---

[1] See comm. *ad loc.* We hope to add a further discussion concerning the difficulties of interpretation presented by this sentence in the introduction to the volume dealing with Amor and Psyche.
[2] See *GCA* 1977, 1.
[3] See *GCA* 1977, 22.
[4] On the way in which Lucius' and Charite's fates are intertwined and paralleled see e.g. Schlam 1968, 40 f.

reactions to the robbery of Milo's house, but it seems preferable to class that scene, together with the other discussions concerning himself overheard by the ass, as a special type of experience, undergone by the ass often in this section, less often elsewhere.[5] The following passages appear to belong to this category:

6, 26 (147, 20)	the robbers discuss the question how to get rid of a useless lame ass.
6, 31-32	the robbers discuss condign punishments for the girl and the ass.
6, 31-32	the robbers discuss condign punishments for the girl and the ass.
7, 1-2	Lucius is accused of robbing the house of Milo.
7, 9	Haemus inquires into the flight of the girl and the ass's part in it.
7, 14 (165, 1)	Charite and her family discuss a proper reward for the ass.
7, 20 (169, 16)	the *puer* accuses the ass of setting fire to his burden on purpose.
7, 21 (169, 20)	the *puer* accuses the ass of sexual assaults on passers-by.
7, 22-23	the herdsmen discuss how to deal with this menace and decide on castration.
7, 25 (174, 16)	the peasant who turns up to perform the operation is told that the ass will be slaughtered the next day.

In addition there are two contrasting passages in which a character says 'if the ass could speak' (173, 18 vs. 175, 14): a clever use of the topos (both philosophical and rhetorical) 'man differs from the brutes in the use of language'.[6] All this creates the strong impression that a major function of the present section is to illustrate the ass's helplessness. Particularly interesting in this respect is the brief mention of roses (165, 12), which are immediately forgotten under the pressure of more immediate concerns.[7]

b. *The time element*

Narrated time in our section of the novel can be accounted for as follows: after the tale of Amor and Psyche the robbers return to fetch the ass to carry booty; the ass escapes with Charite and is captured once more during the following night (151, 24 *ad lunae splendorem*). At dawn the next morning the spy-robber arrives and introduces Haemus/Tlepolemus, who prepares a meal (162, 16), presumably still during the same day. No passage of days and nights is mentioned between

---

[5] The ass finds himself in comparable situations at 8, 23-25 (the market scene), 9, 39 (233, 9 f.).

[6] Cic. *Inv.* 1, 2-4; *de Orat.* 1, 32-33; Quint. *Inst.* 2, 16, 15. In Stoic terms one might say that the ass still possesses the λόγος ἐνδιάθετος but has been robbed of the λόγος προφορικός (This pair of notions became current well beyond the confines of the school: e.g. Philo *Quod det.* 66 (204 M) and 126 (215 M), Theophilus *Ad Autol.* 2, 10 and 22; Clem. Al. *Strom.* 5, 6, 3; see Barth-Goedeckemeyer [5]1941, 235 and 252.) In the early Stoa there is no certainty that man alone possesses the first and instances are quoted of animals making an apparently rational choice. See Pohlenz [5]1978, 39 f. with *idem* 2, [4]1972, 21 f. But most Stoics attribute ἔναρθρος φωνή to man only. Cf. e.g. Sen. *Ira* 1, 3, 7. The opposite opinion appears in Plut. *Sol. anim.* 973 A, where the terminology is the same. See also Statius *Silv.* 2, 4 and Vollmer *ad loc.* The problem is relevant to the wider question of the origin of language (for literature see Schrijvers 1974, 337).

[7] It seems unlikely that either author or narrator implies an absence of roses as vdPaardt believes, *AAGA* 1978, 93 n. 91.

Charite's return home and her actual wedding, but the expression *ipsoque nuptiarum die* (164, 16) implies the passage of at least a few days. The ass is sent to the farm very soon after the wedding night (164, 22 f.). So far, since the time span of Book 4 is at most 24 hours (see *GCA* 1977, 6), only a few days have passed since Lucius' metamorphosis (see also 3, 27: 72, 5 and vdPaardt in *AAGA* 1978, 85): the indicator *ueris initio pratis herbantibus* (165, 11) confirms this.

The description of the ass's labour under the mill's yoke implies a period of several days, possibly weeks (165, 26 *per diem*; 166, 1; 166, 7 *serius*). The episode with the *puer* similarly implies a period of some (unspecified) length (168, 24 *quadam die*; 169, 20 *nec multis interiectis diebus*; 171, 20 *spatio modico interiecto* – add 174, 15; 172, 9). The ass's death is deferred to the next day (174, 23). That day dawns at the beginning of the next book with the report of Charite's death, which saves the ass's life. It is fairly obvious, then, that the time element, which can be accounted for with some accuracy for the first few days of Lucius' life as an ass, becomes much vaguer in Book 7; but it is equally obvious that the low narrative tempo[8] has been stepped up a little, in particular from 7, 15 onwards.

c. *The function of Haemus' tale (7, 5–8)*.

Haemus, Tlepolemus in disguise, tells his tale in order not only to gain admittance to the band of robbers, but to become their chief. They seem to have been without a chief ever since the death of Lamachus.[9] Tlepolemus' aim is to rescue Charite and the operation is brilliantly successful. There are some apparent loose ends in the Charite episode, however. One of these is the fact that there is no mention of an attempt to collect the ransom alluded to in 4, 23 (93, 2); on the other hand the robbers discuss killing Charite after she has been recaptured (152, 21 f.), but eventually prefer Haemus' suggestion that she should be sold to a brothel (161, 21 f.). Another is the question how there could have been *proci* (among them Thrasyllus, 8, 2: 177, 11), when Charite had *iam pridem* (4, 26: 95, 1) been promised to Tlepolemus. A third is the question whether the robbers with whom Thrasyllus had associated (8, 1: 177, 8) were the ones that had kidnapped her – a natural assumption, but one that soon comes to nothing for lack of confirmation or follow-up.[10] To a large extent these loose ends may be explained by pointing out that the narrator cannot present details with which he has not been acquainted: the ego-narrator is limited to what he has witnessed or been told afterwards.[11] However, the question remains why the author should have selected precisely these hints of his narrator's limitations. But the function of the

---

[8] See vdPaardt in *AAGA* 1978, 84 f.
[9] Strictly speaking, Lamachus is never described as the chief of all the robbers, but only of the platoon that attacks Chryseros at Thebes (4, 8: 80, 22 *duce uestro*; 4, 10: 82, 2 *uexillarius noster*; 4, 11: 83, 4 *magnanimi ducis*); nor does the spy-robber mention specifically the loss of the leader (157, 3 *fortissimum quemque*).
[10] Among the most recent discussions of the Charite episode are those of Scobie in *AAGA* 1978, 53, Schlam *ibidem* 98 f. The robbers mention ransom 4, 23 (92, 24 f.) but no attempt to collect it is mentioned; see *GCA* 1977, 178. It is curious that such meager motivation is suggested for the slaves' flight (see 8, 15: 188, 9) after Charite's death; see Junghanns 1932, 84 and against him vThiel I 1971, 123 f.
[11] See vdPaardt in *AAGA* 1978, 76 f.

episode as a whole, as a major instance of bad fortune followed by good fortune, followed once again by bad fortune, is clear enough.

Within this tale the disguised Tlepolemus' speech to the robbers' collective consists largely of an account of the demise of Haemus' band of robbers through the effective outcry raised by one of their intended victims, Plotina. It has been pointed out (Tatum 1969 b, 508) that Plotina's courage as described by Haemus serves as an encouragement for the captive Charite, but it is a moot point whether she can hear the story.[12] Tatum (*ibidem*) also thinks that the tale contains an unheeded warning to the robbers who form the audience, and he notes that eventually the tale will be seen to have foreshadowed Charite's revenge.[13]

It is remarkable that there are three metamorphosis-like disguises in this section. Not only does Tlepolemus, a well-to-do citizen, become Haemus, a notable robber, but Haemus escapes his fate by dressing as a woman, thus becoming the counterpart of Plotina, who dresses in men's clothes and acts with a man's courage. Haemus' disguise and the unheroic manner of his escape somewhat resemble Thrasyleon's disguise in Book 4 and the ironic tale of his 'heroic' end (see *GCA* 1977, 159 f.).[14]

Apart from the structural functions that have been claimed for Haemus' tale, the word 'parody' has been used in connection with the passage, particularly by Eicke 1956, 100 f., Tatum 1969a 141 f.; 1969b, 506 f. and Westerbrink in *AAGA* 1978, 69 f.

Eicke describes the inflated style of the passage as a parody of the epic style, but unlike the others he does not speak of Haemus' tale as a parody of the robbers' tales in Book 4. In fact the elements of style he lists in support of his thesis[15] are to a large extent also present in the earlier robber tales: to that extent an element of parody and/or caricature is certainly present in all of those tales.

Tatum states that this tale includes 'a parody of the values set forth in (the) tales in Book 4, whereas Westerbrink emphasizes that Haemus' speech (which 'may be regarded as a kind of parody by Apuleius of the situation in the robbers' world as he sketched it himself in Book 4') also includes elements which parody earlier authors.

How useful is the notion of parody[16] in the interpretation of the passage? In answering this question it is helpful to see first at what narrative level the parody, if any, is working, and secondly whether what we find is properly characterized

---

[12] See comm. on 160, 23 *deductus* and 161, 25 *quae quidem simul uiderat illum*. See also Walsh in *AAGA* 1978, 21.
[13] See also Tatum 1969a, 141.
[14] See Tatum 1972, 309 with n. 19.
[15] E.g. archaic expressions, neologisms, poeticisms, periphrasis, alliteration, paronomasia, rhyme etc.
[16] Neither Eicke nor Tatum defines parody; Westerbrink uses the definition by Lehmann 1966, 3. Both Tatum and Westerbrink consider exaggeration an important characteristic of parody. Cèbe 1966, 12 on the other hand distinguishes sharply between parody and caricature, the latter being marked mainly by exaggeration. Of course the two may occur in combination.

as parody, using as a guideline J.-P. Cèbe's division of parody into three types.[17]

There are at least three narrative levels: the (implied) author, the narrator (with an element of tension between Lucius and the ass), and the speaker (Tleopolemus in disguise).

The reader obviously is not to take Tlepolemus/Haemus to parody tales he (Tl./H.) has not heard: parody exists to be detected and enjoyed, but at his level detection by the robbers would be fatal; Charite has not heard the robbers' tales of Book 4 and, as we have seen, it is by no means clear that she can hear Haemus' tale, let alone enjoy it; the observing ass does not see through the disguise until later (163, 5). No doubt there is a highly enjoyable comic aspect to the fact that the narrating I is made to depict the experiencing I as often less than clever and more than self-satisfied (e.g. 163, 6 *sed non obscuris prudenti asino*), but this is not parody. If there is parody here, it is at the level of the (implied) author, who winks at the reader. See vdPaardt in *AAGA* 1978, 90 n. 39.

Following Cèbe's scheme[18] we note that the tale cannot be called a literary parody: seen as a literary product it does not parody the literary aspects of the tales in Book 4. If it is parody at all it is rather an instance of Cèbe's third type. This is doubtless what Tatum means when he speaks of a 'parody of values'[19] and it is achieved by both resemblances and differences. All the tales contain a sketch of the intended victim, as well as a characterization of the main robber (including his significant name), and an attempted robbery thwarted by bad luck. Haemus' tale differs from the robbers' tales in two details of perspective: he praises Plotina, and uses the expression *uera enim dicenda sunt*. The robbers do not praise their victims, particularly if they have put up a resistance nor do they need to emphasize their truthfulness, since they are in fact telling the truth. (Indeed, in the context of fiction, insistence on truth often functions paradoxically as an emphatic indication of the fictional character of a tale.[20])

Moreover an element of personal history is included in the portrait of Haemus. There is also an element of inversion: Thrasyleon disguises himself in order not to be recognized as a robber, Tlepolemus so as not to be recognized as a law-abiding citizen. Further items of inversion have been noted in the commentary on 7, 5. Finally, the element of exaggeration is more pronounced in Haemus' tale: obviously the new recruit must impress the robbers' assembly by beating them at their own rhetorical game.

In view of the absence of a clear reason why the reader should laugh here

---

[17] J. B. Cèbe, *La caricature et la parodie dans le monde romain antique des origines à Juvenal* (Paris 1966). He lists three types of parody (and three techniques of literary parody i.e. parody of a literary original). All parody uses contrast or discordance in order to raise a laugh. This contrast may be between content and expression, between a person's activities and his status, or between natural and mimed behaviour. These types are not mutually exclusive (11-12).

[18] This does not differ essentially from Lehmann's definition quoted by Westerbrink in *AAGA* 1978, 64.

[19] Cf. Westerbrink *ibidem* 69 'parody of the situation in the robbers' world'.

[20] See e.g. F. C. Maatje, ³1974, 23.

rather than at the tales of Book 4, it is easier to interpret these differences, in particular the difference in the way the robbers' perspective is maintained, as hints to the reader that things are not quite what they seem to be. Thus they should be taken as an indirect characterization of the narrator (in both his experiencing and narrating aspects) rather than as the elements that constitute parody. The resemblances (including exaggeration) on the other hand may well be taken to give a tinge of parody and caricature to all the robbers' tales, not in comparison with one another, but in comparison with an implied reality.

NOTE TO THE TEXT

Generally we have followed Helm's text, as printed in his latest Teubner-edition (³1931, reprinted with Addenda and Corrigenda 1955). However we have used capitals at the beginning of new sentences and added paragraph numbers throughout. In the following places we have chosen a different reading:

Our text		Helm's text
147, 8	uulnerati⟨s⟩ domi	uulnerati; ⟨his⟩ domi
147, 11	equum meum	equum
148, 7f.	remanserant dudum, recurrunt re⟨s⟩ laturi taedio	remanserant, dudum recurrunt, re⟨liqua ipsi⟩ laturi, taedio
148, 23	. Sed	- sed,
149, 2	secum ?'	secum.'
149, 25	uirginis	uirgini[s]
150,	spirans	⟨su⟩spirans
150, 2	nutu	uu⟨b⟩tu
150, 10	manibus	monilibus
150, 13	compta diligentia perpolibo monilibus bullisque	ampla diligentia perpolibo bullisque
150, 14	ueluti	uelut
150, 16	nucleos,	nucleos⟨et⟩
151, 10	bouem	boue⟨m⟩
151, 13	suspiratus	suspiritus
152, 1	properabas	properas
152, 2	praestabimus	perhibebimus
152, 3	Et unus	et uerbum
153, 1f.	omnium sedato tumultu placido	omnium, sedato tumultu, placido
153, 21	nimis	nim⟨i⟩is
153, 25f.	aestu⟨abit⟩	aestu ⟨cruciante uexabitur⟩
154, 3	cadauer?	cadauer.
155, 9	nanque	namque
155, 17	narrante	enarrante
156, 16	quam	quanquam
157, 19	adsensi[ere]	adsens[i]ere
158, 12	atque	aeque
158, 18	†me orato†	eo fato
158, 22	Inuidia	inuidia
158, 23	Plotina	Plotina,
159, 7	Actiacum	Actiacum,
159, 8	grassabamus	grassabamur,
159, 9	-tabernulam	tabernulam
159, 10	incubabant - inuadimus	incubabant, ⟨cum⟩ inuadimus
159, 12	nanque	namque
160, 17	unanimes	unianimes
160, 18	diuite	diuitem
162, 16	expositionum	expeditionum
163, 13	uinulentiaque	uinolentiaque
163, 17	parati morti	pariter mortui

7

165, 2	facto	pacto
165, 22	mercenariis	merccen⟨n⟩ariis
166, 6	nanque	namque
167, 7	omnibus	⟨ex⟩ omnibus
168, 10	compilabat [cidit] fusti	compilabat ad incitas fusti
169, 19	inigninum	⟨as⟩in⟨um⟩ igninum
170, 6	ferinas uoluptates	ferinas ⟨parans⟩ uoluptates
171, 18	mansues	mites
174, 3	aperitur	⟨r⟩eperitur
174, 15	Interim, dum	Interimdum
174, 18	'Non est', in his	⟨at⟩ 'non est in his'
175, 8	miserae	miseretur
175, 21	derelictoque	deiectoque

TEXT

LIBER VI *(cont.)*

25 ¹Sic captiuae puellae delira et temulenta illa narrabat anicula; sed astans ego non procul dolebam mehercules, quod pugillares et stilum non habebam, qui tam be l⟨l⟩am fabellam praenotarem. ²Ecce confecto nescio quo graui proelio latrones adueniunt onusti, non nulli tamen, immo promptiores uulnerati⟨s⟩ domi relictis et plagas recurantibus ipsi ad reliquas occultatas in quadam spelunca sarcinas, ut aiebant, proficisci gestiunt. ³Prandioque raptim tuburcinato me et equum meum uectores rerum illarum futuros fustibus exinde tundentes producunt in uiam ⁴multisque cliuis et anfractibus fatigatos prope ipsam uesperam perducunt ad quampiam speluncam, ⁵unde multis onustos rebus rursum ne breuiculo quidem tempore refectos ociter reducunt tantaque trepidatione festinabant, ut me plagis multis obtundentes propellentesque super lapidem propter uiam positum deicerent. Vnde crebris aeque ingestis ictibus crure dextero et ungula sinistra me
26 debilitatum aegre ad exurgendum compellunt. ¹Et unus: 'Quo usque', inquit, 'ruptum istum asellum, nunc etiam claudum, frustra pascemus?' Et alius: 'Quid quod et pessumo pede domum nostram accessit nec quicquam idonei lucri exinde cepimus, sed uulnera et fortissimorum occisiones'. ²Alius iterum: 'Certe ego, cum primum sarcinas istas quanquam inuitus pertulerit, protinus eum uulturiis gratissimum pabulum futurum praecipitabo'.

³Dum secum mitissimi homines altercant de mea nece, iam et domum perueneramus. Nam timor ungulas mihi alas fecerat. ⁴Tum qu*ae* ferebamus amoliti properiter nulla salutis nostrae cura ac ne meae quidem necis habita comitibus adscitis, qui uulnerati remanserant dudum, recurrunt re⟨s⟩ laturi taedio, ut aiebant, nostrae tarditatis. Nec me tamen mediocris carpebat scrupulus contemplatione comminatae mihi mortis; et ipse mecum: 'Quid stas, Luci, uel quid iam nouissimum expectas? Mors, et haec acer*b*issima, decreto latronum tibi comparata est. ⁶Nec magno conatu res indiget; uides istas rupinas proximas et praeacutas in his prominentes s[c]ilices, quae te penetrante⟨s⟩, *ante*⟩quam decideris, membratim dissipabunt. ⁷Nam et illa ipsa praeclara magia tua uultum laboresque tibi tantum asini, uerum corium non asini crassum, sed hiru[n]dinis tenue membranu[l]lum circumdedit. Quin igitur masculum tandem sumis animum tuaeque saluti, dum licet, consulis? ⁸Habes summam oportunitatem fugae, dum latrones absunt. An custodiam

9

anus semimortuae formidabis, quam licet claudi pedis tui calce unica finire poteris? Sed quo gentium capessetur fuga uel hospitium quis dabit? ⁹Haec quidem inepta et prorsus asinina cogitatio; quis enim uiantium uectorem suum non libenter auferat secum?"

27 ¹Et alacri statim nisu lorum, quo fueram destinatus, abrumpo meque quadripedi cursu proripio. Nec tamen astutulae anus miluinos oculos effugere potui. Nam ubi me conspexit absolutum, capta super sexum et aetatem audacia lorum prehendit ac me deducere ac reuocare contendit. ²Nec tamen ego, memor exitiabili⟨s⟩ propositi latronum, pietate ulla commoueor, sed incussis in eam posteriorum pedum calcibus protinus adplodo terrae. ³At illa, quamuis humi prostrata, loro tamen tenaciter inhaerebat, ut me procurrentem aliquantisper tractu sui sequeretur. Et occipit statim clamos⟨is⟩ ululatibus auxilium ualidioris manus implorare. ⁴Sed frustra fletibus cassum tumultum commouebat, quippe cum nullus adforet, qui suppetias ei ferre posset nisi sola illa uirgo captiua, quae uocis excitu procurrens uidet hercules memorandi spectaculi scaenam, non tauro, sed asino dependentem Dircen aniculam, sumptaque constantia uirili facinus audet pulcherrimum. ⁶Extorto etenim loro manibus eius me placidis gannitibus ab impetu reuocatum nauiter inscendit et sic

28 ad cursum rursum incitat. ¹Ego simul uoluntariae fugae uoto et liberandae uirginis studio, sed et plagarum suasu, quae me saepicule commonebant, equestri celeritate quadripedi cursu solum replaudens uirginis delicatas uoculas ad⟨h⟩innire temptabam. ²Sed et scabendi dorsi mei simulatione non numquam obliquata ceruice pedes decoros puellae basiabam. Tunc illa spirans altius caelumque sollicito nutu petens:

³'Vos', inquit, 'Superi, tandem meis supremis periculis opem facite, et tu, Fortuna durior, iam saeuire desiste. Sat tibi miseris istis cruciatibus meis litatum est. ⁴Tuque, praesidium meae libertatis meaeque salutis, si me domum peruexeris incolumem parentibusque et formonso proco reddideris, quas tibi gratias perhibebo, quos honores habebo, quos cibos exhibebo! ⁵Iam primum iubam istam tuam probe pectinatam meis uirginalibus manibus adornabo, frontem uero crispatam prius decoriter discriminabo caudaeque setas incuria lauacri congestas et horridas compta diligentia perpolibo ⁶monilibus bullisque te multis aureis inoculatum ueluti stellis sidereis relucentem et gaudiis popularium pomparum ouantem, sinu serico progestans nucleos, edulia mitiora, te meum sospitatorem cotidie saginabo. ¹Sed nec inter cibos

29 delicatos et otium profundum uitaeque totius beatitudinem deerit tibi dignitas gloriosa. ²Nam memoriam praesentis fortunae meae diuinaeque prouidentiae perpetua testatione signabo et depictam in tabula fugae praesentis imaginem meae domus atrio dedicabo. ³Visetur et in fabulis audietur doctorumque stilis rudis

perpetuabitur historia "asino uectore uirgo regia fugiens captiuitatem". ⁴Accedes antiquis et ipse miraculis, et iam credemus exemplo tuae ueritatis et Frixum arieti supernatasse et Arionem delphinum gubernasse et Europam tauro supercubasse. ⁵Quodsi uere Iupiter mugiuit in bouem, potest in asino meo latere aliqui uel uultus hominis uel facies deorum.'

⁶Dum haec identidem puella replicat uotisque crebros intermiscet suspiratus, ad quoddam peruenimus triuium, unde me adrepto capistro dirigere dextrorsum magnopere gestiebat, quod ad parentes eius ea scilicet iretur uia. ⁷Sed ego gnarus latrones illac ad reliquas commeasse praedas, renitebar firmiter atque sic in animo meo *ta*citus expostulabam: 'Quid facis, infelix puella? Quid agis? Cur festinas ad Orcum? Quid meis pedibus facere contendis? Non enim te tantum, uerum etiam me perditum ibis.' ⁸Sic nos diuersa tendentes et in causa finali de proprietate soli, immo uiae herciscundae contendentes rapinis suis onusti coram deprehendunt ipsi latrones et ad lunae splendorem iam inde longius cognitos risu maligno salutant; ¹et unus e numero sic appellat: 'Quorsum istam festinanti uestigio lucubratis uiam nec noctis intempestae Manes Lar*u*asque formidatis? ²An tu, probissima puella, parentes tuos interuisere properabas? Sed nos et solitudini tuae praesidium praestabimus et compendiosum ad tuos iter monstrabimus'. ³Et unus manu secutus prehenso loro retrorsum me circumtorquet nec baculi nodosi, quod gerebat, suetis ictibus temperat. ⁴Tunc ingratis ad promptum recurrens exitium reminiscor doloris ungulae et occip*i*o nutanti capite claudicare. ⁵Sed: 'Ecce' inquit ille, qui me retraxerat, 'rursum titubas et *u*accillas, et putres isti tui pedes fugere possunt, ambulare nesciunt? At paulo ante pinnatam Pegasi uincebas celeritatem'.

⁶Dum sic mecum fustem quatiens benignus iocatur comes, iam domus eorum extremam loricam perueneramus. Et ecce de quodam ramo procerae cupressus induta laqueum anus illa pendebat. ⁷Quam quidem detractam protinus cum suo sibi funiculo deuinctam dedere prae*ci*pitem puellaque statim distenta uinculis cenam, quam postuma diligentia praeparauerat infelix anicula, ferinis inuadunt animis.

31 ¹Ac dum auida uoracitate cuncta contruncant, iam incipiunt de nostra poena suaque uindicta secum considerare. Et utpote in coetu turbulento uariae fuere sententiae, ut primus uiuam cremari censeret puellam, secundus bestiis obici suaderet, tertius patibulo suffigi iuberet, quartus tormentis excarnificari praeciperet; ²certe calculo cunctorum utcumque mors ei fuerat destinata. Tunc unus omnium sedato tumultu placido sermone sic orsus est:

³'Nec sectae collegii nec mansuetudini singulorum ac ne meae quidem modestiae congruit pati uos ultra modum delictique saeuire terminum nec feras nec cruces nec ignes nec tormenta ac

ne mortis quidem maturatae festinas tenebras accersere. ⁴Meis itaque consiliis auscultantes uitam puellae, sed quam meretur, largimini. Nec uos memoria deseruit utique, quid iam dudum decreueritis de isto asino semper pigro quidem, sed manducone summo, nunc etiam mendaci fictae debilitatis et uirginalis fugae sequestro ministroque. ⁵Hunc igitur iugulare crastino placeat totisque uacuefacto praecordiis per mediam aluum nudam uirginem, quam praetulit nobis, insuere, ⁶ut sola facie praeminente ceterum corpus puellae nexu ferino coherceat, tunc super aliquod saxum scruposum insi*cia*tum et fartilem asinum exponere et solis

32 ardentis uaporibus tradere. ¹Sic enim cuncta, quae recte statuistis, ambo sustinebunt, et mortem asinus, quam pridem meruit, et illa morsus ferarum, cum uerm*es* membra laniabunt, et ignis flagrantiam, cum sol nimis caloribus inflammarit uterum, et patibuli cruciatum, cum canes et uultures intima protrahent uiscera. ²Sed et ceteras eius aerumnas et tormenta numerate: mortuae bestiae ipsa uiuens uentrem habitabit, tum faetore nimio nares aestu‹abit› et inediae diutinae letali fame tabescet nec suis saltem liberis manibus mortem sibi fabricare poterit.

³Talibus dictis non pedibus, sed totis animis latrones in eius uadunt sententiam. Quam meis tam magnis auribus accipiens quid aliud quam meum crastinum deflebam cadauer?

LIBER VII

1 ¹Vt primum tenebris abiectis dies inalbebat et candidum solis curriculum cuncta conlustrabat, quidam de numero latronum peruenit; sic enim mutuae salutationis officium indicabat. ²Is in primo speluncae aditu residens et ex an‹h›elitu recepto spiritu tale colleegio suo nuntium fecit:

³'Quod ad domum Milonis Hypatini, quam proxime diripuimus, pertinet, discussa sollicitudine iam possumus esse securi. Postquam uos enim fortissimis uiribus cunctis ablatis c[r]astra nostra remeastis, immixtus ego turbelis popularium ⁴dolentique atque indignanti similis arbitrabar, super inuestigatione facti cuius modi consilium caperet‹ur› et an et quatenus latrones placeret inquiri, renuntiaturus uobis, uti mandaueratis, omnia. ⁵Nec argumentis dubiis, sed rationibus probabilibus congruo cunctae multitudinis consensu nescio qui Lucius auctor manifestus facinoris postulabatur, qui proximis diebus fictis commendaticiis litteris Miloni sese uirum commentitus bonum artius conciliauerat, ⁶ut etiam hospitio susceptus inter familiaris intimos haberetur plusculisque ibidem diebus demoratus falsis amoribus ancillae Milonis animum inrepens ianuae claustra sedulo explorauerat et ipsa membra, in quis omne patrimonium condi solebat,

2 curiose perspexerat. ¹Nec exiguum scelerati monstrabatur

indicium, quippe cum eadem nocte sub ipso flagitii momento
idem profugisset nec exinde usquam compareret; nam et praesidium fugae, quo uelocius frustratis insecutoribus procul ac procul abderet sese, eidem facile suppeditasse; equum nanque illum
suum candidum uectorem futurum duxisse secum. ²Plane seruum eius ibidem in hospitio repertum scelerum consiliorumque
erilium futurum indicem, per magistratus in publicam custodiam
receptum et altera die tormentis uexatum pluribus ac paene ad
ultimam mortem excarnificatum, ³nil quicquam rerum talium
esse confessum, missos tamen in patriam Luci illius multos
numero, qui reum poenas daturum sceleris inquirerent.'

⁴Haec eo narrante, ueteris fortunae et illius beati Lucii praesentisque aerumnae et infelicis asini facta comparatione, medullitus ingemebam subibatque me non de nihilo ueteris priscaeque
doctrinae uiros finxisse ac pronuntiasse caecam et prorsus exoculatam esse Fortunam, ⁵quae semper suas opes ad malos et
indignos conferat nec unquam iudicio quemquam mortalium
eligat, immo uero cum is potissimum deuersetur, quos procul, si
uideret, fugere deberet, ⁶quodque cunctis est extremius, uarias
opiniones, immo contrarias nobis attribuat, ut et malus boni uiri
fama glorietur et innocentissimus contra noxio rumore plectatur.

3 ¹Ego denique, quem saeuissimus eius impetus in bestiam et
extremae sortis quadripedem deduxerat cuiusque casus etiam
quouis iniquissimo dolendus atque miserandus merito uideretur,
crimine latrocinii in hospitem mihi carissimum postulabar. ²Quod
crimen non modo latrocinium, uerum etiam parricidium quisque
rectius nominarit. Nec mihi tamen licebat causam meam defendere uel unico uerbo saltem denegare. ³Denique ne male conscientia tam scelesto crimini praesens uiderer silentio consentire,
hoc tantum inpatientia productus uolui dicere: 'Non feci.' ⁴Et
uerbum quidem praecedens semel ac saepius inmodice clamitaui,
sequens uero nullo pacto disserere potui, sed in prima remansi
uoce et identidem boaui 'non non', quanquam nimia rutunditate
pendulas uibrassem labias. ⁵Sed quid ego pluribus de Fortunae
scaeuitate conqueror, quam nec istud puduit me cum meo famulo
meoque uectore illo equo factum conseruum atque coniugem.

4 ¹Talibus cogitationibus fluctuantem subit me illa cura potior,
qua statuto consilio latronum manibus uirginis decretam me
uictimam recordabar uentremque crebro suspiciens meum iam
misellam puellam parturibam. ²Sed ille, qui commodum falsam
de me notoriam pertulerat, expromptis mille aureum, quos insutu laciniae contexerat quosque uariis ui⟨a⟩toribus detractos, ut
aiebat, pro sua frugalitate communi conferebat arcae, infit etiam
de salute commilitonum sollicite sciscitari. ³Cognitoque quosdam, immo uero fortissimum quemque uariis quidem, sed inpigris casibus oppetisse, suadet, tantisper pacatis itineribus omniumque proeliorum seruatis indutiis inquisitioni commilitonum

13

potius insisteretur et tirocinio nouae iuuentutis ad pristinae manus numerum Martiae cohortis facies integraretur: ⁴nam et inuitos terrore compelli et uolentes praemio prouocari posse nec paucos humili seruilique uitae renuntiantes ad instar tyrannicae potestatis sectam suam conferre malle. ⁵Se quoque iam dudum pro sua parte quendam conuenisse hominem et statu procerum et aetate iuuenem et corpore uastum et manu strenuum, eique suasisse ac denique persuasisse, ut manus ⟨h⟩ebetatas diutina pigritia tandem referret ad frugem meliorem bonoque secundae, dum posset, frueretur ualetudinis ⁶nec manum ualidam erogandae stipi porrigeret, sed hauriendo potius exerceret auro. ¹Talibus dictis uniuersi omnes adsensi[ere] et illum, qui iam comprobatus uideretur, adscisci et alios ad supplendum numerum uestigari statuunt. ²Tunc profectus et paululum commoratus ille perducit immanem quendam iuuenem, uti fuerat pollicitus, nescio an ulli praesentium comparandum — nam praeter ceteram corporis molem toto uertice cunctos antepollebat et ei commodum lanugo malis inserpebat — ³sed plane centunculis disparibus et male consarcinatis semiamictum, inter quos pectus et uenter crustata crassitie reluctabant.

⁴Sic introgressus: 'Ha*u*ete', inquit, 'fortissimo deo Marti clientes mihique iam fidi commilitones, et uirum magnanimae uiuacitatis uolentem uolentes accipite, libentius uulnera corpore excipientem quam aurum manu suscipientem ipsaque morte, quam formidant alii, meliorem. Nec me putetis egenum uel abiectum neue de pannulis istis uirtutes meas aestimetis. ⁵Nam praefui ualidissimae manui totamque prorsus deuastaui Macedoniam. ⁶Ego sum praedo famosus Haemus ille Thracius, cuius totae prouinciae nomen horrescunt, patre Therone atque latrone inclito prognatus, humano sanguine nutritus interque ipsos manipulos factionis educatus heres et aemulus uirtutis paternae. ¹Sed omnem pristinam sociorum fortium multitudinem magnasque illas opes exiguo temporis amisi spatio. Nam procuratorem principis ducenaria perfunctum, dehinc fortuna tristiore decussum, praetereuntem † me orato † fueram adgress*us*. Sed rei noscendae carpo ordinem. ²Fuit quidam multis officiis in aula Caesaris clarus atque conspicuus, ipsi etiam probe spectatus. ³Hunc insimulatum quorundam astu proiecit extorrem saeuiens Inuidia. ³Sed uxor eius Plotina quaedam rarae fidei atque singularis pudicitiae femina, quae decimo partus stipendio uiri familiam fundauerat, spretis atque contemptis urbicae luxuriae deliciis fugientis comes et infortunii socia, ⁴tonso capillo, in masculinam faciem reformato habitu, pretiosissimis monilium et auro monetali zonis refertis incincta inter ipsas custodientium militum manus et gladios nudos intrepida cunctorum periculorum particeps et pro mariti salute peruigilem curam sustine⟨n⟩s aerumnas adsiduas ingenio masculo sustinebat. ⁵Iamque plurimis itineris

difficultatibus marisque terror*ibus* exan*c*latis Zac[h]*y*nthum petebat, quam sors ei fatalis decreuerat temporariam sedem. ¹Sed cum primum litus Actiacum quo tunc Macedonia delapsi grassabamur appulisset, nocte promota — tabernulam quandam litori nauique proximam uitatis maris fluctibus incubabant — inuadimus et diripimus omnia. Nec tamen periculo leui temptati discessimus. ²Simul na*n*que primum sonum ianuae matrona percepit, procurrens in cubiculum clamoribus inquietis cuncta miscuit milites suosque famulos nominatim, sed et omnem uiciniam suppetiatum conuocans, nisi quod pauore cunctorum, qui sibi quisque metuentes delitiscebant, effectum est, ut impune discederemus. ³Sed protinus sanctissima — uera enim dicenda sunt — et unicae fidei femina, bonis artibus gratiosa, precibus ad Caesaris numen porrectis et marito reditum celerem et adgressurae plenam uindictam impetrauit. ⁴Denique noluit esse Caesar Haemi latronis col⟨*h*⟩egium, et confestim interi*u*it: tantum potest nutus etiam magni principis. Tota denique factione militarium uexillationum indagatu confecta atque concisa ipse me furatus aegre solus mediis Orci faucibus ad hunc euasi modum: ¹sumpta ueste muliebri florida, in sinus flaccidos [h]abundante, mitellaque textili contecto capite, calceis femininis albis illis et tenuibus indutus et in sequiorem sexum incertus atque absconditus, asello spicas ordeacias gerenti residens per medias acies infesti militis transabiui. Nam mulierem putantes asinariam concedebant liberos a*bitus*, quippe cum mihi etiam tunc depiles genae leui pueritia splendicarent. ²Nec ab illa tamen paterna gloria uel mea uirtute desciui, quanquam semitrepidus iuxta mucrones Martios constitutus, sed habitus alieni fallacia textus, uilla⟨s⟩ seu castella solus adgrediens, uiaticulum mihi conrasi' et diloricatis statim pannulis in medium duo milia profudit aureorum et: ³'En', inquit, 'istam sportulam, immo uero dotem collegio uestro libens meque uobis ducem fidissimum, si tamen non recusatis, offero breui temporis spatio lapideam istam domum uestram facturus auream.'

¹Nec mora nec cunctatio, sed calculis omnibus ducatum latrones unanimes ei deferunt ueste⟨*m*⟩que lautiusculam proferunt, sumeret abiecto centunculo diuite. Sic reformatus, singulos exosculatus et in summo puluinari locatus cen*a* poculisque magnis inauguratur. ²Tunc sermonibus mutuis de uirginis fuga deque mea uectura et utrique destinata monstruosa morte cognoscit et, ubi locorum esset illa, percontatus deductusque, uisa ea, ut erat uinculis onusta, contorta et uituperanti nare discessit et: 'Non sum quidem tam brutus uel certe temerarius', inquit, 'ut scitum uestrum inhibeam, sed malae conscientiae reatum intra me sustinebo, si quod bonum mihi uidetur dissimulauero. ³Sed prius fiduciam uestri causa sollicito mihi tribuite, cum praesertim uobis, si sententia haec mea displicuerit, liceat rursus ad asinum

redire. ⁴Nam ego arbitror latrones, quique eorum recte sapiunt, nihil anteferre lucro suo debere ac ne ipsam quidem saepe et aliis damnosam ultionem. Ergo igitur si perdideritis in asino uirginem, nihil amplius quam sine ullo compendio indignationem uestram exercueritis. ⁵Quin ego censeo deducendam eam ad quampiam ciuitatem ibique uenundandam. Nec enim leui pretio distrahi poterit talis aetatula. ⁶Nam et ipse quosdam lenones pridem cognitos habeo, quorum poterit unus magnis equidem talentis, ut arbitror, puellam istam praestinare condigne natalibus suis fornicem processuram nec in similem fugam discur⟨su⟩ram, non nihil etiam, cum lupanari seruierit, uindictae uobis depensuram. Hanc ex animo quidem meo sententiam conducibilem protuli; sed uos uestrorum estis consiliorum rerumque domini.'

10   ¹Sic ille latronum fisci aduocatus nostram causam pertulerat, uirginis et asini sospitator egregius. ²Sed in diutina deliberatione ceteri cruciantes mora consilii mea praecordia, immo miserum spiritum, libentes tandem nouicii latronis accedunt sententiae et protinus uinculis exsoluunt uirginem. ³Quae quidem simul uiderat illum iuuenem fornicisque et le⟨n⟩onis audierat mentionem, coepit risu laetissimo gestire, ut mihi merito subiret uituperatio totius sexus, cum uiderem puellam, proci iuuenis amore nuptiarumque castarum desiderio simulato, lupanaris spurci sordidique subito delectari nomine. ⁴Et tunc quidem totarum mulierum secta moresque de asini pendebant iudicio. Sed ille iuuenis sermone repetito: 'Quin igitur', inquit, 'supplicatum Marti Comiti pergimus et puellam simul uendituri et socios indagaturi? Sed, ut uideo, nullum uspiam pecus sacrificatui ac ne uinum quidem potatui adfatim uel sufficiens habemus. ⁵Decem mihi itaque legate comites, quis contentus proximum castellum petam, inde uobis epulas ⟨s⟩aliares comparaturus.'

Sic eo profecto ceteri copiosum instruunt ignem aramque cespite uirenti Marti deo faciunt.

11   ¹Nec multo post adueniunt illi uinarios utres ferentes et gregatim pecua comminantes. Vnde praelectum grandem hircum annosum et horricomem Marti Secutori Comitique uictimant. Et ilico prandium fabricatur opipare. ²Tunc hospes ille: 'Non modo', inquit, 'expositionum praedarumque, uerum etiam uoluptatum uestrarum ducem me strenu⟨u⟩m sentire debetis' et adgressus insigni facilitate nauiter cuncta praeministrat. ³Verrit, sternit, coquit, tuc⟨c⟩eta concinnat, adponit scitule, sed praecipue poculis crebris grandibusque singulos ingurgitat. Interdum tamen [in]simulatione promendi, quae poscebat usus, ad puellam commeabat adsidue, partisque subreptas clanculo et praegustatas a se potiones offerebat hilaris. ⁴At illa sumebat adpetenter et non nunquam basiare uolenti promptis sauiolis adlubescebat. Quae res oppido mihi displicebat. ⁵'Hem oblita es nuptiarum tuique

mutui cupitoris, puella uirgo, et illi nescio cui recenti marito, quem tibi parentes iunxerunt, hunc aduenam cruentumque percussorem praeponis? ⁶Nec te conscientia stimulat, sed adfectione calcata inter lanceas et gladios istos scortari tibi libet? Quid, si quo modo latrones ceteri persenserint? Non rursum recurres ad asinum et rursum exitium mihi parabis? Re uera ludis de alieno corio.'

12 ¹Dum ista sycophanta ego mecum maxima cum indignatione disputo, de uerbis eorum quibusdam dubiis, sed non obscuris prudenti asino cognosco non Haemum illum praedonem famosum, sed Tlepolemum sponsum puellae ipsius. ²Nam procedente sermone paulo iam c⟨h⟩arius contempta mea praesentia qu*a*si uere mortui: 'Bono animo es', inquit, 'Charite dulcissima; nam totos istos hostes tuos statim captiuos habebis' ³et instanti⟨a⟩ ualidiore uinum iam inmixtum, sed modico tepefactum uapore sauciis illis et crapula uinulentiaque madidis ipse abstemius non cessat inpingere. ⁴Et hercules suspicionem mihi fecit, quasi soporiferum quoddam uenenum cantharis immisceret illis. Cuncti denique, sed prorsus omnes uino sepulti iacebant, omnes parati morti. ⁵Tunc nullo negotio artissimis uinculis impeditis ac pro arbitrio suo constrictis illis, imposita dorso meo puella, dirigit gressum ad suam patriam.

13 ¹Quam simul accessimus, tota ciuitas ad uotiuum conspectum effunditur. Procurrunt parentes, affines, clientes, alumni, famuli laeti faciem, gaudio delibuti. ²Pompam cerneres omnis sexus et omnis aetatis nouumque et hercules memorandum spectamen, uirginem asino triumphantem. ³Denique ipse etiam hilarior pro uirili parte, ne praesenti negotio ut alienus discreparem, porrectis auribus proflatisque naribus rudiui fortiter, immo tonanti clamore personui. ⁴Et illam thalamo receptam commode parentes sui fouebant, me uero cum ingenti iumentorum ciuiumque multitudine confestim retro *T*lepolemus agebat non inuitum. ⁵Nam et alias curiosus et tunc latronum captiuitatis spectator optabam fieri. Quos quidem colligatos adhuc uino magis quam uinculis deprehendimus. ⁶Totis ergo prolatis erutisque rebus et nobis auro argentoque et ceteris onustis ipsos partim constrictos, uti fuerant, prouolutosque in proximas r*u*pinas praecipites dedere, alios uero suis sibi gladiis obtruncatos reli[n]quere.

⁷Tali uindicta laeti et gaudentes ciuitatem reuenimus. Et illas quidem diuitias public*a*e custodel*a*e commisere. Tlepolemo puel-
14 lam repetitam lege tradidere. ¹Exin me ⟨su⟩um sospitatorem nuncupatum matrona prolixe cur*i*tabat ipsoque nuptiarum die praesepium meum ordeo passim repleri iubet fae[mi]numque camelo Bactrinae sufficiens apponi. ²Sed quas ego condignas Fotidi diras deuotiones inprecer, quae me formauit non canem sed asinum, quippe cum uiderem largissimae cenae reliquiis rapinisque canes omnes inescatos a*t*que distentos.

17

³Post noctem unicam et rudimenta Veneris recens nupta gratias summas apud suos parentes ac maritum mihi meminisse non destitit, quoad summos illi promitterent honores habituri mihi. ⁴Conuocatis denique grauioribus amicis consilium datur, quo potissimum facto digne remunerarer. Placuerat uni domi me conclusum et otiosum hordeo lecto fabaque et uicia saginari; ⁵sed optinuit alius, qui meae libertati prospexerat, suadens, ut rurestribus potius campis in greges equinos lasciuiens discurrerem daturus dominis equarum inscensu generoso multas mulas alumnas. ¹Ergo igitur euocato statim armentario equisone magna cum praefatione deducendus adsignor. Et sane gaudens laetusque praecurrebam sarcinis et ceteris oneribus iam nunc renuntiaturus nanctaque libertate ueris initio *pr*atis herbantibus rosas utique reperturus aliquas. ²Subibat me tamen illa etiam sequens cogitatio, quod tantis actis gratiis honoribusque plurimis asino meo tributis humana facie recepta multo tanta pluribus beneficiis honestarer. ³Sed ubi me procul a ciuitate gregarius ille perduxerat, nullae deliciae ac ne ulla quidem libertas excipit. Nam protinus uxor eius, aua*r*a *e*quidem nequissimaque illa mulier, molae machinariae subiugum me dedit frondosoque baculo subinde castigans panem sibi suisque de meo parabat corio. ⁴Nec tantum sui cibi gratia me fatigare contenta, uicinorum etiam frumenta mercenariis discursibus meis conterebat, nec mihi misero statuta saltem cibaria pro tantis praestabantur laboribus. ⁵Namque hordeum meum frictum et sub eadem mola meis quassatum ambagibus colonis proximis uenditabat, mihi uero per diem laboriosae machinae adtento sub ipsa uespera furfures apponebat incretos ac sordidos multoque lapide salebrosos.

¹Talibus aerumnis edomitum nouis Fortuna saeua tradidit cruciatibus, scilicet ut, quod aiunt, domi forisque fortibus factis adoriae plenae gloriarer. Equinis armentis nanque me congregem pastor egregius mandati dominici serius auscultator aliquando permisit. ²At ego tandem liber asinus laetus et tripudians graduque molli gestiens equas opportunissimas iam mihi concubinas futuras deligebam. Sed haec etiam spes hilarior in capital ⟨e⟩ processit exitium. ³Mares enim ob admissuram ueterem pasti satianter ac diu saginati, terribiles [alios] alioquin et utique quouis asino fortiores, de me metuentes sibi et adulterio degeneri praecauentes nec hospitalis Iouis seruato foedere riualem summo furentes persecuntur [h]odio. ⁴Hic elatis in altum uastis pectoribus arduus capite et sublimis uertice primoribus in me pugillatur ungulis, ille terga pulposis *t*orulis obesa conuertens postremis uelitatur calcibus, alius hinnitu maligno comminatus remulsis auribus dentiumque candentium renudatis as*c*eis totum me commorsicat. ⁵Sic apud historiam de rege Thracio legeram, qui porrigebat; adeo ille praepotens tyrannus sic pa*r*cus hordei fuit, ut edacium iumentorum famem corporum humanorum largitio-

ut edacium iumentorum famem corporum humanorum largitione sedaret. ¹Ad eundem modum distractus et ipse uariis equorum incursibus rursus molares illos circuitus requirebam. Verum Fortuna meis cruciatibus insatiabilis aliam mihi denuo pestem instruxit. ²Delegor enim ligno monte deuehundo, puerque mihi praefectus imponitur ⟨ex⟩ omnibus ille quidem puer deterrimus. ³Nec me montis excelsi tantum arduum fatigabat iugum, nec saxeas tantum sudes incursando contribam ungulas, uerum fustium quoque crebris ictibus per*dite* dedolabar, ut usque plagarum mihi medullaris insideret dolor; ⁴coxaeque dexterae semper ictus incutiens et unum feriendo locum dissipato corio et ulceris latissimi facto foramine, immo fouea uel etiam fenestra nullus tamen desinebat identidem uulnus sanguine delibutum obtundere. Lignorum uero tanto me premebat pondere, ut fascium molem elefanto, non asino paratam putares. ⁵Ille uero etiam quotiens in alterum latus praeponderans declinarat sarcina, cum deberet potius grauantis ruinae fustes demere et leuata paulisper pressura sanare me uel certe in alterum latus translatis peraequare, contra lapidibus additis insuper sic iniquita*ti* ponderis medebatur. ¹Nec tamen post tantas meas clades inmodico sarcinae pondere contentus, cum fluuium transcenderemus, qui forte praeter uiam defluebat, pero*n*ibus suis ab aquae madore consulens ipse quoque insuper lumbos meos insiliens residebat, exiguum scilicet et illud tantae molis superpondium. ²Ac si quo casu limo caenoso ripae supercilio lubricante [h]oneris inpatientia prolapsus deruissem, cum deberet egregius agaso manum porrigere, capistro suspendere, cauda subleuare, certe partem tanti oneris, quoad resurgerem saltem, detrahere, ³nullum quidem defesso mihi ferebat auxilium, sed occipiens a capite, immo uero et ipsis auribus totum me compilabat [cidit] fusti grandissimo, donec fomenti uice ipsae me plagae suscitarent. ⁴Idem mihi talem etiam excogitauit perniciem. Spinas acerrumas et punctu uenenato uiriosas in fascem tortili nodo constrictas caudae meae pensilem deligauit cruciatum, ut incessu meo commotae incitataeque funestis aculeis infeste me conuulnerarent. ¹Ergo igitur ancipiti malo laborabam. Nam cum me cursu proripueram fugiens acer*b*issimos incursus, uehementiore nisu spinarum feriebar: si dolori parcens paululum restitissem, plagis compellebar ad cursum. ²Nec quicquam uidebatur aliud excogitare puer ille nequissimus quam ut me quoquo modo perditum iret, idque iurans etiam non nunquam comminabatur.

³Et plane fuit, quod eius detestabilem malitiam ad peiores conatus stimularet; nam quadam die nimia eius insolentia expugnata patientia mea calces in eum ualidas extuleram. Denique tale facinus in me comminiscitur. ⁴Stuppae sarcina me satis onustum pro*b*eque funiculis constrictum producit in uiam deque proxima uillula spirantem car*b*unculum furatus oneris in ipso meditullio

reponit. ⁵Iamque fomento tenui calescens et enutritus ignis surgebat in flammas et totum me funestus ardor inuaserat, nec ullum pestis extremae suffugium nec salutis aliquod apparet solacium et ustrina talis moras non sustinens et meliora consilia praeuertitur.

20 ¹Sed in rebus scaeuis adfulsit Fortunae nutus hilarior nescio an futuris periculis me reseruans, certe praesente statutaque morte liberans. ²Nam forte pluuiae pridianae recens conceptaculum aquae lutulentae proximum conspicatus ibi memet inprouido saltu totum abicio flammaque prorsus extincta tandem et pondere leuatus et exitio liberatus euado. ³Sed ille deterrimus ac temerarius puer hoc quoque suum nequissimum factum in me retorsit gregariisque omnibus adfirmauit me sponte uicinorum foculos transeuntem titubanti gradu prolapsum ignem ultroneum accersisse mihi, et arridens addidit: 'Quo usque ergo frustra pascemus inigninum istum?'

⁴Nec multis interiectis diebus longe peio⟨*rib*⟩us me dolis petiuit. Ligno enim, quod gerebam, in proximam casulam uendito uacuum me ducens iam se nequitiae meae proclamans imparem miserrimumque istud magisterium rennuens querelas huius modi concinnat:

21 ¹'Videtis istum pigrum tardissimumque et nimis asinum? Me prae⟨*ter*⟩ cetera flagitia nunc nouis periculis etiam

H. 170 angit. ²Ut que*m*que enim uiatorem prospexerit, siue illa scitula mulier seu uirgo nubilis seu tener puellus es*t*, ilico disturbato gestamine, non nunquam etiam ipsis stramentis abiectis, furens incurrit et homines amator talis appetit et humi prostratis illis inhians illicitas atque incognitas temptat libidines et ferinas uoluptates auersa Venere inuitat ad nuptias. ³Nam imaginem etiam sa*ui*i mentiendo ore improbo compulsat ac morsicat. Quae res nobis non mediocris lites atque iurgia, immo forsitan et crimina pariet. ⁴Nunc etiam uisa quadam honesta iuuene, ligno quod deuehebat abiecto dispersoque, in eam furiosos direxit impetus et festiuus hic amasio humo sordida prostratam mulierem ibidem incoram omnium gestiebat inscendere. ⁵Quod nisi ploratu questuque femineo conclamatum uiatorum praesidium accurrisset ac de mediis ungulis ipsius esset erepta liberataque, misera illa compauita atque dirupta ipsa quidem cruciabilem cladem sustinuisset, nobis uero poenale reliquisset exitium.'

22 ¹Talibus mendaciis admiscendo sermones alios, qui meum uerecundum silentium uehementius premerent, animos pastorum in meam perniciem atrociter suscitauit. ²Denique unus ex illis: 'Quin igitur publicum istum maritum', inquit, 'immo communem omnium adulterum illis suis monstruosis nuptiis condignam uictimamus hostiam'; ³et 'Heus tu, puer', ait, 'obtruncato

H. 171 protinus eo intestina quidem canibus nostris iacta, ceteram uero carnem omnem operariorum cenae reserua. Nam corium adfirmatum cineris inspersu dominis referemus eiusque mortem de lupo facile mentiemur.' ⁴Sublata cunctatione accusator ille meus noxius, ipse etiam pastoralis exsecutor sententiae, laetus et meis insultans malis calcisque illius admonitus, quam inefficacem fuisse mehercules doleo, protinus gladium cotis adtritu parabat.

23 ¹Sed quidam de coetu illo rusticorum: 'Nefas', ait, 'tam bellum asinum sic enecare et propter luxuriem lasciuiamque amatoriam criminatos opera seruitioque tam necessario carere, ²cum alioquin exsectis genitalibus possit neque in uenerem nullo modo surgere uosque omni *me*tu periculi liberare, insuper etiam longe crassior atque corpulentior effici. ³Multos ego scio non modo asinos inertes, uerum etiam ferocissimos equos nimio libidinis laborantes atque ob id truces uesanosque adhibita tali detestatione mansuetos ac mansues exinde factos et [h]oneri ferundo non inhabiles et cetero ministerio patientes. ⁴Denique nisi uobis suadeo nolentibus, possum spatio modico interiecto, quo mercatum proxumum obire statui, petitis e domo ferramentis huic curae praeparatis ad uos actutum redire trucemque amatorem istum atque insuauem dissitis femoribus emasculare et quouis uer*ue*ce mitiorem efficere.'

24 ¹Tali sententia mediis Orci manibus extrac*tus*, set extremae poenae reseruatus maerebam et in nouissima parte corporis totum me periturum deflebam. ²Inedia denique continua uel praecipiti ruina memet ipse quaerebam extinguere moriturus quidem nihilo minus, sed moriturus integer. ³Dumque in ista necis meae decunctor electione, matutino me rursum puer ille peremptor meus contra montis suetum ducit uestigium. ⁴Iamque me de cuiusdam uastissimae ilicis ramo pendulo destinato paululum uiam supergressus ipse securi lignum, quod deueheret, recidebat. Et ecce de proximo specu uastum attollens caput funesta proserpit ursa. ⁵Quam simul conspexi, pauidus et repentina facie conterritus totum corporis pondus in postremos poplites recello arduaque ceruice sublimiter eleuata lorum, quo tenebar, rumpo meque protinus pernici fugae committo perque prona non tantum pedibus, ⁶uerum etiam toto proiecto corpore propere deuolutus immitto me campis subpatentibus, e*x* summo studio fugiens immanem ursam ursaque peiorem illum puerum.

25 ¹Tunc quidam uiator solitarium uagumque me respiciens inuadit et properiter inscensum baculo, quod gerebat, obuerberans per obliquam ignaramque me ducebat uiam. ²Nec inuitus ego cursui me commodabam relinquens atrocissimam uirilitatis lanienam. Ceterum plagis non magnopere commouebar quippe consuetus ex forma concidi fustibus.

³Sed illa Fortuna meis casibus peruicax tam opportunum latibulum misera celeritate praeuersa nouas instruxit insidias. ⁴Pastores enim mei perditam sibi requirentes uacculam uariasque regiones peragrantes occurrunt nobis fortuito statimque me cognitum capistro prehensum attrahere gestiunt. ⁵Sed audacia ualida resistens ille fidem hominum deumque testabatur: 'Quid

me raptatis uiolenter? Quid inuaditis?'

⁶'Ain, te nos tractamus inciuiliter, qui nostrum asinum furatus abducis? Quin potius effaris, ubi puerum eiusdem agasonem, necatum scilicet, occultaris?'; ⁷et ilico detractus ad terram pugnisque pulsatus et calcibus contusus infit deierans nullum semet uidisse ductorem, sed plane continatum solutum et solitarium ob indiciuae praemium occupasse, domino tamen suo restituturum.

⁸'Atque utinam ipse asinus', inquit, 'quem numquam profecto uidissem, uocem quiret humanam dare meaeque testimonium innocentiae perhibere posset: profecto uos huius iniuriae pigeret.'

⁹Sic adseuerans nihil quicquam promouebat. Nam collo constrictum reducunt eum pastores molesti contra montis illius siluosa nemora, unde lignum puer solebat egerere. ¹Nec uspiam ruris aperitur ille, sed plane corpus eius membratim laceratum multisque dispersum locis conspicitur. ²Quam rem procul dubio sentiebam ego illius ursae dentibus esse perfectam et hercules dicerem quod sciebam, si loquendi copia suppeditaret. Sed quod solum poteram, tacitus licet serae uindictae gratulabar. ³Et cadauer quidem disiectis partibus tandem totum repertum aegreque concinnatum ibidem terrae dedere, meum uero Bellerofontem, abactorem indubitatum cruentumque percussorem criminantes, ad casas interim suas uinctum perducunt, quoad renascenti die sequenti deductus ad magistratus, ut aiebant, poenae redderetur.

Interim, dum puerum illum parentes sui plangoribus fletibusque querebantur, et adueniens ecce rusticus nequaquam promissum suum frustratus destinatam sectionem meam flagitat. ⁵'Non est' in his inquit unus, 'indidem praesens iactura nostra, sed plane crastino libet non tantum naturam, uerum etiam caput quoque ipsum pessimo isto asino demere. Nec tibi ministerium deerit istorum.'

¹Sic effectum est, ut in alterum diem clades differretur mea. At ego gratias agebam bono puero, quod saltem mortuus unam carnificinae meae dieculam donasset. ²Nec tamen tantillum saltem gratulationi meae quietiue spatium datum; nam mater pueri, mortem deplorans acerbam filii, fleta et lacrimosa fuscaque ueste contecta, ambabus manibus trahens cinerosam canitiem, heiulans et exinde proclamans stabulum inrumpit meum tunsisque ac diuerberatis uehementer uberibus incipit: ³'Et nunc iste securus incumbens praesepio uoracitati suae deseruit et insatiabilem profundumque uentrem semper esitando distendit nec aerumnae meae miserae uel detestabilem casum defuncti magistri recordatur; ⁴sed scilicet senectam infirmitatemque meam contemnit ac despicit et impune se laturum tantum scelus credit. At utcumque se praesumit innocentem; est enim congruens pessimis conatibus contra noxiam conscientiam sperare securitatem. ⁵Nam pro deum fidem, quadrupes nequissime, licet precariam uocis usu-

ram sumeres, cui tandem uel ineptissimo persuadere possis atrocitate⟨m⟩ istam culpa carere, cum propugnare pedibus et arcere morsibus misello puero potueris? ⁶An ipsum quidem saepius incursare calcibus potuisti, moriturum uero defendere alacritate simili nequisti? ⁷Certe dorso receptum auferres protinus et infesti latronis cruentis manibus eriperes, postremum deserto derelictoque illo conseruo magistro comite pastore non solus aufugeres. ⁸An ignoras eos etiam, qui morituris auxilium salutare denegarint, quod contra bonos mores id ipsum fecerint, solere puniri? ⁹Sed non diutius meis cladibus laetaberis, homicida. Senties, efficiam, misero dolori naturales uires adesse'; ¹et cum dicto subsertis manibus exsoluit suam sibi fasciam pedesque meos singillatim inligans indidem constringit artissime, scilicet ne quod uindictae meae superesset praesidium, ²et pertica, qua stabuli fores offirmari solebant, adrepta non prius me desiit obtundere, quam uictis fessisque uiribus suopte pondere degrauatus manibus eius fustis esset elapsus. ³Tunc de brachiorum suorum cita fatigatione conquesta procurrit ad focum ardentemque titionem gerens mediis inguinibus obtrudit usque, donec solo, quod restabat, nisus praesidio liquida fimo strictim egesta faciem atque oculos eius confoedassem. ⁴Qua caecitate atque faetore tandem fugata est a me pernicies: ceterum titione delirantis Althaeae Meleager asinus interisset.

CHAPTER XXV

The tale is over and the ass's troubles resume.

147, 3-4 Sic captiuae puellae delira et temulenta illa narrabat anicula: "Such was the story told the captive girl by that raving and drunken old woman".
The interpretation of this phrase is closely linked with the interpretation of the story of Amor and Psyche and its function in the *Met*. There are two main questions: (a) has *captiuae* overtones beyond the reminder that the girl is the robbers' captive and (b) does the characterization *delira et temulenta* have a bearing on the story as well as on the storyteller?
As to (a), the emphatic position of *captiuae* suggests that it is more than descriptive, i.e. that it depicts the girl as held captive by the story (for non-corporal captivity see Ov. *Am*. 1, 2, 30 *et noua captiua uincula mente feram*; Macr. *Sat*. 3, 16, 11 *Quid stupemus captiuam illius saeculi gulam seruisse mari*). As to (b), at first sight both *delirus* and *temulentus* seem to distract from the value of the story: if a silly old drunk is telling a story, it cannot be worth much. Walsh 1970, 190 says mildly that Apuleius 'rather incongruously (allots) its telling to the aged crone deputed to the task of bandits' housekeeper'. See also Sandy in *AAGA* 1978, 128 f.; vThiel 1, 1971, 19 n. 54. But at 1, 10 (9, 18) a witch reveals a secret while drunk (cf. Scobie 1975, 102 *ad loc*.) and at 8, 25 (196, 24) a *praeco* is called *delirus* (among other scarcely flattering words), but the reader realizes that the *praeco* – if only he knew it – has just revealed an important truth about the ass he is selling (196, 18 f.: *sed prorsus ut in asini corio modestum hominem inhabitare credas*). It is not impossible, then, that we are faced here with a double meaning typical of Apulein irony: on one level a characterization of the *anus* (see Junghanns 1932, 66 and n. 97) whose function it is to comfort the girl (Junghanns 1932, 160), on the other level a veiled hint that the tale has a deeper meaning.

captiuae puellae: the girl will be named (Charite) at 163, 10. On the delay in naming her see Blanche Brotherton 1934, 36-62; Hijmans in *AAGA* 178, 111 f.

delira: the adj. is used in a context of literary productivity e.g. Hor. *Ep*. 2, 2, 126 f. *praetulerim scriptor delirus inersque uideri e.q.s.*; or myth: Cic. *Tusc*. 1, 48; *Div*. 2, 141.

temulenta: the word is originally used of women only, see Shipp on Ter. *An*. 229. There is an old literary link between wine, truth and song; this link is hinted at by Vergil in *Ecl*. 6, 15 ff. (*Silenum*) *inflatum hesterno uenas, ut semper, Iaccho*, who is the god who sings, 31 f. *uti magnum per inane coacta/semina terrarumque animaeque marisque fuissent/et liquidi simul ignis e.q.s.* Ps. Verg. *Cat*. 9, 59-60 links Bachus and song, cf. Tib. 1, 7, 37; Ov. *Met*. 7, 432; Prop. 4, 6, 76; wine and truth are linked in a variety of proverbial expressions and Plin. *Nat*. 14, 141 is able to state *uolgoque ueritas iam attributa uino est*. Among the *uolgus* we may quote Horace *S*. 1, 4, 89 *condita cum uerax aperit praecordia Liber*; also *Epod*. 11,

13-14; *Carm.* 3, 21, 13-20; *Ep.* 1, 5, 16 f.; Nisbet & Hubbard on *Carm.* 1, 18, 16; see also Wimmel 1960, 225. Several of the above references as well as a number of Greek ones (e.g. Athen. 37 e-f) are collected by Otto 1890, 372; Gow on Theocr. 29, 1 supplies additional material; see also Bury on Plato *Symp.* 217e; Boyancé 1951, 5. Dodds 1960, xiii notes that he who drinks wine becomes ἔνθεος; for this notion see e.g. Rohde 1907, II 20 and n. 1. At Eur. *Bacch* 298 ff. this results in λέγειν τὸ μέλλον (301); see Dodds *ad loc.* and his ref. to Plut. *def. orac.* 432E. The connections between Dionysus and the Muses and Dionysus and Apollo, as well as Dionysus' function as a god of poets and poetry, are discussed in some detail by Kroll 1924 (= ²1964), 30 f. and Kambylis 1965, 166 f.

Closely related (but not entirely the same) is the oxymoron *sobria ebrietas*; see especially Lewy 1929; Dresden 1972, 20 (= 164).

anicula: Callebat 1968, 372 collects the passages in which this word occurs and comments: 'l'emploi du diminutif est gentiment ironique – campant une silhouette en même temps que suggérant un charactère à la fois madré et radoteur'. Cf. 4, 24 (93, 9); 4, 25 (94, 4); 149, 19; 152, 17. In the last-mentioned passage irony is less obvious than a certain tenderness or pity.

sed astans ego non procul dolebam mehercules, quod pugillares et stilum non habebam, qui tam bel‹l›am fabellam praenotarem: 'But, standing not ar away, Iet sad indeed that I had no notebook and pen to take down so fine a story". 147, 4-6

sed... praenotarem: vdVliet proposes *sed ‹dum›... praenotarem, ecce...*; Callebat 1968, 89 has collected 10 out of 19 passages in which *ecce* takes initial position (add to his list: 2, 4 (27, 7); 2, 26 (46, 10); 3, 11 (60, 1); 6, 25 (147, 6); 8, 17 (190, 24); 10, 12 (245, 15); 10, 34 (265, 7); 11, 8 (272, 4); 11, 26 (288, 1)). Though *ecce* in second or third position is more frequent, its usage in first position cannot be called infrequent!

sed astans ego non procul: at 4, 7 (79, 13 f.) the ass had been tied to the entrance of the robbers' cave, at 4, 23 (92, 12 f.) he seems to be free in his movements. In the present passage the important point is that he is able to hear what is being said. See vdPaardt in *AAGA* 1978, 78, who reacts to Helm's scepticism (Helm-Krenkel 1970, 25).

dolebam mehercules: the same expression but in the more forceful present tense at 171, 7 *calcisque... quam inefficacem fuisse mehercules doleo*. For *mehercules* see *GCA* 1977, 175 f.

quod pugillares et stilum non habebam: how an ass would have handled the writing materials is not discussed: the author, as often, is amusing himself (and his readers) at his narrator's expense.

pugillares: the word occurs only here in the *Met.* See e.g. Martial 14, 3 ff. with Friedländer *ad loc.*, Plin. *Nat.* 13, 69 with Ernout *ad loc.* and Plin. *Ep.* 1, 6, 1 with Sherwin-White *ad loc.* For the use of wax tablets see e.g. Foerster 1963, 39 f. (he omits *pugillares* from his list of Latin terms on p. 41).

quod... habebam: is this a noun-clause or an adverbial clause? Callebat 1968, 340 mentions only *quod* + subjunctive after a *verbum sentiendi*, but see 3, 7 (57, 15 f.) *contentus, quod... perhibuit* (and vdPaardt 1971, 68 *ad loc.*) and 9, 15 (214, 17) *unico solacio... recreabar, quod... sentiebam.* See LHSZ 2, 576 f.

qui tam bellam fabellam praenotarem: Callebat 1968, 493 notes several parallels for *qui* as an instrumental ablative, but does not discuss the question whether *qui* here may be taken as a nominative. Indeed, the text appears to offer no indication that a (plural) ablative, not the more common nominative, is intended as it does in Helm's parallels 6, 7 (133, 11) *qui possit agnosci; Apol.* 17 (21, 11) *parum uisum qui uteretur*; but cf. e.g. Cic. *Fam.* 4, 13, 3 qui *antea... opitulari poteram, nunc... ne benigne quidem polliceri possum; Fam.* 5, 1, 2; Ter. *Hau.* 565 *facis adeo indigne iniuriam illi, qui non abstineas manum; ibid.* 1011; Cic. *Fam,* 5, 2, 9; 5, 12, 2. Further examples KSt 2. 2. 286.

bellam fabellam: $\overset{bel}{uela}fabellam$ F; $\overset{b}{uellam}$ φ. There is no doubt about the correction: the interchange of *u* and *b* is quite frequent (cf. 77, 23; 197, 25; 207, 25) and single instead of double consonants are not uncommon; the only surprising aspect is that so common a word should have been corrupted. *Bellus* occurs quite regularly as a qualification of a literary product (*ThLL* notes ca. 25 instances). Callebat 1968, 379 thinks the usage here 'précieux' as against the slight irony at 4, 5 (77, 23); 171, 10 and 8, 26 (197, 25); cf. 9, 7 (207, 25). It is hard to say whether *bellus* was chosen in order to avoid *pulcher*, which may have had a technical connotation (καλόν vs. ἡδύ), cf. C. O. Brink on Horace *Ars* 99; see also Kiessling-Heinze on *S.* 1, 10, 6; *Ep.* 2, 1, 72. Doubtless the opportunity for a pun also affected the choice of adjective (cf. Quint. *Inst.* 9, 3, 66 ff.; Lausberg 1960 par. 637–639).

fabellam: Junghanns 1932, 122 n. 5 (cf. Tatum 1969, 3) notes that all tales in the *Met.* are marked by a formulaic indication. *Fabula* is the word used at 1, 1 (2, 3) (for its range of meaning see Scobie 1975 *ad loc.*); there it applies to the *Met.* as a whole, at 2, 20 (42, 2) e.g. to Thelyphron's tale. *Fabella* occurs in Apuleius only here; it is connected with an *anus* also in Hor. *S.* 2, 6, 78; Tib. 1, 3, 85 (see Kirby Flower Smith and Putnam *ad loc.*); for the usual opinion concerning *aniles fabellae* Smith refers to Quint. *Inst.* 1, 8, 19; 1, 9, 2; Tac. *Dial.* 29 (Gudeman *ad loc.* cites Plato's dislike of the τιτθῶν μῦθοι *Rep.* 377 c–d). Apuleius may be making a playful allusion to a Horatian combination of a Latin and a Greek proverb (*surdo narrare fabulam*, e.g. Ter. *Hau.* 222, and ὄνῳ τις ἔλεγε μῦθον, ὁ δὲ τὰ ὦτα ἐκίνει, Zenob. 5, 42) at *Ep.* 2, 1, 199 f. *scriptores autem narrare putaret asello/fabellam surdo*; see Otto 1890, 335.

praenotarem: cf. 2, 24 (44, 20) and de Jonge *ad loc.*: the compound hardly differs from the simple verb. See also Callebat 1968, 139. In later Latin *prae-* and *per-* were sometimes interchangable (Svennung 1935, 379; LHSz 2, 241; 269: *praerumpere = perrumpere*), but it is not very likely that this was the case as early as Apuleius.

It is hard to cull an indication as to the value or importance of the tale of Amor and Psyche from the ass's reaction[1], but perhaps a noteworthy element of narrative economy may be found in the fact that the ass, as always putting himself forward, notes his own but omits to enlighten us concerning the girl's reaction.

---

[1] See, however, the detailed discussion in Heine 1962, 223–227.

Ecce confecto nescio quo graui proelio latrones adueniunt onusti, 147, 6-10
non nulli tamen, immo promptiores uulnerati‹s› domi relictis et
plagas recurantibus ipsi ad reliquas occultatas in quadam spelunca
sarcinas, ut aiebant, proficisci gestiunt: "Lo and behold, after some
heavy engagement the robbers arrived laden down; but some of them, indeed the
more eager ones, were keen to leave the casualties at home tending their wounds
and – so they said – go off themselves after the rest of the loot, which was hidden
in a cave."

Ecce: according to Robertson and Giarratano-Frassinetti. F has the first *E in rasura*. Helm reads *Ec in rasura*; Castiglioni 1931, 486 implies that F offers enough space for and originally read *Et ecce*: the microfilm leaves us in doubt. If he is right there is no reason to omit *Et* from our text. In itself, however, *et ecce* cannot be regarded as preferable to *ecce*: see Callebat 1968, 89 and 422 f.
For the narrative value of *ecce*, which again and again introduces a sudden change in the situation, see Heine 1962, 172 f., vThiel 1971, 20 n. 56, 21 n. 59. Both authors note that with *ecce* the narrator directly addresses the audience.

confecto ... proelio: see Sal. *Cat.* 61, 1 and Vretska. *ad loc.*; for the military terminology *GCA* 1977, 208 f.

nescio quo: two aspects may be noted; the *proelium* is unimportant from the narrator's point of view and only the results are relevant; the limits of that point of view are underlined both by *nescio quo* and by the fact that only the visible results (*graui*) are mentioned. This indicates that the deviation from the Vorlage is hardly as primitive a procedure as has been thought. Junghanns 1932, 60 n. 103, Lesky 1966, 556, vThiel 1971, 109 f. appear to see Apuleius' more complicated telling of an originally simpler structure as a deterioration, but in view of the major themes in Apuleius' novel the added complication may well be regarded rather as an improvement: both the ass's *curiositas* and his *fortuna* are thus developed in greater detail.

latrones adueniunt onusti: *onusti* may be functional in accounting for an absence long enough for the telling of the 'long' story of Amor and Psyche; see however vdPaardt in *AAGA* 1978, 84 f. on the relationship between narrative and narrated time in the *Met*.

Schlam 1968, a, 44 mistakenly implies that these are other robbers than those who captured Charite.

uulneratis domi relictis: the final *s* of *uulneratis* was added by a second hand. Without that *s* solutions such as Gruter's ‹iis› or Bursian's ‹his› become necessary. With the *s* the need and the precise sense of *ipsi* becomes part of the discussion. Bursian 1881, 132 remarks that the fact that some of the returning *latrones* were wounded is a "dem 'adueniunt onusti' gleichstehendes Moment der Erzählung", hence he prefers *uulnerati*; *ipsi* simply picks up *latrones*. Robertson remarks that Giarratano's *quibus* would be followed by *ceteri* rather than *ipsi*, a remark quoted with approval by Frassinetti. There appears to be no need for more than the simple correction in F: *uulnerati‹s›*. So all modern editors, including Helm in his *Addenda*.

Junghanns 1932, 70 notes that the casualties are added by Apuleius in order to give the second robber at 147, 21 f. a chance to develop the theme of the ass as an οἰωνὸς οὐκ ἀγαθός.

recurantibus: cf. 8, 18 (192, 21) *corporaque sua diuerse laniata... recurare*. The word is fairly rare and Kroll on Catul. 44, 15 thinks it may be 'volkstümlich' Médan 1925, 179 thinks it belongs to the 'langue archaïque'. It occurs e.g. in Stat. *Theb.* 3, 583 (see Snijder *ad loc.*), Aug. *c. Faust.* 19, 7, Isid. *Or.* 19, 22, 23.

ipsi ad reliquas occultatas in quadam spelunca sarcinas: the colon consists almost entirely of long syllables. See Quint. *Inst.* 9, 4, 83 who notes that a high frequency of long syllables gives an impression of stability, whereas frequent shorts create an impression of speed and mobility. See also Hijmans in *AAGA* 1978, 198 f.

quadam: see Graur 1969, 379 f., *GCA* 1977, 38.

ut aiebant: the narrator's limited perspective is maintained with some care if the robbers had not mentioned their destination the ass could not have known about it. (F's original *agebant* has been corrected by a second hand.)

proficisci gestiunt: on the robbers' continual hurry see Junghanns 1932, 65.

gestiunt: the robbers are itching to go; cf. vdPaardt 1971, 107 and *GCA* 1977, 37.

147, 10-12 Prandioque raptim tuburcinato me et equum meum uectores rerum illarum futuros fustibus exinde tundentes producunt in uiam: "And having hurriedly wolfed down their breakfast, they set me and my horse on the road – to be the carriers of that loot – beating us with cudgels all the while".

Prandioque raptim tuburcinato: Non. 179, 21 (= 263, 18 Lindsay) says: *tuburcinari significat raptim manducare* and quotes Titin. (*Com.* 83), Turp. (*Com.* 2) as well as Pl. *Per.* 122. See Flobert 1975, 89 (whose translation "s'empiffrer" does not seem right for our passage). If Non. is right in his definition of the meaning, we have a redundancy comparable to *prioribus inchoatis* 4, 15 (86, 18–19), cf. *GCA* 1977, 124.

me et equum meum: Apuleius seems to have kept the horse carefully in view, cf. 3, 26 (71, 22); 3, 28 (73, 4); 4, 8 (80, 21), without insisting on his presence, wherever possible: in the next chapter, when the robbers set out without Lucius, there is no mention of the horse (except for a possible remnant in *nostrae*, cf. *Onos* 23, 2 καὶ ἀπήδεσαν τὸν ἵππον ἄγοντες). Concerning the horse's possible symbolic function see comm. on 155, 9 and 156, 17, also Gwyn Griffiths on 11, 20 (282, 6 f.), where the horse is restored to Lucius.

uectores rerum illarum futuros: cf. *Onos* 22 6 καὶ ὅσα ἦν τιμιώτατα ἐξελόντες τῷ ἵππῳ κἀμοὶ ἐπέθηκαν. On the future see Bernhard 1927, 45 and comm. on 154, 17–18 below.

fustibus exinde tundentes: cf. *Onos* 22, 5 ἔνθεν ἐπαιόμην τῷ ξύλῳ. The precise sense of *exinde* ("continually") is discussed by Wiman 1927, 57, who compares the present passage with 175, 3–4 *heiulans et exinde proclamans*. Cf. *ThLL s.v.* 1509, 16 (*incessanter, continuo*).

producunt in uiam: cf. 169, 1 *producit in uiam*. Médan 1925, 241 translates "mettre en route" and speaks of an 'expression nouvelle'. The expression *producere in conspectum* occurs in Liv. 27, 17, 16. For a comparable use see *Met.* 1, 23 (21, 21 f.) *hospitem meum produc ad proximas balneas*; cf. Ter. *Ad.* 560 f.; V. Fl. 5, 382 (381).

multisque cliuis et anfractibus fatigatos prope ipsam uesperam per- 147, 12-14
ducunt ad quampiam speluncam,: "and brought us, tired out from the
many hills and turns in the road, towards the very end of day to some cave".

multisque cluis et anfractibus fatigatos: the difficulty of the journey (far more
elaborately described in Apuleius than in the *Onos*) is part of the motivation for
the stumbling described below. For *anfractus* see also vdPaardt 1971, 86.

prope ipsam uesperam: *prope* is rarely used in a temporal sense, cf. e.g. *Bell. Afr.*
42, 1 *cum iam prope solis occasum Caesar expectauisset...*; Suet. *Cl.* 44; LHSz 2,
245. (Médan 1925, 207 mistakenly lists this passage under 'adverbes'.) For the
difficulties concerning the time element see Junghanns 1932, 69 and above,
Introduction p. 2 f.

perducunt: note the paronomasia with *producunt* above (147, 12) and *reducunt*
below (147, 16).

ad quampiam speluncam: for the archaic quality of *quampiam* see LHSz 2, 196;
cf. *Met.* 4, 3 (76, 14). The word is somewhat surprising here, since the *spelunca*
has just been mentioned (147, 9: *in quadam spelunca*), but possibly it is used here
is to produce a euphonic series of *-am* endings.

unde multis onustos rebus rursum ne breuiculo quidem tempore 147, 14-18
refectos ociter reducunt tantaque trepidatione festinabant, ut me
plagis multis obtundentes propellentesque super lapidem propter
uiam positum deicerent: "from there they swiftly took us back again loaded
up with many things, not restored by even the briefest of rests; and they hurried
us with so much agitation, that in pounding me with repeated blows and in
pushing me forward they made me fall on a rock lying beside of the road".

multis onustos rebus: see above on 147, 7 *onusti*.

breuiculo: at *Met.* 1, 11 (10, 24) *grabatulus... breuiculus* the diminutive
restricts, here it enhances the brevity referred to with a kind of plaintive
emphasis. Cf. also Pl. *Merc.* 639; Fronto 146, 16 N (= 140, 9 vdH.); Callebat
1968, 510. On diminutives *GCA* 1977, 96; vdPaardt 1971, 100; Bernhard 1927,
135 f.; LHSz 1, 305 f.

ociter: a very clever and probably acceptable correction in ς for *obiter* F.
Wiman 1927, 48 tried *ob iter* with some older editions, comparing among other
passages 8, 15 (189, 4) *denique ob iter illud... iacere semesa corpora* and arguing
the contrasting variation *producunt in uiam* (12) X *ob iter reducunt* (15/16). For
ociter see Marg. Molt on 1, 23 (21, 21); *ThLL s.v. ocior* 416, 15. *Obiter* does not
occur elsewhere in the *Met. ThLL s.v.* 68, 24; '*fortasse dilatata notione temporali
(i. 'simul, eodem momento'), quae subest plerisque sub 1a allatis: a. referendum vid.
ad momentum continuo subsequens, i.q. statim sim.*: Ps. Quint. *Decl.* 10, 16 *qui
liberos suos sepeliunt flere contenti, ut obiter ab rogo siccis oculis reuertantur
(aliter* Burman *ad* 1.: 'similiter, ut ante')'. (Wieland). *ThLL s.v. ociter*, however,
notes 'obiter trad., vix recte, cf. Helm in app. crit.'; Landgraf 1896, 400 adds Keil,
Gramm. Lat. VII 181, 6: *obiter* κατὰ ταὐτόν.

tantaque trepidatione festinabant: see vdPaardt 1971, 177 on *trepidatio* in the
sense of nervousness.

me plagis multis obtundentes propellentesque: the litany of the ass returns again

29

and again, see *GCA* 1977, 38 f. on 4, 3 (76, 9) *me totum plagis obtundit*. The extended series of long syllables may illustrate the content.

ut ... super lapidem propter uiam positum deicerent: in comparison with the expression in *Onos* 22, 7 κρούω τὴν ὁπλὴν περὶ πέτραν ὀξεῖαν Apuleius has his narrator point an accusing finger. On the local sense of *super* with acc. see LHSz 281; our expression is somewhere between Sall. *J.* 58, 6 *quom alii super uallum praecipitarentur* ("over") and Phaedr. 2, 6, 11 *ut scopulum super / altis ab astris duram inlidat corticem* ("on top of"). It is also possible to take *propellentesque super lapidem propter uiam positum* together as the cause of the fall. Which of the two possibilities was in the author's mind when writing is anyone's guess.

147, 18-20   Unde crebris aeque ingestis ictibus crure dextero et ungula sinistra me debilitatum aegre ad exurgendum compellunt: "Once again they rained blows on me, but they had a hard time forcing me to get up from there, lamed as I was in a right leg and a left hoof".

Unde: the local rather than causal sense seems preferable, but there is a certain vagueness in the expression.

aeque: "just as before": the word occurs in the *Met.* only here and at 5, 26 (123, 23) apart from some restorations: 5, 6 (107, 28 certain), 5, 9 (109, 24 doubtful), 158, 12 (doubtful).

ingestis ictibus: Médan 1925, 181 speaks of "langue familière", but there are closer parallels which he should have cited rather than Ter. *Ph.* 988 *pugnos in uentrem ingere*. Thus Luc. 8, 645 *properas atque ingeris ictus / qua uotum est uicto*. Cf. Curt. 6, 11, 16 *uerbera*, Tac. *Hist.* 3, 85 *uulnera* (see Heubner *ad loc.*), Sen. *Med.* 461 *dira supplicia*. See also *Met.* 9, 11 (211, 20) *plagas* (cf. Paul. Fest. 103 L.).

crure dextero et ungula sinistra: amplification rather than further precision seems to be Apuleius' aim here (cf. *Onos* 22, 7 ὁπλή). The motif of the lamed ass is discussed below on 152, 6.

debilitatum: the verb occurs once more in the *Met.* at 4, 33 (101, 2) in a less physical sense.

compellunt: note the paronomasia with *propellentes* (147, 17) above.

CHAPTER XXVI

The ass decides not to wait for his destined fate.

Et unus: 'Quo usque', inquit, 'ruptum istum asellum, nunc etiam 147, 20-22 claudum, frustra pascemus?': "And one of them said 'How long are we going to waste our time feeding that broken down little ass, especially now he's lame as well?'"

On the liveliness produced by having three robbers discuss Lucius' fate (in the *Onos* 'the robbers' speak) see Junghanns 1932, 70. The conversation, as (afterwards) reported by the intended victim, is clearly worded as a speech for the prosecution (*quousque... pascemus?*). See also 3, 27 (72, 12) and vdPaardt 1971, 194 *ad loc.*, who refers to Gatscha 1898, 154 and Sal. *Cat.* 20, 9. Vretska *ad loc.* questions whether this is parody, but deliberate parody is very likely since the expression occurs three times in the *Met.*: see also below on 169, 18.

ruptum: on *rupta animalia* see Veget. *Mul.* 1, 11, 12 and 4, 1, 9: *nimiam... lassitudinem sequitur aegritudo et omne animal est debile, si rumpitur*; cf. *Dig.* 19, 2, 30, 2 ... *cum maiore onere conductor (mulas) rupisset*.

nunc etiam claudum: on the motif of the lame ass see comm. on 152, 5-7. There may be a suggestion in 6, 18 (142, 1 f.) that the encounter with a lame ass is unlucky, since Psyche is to pass by without speaking. Plin. *Nat.* 8, 183 indicates that lame animals are unfit as sacrificial animals, cf. Hieron. *Ep.* 107, 6. (See Stemplinger 1948, 65 on encounters with cripples in general.)

Et alius: 'Quid quod et pessumo pede domum nostram accessit nec 147, 22-24 quicquam idonei lucri exinde cepimus, sed uulnera et fortissimorum occisiones': "And another 'What about the fact that his arrival at our house has brought terribly bad luck; since he turned up we've had no decent profit – only wounds and the death of our bravest men'."

The second robber elaborates the unlucky aspect of the ass which may have been announced in *claudum*.

pessumo pede domum nostram accessit: in the *Onos* 22, 8 the ass *is* the bad omen: ῥίψωμεν αὐτὸν ἀπὸ τοῦ κρημνοῦ οἰωνὸν οὐκ ἀγαθόν. Throwing him over the edge will serve as a καθαρισμὸς τοῦ στρατοῦ. Cf. Ar. *Aves* 719 f. where ὄνος ὄρνις is mentioned among several other ὄρνιθες; see also Haupt *Opusc.* II 253 f. who quotes (among others) Walther v. d. Vogelweide. Apuleius has chosen an expression denoting a fairly common type of *omen* to replace the Greek idiom, but the expression is his own. Cf. 1, 5 (5, 9) *sinistro pede*.

There appears to be a combination of associations: Aug. *Ep.* 17, 2 (41 Goldb.) speaks of a *boni pedis homo*, the *pedis offensio* is well known as a bad *omen* (Cic. *Diu.* 2, 84 and Pease *ad loc.*) and arrivals/departures are generally surrounded with all manner of ominous associations, as was (and is) the threshold. See further Appendix I.

domum nostram: see *GCA* 1977, 61 on *atria*: there it was the ass-describer who daringly used the word *atrium* for the robbers' abode; now it appears that the robbers also regard their cave as their home (cf. 148, 4) unlike their counterparts in the *Onos* who use στρατός (22, 8).

accessit: *ThLL s.v.* 255, 56 f. gives quite a few instances of *accedere* with acc., thus e.g. Verg. *A.* 5, 732 *infernas accede domos*; *ibid.* 813. See also *Met.* 1, 22 (20, 4) *ostium accedo*; 2, 3 (26, 17 f.) and de Jonge on 2, 2 (25, 20).

idonei: "sufficient"; cf. Cod. Theod. 12, 1, 74 pr. *idonea solius glebae substantia*. *ThLL s.v.* 231, 74 compares Firm. *Math.* 4, 12, 8 *idoneas decernit substantiae facultates*.

exinde: the temporal sense prevails, but there is a slight (?) admixture of the causal "for that reason". See Médan 1925, 148, Callebat 1968, 19 'dès lors'.

cepimus: cf. Cic. *Ver.* 3, 67 *accepto lucro* (the more usual expression is *lucrum facere* e.g. Pl. *Per.* 503).

uulnera: see above on 147, 8.

fortissimorum: Lamachus, Alcimus, Thrasyleon.

occisiones: in Apuleius only here; Médan 1925, 198 ('rare mais classique'); e.g. *Rhet. Her.* 4, 31; Cic. *Inv.* 1, 37; 2, 14 etc. *ThLL* shows that the word is used with increasing frequency in Christian literature.

147, 24-148, 2 Alius iterum: 'Certe ego, cum primum sarcinas istas quanquam inuitus pertulerit, protinus eum uulturiis gratissimum pabulum futurum praecipitabo': "Yet another one: 'I tell you, as soon as he has brought that baggage home, however unwillingly, I am going to throw him straight away into the ravine to be most welcome food for the vultures'."

Once again immediate death is averted: the last of the three critics admits that the ass still has a function.

quanquam inuitus: just as Lucius knows exactly what the other ass is thinking (4, 5) the robber knows Lucius' feelings; see *GCA* 1977, 50. The speaker (whoever he is) interprets from his own point of view.

uulturiis ... pabulum: cf. Pl. *Rud.* 770 *teque ambustulatum obiciam magnis auibus pabulum*; Flor. *Epit.* 2, 17, 7 *adsuetae cadauerum pabulo uolucres castra ... circumuolabant*. (In Verg. *A.* 12, 475 *pabulum* is gathered by a *hirundo*.)

praecipitabo: in 4, 5 the other ass is thrown into a ravine. Here Apuleius has not yet mentioned a ravine (cf. *Onos* 22, 8 ἀπὸ τοῦ κρημνοῦ).

It is clear that the conversation is a sample, and interesting that the narrator should say so in the next sentence; cf. 4, 24 (93, 4) *his et his similibus blateratis*.

148, 3-4 Dum secum mitissimi homines altercant de mea nece, iam et domum perueneramus: "While these gentlest of men quarrelled about my death, we had actually reached home".

secum mitissimi F; *secum immitissimi* ς; *sic immitissimi* Cornelissen; ‹sic› *secum mitissimi* Novák. There is no need for the conjectures. The narrator's irony (still bitter when he is telling his tale) is obvious in *mitissimi*. For the slight distinction between *secum* and *inter se* see LHSz 2, 177, KSt 2, 1, 508.

altercant: for the active form (in Pacuv., Ter., and Apul. only) see Flobert 1975, 291; see also 2, 29 (49, 13) and de Jonge *ad loc*. Actually the phrases quoted from the conversation show climax rather than *altercatio*, which is a description rather of the discussion in chapters 31-32, when the death of the girl rather than of the ass is debated.

iam et domum perueneramus: much more curious than the fact that the robbers regard the cave as home is this designation in the mouth of the narrator, *iam et* connects and accumulates, cf. *ThLL s.v. 126, 69 f.*

Nam timor ungulas mihi alas fecerat: "For fear had made my hooves into 148, 4-5 wings".

The expression is doubtless built on Verg. *A*. 8, 224 *pedibus timor addidit alas*; see Westerbrink in *AAGA* 1978, 68 concerning the parody (*four* wings!). See also Sil. 16, 351 (on the horse Panchates) *sed tum sibi fecerat alas*. See also 16, 506; Man. 5, 160 *quo sidere* (sc. *Lepore*) *natis/uix alas natura negat*; Paul. Nol. *Carm*. 15, 333. The expression *spes addidit alas* in Val. Fl. 7, 546 is a conjecture by P. Wagner (1863); the text is by no means certain.

For the allusion to Pegasus see comm. on 152, 7-10. Here Junghanns' perceptive note (1932, 62 n. 91) concerning the technique of contrasting Lucius' asinine shape and human mind is relevant: 'Besonders seltsam wirken hierbei die Beispiele für Verkoppelung von Vorstellungen, die nicht zu einander passen'.

Tum quae ferebamus amoliti properiter nulla salutis nostrae cura ac 148, 5-9 ne meae quidem necis habita comitibus adscitis, qui uulnerati remanserant dudum, recurrunt re⟨s⟩ laturi taedio, ut aiebant, nostrae tarditatis: "Then having quickly unloaded what we were carrying, without attending to our welfare or even to my death, they rounded up their comrades who had earlier stayed behind because of their wounds and ran back: they would carry the stuff (themselves?), because they were sick, they said, of our slowness".

Translators agree on the order of events: the robbers hastily unload, forget all about the pack animals, take their wounded colleagues, run back. They also take both *nulla cura... habita* and *comitibus adscitis* with *recurrunt*; *nulla cura... habita* as a second qualifier of *amoliti* is less attractive.

tum quae: cumq; F. The correction is doubtless right. The text of the remainder of the period is rather less certain. The content however is reasonably clear: after the journey on which the ass is taken to get the remainder of the booty, a second journey is required. The now lame ass is no good for that journey, but the wounded robbers are. It is only now that we realize 147, 14-15 *multis... rebus* implied '*non omnibus*'.

amoliti properiter: for the deponent see Flobert 1975, 70. The verb has a connotation of heavy effort, see e.g. Liv. 5, 22, 3; 25, 36, 11, Tac. *Ann*. 1, 50, 3. The adverb is rare, but Apuleius seems to like it, see 1, 22 (21, 1) and Marg. Molt *ad loc*.; 5, 29 (126, 11) and Fernhout *ad loc*.; 172, 23; 10, 27 (258, 20). Neue-

Wagener 2, 733 provide further instances; cf. LHSz 1, 499 f. Marg. Molt at 1, 21 (19, 17) on *ampliter* says that adverbs in *-iter* instead of *-e* are *cotidiani sermonis* (cf. vdPaardt 1971, 119). Our instance does not help to prove that thesis; elsewhere it occurs in poetry only: Pacuvius and Accius in Nonius (227 L); Sept. Ser. 16 (Frgm. Poet. Rom. ed. Baehrens) and Aus. *Parent*. 27. See also Callebat 1968, 459.

nulla salutis nostrae cura . . . habita: refers to the 'fact' that the robbers forget to feed the pack animals, except at 4, 1 (74, 15 ff.) and 4, 22 (91, 12 ff.).

ac ne meae necis quidem: refers with beautiful irony to another omission of the thoughtless robbers. Concerning the self-centeredness of the narrator's attitude see comm. on 160, 21 *deque mea uectura*.

qui uulnerati remanserant dudum: Kronenberg's (1892, 16 n. 1) punctuation (after *dudum*) is entirely convincing; he is followed by Robertson and Frassinetti. (Earlier attempts to deal with the passage include the conjectures *actutum* Elmenhorst, Leo, Cornelissen; *indidem* Petschenig; *eodem* Damsté.) For the position of *dudum* cf. e.g. Pl. *Am*. 620; *Mer*. 900; Ter. *An*. 653; Amm. 21, 8, 1; 25, 5, 8.

relatori taedio F; *relaturi taedio* φ; *relaturi taedia* ς; *res laturi, taedio* Petschenig.

Oudendorp rather likes *relecturi taedia* (one ms reads *relectiori*), but he mentions several further solutions, among which *relato anui taedio; relicto me, taedio; prae altiore taedio*. Furthermore he quotes a *uir doctus* who proposed *(in margine) reliqua laturi*, which is the origin of vdVliet's *reliqua ipsi relaturi* and Helm's *reliqua ipsi laturi* which is printed by Robertson. The latter also tried *reliqua suis umeris laturi*; cf. *Onos* 23, 1 f.: ἀπήεσαν ὡς τὰ λοιπὰ τῶν σκευῶν ἀνασῶσαι. "τὸν δὲ ἄθλιον τοῦτον ὄνον",ἔφη τις αὐτῶν, "τί ἐπάγομεν ἄχρηστον ἐκ τῆς ὁπλῆς; τῶν δὲ σκευῶν ἃ μὲν ἡμεῖς οἴσομεν, ἃ δὲ καὶ ὁ ἵππος." Luetjohann proposed *reliquam praedam ipsi relaturi*, in which he is followed by Giarratano and Scazzoso.

F's reading cannot be forced to yield sense. The ancient correction *relaturi* may be right, but scholars are unanimous that it cannot stand by itself. An old attempt at solving the problem is the economical *taedia*, explained by Floridus as *reportaturi fastidia nostrae tarditatis*. Hildebrand objects and, indeed, it is hard to find a parallel for the sense "res quarum Tarditatem Nostram taeduerat". We prefer Petschenig's as a palaeographically sound solution, with a slight hesitation: *ipsi* is lacking. Two further possibilities deserve consideration: *relicturi taedia nostrae tarditatis* (Schoonhoven, with ic/a confusion) and *non laturi taedia, ut aiebant, nostrae tarditatis* (more or less collective *taedia* also in e.g. Ov. *Met*. 13, 213; *Pont*. 3, 7, 3. But *non* for *re-* is hazardous). The *Onos* too emphasizes the notion that the robbers are no longer willing to put up with a lame ass.

ut aiebant: once again the phrase serves to remind the reader of the narrator's point of view, cf. 147, 10. As at 156, 25 below, the expression is enclosed by the indirect quotation it refers to. The *Onos* is more precise with ἔφη τις.

nostrae tarditatis: the narrator includes the horse in the robbers' *taedium*, though previously no mention had been made of the horse's slowness. Thus Apuleius manages at once to put his narrator in a characteristically too central

Nec me tamen mediocris carpebat scrupulus contemplatione comminatae mihi mortis: "And yet a more than ordinary anxiety fretted me as I contemplated the death that threatened me". 148, 9-10

nec ... mediocris: it is not surprizing that litotes, characterized by Lausberg 1960, 304 as a periphrastic combination of emphasis and irony, should occur frequently in Apul. Strilciw 1925, 108 f. gives an incomplete list; in addition to the present example we have noted the following omissions in 6, 25-7, 28; 148, 13 *nec magno conatu res indiget*; 152, 4 *nec ... temperat*; 161, 12 *nec ... leui pretio*; 170, 8 *non mediocris lites*; 171, 19 *non inhabiles*; 172, 24 *nec inuitus*. See also vdPaardt 1971, 49.

tamen: the thought is something like "it was very nice that the robbers had left again, and yet ..."

carpebat scrupulus: cf. 182, 10 *luctu ac maerore carpebat animum. Carpere* is used in the sense of "vex" (*ThLL s.v.* 495, 12 f.) which is usually poetic (Médan 1925, 194), cf. e.g. Verg. *A.* 4, 2 *caeco carpitur igni* and Pease *ad loc.*; ibid. 32 *solane perpetua maerens carpere iuuenta.* The first prose instances under this heading (Sen. *Ira* 2, 29, 1; *Ep.* 26, 4 and 120, 18) show a close metaphor of the basic sense of taking a part from a whole (cf. *ThLL s.v.* 491, 54 f.). *Scrupulus* is originally a sharp little rock (see comm. on 153, 16-18). The combination shows that *scrupulus*, too, is used in a more abstract sense ("anxiety", "uneasiness"). At the same time the sounds *c* and *cr* appear to function as some kind of illustration.

On passive *comminatae* see Médan 1925, 11, cf. 10, 6 (241, 9); further instances in Flobert 1975, 363.

et ipse mecum: 'Quid stas, Luci, uel quid iam nouissimum expectas?: 148,10-11 "and I said to myself: 'Why are you standing here, Lucius? Why are you just waiting for the worst?'"

Sandy 1968, 137 deals with the soliloquy as a topos and notes that the hortatory soliloquy is specifically Apuleian, cf. e.g. Venus at 4, 30 and Psyche at 6, 5 (they differ slightly in that Venus gives vent to her indignation, whereas Psyche's speech is more strictly an exhortation), and Lucius himself at 2, 6. The first instance of a self-admonishing soliloquy in the strict sense is Eur. *Medea* 401–409, see Page *ad loc.*; Leo 1908, 18 and 94 ff., Schadewaldt 1926, 192. On monologue and soliloquy in comedy see Duckworth 1952, 103 f.; in Vergil, see Highet 1972, 228 ff. and *passim*. In prose Cato's address to his *animus* in Sen. *Prou.* 2, 10 is very close (cf. Hom. *Od.* 20, 18).

This particularised expression of the inside view of the character (see e.g. Hägg 1971, 112 and *passim*) functions at once within the immediate context (underscores a dramatic decision, see also Lämmert [5]1971, 71 f.) and, in the case of 2, 6 and our present passage, serves to increase the distance between the narrator and his object, i.e. himself-at-that time. Junghanns 1932, 27 n. 34 notes the retarding and thereby dramatizing function of the soliloquy.

nouissimum: either "your last moment" or "the worst"; cf. Vulg. *Prou.* 23, 18 *nouissimum* (= the end); Tac. *Ann.* 6, 50, 5 *Caesar... a summa spe nouissima expectabat*.

quid stas..., uel quid... expectas: an instance of rhyming cola, see Bernhard 1927, 224 f. Callebat 1968, 102 regards *stas* and *expectas* as deliberative indicatives, but the notion of deliberation seems singularly inappropriate to the impatient and urgent questions.

148, 12-13 Mors, et haec accerbissima, decreto latronum tibi comparata est: "Death, and a most cruel death at that, has been devised for you by the robbers' decree".

et haec acerbissima: the *praecipitatio* threatened above (148, 2) had been applied to Lucius' fellow ass at 4, 5 (78, 8) *etiam nunc spirantem praecipitant* (see *GCA* 1977, 52).

et haec: parallels for this explicative combination are found in ThLL *s.v. hic* 2725, 5 f., e.g. Cic. *N.D.* 1, 4 *sunt autem alii philosophi, et hi quidem magni..., qui*; Plin. *Ep.* 1, 14, 9 *Et sane de posteris et his pluribus cogitanti...* See KSt 2, 1, 619 Anm. 3 and comm. on 156, 2 below.

decreto latronum: a slight exaggeration (at 148, 2 only one of the robbers is speaking) seems natural in the rhetorical circumstances, but the habit of exaggerating adversity when it applies to himself is one of Lucius' main characteristics (though not his alone).

comparata est: the verb is frequently used for mental activities (here a mere plan); cf. Cic. *Catil.* 2, 1 (*pernicies*); 3, 21 (*interitum*); *Sul.* 33 (*exitum*).

148, 13-16 Nec magno conatu res indiget; uides istas rupinas proximas et praeacutas in his prominentes s[c]ilices, quae te penetrante‹s, ante›quam decideris, membratim dissipabunt: "Nor does the job need much effort; you see those clefts nearby and the sharp rocks sticking out of them. They will penetrate you before you reach bottom and tear you limb from limb".

Nec magno conatur res indiget: *res* refers to the ass's execution. The phrase recalls Seneca's argument that gaining one's freedom through suicide is easy (e.g. *Prou.* 6, 7-10). As an argument for trying to escape execution it is incongruous enough to be funny.

uides istas rupinas...: one element of the description of the robbers' haunt at 4, 6 (78, 24), *qua saxis asperrimis... cingitur*, is put to good use here, and again at 7, 13 (164, 10 f.).

uides: Bernard 1927, 11 notes that Apuleius likes to place the verb at the beginning in order to emphasize the direct link with the previous sentence and quotes a number of instances with *uidere*; add e.g. 2, 23 (44, 1).

rupinas: apart from the Glossaria (see below) the word occurs only in Apul. At 7, 13 (164, 10) it is restored by ς with great probability from F *rapinas: prouolutosque in proximas rupinas praecipites dedere*. At *Flor.* 11, 2 (16, 13) the sense "clefts" is rather awkward: *... qui herediolum sterile et agrum scruposum, meras rupinas et senticeta miseri colunt*; hence Stewech conjectured *spinas*. For the meaning see *CGL* 4, 165, 40a *rupinas abruptas montium*; cf. 5, 609, 52; 636, 48. Schlutter 1898, 192 casts doubt on these entries in the glossaries. See however Birt 1897, 78; LHSz 1, 328.

proximas... praeacutas... prominentes: note the alliteration, the sound of which seems to be singularly apt.

scilices F; the correction in φ is obvious. Unlike the earlier *scrupulus*, these stones are large and concrete.

penetrante quã F; *pene antequam* φ (2nd hand in mg.); *penetrantes antequam* Pricaeus. This brilliant solution was preceded by Colvius' *quae te penetrantes quaqua decideris*. Oudendorp prefers the marginal reading in φ, but Hildebrand is right in rejecting it, precisely because it is a marginal reading. He compares the description of the fate of Psyche's sister at 5, 27 (124, 18 ff.) *Nec tamen ad illum locum uel saltem mortua peruenire potuit. Nam per saxa cautium membris iactatis atque dissipatis et proinde, ut merebatur, laceratis uisceribus suis alitibus bestiisque obuium ferens pabulum interiit*. The ass has just heard the story...

membratim dissipabunt: the expression is as picturesque as the one just quoted; a similar picture occurs in Enn. *scen.* 117 f. *alia fluctus differt dissupat/uisceratim membra*, see Jocelyn *ad loc.*; cf. also e.g. Ov. *Tr.* 3, 9, 27 (dealing with Medea) *atque ita diuellit diuulsaque membra per agros / dissipat in multis inuenienda locis eqs.* (*ThLL s.v.* 1488, 12 f.). On Apuleius' penchant for adverbs in *-tim* see *CGA* 1977, 26 and 71.

Nam et illa ipsa praeclara magia tua uultum laboresque tibi tantum 148, 16-19 asini, uerum corium non asini crassum, sed hiru[n]dinis tenue membranul[l]um circumdedit: "For that very magic of yours, too, has for all its brilliance given you only the appearance and troubles of an ass, but has invested you not with an ass's thick hide, but the thin skin of a leech".

Nam et introduces the second part of the argument why the ass should escape such a fate. It strikes one as a very forced effort to underscore the previous sentence, especially if one remembers 3, 24 (70, 11) *cutis tenella duratur in corium*. Perry 1926, 241 n. 11 lists this as an instance of self-contradiction on the part of the author, though he admits that it might be a witticism. Vallette *ad loc.* disagrees and takes the leech's membrane metaphorically – the ass's hide will not protect Lucius any more than would a leech's membrane; Feldbrugge 1938, 57 says that the ass's sensitivity is underscored. The situation is bad enough to warrant a rather bitter rhetorical wit.

illa ipsa praeclara magia tua: the anger of 3, 26 (71, 8 ff.) – which was checked by self-interest – is replaced here by a certain scorn for his earlier interest in magic: there is no need to read *maga* with Helm *in app. crit.*

illa... tua: with the slightly redundant *ipsa* we have one of many instances of strong reinforcement in the *Met.*, see Callebat 1968, 279 f. Here the combination has a palpably ironic-pejorative flavour.

uultum... corium... membranulum: for Apuleius' employment of similar contrasts see Junghanns 1932, 62 n. 91; cf. above 148, 4-5 *ungulas-alas*.

F's *hirundinis* was corrected in ς; *hirudo* "leech", "sangsue" (Vallette) is also restored at *Apol.* 8 (9, 22); Plin. *Nat.* 8, 29 *Cruciatum in potu maximum sentiunt*

37

(sc. elephanti) hausta hirudine, quam sanguisugam uulgo coepisse appellari aduerto. This statement indicates that *hirudo* is a more literary word than *sanguisuga*, see Ernout's note on the Pliny passage just quoted.

VdVliet's *hominis* for *hirudinis* destroys the wit; Kronenberg's *harundinis* (cf. Plin. *Nat.* 16, 126 *cortex... quibusdam... membranaceus, ut uiti, harundini*) is very learned, but in comparison with *hirudinis* certainly the *lectio facilior*.

membranulum: for the form (side by side with the more common *membranula*, cf. *membranum/membrana*) see Isid. *orig.* 7, 6, 4C where C' exhibits much the same error as found in F: *membra nullam*.

148, 19-20 Quin igitur masculum tandem sumis animum tuaeque saluti, dum licet, consulis? "So why don't you finally pluck up your manly courage and do something to save yourself while you can?"

Here we come to the kernel of the soliloquy, the actual decision; so far the dangers have been described, presently the opportunities will be seen to outweigh the difficulties.

quin igitur gives a particular intensity to this central question of Lucius' soliloquy. See Callebat 1968, 92.

masculum... animum: cf. Psyche at 6, 5 (132, 8). *Physiogn,* 4 (7, 4) specifies: *masculinus animus est uehemens*, but *masculus* in our passage refers to courage rather than violence, cf. Pers. 5, 144 *calido sub pectore mascula bilis / intumuit* and Villeneuve *ad loc. (= uirilis)*.

At 6, 5 (132, 8-9) Psyche uses the same words, whereas at 159, 3-4 Plotina is characterized by the words *aerumnas adsiduas ingenio masculo sustinebat* and at 8, 11 (186, 6) Charite performs her action *masculis animis*. Our phrase is curious in so far as no doubt exists concerning Lucius' masculinity, but the decision to be taken belongs to Lucius' human aspect, and therefore the phrase is to be taken in contrast with his asinine shape.

There is no parallel phrase in the *Onos*.

148, 20-21 Habes summam oportunitatem fugae, dum latrones absunt: "You have a perfect opportunity for escape, while the robbers are away".

summam oportunitatem: the phrase develops the preceding words *dum licet*. It appears to replace a time indicator in the *Onos* 23, 4: νὺξ μὲν αὕτη καὶ σελήνη πολλή, which is followed by οἱ δὲ οἴχονται ἀπιόντες: *dum latrones absunt*. The reference to the moon was presumably regarded as superfluous since it occurs again when girl and ass are captured, both in the *Onos* (24, 2) and in the *Met.* (151, 24).

oportunitatem: scholars are generally agreed that the spelling *opportunus* would reflect the origin of the word as a sailors' term, cf. Fest. 207 L *opportune dicitur ab eo, quod nauigantibus maxime utiles optatique sunt portus*. See also Walde-Hofmann and Ernout-Meillet *s.v.*; *ThLL s.v. opportunus* 775, 47 f. and the dictionaries suggest that the spellings *opport-* and *oport-* occur equally often. The best attested spelling is to be preferred in each case.

An custodiam anus semimortuae formidabis, quam licet claudi pedis 148, 21-23
tui calce unica finire poteris?: "Are you going to be afraid of the surveillance of a half-dead old hag that you could put an end to with a one kick of your foot, however lame?"

The old woman, at 6, 25 (147, 3) *delira et temulenta* after telling the tale of Amor and Psyche, in Book 4 a vigorous housekeeper and cook (even if the robbers call her unflattering names in 4, 7), is here *semimortua,* which fits Lucius' self-persuasion. That it is mere rhetoric will appear in the next chapter. At the same time Apuleius may have chosen this adjective in order to foreshadow the woman's death, which follows in ch. 30.

semimortuae: also 1, 14, (13, 8); see *GCA* 1977, 112 f. on *semiuiuus* and Médan 1925, 174. The Thesaurus Inst. at Munich has provided the following references: Cat. 50, 15; Sen. *Con.* 1, 7, 9 (?);[Quint.] *Decl.* 364, 5 Lehnert; Hyg. *Astr.* 2, 4 (35, 16); Avit. Brac. *Lucian. epist. rec. B 3*.

licet claudi pedis tui calce unica: the ass was injured at 147, 19; fear gave him wings for hooves at 148, 4-5; presently he will run away *quadripedi cursu* (149, 4 and 25), but when caught (152, 3 f.) he will immediately remember his injury: the reader is never sure at what level of fiction he is to place this lameness, the author's or that of Lucius himself. For *licet* see vdPaardt 1971, 80.

formidabis: future simple in a deliberative question ('unwillige Frage') occurs several times in Latin, see KSt 2, 2, 511, LHSz 2, 311, who give instances with first person only; in the soliloquy the second person is not surprizing.

quam: most translators take the relative with *anus,* but Vallette and Vitali manage to retain the ambiguity of a relative that also may refer to *custodiam.*

unicus in the sense of "one only" also (e.g.) at 4, 22 (92, 8), 156, 7-8.

finire: used in the sense of *occidere*; see Médan 1925, 150, who refers to *finis* = death. For *finire* this sense is not uncommon, though it occurs more frequently in the passive, see *ThLL s.v.* 783, 45 f.; cf. e.g. Sen. *Prou.* 6, 6 *contemnite mortem, quae uos aut finit aut transfert; Ep.* 24, 24; Tert. *scorp.* 10 (168, 24) *si bestiis finiendus* (sc. *Christianus*).

Sed quo gentium capessetur fuga uel hospitium quis dabit?: "But 148, 23-24 where on earth can one take flight to and who will provide shelter?"

On *quo gentium* see Médan 1925, 40; Callebat 1968, 488 who cites Pl. *Bacch.* 831; *Rud.* 824.

capessetur: the passive is striking: it is not clear whether the author intended to highlight the action rather than the actor (see e.g. Serbat 1975, 131) or, in view of the lessening frequency of the passive in popular language, wished to colour Lucius' speech as bookish (see Löfstedt 1933, 2, 367). There is also an element of *uariatio* in the sentence and the passive/active *capessetur/dabit* is part of that scheme.

The questions parody such series of questions as asked by Ariadne in Catul. 64, 177 f., which in turn recall Eur. *Medea* 502 f. See also Ov. *Met.* 8, 113 (Scylla) and Bömer's numerous parallels *ad loc.*; Sen. *Med.* 451 and Costa *ad loc.*

148, 24-149, 2 Haec quidem inepta et prorsus asinina cogitatio; quis enim uiantium uectorem suum non libenter auferat secum?"': "That is a silly and thoroughly asinine thought; for what traveller would not gladly take his mount along with him?'"

Kronenberg 1908, 304 inserted *at* before *haec*. However, the *vis adversativa* he misses is to some extent represented by *quidem,* which opposes the thought to the frequent protestations of the humanity of this ass's mind, see *GCA* 1977, 23. The self-correction in connection with the *conditio asinina* is the funnier since this very human thought is termed an *asinina cogitatio:* see Junghanns 1932, 62 n. 91.

asinina: the word also at 8, 28 (199, 23), see Médan 1925, 202 who regards it as rare and belonging to the 'langue postérieure'. It occurs from Var. *R.* 2, 8, 2 onwards. In the subjective sense of "asinine", "stupid" *ThLL* cites only two other instances: Aug. *c. Jul. op. imp.* 4, 56 *quem tantae stoliditatis perdere deberet, etiamsi tibi asinina frons esset*; *quant. anim.* 14, 24. But cf. Tert. *Nat.* 1, 11, 1; Aug. *Epist.* 187, 24.

uiantium: partit. gen. instead of *uiator*. Apul. has the verb three times, always in the present part.: see 10, 5 (240, 14), *Flor.* 1, 1 (1, 1), Callebat 1968, 143.

quis enim ... secum: later on the ass is in fact quite ready to go with a chance *uiator* (7, 25: 172, 22 ff.) but, as usual, that chance of an escape from a bad situation is cut off by an evil Fortuna.

Note the joke in *uectorem ... auferat*.

CHAPTER XXVII

Ass and girl aid and abet each other in escaping.

Et alacri statim nisu lorum, quo fueram destinatus, abrumpo meque   149, 3-4
quadripedi cursu proripio: "And with a vigorous pull I immediately broke
the thong by which I was tied and made off at a four-footed run".

A sequence of events similar to those in chapter 27-29 (the ass escapes, someone mounts him, the two are caught) occurs at 7, 25. See for the 'Motivwiederholung' Junghanns 1932, 102 n. 160, vThiel 1971, 119 f. On the question of repetition of motifs in general, see Anderson 1976b, 53.
   alacri nisu: usually in Apuleius *alacer* directly describes a state of mind (e.g. 1, 17 (15, 18) *emergo laetus atque alacer*; it does so indirectly here, and at 2, 11 (34, 4) *alacrem uigorem libidinis incutiat*; 3, 5 (55, 24); 9, 11 (211, 22).
   lorum quo fueram destinatus: in the *Onos*, also after a soliloquy (however different), the ass notices suddenly that he is not tied up at all (23: ὁρῶ ὅτι οὐδὲ προσεδεδέμην οὐδενί), a curious difference that is explained by Bianco 1971, 149 as follows: "forse, per rendere movimentata l'azione, fa spezzare a Lucio il capestro, prima di avventurarsi nella corsa liberatrice". Bianco of course argues that Apuleius is dependent on the *Onos*, but even if that were so we doubt whether the explanation is sufficient. However this may be, the author has his fun with the *lora*, whose quality appears to vary with his need to allow or not allow the ass to escape, cf. 4, 3 (77, 1).
   fueram destinatus: for the 'verschobenes Plusquamperfectum' see vdPaardt 1971, 54, *GCA* 1977, 121 f.
   meque ... proripio: the situation is rather similar to the one at 4, 2 where the ass sees a way out from his asinine situation and where we read *cursu me concito proripio* (75, 16). In that passage his (horse-like) speed precedes a disappointment in the shape of poisonous flowers; here his quadruped speed is checked by the old woman. Feldbrugge 1938, 57 speaks of the 'Pechvogel' theme. On similar reversals *GCA* 1977, 110, where (the) Envy (of the gods) is the cause.
   quadripedi cursu: in itself neutral, the word *quadripes* is here used in a favourable, elsewhere, e.g. 7, 3 (156, 2); 7, 27 (175, 14); 11, 2 (267, 22), in an unfavourable sense. Both spellings (with *-i-* and *-u-*) are found; with *-u-* at 8, 5 (180, 6) and 7, 27 (175, 14). It is both used as an adj. and a noun. The form *quadripedus* also occurs, cf. Fro. *Aur.* 1(p. 122) *quadripedo cursu*; Amm. 14, 2, 2 *quadripedo gradu*. See also Morelli 1913, 179; Médan 1925, 323.

Nec tamen astutulae anus miluinos oculos effugere potui: "And yet I   149, 4-5
could not escape the kite-like eyes of the sharp little old bag."

41

On the narrative function of *nec tamen ... potui* see Junghanns 1932, 58, n. 87: 'Apuleius leitet solche Umschläge mit Vorliebe durch einen allgemeinen Satz ein'. Note the contrast between *custodiam anus semimortuae* (148, 21–22) and *astutulae anus miluinos oculos*: as so often, the ass's subjective point of view determines the description.

acutulę F, *astutulę* F in mg. (same hand), *astutulae* φ ς. The editors are agreed that the correction should be adopted, with the exception of Hildebrand, Eyssenhardt and van der Vliet. The latter indeed wishes to read *acutule asine* at 9, 30 (225, 11), which we regard as unnecessary. The word *astutulus* is confined to Apul.: 9, 1 (203, 9 *ex coniectura Roaldi*) and 9, 30 (225, 11). Cf. also *perastutula* 9, 5 (206, 10). *Acutulus* also occurs in Cicero (*N.D.* 3, 18) and Gellius (17, 5, 3). *Astutus* seems to have the connotation of (sometimes malicious) cleverness that is slightly more general than the rather intellectual *acutus*. Since the reading *astutulae* not only appears in F, but is the *lectio difficilior* as regards frequency, and has the preferable connotation, we follow the majority of the editors. (Vallette translates "maligne"; cf. e.g. Cic. *Mur.* 8 *hominis et astuti et ingrati*.) See further Helm Praef. *Fl.* xxxviii; Médan 1925, 135.

astutulae anus: for *astutae aniculae* – diminution by enallage. Diminutive adjectives are discussed in LHSz 1, 308 f.

miluinos oculos: the connotation is doubtless sharp sight; see Otto 1890, 223, but ours is the only instance of the *miluus* being employed in this sense, for which the *aquila* is commonly used (Otto 1890, 32 f., Nachträge zu Otto 1968, 52; 135; 233; 261). Cf. 2, 2 (26, 8); *Fl.* 2 (2, 6–7): *ceterum si magis pollerent oculorum quam animi iudicia, profecto de sapientia foret aquilae concedendum*. In Plautus the *miluus* has a reputation for rapacity; see *Poen.* 1292 and Maurach *ad loc.*, cf. *Ps.* 852 *an tu inuenire postulas quemquam coquom nisi miluinis aut aquilinis unguibus?* (If there is caricature here as with Lucian's vulture (see Anderson 1976b, 52 f.) the details escape us.)

149, 5-8 Nam ubi me conspexit absolutum, capta super sexum et aetatem audacia lorum prehendit ac me deducere ac reuocare contendit: "For when she saw me loose, she assumed a boldness beyond her sex and age, snatched the thong and struggled to pull me round and call me back."

nam ... contendit: in discussing Brant's *reducere* Hildebrand argues that the ass had not yet moved ("Neque enim adhuc processerat asinus"). This is most unlikely in view of *meque quadripedi cursu proripio*. The remainder of the chapter is doubtless meant as a detailed description of a very fast development (more or less comparable to a slow motion sequence in an action picture).

capta super sexum et aetatem audacia: Heine 1962, 237 n.1 discusses the passage in connection with Psyche's metamorphosis at 5, 22 (120, 2): *sexum audacia mutatur*. Here we have an unexpected activity which is no more than compared with masculine behaviour, not really meant as a metamorphosis, cf. the parallels quoted above on 148, 19-20 with *masculum ... animum*. See also Just. 2, 12, 24 ... *ut in uiro muliebrem timorem, ita in muliere uirilem audaciam cerneres*. Cf. Stat. *Theb.* 5, 105 *firmate animos et pellite sexum*.

prehendit ... contendit: Bernhard 1927, 226 notes 'Gliederrreim'. See also

Callebat in *AAGA* 1978, 181 f. In the *Onos*, where the ass was not tied up, the woman grabs him by the tail and hangs on.

diducere F, *deducere* ς and edd. On the confusion of i/e see *GCA* 1977, 52 and Helm Praef. *Fl.* xxxiv. *Diductum* occurs at 10, 1 (236, 13) (Helm notes that φ reads *deductum*; this is not confirmed by the other editors); *deducere* occurs some twenty times. It is difficult to defend *diducere* in our passage.

reuocare: if one is to believe the majority of the translators the word is used here in the sense of "pull back". Helm, however, is right in translating "zurückrufen". There is no reason to suppose that the woman at first keeps silent.

Nec tamen ego, memor exitiabili‹s› propositi latronum, pietate ulla commoueor, sed incussis in eam posteriorum pedum calcibus protinus adplodo terrae: "But remembering the fatal proposition of the robbers, I was not moved by any sense of pity, but kicking at her with the hoofs of my hind feet immediately threw her to the ground with a thud". 149, 8-10

The final *s* of *exitiabilis* in F has been added by a second hand.

memor ... latronum: the *Onos* passage (23, 7) is quite different: ἐγὼ δὲ ἄξιον κρημνοῦ καὶ θανάτων ἄλλων εἰπὼν εἶναι τὸ ὑπὸ γραίας ἁλῶναι ἔσυρον αὐτήν.

pietate: here in the general sense of pity (Mitleid); cf. e.g. 6, 18 (142, 15) *nec tu tamen inlicita adflectare pietate* and 4, 26 (94, 18) *pietatis humanae memor*, where however the aspect of duty has not faded entirely. See Wagenvoort 1924, 10 f.; Liegle 1932, 59–100.

incussis in eam posteriorum pedum calcibus: see 4, 3 (76, 11–12), where the ass uses similar measures in order to escape the *hortulanus*, and *GCA* 1977, 39.

adplodo terrae: Oudendorp notes "*adplodere* videntur amasse in grauiore adlisione ... *adplaudere* uero de leuiore percussione". Cf. e.g. 3, 9 (58, 20) *his dictis adplauditur*; 9, 40 (233, 27) *sublimem elatum terrae grauiter adplodit*. The instances quoted in *ThLL s.v.* 295, 10 f. appear to confirm this impression. A noise is implicit in the word *adplodere*. Vallette's "je l'applique droit contre le sol" therefore is not nearly as apt as Helm-Krenkel's "klatsche sie geradeswegs auf die Erde". Cf. Arnob. *Nat.* 5, 16 *pectoribus adplodentes palmas*.

At illa, quamuis humi prostrata, loro tamen tenaciter inhaerebat, ut me procurrentem aliquantisper tractu sui sequeretur: "But she, though flat on the ground, hung on to the thong tenaciously, so that she followed me for a little while by letting herself be dragged along as I tried to run forward". 149, 10-13

at illa ... sequeretur: the old woman apparently has not only a man's audacity but her own tenacity: once again she does not react as might have been expected. Médan 1925, 204 mistakenly regards *tenaciter* as a rare word of later Latinity. In the *Met.* it occurs only here (it was conjectured at 222, 3–4 by Beite). Cf. Ov. *Ep.* 3, 43; 9, 21 and e.g. Symm. *Ep.* 3, 31, Macr. *in Somn. Scip.* 1, 6, 23. The Thes. Inst. at Munich provides another three dozen instances.

aliquantisper: the word may belong to the 'langue familière' as Médan 1925, 185 suggests. It occurs also e.g. at 1, 11 (10, 20); see Marg. Molt *ad loc.*, who notes its relative frequency in Plautus (e.g. *Ps.* 571) and Terence (*Ad.* 639).

tractu sui: "en se faisant trainer" (Vallette) "so dasz sie sich ... mitschleppen liess" (Helm). Abl. of means of a verbal noun construed with objective genitive. *Tractus* in the literal sense also e.g. Sal. *Jug*. 78, 13; Verg. *G*. 3, 183; Plin. *Nat*. 36, 51; Tac. *A*. 15, 37; obj. gen. LHSz 2, 66 f. *sui* is here used for *suo*, a regular phenomenon: LHSz 2, 61; cf.*fatigotionem sui* 1, 20 (19, 3) and Marg. Molt *ad loc.*; 5, 3 (105, 5) and Fernhout *ad loc.*; *inuidiam mei Apol*. 25 (29, 15). Oudendorp and Hildebrand take *tractus* 'passiva sententia de motu' and quote *Mun*. 10 (145, 20) in support, but the force there is active rather than passive. Indeed it is hard to find a parallel for *tractus* = "a being drawn"; but there is no need to adopt the conjectures *tracta humi* (Groslot) or *tractus ui* mentioned by Oudendorp, though the second ("by the force of her dragging") merits an honourable mention.

149, 13-14   Et occipit statim clamos⟨is⟩ululatibus auxilium ualidioris manus implorare: "And with loud wails she started immediately to cry out for the help of a stronger hand".

occipit: Fernhout on 5, 15 (115, 9) and vdPaardt 1971, 30 follow Médan 1925, 182 in classifying the word as belonging to the *sermo cotidianus*. Devoto 1944, 178 thinks its use by Sallust reflects a stylistic aim for which the labels 'archaic' or 'familiar' give insufficient descriptions (see also Devoto-Opelt 1968, 157 and Callebat 1972, 1104). In fact the word occurs frequently in Plautus (e.g. *Stich*. 380) and Terence (e.g. *An*. 79) and reappears with some frequency in the historians, e.g. Sal. *Hist*. fr. 2, 87, Livy (e.g. 1, 7, 6 see Weissenborn-Müller *ad loc.*) and Tacitus (e.g. *Ann*. 3, 2, 3: see Furneaux *ad loc.*). There can be little doubt that Apuleius regards the word as archaic. In 9 of the 13 Apuleian instances[1] of the word it is constructed with the inf. as here; cf. e.g. below 152, 6-7; it is used absolutely at 9, 14 (213, 8); with *a* at 7, 18 (168, 9) and *Apol*. 51 (58, 5); with an abl. at *Flor*. 13 (18, 4-5).

clamos⟨is⟩: φ. F has *clamos*, changed to *clamās* by a second hand. The correction in φ is generally accepted.

clamosis ululatibus auxili(um): Médan 1925, 270 notes the dactylic sequence and *ibid*. 363 the redundant adj.; see also Bernhard 1927, 175; cf. *stellis sidereis* (150, 14) and comm. *ad loc*. Comparable expressions with *clamosus*: 8, 28 (199, 10) *uaticinatione clamosa*; 9, 42 (235, 23) *clamoso strepitu*.

ualidioris manus: in the *Onos* (23, 7) the old woman calls the girl directly. Apuleius uses the opportunity to indicate that there is no one else present.

149, 14-20   Sed frustra fletibus cassum tumultum commouebat, quippe cum nullus adforet, qui suppetias ei ferre posset nisi sola illa uirgo captiua, quae uocis excitu procurrens uidet hercules memorandi spectaculi scaenam, non tauro, sed asino dependentem Dircen aniculam, sumptaque constantia uirili facinus audet pulcherrimum: "But in vain she tried to stir up a useless tumult with her sobbing, since there was no one present

---

[1] Helm notes *occeperat* as the reading of φ at 1, 3 (3, 9) but this is not confirmed in either Robertson or Giarratano-Frassinetti.

who could render her aid, with the one exception of that captive girl, who at the summons of her voice came running up and saw by Hercules the spectacle of a memorable scene, an old woman in the rôle of Dirce hanging not from a bull but an ass. Assuming the courage of a man, the girl dared a very splendid feat."

frustra ... cassum: on the redundancy see Médan 1925, 365.

tumultum commouebat: Vallette may be right in taking the imperfect *de conatu*. *Tumultus* is very close here to the more abstract sense of "alarm" but the Apuleian passages in which the word occurs (12 instances) all have a connotation of actual noise as well; possible parallels for "alarm": 4, 11 (82, 23) *ac dum ... urguemur graui tumultu*; 10, 28 (259, 11) *populi concitato tumultu*.

quippe cum: see comm. on 155, 4–6.

suppetias: the word occurs in Plautus (8 times e.g. *Epid.* 659; *Men.* 1003); in Varro (fr. *Men.* 509); *B. Afr.* (7 times e.g. 68, 2; 75, 4); Suet. *Vesp.* 4, 5; 5 times in Apuleius, later in Ammianus Marcellinus (ten times) and others. As with *occipere* above it is hard to decide whether to classify the word as belonging to the *sermo cotidianus* or as archaic. Benhard 1927, 132 regards the word as 'vulgar'. Callebat 1968, 186 says *accurrere suppetias* at 9, 37 (231, 6) belongs to the *sermo cotidianus*, cf. Landgraf 1914, 71. Indeed the expressions *ire, uenire, occurrere* (etc.) *suppetias* occur in Plautus (*Men.* 1020 *tibi suppetias ... adueni*), Varro (see above) and in particular *B. Afr.* (25, 5; 39, 4; 41, 2; 66, 2; 68, 3; cf. 75, 4 *eos ... suppetias mittit*). *Suppetias ferre (alicui)*, however, is more common in Plautus (*Am.* 1106; *Epid.* 659; *Men.* 1003; *Mil.* 1053; *Rud.* 624; 1083), but occurs before Apuleius only in Suet. *Vesp.* 4, 10. It looks, then, as if this expression must be regarded rather as an archaism, possibly borrowed directly from Plautus. In Apul. cf. *Soc.* 6, 133 (14, 2) *qui ultro citro portant hinc petitiones inde suppetias*.

excitu: hapax. The expression *uocis excitu procurrens* is, of course, highly artificial, and part of the art of Apuleius' picture is that he presents within his slow motion movie a neatly framed (*uidet!*) caricature (see Feldbrugge 1938, 58) of a well-known pictorial group – a caricature since bull has changed to ass and Dirce to an *anicula*. At the same time it is to be remembered that Dirce was dragged to her death and that the picture may therefore be a last, emphatic foreshadowing of the death of the old woman.

memorandi spectaculi scaenam: curiously enough, as Mrs. Goold kindly points out to us, the value of the words "scene" and "spectacle" in English is exactly the reverse of their Latin counterparts. For the redundancy see Bernhard 1927, 174; for *scaena* in the sense of the enacted scene *GCA* 1977, 151.

When myth is next mentioned (151, 1 f.), A. introduces an interesting *variatio*: a painting will illustrate and perpetuate a new myth.

non tauro sed asino dependentem Dircen aniculam: once again we must consider the possibility that, while the author intends the reader to recognize the caricature, he does not make the narrator responsible for or conscious of it. The caricature, which also occurs in the *Onos* 23, 8, refers to the story of Dirce tied to a bull by Amphion and Zethus, to punish her for planning the same fate for their mother Antiope. There are two versions of the story which are found in Hyg. *Fab.* 7 and 8. The second of these originates from Euripides' Antiope. In both versions Dirce is torn to pieces by the bull; cf. Euripides, *Antiope* fr. 48, 62 Kambitsis. See also e.g. Pl. *Ps.* 199 f.; Prop. 3, 15, 37 *puerique trahendam/uinxerunt Dircen sub trucis ora bouis* (see Butler and Barber *ad loc.*); Ov. *Ib.* 535 f.; Sen. *Phoen.* 19 f.; Schol. on Apoll. Rhod. 4, 1090; Schol. on Stat. *Theb.* 4, 570; Apollod. *Bibl.* 3, 5, 5; *Anthol. Pal.* 3, 7; Nemes. *Cyn.* 22. On the numerous representations in art see Lauter-Bufe 1967, 29-33; van der Meer 1978, 35-41. The best known, the Farnesian Bull (after an original by Apollonius and Tauriscus of Tralles, see Plin. *Nat.* 36, 34), is contemporary with Apul.

sumptaque constantia uirili: see above on 149, 6-7 *capta... audacia* and note the contrast between the treatment of the *anus* and the *puella*, who respectively oppose and aid Lucius' flight. Such subjective value judgments in the *Met.* are entirely consistent with the point of view of the narrator, and serve to remind us of that point of view. In the *Onos* (23, 8) the situation is not nearly as clear: τολμᾷ τόλμημα γενναῖον καὶ ἄξιον ἀπονενοημένου νεανίσκου.

149, 20-22 Extorto etenim loro manibus eius me placidis gannitibus ab impetu reuocatum nauiter inscendit et sic ad cursum rursum incitat: "For she twisted the thong from her hands, called me back with soothing whispers from bolding, briskly climbed on my back and so urged me into a gallop again".

For the motif of a girl riding a donkey back to her lover see Phaed. *App.* 14 and Anderson 1976 b, 48.

In comparison with the brief description in *Onos* 23, 9: (ἀναπηδᾷ γὰρ εἰς ἐμὲ καὶ ἐπικαθίσασά μοι ἤλαυνεν), we find here, as elsewhere, an interesting addition of picturesque detail in *extorto... reuocatum*.

Extorto etenim loro manibus: Médan 1925, 227 remarks on the unusual wordorder (*etenim* more usually occurs in first position) and *ibid.* 48 on the abl. *manibus* which he regards as poetic. *ThLL s.v.* 2040, 5 f. does not support that opinion. Cf. *Fl.* 19 (40, 15 f.) *ita uispillonum manibus extortum*.

placidis gannitibus: see *GCA* 1977, 24 (*secretis gannitibus*); Bernhard 1927, 200 gives a list of expressions similarly transferred from their proper animal reference to human use.

reuocatum: the word echoes *reuocare* (149, 7) and so underlines the contrast between the intentions of the *anus* and those of the *uirgo*.

nauiter: the form is discussed below on 162, 19. Apuleius uses it twelve times: 2, 6 (30, 2); 2, 17 (39, 3) cf. de Jonge *ad loc.* ("strenue", "industrie"); 4, 12 (83, 15) cf. *GCA* 1977, 95 *ad loc.*; 6, 1 (129, 9); 6, 16 (140, 15); 6, 21 (144, 22); 10, 24 (256, 6); 11, 23 (284, 22 Gwyn Griffiths: "with a will"); *Pl.* 1, 12 (96, 10). The word occurs from Terence onwards (e.g. *Eu.* 51); Cic. *Fam.* 5, 12, 3, several times in Livy (e.g. 24, 23, 9) but also in Lucr. 1, 525 and Hor. *Ep. 1, 1, 24*. See also Sis. *Mil.* 4; Gel. 7, 10; 15, 4, 3; Tert. *Herm.* 3 (129, 11). These instances (a selection from those provided by the Thes. Inst. at Munich) may suffice to confirm Callebat's impression (1968, 175) that the word may be classified with the *sermo familiaris*.

cursum rursum incitat: Bernhard 1927, 245 insists that the clausula makes synaloephe unlikely. Hence he notes rhyme (*ibid.* 224). We are not so sure: the clausula _ _ _ _ ⌣ _ is sufficiently frequent (3,9 %) to admit synaloephe, in which case the rhyme is much less marked than it looks at first sight. See Hijmans in *AAGA* 1978, 199.

CHAPTER XXVIII

Lucius escapes with the girl. A prayer full of promises.

Ego simul uoluntariae fugae uoto et liberandae uirginis studio, sed 149, 22-26
et plagarum suasu, quae me saepicule commonebant, equestri celeritate quadripedi cursu solum replaudens uirginis delicatas uoculas ad⟨h⟩innire temptabam: "Because of both my wish to escape myself and my eagerness to free the girl, but also because of the encouraging raps which exhorted me pretty often, I galloped along, beating the ground like a race-horse, and tried to whinny a reply to the girl's sweet words".

Ego: Kronenberg suggested ⟨at⟩ *ego*. The addition is paleographically tenable (Robertson: 'fort. recte') on account of the preceding *incitat*; moreover, the combination *at ego* is often found in the *Met.* (see Callebat 1968, 89). Still, the conjecture is not absolutely necessary, since there is no question of an adversative or an affective element. Cf. *Onos* 23, 9 κἀγὼ τῷ τε ἔρωτι τῆς φυγῆς καὶ τῇ τῆς κόρης σπουδῇ ἔφυγον ἵππου δρόμῳ.

simul uoluntariae fugae uoto et liberandae uirginis studio, sed et plagarum suasu: modifiers of *equestri celeritate... replaudens*, not of the main verb. *Simul... studio*, the rendition of ἔρωτι τῆς φυγῆς, is a typical Apuleian reduplication (assuming, at least, that the *Onos* represents 'the original' here). Observe the parallelism in the construction and the almost equal number of syllables in the cola. Feldbrugge 1938, 58, may be right in regarding *sed et plagarum suasu* as 'kostelijk nuchter' ("delightfully down-to-earth"), but it seems doubtful whether it is an 'addition" (Feldbrugge *ibid.*): rather, the contrast already present in the Greek original is accentuated here. Quite unusually the *fuga* is here *uoluntaria*, i.e. "of my own will", cf. Cic. *Att.* 9, 13, 4 *discessus uoluntarius*.

suasu: according to Médan 1925, 174, 'langue familière'.

saepicule: cf. Pl. *Cas.* 703. Desertine 1898, 17 and Callebat 1968, 520 assume a derivation from Plautus. See further Marg. Molt 1938, 73; De Jonge 1941, 24; Médan 1925, 136. The diminutive adverbs are treated by Bernhard 1927, 137.

commonebant: this correction by ς of *commouebant* is generally accepted, and rightly so: Oudendorp already observed that *commonere* is used especially of those 'qui incitant tum homines, tum bestias suis votis non satis respondentes'; Hildebrand uses words to the same effect. In 9, 17 (215, 24) the object of *commonere* is the *seruulus* Myrmex.

equestri celeritate: does Lucius regard himself as an *eques* rather than an *equus*? It seems precarious to draw such a far-reaching conclusion from the use of *equester*, the more so as *equester* is used as an adjective with *equus* more than once: cf. Liv. 40, 31, 5 *fremitum equestrem* (a conjecture of Gronovius for *equestrium* in the mss.). Livy also mentions (1, 9, 6) *Neptunus Equester* (Ogilvie *ad loc.* refers to *Neptunus Equestris*, without further explanation); here the adjective clearly is a

47

translation from the Greek epithet ἵππιος, which can mean both *equinus* and *equester*; the former meaning is more appropriate to Neptune. (Besides, *eques* can stand for *equus*, although there are textual problems in most of the passages where this meaning seems the right one; see *ThLL s.v.* 717, 20 f.) Cf. also Apul. *Met.* 4, 2 (75, 17-18) *equum currulem... effectum*.

quadripedi cursu solum replaudens: Feldbrugge 1938, 59 speaks of a 'comical Vergilian reminiscence', undoubtedly referring to the famous onomatopoeic verse *quadripedante putrem sonitu quatit ungula campum* (*A.* 8, 596; cf. *A.* 11, 875); see Westerbrink *AAGA* 1978, 68.

quadripedi cursu: "at a gallop", deleted by vdVliet because it has already occurred at 149, 4 – hardly a convincing argument; see further comm. *ad loc.*

replaudens: replaudere "to strike against" occurs in Apul. only. Cf. 1, 7 (7, 1) *frontem replaudens*; see Marg. Molt 1938, 59; Scobie 1975, 95; Médan 1925, 132; Bernhard 1927, 120.

uirginis delicatas uoculas adhinnire: the terminology is clearly erotic. For *adhinnire* cf. Pl. *Cist.* 307-8 *quamquam uetus cantherius sum, etiamnunc, ut ego opinor, / adhinnire equolam possum ego hanc, si detur sola soli;* Ov. *Ars* 1, 279-280 *admugit femina tauro, / femina cornipedi semper adhinnit equo;* Ov. *Rem.* 634 *fortis equus uisae semper adhinnit equae.* In Cic. *Pis.* 69 the verb is used in a figurative sense, but its original erotic meaning can still be felt. The passage from Plautus shows us that the reading of the mss. *uirginis* should be retained here (with Giarratano, Terzaghi, and Scazzoso; cf. Médan 1925, 330; Augello 1977, 159): vdVliet's conjecture *uirgini*, accepted by most editors, yields a syntactical construction not found anywhere else. The *delicatae uoculae* repeat the *placidi gannitus* of 149, 20-21. *Delicatus* fits into this erotic context excellently: see Fordyce on Cat. 50, 3 *conuenerat esse delicatos;* Rudd 1959, 241. For the diminutive *uocula* see comm. on 4, 7 (79, 23).

149, 26-150, 1 Sed et scabendi dorsi mei simulatione nonnumquam obliquata ceruice pedes decoros puellae basiabam: "But, in addition, under the pretense of scratching my back, I sometimes bent my neck and tried to kiss the girl's pretty feet".

scabendi: F has *scauendi*; in φ, which initially had the same reading, this has been emended into *scabendi* (in F it has been 'corrected' into *scalpendi*, which presupposes a less simple corruption). For the frequent confusion in the mss. of *b* and *u* see Helm, Praef. *Flor.* XLVI. The verb belongs to colloquial speech: see Callebat 1968, 38. Médan 1925, 319 sees the construction *scabendi... simulatione* as an instance in which 'un substantif abstrait remplace une proposition complétive'. Although the expression cannot be denied some artificiality (by which, incidentally, the comical effect is enhanced; cf. Feldbrugge 1938, 59), still one should, in making such judgements as this, guard against taking one's own language as normative. See vdPaardt 1971, 158, n. 1.

obliquata ceruice: correction by ς of *obliquat a ceruice* (in F another hand added ; after the *t*); cf. 3, 2 (53, 4) *obliquato... aspectu*.

basiabam: probably used *de conatu*, an aspect already indicated by the preceding *temptabam*. Kissing a person's feet is usually an erotic gesture denoting submission, in this case rather to Eros/Amor than to Charite herself.

Tunc illa spirans altius caelumque sollicito nutu petens . . . inquit: 150, 1-3
"Next, heaving a deep sigh and turning her distracted gaze toward heaven, she spoke".

Tunc: much more frequent in the *Met*. than *tum* (120 to 13); here it is used as a transitional particle. See Callebat 1968, 326 f.; vdPaardt 1971, 65 f. The colloquial *tunc* contrasts with the highly poetical words which follow.

spirans: this reading of the mss. is accepted only by Hildebrand, Eyssenhardt, and Robertson; most editors follow ς and read *suspirans* (Helm refers to 9, 23 (220, 19 f.) *at ille dolenti prorsus animo suspirans adsidue . . . inquit*), but this is certainly unnecessary. Hildebrand defended *spirans altius* as meaning 'tiefer, freier Athem holend'; in that case these words would indicate Charite's optimism, but this is in conflict with *sollicito nutu*. If one sees Apuleius *iocans* behind this expression, one might explain "taking a deep breath" by pointing out the 'breathtakingly' long prayer that follows.

But it is most probable that *spirare* is used here for *suspirare* (thus – with some reservation – Wiman 1927, 48 and Robertson; more positively Armini 1928, 303; Bernhard 1930, 307; Augello 1977, 160). Cf. Mart. 2, 26, 1 *querulum spirat*. The noun *spiritus* in the sense of *suspirium* or *suspiritus* is found in Prop. 1, 16, 32 *surget et inuitis spiritus in lacrimis*; Enk *ad loc*. refers to Hor. *Epod*. 11, 10. Therefore we wonder whether the conjecture *suspiritus* is absolutely necessary in *Met*. 8, 15 (188, 7) *longos trahens ‹su›spiritus* (Helm and other editors following Brantius). Bernhard (1930) sees *spirans* as a 'bewusst gesuchte Ausdrucksweise' and refers to his own remarks in 1927, 119 f. (*simplex pro composito*).

nutu: this reading is not accepted by vdVliet, Helm, Gaselee, Robertson, Brandt-Ehlers, vThiel, who all read with Colvius *uultu* (Roaldus: *obtutu*). But *pace* Dowden 1979, 69 *nutus* in Apuleius means not only "nod", "beckoning", but also "glance" or even "eyes"; cf. 2, 30 (50, 13) *ac dum directis digitis et detortis nutibus praesentium denotor*; 10, 24 (255, 17 f.) *sed haec bene atque optime plenaque cum sanctimonia disposita feralem Fortunae nutum latere non potuerunt*; 11, 16 (278, 7) *digitis hominum nutibusque notabilis*. See Wiman 1927, 48 f. (with the approval of Armini and Bernhard); de Jonge 1941, 118; Augello 1977, 160.

'Vos', inquit, Superi, tandem meis supremis periculis opem facite, et 150, 3-5
tu, Fortuna durior, iam saeuire desiste. Sat tibi miseris istis cruciatibus meis litatum est: "You gods above, come to my help at last in my ultimate peril and you, Fortune, too hard on me, cease raging now. Enough propitiation has been made to you by those miserable torments of mine".

The *Onos* (23, 10) has ἡ δὲ παρθένος τοῖς μὲν θεοῖς ηὔχετο σῶσαι αὐτὴν τῇ φυγῇ. In Apul. we find the tripartition which is typical of prayers (*superi . . . et tu, Fortuna . . . tuque*), but it is possible – and even probable – that this tripartion existed in the original novel as well, especially if we assume with Perry and others that Lucian is the author; for parody of prayers in Lucian see Kleinknecht [r]1967, 137 f. Another formal characteristic of prayer found here is alliteration: in the

49

address to the *superi* sigmatism, in that to Fortuna sigmatism plus *t*-iteration, culminating in the final words *litatum est*; see Kleinknecht 159. Mark the prayer's 'Du-Stil'; see Norden[r] 1956, 144 f.

Superi: the gods of heaven are invoked first; cf. *caelum . . . petens* (150, 2).

supremis periculis: perhaps an ambiguity: things are at their worst now, but Charite hopes, of course, that these *pericula* will be the last; cf. 11, 2 (267, 19).

opem facite: for *facere* instead of the usual *ferre*, see Callebat 1968, 172; Médan 1925, 241.

Fortuna: on the relationship between Fortune and other divine powers who determine the events in the novel, see Heine 1962, 137 f. It seems that Fortune is assumed to be subordinate to the *prouidentia diuina* (Heine 1962, 139), just as in 8, 31 (202, 11 f.), where the distracted cook is thus adressed by his wife: *fortuitum istud remedium, quod deum prouidentia subministrat, intueris? Nam si quid in ultimo fortunae turbine resipiscis . . .* See further Riefstahl 1938, 30 f.; Tatum 1969[a], 155, n. 62; Walsh 1970, 181; vdPaardt 1971, 108, n. 2 (for Ciaffi 1960, 195 read Ciaffi 1960, 145).

iam saeuire desiste. Sat . . . litatum est: cf. Cat. 23, 26-27 *et sestertia quae soles precari / centum desine: nam sat es beatus*. This poem contains elements of parody, as do Cat. 36 (see Kleinknecht [r]1967, 178 f.) and 44 (see Jones 1968, 379 f.). The use of *sat*, which occurs only five times in the *Met.* while *satis* is quite frequent, is probably not accidental here, for it has poetical connotations and therefore fits the supplicatory style of this passage. See Neue-Wagener 2, 595 f.; Landgraf on Cic. *S. Rosc.* 89; Pease on Cic. *N.D.* 3, 68. As to *sat* in Cat. 23, 27, its reading is not certain; see Fraenkel 1966, 114 f.

istis . . . meis: for the combination of *iste* with the personal pronoun of the first person, see Médan 1925, 218; Bernhard 1927, 171; Callebat 1968, 272.

litatum est: a metaphor from the language of cult. It is, of course, highly functional in this prayer to the goddess Fortune. See vdPaardt 1971, 72 f.; to the literature mentioned there add Médan 1925, 257.

150, 5-9 Tuque, praesidium meae libertatis meaeque salutis, si me domum peruexeris incolumem parentibusque et formonso proco reddideris, quas tibi gratias perhibebo, quos honores habebo, quos cibos exhibebo: "And you, bulwark of my freedom and my salvation, if you take me home safe and sound and restore me to my parents and handsome suitor, what thanks shall I render you, what honours pay you, what dishes serve up to you!"

The 'third divinity' turned out to be the ass, which makes this prayer clearly a parody; see Westerbrink *AAGA* 1978, 69. The repetition *tu . . . tibi* is entirely in style; Callebat 1968, 109 f. is wrong in assuming that the repetition is due to the spontaneous character of the 'langue familière'. Observe also the alliterations (Médan 1925, 307), the anaphora of *meae* and of *quos*, and the homoioteleuta (Strilciw 1925, 112).

praesidium salutis: functions here as an *epiklesis*. The ass still has to prove that he is, indeed, her *praesidium*. For the combination of *libertas* and *salus* see *GCA* 1977, 152.

si . . . reddideris: unlike its use in this passage, *si* in a prayer generally has no purely conditional meaning (see e.g. Kroll and Fordyce on Cat. 76, 17), but rather that of "as truly as". Again Charite (or Apuleius) uses the formulaic diction, but the meaning is changed.

parentibus: cf. *Onos* 23, 10 ἦν με, ἔφη, κομίσῃς πρὸς τὸν πατέρα. In Apul. the father does not play a prominent part; see vThiel 1971, 11, n. 126.

formonso proco: the *Onos* does not even mention him! His status seems less fixed here than in 4, 27 (95, 21), where he was referred to as *maritus*. *Formonsus* is treated by Callebat 1968, 383.

perhibebo . . . habebo . . . exhibebo: the simplex is framed by the compounds; see Bernhard 1927, 237. The objects of these verbs become gradually more concrete: *gratias* is purely abstract, but the *honores* are likely to be more tangible; cf. 164, 24 f. where Charite keeps bringing up Lucius' merits *quoad summos illi (sc. parentes eius et maritus) promitterent honores habituri mihi* (see comm. *ad loc.*).

Iam primum iubam istam tuam probe pectinatam meis uirginalibus 150, 9-11
manibus adornabo: "To begin with, I shall properly comb and arrange that mane of yours with my maidenly hands".

With Oudendorp, Hildebrand, and vdVliet we prefer the reading *manibus* (Cod. Dorv. and older editions) to *monilibus*, which, according to recent editors, is to be found in F. Actually, the latter tradition is not very reliable: vdVliet mentions in his app. crit. that *mo-* seems to be a correction of *ma-*, and that *nilib* is written by a more recent hand. Hildebrand points out that the words are easily interchanged in their abbreviated forms. Contextual arguments also plead for *manibus* (and against *monilibus*). In the first place *monilia* are certainly used to adorn animals, especially horses (cf. Verg. *A.* 7, 278; Stat. *Theb.* 9, 689; Apul. *Soc.* 23; 33, 11), but in those cases what is adorned, is always the neck, the chest, or the forehead – never the mane. See also *RE s.v. monile*. Secondly, it may have escaped the attention of most editors that the passage *iam primum . . . saginabo* is an expansion of the preceding sentence: first the *gratiae* are specified, then the *honores*, and finally the *cibi*. The reading *monilibus adornabo* takes us directly to the category of the *honores*, which are treated later (150, 13-15). *Virginalibus manibus adornare* – the verb being equivalent not to *exornando augere* but to *praeparare* or the simple *ornare* – is a clear proof of the girl's gratitude:'Hic promittit puella se ipsam suis, non equisonis alicujus, manibus, licet tenera esset virgo, ejus iubam pexuram et adornaturam; se ipsam ejus ornatricem fore' (Oudendorp).

For *probe* as a synonym of *bene*, see vdPaardt 1971, 62; Callebat 1968, 57 discusses the verb *pectinare*, which has gradually replaced *pectere*.

frontem uero crispatam prius decoriter discriminabo caudaeque se- 150, 11-13
tas incuria lauacri congestas et horridas compta diligentia perpolibo: "first I shall curl the hair of your forehead and then part it elegantly in the middle; and the hairs of your tail, matted and shaggy for lack of washing, I shall smooth with elaborate care".

Two serious textual problems occur in this passage.

51

1. *compta*[1] is the reading found in F and, although frequently challenged, most probably correct. Gruterus defended *compta diligentia* as synonymous with *accurata diligentia*; it was retained by Oudendorp and Hildebrand (the latter with somewhat less conviction) and in the twentieth century by Giarratano-Frassinetti, Terzaghi, Helm-Krenkl, Brandt-Ehlers, Scazzoso, vThiel. See also Augello 1977, 160 f. The best interpretation is by Armini 1928, 303: 'Nam ut quis pro *anxie* potest scribere *anxia cura,* ita nihil obstat, quo minus pro *compte* scribat *compta cura* uel *compta diligentia.* Cf. *Met.* III, 3 (54, 11) *peruigilem diligentiam.* Et certe inest lusus uerborum: diligentia ipsa *compta* uocatur, quod in *comendis* setis adhibetur'. This ambiguity – rightly pointed out by Armini – is generally lost in translation; instead, emphasis is given to one of the aspects: compare "in peinlicher Sorgfalt" (Helm-Krenkel) with "mit Frisierkunsten" (Brandt-Ehlers). Cf. also *Met.* 9, 14 (213, 6 f.) *fabulam denique bonam prae ceteris, suaue⟨m⟩, comptam ad auris uestris adferre decreui* where *comptam* almost becomes a technical term of literary criticism; cf. Luck [2]1969, 104, n. 1.

2. We have less certainty as to the correctness of *perpolibo.* This reading of α may, according to Robertson, be derived from F, because in F this passage has been tampered with; now it reads *monilibus,* which is not accepted by most editors. *Perpolibo* by itself is not in disharmony with the context. The future in *-ibo* is unique for this verb, but not within the category of verbs of the fourth conjugation (see e.g. LHSz 1, 578). Its meaning, too, fits well (cf. Vell. 2, 22, 4 *loco nuper calce harenaque perpolito*). The strongest argument against *perpolibo* (as against Leo's conjecture *mollibo* which is accepted by Helm[1-2] and Gaselee and approved of by Armini 1928, 303) is its unconvincing tradition. An additional argument is offered by Beyte and Bernhard 1927, 226 n. 48, viz. that a verbal form in *-abo* would be preferable because *adornabo* (10-11) and *discriminabo* (11) suggest the desirability of a third verb to rhyme with them. If we reject *perpolibo,* we may choose among *pectinabo* (φ), *extricabo* (vdVliet, who in his apparatus also mentions *enodabo*), and *ornabo* (Simbeck in *ThLL s.v. comptus*). None of these possibilities is particularly attractive. *Pectinabo* (added by another hand) and *ornabo* are too bland, and they repeat the already used verbs *pectinatam* and *adornabo* which are out of place here, not so much stylistically as contextually. vdVliet's proposals are not sufficiently supported by the manuscript tradition to be taken seriously. For these reasons we prefer *perpolibo,* after all.

With Hildebrand, vdVliet regarded *incuria lauacri,* too, as corrupt. He deleted the genitive and read, after *Apol.* 4 (6, 12), ⟨diutina⟩ *incuria*; by way of explanation it should be mentioned that *lauacri* is an addition in F, and is completely lacking in φ. But this combination seems to be excellent Apuleian Latin: for the abstract *lauacrum* (i.e. synonymous with *lauatio*) see Médan 1925, 152 and Callebat 1968, 132; *incuria* with an objective genitive occurs from Cato *Dict.* 78

---

[1] There are many conjectures. ς has *cuncta*; Sopingius proposed *prorupta* and, according to Oudendorp and Hildebrand, also *prompta* which is included in Helm[1-2], Robertson, and Vitali (as a conjecture of Helm). Kronenberg's emendation *comptas* (with *setas*) is approved of by vdVliet and Gaselee, both of whom also read *diligenter,* and by Eyssenhardt, who replaced *compta diligentia perpolibo* with *comam diligenter.* Mention should further be made of *comptus* (gen. sing.) proposed by Leo; *apta* by Giarratano (only in app. crit., not in text); *ampla* in Helm[3]; *cum pia* by Beyte, who later proposed *comperta.*

magna cura cibi magna uirtutis incuria onward.

frontem . . . crispatam: metonymy for "the curled hairs of the forehead"; see Médan 1925, 349.

prius: taken with *crispatam* in our translation. Another possibility is to take it with *discriminabo*, but there are arguments against it: first, *discriminabo* already has a modifier in *decoriter* and, secondly, *prius* would then be a self-correction with respect to *iam primum*, which seems inappropriate here.

decoriter: this synonym of *decore* occurs for the first time in Apul.; see also 5, 22 (120, 16) and 11, 4 (268, 22); later in Jul. Val. 1, 24; 2, 29. For adverbs in *-iter* from adjectives of the second declension see vdPaardt 1971, 46 and 119.

setas: for its spelling see *GCA* 1977, 121.

congestas: an interesting parallel for this entire passage is *Apol.* 4 (6, 11 f.) *(capillus)* hirtus et globosus et congestus, prorsum inenodabilis diutina incuria non modo comendi, sed saltem expediendi et discriminandi. The second century's interest in hair-styling is known from literature and the arts; see vdPaardt 1971, 124 (126).

monilibus bullisque te multis aureis inoculatum ueluti stellis sidereis 150, 13-17 relucentem et gaudiis popularium pomparum ouantem, sinu serico progestans nucleos, edulia mitiora, te meum sospitatorem cotidie saginabo: "adorned with chains and many gold medallions you will shine as if with celestial stars, and among the cheers of the people's procession you will triumph; and carrying nuts and softer delicacies in my silk garment I will daily feed you as my saviour".

This passage, too, contains some textual problems:

1. *monilibus* has been added by a later hand in F, perhaps over a faded *perpolibo*. Most editors omit it, but since we read *manibus* in 150, 10 the major objection against *monilibus* has disappeared. Because contextually there are no objections either (see comm. on 150, 10) we can maintain *monilibus*, as did Oudendorp, Hildebrand, Eyssenhardt, and vdVliet; *inoculatum* admittedly goes better with *bullis* than with *monilibus*.

2. *inoculatum* is the reading of a few younger mss. and of the editio princeps; φ has *inaulatum* which, according to Robertson, is also the reading of F. The emendation seems necessary, however, since *inaulatum* does not make sense.

3. Robertson argues that *ueluti* (φ, α) could well have been the reading of F (Helm disagrees in his app. crit.; cf. Augello 1977, 161), and therefore he accepts it, as do Brandt-Ehlers, and as did the older editors. *Veluti* accords better than *uelut* with the poetic-archaic vocabulary of this prayer, see LHSz 2, 632.

4. Most editors (and with them Bernhard 1927, 56, n. 17) accept the addition ⟨*et*⟩ between *nucleos* and *edulia mitiora*, proposed by Salmasius; vdVliet reads ⟨*et siqua sunt*⟩; Scriverius wanted to erase *edulia mitiora* as a gloss; Haupt prefers the abl. sing. *edulio mitiore*. But the asyndeton is justifiable in consideration of the supplicatory style; cf. Pl. *Curc.* 90 *uoltisne olius [aut] pulpamentum [aut] capparim*, where *aut* is deleted by Lindsay and Ernout after Muretus. See Collart *ad loc.* (who maintains the second *aut*); Kleinknecht [r]1967, 159; Blomgren 1937, 4, n. 3.

53

5. *saginabo* is the reading of ϕ^2, and is generally preferred to *saturabo*, which is written over an erasure in F *(sa**turabo)*; Damsté 1928, 20 proposes *salutabo*, which has the attraction of producing an ironical repetition in 151, 24 *risu maligno salutant*. *Saginabo* seems the most likely reading: Helm thinks he reads a g in the erasure in F, and also points out that Apul. frequently uses *saginare*, while *saturare* does not occur elsewhere in this work. The verb *saginare*, moreover, can be used both of animals ("to fatten") and of humans "feasting to their hearts' content"; see *GCA* 1977, 26.

bullis: originally the *bulla* is a gold medallion, heart-shaped or round (thence its name: "waterbubble") containing a charm. It appears from both material and contents that the *bulla* had an apotropaic function. They were worn by well-born boys until they received the *toga uirilis*, and by girls until they married, in all likelihood. It seems important in this connection *(ouantem)* that the *bulla* was also worn by the Roman *triumphator*, although its primary function in that case may have been ornamental. Cf. Ov. *Met*. 10, 112 f. See Vallette 97, n. 1; Marquardt 1886, 84; Versnel 1970, 65; 380.

inoculatum: ThLL regards this as a 'uix forma uerbalis'; as an adjective it would be a *hapax legomenon*. Médan 1925, 167 and *OLD* take it as the participle of *inoculare* ("to engraft"), which seems to be used only as an agricultural technical term. The association of *oculus* with *stella* is quite common, as Oudendorp and Hildebrand observe.

stellis sidereis: the pleonastic adjective strengthens the poetic element. See Médan 1925, 363; Bernhard 1927, 175 f.

gaudiis: the plural is quite frequent in the *Met*. See Bernhard 1927, 103; Fernhout 1949, 94.

ouantem: Lucius is represented here as a *triumphator* (see above on *bulla*) rather than the *triumphator*'s mount.

progestans: the files of the *ThLL* Institute show that this verb is found in Apul. only.

nucleos: "nuts", "kernels". According to Callebat 1968, 42 it means especially "almonds" (cf. Rode: "Mandelkernen") and not "gâteaux" (Vallette and Grimal); another possibility is that the word refers to the kernels of pine-cones, which were appreciated as delicacies but are less hard than almonds.

edulia mitiora: the comparative does not necessarily indicate an opposition to another term (*mitiora* sc. *nucleis*) although this would produce a nice effect here. The alternative is "(rather) soft delicacies", which most translators take as "cookies". For *edulia* see Callebat 1968, 27.

CHAPTER XXIX

Pretty promises are made to Lucius, but the escape fails.

Sed nec inter cibos delicatos et otium profundum uitaeque totius beatitudinem deerit tibi dignitas gloriosa: "But more: in the midst of delicious food, total leisure, and life-long happiness you will not want for glorious prestige". 150, 17-151, 1

Sed: in Apul. it often indicates an addition or a correction, rather than an opposition; see Callebat 1968, 91 and 326; LHSz 2, 487 (with bibliography). The adversative force is not completely absent here; hence our translation: "but more".

cibos delicatos: cibos refers to 150, 16; *delicatos* is a significant echo of *delicatas (uoculas)* in 149, 25: anything coming from Charite is delicious.

otium: here used in the meaning "leisure", "inactivity", but we are reminded of its political connotation by the proximity of *dignitas*. For *otium* see Burck (ed.) 1967, 503 f.; at 509, n. 14 he gives a bibliography on *otium cum dignitate*, an idea introduced by Cicero (*Sest*. 98).

beatitudinem: this noun is not frequent in classical Latin (Cic. *N.D.* 1, 95) but is a favourite of Christian authors. Apuleius is the first to use it often; cf. 5, 3 (105, 3); 9, 11 (211, 4); 10, 33 (264, 20); 11, 15 (277, 12); see Médan 1925, 198.

dignitas gloriosa: a fine clausula (cretic + ditrochee). *ThLL s.v. gloriosus* (2103, 22) gives as parallels Firm. *Mat*. 6, 12, 1 and Sacr. Leon. 308 Petri apostoli; Bernhard 1927, 175 classes the combination under pleonastic use of the adjective. For *gloria* in Apul. see Knoche in Burck (ed.) 1967, 421, n. 6.

Nam memoriam praesentis fortunae meae diuinaeque prouidentiae perpetua testatione signabo et depictam in tabula fugae praesentis imaginem meae domus atrio dedicabo: "For I shall put on record for ever the memory of my present good fortune and of this divine providence: I shall consecrate a painting of this escape in the atrium of my house". 151, 1-4

praesentis: in later Latin, especially by jurists and Christian authors, *praesens* is used as an equivalent of *hic*; see Callebat 1968, 291; LHSz 2, 183; *GCA* 1977, 41.

diuinae prouidentiae: cf. Heine 1962, 138: 'auch die "prouidentia diuina" hat wenig Erhabenes, sondern ist zur unverbindlichen Floskel herabgesunken'; for the passages in the *Met*. where *prouidentia diuina (caelestis)* occurs, see Heine 1962, 138, n. 6.

signabo et ... dedicabo: the two parts of the sentence connected by *et* do not indicate two different promises but rather two aspects of one promise (i.e. parataxis instead of hypotaxis; see LHSz 2, 482).

depictam in tabula... imaginem: the custom of dedicating a picture of the danger from which one has escaped is known to us from literature and art; it often refers to an escape from the dangers of the sea. Cf. Hor. *Carm.* 1, 5, 13 f. *me tabula sacer / uotiua paries indicat uuida / suspendisse potenti / uestimenta maris deo* (or *deae*, with Zielinski, a notorious textual question; see Nisbet and Hubbard *ad loc.*); Hor. *S.* 2, 1, 32 f. *quo fit ut omnis / uotiua pateat ueluti descripta tabella / uita senis*; Tib. 1, 3, 27 f. *nunc, dea, nunc succurre mihi (nam posse mederi / picta docet templis multa tabella tuis)*; see Smith *ad loc.*; Pease on Cic. *N.D.* 3, 89; Mayor on Juv. 12, 27; Weinreich 1931, 20 f., who also reproduces a Pompeian Isis-Epona riding an ass.

atrio: for the *ablatiuus loci* see Médan 1925, 57.

151, 4-6 Visetur et in fabulis audietur doctorumque stilis rudis perpetuabitur historia 'asino uectore uirgo regia fugiens captiuitatem': "People will look at it, in tales they will hear about it, the pens of men of letters will immortalize it: the unheard-of story of 'a princess escaping captivity on an ass's back'".

fabulis: much has been written on the meaning of *fabula* in Apul., especially on the distinction between *fabula* and *historia*. Reitzenstein says that 'die *historia* das literarisch ausgebildete Werk ist, die *fabula* zunächst der mündlichen Mitteilung angehört oder sie nachahmt' (in Binder-Merkelbach 1968, 144). An important argument against this distinction seems to be *Met.* 2, 12 (35, 9), in which Lucius – referring to the prophecy of the soothsayer Diophanes – says to Milo: *nunc historiam magnam et incredundam fabulam et libros me futurum*; here the words are practically synonymous, as Vallette (1, 40, n. 1) remarks.

Here, at any rate, we find a clear allusion to three different things: the escape will be immortalized in art (*uisetur*), in stories told by people (*fabulis*), and in literature *(historia)*.

rudis: according to Helm and to several translators it has here the meaning "new"; exact parallels are not easily found, but an approximate one e.g. Cat. 64, 11 *illa rudem cursu prima imbuit Amphitriten* ("as yet untried"). More natural here seems the sense of "uncultivated", "unpolished" (cf. Hor. *S.* 1, 10, 66 *rudis et Graecis intacti carminis*), which produces an implied antithesis between the raw material and the refined art of the *docti*. A third possibility is "simple" in the sense of "not learned", as is found in Graves' translation of the passage: "I'll get some clever author to write the story out in a book for future generations to read. The title will be, let me see: 'Flight on Ass-back: or, How a Young Lady of Royal Blood Escaped from Captivity.' It's not a very learned subject, of course, but you'll have your niche in history". Finally this *historia* may be called *rudis* in a quite different respect: cf. 163, 24 *nouumque et hercules memorandum spectamen, uirginem asino triumphantem*, with reference to which Grimal 1958, 1449 remarks: 'L'âne, animal réputé pour sa lubricité, était une monture peu convenable pour une vierge'; see also Scobie 1969, 53, n. 2.

The conjectures *iugis* (De Rooy) and *eruditis* (Hertz) are unnecessary, at any rate.

historia: Scobie 1975, 76 maintains that Apuleius uses *historia* here (and elsewhere) in the sense of 'fictional narrative', but within the framework of fictional narrative this *historia* is 'reality'.

uirgo regia: Charite is not a real princess, of course, so *regius* is here a synonym of *nobilis*; cf. 4, 2 (75, 15) *regius nitor* and *GCA ad loc.*

The choice of words in this passage does not necessarily imply an allusion to a literary work which dealt with a princess suffering a similar fate (Rode-Burck 1961, 236). Such a 'Vorlage' was supposed by Weinreich 1931, 9 f., who related it to a fable of Phaedrus (*App.* 14) and suggested that both Phaedrus and the original ass-novel had their origin in an aretalogical novel. Van Thiel's refutation of this theory (1971, 110 n. 126) seems to be conclusive.

Griffith 1968, 762 points out that the title of the *rudis historia* 'ganz wie ein Bruchstück eines iambischen Versmasses klingt'; moreover, iambic elements can be found in the preceding prayer. Hence Griffith supposes a metrical fable was copied here ('dort aber war die Belohnung des Esels nicht, wie bei Phaedrus App. 14, ausgelassen'). It does not seem necessary to accept this theory either, if we remember that the story is immortalized on the spot, viz. by Lucius (or Apuleius); it is an ironical circumstance that the escape actually fails.

Accedes antiquis et ipse miraculis, et iam credemus exemplo tuae 151, 6-9 ueritatis et Frixum arieti supernatasse et Arionem delphinum gubernasse et Europam tauro supercubasse: "You yourself, too, will find your place among the miraculous stories from the past, and we will now believe, by your example from real life, that Phrixus swam across the sea on a ram, that Arion steered a dolphin, and that Europa reclined on a bull".

Cf. Weinreich 1931, 18: 'Die Pointierung, dass die neue Wirklichkeit alte Wunder und Mythen beglaubigt, kennen wir z. B. aus Martial, der darin griechischer Technik folgt.' For this see Weinreich 1928, 30 f.; 34; 72; 74, n. 1; 77 f.; Schrijvers 1973, 16.

et iam: F and φ have *etiam*. The correction is not by Petschenig, as Helm assumes with his predecessors; it is already found in ς.

exemplo tuae ueritatis: Wower proposed *exemplo tuo veritati*, wrongly, as Oudendorp points out, 'quia constructio nequit esse: *Credemus veritati sed credemus, Phryxum supernatasse arieti* etc. *exemplo tuae veritatis* sive tuo vero exemplo'. Médan 1925, 316 regards *ueritas* as *abstractum pro concreto*; one may also take it as a genitive of quality in place of an adjective.

Frixum: Robertson and Brandt-Ehlers prefer the spelling with *Ph* (ς), as in *Photis*, but there seems to be no reason not to maintain the spelling with *F-*, found in F.

The story of Phrixus and Helle, children of king Athamas of Thebes, is a well-known myth, often referred to in literature: they escaped their evil stepmother by fleeing on a ram, a gift from Hermes. This golden-fleeced ram took them across the sea to Colchis, but Helle fell into the Hellespont, named after her.

Robertson 1940, 1-8 establishes beyond doubt that in the original version of the myth the ram swam rather than flew across the sea. Among Roman authors only Aug. *C.D.* 18, 13 (p. 272, 14D) has a flying ram. Though *supernatare* does occur in the meaning "fly across" (Stat. *Silv.* 3, 2, 47; Aug. *C.D.* 15, 27 (p. 118,

28D)) there is no reason not to take the verb in its usual sense. In all three myths, then, a journey across the sea is referred to.

Arionem: Herod. 1, 24 tells us the story of Arion: travelling from Italy to his native Corinth, this singer/poet was threatened by sailors who coveted his riches. He requested permission to sing one last time, threw himself in full regalia into the sea after this performance, and was picked up and delivered home by a dolphin.

delphinum gubernasse: F has in the margin as a variant *delphino* (the reading of φ), which fits in badly with *gubernasse*. Oudendorp is enthusiastic about Mercerus' conjecture *delphino supernasse* and expatiates on the difference between *nare* (ships, fish) and *natare* (all animals except fish). His theory, already strongly challenged by Hildebrand, is disproved by the material of the *ThLL* Institute. *Delphinum* should be retained.

Europam: this daughter of king Phoenix of Tyre was abducted by by Zeus/Jupiter in the shape of a bull, and brought to Crete (or, according to other versions, to Boeotia). See Ovid *Met.* 2, 833 f. It is clear from what follows that Charite identifies herself most closely with Europa. Note the anaphoric tricolon with parallelism in the number of syllables, and the homoeoteleuton (Strilciw 1925, 112 curiously enough speaks of a homoeoteleuton '*duorum membrorum*'). On mythology in the *Met.*, in particular Charite's references to it, see *GCA* 1977, 199 f.

151, 9-11 Quodsi uere Iupiter mugiuit in bouem, potest in asino meo latere aliqui uel uultus hominis uel facies deorum': "And if Jupiter really bellowed like a bull, a human shape or a divine appearance may well be hidden in my ass!' "

migiuit in bouem: the reading of F and φ should be maintained; the "emendation" of ς (*in boue*, accepted as the correct reading by Helm and a few others) and the conjectures *mugiens iuit* (Walter) and *in boue(m) reformatus* (Lütjohann) are unnecessary; see vdPaardt 1971, 179, n. 1 and the literature mentioned there; *GCA* 1977, 51. The reading is rightly accepted by Oudendorp, Hildebrand (with the correct argumentation), Eyssenhardt, vdVliet, Gaselee, Giarratano-Frassinetti, Brandt-Ehlers, Scazzoso; see also Augello 1977, 161 f.

potest... latere: 'a grotesque assumption, which is extremely piquant for Lucius himself' (Feldbrugge 1938, 59). vThiel 1971, 14 finds this less witty than the corresponding passage in the *Onos*, where this assumption is not made: 'In der Epitome 23, 10 redet die Jungfrau auf der Flucht mit dem Esel wie mit einem Menschen, bei Apuleius VI 29, 5 spricht sie diesen Gedanken platt aus'. Walsh 1970, 60 recognizes the dramatical irony and *ibidem* 160 points out the parallel in 8, 25 (196, 18 f.), where the *praeco* recommends the ass as being so tame *ut in asini corio modestum hominem inhabitare credas*.

aliqui: according to Hildebrand *aliqui* is used here in the sense of *aliquis*, but why should it not be taken as an adjective modifying *uultus*?

uultus hominis...facies deorum: 'dicta sunt pro simplici substantivo: *homo* vel *deus*' (Hildebrand). Médan 1925, 336 points out the *uariatio* in the use of the number. For *uultus* meaning "shape", "appearance", see LS *c.v.* II 3.

Dum haec identidem puella replicat uotisque crebros intermiscet 151, 12-15
suspiratus, ad quoddam peruenimus triuium, unde me adrepto capistro dirigere dextrorsum magnopere gestiebat, quod ad parentes eius ea scilicet iretur uia: "While the girl repeated this again and again and mingled many sighs with her vows, we arrived at a fork in the road; there she grasped my halter and tried her hardest to make me turn to the right, because – so she reasoned, of course – one went that way to her parents".

Dum haec identidem... replicat: cf. 1, 14 (13, 18) *haec identidem mecum replicabam*; 3, 1 (52, 19) *haec identidem mecum replicans*. Not only the formulation is strikingly similar, but also the situation in which the *replicantes* are: Aristomenes, Lucius, and Charite are all in a critical situation.

In our passage *secum* is lacking and *replicare*, therefore, does not mean "think", "reflect upon" (for how can Lucius know what Charite thinks?) but "repeat"; the following *intermiscere suspiratus* points that way, too. See Callebat 1968, 158, who does not distinguish between the two meanings, but correctly assumes that in both meanings the word is a 'neologism'; the material from the *ThLL* Institute confirms this.

uotis... intermiscet suspiratus: *intermiscere* is found either with a dative or an ablative (for the dative cf. Verg. *Ecl.* 10, 4 f. *tibi... / Doris amara suam non intermisceat undam*) but, as here, it is often hard to say which case is being used; the *Index Apul.* and the *OLD* opt for an ablative, the *ThLL* is more cautious.

suspiratus: this is the spelling in α; F and φ have *suspirit(us)*, but in the margin of F is written *rat*, according to Giarratano and Robertson. The latter refers to Ov. *Met.* 14, 129 f. *respicit hunc uates et suspiratibus haustis / ... dixit*, which is the only place where the word is spelled in this qay. With Robertson, Terzaghi, Brandt-Ehlers, Vitali, Frassinetti, and vThiel we prefer *suspiratus* because of its poetic connotations; moreover, it is the *lectio difficilior*.

quoddam... triuium: in view of what follows this *triuium* in Apul. is functional; it is not so in *Onos* 24, 1: ἐπεὶ δὲ ἥκομεν ἔνθα ἐσχίζετο τριπλῆ ⟨ἡ⟩ ὁδός, οἱ πολέμιοι ἡμᾶς καταλαμβάνουσιν ἀναστρέφοντες. Cf. Macleod in his Loeb edition of the *Onos*, 91, n. 1: 'This pointless mention of the three roads is an indication that this work is an abridgement of another version. In Apuleius 6, 29 they are caught because they have stopped and are arguing about what road to take'. See also vThiel 1971, 111.

Petrarch interpreted this passage allegorically, namely as a reference to the choice between divine and human providence; see Scobie, *AAGA* 1978, 212.

gestiebat: for this frequently used verb see vdPaardt 1971, 107.

quod... scilicet iretur: unlike *replicat* this passage reflects the thought of a different person, i.e. Charite: 'vision du dedans'. This is shown by the use of *quod*+subjunctive and by *scilicet*, which certainly is appropriate here. We disagree with Elmenhorst, who deletes *scilicet*. See vdPaardt, *AAGA* 1978, 77.

Sed ego gnarus latrones illac ad reliquas commeasse praedas, renite- 151, 16-18
bar firmiter atque sic in animo meo tacitus expostulabam: "But, because I knew that the robbers had gone that way to fetch the rest of their booty, I put up a stubborn resistance and in my mind I silently remonstrated with her as

follows".

gnarus: only here in the *Met.* (Beroaldus conjectured *gnarae* in 5, 31 (128, 5)); the construction with the *accusatiuus cum infinitiuo* occurs from Sall. *Hist. fragm. 3, 98* onward.

illac: according to Médan 1925, 56 and 225 *illac* here means *illuc*. This seems improbable.

firmiter: Apul. always uses this form, rather than *firme*; see Callebat 1968, 175.

tacitus expostulabam: cf. 3, 24 (70, 22) *oblicum respiciens ad illam tacitus expostulabam*, where Fotis is the one rebuked. In both cases Lucius is the victim of a woman's mistake. For the predicative use of *tacitus*, see Callebat 1968, 415. vdPaardt 1971, 182 discusses the verb *expostulare*.

151, 18-20 'Quid facis, infelix puella? Quid agis? Cur festinas ad Orcum? Quid meis pedibus facere contendis? Non enim te tantum, uerum etiam me perditum ibis': "'What are you doing, unhappy girl? What are you up to? Why are you hurrying to Orcus? Why are you trying to do it with my feet? You know you are going to destroy not only yourself, but me too".

infelix puella: for *infelix* see *GCA* 1977, 156. Charite is called *infelix* in 8, 6 (181, 2), too; cf. also 4, 24 (93, 13) *infelicis rapinae praeda*. The use of *infelix* characterizes Charite as a Dido-figure, who is called *infelix* 8 times in the Aeneid; cf. Pease on Verg. *A.* 4, 68: 'The word is ... almost a permanent epithet, like *pius* used of Aeneas'. See Forbes 1943/4, 39; Walsh 1970, 53 f. There are also similarities of composition between the Dido-story and the Charite-story: both frame an inserted narrative which is told by a sub-narrator, consists of two books (although in the *Met.* the narrataive is not confined within actual book-limits), and contains both prospective and retrospective elements. In the stories of both Dido and Charite dreams play an important role; see *CGA* 1977, 204.

Orcum: see Callebat 1968, 405 f.; vdPaardt 1971, 80 f.

Quid meis pedibus facere contendis?: Rohde 1885, 103 proposed the insertion of *uim* after *pedibus*, which was accepted by vdVliet and Helm[1,2]; Bursian wanted to read ⟨me⟩ *meis pedibus facere*. Neither emendation is necessary, for the sentence can be read with *id* understood (Helm[3], *app. crit.*). See Kronenberg 1928, 37; Wiman 1927, 49 f. A somewhat different explanation is given by Damsté 1928, 20, who takes *quid* as a direct object rather than as an adverbial accusative: 'Non perspexerunt salem esse loci, quod asinus de pedibus suis loquitur tamquam de instrumentis, quod non sui iuris sunt'.

Non enim te tantum...: the ass's concern appears to have its ultimate origin in self-interest; see also comm. on 154, 2 f.

perditum ibis: possibly an archaizing periphrasis for *perdes*; see LHSz 2, 381. Yet *ibis* does retain some of its original force.

According to Bernard 1927, 247 this is one of the ten instances where elision gives a better clausula.

151, 21-25 Sic nos diuersa tendentes et in causa finali de proprietate soli, immo uiae herciscundae contendentes rapinis suis onusti coram deprehendunt ipsi latrones et ad lunae splendorem iam inde longius cognitos risu maligno salutant: "While we were thus pulling different ways and quarrelling in this boundary dispute about landownership or rather about road-division, we were taken in the very act by the robbers themselves, burdened with their loot: they had already recognized us from afar by the light of the moon and greeted us with malicious laughter".

Not everyone appreciates the jokes of Apuleius Juridicus. Norden 1912, 162 quotes Rode's opinion: 'eine elende Pedanterie, die ausgemerzt zu werden verdiente'. But Norden himself rightly reminds us of the fact that Apuleius wrote for a public 'das dem Rechte nicht so verständnislos gegenüber stand, wie dies in den weiteren Volkskreisen unserer Zeit die Regel ist'. The *lector doctus* of the *Met.*, therefore, will have known that a *causa finalis* is a boundary dispute between two neighbours. In such cases it is difficult to ascertain who is the plaintiff and who the defendant; hence the stipulation in *Dig.* 10, 1, 10: *iudicium communi diuidundo, familiae erciscundae, finium regundorum tale est, ut in eo singulae personae duplex ius habeant agentis et eius quocum agitur.* For this reason an *arbiter* was often appointed; ironically, fate (i.e. Apuleius) wills that the *arbitri* in this case are the robbers, who are little concerned about who is right and who is wrong.

de proprietate soli, immo uiae herciscundae contendentes: its meaning is, of course, "disputing as to which way we should take" (LS), not "the division of a 'chemin mitoyen' " (Vallette *ad loc.*). *(H)erciscere* (perhaps a deponent, thus *OLD*) means "divide an inheritance"; another instance of Apul.' playful use of this technical term is 9, 27 (223, 28) *nec herciscundae familiae sed communi diuidundo formula dimicabo, ut sine ulla controuersia uel dissensione tribus nobis in uno conueniat lectulo.* See Norden 1912, 155; Summers 1967, 239 f.

tendentes ... contendentes: Callebat 1968, 471 regards this word-play with the simple and the compound verb as an influence from Plautus, who uses this form of paronomasia quite often; cf. LHSz 2, 710.

rapinis suis onusti: emphasis is put on the fact that in Lucius' absence the robbers have to act as their own beasts of burden.

ad lunae splendorem: cf. *Onos* 24, 1 καὶ πόρρωθεν εὐθὺς πρὸς τὴν σελήνην ἔγνωσαν τοὺς δυστυχεῖς αἰχμαλώτους. In *Onos* 23, 4 Lucius takes advantage of the full moon to make an attempt at escape; this motif is absent in Apul.

risu maligno: Heine 1962, 251 discusses the motif of 'Schadenfreude' in the *Met.*

CHAPTER XXX

Lucius and the girl are led back to the robbers' cave, where the old woman appears to have hanged herself.

151, 25-27 et unus e numero sic appellat: 'Quorsum istam festinanti uestigio lucubratis uiam nec noctis intempestae Manes Laruasque formidatis?: "and one of them hailed us as follows: 'Where are you going at such a hurried pace on that moonlit road? Are you not afraid of spirits and ghosts in the dead of night?"

unus: see comm. on 152, 3 below.

festinanti uestigio: cf. 1, 14 (13, 20) *trepido uestigio*; 3, 21 (68, 2) *suspenso et insono uestigio*; 5, 26 (123, 12) *laboranti uestigio*. In view of their disagreement on which road to take, Charite's and the ass's *uestigium* (= *gradus*) can hardly be called *festinans*.

lucubratis uiam: according to Médan 1925, 346 *uiam lucubrare* means no more than "to be on one's way", but this interpretation does not do justice to the humour in the expression: *lucubrare* means "to make by lamp-light" and *uiam lucubrare*, consequently, means "to travel a road in the light (here: of the moon)". Bétolaud (461) rightly calls it an 'expression... bien remarquable et bien heureuse'.

noctis intempestae: the expression is also found at 1, 10 (10, 1) and 2, 25 (45, 16); when used in the ablative, it is generally regarded as a rendering of the Greek νυκτὸς ἀωρί or ἀωρίᾳ, which is actually found in the corresponding passage of the *Onos* (24, 2): ποῖ βαδίζεις ἀωρίᾳ, ταλαίπωρε; (note the bland βαδίζεις). The ancient grammarians disagreed on the meaning of *intempestus*: see Hildebrand *ad loc*. Probably Apul. agreed with Varro *L.L.* 6, 7, who quotes Aelius (?): *cum tempus agendi est nullum*, for it is typical of robbers to be active at that time; cf. Servius on Verg. *A*. 3, 587 *inactuosa: carens actibus*.

Manus Laruasque: F first had *Larbas*, which a later hand has corrected to *Laruas*; see Helm Praef. *Flor*. XLVI on the confusion between *b* and *u*. *Manes* are the souls of the dead, who are feared and whose propitious disposition is sought; see Nisbet-Hubbard on Hor. *Carm*. 1, 4, 16; *R.E*. 14, 1051, 43 f. For *Laruae* see *GCA* 1977, 170 f.

151, 27-152, 1 An tu, probissima puella, parentes tuos interuisere properabas?: "Were you on your way to make a quick, secret visit to your parents, you good girl, you?"

There are a few small textual problems, which are connected with the fact that F has been completely rewritten from *laruasque* through *loro* (152, 4) and that a lacuna in φ has been fitted by a different hand, according to Robertson. These problems are:

1) *an* is the reading of φ, F has *at*, and Plasberg proposed *ain*. The ironical *an* seems the most appropriate here.

2) F's reading *interuisere* is much to be preferred to *furtim uisere* in φ, which has all the characteristics of a gloss. *Interuisere* here means "to visit secretly" (compare 1, 24: 22, 14 and 6, 19: 134, 14, where the prefix carries no meaning); in Plautus, too, the element of discretion/secrecy is clearly expressed by the prefix, e.g. *Aul.* 363, *St.* 456. See Callebat 1968, 174, who rightly mentions this notion; *ThLL* and *OLD s.v.* omit it.

3) *properabas* in F *rescriptus* is preferable to the present tense *properas* in α and φ: at this moment the girl has come to a complete halt.

probissima: κατ' ἀντίφρασιν, see Bernhard 1927, 239; Callebat 1968, 399 and 468.

For the infinitive depending on *properabas* see Médan 1925, 76; LHSz 2, 346.

Sed nos et solitudini tuae praesidium praestabimus et compendiosum ad tuos iter monstrabimus': "But we shall offer you protection in your solitude and show you a good way to your people' ". 152, 1-3

Sed nos: Westendorp Boerma / Hijmans 1974, 407 take *nos* as a reflexive pronoun with *praestabimus*, and *praesidium* consequently as a predicate accusative. But it is possible to take *nos* as the subject (antithesis: *an tu ... sed nos*), and *praestare* in the sense of *praebere*; see *ibid.* 406, n. 2.

solitudini tuae praesidium: protection will be offered not by the ass (whom Charite, unknown to the robbers, had called her *praesidium* only a short while ago) but by the robbers. Helm does not mention the reading *sollicitudini* in AE: at first sight this reading seems attractive because Charite is not, strictly speaking, *in solitudine*. But we prefer the reading of F and φ for the very reason that the robbers treat the ass as quantité négligeable.

praestabimus: this reading of F is certainly the best; it is found in Hildebrand, Eyssenhardt, vdVliet, Helm[1-2], Gaselee, Brandt-Ehlers, and vThiel; Helm[3] and Helm-Krenkel revert to the reading of ς, *perhibebimus*, also preferred by Oudendorp, Giarratano, Terzaghi, Vitali, and Scazzoso. Robertson reads, with the *editio princeps*, *praebebimus*; Frassinetti ventures the conjecture *praehibebimus*. Oudendorp, strangely enough, finds the reading of F objectionable because of the homoeoteleuton *praestabimus ... monstrabimus*; this, however, argues not against, but rather for the reading, and not 'aliquatenus' (Robertson in his *app. crit.*) but *magnopere*; cf. Bernhard 1927, 227: 'Auch der Räuber, der Charite auf ihrer Flucht ertappt hat, bedient sich in seinen ironischen Worten eines Reims'; see also Strilciw 1925, 112 f.

et compendiosum ad tuos iter monstrabimus: this reading of AUS is now generally preferred to that of F *et ad parentes tuos iter* (Hildebrand, Eyssenhardt, Helm[1-2], Gaselee). With *tuos* the robbers probably do mean *parentes* but not her real ones! *Parentes* in F and in the reading of the Cod. Burn 128 Mus. Brit. *compendiosum ad parentes tuos iter* (accepted by Vitali) has all the characteristics of a gloss.[1] *Compendiosum* contains a typically Apuleian ambiguity: it means not only "shortened", as in 11, 22 (284, 17 f.), but also "advantageous", i.e. for the robbers themselves (cf. 161, 9 *sine ullo compendio*): see Callebat 1968, 387.

Callebat 1968, 144 points out that *monstrare* occurs in the *Met.* 5 times as often as its synonym *ostendere* (15: 3), whereas it does not occur at all in the *Flor.* and *Apol.* (*ostendere* 12 times in *Apol.*, twice in *Flor.*). It is clearly a word from colloquial language, as is proved by its survival in the Romance languages; see also Svennung 1936, 542, n. 1.

152, 3-5 Et unus manu secutus prehenso loro retrorsum me circumtorquet nec baculi nodosi, quod gerebat, suetis ictibus temperat: "And another, suiting the action to the word, took my strap and pulled me around; he did not spare the usual blows with the knotty cudgel he carried".

Et unus manu secutus: this is the reading of F; generally the reading of α *et uerbum manu secutus* is followed, which has, indeed, striking parallels: 1, 26 (24. 1) *et dictum iure iurando secutus*; 2, 11 (34, 17) *quod dictum ipsius Milo risu secutus*; 3, 16 (64, 10) *et uerbum facto secutus*. The following conjectures keep close to F: Hildebrand's *ea unus manu secutus* and Leo's *at minas manu secutus*. The following objections against F may be raised:
1) *unus* in 152, 3 cannot refer to the robber who was called *unus* in 151, 25, but must refer to someone else; therefore *unus... unus* is used here for *unus... alius* or *alius... alius*. That two robbers are active in this scene is implied also by *ille qui me retraxerat* below, a defining relative clause.
2) the lack of an object with *secutus*. This argument was countered by Hildebrand as follows: '*Verbum* vero vel simile quid cogitatione addi poterat, quia praecedit, latronis oratio, quam statim factum sequitur'.

We conclude that the arguments against the reading of F are not decisive, and that, therefore, it should be retained.

prehenso loro: cf. 149, 3 *lorum, quo fueram destinatus, abrumpo*; 149, 7 *(anus) lorum prehendit*; 149, 20 *(puella) extorto... loro manibus eius* (sc. *anus*) *me... inscendit*. Now that the strap is in the robbers' hands again, the *status quo ante* has been restored. It is possible that in the above-mentioned passages we have the masculine *lorus* (not the neuter *lorum*) "lash", "strap", as is certainly the case in 3, 13 (61, 26) and 3, 14 (62, 11). See vdPaardt 1971, 104.

nodosi: see Ernout 1949, 45 and 82; Callebat 1968, 385.

suetis: according to Bernhard 1927, 120 '*simplex pro composito* (= *consuetis*)'; cf. 172, 10 *suetum... uestigium*; 11, 23 (284, 26) *sueto lauacro*. *Suetus* for *consuetus* is already found in Tacitus (*Ann.* 1, 64; *Hist.* 2, 80), so that the suggestion made by Médan 1925, 146, that the word has here a completely new meaning, is incorrect.

152, 5-7 Tunc ingratis ad promptum recurrens exitium reminiscor doloris

[1] Too far-fetched is vdVliet's *compendiosum ad ⟨domesticos⟩ iter*, a rendering of the parallel passage in *Onos* 24, 3 ἡμεῖς σε τοῖς οἰκείοις ἀποδώσομεν; cf. φ *et compendiosum ad domos iter*.

ungulae et occipio nutanti capite claudicare: "At this point, as I returned reluctantly to an immediate death, I remembered my sore hoof and started to limp with a nodding head".

ingratis: see vdPaardt 1971, 80.

reminiscor doloris ungulae: Lucius sustained this *dolor ungulae* during the activities of the previous day; cf. 147, 18 *unde crebris aeque ingestis ictibus crure dextero et ungula sinistra mē debilitatum aegre ad exurgendum compellunt*. One cannot, therefore, agree with Gertrude Drake 1968, 106 that Lucius only pretends to be injured; he had forgotten the *ungula* in the excitement for a moment (148, 4 *nam timor ungulas mihi alas fecerat*), but the pain has returned now that his flight has failed.

occipio: see comm. on 149, 13.

claudicare: the limping ass is a recurrent motif in the *Met.*; not only Lucius himself limps, but also the ass in the underworld (6, 18: 142, 1) which Psyche has to pass in silence, following the directions of the *turris*; this similarity has persuaded Nethercut 1968, 114 that this ass and Lucius are identical. A striking feature is that the pastophore who is to initiate Lucius into the Osiris-cult (11, 27: 288, 19f.), and whose name is Asinius Marcellus, limps because of a deformed left foot; see Gwyn Griffiths *ad loc.*

Sed: 'Ecce', inquit ille, qui me retraxerat, 'rursum titubas et uaccil- 152, 7-10 las, et putres isti tui pedes fugere possunt, ambulare nesciunt? At paulo ante pinnatam Pegasi uincebas celeritatem': "But 'Look at you', said the man, who had pulled me back, 'you're stumbling and staggering again! Those rotten feet of yours can run away all right – can't they walk? Just now you were outdoing the winged speed of Pegasus'".

Ecce: shows the robber's indignation, as does the alliteration of *p* further on (the plosives echo his explosion of anger). Heine 1962, 173 follows Macrobius in distinguishing between the use of *ecce* by the narrator (32 times) and by a character which the narrator has put upon the scene (29 times); for further literature see vdPaardt 1971, 87.

titubas et uaccillas: both verbs are often used of the reeling gait of an intoxicated person (e.g. Lucius in 2, 31: 51, 8 *titubante uestigio*; another instance is 4, 8: 80, 15 f., at least if our reading is correct), but they also denote mental instability (Sen. *Ep.* 114, 23 *cum ille* (sc. *animus*) *paulum uacillauit*). Lucius 'vacillates' here in both respects, of course.

putres isti tui pedes: the contempt appears from *isti tui* (see Bernhard 1927, 171) and is illustrated by the alliteration. The figurative use of *puter* is not infrequent in the poets; cf. Hor. *Epod.* 8, 7 *mammae putres*.

fugere possunt, ambulare nesciunt: not synonyms, as Bernhard 1927, 148 maintains, but an adversative asyndeton. For a discussion of the use of *ambulare*, see Callebat 1968, 142 f.

pinnatam Pegasi... celeritatem: a remarkable enallage; see Bernhard 1927, 215; Médan 1925, 323, 348; Strilciw 1925, 122.

Pegasus is the winged horse born from the drops of blood which fell into the sea from Medusa's head, severed by Perseus (Ov. *Met.* 4, 785 f. *pennisque fugacem / Pegason et fratrem* (sc. *Chrysaorem*) *matris de sanguine natos*); with his help the Corinthian Bellerophon fought the Chimaera. The Muses' spring, Hippokrene, was struck from Mount Helicon by Pegasus' hoof (Ov. Met. 5, 262 f.); hence Pegasus later becomes a symbol of poetic inspiration. See *R.E.* 19, 56 f.; Roscher 3, 1735 f.

Pegasus and/or Bellerophon are mentioned at three other places in the *Met.* In 7, 24 Lucius escapes a fierce bear by taking to flight (172, 17 f. *meque protinus pernici fugae committo*). A passer-by appropriates him as a mount; the rider is referred to at 174, 10 as *meus Bellerofon*; implicitly Lucius has become Pegasus.

In 8, 16 (189, 22 f.) Lucius outruns the horses in whose company he finds himself. His speed is the result of fear, but according to him fear must also have inspired Pegasus: *denique mecum ipse reputabam Pegasum inclutum illum metu magis uolaticum fuisse ac per hoc merito pinnatum proditum, dum in altum et adusque caelum sussilit ac resultat, formidans scilicet igniferae morsum Chimaerae.*

In 11, 8 (272, 18) Lucius sees in the Isis-procession (the *anteludia*) an *asinum pinnis adglutinatis adambulantem cuidam seni debili ut illum quidem Bellerophontem, hunc autem diceres Pegasum, tamen rideres utrumque.* See Gwyn Griffiths 1975, 180 and 353 (addendum); id., *AAGA* 1978, 159.

152, 11-12 **Dum sic mecum fustem quatiens benignus iocatur comes, iam domus eorum extremam loricam perueneramus:** "While my kindly companion, brandishing his club, was still jesting thus with me, we had already arrived at the outermost enclosure of their house".

quatiens: '*quatere fustem* dicitur pro concutere et vibrare eum crebro verberando, ut passim *quatere hastam*' etc., (Oudendorp).

mecum ... benignus iocatur comes: cf. Nisbet and Hubbard on Hor. Carm. 1, 9, 6: '*benignus* sometimes implies not so much kindness and amiability as objective openhandedness of a material sort'. Of course *benignus* is highly ironical here, as *bonus* often is; see Callebat 1968, 467; vdPaardt 1971, 53.

iam ... perueneramus: a variation on 148, 3 f. *Dum secum mitissimi homines altercant de mea nece, iam et domum perueneramus.* For the usage of *domus*, see comm. on 147, 22 f.

extremam loricam: the accusative (without preposition) with *peruenire* is also found at 1, 5 (4, 20) *si Thessaliam proximam ciuitatem perueneritis*; see Marg. Molt *ad loc.* With *lorica* (cf. Greek θώραξ) is meant the enclosure, extensively described in 4, 6.

152, 13-14 **Et ecce de quodam ramo procerae cupressus induta laqueum anus illa pendebat:** "And look, from a branch of a high cypress the old woman – you know – was hanging with a noose around her neck".

Et ecce: again surprise, this time the narrator's; see on 152, 7 f.

de quodam ramo procerae cupressus: vThiel 1971, 12, n. 32 observes that Apul. has given a more concrete and precise form to the corresponding passage in the *Onos* (24, 6) τὴν μὲν γραῦν εὕρομεν ἐκ τῆς πέτρας κεκραμένην ἐν καλῳδίῳ. The cypress may seem a little odd in view of the scant opportunities it provides for hanging: perhaps the symbolism of the cypress as the tree of death effected the choice. Cf. Murr 1890, 118: 'Wie alle immergrünen Bäume eigneten sich insbesondere auch die Nadelhölzer für die Vorstellung der immerwährenden Fortdauer des Lebens... und konnten so leicht zu den Unterirdischen in Beziehung gesetzt werden'; see further Cumont 1942, 219 and 292; Tatum 1969a, 168, n. 71.

quodam: see Graur 1969, 379.

cupressus: this genitive form also occurs in 8, 18 (191, 11); in *Mund.* 36, 12 the genitive plural *cupressorum* is used; see Callebat 1968, 122.

induta laqueum: for the 'middle' construction cf. 9, 20 (218, 6) *tunicas iniectus*; 11, 14 (277, 1) *superiorem exutus tunicam*. The phrase *laqueum induere* is found also at 1, 16 (15, 4); see vGeisau 1916, 78. Observe that here no motive is given for the suicide, unlike *Onos* 24, 6: δείσασα γάρ, οἷον εἰκός, τοὺς δεσπότας ἐπὶ τῇ τῆς παρθένου φυγῇ κρημνᾷ ἑαυτὴν σφίξασα ἐκ τοῦ τραχήλου. For the suicide motif see *GCA* 1977, 187 f.

Quam quidem detractam protinus cum suo sibi funiculo deuinctam 152, 14-18
dedere praecipitem puellaque statim distenta uinculis cenam, quam
postuma diligentia praeparauerat infelix anicula, ferinis inuadunt
animis: "Immediately they pulled her down and threw her, tied with her own rope, into the ravine; at once they tied the girl up some distance away; then, with bestial greed, they attacked the meal, which the poor old woman had prepared with posthumous care".

cum suo sibi funiculo deuinctam: for *suus sibi* see Callebat 1968, 258, f.; Scobie 1975, 93. A parallel may be found in the story borrowed by Aulus Gellius from Plutarch, about the suicide mania which had taken possession of the girls in Miletus (*N.A.* 15, 10): *decreuisse Milesios ut uirgines quae corporibus suspensis demortuae forent, ut hae omnes nudae cum eodem laqueo quo essent praeuinctae efferrentur. Post id decretum uirgines uoluntariam mortem non petisse pudore solo deterritas tam inhonesti funeris.* Cf. Plin. *Nat.* 2, 156; Luc. 6, 538 f.

dedere praecipitem: F is uncertain (*.d.* in the margin, see Helm Praef. *Flor.* XXXIV), but this reading of φ is correct; cf. 164, 10 *praecipites dedere*, where the robbers themselves, killed with their own swords, are thrown into the ravine.

distenta uinculis: *distenta* from *distinere* "to keep apart" (cf. 6, 11: 136, 14 f.) *sic ergo distentis et sub uno tecto separatis amatoribus tetra nox exanclata*) i.e. separated from both the robbers and the meal (Oudendorp). The conjectures made by Colvius (*destinata*) and Robertson in his *app. crit.*: *(distenta ‹in› uinculis)* are superfluous.

postuma diligentia: "in ihrer über den Tod hinauswirkenden Fürsorge" (Helm-Krenkel); see further *GCA* 1977, 51.

infelix anicula: according to Callebat 1968, 372 ironically used; but a mild rehabilitation by the narrator is more probable. See *GCA* 1977, 63 f.

cenam ferinis inuadunt animis: *cenam inuadere* on the analogy of *hostem inuadere* (Médan 1925, 247); cf. Aur. Vict. *Epit.* 20, 9 *cibum auidius inuadere*; Heine 1962, 154 observes 'die... grosse Gier der Räuber beim Essen und Trinken'. Much duller is the parallel passage in *Onos* 24, 7: εἶτα ἐδείπνουν, καὶ πότος ἦν μακρός.

CHAPTER XXXI

Deliberation on how to punish the girl and the ass.

152, 19-20 Ac dum auida uoracitate cuncta contruncant, iam incipiunt de nostra poena suaque uindicta secum considerare: "And while they gobbled up everything with greedy voracity, they already started to consult together about our punishment and their own revenge".

The combination of *dum*, which indicates the concomitance of two actions (Ernout-Thomas ²1964, 371), and *iam* "already" illustrates the robbers' conflict between hunger for food and thirst for revenge; one can see (in the alternation of open *a* with closed *u* or semi-closed *o*) their jaws moving and hear (in the five-fold alliteration of *c*) them crunching – the robbers are carrying on their discussion with their mouths full.

uoracitate: Médan 1925, 202 calls this a 'mot rare de la langue postérieure'; the same quality is ascribed to the ass in 175, 5 *nunc iste securus incumbens praesepio uoracitati suae deseruit*. In the robber-stories much attention is paid to eating, both the robbers' – 4, 8 (80, 5 f.); 6, 25 (147, 10); 7, 11 (162, 15) – and the ass's – 4, 1 (75, 1 f.); 4, 22 (91, 12 f.); 6, 29 (150, 17); 7, 14 (164, 16 f. and 165, 3 f.).

contruncant: the object of *contruncare* " to cut to pieces" can be a living creature (Pl. *Ba.* 975 *eos ego hodie omnes contruncabo duobus solis ictibus*) as well as food (Pl. *St.* 554 *meum ne contruncent cibum*). Apul. always uses the verb in the latter meaning; see Marg. Molt 1938, 43.

de nostra poena suaque uindicta: *nostra* has the value of an objective genitive of the personal pronoun, *sua* that of a subjective genitive.

secum considerare: cf. Ter. *Hau.* 385 *et quom egomet nunc mecum in animo uitam tuam considero*; Cic. *Prou.* 1 *consideret ipse secum*. In both these passages *secum considerare* means "to take counsel with oneself", but here in Apul. "to take counsel with each other". Oudendorp already remarks 'quod videndum an ita alibi occurrat'; according to *ThLL* this question must be answered in the negative, but a comparable construction occurs at 10, 5 (239, 27) *ac dum de oblationis opportunitate secum noxii deliberant homines*. Examples of Apul.'s use of *secum* as a synonym of *inter se* are given in Callebat 1968, 259; see also comm. on 148, 3.

152, 21 Et utpote in coetu turbulento uariae fuere sententiae: "And – as usual in a turbulent meeting – the opinions varied".

On the elliptic use of *utpote* see Médan 1925, 238. Summers 1967, 241 points out that 'the penalties discussed by the robbers are those applicable to the *humiliores* – plebeians, freedmen, slaves – under Roman law. The terms are especially appropriate here because of the girl's wretched position'. Indeed they regard her as – to use her own words (4, 24: 93, 14) – *mancipium effecta*. Norden 1912, 81 points out that *iure* this is not the case.

ut primus uiuam cremari censeret puellam, secundus bestiis obici suaderet, tertius patibulo suffigi iuberet, quartus tormentis excarnificari praeciperet: "that is, the first proposed that the girl should be burned alive, another advised that she should be thrown to wild beasts, a third ordered that she should be nailed to the cross, and a fourth instructed that she should be tortured to death". 152, 21-24

ut is used explicatively ("that is", "namely"). Here it explains a whole sentence and not – as is more usual – a pronominal expression within the main clause; see LHSz 2, 645 and Schrijnen-Mohrmann 1937, 2, 126 f.

primus... secundus... tertius... quartus: cf. 147, 20 f. *unus... alius... alius iterum.*

censeret... suaderet... iuberet... praeciperet: observe the climax. *Censeret* describes the speaker's personal view; *suaderet* implies that he would like to transmit his opinion to others; *iuberet* suggests the relationship between an officer in command and private soldiers; *praeciperet* corresponds with the attitude of an expert teacher versus inexpert pupils (might the last speaker be the same as in 4, 12, who 'has some of the tone of an unregenerate schoolmaster'? See *GCA* 1977, 94).

Another climax may be observed in the duration and gruesomeness of the tortures: burning soon results in suffocation; in the case of abandonment to wild animals death will be slower; crucifixion means a most painful and prolonged agony ('die physischen und seelischen Leiden des langsam am Kreuze Hinsterbenden sind unvorstellbar', Schneider in *Th. Wb. NT* 7, 1964, 573); as for *tormentis excarnificare*, the duration and intensity of the torments can, of course, be increased at will.

Yet another climax is to be found in the increasing number of syllables:

uiuam cremari censeret	8 syll.
bestiis obici suaderet	9 syll.
patibulo suffigi iuberet	10 syll.
tormentis excarnificari praeciperet	13 syll.

Except with *iuberet*, the use of the passive infinitive is remarkable. For *censere*, however, a parallel passage is Pl. *Aul.* 528 *aes censet dari*; for *praecipere* cf. *Dig.* 31, 1, 89, 7 *codicillos aperiri testator praecepit*.

excarnificari: this word is found for the first time in Ter. *Hau.* 813; later in Cicero, Seneca, and Suetonius. Chr. Mohrmann 1932, 255 f. (cf. 1965, 3, 211 f.) observes that in Christian authors verbs in *-ficare* are directly derived from any kind of noun or adjectives, whereas in earlier Latin they are derived from nouns and adjectives in *-fex* and *-ficus* only.

certe calculo cunctorum utcumque mors ei fuit destinata: "at any rate she had certainly been unanimously sentenced to death". 152, 24-153, 1 *certe calculo cunctorum*: again, as in line 19, alliteration of the *c*: the jaws go on crunching.

certe ... utcumque: these words are more or less synonymous and confirm each other.

fuerat: for *fuerat* instead of *erat* see Médan 1925, 6 and LHSz 2, 321; here probably also used to avoid hiatus.

calculus: this is a white or black voting-pebble with which one voted for acquittal or conviction, for approval or disapproval respectively: *Met.* 10, 8 (243, 5); 10, 32 (263, 24). In its figurative sense of "opinion", "judgment" the word occurs in Apul. also at 160, 16 *calculis omnibus ducatum latrones unanimes ei deferunt*.

153, 1-2 Tunc unus omnium sedato tumúltu placido sermone sic orsus est: "Then, after the general tumult had died down, one started to speak as follows in a quiet strain:"

Since we think that the progressive link with *omnium* is more meaningful than the regressive, we have in our translation chosen the former with Brandt-Ehlers. Of course we cannot be certain.

placido sermone sic orsus est: cf. Verg. *A.* 1, 521 *maximus Ilioneus placido sic pectore coepit*; *A.* 7, 194 *atque haec ingressis* (sc. *Teucris Latinus*) *placido prior edidit ore*; *A.* 11, 251 *auditis ille* (sc. *Diomedes*) *haec placido sic reddidit ore*. The words with which the following argumentation is introduced suggest the atmosphere of Verg. *A.* 1, 147-153 and raise the expectation (as does the beginning of the speech itself) that the speaker will make a much milder proposal than his predecessors did – but soon the opposite will prove to be true.

153, 3-7 'Nec sectae collegii nec mansuetudini singulorum ac ne meae quidem modestiae congruit pati uos ultra modum delictique saeuire terminum nec feras nec cruces nec ignes nec tormenta ac ne mortis quidem maturatae festinas tenebras accersere: "'It is not in accord with the principles of our society, nor with the gentleness of its individual members, and least of all with my moderation, to allow you to vent your rage beyond measure and beyond the limits of the offense, and to invoke wild beasts and crosses and fires – not to mention the untimely darkness of a hasty death".

nec ... nec ... ac ne ... quidem: a threefold polysyndeton, immediately followed by a fivefold one (153, 5f. *nec ... nec ... nec ... nec ... ac ne ... quidem*); see Bernhard 1927, 124; Callebat 1968, 99; LHSz 2, 805; vdPaardt 1971, 62.

ne ... quidem: here and 153, 6: "let alone", "not to mention", rather than "not even"; see *GCA* 1977, 80.

secta: see *GCA* 1977, 136 f.

mansuetudini: this word occurs at two more places in the *Met.* (8, 24: 196, 15 and 10, 16: 249, 7); there it is used by the narrating Lucius in reference to the *mansuetudo* of the experiencing Lucius.

ultra modum delictique saeuire terminum: cf. 3, 9 (58, 19) *(ut) pro modo facinoris saeuiatis*.

festinas: in the sense of "early", "premature" the adjective is not used until the second half of the first century A.D.: Val. Fl. 4, 469 f. *quam te | exedit labor et miseris festina senectus!* Auson. *Ecl.* 8, 32 *grauidos sentit subrepere nixus | ante expectatum festina puerpera uotum.*

accersere: this is the reading of F, cf. 7, 20 (169, 18) *accersisse*. Bücheler 1884, 414 f. thinks that editors are wrong in deleting the forms of *accessere*, which have not infrequently been transmitted in the mss. (see *ThLL* 2, 448, 36 f.). But following ç (cf. also 235, 2 and 244, 14) modern editors read the form with -*rs*-, both here and at 169, 18.

Meis itaque consiliis auscultantes uitam puellae, sed quam meretur, largimini: "So listen to my advice and grant the girl life – but the one she deserves". 153, 7-8

auscultantes: used absolutely or constructed with a dative, *auscultare* means "give heed to", "obey": Caecil. *com.* 196 *audire ignoti quom imperant soleo, non auscultare.* In addition to this passage, Apul. uses the verb in this meaning also at 5, 25 (123, 5) *ergo mihi ausculta nec te ... perimas* and 8, 31 (202, 14) *mi ausculta* (but 6, 18: 141, 17 *mihi ausculta* "hearken to me"). According to Médan 1925, 178 the verb belongs to the 'langue archaïque'; according to *ThLL* it is a 'verbum imprimis priscorum scaenicorum et sermonis vulgaris' ("listen", "keep your ears open"). Callebat 1968, 171 calls it 'un terme évité par le purisme littéraire mais vivant dans les diverses classes sociales'.

sed quam meretur: the girl has to pay a high price for her attempt at escape! The robbers do not seem to realise that the new plan rules out their original intention of exacting a ransom; they are reminded of it by Haemus at 161, 8 f. (see comm. *ad loc.*).

sed, followed by the clause *quam meretur*, is used here in opposition not to another (previously mentioned) clause, but to the unqualified noun *uitam*. Cf. Sen. *Ep.* 85, 7 *habet pecuniae cupiditatem, sed modicam* (with four parallel constructions!).

quam in the sense of *qualem*.

largimini: ironically used; *largiri* means not merely "give", but "give generously".

Nec uos memoria deseruit utique, quid iam dudum decreueritis de isto asino semper pigro quidem, sed manducone summo, nunc etiam mendaci fictae debilitatis et uirginalis fugae sequestro ministroque: "Certainly it has not altogether slipped your memory what you long since decided to do about that ass – always lazy but still a consummate glutton and now a liar too with his fictitious disability, and a trustee and servant of the girl in her escape". 153, 8-12

nec uos memoria deseruit: a mannered expression (which does not seem to occur elsewhere) instead of the more customary *aliquid de memoria excidit* or *aliquid (e) memoria (ex)cedit*.

nec ... utique = nec ... omnino; see Callebat 1968, 97.

semper pigro... manducone summo... mendaci: for the combination of these negative qualities cf. Epimenides in St. Paul *ad Tit.* 1, 12 Κρῆτες ἀεὶ ψεῦσται, κακὰ θηρία, γαστέρες ἀργαί. Cf. Diels *VS* 1, 31.

manducone: Fest. 115 L says on *manducus* (= *manduco*; see Non. 25 L) *manduci effigies in pompa antiquorum inter ceteras ridiculas formidolosasque ire solebat magnis malis ac late dehiscens et ingentem sonitum dentibus faciens, de qua Plautus (Rud. 535) ait: "Quid si ad ludos me pro manduco locem? Quapropter? Clare crepito dentibus".*

The pot calls the kettle black: the robbers are themselves characterized by *auida uoracitate* (152, 19) – according to Lucius, at least.

nunc etiam mendaci fictae debilitatis: for the genitive of relation cf. Pl. *Asin.* 855 *si huius rei me esse mendacem inueneris*; Médan 1925, 36.

uirginalis fugae: "the girl's flight"; for the use of an adjective instead of the genitive of a noun, see Bernhard 1927, 110 f.

sequestro: a *sequestrum* or *sequestre* is an agreement where a subject of dispute is deposited with a third person; after the sentence it is awarded to the winner of the lawsuit. The person who administers the deposit is called a *sequester*. Apul. uses this word here (likewise the feminine *sequestra* in 9, 15: 214, 11) in the metaphorical sense of "mediator", "go-between": Charite has entrusted the ass with the execution of the plan of flight, just as litigants entrust the subject of dispute to a *sequester*. See Norden 1912, 180 f.; Summers 1967, 241.

153, 12-16 Hunc igitur iugulare crastino placeat totisque uacuefacto praecordiis per mediam aluum nudam uirginem, quam praetulit nobis, insuere, ut sola facie praeminente ceterum corpus puellae nexu ferino coherceat: "May it therefore please you to slaughter him tomorrow, to take out all his guts, and to sew the girl, whom he has preferred to us, naked into his belly – so that, with only the girl's face showing, he holds the rest of her body in a bestial bond".

iugulare is generally (but not exclusively; see e.g. Aug. *Serm.* 178, 9, 10 *lupus uenit ad ouile ouium, ...quaerit iugulare, quaerit deuorare*) used of people; our Lucius/ass is threatened by a similar danger at 8, 31 (202, 14 f.) *aduenam istum asinum remoto quodam loco deductum iugula*.

crastino = *cras* (which does not occur in Apul.); likewise 2, 11 (34, 15) and 7, 26 (174, 19); cf. 1, 24 (22, 17) *crastino die*. See Callebat 1968, 167.

totisque: for *totis* = *omnibus* see Callebat 1968, 287; vdPaardt 1971, 121. Observe the double hyperbaton *totis... praecordiis, uacuefacto... insuere*. On several grounds – first, because of the extensive hyperbaton; second, because a pronoun like *ei* has been omitted with *uacuefacto* (see Bernhard 1927, 160); third, by the addition *quam praetulit nobis* – the auditors of the narrator and the readers of the story are left in a suspense that is more than merely grammatical.

uacuefacto: the verb *uacuefacere* is found first in Cic. *Cat.* 1, 16 *aduentu tuo ista subsellia uacuefacta sunt,* and occurs not infrequently in later authors. In Apuleius it occurs only here.

per mediam aluum nudam uirginem... insuere: possibly the speaker has been inspired to his proposal by Thrasyleon's example.

Both the use of *per* instead of *in* and the addition of *mediam* and *nudam* tend to make the proposal more vivid; see Callebat 1968, 219. For the use of *per* to emphasize extent, see Quint. *Inst.* 8, 3, 84 *Idem* (*sc.* Verg. *A.* 3, 631) *Cyclopa cum iacuisse dixit 'per antrum' prodigiosum illud corpus spatio loci mensus est*; cf. Hand, *Turs.* 4, 430. Whether the respective dimensions of Charite and the ass permit the recommended operation is not considered in the *Met.*; it is considered, however, in the description which SHA, Jul. Cap. *Macr.* 12, 4 gives of a similar punishment: *Cum quidam milites ancillam hospitis iam diu praui pudoris affectassent idque per quendam frumentarium ille didicisset, adduci eos iussit interrogauitque utrum esset factum. Quod cum constitisset, duos boues mirae magnitudinis uisos subito aperiri iussit atque his singulos milites inseri capitibus, ut secum conloqui possent, exertis; itaque poena hos affecit, cum ne adulteris quidem talia apud maiores uel sui temporis essent constituta supplicia.*

Perhaps one may assume that Macrinus has read the *Met.*, as has his older contemporary, the anti-emperor Clodius Albinus, about whom Septimius Severus makes the following remark (in a letter to the Senate, in which he complains that Albinus has been preferred to him, *SHA*, Jul. Cap. *Albin.* 12, 12): *maior fuit dolor quod illum pro litterato laudandum plerique duxistis, cum ille naeniis quibusdam anilibus occupatus inter Milesias Punicas Apulei sui et ludicra litteraria consenesceret.* (But Herrmann 1972, 576 thinks that these words certainly do not refer to the *Met.*; moreover, one should keep in mind that the authenticity of the letter is disputed, see Scobie 1975, 49 n. 10).

nudam: Rohde 1885, 103 wonders: 'wozu *nudam?*' For the word is not borrowed from *Onos* 25, 6, which merely says τὴν δὲ ἀγαθὴν ταύτην παρθένον τῷ ὄνῳ ἐγκατοικίσωμεν. Assuming that the *nuditas* will add a piquant flavour to the story, one would expect *nudam* to be in a different position, i.e. predicatively before *insuere*. Therefore Rohde thinks that Apul. may have written *mundam*, thus – with the adjective used ironically – motivating the addition *quam praetulit nobis*. Several arguments can be found against this. First, the vague, general qualification of morality ('good') in the *Onos* is replaced by a description with an obvious sexual connotation ('pure'). Secondly, the element of nudity is often introduced by Apul. (24 forms of *nudus*, 14 forms of *nudare* in the *Met.*). Thirdly, the adjective *mundus* occurs nowhere else in the *Met.* Therefore it seems preferable to retain the reading of F, even if the position of *nudam* is, indeed, somewhat puzzling.

quam praetulit nobis: i.e. "whose side he chose rather than ours"; *Onos* 25, 5 says more explicitly καὶ υἱὴν καὶ τῆς φυγῆς τῆς παρθένου γενόμενον ὑπηρέτην καὶ διάκονον. Apul.'s vaguer formulation is witty because it presupposes a conscious choice on the part of the ass; one might even think of an erotic preference (cf. Ov. *Met.* 4, 56 (sc. *Thisbe*) *praelata puellis*), especially if one remembers the ass's attempts to kiss the girl's feet (149, 27 f.).

facie praeminente: the object of this measure is evident from *Onos* 25, 7: ὡς ἂν μὴ εὐθὺς ἀποπνιγείη. Cf. also 153, 6 f. *ne mortis quidem maturatae festinas tenebras accersere*.

ceterum corpus puellae: cf. 4, 11 (82, 21) *ceterum Lamachum*.

ferino: Damsté 1928, 20 f. conjectures *uterino*, which draws an amusing parallel with 7, 4 (156, 21) *uentremque crebro suspiciens meum iam misellam puellam parturibam* but is unnecessary.

coherceat: even in death the ass will take an active part in the girl's punishment.

153, 16-18 tunc super aliquod saxum scruposum insiciatum et fartilem asinum exponere et solis ardentis uaporibus tradere: "then, on top of a jagged rock, to expose the stuffed and crammed ass and to expose him to the blaze of the burning sun".

Note the s/c alliteration in *super aliquod saxum scruposum insiciatum*.

super aliquod saxum... exponere: cf. 4, 33 (100, 21) *montis in excelsi scopulo, rex, siste puellam* (more s/c alliteration); 6, 25 (147, 16) *ut me... super lapidem... deicerent*.

scruposum: in addition to this passage, Apul. uses the word only in *Fl.* 11 (16, 13). Médan 1925, 175 regards it as a word from the 'langue archaïque', see e.g. Pl. *Capt.* 185 *nam meus scruposam uictus commetat uiam*. For Apul.'s use of adjectives in *-osus*, see Luisa Gargantini 1963, 38. Isid. *Orig.* 16, 3, 5 contrasts *scrupus with calculus: Calculus est lapillus terrae admixtus, rotundus atque durissimus, et omni puritate lenissimus. Dictus autem calculus quod sine molestia breuitate sui calcetur: cuius contrarius est scrupus, lapillus minutus et asper, qui si inciderit in calciamentum, nocet et molestia est animo; unde et animi molestiam scrupulum dicimus: hinc et scrupea saxa, id est aspera*.

insiciatum: F has *insiticium* ("introduced by hybridization", "foreign", "imported"); this reading is adopted by Gaselee and defended by Armini 1932, 82; but Robertson (with Frassinetti's approval) rightly rejects it as follows: 'nec bene cum *fartilem* sociatur nec apte de asino hic dicitur'. Heinsius' conjecture *insiciatum* ("stuffed") is accepted by modern editors. Var. *L.* 5, 110 explains *insicia ab eo quod insecta caro*. Macr. *Sat.* 7, 8, 1 remarks: *isicium, quod ab insectione insicium dictum amissione N litterae postea quod nunc habet nomen obtinuit* (*ThLL* has, therefore, the lemma *isicium* rather than *insicium*); the mss. of Apicius (whose second book is wholly devoted to *isicia* and dishes prepared with these) almost always have the form *esicium*; see André 1965, 51 f. (on Apic. 2, 42).

fartilem: a rare adjective. *ThLL* mentions, besides our passage, Plin. *Nat.* 10, 52 *fartilibus in magnam amplitudinem crescit* (sc. *anseris iecur*), taking *fartilibus* as an ablative plural of the nominalized adjective ("fattening feed"). *OLD* quotes the same passage as follows: *fartilibus* (sc. *anseribus*) ..., taking *fartilibus* as a plural dative of the adjective ("fattened"). The word further occurs also at Tert. *Val.* 27 *Nunc reddo de Christo; in quem tanta licentia Iesum inserunt quidam, quanta spiritale semen animali cum inflatu infulciunt, fartilia nescio quae commenti et hominum et deorum suorum*.

In the quotation from Tert. *fartilia* can only be taken as the plural of a nominalized adjective ("stuffing"). In the Pliny passage *fartilis* can have two meanings, namely "stuffing" (*ThLL s.v.* 286, 76) and "stuffed" (*OLD*). In our passage only the meaning "stuffed" makes sense. Adjectives in *-ilis* tend to be passive; *farcio* has two meanings ("stuff" and "stuff into") and therefore *fartilis* can both describe a roast turkey and its chestnut stuffing as Prof. Philippa Goold kindly points out to us. See also *ThLL s.v.* 286, 73 *idem quod fartus (per iocum)*. On adjectives in *-ilis* in Apuleius see Luisa Gargantini 1963, 36.

solis ardentis uaporibus: uapor means "heat" here, not "vapour"; cf. Ov. *Met.* 10, 126 f. *solisque uapore / concaua litorei feruebant bracchia cancri*. This meaning of the noun seems to originate from Lucretius, who uses it more than forty times, always (according to Bailey on 1, 1032) as a synonym of *calor*. After Lucr. this use is found in prose, too: Cic. *Sen.* 15, 51 (sc. *terra semen*) *tepefactum uapore et compressu suo diffundit*.

CHAPTER XXXII

Everyone agrees with the last speaker.

153, 18-23 Sic enim cuncta, quae recte statuistis, ambo sustinebunt, et mortem asinus, quam pridem meruit, et illa morsus ferarum, cum uermes membra laniabunt, et ignis flagrantiam, cum sol nimis caloribus inflammarit uterum, et patibuli cruciatum, cum canes et uultures intima protrahent uiscera: "For in this way they will both endure all the things that you so rightly decided upon: the ass will suffer the death he has long since deserved, and she will feel the bites of wild animals when worms tear her limbs apart, the blaze of fire when the sun with its heat sets the belly utterly aflame, and the agonizing torture when dogs and vultures pull forth the inner guts".

quae recte statuistis: whereas in 153, 4 the speaker created the impression of objecting to his comrades' proposals on the ground that they were *ultra modum*, he now evidently fully agrees with them. About the use of *statuere* see comm. on 156, 20. That this relative clause is non-restrictive appears from the fact that the speaker adopts all the proposals and, by making some variations, manages to combine and even expand them:

morsus ferarum (153, 20)	– *bestiis obici* (152, 22)
ignis flagrantiam (153, 21)	– *uiuam cremari* (152, 22)
patibuli cruciatum (153, 22)	– *patibulo suffigi* (152, 23)
ceteras eius aerumnas et tormenta (153, 23)	– *tormentis excarnificari* (152, 24)

About the variations we may remark the following. The man who proposed to throw Charite to the animals will have had in mind lions, bears, etc. (see Friedländer 1921/23 2, 409 f.); the last speaker apparently means by *ferae* the *uermes*, who *membra laniabunt*. Nowhere in the extant literature is there an example of *uermes* as the subject of *laniare*; one does find e.g. *aquila* Cic. *Carm.* frg. 7, 5 Morel; *draco* Cic. *Carm.* frg. 22, 16; *lupus* Ov. *Ep.* 10, 84. – *Viuam cremari* conveyed the meaning of being literally abandoned to the flames; *ignis flagrantia* in this passage refers to the unbearable heat of the sun. – *Patibulo suffigi* refers to actual crucifixion (not common for women; see Mommsen 1899, 923); the agony referred to in this passage is not caused by mere crucifixion but rather by an additional torment, as appears from the explicatory *cum*-clause. A similar torture was undergone by the robber-chief (!) Laureolus: while hanging to the cross he was torn apart by wild animals. The mimic poet Catullus (under Caligula) wrote a play on this subject, which (as Martial tells us in *Sp.* 7) was performed in a realistic way: at the end of the play Laureolus' part was taken over by someone sentenced to death; see Friedländer 1921/23 2, 413; Schanz-Hosius 1935 2, 564 f.

sustinebunt: on the notion of 'must', which is not explicitly expressed here, see Nägelsbach 1905, 430 f.

et mortem asinus ... et illa ... uiscera: chiasmus. The structure of the sentence is unbalanced: one colon referring to the ass, versus three devoted to the girl (see Bernhard 1927, 58). This shows that the ass is something of a 'quantité négligeable' to the speaker; thus Lucius is not only threatened with death, but scorned as well.

mortem ... quam pridem meruit: cf. 153, 8 *uitam puellae, sed quam meretur, largimini*; like the girl, the ass will get his deserts!

ferarum: *ferae* generally means four-footed, undomesticated animals: Serv. auct. on Verg. *A*. 11, 571 *ueteres ... omnes prope quadrupedes feras uocabant*; August. *Gen. litt*. 15, 496, 24 f. (Zycha) *quadrupedes accipiamus omnia iumenta ... bestias uel feras omnia quadrupedia indomita*. The explicatory *cum*-clause reveals that *ferae* in this passage refers to *uermes* – a humorous ἀπροσδόκητον.

uermes laniabunt: at 8, 22 (194, 12 f.) a comparable torture is described: a slave, smeared with honey and tied naked to a hollow tree, is eaten by the ants living in the tree.

nimis: this reading of F is adopted by vdVliet and Gaselee; all other authors read *nimiis* (φ). One should bear in mind, however, that *nimis* means not only "too (much)" but also "to an excessive degree" (see Hand *Turs*. 4, 207 f.); in the latter meaning the adverb can very well be connected with *inflammarit*. A scribe, not observing the hyperbaton, might easily have inserted an *i* in order to connect the resulting adjective with *caloribus*.

caloribus: the plural form occurs in Apul. only here; cf. Sen. *Ep*. 90, 17 (sc. *Syrticis gentibus*) *propter nimios solis ardores nullum tegumentum satis repellendis caloribus solidum est nisi ipsa arens humus*.

canes et uultures: from Homer on one can find the combination of dogs and birds (of prey), especially dogs and vultures; they feed on corpses which are often abandoned to them intentionally. Cf. *Il*. 1, 4 f. αὐτοὺς δὲ ἑλώρια τεῦχε κύνεσσιν οἰωνοῖσί τε πᾶσι...; 18, 271 πολλοὺς δὲ κύνες καὶ γῦπες ἔδονται...; Liv. 41, 21, 7 *Cadauera intacta a canibus ac uolturibus tabes absumebat*: Ov. *Ib*. 169 f. *unguibus et rostro tardus trahet ilia uultur, / et scindent auidi perfida corda canes*; Plin. *Nat*. 36, 107, *inexcogitatum ante posteaque remedium inuenit ille rex* (sc. *Tarquinius Priscus*), *ut omnium ita defunctorum corpora figeret cruci spectanda ciuibus simul et feris uolucribusque laceranda*; see also Catul. 108, 4 f. with Kroll's note.

intima protrahent uiscera: a grimly humorous double entendre. *Viscera*, in all probability, primarily refers to the entrails of the girl herself, but at the same time her body as a whole forms the ass's entrails; the gruesomeness of this scene is emphasized by the hyperbaton.

Sed et ceteras eius aerumnas et tormenta numerate: mortuae bestiae 153, 23-27
ipsa uiuens uentrem habitabit, tum faetore nimio nares aestu⟨abit⟩ et
inediae diutinae letali fame tabescet nec suis saltem liberis manibus
mortem sibi fabricare poterit': "But count up further tribulations and
torments, too: alive herself, she will dwell in the belly of a dead beast; moreover,

her nostrils will burn with the excessive stench, she will waste away with the deadly hunger produced by long fasting, and, through not having even her hands free, she will not be able to prepare her own death' ".

aerumnas et tormenta: the mental and physical agonies respectively. In reference to *antiquitas* (sc. *uerborum*) Quint. (*Inst.* 8, 3, 24 f.) remarks that archaisms *sanctiorem et magis admirabilem faciunt orationem ... sed utendum modo nec ex ultimis tenebris repetenda*; among the examples of such improper use he writes: *aerumnas quid opus est, tamquam parum sit si dicatur quod horridum* (according to Cousin's text, but the proper reading is much debated). Tatum 1969 b, 489 n. 10 observes that 'the word *aerumna* in particular is often used to describe Lucius' tribulations'; cf. comm. on 155, 18.

numerate: in the address to the audience, the speaker himself starts to "sum up": another four torments are added – if our reading is correct – to the four already mentioned.

mortuae bestiae ipsa uiuens: another chiasmus.

faetore nimio nares aestuabit et: the reading in F *aestuet* is obviously corrupt: the present subjunctive in the midst of the future indicatives *habitabit, tabescent, poterit* is out of place. Médan's opinion (1925, 6) that a 'confusion dans les conjugaisons' has taken place here, has not met with approval and rightly so: Lausberg 1962, 3, 175 f. gives examples only of transition from second to third and from third to second conjugation. The most attractive of the proposed conjectures is that by Robertson (followed by Vitali, whose text wrongly uses [ ] instead of ‹›), namely *aestu‹abit› et* (cf. the reading *aestuabit* or *aestuabunt* in ς). Most conjectures retain *aestu*, which necessitates the addition of a finite verb. Castiglioni (followed by Giarratano, Frassinetti, vThiel, and Scazzoso) reads ‹*excruciata*› *aestu et*; but this results in only three torments, whereas *Onos* 25, 8 (the parallelism with which is especially striking in this passage) mentions four. This argument is already advanced by Robertson in his *app. crit.*; his second consideration, namely that the words *tormenta numerate* necessitate more than three torments, is less valid: *numerare* here may well be restricted to three objects. Brakman's *nares aestu ‹marcescent› et* is paleographically improbable; moreover, it causes an unacceptable change of subject (in our translation we have not been able to avoid this change).

For the use of the causal ablative *faetore nimio* instead of e.g. *propter faetorem nimium* cf. Pl *Am.* 1118 *mihi horror membra misero percipit dictis tuis*; see LHSz 2, 132.

inediae diutinae: this is explained by the remark of Hier. *Orig. Ez.* 11, 283 *homini non utique septimo die letalis inedia*. Later in the story the ass wishes to end his life by *inedia*: 7, 24 (172, 5); Charite, too, considers it: 8, 7 (181, 28); Thrasyllus actually does it: 8, 14 (188, 6).

mortem sibi fabricare: Médan 1925, 241 calls this an 'expression nouvelle'. Apul. uses the verb in the *Met.* three times in the active and twice in the passive, but never as a deponent; outside the *Met.* he uses it six times in the passive, three times as a deponent, but never in the active. See Callebat 1968, 295; vdPaardt 1971, 98; Flobert 1975, 305.

Talibus dictis non pedibus, sed totis animis latrones in eius uadunt 154, 1-2
sententiam: "After words like these the robbers sided with him – not by ballot,
but by acclamation".

Talibus dictis: causal or ablative absolute? *Index Apul.* mentions our passage
not *s.v. dictum (subst.)* but *s.v. dicere*, apparently taking the words as an ablative
absolute. Cf. 1, 13 (12, 23) *His editis abeunt*; 6, 21 (144, 23) *His dictis amator leuis
in pinnas se dedit*. On account of these passages the ablative absolute seems
preferable.

non pedibus ... in eius uadunt sententiam: cf. 2, 7 (30, 13) *et quod aiunt, pedibus
in sententiam meam uado*. The usual term, in spite of Apuleius' *quod aiunt*, is
pedibus ire in alcs sententiam (e.g. Liv. 9, 8, 13). The words contain an allusion to
the formula by which the *princeps senatus* puts a proposal to the vote: *qui hoc
censetis, illuc transite; qui alia omnia, in hanc partem*. Cf. Festus 314 L; Plin. *Ep.* 8,
14, 19 and Sherwin-White *ad loc.*; see Willemse 1910, 195 f. and Otto 1890, 276.
For the parodying element see Westerbrink in *AAGA* 1978, 65.

In view of 2, 7 (30, 13) and the fact that as early as Cic. *uadere* is used as a
synonym of *ire*, we disagree with Callebat 1968, 143, who assumes that the use of
uadere in this passage introduces an element of swiftness and violence.

Quam meis tam magnis auribus accipiens quid aliud quam meum 154, 2-3
crastinum deflebam cadauer? "When I heard that with my large ears – what
else could I do but weep for myself: the corpse of tomorrow?"

quam: the antecedent *sententiam* in the previous sentence meant "proposal";
in the relative clause this meaning has shifted to "resolution" or (as a juridical
technical term) "sentence". Bernhard 1927, 54 mentions this clause as an
example of 'Verschränkung der Relativsätze' and consequently puts a comma
after *sententiam*; all modern editors, however, put a period. LHSz 2, 569 point
out that the choice between 'relative Verschränkung" and *'coniunctio relativa'* is
often a matter of punctuation only.

tam magnis auribus: the ass's ears are large in comparison to those of a human
being. The words emphasize that this ass is a metamorphosed human being,
while at the same time they explain the fact that he is able to understand
everything perfectly: his *crastinum* (154, 3) shows that he has properly taken in
crastino (153, 12). For *tam magnis = tantis* cf. 4, 7 (79, 19) and *GCA* 1977, 65. For
the deictic use of *tam* see Nägelsbach 1905 (= [r]1963), 404.

quid aliud ... deflebam: if this pathetic exclamation is meant as an invitation to
the reader to answer the question, his answer might be simply: *miserrimam
puellam deflere poteras*. The conceivability of such a reaction adds a touch of
humour to the desperate-sounding sentence. Smith 1968, XX n. 2 observes that
Lucius' speculations on his future (here and 253, 20 f.) will prove incorrect; the
narrator in the *Onos*, on the other hand, sometimes makes a 'Vorausdeutung'
which proves correct (see Lämmert 1955, 143 f.), e.g. at the end of ch. 15 ταῦτα
ἐννοῶν ἠγνόουν (Smith wrongly reads ἠγνοων)ὁ δυστυχὴς τὸ μέλλον κακόν.

Note, finally, that the sixth book ends with the ominous word *cadauer* (with
which the first words of the seventh book will form a striking contrast; one may
wonder whether the author is pulling the narrator's leg, cf. Scobie in *AAGA* 1978,
47).

CHAPTER I

One of the robbers reports on the events in Milo's house.

154, 5-8 Vt primum tenebris abiectis dies inalbebat et candidum solis curriculum cuncta conlustrabat, quidam de numero latronum peruenit; sic enim mutuae salutationis officium indicabat: "At soon as the day, having cast off the dark, was beginning to brighten, and the shining chariot of the sun was illuminating everything, one of the robbers arrived; that was evident from the manner in which they greeted each other".

The previous book ended in a minor key (Lucius expected that the next day would bring him death), but now day breaks with brilliant sunlight everywhere. The first words of this chapter form the first four feet of a hexameter; observe also the balanced dicolon of fifteen and sixteen syllables, which may also contribute to the suggestion of a harmonious situation. The poetic description of dawn is a topos (mocked at by Sen. *Ep.* 122, 11 f.) from Homer on: ἦμος δ' ἠριγένεια φάνη ῥοδοδάκτυλος Ἠώς. See vdPaardt 1971, 23 f.; Scobie 1975, 116; Westerbrink in *AAGA* 1978, 65 f. The initial words of this chapter are often compared to Enn. *Ann.* 212 V (= 6, 19) *ut primum tenebris abiectis in‹d›albabat*; according to Norden 1915, 78 n. 2 (following Bergk 1861, 308) this is an 'elende Fälschung des Portugiesen Achilles Statius' (viz. in his commentary written in 1566 on Catul. 63, 40). Ethel M. Stewart, nevertheless, notes (1925 *ad loc.*) that 'there is a reminiscence of our line in Apul. *Met.* 7' and maintains that 'the reference is to the second day of ‹the battle of› Asculum' (278 B.C.); Calboli 1968, 75, too, assumes that Apuleius' words are a reminiscence of Ennius.

ut primum with imperfect indicative: cf. 9, 23 (220, 9) *ut primum occursoriam potionem et inchoatum gustum extremis labiis contingebat adulescens*. Médan 1925, 93 remarks that '*ubi* et *ut* sont construits régulièrement avec l'impf. de l'indic.', but our passage and the one quoted above are the only occurrences (of twelve) in the *Met.* where *ut primum* is constructed with the imperfect indicative.

tenebris abiectis: the (more or less) personified day throws off darkness like a garment; cf. 3, 20 (67, 13) *omnibus abiectis amiculis*. The metaphor is different in Eur. *Ion* 1150 μελάμπεπλος νύξ, where night is not identified with the garment.

inalbebat: a *hapax legomenon* with, perhaps, an ingressive connnotation, cf. *ThLL s.v.* 816, 16: '*i.q. album esse (fieri?)*'; one might compare *rubēre* (= *rubescere*) in Lucr. 5, 461 f. *aurea cum primum geminantis rore per herbas / matutina rubent radiati lumine solis*. The transitive *inalbare* occurs 9, 24 (221, 11 f.) *uiminea cauea, quae ... lacinias circumdatas suffita*[1] *candido fumo sulpuris inalbabat*; 10, 20 (252, 14 f.) *cerei praeclara micantes luce nocturnas nobis tenebras*

---

[1] This is the reading of *ThLL s.v.* 816, 30, following Colvius; F has *suffisa*; ς (followed by Helm, Robertson, and Frassinetti) has *suffusa*.

inalbabant. Inalbare is used in a figurative sense ("to cleanse") by Christian authors.

solis curriculum: this poeticism does not fit in very well with *conlustrabat*; comparable to our passage is 9, 28 (224, 9) *cum primum rota solis lucida diem peperit*. The metaphor is purer in 10, 35 (266, 8) *ultimam diei metam curriculum solis deflexerat*; cf. Q. Cic. poet. *Fr.* 1, 16 *at dextra laeuaque ciet rota fulgida solis / curriculum*. On the other hand it might be argued that Apul. achieves a parodic effect by the choice of his words.

curriculum cuncta conlustrabat: alliteration. Curiously enough, the three occurrences in the *Met.* of the verb *conlustrare* are all combined with *cuncta*: 1, 18 (16, 8) *iam iubaris exortu cuncta conlustrantur*; 11, 2 (267, 16) *ista luce feminea conlustrans cuncta moenia*; this is not the case in Apul.'s other works.

quidam: refers to the robber mentioned 3, 28 (73, 6).

peruenit: all the occurrences of this verb which are mentioned by LS are constructed with *huc, in,* or *ad* with the accusative, indicating direction. Perhaps this is why Stewech proposes the conjecture *reuenit* and Vulcanius (followed by Robertson) *superuenit*; cf. 11, 20 (281, 17 and 282, 3), where *superuenire* is used without any phrase denoting direction.

mutuae salutationis officium: what this *officium* consists of we learn from 4, 1 (74, 1 f.): *sermo prolixus et oscula mutua*; cf. Suet. *Jul.* 82, 1 *assidentem conspirati specie officii circumsteterunt*.

Is in primo speluncae aditu residens et ex an‹h›elitu recepto spiritu   154, 8-10
tale collegio suo nuntium fecit: "He sat down at the front of the entrance of the cave and, having recovered his breath after panting, he made the following report to his comrades".

residens et ... recepto spiritu: on the connection of *participium coniunctum* and *ablatiuus absolutus,* see Bernhard 1927, 43 and LHSz 2, 140.

residens: from **residēre** or from *residĕre*? The former alternative seems preferable because of the sequence of events (*residens... recepto spiritu... nuntium fecit*), especially with preterite use of the present participle; see LHSz 2, 386 f.

recepto spiritu: Gatscha 1898, 158 refers to Serv. on Verg. *G.* 1, 437. Although he may well be right, one has to bear in mind that the reference is to fish which have been caught and are lying on the beach but, after eating some herbs which grow there, *recepto spiritu* are able to return to sea. Morelli 1913, 184 compares *Hist. Apoll.* 37 *tremebundus toto corpore expalluit diuque maestus constitit. Sed postquam recepit spiritum ...*, where the expression refers not to a physical but a psychological condition. – Observe the alternation in *ex anhelitu recepto spiritu tale*.

tale nuntium: Servius comments twice on the gender of this word: first on Verg. *A.* 6, 456 *qui nuntiat genere tantum dicitur masculino; quod autem nuntiatur, licet neutro dicatur, tamen inuenitur etiam masculino*; secondly on Verg. *A.* 11, 896 *nuntius est qui nuntiat, nuntium quod nuntiatur* (Ernout-Meillet are wrong when they note: 'toutefois *nuntium* dans ce sens n'est que l'adj. accompagnant un nom neutre'); Hildebrand objects to this remark. It seems that Apul. adheres to Servius' lattter definition: cf. 8, 6 (181, 3 f.) *quae quidem simul percepit tale*

81

nuntium, quale non audiet aliud; it may also be true for 9, 28 (224, 20) *pistor ille nuntium remisit uxori*, which *Index Apul.* and *OLD* enter *s.v. nuntius*. Cf., too, Isid. *Orig.* 10, 189 *Nuntius est [et] qui nuntiat et quod nuntiatur, id est* ἄγγελος καὶ ἀγγελία. *Sed nuntius ipse homo genere masculino; id uero, quod nuntiat, genere neutro.* The neuter is found, too, in Catul. 63, 75 *deorum ad auris nova nuntia referens*; Var. *L.* 6, 86 *ubi censor auspicauerit atque de caelo nuntium erit.*

154, 11-13 Quod ad domum Milonis Hypatini, quam proxime diripuimus, pertinet, discussa sollicitudine iam possumus esse securi: "'As to the house of Milo of Hypata, which we recently plundered, we can shake off our worry and feel safe now".

To plunge into the matter without an introduction is quite usual among acquaintances who already know the situation, cf. 4, 8 (80, 17) *nos quidem... Milonis Hypatini domum fortiter expugnauimus.*

quam proxime diripuimus: viz. three days ago, cf. 3, 28 (72, 21 f.); see vdPaardt in *AAGA* 1978, 84 f.

quod ad... pertinet: cf. 3, 23 (69, 21) *bono animo es, quod ad huius rei curam pertinet.*

discussa sollicitudine: cf. 4, 21 (90, 11) *timore discusso*; Amm. 30, 10, 6 *sollicitudine discussa uixere securius.*

154, 13-18 Postquam uos enim fortissimis uiribus cunctis ablatis c[r]astra nostra remeastis, immixtus ego turbelis popularium dolentique atque indignanti similis arbitrabar, super inuestigatione facti cuius modi consilium caperet‹ur› et an et quatenus latrones placeret inquiri, renuntiaturus uobis, uti mandaueratis, omnia: "For when – after carrying everything off with great stoutness of heart – you had gone back to our camp, I mingled with the knots of people; and under the pretense of being sad and indignant I noted what kind of measures would be taken concerning the investigation of the deed, and whether – and to what extent – it would be decided to trace the robbers, with the intention of reporting everything to you, as you had instructed".

uos... ego: the personal pronouns are used here to emphasize the contrast; according to Bernhard 1927, 112 this use is quite rare in Apul.

fortissimis uiribus: there has been some doubt as to the correctness of this reading in F, which has resulted in some ingenious conjectures: *fortissimi uiri* (Scaliger) and *fortissimi uiri; rebus* or *fortissimi, ui rebus* (Oudendorp). Helm's comment on Scaliger's conjecture is *'fort. recte'*; Robertson remarks, about the former conjecture of Oudendorp and that of Scaliger, *'alteruter fort. recte'*. But Frassinetti rightly considers emendation unnecessary, referring to 2, 32 (51, 15) *ex summis uiribus*; 3, 5 (55, 24) *uiribus alacribus*; 3, 6 (56, 10) *ualidis... uiribus.* Perhaps Oudendorp's objection is to the use of a nominalized neuter adjective (*cunctis*) in an ambiguous case form; Helm refers for this to 5, 20 (119, 1) *cunctis istis foras tecunt relatis.* See also Summers ʳ1965, LX; Wagenvoort 1967, remark 18[a] for similar instances in Seneca.

castra nostra remeastis: the accusative of direction with *remeare* is not found elsewhere in Apul. (except 10, 26: 257, 23 *medicus... domum remeabat*). See e.g. Verg. *A.* 11, 793 *patrias remeabo inglorius urbes*; Stat. *Silv.* 3, 5, 12 *Euboicos fessus remeare penates / auguror*; Amm. 17, 13, 34 *destinatas remearunt urbes*.

turbelis: vdPaardt 1971, 203 says that *turbela* = *turba* and that the suffix *-ela* is vulgar; Callebat 1972, 1105 objects to this opinion. Because the word is used in the plural it seems to have some diminutive force, at least here: *small* groups, "folla del poplino" (Pagliano), have been formed in which the 'spy' listens for information; cf. the situation in 4, 20 (90, 4) *populi circumfluentis turbelis immisceor*. See also *GCA* 1977, 154 f., where, however, our passage is judged differently.

Médan 1925, 24 on 11, 9 (272, 22) finds the nominal use of *popularis*, meaning "people" ("des bourgeois"), 'rare et de la langue postérieure'.

dolenti atque indignanti similis: for nominalized participles see Callebat 1968, 252. *Indignanti similis*: cf. 8, 25 (196, 23) *similis indignanti*. Gatscha 1898, 147 refers to Verg. *A.* 8, 649 *illum indignanti similem similemque minanti / aspiceres*, where in similar words a completely different situation is described.

arbitrabar: for *arbitrari* in the sense of "observe", "pay attention", see vdPaardt 1971, 159.

super: for its use instead of *de* see *GCA* 1977, 101 f.

caperetur... placeret: imperfect subjunctive referring to the future; see LHSz 2, 550. *Caperetur* is a correction by ς, followed by Helm, Robertson, Frassinetti, and vThiel; F has *caperet*. Plasberg's conjecture ‹*ciuitas*› *caperet* gives a fourfold *e*-alliteration, but seems somewhat far-fetched.

an: see vdPaardt 1971, 166 for the use of *an* instead of *num* or *-ne*.

inquiri: *inquirere* means here "to trace (a criminal)"; cf. Sen. *Con.* 10, 1, 2 *non desinam inquirere percussorem*. An *inquisitor* is a detective; cf. Suet. *Iul.* 1, 2 *ut commutare latebras cogeretur seque ab inquisitoribus pecunia redimeret*.

renuntiaturus: for Apul.'s use of the future participle see Bernhard 1927, 45.

uti: for the use of this archaic disyllable see LHSz 2, 632.

mandaueratis: Summers 1967, 243 and 212 is wrong in supposing that a reference is made here to the technical (viz. juridical) term *mandatum*; *mandare* means here "to give instructions", "to command", etc. (see *OLD s.v.*, 6).

Nec argumentis dubiis, sed rationibus probabilibus congruo cunctae multitudinis consensu nescio qui Lucius auctor manifestus facinoris postulabatur,: "And on the ground not of dubious indications but of probable arguments a certain Lucius was accused – with the unanimous agreement of the whole crowd – as the evident perpetrator of the crime". 154, 18-21

Nec... sed: for the antithesis see Bernhard 1927, 60 f.; vdPaardt 1971, 141.

argumentis and *rationibus* are synonyms here, distinguished from each other only by their respective adjectives *dubiis* and *probabilibus*. Quint. *Inst.* 5, 10, 11 makes the following distinction: *cum sit argumentum ratio probationem praestans, qua colligitur aliquid per aliud et quae quod est dubium per id, quod dubium non est, confirmat, necesse est esse aliquid in causa, quod probatione non egeat*. Thus, according to Quint.'s definition, it is impossible for an *argumentum* to be *dubium*; this is contrary to Apul.'s use.

   congruo consensu: alliteration. The frequency of *co-* or *cu-* in this chapter is striking: at the beginning of a word *curriculum cuncta conlustrabat* (154, 6), *cunctis* (13), *cuiusmodi consilium* (16), *congruo cuncta... consensu* (10), *commendaticiis* (21), *commentitus* (22), *conciliauerat* (23), *condi... curiose* (155, 3); within a word *discussa* (154, 12), *securi* (13), *plusculisque* (24).

   congruo: this adjective (found in both ante- and postclassical Latin) is especially frequent in Christian authors from the time of Apul. onwards. When used absolutely (without a dative or ablative) it can mean "in accord with the norms": Vet. Lat. *Luc.* 15, 12 *da mihi congruam partem substantiae* (τὸ ἐπιβάλλον μέρος) and "mutually agreeing": Cens. 6, 6 *quorum opiniones ut de hac specie congruae, ita... dispariles*.

   postulabatur = accusabatur, cf. 3, 6 (56, 18) *tantillo crimine postulatis*; 7, 3 (156, 4) *crimine latrocinii postulabar*. See Löfstedt 1911, 239; vdPaardt 1971, 61 f.

154, 21-155, 4 qui proximis diebus fictis commendaticiis litteris Miloni sese uirum commentitus bonum artius conciliauerat, ut etiam hospitio susceptus inter familiaris intimos haberetur plusculisque ibidem diebus demoratus falsis amoribus ancillae Milonis animum inrepens ianuae claustra sedulo explorauerat et ipsa membra, in quis omne patrimonium condi solebat, curiose perspexerat: "because, during the previous days, by means of a forged letter of recommendation, he had passed himself off to Milo as an honest man and had thoroughly ingratiated himself with him, so that he was even hospitably received and reckoned among his intimate friends. After staying there for several days and winning the heart of Milo's servant-girl with false professions of love, he had closely examined the locks on the door, and carefully inspected the very rooms in which all the valuables used to be stored".

   This information has obviously been gathered from the *turbelae popularium*.

   fictis commendaticiis... commentitus: a subtle play on words. *Fictis* is synonymous with *commenticiis*, which Apul. does not use here, probably because it resembles the immediately following *commendaticiis* (this leads to confusion in the mss. of Gell. 3, 19, 4 *nam si licet res dicere commenticias* (recc., *commendaticias* P)), and also because it is derived from the same stem as *commentitus*. Lucius' own words in 1, 22 (20, 12) *litteras ei a Corinthio Demea scriptas ad eum reddo* do not at all create the impression that the letter was forged. A counterfeit letter of recommendation occurs 4, 16 (86, 21 and 25) in the story of the robbers' attack on Demochares' house.

   commendaticiis litteris: "letter of recommendation", cf. Cic. *Fam.* 5, 5 *statueram nullas ad te litteras mittere nisi commendaticias*. Pricaeus points out Vulg. 2 Cor. 3, 2 (read 3, 1) *numquid egemus commendaticiis epistolis ad uos aut ex uobis*, where the Greek text has συστατικῶν ἐπιστολῶν.

   sese is the object both of *commentitus* and of *conciliauerat*.

   artius: for the comparative with the function of the positive, see LHSz 2, 168 f.

   conciliauerat... explorauerat.. perspexerat: these indicatives in a relative clause have a causal meaning; see LHSz 2, 559.

inter familiares... haberetur: cf. 2, 26 (46, 17) *inter ceteros familiares dehinc numerabimus*.

plusculis diebus: for the ablative indicating the duration of time, see Löfstedt 1911, 55; LHSz 2, 148. The adjective *plusculus* "several" occurs frequently in Apul. *Met.*; see Bernhard 1927, 137; vdPaardt 1971, 130 and 159.

ibidem = ibi, cf. Tac. *Ann.* 14, 16 (sc. *conuiuae Neronis*) *considere simul et adlatos uel ibidem repertos uersus conectere*; Suet. *Dom.* 23, 1 *senatus adeo laetatus est, ut... non temperaret, quin... imagines eius coram detrahi et ibidem solo affigi iuberet*.

falsis amoribus: Apul. often uses the plural of abstract nouns; see Bernhard 1927, 100 f.

ancillae Milonis animum inrepens: Lucius himself (in human shape again) expresses a completely different view on this matter in 11, 20 (282, 4 f.) *cum me Fotis malis incapistrasset erroribus*; this is, however, in contradiction with his first private conversation with Fotis 2, 7 (31, 1 f.).

animum inrepens: for *inrepere* with the accusative without *in* (a construction not mentioned by *ThLL*) cf. 3, 24 (70, 4) and 8, 11 (185, 27) *inrepit cubiculum*; 4, 15 (86, 18) *quam (sc. caueam) inrepsit*. Cf. Tac. *Ann.* 4, 2 (sc. *Seianus*) *inrepere paulatim militares animos* with Nipperdey-Andresens's note: '*inrepere* veilleicht bei Tac. zuerst mit dem Akk.'.

sedulo: here, as often, the adverb has lost its original meaning mentioned by Nonius 54 L *sedulum significat sine dolo*; cf. Don. Ter. *Ad.* 413; Serv. on Verg. *A.* 2, 374; Isid. *Orig.* 10, 244 and 247. Charisius (p. 250 Barwick) criticizes this definition as follows: (sc. Helenius Acro) *commentarius, quos Adelphis Terenti non indiligenter attulit... ita disserit: 'ut falso' inquit 'et consulto, ita sedulo dictitatum', nisi forte sine dolo putat esse sedulo nec cum industria, cum sit utique diuersum*. Vanicek 1881, 295 explains: '*sed-u-lus* versessen auf etwas = emsig, eifrig, sorgsam'; LS *s.v. sedulus* are of the opinion that 'the derivation from *se-dolo*... is an error'. But Walde-Hofmann [3]1954, 509 and Ernout-Meillet [3]1951, 325 still accept the ancient explanation; see also Lindsay 1894, 563.

membra: "rooms"; see vdPaardt 1971, 197.

quis = quibus; see vdPaardt 1971, 159 f.

CHAPTER II

The ass Lucius, full of astonishment, continues to listen to one of the robbers giving an account of the gossip in Hypata about the man Lucius.

155, 4-6 Nec exiguum scelerati monstrabatur indicium, quippe cum eadem nocte sub ipso flagitii momento idem profugisset nec exinde usquam compareret: "There was no small indication of a criminal being involved, it was pointed out: for that same character had that same night, at the very moment of the offense, made off and had not been in evidence anywhere since".

Nec exiguum: litotes is a figure of speech seldom used by Apul., but cf. 148, 9 *nec... mediocris*. See vdPaardt 1971, 49.

scelerati... indicium: with *indicium* the objective genitive is usually that of an abstract noun, e.g. *timoris, pietatis, beneuolentiae*, etc., but cf. Cic. *Fin.* 5, 4 *multa in omni parte Athenarum sunt indicia summorum uirorum*; Quint. *Inst.* 9, 2, 4 *docti hominis indicium*. Cf. *ThLL s.v.* 1148, 59.

quippe cum: generally a rather rare combination, although quite frequent in Apul., see Fernhout 1949, 55. It does also occur in Classical Latin, e.g. Nep. *Praef.* 4 *quippe cum ciues... uterentur*; Liv. 26, 39, 9 *quippe cum... pugnarent*. See LHSz 2, 560.

idem: this pronoun (or formations related to it) occurs unusually often in this page: 5 *eadem nocte*, 8 *eidem*, 10 *ibidem* (154, 24 without an apparent difference in meaning from *ibi*). It is hard to resist the impression that Apul. wishes to characterize this robber by a somewhat mannered style; see also e.g. 154, 15 *dolentique atque indignanti similis*; 154, 16 *cuius modi consilium... et an et quatenus*; 154, 18-19 *argumentis... rationibus probabilibus* (two notions with practically identical meaning); the alliteration at 154, 19 *congruo cunctae... consensu*; the word-play at 154, 21-22 *commendaticiis... commentitus*; the accumulation of participles at 155, 10-16; the exaggeration at 155, 13 *ad ultimam mortem*.

Furthermore, these stylistic nuances fit in well with the somewhat pompous legal reflections at the end of his story. One should, however, not come to such conclusions too hastily: Apul. has a definite tendency to indulge his taste for the spectacular and bizarre, and repeatedly shows his delight in legal subtleties. On this subject see Bernhard 1927, 194-195; Eicke 1956, *passim*; Walsh 1970, 63 f.; Gwyn Griffiths 1975, 55 f.

sub ipso... momento: according to LHSz 2, 279 this 'temporal-modal-instrumentales *sub*' in the sense of *simul cum* already occurs in Classical Latin, but is definitely in vogue in Late Latin. Disregarding the instances in which the modal element predominates (e.g. Lucr. 4, 543 *tuba depresso... sub murmure mugit*; Prop. 2, 28, 35 *magico sub carmine rhombi*), one finds that Cicero does not use temporal *sub*, but that Caesar does, e.g. *Gal.* 5, 13, 3 *sub bruma*, as do Nepos and the Augustan poets.

exinde: temporal "since", see comm. on 147, 12.

compareret: "had been seen"; *comparēre* is often combined with a negation in the sense of "to be missing", "to be lost", e.g. Cic. *Tul.* 54 *seruus meus non comparet*.

nam et praesidium fugae, quo uelocius frustratis insecutoribus pro-   155, 6-8
cul ac procul abderet sese, eidem facile suppeditasse: "in fact an aid to flight, by which he could thwart his pursuers more quickly and hide himself farther and farther away, had been readily available to him".

nam: explains how Lucius could disappear so fast without a trace; consequently there is no need for Eyssenhardt's conjecture *iam* which did not merit a place in Helm's *app. crit.* for that reason. The indirect discourse sums up the contents of the gossip in town. The robber himself, of course, knows almost as well as the ass what actually happened: the robbers had (3, 28: 73, 3-8) loaded the horse and the two asses with the loot from Milo's house and driven them away. A special flavour is added by the fact that the robber, who tells the story, knows nothing about the mysterious Lucius, but the ass, who listens, knows everything.

On *nam et* = *nam* see vdPaardt 1971, 87-88.

praesidium fugae: this objective genitive with *praesidium* is quite rare; perhaps comparable to Cic. *Sul.* 77 *ubi erit ... illud firmissimum praesidium pudoris*. Elsewhere Cicero prefers a prepositional construction, probably for the sake of clarity, e.g. *Tusc.* 2, 2 *magnum is sibi praesidium ad beatam uitam comparauit*.

frustratis insecutoribus: although the verb usually occurs as a deponent, forms with passive meaning are not infrequent, e.g. Sil. 2, 247 *frustrato proditus ictu*; Apul. himself says *Apol.* 25 (29, 15) *frustrata expectatione omnium*. Flobert 1975, 294 gives a series of examples in which this verb has an active meaning.

procul ac procul: a similar *geminatio*, which was – and is – especially in vogue in colloquial language (Hofmann ³1951, 58; LHSz 2, 808-809), is also found in highly poetic language, cf. Verg. *A.* 6, 258 *procul, o procul este, profani*. All occurrences of rhetorical *geminatio* in Apul. which clearly aim at a stylistic effect are discussed by Bernhard 1927, 232-238; see also Gwyn Griffiths 1975, 274 commenting on *diu diuque* at 11, 20 (281, 18). In F *ac procul* has been deleted by another hand.

suppeditasse: "had been at hand", cf. Cic. *Brut.* 245 *cui si uita suppeditauisset*; Liv. 28, 27, 3 *nec consilium, nec oratio suppeditat*.

equum nanque illum suum candidum uectorem futurum duxisse   155, 8-10
secum: "for he had taken along that white horse of his to be his mount".

equum ... candidum: Lucius' horse, which is called here *candidus* because of its white colour, and which is going to change owners many times in the course of the book, is finally (11, 20) restored to its original proprietor. Lucius has there, to his own astonishment, dreamt of a slave Candidus whom he never owned. When the dream is interpreted this Candidus turns out to be his horse, cf. Gwyn

Griffiths 1975, 277 and 355, and recently Dowden 1977, 142-143. Whether or not a symbolical value should be attached to this adjective is difficult to determine; Gertrude Drake 1968, 104 is one of those who advocate an allegorical interpretation of the white horse. See also Nethercutt 1968, 111.

nanque: for the spelling see comm. on 159, 12.

illum: it is uncertain whether this accusative denotes the subject or the object of *duxisse*; ambiguities such as this are not uncommon in our author.

futurum: at first sight, this participle seems superfluous here; but in 155, 11 below it is functional; see also comm. on 165, 6.

155, 10-16 Plane seruum eius ibidem in hospitio repertum scelerum consiliorumque erilium futurum indicem, per magistratus in publicam custodiam receptum et altera die tormentis uexatum pluribus ac paene ad ultimam mortem excarnificatum, nil quicquam rerum talium esse confessum, missos tamen in patriam Luci illius multos numero, qui reum poenas daturum sceleris inquirerent: "His slave, who had been found there at his lodgings, would certainly be a source of information about his master's crimes and intentions. By order of the authorities he had been locked up in the public prison; and the next day he had been tormented in various ways and almost been tortured to death. He had not confessed anything of the kind: nevertheless many men had been sent to that Lucius' native town to search for the culprit in order to make him pay for his crime".

plane: to be connected with *futurum indicem*, rather than with *repertum*.

seruum: at 2, 31 (51, 6) Lucius appears to have brought one slave along on his journey; at 3, 27 (72, 10) as well he speaks of *seruulus meus*. But at 2, 15 (37, 11) mention is made of *pueri* and at 11, 20 (282, 3-4) of *famuli*. An extensive discussion of this problem can be found in vdPaardt 1971, 74. The inconsistency may be due to carelessness on the author's part, who now seems also to have forgotten that at 3, 27 (72, 20-21) he had allowed this slave to flee: *profugit territus*; yet now he is found in Milo's house, although no mention has been made of his return. See vdPaardt 1971, 196. On the other hand Apul. may have done so intentionally: the unscrupulous robber invents the larger part of his story.

Summers 1967, 245-248 enters into the legal aspects of this passage. By leaving his slave in Milo's hands Lucius would have forfeited his ownership. In that case the magistrate can order the slave to be sold: a slave may not bear witness against his own master (in this case Lucius), but after this public sale he is free to do so. It is, indeed, quite possible that Apul., well acquainted as he was with Roman law, had this in mind even though he does not mention such a sale.

in hospitio: i.e. Milo's house, which had been assaulted by the robbers (3, 28). This concrete usage of *hospitium* was in vogue in Latin of all periods; Apul. employs it in this sense at 1, 7 (6, 18). But the noun may have an emotional value here, indicating the relationship between the two men.

scelerum consiliorumque: it is hard to decide whether the author means "crimes and preparations" (Vallette) or, with a hendiadys, "criminal designs" (Helm). We have a slight preference for the former translation because it is simpler. Arguments for the latter are two: from now on the issue seems to be the punishment for committed crimes; moreover Apul. uses hendiadys more than once, e.g. 3, 20 (67, 11) *fidem silentiumque*. See vdPaardt 1971, 151.

indicem: the slave could disclose his master's misdeeds and plans – if any – at the impending trial. One of the meanings given by *OLD* is "one who reveals or points out", cf. Cic. *Clu*. 21 *interim uenit index... qui nuntiaret ei filium eius uiuere*.

repertum... receptum... uexatum... excarnificatum... esse confessum: instead of this accumulation of participles, classical prose-writers might have preferred some variation in the form of dependent clauses. See Bernhard 1927, 41 f. on 'Die Partizipialkonstruktionen' and *GCA* 1977, 82. But it is precisely by means of these participles, each of them indicating a new phase, that the author has managed to reach a true climax.

per magistratus: one may wonder whether *per* stands here for *a* with the ablative = *a magistratibus*, as Callebat 1968, 220 claims. If so, this would be the only place in Apul. where this usage – frequent though it is in later Latin – is found. Callebat's view is given support by the fact that, when preceded by *per* "by means of", nouns denoting persons often refer to inferiors *(per legatos, per nuntium)*. See also Médan 1925, 73, and LHSz 2, 240 on *per* 'als Agens beim Pass. statt *ab*'. Neither in the material of the *ThLL* nor in legal texts can a clear distinction be detected between *per m.* and *a m.*

altera die: feminine, cf. *GCA* 1977, 22.

pluribus = *multis* or *plurimis* or *compluribus*, cf. LHSz 2, 168 f.

ad ultimam mortem: a not very usual combination for the outcome of this harsh punishment, fortunately tempered by *paene*. Much more traditional is *extrema mors* or *suprema mors*, both in Apul. 8, 30 (201, 12-13) *paene ad extremam confecerant mortem* (mitigated by *paene* here as well) and in other authors; Verg. *A*. 2, 446-447 *quando ultima cernunt / extrema iam in morte parant defendere*; Sil. 5, 416 *iam morte suprema*. There are exceptions e.g. Hor. *S*. 1, 7, 13 *ut ultima diuideret mors* and Amm. 28, 1, 55 *mancipia ad usque ultimum lacerabat exitium*.

excarnificatum: this verb, which also occurs at 152, 24 (*tormentis excarnificari*) is found in Classical Latin, e.g. Cicero *N.D*. 3, 82 *a Cyprio tyranno excarnificatum*; it is a well-known fact that Christian Latin has a preference for verbs in -*ficare*, cf. Chr. Mohrmann 1961, 1, 92-93.

nil quicquam: a strong expression for "nothing whatsoever". On the expressiveness of similar negatives see Marouzeau 1946, 158-159.

in patriam Luci: it does not become quite clear in the novel which this native town is, but Corinth is often emphasized: 1, 1 (1, 7) *Isthmos Ephyrea*; 1, 22 (20, 12) *litteras ei a Corinthio Demea... reddo*; 2, 12 (35, 1) *nam et Corinthi... apud nos*. In 10, 19 (251, 11-12) the ass returns, partly by land, partly by sea, to Cenchreae, the sea-port near Corinth, where he will recover his human shape. See Marg. Molt 1938 on 1, 22; Walsh 1970, 172 suggests that Apul. is well acquainted with this town and its religious life because he may have been initiated there himself. See further Mason 1971, 160-165; Scobie 1975, 72; Gwyn Griffiths 1975, 14 f.

Luci: at 155, 18 and 9, 13 (212, 21) the principal mss. have the spelling *Lucii*.

multos numero: cf. *GCA* 1977, 42 and 64.

inquirerent: we are not told whether these messengers are also allowed to arrest the culprit in what is not their own country. Of course there are no problems as to extradition because in the 2nd century A.D. both Hypata and Corinth are under Roman jurisdiction.

155, 17-156, 1 Haec eo narrante, ueteris fortunae et illius beati Lucii praesentisque aerumnae et infelicis asini facta comparatione, medullitus ingemebam subibatque me non de nihilo ueteris priscaeque doctrinae uiros finxisse ac pronuntiasse caecam et prorsus exoculatam esse Fortunam, quae semper suas opes ad malos et indignos conferat nec unquam iudicio quemquam mortalium eligat, immo uero cum is potissimum deuersetur, quos procul, si uideret, fugere deberet, quodque cunctis est extremius, uarias opiniones, immo contrarias nobis attribuat, ut et malus boni uiri fama glorietur et innocentissimus contra noxio rumore plectatur: "As he told this story, I made a comparison between the erstwhile prosperity of that blessed Lucius and the present hardship of the unfortunate ass; I fetched a sigh from deep within me and the thought occurred to me that it was not for nothing that the sages of yore had imagined and proclaimed Fortune to be blind and entirely eyeless. She always bestowed her riches – so I reasoned – on the wicked and unworthy, and never selected any mortal judiciously. On the contrary: she liked best to dwell with those to whom she ought to give a wide berth, if she were able to see at all. And worst of all, she imputed to us different reputations even contrary to the facts, with the result that the wicked man glories in the fame of a good man, but the most innocent man, on the other hand, is punished with the reputation of a criminal".

eo nărrante: according to Robertson and Frassinetti this was the original reading of F, which was changed by another hand into *eo enarrante* (according to Helm the addition of *eo* took place by the same hand, while the first *a* in *enarrante* was deleted); φ and α read *eo narrante*. In making a choice one may consider the fact that in Classical Latin *enarrare* is somewhat stronger than *narrare* (already in Pl. *Am.* 525 *ea tibi omnia enarraui*) – consequently *ThLL* speaks of *plene aut accurate narrare* – but the preposition's force is often weakened. Thus one could opt for *enarrante*, the more so as Apul. frequently shows a preference for compounds (cf. 154, 6 *conlustrabat* and see Bernhard 1927, 120-122), but we are of the opinion that the authority of F should turn the scale.

ueteris fortunae e.q.s.: the ass Lucius' self-pity has been moulded into a beautiful, ingeniously built period: *ueteris* (3) *fortunae* (3) *(et) illius* (3) *beati* (3) *Lucii* (3) *praesentis(que)* (3) *aerumnae* (3) *(et) infelicis* (4) *asini* (3). This sentence has a strongly harmonious composition, both with respect to the number of syllables and to the thematic correspondence between its constituent pairs: the first with the third, the second with the fourth; see Bernhard 1927, 89 f. on 'Parallelismus der Gliederung'. Apul. uses the motif of Lucius' self-pity repeatedly, e.g. 9, 13 (212, 21-23) *ueteris... Lucii fortunam recordatus... maerebam.*

aerumnae: the word strikes one as being somewhat archaic, Quint. *Inst.* 8, 3, 26 mentions it as such in a famous tirade. From Cicero onwards it is found in prose but with a poetic colouring; in the 2nd cent. A.D. it becomes scarce in poetry but more and more frequent in prose (see *ThLL s.v.* 1066, 47 f.). At 1, 1 (1, 11) and 9, 15 (214, 17) Apul. uses the Lucretian (6, 1231) adjective *aerumnabilis*.

medullitus: "in my very marrow", a comparatively rare adverb. Varro still uses it in its literal sense, as appears from Nonius 202, 8 L; but even in early Latin it can have a figurative meaning: Enn. *Sat.* 3, 7 *Enni poeta salue qui mortalibus uersus propinas flammeos medullitus*. After that it is not found until in Apul.: *Fl.* 18 (39, 3) *summis medullitus uiribus contendunt*. Later it appears in Amm. 30, 8, 10, 14, 1, 9 (here also combined with *gemere*) and 15, 2, 3.

subibatque me: "and the thought occurred to me". The mss. disagree: F *subiit*q*; (*iit* by another hand *in ras.*), φ *subiliatque* (according to Robertson and Frassinetti in two words), but here a different hand wrote in the margin *subiit itaque*; a group of recentiores has *subibatque*. This last form seems clearly preferable: the imperfect suits the gradually developing comparison better than a perfect would. Another argument for the imperfect is the use of *-que* as a connection between the two verbs *ingemebam* and *subibat*. The expression is used here impersonally, unlike the use at 156, 19.

me: an accusative with *subire* in this meaning is also found at 3, 29 (74, 1-2) *consilium me subit* and 156, 19 *subit me illa cura,* at 161, 27 the verb takes a dative, for no obvious reason: *mihi merito subiret*. Liv. 45, 5, 11 has *subit... animum* followed – as in Apuleius' phrase – by an acc. c. inf.

ueteris priscaeque doctrinae uiros: here *doctrina* must be practically identical with *philosophia*, as in e.g. Cic. *Mur.* 60 *accessit... doctrina non moderata nec mitis (sc. Stoica); Tusc.* 4, 2 *Pythagorae... doctrina cum longe lateque flueret...;* Lucr. 2, 8 *doctrina sapientum*

ueteris priscaeque: this 'Synonymik koordinierter Begriffe' (Bernhard 1927, 164 f.) is frequently used by Apuleius; see also Médan 1925, 362 (who does not mention our place).

Hildebrand *ad loc.* makes a comparison with the Greek combination ἀρχαῖος καὶ παλαιός (see e.g. Soph. *Tr.* 55 παλαιὸν δῶρον ἀρχαίου ποτὲ θηρός) and also quotes Vell. 1, 16, 3 *priscam illam et ueterem... comoediam*.

caecam et... exoculatam: the verb is, prior to this passage, only found at Pl. *Rud.* 731 *ni ei caput exoculassitis... ego uos uirgis circumuinciam*. Apul. also uses it at 8, 13 (187, 4) *(Thrasyllum) prorsus exoculatum relinquens*. A similar verb is *edentare* (Pl. *Rud.* 662).

Helm-Krenkel 1970, 411 suggest that Apul., in referring to a blind Fortune, is following Pac. *fr.* 366 Ribbeck (quoted by *Rhet. Her.* 2, 36) *Fortunam insanam esse et caecam et brutam perhibent philosophi*. This notion, however, was widely spread: cf. Plin. *Nat.* 2, 22 quoted by Vallette 7, n. 3 *(Fortuna) uolubilis... a plerisque uero et caeca existimata, uaga, inconstans, incerta, uaria indignorumque fautrix*. Juvenal, too, repeatedly complains about her capriciousness (6, 605 *Fortuna improba*; 7, 197 f. without the notion of blindness). See also Juv. 3, 40; Hor. *Carm.* 3, 29, 50; Plin. *Ep.* 4, 11.

The Greeks as well reflected on the fickleness of Τύχη; see the extensive discussions in Daremberg-Saglio 2, 1273 *s.v. Fortuna*; the article *Fortuna* in *R.E.*;

Roscher 1, 1503 f. and 5, 1320 f. on Τύχη (col. 1324 she is compared to a blind helmsman).

In Menander's *Apsis* the goddess Τύχη speaks the prologue (97-148); in *fr.* 463 Koerte, from another of his comedies, she is called blind as well: τυφλόν γε καὶ δύστηνόν ἐστιν ἡ Τύχη. Gomme-Sandbach 1973, 74 remark: 'The workings of chance should be blind (e.g. frag. 463) and are usually so regarded, but human inconsistency cannot avoid the idea that the force that brings luck, good or bad, can be influenced or propitiated'.

It is fully comprehensible that the concept of chance eventually developed into a personality with its own thoughts and emotions, and that Τύχη / *Fortuna* thus became a goddess. One gets the impression, while a sense of the deity's fickleness (or even hostility, as Apul. and others often explicitly mentioned) already existed in the Greek world, the notion of her redemptive function increased as traditional belief declined or blurred. While the cult of Τύχη was always regarded in Greece as positive in value, this was not the case in Roman religion, where too the goddess Fortune had her own cult: we know of a *mala* (or *aduersa*) *Fortuna*, to whom an altar on the Esquiline was dedicated (Cic. *N.D.* 3, 63; *Leg.* 2, 28; Plin. *Nat.* 2, 16). See Latte 1960, 182; kl. Pauly 2, *s.v. Fortuna* 597, 15 f.

The image of a blind Fortune continues to exist well into the Middle Ages; see Patch 1974, 44: 'Fortuna is blind, or more often blindfolded, to show that she has no regard for merit. Yet sometimes her eyes appear, and very expressively, as when one of them weeps and the other laughs'.

Her blindness is further mentioned by Apul. 5, 9 (109, 23) *En orba et saeua et iniqua Fortuna*; 8, 24 (195, 21) she is called *Fortuna mea saeuissima* (her *impetus* is qualified as *saeuissimus* at 156, 1 as well). At 11, 15 (277, 18) she is called *nefaria*, but the next line mentions the *(tutela) Fortunae, sed uidentis*: there she has, in the shape of Isis, regained her eyesight; see Gwyn Griffiths 1975, 253; Penwill 1975, 74-75.

The emphasis on Fortune's blindness in this passage is especially interesting, since it is obvious from what follows (155, 22 f.) that she is quite able, indeed, to distinguish between right and wrong: she always gives everything to the wicked. This is consistent with the ironical-exaggerating picture drawn by Apul. of his narrator.

The literature on Fortune's function in the *Met.* is extensive; see e.g. Rohde [3]1914, 300; Junghanns 1932, 163-164; Ciaffi 1960, 151; Schlam 1968, 120 f.; Tatum 1969, 61 f., 88 f., with a detailed exposition and a complete list of her epithets 94, n. 184; Chr. Harrauer 1973, 97.

It is equally understandable that Ploutos, too, is sometimes pictured blind (Roscher 3, 2583, 19): the underlying idea is that wealth is irrationally distributed among mortals.

conferat: in accordance with the rules of *consecutio temporum* one might expect an imperfect subjunctive after *subibat*, both in this case and in those following. The narrator presumably uses the present subjunctive in order to represent Fortune's unfairness as everlasting and permanent.

iudicio: "with good judgment", "judiciously", almost "deliberately"; cf. Caes. *Gal.* 6, 31, 1 *Ambiorix copias suas iudicione non conduxerit... an tempore exclusus... dubium est*; likewise Nep. *Att.* 15, 3.

immo uero: Apul. is very fond of the particle *immo*, which occurs 70 times in the *Met.*, 9 times in the *Apol.*, and 4 times in the *Fl.* He uses it in particular to introduce a climax, see Bernhard 1927, 127-128. According to Callebat 1968, 327 he is influenced by the language of the comic poets. But it is clear that the use of *immo*, and in particular that of *immo uero*, has developed especially through rhetorical education, cf. Cic. *Cat.* 1, 2 *uiuit? immo uero etiam in senatum uenit;* see also Cic. *Off.* 3, 90. This rhetorical element is evident in Apul. as well, e.g. 1, 12 (11, 21-12, 1) *faxo eum sero, immo statim, immo uero iam nunc* ...; see also 10, 33 (264, 1-2) *immo ... immo uero.* See further *GCA* 1977, 201.

is: the reading of F (φ has the more usual *his*) seems quite defensible in view of 9, 41 (234, 24) *is tantum clades enarrat suas.*

deuersetur: the verb usually means "to make one's abode"; Fortune prefers to live with the wrong customers and keep them company.

extremius: the first occurrences of this curious comparative, formed from the superlative *extremus*, are in Apul. 1, 8 (8, 1) *si quid est tamen nouissimo extremius* (see Marg. Molt. *ad loc.*) and in this passage; later in Tert. *An.* 33, 10 *quia nihil plenius quam quod extremius, nihil autem extremius quam quod diuinius;* finally in the 5th cent. author Salvianus, *Gub.* 5, 9 45 *ferenda ... erat extrema haec sors eorum, si non esset aliquid extremius*, a passage which is strongly reminiscent of Apul. 1, 8.

Apul. has similar formations: *Soc.* 3(10, 12) *postremius* and *Apol.* 98 (108, 23) *postremissumus.* Tert. *Apol.* 19 even has *extremissimus.* Neue-Wagener 2, 243 f. list a whole series of such comparatives and superlatives formed from anomalous superlatives, and offer as an explanation that the meaning of these superlatives has worn off by constant use, so that they are no longer felt as superlatives. Gel. 15, 12, 3 mentions as the oldest example *postremissimus* in an oration of C. Gracchus.

Callebat 1968, 403 wonders whether the degrees of comparison here have merely undergone a weakening in sense (a frequent phenomenon in the second century A.D., see Löfstedt 1933, 2, 205) or whether Apul. makes use of this curious formation in order to accentuate an emphatic statement. Undoubtedly the latter is the case, as in the passage quoted from Tert. *An.*; Waszink quotes there the introduction to the *Passio Perpetuae* (1, 3), which may also have been written by Tert. and where a similar word-play on *nouitiora ... nouissimiora* ("nearer to the end of the world") occurs.

In addition to Médan 1925, 213, cf. Koziol 1872, 304 and Leky 1908, 66; they all use the now obsolete concept of Africanism.

opiniones: i.e. the esteem in which one is held by others. The ass Lucius is annoyed at the fact that the reputation of an honest citizen – he still regards himself as such! – is impaired by Fortune's arbitrary and, on reflection, even perverse behaviour. See also the remark on irony in this passage at 155, 21. *Contrarias* sc. to reality.

ut ... plectatur: again a carefully and symmetrically constructed antithesis, ending in a beautiful clausula of cretic + trochee.

noxio rumore: F and φ offer *noxio2 ore.* Consequently one has a choice between *noxio rumore*, which already Casaubonus preferred (now followed by Helm, Giarratano-Frassinetti, Scazzoso, and others), and *noxiorum more*, which

Colvius proposed (followed by Robertson). One of the arguments used for the latter alternative is the passage from Tert. *Fug.* 2, 1 (already quoted by Pricaeus) *sectatores ueritatis nocentissimorum more tractari*. Taken by itself it would, indeed, be a good parallel, except for the fact that it would make this passage in Apul. somewhat colourless. We prefer *noxio rumore* because of the quite pointed contrast with *boni uiri fama*. Another argument for this reading is the construction with the ablative of the penalty; cf. *Cod. Just.* 9, 20, 7 *capite aliquem plectere*; *Vulg. Deut.* 21, 22 *morte plectendum est*.

plectatur: in the sense of "punish" this verb usually occurs in the passive, e.g. Cic. *Leg.* 3, 46 *ut in suo uitio quisque plectatur*.

CHAPTER III

After his general lamentation Lucius now presents his personal predicament.

Ego denique, quem saeuissimus eius impetus in bestiam et extremae 156, 1-5
sortis quadripedem deduxerat cuiusque casus etiam quouis iniquissimo dolendus atque miserandus merito uideretur, crimine latrocinii in hospitem mihi carissimum postulabar: "Take me, for example: a most cruel attack of hers had degraded me to an animal, indeed a four-footed creature of the lowest sort. Surely my misfortune would fill even the most unfeeling with sorrow and pity, and rightly so: I was being accused of robbing my beloved host".

denique: "indeed", "for example", cf. Marg. Molt 1938, 41-42; 1943, 129 f.; vdPaardt 1971, 42-43.

impetus: the meaning "attack" is made probable by its modifier *saeuissimus*: the same combination is found e.g. in Hor. *Carm.* 3, 1, 27 *saeuus Arcturi cadentis impetus* and in Apul. 8, 4 (179, 10) *(aper) ... impetu saeuo frementis oris totus fulmineus*. Its meaning is also suggested by the irony of the preceding passage. The connection of the noun *impetus* with *fortunae* is found in other authors, e.g. *Rhet. Her.* 4, 24 *omnis impetus fortunae se putant fugisse*; Cic. *Q. fr.* 1, 1, 5 *impetum fortunae superare*.

et: = *et quidem*, cf. 1, 23 (21, 9) *et recte*. Médan 1925, 230 points out that the usage of *et* or *-que* 'remplaçant une apposition' is frequent in the comic poets as well, e.g. Pl. *Truc.* 111; Ter. *Ph.* 199. Other well-known examples are Catul. 17, 14-15 *puella / et puella tenellulo delicatior haedo*; Cic. *Ver.* 2, 3, 65; *Lig.* 24. See also comm. on 148, 12.

extremae sortis: Apul. frequently uses the superlative *extremus* in order to express the most ignoble and contemptible degree, e.g. 1, 17 (15, 24) *fetòrem extremae latrinae*; 1, 21 (19, 18) *extremae auaritiae*.

deduxerat: "had degraded", as in Liv. 9, 34, 18 *antiquissimum sollemne ... ab nobilissimis antistitibus ... ad seruorum ministerium ... deduxisti*.

quouis: this dative, found in F, has been accepted by Helm and Frassinetti. The emendations *quoiuis* (Seyffert, accepted by Robertson) or *cuiuis* ς seem unnecessary, since dative forms like *quouis* are found more than once in Apul.; cf. 3, 3 (53, 24) *uasculo quodam ... infusa* and vdPaardt *ad loc.*, who also quotes 4, 17 (87, 13) *lacu aliquo conterminum*. See *GCA* 1977, 132; Leumann 1977, 480 refers to these dative forms as 'meist späte Zeugnisse. Bei Apuleius als Pseudo-archaismen *quō* mit *quō-vīs* sowie *illo isto ipso utroque*'.

dolendus atque miserandus: practically a tautology. It does not occur in the list of 'Synonymik koordinierter Begriffe' in Bernhard 1927, 164 f.

merito: the narrator strongly emphasizes the pathos of his situation even before this latest blow.

uideretur: one does not need to be surprised at this subjunctive alongside *deduxerat* in the parallel relative clause. The author clearly feels a consecutive notion in the second part: "such a wretch that...", while *deduxerat* is rather a piece of actual information. Callebat 1968, 343 distinguishes between a 'fait réel' and an 'éventualité'.

latrocinii in hospitem: a prepositional construction instead of an objective genitive with the noun *latrocinium* does not occur elsewhere, according to *ThLL s.v.* 1017. The construction itself is quite common in classical Latin, especially with *in, erga, aduersus*, evidently for the sake of clarity.

postulabar: cf. 154, 21.

156, 5-7 Quod crimen non modo latrocinium, uerum etiam parricidium quisque rectius nominarit: "Why, that crime shouldn't just be called robbery, but, more correctly, actual parricide".

non modo... uerum etiam... rectius: a sort of contamination of *non modo..., uerum etiam* and *non..., uerum rectius*. Thus *rectius* is somewhat redundant.

parricidium: although etymologically this word is not related to *pater* (its meaning is broader: "murder of a relative"), yet this association was generally made by the Romans: Ernout-Meillet 1967 *s.v. pār(r)icīda(s)* quote e.g. Cic. *S. Rosc.* 70; *Mil.* 17; *Phil.* 3, 18, etc. During the Empire *par(r)icida(s)* as a legal term always means "murderer of a relative", cf. Paul. *Sent.* 5, 24, 1 *lege Pompeia de parricidiis tenetur qui patrem, matrem, auum, auiam, fratrem, sororem, patruelem, matruelem, patronum, patronam... occiderit*. In the *Glossaria Latina* the word is generally rendered by πατροκτόνος. Cf. on its etymology Walde-Hofman *s.v.*

Apul. will certainly have associated the word with *pater* and consequently lets Lucius respond to the accusation as to that of having murdered his father; this agrees with his feelings toward Milo: 3, 7 (57, 11) *illum bonum hospitem parentemque meum Milonem*. For that reason he takes the charge extremely seriously. Moreover, Milo had been his host, and the sacredness of hospitality throughout antiquity is well-known (it may suffice to mention Homer). Thus, to lay hands on a host to whom one also ascribes fatherly feelings is outrageous. The interesting treatise *De officiorum gradu* in Gel. 5, 13 gives an impression of how great a value was attached to sense of duty.

On the penal implications of a charge of *latrocinium* see Summers 1967, 150 and 248; on *parricidium* Norden 1912, 130; Summers 1967, 166.

quisque = quis "someone", with weakening of the element -*que*; cf. LHSz 2, 199.

156, 7-8 Nec mihi tamen licebat causam meam defendere uel unico uerbo saltem denegare: "And yet I could not defend my cause or, even with one single word, deny it".

It is amusing that the ass imagines himself standing trial and having to prove his innocence. Obviously nobody else expects him to appear in the court room!

licebat: as becomes evident from what follows, he means that his inability to exonerate himself is not moral, but physical, the result of Fortune's animosity. This non-moral sense of *licet* is frequently found in Apul., e.g. 1, 23 (21, 7); 6, 26 (148, 20); 10, 8 (243, 6); 11, 14 (276, 28), etc.

Denique ne mala conscientia tam scelesto crimini praesens uiderer silentio consentire, hoc tantum inpatientia productus uolui dicere: 'Non feci': "Finally, in order not to create the impression that because of a bad conscience I, though present, tacitly admitted such an infamous charge, I wanted to say only this – unable to restrain myself –: 'not guilty' ". 156, 8-11

praesens: Helm-Krenkel leave this word untranslated, although it must have a function in this connection: if one is present at one's own trial and remains silent at the accusation, it will look much like a confession. Cf. Ambr. *Serm.* 49 *taciturnitas pro consensu habetur*. A similar sense of guilt, expressing itself by silence, is found in Hor. *Epod.* 7, 15 *(an culpa) ... tacent, et albus ora pallor inficit*. It is of old a proverbial notion, cf. Otto 1890 (^{r}1965), 339, who quotes, among others, Sen. *Con.* 10, 2, 6 *sed silentium uidetur confessio* and Paul. *Dig.* 50, 17, 142 *qui tacet, non utique fatetur, sed tamen uerum est eum non negare*.

inpatientia productus: its meaning must be that the ass cannot bear it any longer: he simply has to do something. Seneca in Tac. *Ann.* 15, 63, 3 asks his wife at the moment of his suicide to leave the room *ne dolore suo animum uxoris infringeret atque ipse uisendo eius tormenta ad impatientiam delaberetur*. *Producere* in the sense of "to induce a person to do something" is not uncommon, e.g. *Rhet. Her.* 1, 3, 4 *producti sumus, ut... loqueremur*; 4, 47, 60 *productus studio*; Plin. *Nat.* 9. 59, 122 *nulla sponsione ad hoc producto* (sc. *histrioni*). Floridus' *perductus* is therefore unnecessary.

non feci: this passage shows a clear parallel with 8, 29 (200, 25), and especially with 3, 29 (73, 16-18), where the ass wants to invoke the emperor with the words *O Caesar* but does not get any further than *O*. For the polemics on this subject see vdPaardt 1971, 204-205. From the Greek text of the *Onos* corresponding to that passage it is evident that Lucius had wanted to bray in Greek ὦ Καῖσαρ, for our passage, which completely lacks a Greek parallel (*Met.* 7, 1-12 has no equivalent in the *Onos*), it has therefore been assumed that the 'Vorlage' must have read οὐ τοῦτο ἐποίησα and that the ass did not get further than οὐ (Snell 1935, 355-356 = *Ges. Schr.* 1966, 200-201). This viewpoint is challenged by Bianco (extensively 1956, 47-62, briefly 1971, 73), who argues that the ass did, in fact, wish to say *non feci* in Latin but had trouble pronouncing the *f*; this would be explained by the sentence 14-15 *quanquam... labias*. If so, this episode would be Apul.'s own invention; it would not have been part of the Greek original and thus it would be absent from the *Onos*, too. A dubious argument: rounding of the lips is not necessary for the articulation of the sound *f*, but rather the expulsion of breath between teeth and lower lip; cf. Marius Victorinus *Ars.* 1, 6 (6, 34, 9 K): *F litteram imum labium superis imprimentes dentibus reflexa ad palati fastigium lingua leni spiramine proferemus*; see Sturtevant 1940, 162-163. For the articulation of the sound οὐ, however, this rounding is essential.

It seems therefore better to follow Heller 1941/42, 533 and 1942/43, 98 merely assuming that at 3, 29 Apul. follows his Greek predecessor quite closely with this witticism, and that later, confident that his readers have understood the joke, he can count on success when he repeats it at 7, 3 and 8, 29.

See further on these problems Goldbacher 1872, 333; Junghanns 1932, 77; Rice 1950, 71; Nehring 1952, 229; Walsh 1970, 159; Van Thiel 1971, 96.

The philologist will do well to observe and listen to a live ass. He will be surprised to find that these long-eared animals produce a sound which, at least in the Netherlands, does not even remotely resemble the traditional *ia* of the German asses (wittily discussed by Snell); neither does it come close to Greek ὤ or οὖ, nor to Latin *non* or *o*; instead, it is a heartrending discord. The description of the ass's braying at 164, 1-2 comes close to reality.

It seems to us that Apul., knowledgeable as he is about Roman law, would have used the formula *non feci* intentionally, because it is traditional for a defendant who denies his guilt. Cf. Cic. *Lig.* 30 *Ad parentem sic agi solet, ad iudices: "non fecit; non cogitauit..."*; Ov. *Am.* 2, 5, 9; Quint. *Decl.* 11, 10; the opposite e.g. Cic. *Ver.* 5, 14 *fecisse uideri pronuntiat*, with Levens' note: 'the actual formula in which a verdict of "guilty" was pronounced'; Juv. 6, 638 *sed clamat Pontia 'feci | confiteor...'*.

156, 11-15 Et uerbum quidem praecedens semel ac saepius inmodice clamitaui, sequens uero nullo pacto disserere potui, sed in prima remansi uoce et identidem boaui 'non non', quanquam nimia rutunditate pendulas uibrassem labias: "And the first word I brayed with exceeding loudness, over and over again, but the next I could not utter at all. I came to a stop at the first word and repeatedly bellowed 'not, not', although I made my pendulous lips quiver with as much rounding as possible".

prāecēdēns sĕmĕl āc | saēpiŭs īnmŏdīcē: whether or not this pentameter is intentional, is a vexed question. Bernhard 1927, 250 n. 84 believes that it is coincidental and opposes Schober 1904, 10 f., who regards it as intentional. Our opinion is that the truth is somewhere in between: the fact that a dactylic pentameter occurs in a clause like this, which does not even form a syntactical unity (the colon, for example, ends with *praecedens*), is due to Apul.'s aim for rhythm. This rhythm is immediately interrupted by a conventional clausula, namely the ditrochaic *clamitaui*.

For additional examples of verse units or verse parts see vdPaardt 1971, 35; comm. on 154, 5 (the first four feet of an hexameter).

semel ac saepius: "once and more often", i.e. "over and over again". Cf. Var. *L.* 10, 2, 33 *semel et saepius*; Cic. *Phil.* 14, 22 *semel et saepius sententiam meam... sustulerunt*.

disserere: if its basic meaning is, indeed, "to dispose, set in order" *(OLD)*, as in Col. 10, 165 *tu cinge comas, tu dissere crines*, then the verb has been luckily chosen: "to arrange the words in the proper order", i.e. "pronounce"; see also *ThLL s.v.* 1459, 29. The verb generally refers to an exposition at a meeting, e.g. Cic. *Fam.* 12, 7, 2 *quod... in senatu pluribus uerbis disserui*. In the philosophical sense it means "to reason logically about", i.e. it translates διαλέγομαι; cf. Cic. *Fat.* 1; *De Orat.* 1, 68, etc.; Ernout-Meillet 1951, 1092. Colvius' conjecture *edissere* is less suitable: "to set forth in words, expound or relate" *(OLD)*.

boaui: a variant of *clamitaui*, possibly chosen for the sake of assonance. It may have been chosen for humorous purposes, too: although the verb is a Greek loan-word (= βοᾶν), Roman folk etymology derived it from *bos*, as is mentioned explicitly by Nonius 79, 5 L (110 L) *bount a boum mugitibus* (cf. Var. *L.* 7, 104). A gloss on *boatus* gives this derivation, too: *CGL* 4, 26, 37 *uox plena siue mugitus boum*.

In early Latin poetry, to which the verb is primarily confined, it can be used in a broader sense, e.g. of persons, as in Pl. *Am.* 232 *boat/caelum fremitu uirum*, also Var. *Men.* 386 *bount*; Ov. *Ars* 3, 450 *"redde meum" toto uoce boante foro*. After the classical period it becomes rare.

Apul. uses this verb four times and, in our opinion, always with humorous intentions: in *Fl.* 17 (32, 4) he says about *tragoedi* that they *identidem boando purgant rauim*; in *M.* 5, 29 (126, 13) he disrespectfully describes the raging Venus as *quam maxime boans*; *M. 9, 20 (218, 8)* the cuckolded husband loses his temper in the following way: *fidem deum boantem dominum*. So, when the ass begins to *boare* like a bull, it may elicit a smile from the reader.

See on *boare* Ernout-Meillet *s.v. boō*; Callebat 1968, 513-514.

quanquam ... uibrassem: for *quanquam* followed by a subjunctive see vdPaardt 1971, 3.

uibrassem: a graphic expression; it is understandable that the long and flabby lips begin to quiver at the strenuous attempt to form the rounding for the o-sound. *Pendulas* is therefore functional, cf. 3, 24 (70, 15) *labiae pendulae*.

nimia = *magna*, just as the adverb *nimium* in Apul. is often equivalent to merely *ualde*; cf. *GCA* 1977, 58. *Nimia rutunditate* is hardly to be connected with *pendulas*, as this would connote a physically precarious achievement. It seems better to have *nimia rutunditate* modify *uibrassem*.

The motif of the voice suddenly breaking off as a result of a metamorphosis is, of course, repeatedly found in Ovid, e.g. *Met.* 1, 647 (about Io) *si modo uerba sequantur / oret opem*; 2, 485 (about Callisto) *mens antiqua manet ... assiduoque suos gemitu testata dolores* (see Fränkel 1945, 79-81); 3, 201 (about Actaeon) *'me miserum' dicturus erat: uox nulla secuta est*. Philemon and Baucis are granted the time to say *uale* simultaneously (*Met.* 8, 717-718; see Galinsky 1975, 201). See further e.g. Segal 1969, 91 f.

labias: feminine, which is not unusual in early Latin, e.g. Pl. *St.* 723a; cf. vdPaardt 1971, 180. Callebat 1968, 52 remarks that it is avoided by the classical authors as 'appartenant vraisemblablement au parler commun'. See also LHSz 2, 11.

Sed quid ego pluribus de Fortunae scaeuitate conqueror, quam nec istud puduit me cum meo famulo meoque uectore illo equo factum conseruum atque coniugem: "But why am I adding to my complaints of Fortune's disfavour, who was not even ashamed of the fact that I had become a fellow-slave and yoke-mate of my servant and carrier, that horse". 156, 15-18

scaeuitate: "warped, unfavourable disposition" or even "perversion", a notion commonly linked with Fortune in Apul.'s *Met.*, cf. 3, 14 (62, 15) ‹*fortunae*› *scaeuitas* and vdPaardt 1971, 108 *ad loc.*; 4, 2 (75, 19) *fortunae meae scaeuitatem* and *GCA* 1973, 33 *ad loc.* φ's reading *seuitate* is somewhat less attractive because the combination *saeuitas fortunae* does not seem to occur elsewhere; cf., on the other hand, 5, 5 (106, 16) *fortuna saeuior* and 5, 22 (119, 20) *fati saeuitia*. At 2, 13 (35, 18) both notions are combined: *fortunam scaeuam an saeuam uerius dixerim*; cf. De Jonge 1941, 60-61. On Fortune's role see comm. on 155, 17 f.

[quan] quam: this emendation is already found in Beroaldus, who evidently ascribed the mistake to dittography. Pricaeus saw its origin in a misread abbreviation and proposed *quam quidem*, supported by places like *Apol.* 62 (70, 24) and 37 (43, 8), where similar corrections are needed. Oudendorp's idea, to read *quam nequam (= nequissimam)*, is ingenious indeed. All of them undoubtedly realized that *quanquam* is not tenable, because it renders the purport of the sentence unintelligible. Armini 1932, 83 makes an attempt at defending it: '... the main clause contains a rhetorical question, identical to a negative statement. (What is the use of complaining =) I am not going to complain of Fortune's hostility, although (I had reasons enough because) she was not even ashamed...' (our translation). This somewhat forced reasoning neglects *pluribus*, which makes a vast difference: Lucius did complain about Fortune's unreasonableness previously. We are of the opinion that a relative clause ties in most logically with the preceding text. An additional argument, which may be the strongest of all, is that Apul. does not use the conjunction *quanquam* with an indicative elsewhere. We believe, therefore, that Beroaldus' emendation is correct and palaeographically least drastic.

istud: somewhat redundant; it anticipates the *accusativus cum infinitivo* construction *me ... factum (esse)*. Cf. Bernhard 1927, 180 on 'Setzung überflüssiger Worte'.

illo equo: it seems most plausible to regard these words as an apposition to *meo famulo meoque uectore,* in which case they can hardly be dispensed with (although Koziol wanted to delete *equo*). Otherwise one would be inclined to think – erroneously – that *meo famulo* refers to the servant of 155, 10, who, however, was captured. With *meo famulo* Lucius alludes here to his horse Candidus, cf. comm. on 155, 9; for the apposition cf. 3, 26 (71, 15) *ad equum meum illum uectorem*. This interpretation is more attractive than taking *-que* to be explicative.

It is clear that the ass-narrator is exaggerating again: nowhere in the novel does he have to suffer the humiliation of being put to the yoke together with his horse.

coniugem: "yoke-mate", a playful use of this word, which, of course, usually means "spouse". The *ThLL* has no other example of a *iumentum* styled like this. Gertrude Drake 1968, 108 comments as follows on this concluding sentence: 'This seems to be a parody of Plato's myth of the soul, which consists of a charioteer who must drive two horses to heaven, a white thoroughbred that tries to soar aloft, and an unruly black horse that keeps pulling the other down (Phaedrus 246a-b; 247b;253d-255a)'; this supposition fits in with her total hypothesis on the interpretation of our novel.

Thibau 1965 does not discuss this passage, but he, too, emphasizes the influence of the *Phaedrus* on the novel in connection with the horse Candidus; he even goes so far as to say (103): 'il ne subsiste plus aucun doute que tout le roman sera sous le signe de la théorie platonicienne de l'Erôs'.

CHAPTER IV

Fortunately for Lucius events will prove him wrong.

Talibus cogitationibus fluctuantem subit me illa cura potior, qua statuto consilio latronum manibus uirginis decretam me uictimam recordabar uentremque crebro suspiciens meum iam misellam puellam parturibam: "While I was tossed about on such reflections, this even more urgent concern occurred to me: I recalled that the robbers' mind was made up and that I was appointed as a sacrifice to the girl's Shade. Yes, while looking up at my belly again and again, I already felt pregnant with the poor baby".

fluctuantem: "to move in the manner of waves" (*OLD*), a metaphor often used by Apul. Cf. *GCA* 1977, 28 on 4, 2 (75, 9).

subit me: the historical present suggests a suddenly occurring thought, while the imperfect subibat at 155, 19 connotes a reflection which is gradually taking shape. The notion of suddenness is maintained if *subit* is regarded as a contracted perfect. Cf. Kieckers 1930 ([1]1960), 2, 329 and LHSz 1, 600; but not all of the latter's examples are convincing (e.g. Verg. *A.* 1, 171; 2, 275; 10, 149).

potior: "more important", because it relates to an immediate danger.

statuto consilio: an instrumental ablative: "because of the decision made". *Statuere* has a somewhat legal connotation because it is used especially of punishments: *poenam statuere*, e.g. Cic. *Inv.* 2, 145; Tac. *Ann.* 14, 49, etc. Cf. 5, 21 (119, 11).

manibus: the plural is of course invariable; e.g. Verg. *A.* 4, 427 *nec patris Anchisae cinerem manisque reuelli*; Tib. 1, 1, 67 *tu manes ne laede meos*, etc. See Latte 1960, 99: 'Selbst als man sich daran gewöhnt, den einzelnen Toten mit dem Wort zu bezeichnen, setzt man grammatisch widersinnig Dis Manibus im Plural vor den Individualnamen'.

Again the author's sense of humor runs away with him: it is not the girl whom the robbers intend to kill at once (so the *Manes* are premature); it is the ass, who will be eviscerated so that Charite can be sewn into his skin (6, 31). Thus the chronological order of events is reversed, and the ass, wretched as he is, sees his immediate future in too golden a light: he will not even live long enough to become aware of his 'pregnancy'.

suspiciens: Oudendorp had difficulties understanding how the ass can *suspicere* at his own belly: 'nec enim (venter) altior est capite', and suggests that *suspicere* means here 'obliquum et a latere adspicere'. He cannot give any parallels for this; neither can Hildebrand, who thinks that the ass looks over his whole body 'von unten bis oben'.

Vallette is closer to the truth with his translation 'en me baissant je regardais mon ventre'. For, if the ass bends forward with his head between his forelegs, one could say that he looks *up* at his belly.

iam misellam puellam parturibam: with obvious alliteration (*p* ... *p* ...), assonance (*-ellam* ... *-ellam*) and homoeoteleuton *-am* ... *-am* ... *-am* ... *-am*). More examples of this can be found in Strilciw 1925, 113 and Bernhard 1927, 224. It is amusing that a male creature feels himself *parturire,* and also that the imagined *parēre* has to take place in a direction contrary to that which is customary in nature.

misellam: Koziol 1872, 260 f. gives the complete list of diminutives in Apul.; they are also discussed by Bernhard 1927, 135 f. Koziol may contend that most diminutives are 'blosses Putz- und Flitterwerk des Ausdrucks', yet nobody can escape the impression that Lucius expresses here his genuine compassion for the poor girl and her cruel fate. The adjective suits Charite very well; the author uses it of her at 8, 1 (176, 22) as well, when a slave describes her death to his cronies. Charite herself uses the attribute with reference to her groom at 4, 27 (96, 2). Psyche, too, is repeatedly called *misella,* and always in situations in which she is, indeed, pathetic: e.g. 5, 5 (107, 2); 5, 18 (117, 11) rhyming with *tenella*; 4, 34 (101, 17); 5, 26 (123, 21) when she laments her own fate; 6, 9 (134, 19) where it contrasts with the atrocious punishments that are inflicted upon her; 6, 17 (141, 13) and 6, 21 (144, 20) both in the vocative, with a mixture of pity and reproach.

The sadistic little fellow who has departed this life is mourned by his mother with this word at 175, 17. It is used in a beautifully ironical way of the covetous Myrmex at 9, 19 (217, 4).

It seems to us that the diminutive has an obvious function in the passages mentioned above: it disarms or at least diverts the reader. See further on this question vdPaardt 1971, 100 and *GCA* 1977, 67.

parturibam: for imperfects on *-ibam* see Médan 1925, 5-6; Callebat 1968, 126; *GCA* 1977, 59. They occur in Latin of all periods.

156, 22-157, 2 Sed ille, qui commodum falsam de me notoriam pertulerat, expromptis mille aureum, quos insutu laciniae contexerat quosque uariis ui⟨a⟩toribus detractos, ut aiebat, pro sua frugalitate communi conferebat arcae, infit etiam de salute commilitonum sollicite sciscitari: "But the man who had just made the slanderous report on me brought out a thousand gold coins, which he had hidden by sewing them into his cloak. He had, he said, robbed them from various travellers, and thanks to his sterling character he was now depositing them in the common purse. Then he started to inquire after his comrades' health, too".

ille, qui: it is not entirely certain whether *ille* has already lost its demonstrative force, and means little more than *is*. Perhaps the author uses it in order to call our attention to the narrating robber.

commodum: "just now"; see *GCA* 1977, 69.

falsam de me notoriam pertulerat: it is not clear whether the meaning is "who had falsely accused me" or "who had made the slanderous report on me". From the files of the *ThLL* Institute it appears that this is the first occurrence of the noun *notoria*, which will re-appear some two centuries later. From these sparse occurrences in late Latin one gets the impression that the origin lies in the adjective *notorius* "informing", which is used with *epistula*: "a letter with information". Later on *notoria* is used as a noun, e.g. Aug. *Ep.* 129, 1 *multum nos sollicitos reddidit notoria uel litterae fratrum nostrorum*; cf. Aug. *Ep.* 129, 7 (*Ep.* 133, 1 is uncertain because of the disagreement of the mss.). In other texts the word seems to have entered the legal sphere, e.g. *SHA* 25 Treb. Pollio *Claud.* 17 *nihil me grauius accepit quam quod notoria tua* ("by your information, by your tip") *intimasti Claudium... grauiter irasci*; see also Symm. *Ep.* 9, 125 (10, 4). The word occurs once in the *Digesta* at 48, 16, 6, 3 *Nuntiatores, qui per notoriam indicia produnt, notoriis suis adsistere iubentur* ("denunciation"). In the *Glossaria Latina* it is often rendered by μήνυσις or ἀναφορά(-ία).

Because of this, and in view of Apul.'s preference for legal jargon, one may be inclined to interpret these words as "who had falsely accused me". But *de me* and *pertulerat* cause us to believe that he means no more than "who had made the slanderous report on me".

mille aureum: on plural genitives such as this see *GCA* 1977, 143 and *M.* 2, 23 (43, 30) *"Mille", inquit, "nummum deponentur tibi"*.

At 160, 10 Haemus produces two thousand gold coins, in both cases respectable sums, with correspondingly considerable weights. If the (*aureus*) *solidus* (cf. 10, 9: 243, 19) at this time still had the weight which was customary under Nero, viz. 1/45 pounds = 7,28 grams (presumably the weight increased to 1/42 pounds towards the end of the second century, cf. Thompson 1961, 243 f), then this robber would carry more than 7 kilograms of gold in his cloak, and Haemus more than 14 kilograms (in that case *diloricatis... pannulis* (160, 10) becomes more significant!).

But one would be well-advised not to take these numbers too literally. Jones 1974, 69 points out the difficulties in establishing the exact weight and value of ancient coins. Moreover, both Petronius and Apuleius often use numbers and prices in order to achieve a comic or surprising effect; and often these are in round figures, as is the case here. Duncan-Jones 1974, 251 properly observes: 'Both novelists (viz. Petr. and Apul.) evidently sometimes used prices for comic effect. Where this is so their figures have little positive value for economic history. It is equally difficult to show that they sought to achieve realism by choosing a plausible amount even when the context was quite neutral'.

Junghanns 1932, 149, n. 49 rightly remarks: 'Zwischen diesen 1000 Goldstücken und den 2000, die 160, 10 Haemus selbst spendet, besteht deutliche Beziehung (Steigerung)'. The robbers will, indeed, be impressed and listen more attentively when so large a sum of gold is shown; even more so when Haemus comes up with the double amount.

insutu laciniae: the noun *insutus* is a *hapax legomenon*. On *lacinia* see vdPaardt 1971, 83; here it is probably a robber's cloak. In Petr. 13, too, coins are hidden in a *sutura* of a *lacinia*.

pro sua frugalitate: "of sterling character as he was"; he does indeed know how to display his social conscience. The perspective is maintained with the words *ut aiebat*.

communi arcae: it had already been suggested at 4, 8 (80, 24) and 4, 21 (91, 8) that the robbers live in a kind of commune with communal funds; here it is said so explicitly. Oudendorp even quotes Papinianus in *Dig.* 17, 2, 82 *Iure societatis per socium aere alieno socius non obligatur nisi in communem arcam pecuniae uersae sint*, which shows that a *communis arca* is a legal term with fixed rules.

infit: a poetic verb with an archaic sound; cf. *GCA* 1977, 186.

salute... sollicite sciscitari: strong alliteration of the *s* (see the long list at Strilciw 1925, 112), combined with assonance of *c* and *t*.

157, 2-11 Cognitoque quosdam, immo uero fortissimum quemque uariis quidem, sed inpigris casibus oppetisse, suadet, tantisper pacatis intineribus omniumque proeliorum seruatis indutiis inquisitioni commilitonum potius insisteretur et tirocinio nouae iuuentutis ad pristinae manus numerum Martiae cohortis facies integraretur: nam et inuitos terrore compelli et uolentes praemio prouocari posse nec paucos humili seruilique uitae renuntiantes ad instar tyrannicae potestatis sectam suam conferre malle: "When he had learned that some of them, in fact the very bravest, had perished in various but always dashing enterprises, he recommended that they should rather, by peaceful marches for the time being and while observing an armistice on all fronts, concentrate on the enlistment of comrades in arms; by levying young recruits they should restore the force's manpower to the former troop figure. Those who were reluctant, he said, could be forced by intimidation, those who were willing could be incited by a reward, and not a few would rather give up their humble life of slavery and direct their way of life towards something like the life of a prince".

cognitoque: an ablative absolute without a nominal ablative is quite common in Apul., see *GCA* 1977, 135; LHSz 2, 141-142. It is a normal linguistic phenomenon, the oldest example of which is considered to be Quad. *Hist.* 12 *impetrato prius a consulibus, ut... permitterent*. It is very much in vogue with historians like Livy, Tacitus, and in later Latin; e.g. Liv. 33, 41, 5 *cognito uiuere Ptolemaeum*; Tac. *Ann.* 1, 46, 1 *At Romae nondum cognito, qui fuisset exitus...*

inpigris: the brigands' activities are, of course, greatly glorified and pictured as favourably as possible. This was not difficult in Thrasyleon's case, considering his courageous conduct when he was disguised as a bear, and his painful death (4, 21). Glorious feats and a spectacular demise can certainly be attributed to Lamachus as well (4, 11). But it is considerably more difficult to make such a claim for Alcimus, who was craftily manoeuvred out of the window by an old woman and thus fell to his death (4, 12). It must be said that the robber who gives the account of these casualties executes his difficult task magnificently: in his version they are all indeed depicted as *inpigri casus*, although inpigri may be somewhat too euphemistic.

oppetisse: this is undoubtedly the correct reading: F has *op* written over *ad* by the same hand, and *oppetisse* is found in φ, too. The lack of a direct object such as *mortem* is poetic or (in prose) post-Augustan; cf. Verg. *A.* 1, 95-96 *quis ante ora patrum Troiae sub moenibus altis / contigit oppetere*. The solemn ring of this verb accentuates the heroism with which these bravos died.

suadet is followed by a subjunctive without *ut*. Similar constructions after verbs of exhorting, obtaining, etc. occur in Latin of all periods, but especially in colloquial language, cf. Bernhard 1927, 51-52; Callebat 1968, 359; LHSz 2, 530.

In Apul. see also e.g. 10, 4 (239, 5-6) *bonum caperet animum refectionique se ac saluti redderet, impendio suadet.*

pacatis itineribus omniumque proeliorum seruatis indutiis: one's first inclination is to read two parallel absolute ablatives and to translate *pacatis itineribus* with "after having left the roads alone (for a while)"; this is the translation found most often. From the cards of the *ThLL* it appears, however, that *pacare itinera* never means "to leave the roads alone" but always "to clear the roads of enemies" or "to pacify the roads by the use of arms". In that case it seems better to regard *pacatis itineribus* as an instrumental ablative, in which *pacatus* has the adjectival meaning of "quiet", "peaceful", and *itineribus* means "expeditions", "marches". As a consequence, *tantisper* must be taken more closely with *insisteretur*. For a more detailed argumentation we refer to *Apuleiana Groningana* IV, *Mnem.* 1977, 431 f.

Observe how often this narrator uses military terms: *pacatis itineribus, proeliorum seruatis indutiis, inquisitioni commilitonum, tirocinio, Martiae cohortis*, etc. See *GCA* 1977, 208-209.

insisteretur: constructed with a dative, this verb – in the sense of "to apply oneself to", "to concentrate on" – is also found in Tib. 3, 7, 135 *magnis insistere rebus / incipe* and in Tac. *Ann.* 2, 21 *orabatque insisterent caedibus*. But the impersonal passive, as found in this passage, is rather unusual.

tirocinio: one is tempted to translate this with "by recruitment" but it is extremely difficult to find a clear example of this meaning in the lexica, except perhaps Amm. 21, 6, 6 *indictis per provincias tirociniis*. The alternative is to regard *nouae iuuentutis* as an explicative genitive, and to take *tirocinium* in its rather frequent meaning of "raw troops", "recruits", i.e. a concrete collective. Cf. Liv. 40, 35, 12 *cum contemptum tirocinium etiam mitiores barbaros excitare ad rebellandum possit*, with Weissenborn-Müller's note 'abstractum pro concreto'; cf. in general LHSz 2, 745 f.

numerum: three men had been lost: Lamachus, Alcimus, and Thrasyleon.

Martiae cohortis: this pompous term, meaning "a regiment sprung from Mars", reminds one of Cicero's references in the *Philippics* to the third legion, which had been given the epithet Martia: *Phil.* 4, 5 *legio Martia, quae mihi uidetur diuinitus ab eo deo traxisse nomen, a quo populum Romanum generatum accepimus*; see also *Phil.* 3, 6.

facies: "the external appearance"; even after the numerical strength is made up, it will take time to recover the bands' former effectiveness in action.

et inuitos terrore compelli et uolentes praemio prouocari posse: the parallellism and the alliteration of *p* are noteworthy.

renuntiantes: with a dative: "renouncing", giving up". Cf. Quint. *Inst.* 10, 7, 1 *ciuilibus officiis renuntiabit.*

ad instar tyrannicae potestatis sectam suam conferre malle: Apul. generelly uses the expression *ad instar*, followed by a genitive, in the sense of "like", e.g. 2, 21 (42, 11) *ad instar oratorum conformat articulum*; 4, 26 (95, 15) *ad instar Attidis ... disturbatae ... nuptiae*. But this meaning does not seem to suit our passage since it leaves the rest of the sentence *sectam ... malle* hard to translate. Unless the text is corrupted, it seems more probable that Apul. has taken *instar* here in its original substantival meaning ("balance", "equivalence") assumed by LHSz 2, 218: 'als t(erminus) t(echnicus) der Kaufmannssprache ein substantivierter Inf. instār(e) "das Einstehen (der Waage beim Wiegen)"'. Thus *instar* can acquire, via "counterweight", the meaning of "equivalent", "value", "power", "authority". The most famous illustration of this is Verg. *A.* 6, 865 (on Marcellus) *quantum instar in ipso,* which Norden paraphrases with '*quantum in eo inest ponderis atque amplitudinis*' and Austin 1977 *ad loc.* with 'how great his single worth'; Servius explains it as 'similitudo'. A good parallel of this somewhat archaic usage is given by Gel. 20, 1, 39 (already quoted by Kronenberg) *populus Romanus e parua origine ad tantae amplitudinis instar emicuit.* Cf. also Iust. 4, 4, 7; Ov. *Am.* 3, 11, 47. On the etymology see Wölfflin 1885, 581 f.

sectam suam: "their life style", "line of conduct", "mode of life", as in Cic. *Cael.* 40 *nos, qui hanc sectam rationemque uitae ... secuti sumus*; Quint. *Inst.* 3, 8, 38 *exprobrare diuersam uitae sectam.* For some observations on *secta* in Apul. see *GCA* 1977, 136-137.

ad ... conferre: in consequence of our translation of *instar*, these two words can now be connected: "to direct towards", possibly "to adapt to". The author's intention may be rendered with "live like a prince", since *tyrannica potestas* is here presented as an attractive alternative to its opposite, namely a *seruilis uita.* It is the unrestricted power of an absolute monarch, exercised at will; cf. Apul. 10, 6 (241, 21) *tyrannica impotentia*; 9, 36 (230, 13) *tyrannica superbia*; 7, 16 (166, 23) *praepotens tyrannus* (none of these passages have a parallel in the *"Ονος*). Thus a free robber's life is compared with *tyrannica potestas.*

157, 11-18 Se quoque iam dudum pro sua parte quendam conuenisse hominem et statu procerum et aetate iuuenem et corpore uastum et manu strenuum, eique suasisse ac denique persuasisse, et manus ⟨h⟩ebetatas diutina pigritia tandem referret ad frugem meliorem bonoque secundae, dum posset, frueretur ualetudinis nec manum ualidam erogandae stipi porrigeret, sed hauriendo potius exerceret auro: "He himself, too, had recently met with a man, stately of stature, young in years, huge of body, and fast of fist. He had urged and eventually persuaded him to turn his hand, weakened by prolonged sloth, to a more profitable goal, and to enjoy the benefits of good health while he could. Then he would not need to stretch out his strong hand to beg for alms, but rather might exercise it by raking in gold".

iam dudum: dudum often means "a little while ago", e.g. Pl. *Rud.* 1079 *milieris, quam dudum dixi fuisse liberam.* In the combination *iam dudum* that meaning, although less common, is still possible, e.g. Apul. 8, 22 (194, 9) *infantulumque, quem de eodem marito iam dudum susceperat,* where its meaning has to be "a short time ago"; the same holds for Pl. *Am.* 491 *ut iam dudum dixi* (i.e. some 15 verses earlier); see also Pl. *Epid.* 407-408 *quia dixit mihi / iam dudum.* The meaning is necessary for this passage, too, the speaker cannot have met Haemus until after the girl was kidnapped, i.e. the previous day (cf. 4, 26). On the other hand, the possibility of an intentional vagueness on Apul.'s part should not be entirely excluded: Junghanns 1932, 150, n. 51 may be right in his belief that it really happened "already a long time ago" and that it is 'unbedachte Übertreibung des

Räubers oder Unbedachtsamkeit des Apuleius', who has apparently forgotten the exact lapse of time.

hominem et statu procerum et aetate iuuenem et corpore uastum et manu strenuum: a fine and impressive description of Haemus' qualities in a fourfold parallelism; Bernhard 1927, 23 calls it a 'schwülstige Häufung der Adjektiva'. That the words are actually not much exaggerated becomes evident in 157, 21 f., when Haemus himself appears, this time described by the narrating Lucius-ass.

The robber uses the word *manus* three times in this sentence, qualifying it alternately as strong – weak – strong.

suasisse ac denique persuasisse: a similar paronomasia occurs 9, 25 (222, 4) *suasi ac denique persuasi*. Also Jul. Val. 2, 5 *cum tu suaseris et... persuaseris*.

ad frugem meliorem: from the robbers' point of view, of course. The expression *ad bonam frugem* is proverbial: Cicero adds ut dicitur in *Cael*. 28 *et se ad frugem bonam, ut dicitur, recepisse*; see Austin *ad loc.* and Otto 1965, 147 *s.v. frux*. Apul. uses a variant of this expression in 4, 5 (78, 10) *asinum... bonae frugi*; see *GCA ad loc.*

We have here another excellent example of Apuleius' irony: Haemus is determined to exterminate the whole gang of robbers and to free Charite. See Junghanns 1932, 150.

erogandae stipi: cf. 1, 6 (5, 15) *stipes in triuiis erogare*.

hauriendo... auro: Haemus will do that very thing (cf. 164, 7-8), only in a different way from what is suggested here. The metaphor is not very common, but cf. Cic. *Sest*. 93 *haurire cotidie ex pacatissimis... Syriae gazis innumerabile pondus auri*. Tlepolemus appears here as a sort of beggar, although it will soon (160, 10) turn out that he carries two thousand pieces of gold in his cloak.

Observe the hyperbaton *bono... frueretur* and *secundae... ualetudinis*.

CHAPTER V

The robber introduces Haemus to his colleagues; Haemus starts on the tall story of his previous bloody career.

On the place and function of chapters 5-8 in Apuleius' narrative see the introduction.

157, 18-20 Talibus dictis uniuersi omnes adsensi[ere] et illum, qui iam comprobatus uideretur, adscisci et alios ad supplendum numerum uestigari statuunt: "They all to a man agreed with these utterances and decided both to accept that fellow, who already seemed to have been approved, and to look for others to make up their numbers".

uniuersi omnes: Callebat 1968, 526 notes that this redundancy occurs in Pl. *Trin.* 1046; Var. *L*, 10, 10, and later reappears in Fronto (p. 121, 14 vdH.) and Aulus Gellius (19, 12, 1). The expression is only logically redundant; at 160, 16 f. Apuleius even more emphatically underlines the robbers' unanimity.

adsensi: adsensiere F, adsensere φ. Robertson follows vdVliet in reading *adsensi*; the latter explains that F simply combined *adsensi* and *adsensere*. That explanation is quite possibly right, but it does not indicate that either reading is preferable to the other. An argument in favour of the deponent participle may be found in the relative frequency of the deponent and active forms of the verb. Flobert 1975, 201 notes that in Apuleius this is 2:1 but adds that his statistics are 'faussées par le groupement de l'infectum et du perfectum; ce dernier en effet est rarement déponent'. Since the verb occurs only six times in Apuleius, statistics do not mean much in his case; nevertheless the perfect deponent constitutes a *lectio difficilior*, though it is not without parallels: 4, 17 (87, 18) *non difficulter adsensus... permisit* (cf. *As.* 23: 59, 19 f. *tuis uerbis libenter adsensus felicissimum hominem iudico, qui sit tantam felicitatem consecutus*).

qui iam comprobatus uideretur: the approval is a little hasty. Presently it will be noticed that the young man's story referred to does not altogether tally with what the robber has just said about him; cf. 160, 11 ff., where this young man who is to be rescued from the poverty of a beggar's life produces 2000 *aurei*, thus furthering his claim to leadership. For the subjunctive there are three possibilities: a. there is no reason at all (cf. LHSz 2, 560), b. it gives a causal aspect to the clause, c. it is due to the fact that the relative clause is virtually in *oratio obliqua*. The last-mentioned possibility seems most likely: the narrator gives a reason from which he detaches himself, since he has not himself heard the actual approval.

comprobatus: the word occurs in this sense in a military context in Suet. *Gal.* 16, 2 (cf. Cic. *Phil.* 5, 28), but cannot count as a technical term; see e.g. Cic. *Arch.* 31; Quint. *Inst.* 10, 1, 130.

adscisci: the verb has a somewhat formal flavour in both military and political contexts; see e.g. Sal. *Cat.* 47, 1 and *ThLL s.v.* 764, 2 ff.

supplendum: also often used in a military context, e.g. Cic. *Phil.* 8, 27; Tac. *Hist.* 4, 19.

uestigari: also at 10, 14 (247, 5): *cotidiani damni studiose uestigabant reum*; cf. *Soc.* 1 (6, 9); *Apol.* 16 (18, 18); 27 (31, 21); 41 (48, 16). The word is rather rare in Apuleius' time (see e.g. Gel. 6, 16, 4; Minuc. 22, 2), but occurs fairly frequently in the classical period (the Thesaurus material at Munich totals well over a hundred instances).

Tunc profectus et paululum commoratus ille perducit immanem quendam iuuenem, uti fuerat pollicitus, nescio an ulli praesentium comparandum – nam praeter ceteram corporis molem toto uertice cunctos antepollebat et ei commodum lanugo malis inserpebat – sed plane centunculis disparibus et male consarcinatis semiamictum, inter quos pectus et uenter crustata crassitie reluctabant: "Then having gone off and stayed away for a little while, he brought along a huge young man, as he had promised, to whom I think not one of those present could be compared – for, apart from the massive size of the rest of his body, he towered above them all by the whole of his head, and just recently a down had begun to cover his cheeks, – but he was unmistakably only half-covered by the patches of an ill-fitting and badly sewn-up cloak; between these patches his chest and belly, embossed with muscles, were having a wrestling match". 157, 21-158, 2

Tunc profectus et paululum commoratus: Junghanns 1932, 52 n. 74 says that these words indicate a 'Spannungspause'. He is right in so far as the sponsor of Haemus inserts such a moment to allow the tension among the robbers to mount, but the words themselves, discussing this device, are directed at a different audience by the narrator, Lucius.

perducit: vdVliet prints *producit* from Gudianus 172, a manuscript without independent authority. There is no reason to adopt its conjecture (or mistake); *perducere* is employed for "bringing into the presence of" both with and without prepositional phrase (with: Suet. *Tib.* 65, 1 *qui se ... in conspectum eorum ... perduceret*; without: Tac. *Hist.* 1, 25, 1 *a quo Barbium Proculum ... et Veturium optionem ... perductos*).

uti fuerat pollicitus: on the form and function of the pluperfect see vdPaardt 1971, 54; cf. *GCA* 1977, 122; comm. on 149, 3 above.

– *nam praeter ceteram corporis molem toto uertice cunctos antepollebat et ei commodum lanugo malis inserpebat* –: see Bernhard 1927, 92 on the frequency of parenthesis in the *Met.* He finds 18 instances; see also vdPaardt 1971, 67; *GCA* 1977, 38, 40. For a systematic discussion of parenthesis in a single author see von Albrecht 1964, who discusses causal parentheses introduced by *nam* 59 f. Epic colouring is evident in several details of the parenthesis.

toto uertice: in Verg. *A.* 7, 784 (*Turnus*) *toto uertice supra est*. The picture is Homeric, cf. *Il.* 3, 210 and 227. See also Verg. *A.* 8, 162 *sed cunctis altior ibat / Anchises* and P. T. Eden *ad loc.*

antepollebat: Médan 1925, 32 notes that here the verb takes an acc., at 1, 5 (5, 6) a dative. For the prefix *ante-* see *ibidem* 126. The verb does not occur anywhere else.

et ei: Blümmer 1905, 31 proposed an unnecessary *etsi*: the two elements here correspond perfectly with *et statu procerum et aetate iuuenem* (lines 12-13 above).

commodum ... inserpebat: Bernhard 1927, 200 quotes 5, 16 (115, 20) *modo florenti lanugine barbam instruens* and 5, 8 (109, 13) *commodum lanoso barbitio genas inumbrantem,* and refers to Vergil *A.* 10, 324 *flauentem prima lanugine malas.* The motif has its startingpoint in Homer. *Od.* 11, 320 πυκάσαι τε γένυς εὐανθέι λάχνῃ, cf. *Il.* 24, 348. It occurs with some frequency, cf. Lucr. 5, 889 with Merrill and Bailey *ad loc.*; Vergil *A.* 8, 160 with P. T. Eden *ad loc.*; see also *Apol.* 63 (71, 21) *ut decenter utrimque lanugo malis deserpat.* Weyman 1893, 368 notes Amm. 31. 10, 18. The loveliness of this age (noted by both Homer and Vergil) is not supposed to affect the robbers, but the readers will soon realise that it is Charite's attractive bridegroom who is here described. On the other hand the immense, towering shape with a fresh growth near the top seems to provide a neat explanation for the name Haemus. See below on 158, 10-15.

sed plane ... semiamictum: it is only at 163, 6-8 that we are informed that this is a disguise – an exaggerated one at that – but the reader who knew his Plautus might guess the truth even now, see *Epid.* 455 *Proin tu alium quaeras quoi centones sarcias*; cf. Otto 1890 *s.v. cento* Nachtr. 147; *cento* and *centunculus* refer to a "patchwork quilt"; the combination *centones sarcire* in Plautus refers to telling lies. Cf. Lucil. 747 (Marx) *sarcinatorem esse summum, suere centonem optime.* The image of sewing is used for machinations, lies, strategems and the like from Homer onwards, cf. H. Fränkel 1925, 3 f.; E. Fraenkel on Aesch. *Agam.* 1604; see also Pl. *Capt.* 692 ... *atque ob sutelas tuas te morti misero* and Lindsay *ad loc.*; cf. *Am.* 367 and Ussing *ad loc.*; *Cas.* 95; *Ps.* 353; 540. The verb *consarcinare* is used in a similar context by Amm. Marc. e.g. 14, 5, 6; 14, 9, 2; 16, 8, 4, see de Jonge on the first of these for further parallels. If Apuleius does give a hint as to the fictitious, or disguised, nature of the character by means of these words, it is not the first time: cf. 1, 6 (6, 7) *et cum dicto sutili centunculo faciem suam iam dudum punicantem prae pudore obtexit* (sc. the inverted Socrates; cf. e.g. Schlam 1970, 486; vdPaardt in *AAGA* 1978, 84). At 9, 12 (212, 3) and 9, 30 (225, 19) the element of sewing is lacking; for the same reason we do not think *mimi centunculo* in *Apol.* 13 (15, 21) is relevant here.

plane: see *GCA* 1977, 25.

centunculis disparibus: the word *dispar* may refer to the uneven size of the patches; *centunculis* (cf. 160, 18) hardly refers to more than one garment; the plural for a single garment occurs nowhere else: possibly the patches are referred to.

semiamictum: cf. 9, 30 (225, 19) *flebili centunculo semiamicta*; 9, 12 (212, 3) *scissili centunculo magis inumbrati quam obtecti.*

inter quos pectus et uenter crustata crassitie reluctabant: the alliteration of *ct* and *cr* is noteworthy.

crustatus: Médan 1925, 146 translates "épais" (new meaning). *OLD* however proposes the much more attractive meaning "to carve in relief, emboss" for *crustare* and quotes the present passage (*ThLL* interprets *crusta obducere*).

crassities is rare: it occurs here and Cael. Aur. *Chron.* 5, 10, 123; Oribas. *syn.* 5, 43 (*crossicie*).

The main problem of the phrase is presented by *reluctabant*. Armini 1928, 303 takes *reluctabant* in the sense of *relucebant* ('notione relucendi'), vdVliet considered *relucebant* (Gruter), Robertson printed *relucitabant* (equally Gruter), see also Giarratano-Frassinetti. The Thesaurus material at Munich could not produce any parallel for this verb. Helm (*app. crit.*) explains *reluctabant* as "specie discrepabant". The translators are divided in their interpretations; several side with Armini (e.g. Adlington-Gaselee, Butler, Augello), several others take *reluctabant* more literally (e.g. Byrne "came bursting through", Brandt-Ehlers, Pagliano), Scazzoso suggests a tight fit ("nei quali erano a stento contenuti il suo petto ed il ventre"), Carlesi-Terzaghi suggest the most literal rendering ("facevan la lotta") which we have adopted as the most playful. For *reluctari* cf. Verg. *G.* 4, 301 and Hor. *Carm.* 4, 4, 11 (*reluctantis dracones*); for the active Flobert 1975, 124 f. See Augello 1977, 164.

158, 3-160, 15: some introductory remarks.

Haemus' speech differs from the robber's speech (4, 9-21) in so far as the latter reports what has occurred; during the robber's tale – notwithstanding the obvious intention to present his audience with the most favourable version possible – the reader nowhere receives a signal that it is all lies. Haemus' story on the other hand is made up out of whole cloth. This becomes clear to the reader as soon as his identity as Tlepolemus is revealed. Its main purpose is for him to be accepted into the robbers' company[1]. Quite in keeping with this difference the robber's tale in book 4 is presented as part of a dialogue (see 4, 8), whereas Haemus' words constitute an address consisting of three main parts: he introduces himself (158, 3-15), tells the story of the loss of his band and his own escape (158, 15-160, 6), and with a grand gesture he offers to become the robbers' leader (160, 6-15). This arrangement is not unlike that of the speech for the prosecution at 3, 3, cf. vdPaardt 1971, 46 f., Bernhard 1927, 275. In addition to the differences from the robber's tale mentioned in the Introduction (above p. 4 f.) we note that Haemus does not just compete with the robbers at their own game, he wins hands down and in all respects. He is bigger, bloodier, cleverer: he is presented as successful where the other robbers were not. Such exaggerations as *totamque prorsus deuastaui Macedoniam* and *cuius totae prouinciae nomen horrescunt* immensely impress his audience, but make the reader smile. The words *libentius uulnera corpore excipientem quam aurum manu suscipientem ipsaque morte quam formidant alii, meliorem* recall in an exaggerated way the attitudes of a Lamachus or a Thrasyleon. On the other hand there are some features that look like deliberate inversions: Thrasyleon dresses up as a bear in order to get in and as a

---

[1] Junghanns 1932, 74 n. 111 discusses the *dissimulatio*. See also the introduction of the bear Thrasyleon into the house of Demochares (4, 16 ff.). The reader gets a hint concerning the *dissimulatio* at 161, 2-3, cf. comm. *ad loc.* and on 157, 16 above. See Lausberg 1960, 561 and in particular 585 f. on *dissimulatio* and *anagnorisis* in the ancient novel.

result loses his life, bloody Haemus dresses up as a woman in order to get out and so retains his life. Haemus' band dies but he escapes, Lamachus' band escapes but he dies. In addition a few direct links with the robber stories have been noted below *ad loc*. Finally there is the curious piece of one-upmanship in that Haemus offers 2000 pieces of gold, whereas the other robber gave only 1000.

158, 3-7 Sic introgressus: "Hauete", inquit, "fortissimo deo Marti clientes mihique iam fidi commilitones, et uirum magnanimae uiuacitatis uolentem uolentes accipite, libentius uulnera corpore excipientem quam aurum manu suscipientem ipsaque morte, quam formidant alii, meliorem: "Having entered in this way he said: 'Hail, followers of the most valiant god Mars and from now on my trusted fellow-soldiers! Willingly accept a willing man of great-hearted courage, one who is more ready to take wounds on his body than pick up gold with his hand and who actually has the better of death, which other men fear".

sic: there appear to be two main possibilities: *sic* expresses either a backward or a forward link. If it is the former the choice lies between a reference to the preceding description of the disguise (*'talis'*, cf. Forcellini *s.v.* 8, LS *s.v.* I 5; this use however is ordinarily predicative with *esse*) and a reference to the manner of introduction (157, 21-22); if the latter, it is to be taken with *inquit*. See also *GCA* 1977, 182; as there we feel a slight preference for the backward link ("having entered in this manner"); cf. e.g. 4, 24 (93, 20) *lamentata sic* and *GCA* 1977, 184 *ad loc.*; 4, 25 (94, 5).

introgressus: the word, which first occurs as an intransitive in Verg. *A.* 1, 520 and later in transitive sense in Stat. *Theb.* 3, 345, becomes somewhat more common from Apuleius' time onwards (in both trans. and intrans. senses, e.g. Gel. 12, 1, 3; Tert. *ieiun.* 10, 3 p. 286, 17).

habete F; *hauete* ς. The reading of F can hardly be defended without surgery. The correction in ς is both simple (cf. Helm. Praef. *Fl.* 46 for the interchange of *u* and *b* and produces an acceptable opening. For the spelling *hauete* see Ernout-Meillet *s.v. aue*. They refer to the statement by Quintilian (1, 6, 21) that the pronunciation *auē* is highly cultured. The opposite conclusion, that in his (and Apuleius' ?) time *hauĕ* was low and unacceptable may not be drawn.

fortissimo deo Marti clientes: thus F; Petschenig proposed *fortissimi* and Robertson comments: 'fortasse recte'. Indeed the robbers are addressed as *fortissimi fidelissimique mei hospitatores iuuenes* by the *anus* at 4, 7 (79, 24) but on the other hand Venus speaks to her son about Mars as *uitricum tuum fortissimum illum maximumque bellatorem* at 5, 30 (127, 7-8). Neither phrase being clearly preferable to the other, there is insufficient reason to change the ms. reading. For the etymological link *cliens-clueo* cf. Pl. *Men.* 574 ff. There is no proper parallel for this dative with *cliens* (sympathetic dative) but Callebat 1968, 490 f. notes that a dative substituted for an expected genitive is not uncommon in specialists' language, poets, Tacitus etc. (cf. Löfstedt I ²1942, 209 f.; LHSz 2, 95 f.); in Apuleius, see, e.g. 5, 13 (113, 16-17) *fidei atque parciloquio meo perpendisti documenta* and Fernhout 1949, 86 *ad loc.*; cf. also Médan 1925, 42. As a circumlocution for *latrones* (Médan 1925, 346; Strilciw 1925, 110) the phrase has various advantages: it strengthens the military flavour and underlines the robbers' dependence on violence, but also reminds the reader of 4, 22 (91, 11) *Marti deo blanditi*; thus it is one of several direct references to the robber stories of book 4.

mihique iam fidi commilitones: Médan 1925, 230 remarks that *-que* 'remplaçant une apposition' also occurs in Plautus and Terence. He is right, of course, but here *-que* links *mihi* with *Marti* (with some considerable effect), and there is no question of a replaced apposition. *commilitones*: Callebat 1968, 74 seems to be wrong in stating that the meaning 'compagnons d'armes' does not occur in Apuleius: the fiction that the robbers' band is a military unit is, on the contrary, sustained precisely by words like these. See *GCA* 1977, 208 f.; cf. Rode-Burck 1961, 237. In the parallelism *fortissimo deo Marti clientes mihique iam fidi commilitones* the words *mihique iam fidi* are an almost naked hint that Haemus is not merely asking admittance but is making for the leadership.

uirum magnanimae uiuacitatis uolentem uolentes accipite: for *uiuacitas* in the sense of "courage" several parallels can be cited from later authors, e.g. [Quint.] *Decl*. 4, 8 *inde est quod inter luctus et desperationes foeda uiuacitate duramus*; Cypr. *Epist*. 22, 1; Ios. *Antiq*. 7, 7 p. 194, 13 *impetum eorum sua uiuacitate suscipiens ... interiit*. The addition of the adj. *magnanimae* strengthens this interpretation. And indeed, when the whole story is over and done with, Haemus-Tlepolemus has proved his manly courage by entering the lions' den and coming through unscathed. Yet he does so by means of a clever stratagem, paying a liberal entrance fee, and a perceptive reader may well have realized that *uiuacitas* may mean "intelligence", "cleverness" (see e.g. Claud. Donat. *A*. II 520, 7 on *A*. 11, 690 ff. *sequentis Camillae uiuacitas partem qua hominem penetraret inuenit*; cf. II 46, 13; II 157, 16; Arnob. Maior V 32 *nec quas (rationes) facile quiuis possit ingenii uiuacitate pernoscere*) and that *magnanimus* may mean "liberal" (e.g. *SHA* Jul. Cap. *M. Ant. Phil*. 17, 7: *in munere autem publico tam magnanimus fuit, ut centum leones una missione simul exhiberet*; cf. Symm. *Epist*. 4, 31; *Cod. Iust*. 10, 15, 1, 1). The alliteration is noteworthy (see Médan 1925, 306); in addition there may be some deliberate arranging of the vowel sounds. See Hijmans in *AAGA* 1978, 201 f. In *uirum magnanimae uiuacitatis* there appears to be another reference to book 4, e.g. to the description of Lamachus 4, 11 (82, 25) *uir sublimis animi uirtutisque praecipuus* and Thrasyleon 4, 21 (90, 17 f.) *praesentem casum generoso uigore tolerans*; cf. also the discussion of *uolentem uolentes* below.

uolentem uolentes: cf. e.g. Aesch. *Prom*. 19 ἄκοντα σ' ἄκων, 192 σπεύδων σπεύδοντι, 218 ἑκόνθ' ἑκόντι and Groeneboom *ad loc*. Pease on Verg. *A*. 4, 83 *illum absens absentem auditque uidetque* gives more instances and literature. Polyptoton occurs on several occasions in Apul., e.g. 5, 20 (119, 2) *hominem iungemus homini*. See Strilciw 1925, 116; Bernhard 1927, 236 f. adds further instances. On the term in ancient literary criticism see Lausberg 1960, 328.

libentius uulnera corpore excipientem quam aurum manu suscipientem: Médan 1925, 271 notes the two heroic clausulae, but perhaps the effect is attributable to the homoeoteleuton rather than to the rhythm. See also below on *ipsaque ... meliorem*. For the exaggeration see above. Tatum 1969[b], 506 is quite right in remarking that these gullible robbers 'are deceived even as they hear the truth'.

Upon re-reading the words *libentius... excipientem* the ancient reader may well have remembered with a chuckle that Haemus' real name was Tlepolemus.

ipsaque morte, quam formidant alii, meliorem: the last three words form part of an hexameter. Together with the two heroic clausulae in the previous phrase, they may give an epic quality to the speech; but without an overall survey of Apuleius' use of rhythm such a remark is hazardous. There may be a reminiscence (and exaggeration) here of the proverbial 'safety in fortitude' common in generals' speeches before the battle, see e.g. Xen. *Cyr.* 3, 3, 45; Sal. *Iug.* 87, 2 (*fortissumum quemque tutissumum*), 107, 1 (*quanto sibi in proelio minus pepercissent, tanto tutiores fore*), Cat. 58, 17 (*audacia pro muro habetur*); Liv. 25, 38, 18; Curt. 4, 14, 25. Cf. also the proverbial *fortibus est fortuna uiris data* in Enn. *Ann.* 257 (see Otto, 1890, 144; Ov. *Fast.* 2, 782 and Bömer *ad loc.*). The fun of the phrase lies in the double or triple possibilities of interpretation: (1) Haemus may be indifferent to death (like Lamachus, thus *OLD s.v. melior* 10 a) or (2) he may conquer death (such death as is threatening Charite: cf. Heracles in Eur. *Alc.*; see for this common motif Lesky in *RE s.v. Thanatos* 1245 ff.) or even: (3) Haemus outdoes death in killing – losing as he does his entire band in his own story *and* (later) killing the entire robbers' band whose leadership he pretends to seek here. The first represents what the robbers will assume Heamus means, the second what may be in his mind, the third what the reader may realise in retrospect.

quam formidant alii: on the word order see Bernard 1927, 16, who notes Apuleius' tendency to place the verb second- or third-last in the sentence.

158, 8-9 Nec me putetis egenum uel abiectum neue de pannulis istis uirtutes meas aestimetis: "And do not think me destitute or contemptible nor judge my prowess by these rags".

nec... neue: LHSz 2, 517 note that the combination occurs in the language of poets; it is e.g. Servius' reading at Verg. *G.* 3, 435 f.; see also Prop. 1, 8, 11 f.; Ov. *Met.* 8, 709 f.; Juv. 14, 201-3 and Friedländer *ad loc.* On the form of the prohibition see Médan 1925, 21; Callebat 1968, 101; the latter *ibid.* 96 remarks that there are only three instances of *neue* in the *Met.*

egenum: on the absolute sense of "poor" see Callebat 1968, 164, who cites e.g. Stat. *Th.* 12, 495.

pannulis: the word occurs also below 160, 10; 9, 12 (212, 6); later in Amm. 19, 8, 8; 22, 9, 11; 26, 6, 15; 31, 2, 5 and perhaps in Hier. *in Ezech.* 7 praef. (but ed. Glorie (Corp. Christ. p. 277, 21) reads *pannos*) and in the *Vita Caes. Arel.* 2, 15 ed. Krusch (*MGH*).

istis: vdPaardt 1971, 89 agrees with Callebat 1968, 270 that this use of *iste* suggests a gesture on the part of the speaker. See also *GCA* 1977, 165 on 4, 21 (91, 8) where the value of the gesture is somewhat different.

On *aestimare de* see Médan 1925, 67; Ruiz de Elvira 1954, 114: only here in Apuleius and in Tertullian *Nat.* 1, 10, 25 (*de contemptu aestimanda*) (*ThLL s.v.* 1103, 67), cf. Callebat 1968, 202.

The interest of the sentence lies in the fact that Haemus indicates here that the robber who introduced him was misinformed. The fact that all the robbers remain misinformed concerning his real self for a little while longer materially adds to the reader's enjoyment.

Nam praefui ualidissimae manui totamque prorsus deuastaui 158, 9-10
Macedoniam: "For I have commanded a most valiant troop and I have utterly ravaged the whole of Macedonia".

Rode-Burck 237 note 'mit ihrem Beutegebiet Makedonien and Thrakien ist der ganze Norden der Balkanhalbinsel gemeint'. It may be thought that Burck is exaggerating the exaggeration, but the problem of brigandage in the Roman empire appears to have been immense. For details concerning various areas and periods Mac Mullen 1966, 255-268; for the *Met.* as one of his sources *ibid.* 256, 264. See also MacKay 1963, 150, who appears to discount the realism of the present tale. See also below on 159, 22 f.: *tantum potest nutus etiam magni principis.*

On the frequency of *prorsus* in the *Met.* see Callebat 1968, 538, who notes several instances where it reinforces such words as *totus, cunctus* and the like, e.g. 10, 21 (252, 15); 10, 27 (258, 20); here however it may just as well be taken with *deuastaui.*

deuastaui Macedoniam: Bernhard 1927, 18 notes this instance in his discussion of Apuleius' penchant for having the verb in second last place; see also above on line 7.

Ego sum praedo famosus Haemus ille Thracius, cuius totae 158, 10-15
prouinciae nomen horrescunt, patre Therone atque latrone inclito prognatus, humano sanguine nutritus interque ipsos manipulos factionis educatus heres et aemulus uirtutis paternae: "I am that famous brigand Haemus the Thracian, upon hearing whose name all provinces shudder. Sired by a father called Theron, a famous robber, nourished on human blood and brought up among the very platoons of our troop, I am the heir and imitator of my father's valour".

Ego sum: the personal pronoun is not used 'sans raison spéciale' (Médan 1925, 215) but occurs fairly often in contexts where the contrast with others is implicit in the dramatic situation. See e.g. Pl *Aul.* 2 *ego Lar sum familiaris*; *ibidem* 704 *ego sum ille rex Philippus*; *Bac.* 573 *parasitus ego sum hominis nequam*; Ps. 1209 f. Westerbrink in *AAGA* 1978, 70 notes an element of parody of passages such as Hom. *Od.* 9, 19 f. and Verg. *A.* 1, 378.

praedo: the common word for the robbers is *latrones* (used more than 60 times in the *Met.*); the present formula is repeated at 7, 12 (163, 7); otherwise the word *praedo* occurs only once in the *Met.* at 8, 2 (177, 21), where a *famulus* of Charite employs it to refer to the robbers whom Haemus is now addressing. The formula here may be due to a simple desire for variation, since *latro* was required below for the group *patre Therone atque latrone inclito* with its deliberate sound effects.

famosus: for the sense of "famous" rather than "ill-famed" see *GCA* 1977, 105.

Haemus ille: for the triple significance of this name see Hijmans in *AAGA* 1978, 115, where it is argued that there is a connection with the Thracian mountain range (cf. 157, 24), and with αἵνα (*humano sanguine nutritus*), but also a pun on *aemulus,* since this robber is his father's rival hunter (*Theron*): is he not in effect hunting the robbers? (He will also die during a hunting party, and there may be an ominous, though remote, foreshadowing here.) It may be that Apuleius chose this particular name because of a number of mythical and literary associations, such as occur in Callimachus (*Hymn. in Del.* 63 f.: Mars), in Vergil (*G.* 1, 491 f.: blood), Ovid (*Met.* 6, 87 ff.: metamorphosis), and perhaps Juvenal (3, 99: an actor). For a survey of the possibilities see Hijmans 1978, 407 f. For emphatic *ille* see Callebat 1968, 277, LHSz 2, 185.

cuius totae prouinciae nomen horrescunt: Callebat 1968, 287 discusses *totae* = "all"; see also vdPaardt 1971, 121; *GCA* 1977, 51; 165. Of course it is possible to defend the sense "entire" here by referring to *totamque ... Macedoniam* above.

patre Therone atque latrone inclito prognatus: editors print Lipsius' *aeque*; Robertson points out that the same *corruptela* occurs at 5, 6 (107, 28). However, in view of Apuleius' high consciousness of the meaning of several of the names he uses (see *GCA* 1977, 102 ff., *AAGA* 1978, 107), the conjunction may be defended as a simple link between two equal-level expressions.

humano sanguine nutritus: the main function of the phrase, apart from its sensationalism, is to provide an etymology for the name Haemus.

manipulos factionis: the first word reinforces the military flavour, see *GCA* 1977, 209; the second, with its unfavourable connotation, provides a touch of humour in the contrast. See *GCA* 1977, 120; 175.

heres et aemulus uirtutis paternae: the second etymological hint in one sentence.

CHAPTER VI

Haemus starts on the explanation of his losses: the story of Plotina.

Sed omnem pristinam sociorum fortium multitudinem magnasque 158, 15-16
illas opes exiguo temporis amisi spatio: "But the whole of this original multitude of brave allies and those large amounts of wealth – I lost them all within a short space of time".

omnem ... multitudinem: hyperbaton is quite common in Apuleius (Bernhard 1927, 24 ff.; *GCA* 1977, 22 etc.); the double hyperbaton in this sentence (cf. *exiguo ... spatio*) draws attention to the contrast of large and small.

exiguo temporis ... spatio: with the combination may be compared 2, 28 (48, 17) *exiguum uitae spatium*; Gel. 14, 1, 5 *in tam breui exiguoque uitae spatio*.

Van Thiel 1971, 20 n. 58 gives the list of similar indications of theme at the beginning of a story.

Nam procuratorem principis ducenaria perfunctum, dehinc fortuna 158, 17-19
tristiore decussum, praetereuntem† me orato† fueram adgressus. Sed rei noscendae carpo ordinem: "An imperial Procurator — one who had held the rank of *ducenarius* but had since, through rather bad luck, been toppled — this man I had attacked as he passed by (?..?). But I'll make things clear by taking them in order".

Nam procuratorem principis ducenaria perfunctum: *ducenaria* as an abstract noun (office of a *procurator ducenarius*) occurs only in Apuleius. Helm-Krenkel note that the term refers to both rank and salary (200,000 HS). See also Callebat 1968, 131, Vallette *ad loc.*; also Hirschfeld 1905, 432, 438; Pflaum 1960-1961, 950 f.

dehinc fortuna tristiore decussum: for *fortuna* see above on 155, 21. This *tristior fortuna* will presently turn up in the guise of *saeuiens Inuidia* (158, 22). The transferred sense of *decutere* is rare, see e.g. Cic. *Fam.* 8, 13, 1.

Haemus does not tell his audience how he knows these details.

praetereuntem me orato is probably the first reading in F (*ptereunte* with something erased above the final *e*); φ and a* have *praetereunte me orato*. The passage has been the object of emendators' zeal for many centuries. Their efforts may be classified as follows:

1. The entire group *praetereuntem me orato* is regarded as corrupt. In the margin of his copy of the Colvius edition (1588) Oudendorp found *praeter uiam de meo irato* (mistake for *deo*?); Oudendorp mentions two further anonymous conjectures in this class: a highly imaginative *praeeunte meo patre* and *praetereuntium incoram*. *Incoram* occurs with gen. 4 times in the *Met.*, twice *incoram omnium* (7, 21: 170, 13; 9, 10: 209, 23), twice *incoram sui* (9, 15: 214, 1; 10, 5: 240,

25). *ThLL* gives no instances where it follows the genitive. See Callebat 1968, 240. Cornelissen 1888, 166 proposes *proterua temeritate*, Petschenig 1888, 765 *properante meo fato*. Through it may be argued that Haemus does not attack the *Procurator* as he passes by, but when he spends the hight ashore at an inn, there is no reason to suspect *praetereuntem*, since *praeterire* does not exclude the notion of an intermediate stop, cf. e.g. Lucil. 898 *huc alio cum iter haberet praeteriens uenit*.

2. The corruption is confined to *me orato*.

a. The words hide a geographical indication: thus Wower (1606) proposes an otherwise unknown city *Orato* approved by Elmenhorst and Scioppius; Unger's *Orico* was attacked by Hildebrand since (1) it is too far from the coast at Actium and (2) the dative or ablative does not fit *praeterire*. (This objection also applies to *Orato*). Oudendorp (1786) suggests *oram*, which is palaeographically rather less attractive than *Orico*.

b. The words hide an indication of time: Bétolaud and Clouard print *praetereunte noctu* (Clouard translates as if he read *praetereuntem noctu*: "...était sur les routes; je l'attaquait de nuit"). This conjecture is not very attractive either palaeographically or from the point of view of sense.

c. The words hide a noun or adjective to be construed with *praetereuntem*. Wasse's *rate* or *oria*, though attractive, are vitiated by the details of the account that follows: Haemus does not attack as the procurator is sailing by on a ship, but when the ship has landed (159, 7 f.). Oudendorp also quotes an anonymous conjecture *inoratum*, which underlines the bad treatment of the procurator. *Memoratum* ("on everybody's lips", cf. *Fl.* 18: 37, 10) is palaeographically more attractive, and would indicate how Haemus came to know about the procurator and thus suggest a reason for the attack, but is harsh without e.g. *omnibus*.

d. The words hide an adverb or adverbial expression with *praetereuntem*: Oudendorp (1786) proposes *cum consorte tori* (palaeographically unlikely), Purser (1906) *morato* (= slowly) with one of the *recentiores*; the adverb is not attested elsewhere.

e. The words hide an adverb or adverbial expression with *fueram adgressus*: Beroaldus (1500) proposes *coram*, Stewech (1586) *incoram*. The objection is that the attack is not *coram* but at night. Soping proposed *inopinato*, Haupt (1872) has *deo meo irato*, quoting in support Ter. *Ph.* 74 *memini relinqui me deo irato meo*; cf. Pl. *Poen.* 452 and Maurach *ad loc.*, Naev. *com.* 70. This conjecture is more attractive from a literary than from a palaeographical point of view. It was adopted by Giarratano and Scazzoso. Variations on Haupt's conjecture (itself probably suggested by an anonymous scholar in Oudendorp, see above under 1) were produced by Crusius (1890) *deo irato* (adopted by Helm 1907, 1913 and Gaselee); vdVliet (1897) *Marte deo irato*; and Robertson (1945) *Ioue irato* (presented with the palaeographical explanation: *pro iŭei uid. libr.* mei *legisse*). Bursian (1881) proposes *meo fato*, approved by Giarratano-Frassinetti; Thomas 1928, 214; Carlesi-Terzaghi; Pagliano. It is very attractive palaeographically, and the sense – "to my misfortune" – fits the context. The conjectures of Haupt (including its variants) and Bursian have in common that the expression gives an explicit reason for the failure of the undertaking; but their proposals do not suggest a reason for the corruption as Helm's proposal (1931) does: *eo fato* (with aposiopesis after *adgressus*). He supports the expression *eo fato... ut* with references to Cic. *Font.* 45, *Mil.* 30 and *Phil.* 10, 14 but gives no parallels for the aposiopesis which does not occur elsewhere in the *Met.*, except perhaps at 8, 8 (183, 13) where Haemus/Tlepolemus is addressing Charite in a dream (a very natural instance, if it is one). For the frequency of the figure in various authors see LHSz 2, 823 f. and the literature collected there; they emphasize the fact that aposiopesis is often verbally signalled.

Another old conjecture (Modius *in mg.* Colv.), *inconsiderato*, presents an implicit rather than an explicit reason for the failure. However, it sounds too self-critical a note for the robbers to swallow. Perhaps *maturato* (see Schol. Veron. Verg. *A.* 7, 266; Heges. 1, 44, 3; also Pl. *Ps.* 1157, where editors read *maturate*, but A has a doubtful *maturate*) gives the right shade of meaning. Apuleius has emphasized the robbers' hurry on previous occasions (e.g. 147, 10); a hurried attack on a rich traveller passing through would recommend itself to Haemus' audience. For the numerous words Apuleius shares with Plautus only (or very few others) see Desertine 1898, *passim*.

Médan 1925, 247 notes that expressions of the type *iter carpere* have served as a model for the combination *carpo ordinem*; cf. *OLD s.v. carpo* 8. The expression is found again in Hier. *Ep.* 108, 3: *Carpamus igitur narrandi ordinem*, see *ThLL s.v.* 494, 15 f.

Fuit quidam multis officiis in aula Caesaris clarus atque conspicuus, 158, 19-21
ipsi etiam probe spectatus: "There was a man, through many offices famous and prominent at Caesar's court and highly esteemed also by the emperor himself".

Fuit quidam: Haemus begins his tale (after the false start) as a separate story; cf. 4, 28 (96, 16) *Erant in quadam ciuitate*; 8, 1 (177, 5) *Erat in proxima ciuitate*; 8, 26 (198, 1); 10, 19 (251, 20). Cf. Hist. Apol. 1, 1 *Fuit quidam rex Antiochus nomine* (RB), *in ciuitate Antiochia rex fuit quidam* (RA); see Weyman 1893, 330; Bernhard 1927, 12 f. *Fuit* and *erat* are both equivalents of ἦν, cf. Xen. Eph. 1, 1 ἦν ἐν Ἐφέσῳ ἀνήρ... For the interchange of perfect and imperfect see LHSz 2, 317. For the position of *fuit* see K St 2, 601 Anmerk. 4 (*esse* is commonly placed in front when new narrative elements or episodes are introduced). The narrative situation has been discussed in the introduction, above p. 3.

multis officiis... clarus atque conspicuus: conspicuous alliteration. For *officia* compare Pl. 2, 230 *ad hoc bonus quisque natura et industria in honoribus et officiis praeferatur*. Whether in our passage "posts" are meant or rather "services" is not made explicit. Suetonius sheds an interesting light on posts held by *procuratores*, *Vesp.* 16, 2: *Creditur etiam procuratorum rapacissimum quemque ad ampliora officia ex industria solitus promouere, quo locupletiores mox condemnaret*. Hildebrand discusses an old controversy whether *officia* here means the officer rather than the office. There is no doubt that office is meant. Function and performer are not clearly distinguished in Suet. *Vesp.* 21: *perlectis epistulis officiorumque omnium breuiariis*, a late development (also e.g. Ulp. *dig.* 1, 18, 6, 5; see *ThLL s.v.* 522, 70 f.) that parallels the much older double meaning of *magistratus* (see e.g. Kübler in *RE* 14, 400 f.).

in aula Caesaris: *aula* (in the *Met.* here only) was borrowed from Greek in the republican era. In the sense of a ruler's palace it is first used in Verg. *G.* 2, 504; (see also *A.* 4, 328; Sen. *Ep.* 29, 5).

clarus atque conspicuus: no official titles are implied by these words (see Summers 1967, 249 who quotes *uir egregius* and similar titles; also Millar 1977, 289). *uir clarissimus* is the title for a senator, see *ThLL s.v.* 1275, 8 f. and Gagé 1964, 85. A similar combination occurs at 11, 16 (278, 6 f.): *totae ciuitati notus ac conspicuus*.

ipsi etiam probe spectatus: cf. 3, 6 (56, 19) *probe spectatus apud meos* and vdPaardt 1971, 62 *ad loc.*, who gives the relevant literature for colloquial *probe*. *Spectatus* finds a comment in Non. 437 M. (703, 13 Lindsay), who illustrates his contention that *spectatus* has greater weight than *probatus* by quoting Lucil. 617: *tuam probatam mi et spectatam maxume adulescentiam. Ipsi* is *dat. auctoris* or *iudicantis*, see LHSz 2, 96 f., who note that this dat. is less frequent in the *Met.* than in the *Fl.*

158, 21-22 Hunc insimulatum quorundam astu proiecit extorrem saeuiens Inuidia: "He was traduced by certain men's guile, and savage Envy sent him into Exile".

Heine 1962, 148 n. 3 notes that we have here one of the many instances in the *Met.* of wanderers who are, or have become, homeless. Certainly the story told by Haemus helps to create an impression of a hostile and unpleasant world in which contrasts between high and low, past and present play an important part, see also Heine in *AAGA* 1978, 36.

astu: the final *u* has been tampered with in F. See 4, 12 (83, 21-22) *deceptus astus*.

proiecit extorrem: for *proicere* in the sense of "throw out", "banish" see 9, 36 (230, 9) ...*sublatum de casula longissime statimque proiectum iri*. Though it occurs but twice in the *Met.*, it is not an uncommon meaning of *proicere*; cf. e.g. Sen. *Prou.* 3, 2 *pro ipsis est, inquis, in exilium proici*; Ov. *Tr.* 5, 1, 13; Tac. *Ann.* 4, 71. The word is usually construed with an indication of place: cf. Cic. *Cat.* 2, 1, 2 *quod tantam pestem euomuerit forasque proiecerit*; however Ov. *Pont.* 2, 3, 30 uses it absolutely: *uix duo proiecto tresue tulistis opem*; Amm. 22, 7, 5 in the specialized sense of "discharge": *duo agentes in rebus ex his qui proiecti sunt*.

extorrem: the word occurs once more in Apul.: 5, 9 (110, 1) *extorres et lare et ipsa patria*; cf. Cod. Theod. 16, 5, 31 *e ciuitatibus pellantur extorres*.

saeuiens has the effect of practically personifying *inuidia*, see *GCA* 1977, 110. Summers notes that 'here too Apuleius seems to be disparaging the regime at Rome in a very subtle manner'. Very subtle?

It would be possible to take *inuidia* as an abl. and *saeuiens* with the subject (Caesar) of *proiecit*, but for *inuidia* on the part of Caesar we have not been prepared; for *inuidia* on the part of *quidam*, however, we have: the *procurator* was, after all, *Caesari probe spectatus*. Seneca mentions a similar situation: *Ep.* 74, 4 *occurrent naufragi similiaue naufragiis passi, quos aut popularis ira aut inuidia, perniciosum optimis telum, inopinantis securosque disiecit*...

Sed uxor eius Plotina quaedam rarae fidei atque singularis pudicitiae 158, 22-25
femina, quae decimo partus stipendio uiri familiam fundauerat,
....: "But his wife Plotina, a woman of rare fidelity and singular chastity, who
had given her husband's family a firm foundation by a ten-fold contribution of
births, ...".

It is hard to decide whether a comma should be placed after *eius*, after Plotina,
or after both *eius* and *quaedam*. Most edd. follow Colvius in placing a comma
after *Plotina*. Robertson prints *Plotina quaedam, rarae ... femina*. Oudendorp
appears to agree in his comm. but prints a comma before *quaedam*. Hildebrand
quotes as an example of a name + *quidam Met.* 2, 13 (35, 21) *Cerdo quidam
nomine*, but prints *Plotina, quaedam*. For *eius, Plotina quaedam rarae fidei...
famina*, 4, 9 (81, 16 f.) *Chryseros quidam nummularius* may be cited as a parallel,
but a reasonably independent phrase like *quidam intro currens famulus* also
occurs in the *Met.* (3, 12: 60, 23 f.). The clausula rhythms provide little help.

We shall probably never know whether Apuleius adopted the name Plotina for
this chaste and true wife of a Procurator in order to recall Trajan's equally chaste
and true Pompeia Plotina. She married Trajan when young and stayed with him
till his death; apparently she exercised great personal influence. For her praise see
Plin. *Paneg.* 83–84; Dio Cassius 68, 5, 5. See also Balsdon 1962, 133 f. There are
two contrasting features: Pompeia Plotina was childless and, if we are to believe
Ps. Aur. Victor *epit. de Caes.* 42, 21, intensely disliked the dishonesty of the
imperial *procuratores*.

quae ... fundauerat: for a similar eulogy see Sen. *Marc.* 16, 3 where the mother
of the Gracchi is mentioned: *duodecim illa partus totidem funeribus recognouit*.
Cf. Plut. *TiGr.* 1, 3 ff., Plin. *Nat.* 7, 57–60; Martial 10, 63 is an epitaph for a
woman with five sons and five daughters. See for large families in general
Balsdon 1962, 193. Childlessness was felt to be a threat to the social system in the
early empire. On Augustus' legislation (*lex Julia de maritandis ordinibus* of 18
B.C. and *lex Papia Poppaea* of 9 A.D.) and its effects see Gardthausen 1891 1,
902 f.; Balsdon 1962, 202. Among the women of the imperial court Agrippina
with nine children by Germanicus held the record until Faustina, Marcus
Aurelius' wife, gave birth to at least thirteen (see *RE* 1, 2287).

decimo stipendio: the expression may well be a metaphor from military service
with *stipendium* (in view of the yearly event) in the precise sense of "year of
service"; e.g. Hirt. *Gal.* 8, 8, 2 *octauo iam stipendio*; cf. 1, 1 (1, 10) *primis pueritiae
stipendiis*, where we think years of in-service training are meant rather than
campaigns. Elsewhere in the *Met. stipendium* is used more generally in the sense
of "service", "act of service": 9, 20 (217, 22) *commodum prima stipendia Veneri
militabant nudi milites*; 11, 30 (291, 6).

uiri: in the sense "husband" *uir* gradually gives way to *maritus*, see Callebat
1968, 146.

fundauerat: said of a woman, unlike the other instances of this meaning: Stat.
Silv. 4, 7, 30; Plin. *Ep.* 4, 21, 3; [Sen.] *Oct.* 532.

... spretis atque contemptis urbicae luxuriae deliciis fugientis co- 158, 25-28
mes et infortunii socia, tonso capillo, in masculinam faciem reforma-

to habitu, pretiosissimis monilium et auro monetali zonis refertis incincta...: "... spurned and scorned the delights of Roman luxury and became the companion of his exile and sharer of his misfortune. With cropped hair, her clothing changed to a male appearance, girt with a belt stuffed with the most precious of her necklaces as well as one with gold coins.."

... *spretis atque contemptis urbicae luxuriae deliciis*: Hildebrand discusses the question whether *spretis atque contemptis* are placed in a particular order; he concludes (with the aid of many parallels) that this is not the case. Bernhard 1927, 168 says 'zwei speziellere Begriffe dienen zur Bezeichnung eines allgemeinen'. Médan 1925, 363 regards the expression as a juxtaposition of synonyms. There seems to be no reason to disagree. Cf. Ter. *And.* 248 *quot modis contemptus spretus*.

urbicae luxuriae refers to the amenities that Rome offers its inhabitants just as at 11, 28 (289, 13) *erogationes urbicae* refer to the cost of living in that city; *urbicus* occurs for the first time in Martial (1, 41, 11; 1, 53, 5; 12 *praef.*), several times in Suet. (*Jul.* 49, 2; *Aug.* 18, 2; 46; *Nero* 23, 1; *Dom.* 8, 2) and once in Gel. 15, 1, 3, always with reference to the city of Rome and usually in contrast to either the countryside or the provinces.

fugientis comes et infortunii socia: for *fugientis* in the sense of "being exiled" see e.g. Hor. *S.* 1, 6, 13 *Tarquinius regno pulsus fugit*; Paul. Fest. 279 M (= 347 L.); Val. Max. 4, 6 ext. 2 quoted below under *tonso capillo*; *ThLL s.v.* 1477, 20 f. Cf. φεύγω. For the difficult question of the terminology of exile (our *procurator* is sent to a specific island, but possibly only temporarily (159, 6) unless the term *temporariam sedem* refers to the outcome of the adventure rather than to the sentence) see Mommsen 1899, 974 f.; 1010 f. The two main possibilities are *relegatio*, which does not, and *deportatio*, which does involve *deminutio capitis*. Mommsen argues that the term *deportatio* was introduced in the early principate; P. Garnsey 1970, 111 f. thinks it was later. Here the relevant punishment may be *relegatio in insulam*, which did not carry confiscation of all property with it. Since *infortunii socia* adds pathos (she is not just a companion of her exiled husband, but in addition an associate of his *infortunium*), Strilciw 1925, 116 is mistaken in citing it as an instance of *perissologia* (for the definition see Lausberg 1960, 268, par. 502).

Quite a few of Plotina's historical sisters acted as she did: Tac. *Ann.* 15, 71, 3 *Priscum Artoria Flaccilla coniunx comitata est, Gallum Egnatia Maximilla* (see Koestermann *ad loc.*); Tac. *Hist.* 1, 3, 1 *comitatae profugos liberos matres, secutae maritos in exilia coniuges* (see Heubner *ad loc.*); Sen. *Helv.* 16, 7 *Rutilia Cottam filium secuta est in exilium*; Plin. *Ep.* 7, 19, 4 on Fannia: *Bis maritum secuta in exilium est, tertio ipsa propter maritum relegata*; see also Balsdon 1962, 58; more in general Friedländer [10] 1921, 1, 517. Sen. *Ep.* 9, 10 cites following one's friend into exile as one of the duties of *amicitia*.

infortunii: Oudendorp reads and Hildebrand reports a reading *infortuniis (ς)*. Since both gen. and dat. are possible with *socius*, there is no reason to deviate from F. On *infortunium* see *GCA* 1977, 201.

tonso... reformato... refertis incincta... sustinens: Apuleius' use of 'Partizipialkonglomerat' is discussed by Bernhard 1927, 41 f. See also *GCA* 1977, 82. Here so much information concerning Plotina is packed closely together that as a result we hesitate whether the husband or the wife is subject of *petebat* (159, 6) and *appulisset* (159, 8). Therefore our translation is deliberately vague.

tonso capillo: Plotina's hair is clipped or cropped in order to give her a masculine appearance, cf. Mart. 9, 36, 11 *at tibi si dederit uultus coma tonsa uirilis*. She had a predecessor in Hypsicratea, wife of Mithridates, if we are to believe Val. Max. 4, 6 ext. 2. Hypsicratea loved her husband very much: *tonsis ... capillis equo se et armis adsuefecit, quo facilius laboribus et periculis eius interesset. Quin etiam uictum a Cn. Pompeio per efferatas gentes fugientem animo pariter et corpore infatigabili secuta est*. Cf. Plut. *Pomp*. 32, 8; Eutr. 6, 12, 3.

in masculinam faciem reformato habitu: *in* (in consecutive sense) is discussed at length by Callebat 1968, 227 f.; its particular use with the notion of transformation *ibid*. 229. For *reformare* and *reformatio* in the sense of "transform" rather than "restore" see *ibid*. 153; *GCA* 1977, 171.

pretiosissimis monilium et auro monetali zonis refertis incincta: see Casson, 1974, 177 who cites a Mich. papyrus (*P. Mich*. 214) in which a soldier advises his wife to travel with her gold ornaments out of sight. The use of *monetalis* with *aurum* is rare, cf. Ambr. *parad*. 3, 15 *hoc ergo bonum aurum dicere licet, non monetale, quod corruptibile ac terrenum est*; it is more common, in particular on inscriptions, in the phrase *triumuir monetalis*. For the origin of *moneta, monetalis* cf. *Suda s.v.* Μονήτα; Regling in *RE s.v.* Münzwesen 479, 32 (originally the mint was situated in Rome near the temple of Juno Moneta), for the *tresuiri* in imperial times see *ibid*. 484, 18 ff.

zonis: the word here refers to the belt in which travellers stored their money (as distinct from *crumena*, βαλλάντιον). The plural probably indicates that Plotina travelled with two belts, one for her *monilia*, one for her coins. *Zona* is a Greek loan word, in common use since Plautus. See e.g. Pl. *Mer*. 925 and Enk *ad loc.*; *Truc*. 954 and Enk *ad loc.*; C. Gracchus *ap*. Gel. 15, 12: *"Itaque" inquit "Quirites, cum Romam profectus sum zonas, quas plenas argenti extuli, eas ex prouincia inanes retuli*. Emperor Vitellius, trying to avoid his enemies, *zona se aureorum plena circumdedit* (Suet. *Vit*. 16). See also Bernard 1927, 144; Callebat 1968, 68.

The fact that she is carrying money is one of several resemblances between Plotina and Haemus: both are wearing a disguise (Haemus' second disguise is, like Plotina's, transsexual: 159, 26 f.), and both are engaged in helping their partners.

incincta: Médan 1925, 191 regards the word as poetic. He may well be right. *ThLL s.v. incingo* cites 15 instances in poets before Apuleius (e.g. Enn. *scen*. 30; *Catul*. 64, 258 and 308) against 4 in prose. Liv. 8, 9, 9 *incinctus cinctu Gabino* has a solemn sound, referring as it does to a particular religious way of draping the toga. Cf. Quint. *Inst*. 11, 3, 146 (in a description of how the orator plays with his toga): *laeuam inuoluere toga et incingi paene furiosum est*. Val. Max. 3, 1, 1 refers to the statue of Aemilius Lepidus as *bullata et incincta praetexta*. See also Petr. *Sat*. 135, 4. In the *Met*. the word occurs also at 8, 13 (187, 7) and 11, 8 (272, 5 f.).

.... inter ipsas custodientium militum manus et gladios nudos 158, 28-159, 4
intrepida cunctorum periculorum particeps et pro mariti salute
peruigilem curam sustine⟨n⟩s aerumnas adsiduas ingenio masculo

sustinebat: "... intrepid in the midst of troops of military guards and naked swords, sharing all dangers and keeping up a careful vigilance for her husband's safety, she sustained continual hardships with a masculine spirit".

inter ipsas custodientium militum manus et gladios nudos intrepida: a similar military escort, but in the opposite direction, is given to St. Paul: *Acts* 27, 1 f. Though the naked sword occurs in the form *ense...nudo* in Verg. *A.* 12, 306 and *nudo...ferro* in Ov. *Ep.* 13, 81, Apuleius seems to be the first to use the combination *gladius nudus*: 1, 12 (11, 9), 8, 13 (187, 6), 10, 31 (262, 16). *Intrepida*: some slight ironies may be suspected. Plotina is intrepid in the face of what ought not to be a danger (*custodientium militum*), but the presence of this force does not preclude the robbers' attack.

et pro mariti salute peruigilem curam sustine⟨n⟩s
aerumnas adsiduas ingenio masculo sustinebat

The two clauses which conclude the praise of Plotina show an almost equal number of syllables, end with the same verb (polyptotic epiphora), and exhibit a careful chiastic arrangement:

pro mariti salute ⟶ × *ingenio masculo*
peruigilem curam ⟶ × *aerumnas adsiduas*

Helm's earlier conjecture *suscipiens* (cf. *Apol.* 15 (17, 28) *curam...suscipiendam*) is unnecessary: the collection of parallels in Wiman 1927, 50 includes such instances of repetition as 1, 9 (9, 6 ff.) *iam in sarcina praegnationis obsepto utero et repigrato fetu perpetua praegnatione damnauit*, and 5, 10 (110, 18 ff.) *ego uero maritum articulari etiam morbo complicatum... sustineo plerumque... digitos eius perfricans... nec uxoris... faciem, sed medicae... personam sustinens*; cf. von Albrecht 1971, 18.

peruigilem curam: cf. (e.g.) *peruigil...labor* V. Fl. 5, 141; *peruigili...cura* Stat. *Silv.* 3, 5, 2; cf. Luc. 4, 6-7. An even bolder usage is found *Met.* 9, 11 (210, 21) *lucubrabant peruigilem farinam*. See Bernhard 1927, 109 for Apuleius' use of *per-*.

ingenio masculo: see 6, 27 (149, 19) *constantia uirili* (of Charite) and *ibidem* 149, 6-7 *capta super sexum et aetatem audacia* and comm. *ad loc*. See also Heine 1962, 237 n. 1 on the context in which Apuleius speaks of male courage in a female person (Heine deals with the situation of Psyche in 5, 22). On Plotina see e.g. Schlam in *AAGA* 1978, 100.

159, 4-7 Iamque plurimis itineris difficultatibus marisque terroribus exanclatis Zac[h]ynthum petebat, quam sors ei fatalis decreuerat temporariam sedem: "And now, after very many difficulties on the journey and terrors of the sea had been endured, they were making for Zacynthus, an island which the decree of fate had assigned him as a temporary abode".

On the function of *iamque* in dramatic narrative see Chausserie-Laprée 1969, 497 f.

terroribus: *-bus* in *ras*. F. Robertson notes 'quid fuerit non liquet' but Helm thinks the ms. may originally have shown *terrorisque*; *terrorique* φ. The correction appears to be right.

exanclatis: the basic meaning of the verb is "to drain", "to draw off a liquid" but in the sense "endure" it occurs from Ennius *Scen.* 102 onwards. Cf. 1, 16 (14,

19) *qui mecum tot curas exanclasti* and Marg. Molt *ad loc*; 11, 2 (267, 20) *saeuis exanclatis casibus* and Gwyn Griffiths *ad loc*. *OLD* mistakenly creates the impression that before Apuleius the word in this sense is used only in poetry, see Cic. *Ac*. 2, 108 and *Tusc*. 1, 118, though a certain poetic flavour cannot be denied those passages. On the spelling see Walde-Hofmann *s.v. anclo* (' -t- durch Neuanknüpfung an ἀντλῶ'); *ThLL s.v. exanclo* 1171, 22 notes the spelling *-tl-* in Serg. *Gramm*. 4, 477, 11. F gives *-tl-* here and at 131, 14; elsewhere *-cl-* (four times), or a doubtful reading (twice). Quint. *Inst*. 1, 6, 40 condemns the word as altogether too archaic.

Zacynthus is now called Zante. For the literary contexts in which the island figures see Williams on Verg. *A*. 3, 270. According to Plin. *Nat*. 4, 54, it was quite fertile. A full description in Philippson-Kirsten, *Die griechischen Landschaften*, 1950-1959, 2, 528-540. The reference to the *litus Actiacum* (159, 7) makes it likely that what is implied is a journey overland from Rome to Brundisium, followed by a ship from there to the final destination. It is not clear whether the stopover on land indicates a very light ship of the kind used to convey officials or whether we should assume that the party boarded a ship making the regular Brundisium-Corinth run. For both possibilities see Casson 1974, 150 f.

quam sors ei fatalis decreuerat temporariam sedem: on *sors fatalis* see Heine 138 n. 1 (*fortuna, sors, fatum* often synonymous), also Gwyn Griffiths on 11, 15. Here the *sors fatalis* is coextensive with *Inuidia*, above 158, 20. By using these two expressions the narrator manages to avoid involving the emperor. Callebat 1968, 165 thinks the word *temporaria* is borrowed from the 'parler commun'. The material at the Thesaurus Institute (Munich), however, includes, apart from the instances mentioned by Callebat, such passages as Curt. 4, 5, 11 ("adaptable to circumstances"), Plin. *Nat*. 11, 223; 18, 249 ("temporary"), Plin. *Ep*. 6, 13, 5 ("improvised"), *Paneg*. 91, 7 ("temporary"). The case for its being 'parler commun', therefore, is doubtful. Even more dubious is the question whether the *sedes* is *temporaria* because the narrator knows that Plotina's appeal to the emperor will be successful or because we have to do with a *relegatio ad tempus* (thus Rode-Burck 237).

CHAPTER VII

The story of Plotina continued; the emperor is begged to intervene, the robbers' band is destroyed, but Haemus escapes.

159, 7-11 Sed cum primum litus Actiacum quo tunc Macedonia delapsi grassabamus appulisset, nocte promota — tabernulam quandam litori nauique proximam uitatis maris fluctibus incubabant — inuadimus et diripimus omnia: "But as soon as they had landed on the coast of Actium where we were on the prowl just then, having slipped down from Macedonia, we made our attack at dead of night — to escape the motion of the sea they slept in an inn close to shore and ship — and pillaged everything".

The syntax of the period is not entirely satisfactory in F, which, apart from the punctuation, reads as above. A number of scholars have thought an emendation was needed. Others have felt that judicious punctuation would solve the problem. Oudendorp and Hildebrand take *nocte promota* with *incubabant* after which they print a full stop. Luetjohann 1873, 482 argues that the asyndeton is offensive ('anstössig') and that *nocte promota* is more naturally taken with the attack of the robbers. He proposes to insert a relative: *tabernulam quandam, ⟨quam⟩ ... incubabant, inuadimus*. He is followed by vdVliet with the difference that the latter inserts ⟨quam⟩ after *proximam*. Giarratano inserts *ubi* at the same place, Armini 1928, 304 prefers ⟨cui⟩ if any insertion is necessary, whereas Helm prints *incubabant, ⟨cum⟩ inuadimus*. Leky 1908, 42 prefers to treat *uitatis ... incubabant* as a parenthesis, Robertson *nocte ... incubabant*. We follow a suggestion by E. R. Smits to take *nocte promota* with *inuadimus* (the same indication of time occurs at 4, 22: 92, 3 and 9, 20: 217, 20 in comparable circumstances) and *tabernulam ... incubabant* as the parenthesis. There is no need for a dative with *incubabant*, see 4, 17 (87, 14-16) *an ignoras hoc genus bestiae lucos consitos ... semper incubare* and *GCA* 1977, 132 f. *ad loc*. On parenthesis in Apuleius see Bernhard 1927, 92 f., who insists that he has collected all 18 instances. Most of them are introduced by *autem, enim* or *nam*, but this is not always the case, see 3, 7 (57, 10) and vdPaardt 1971, 67 *ad loc*. See also below (lines 17-18) *uera enim dicenda sunt*.

cum primum with pluperfect subjunctive is not attested before the second century. See Callebat 1968, 343, who quotes 8, 2 (177, 10 f.) *cum primum Charite nubendo maturuisset*; also LHSz 2, 620; 626. (With plupf. ind.: 11, 14: 276, 25).

Macedonia delapsi: ThLL s.v. *delabor* mistakenly reads *Macedoniam* and notes that the robbers are sailing. For the ablative of separation with *delapsi* cf. 5, 20 (118, 20) *toro delapsa*; Verg. *A*. 7, 620 *caelo delapsa*; 10, 596 *curru delapsus*; Ov. *Met*. 1, 212.

F has *grassabamus*. Most scholars (not Giarratano) are in favour of *grassabamur* (ς) and they may be right since (1) this is the only occurrence of the active form in Apuleius against 2, 17 (39, 3) *grassare* (imperative); 8, 17 (190, 19) *grassati* and *P.* 2, 17 (244) *grassari*. It does not find much support elsewhere: Optat. 2, 21 (57, 21) has *crassant* in cod. R and *CGL* cites *grassare* 4 times (4, 242, 5; 521, 28; 587, 23; 5, 299, 17); as a true passive it occurs Hil. *Hymn. Christ.* 34 (*CSEL* 65, 220); and (2) it is but a slight copying error; furthermore (3) Flobert 1975, 304, specialised as he is in problems concerning deponent verbs, suspects *grassabamur*. In favour of the active form it may be argued that (1) there was a general tendency towards the disappearance of deponent verbs, a tendency checked by conscious archaisms on the part of authors such as Apuleius; the resulting situation was one of confusion (Callebat 1968, 294 ff.; Flobert 1975, *passim*); (2) the authority of ς is very slight, since the correction is as easily made as the error; (3) the situation at 4, 11 (82, 17) *comminiscimus* is very similar. In fact Flobert 1975, 308 cites twelve instances in which Apuleius is the first to use a verb as an active which is elsewhere deponent[1], and another thirteen in which he revitalizes such an active. Flobert's suspicion concerning some of the readings may be partly explained by his concern to present conservative statistics and to exclude all dubious instances. We feel a slight preference for the reading of F.

tabernulam ... incubabant: spending the nights on shore was not uncommon when making a sea voyage in ancient times. See Casson 1974, 151 and his discussion of Cicero's voyage to Ephesus in 51 B.C. (*Att.* 5, 11 and 12); *ibid.* 197 f. on inns in general.

inuadimus et diripimus: the robbers listening to Haemus' tale recognize the method: cf. e.g. 3, 28 (72, 21 f.) *ui patefactis aedibus globus latronum inuadit omnia*.

Nec tamen periculo leui temptati discessimus: "But harassed by no slight 159, 11 danger we made off".

nec ... leui: the litotes is strong. Strilciw 1925, 109 collects numerous further instances with *nec*. See above on 148, 9.

periculo ... temptati: it is hard to find a precise parallel for the combination. Apuleius appears to try out a conflation of *temptare periculum* (e.g. Verg. *A.* 11, 505) and *temptari morbo* (e.g. Hor. *Ep.* 1, 6, 28) or *scelere* (Cic. *Cael.* 55).

Simul nanque primum sonum ianuae matrona percepit, procurrens in 159, 11-17 cubiculum clamoribus inquietis cuncta miscuit milites suosque famulos nominatim, sed et omnem uiciniam suppetiatum conuocans, nisi quod pauore cunctorum, qui sibi quisque metuentes delitiscebant, effectum est, ut impune discederemus: "For as soon as the lady noticed the first sound of the door, she ran into the (main?) bedroom and filled the whole place with her cries of alarm, summoning the soldiers and her servants by name to help her, and the entire neighboorhood as well, except that as a result

---

[1] *aduenero Socr.* 5 (13, 2); *aemulo* 1, 23 (21, 16); *blandio Apol.* 87 (96, 6); *comminisco* 4, 11 (82, 17); *commino* 7, 11 (162, 13) (but see comm. *ad loc.*); *consauio* 6, 22 (145, 6); *grasso* here (*mino* 3, 28: 73, 5 but see vdPaardt 1971, 200 *ad loc.*); *pignero* 3, 22 (68, 27); *pugilo Socr.* 21 (31, 15); *relucto* 4, 20 (89, 16 f.); *supergredio* 10, 2 (237, 9: doubtful: F has *supergesserat*).

of the general panic – they all hid, each frightened for his life – we were enabled to escape scot-free".

Callebat, 1968, 432 f. discusses the weak temporal link between the main clause and the subordinate clause introduced by *simul*. On *simul* see also below 161, 25.

F has *nanque* though apparently something has been erased above the second *n*. The spelling *nanque* occurs 3 times in the *Met.*, against *namque* 19 times. The older lexica give *nanque* as an alternative spelling without mentioning instances. Sidney Allen 1965, 30 notes that in such positions 'we may assume ... assimjlati-on to the following velar.' See also Sommer 1914, 237. On the position of *namque* see Draeger 2, 158 (30 times in first, 19 in second or later position in Apuleius); Neue-Wagener 2, 976 f.; Médan 1925, 227; Bernhard 1927, 28.

matrona percepit: the word *matrona* here cannot be used as an argument that in the case of *petebat* (159, 6) and *appulisset* (159, 8) the *procurator* was subject: see e.g. 5, 22 (120, 7), where a new sentence starts with *At uero Psyche* although she was the subject of the main clause of the previous sentence as well.

in cubiculum: perhaps a common dormitory for soldiers and servants, but (as often) Apuleius leaves some details to the imagination of his readers. A more interesting instance is found in 4, 18 (88, 7 f.), where the reader is allowed to imagine for himself how Thrasyleon comes by a sword. See *GCA* 1977, 138 *ad loc.*

clamoribus inquietis cuncta miscuit: the picture is one of space filled with noise, as at 8, 4 (179, 5) *latratibus feruidis dissonisque miscent omnia*. It is not uncommon: cf. Sall. *Jug.* 12, 5 *strepitu et tumultu omnia miscere* and Koestermann *ad loc.*, who notes that this use of *miscere* is poetic. See also *ThLL s.v.* 1094, 32 f. The alliteration (i.a. *cu-* 5 times) is remarkable.

nominatim: see Callebat 1968, 477 for Apuleius' penchant for adverbs in *-tim*; also *GCA* 1977, 26. If the word refers to both soldiers and slaves (as we think it does) it conveys a neat characterization of Plotina. Apuleius likes to add such small characterizations of a relationship. Cf. e.g. Chryseros who calls his neighbours by name (4, 10: 82, 12); both characters are shown as efficient people.

sed et omnem uiciniam suppetiatum conuocans: Chryseros does the same in the passage just quoted above. *Sed et* has its proper adversative force (Plotina could not call the neighbours *nominatim*; Callebat 1968, 326 should not have included the present passage among those in which *sed et* is employed as a non-adversative transitional phrase).

omnem: apparently the scribe of F corrected his own mistake (*omnia › omnem*).

uiciniam: Callebat 1968, 58 f. lists the word among a group of abstracts that have gained a concrete sense in Apuleius. See also LHSz 2, 747 f.; vdPaardt 1971, 37; *GCA* 1977, 80.

suppetiatum: see *GCA* 1977, 85. The verb *suppetiari* occurs five times in Apuleius, four times in the form of a supine and once (8, 20: 192, 25) in the infinitive. The material collected at the *ThLL* institute at Munich shows that the verb remains fairly rare. It occurs four times in the *Itin. Alex.* (25, 26, 34, 52), twice in *Jul. Val.* (1, 43 and 2, 27). See also Scobie 1975, 111.

conuocans: see Bernhard 1927, 44 on 'Nachstellung der Partizipia'.

nisi quod: ellipsis of some such thought as "and she would have caused the immediate destruction of our band". No similar ellipsis occurs with *nisi quod* in the *Met.*: 3, 24 (70, 17); 5, 21 (119, 9); 9, 13 (212, 24); 10, 2 (237, 25); 10, 30 (261, 11); 10, 31 (261, 28). See also LHSz 2, 587 for the history of the combination.

pauore ... delitiscebant: at 4, 9 (81, 8) much the same thought is used in order to show that large houses are particularly vulnerable to robbers. One also remembers how Lucius' *seruulus*, when the robbers attacked, *profugit territus* (3, 27: 72, 20 f.).

Sed protinus sanctissima – uera enim dicenda sunt – et unicae fidei femina, bonis artibus gratiosa, precibus ad Caesaris numen porrectis et marito reditum celerem et adgressurae plenam uindictam impetrauit: "But the woman, most virtuous – for the truth must be told – and of a singular faithfulness, was influential through her fine behaviour; she immediately addressed a petition to Caesar's divinity and obtained for her husband a speedy return and for the attack a complete revenge". 159, 17-21

protinus: it is not entirely clear whether *protinus* is to be taken with *porrectis* or *impetrauit*; in both cases *protinus* is far removed from the verb it qualifies, but this is not uncommon in the *Met.*, cf. e.g. 3, 18 (65, 14 f.); 4, 16 (86, 27 f.); 6, 16 (140, 17 f.).

uera enim dicenda sunt: the parenthesis is placed in much the same position as at 5, 10 (110, 25 f.) *quam patienti uel potius seruili – dicam enim libere quod sentio – haec perferas animo* and is clearly intended to excuse the preceding word. Tatum 1969[b], 507 deals with these words as follows: 'H. justifies this praise of her virtue, which seems out of place amidst robbers, by saying piously that he must tell the story because 'the truth has to be told'.' In his view the phrase echoes 4, 12 (83, 22) *uera quae dicta sunt credens*. There the robber Alcimus is caught by words in much the same way as Haemus hopes to catch his audience. (Tatum speaks of echolalic responsions; see also *ibid.* 501.) Tatum also suggests that Haemus/Tlepolemus is having a private joke with Charite, but Charite does not appear to become aware of his presence until later. On the other hand he may well be right in stating that Plotina's virtuous role foreshadows Charite's own in book 8. Concerning the insistence on truth in fiction see also Introduction p. 5. On parenthesis in the *Met.* see Strilciw 1925, 120 f.; and above on lines 7-11.

unicae fidei: *unicus* in the transferred sense "unparalleled, excellent" is rare in the *Met.*: see 3, 11 (60, 18) *splendidissima et unica Thessaliae ciuitas* and 10, 5 (240, 10) *malitiae nouercalis exemplar unicum*. In the other 24 instances it always refers to something that occurs once only, as e.g. at 11, 5 (269, 17 f.) *cuius numen unicum ... totus ueneratur orbis* (see Gwyn Griffiths 1975, 145 *ad loc.*).

bonis artibus gratiosa: the translators offer two possibilities for *artibus* ("conduct" – e.g. Vallette, Grimal – and "qualities, merits" – e.g. Butler, Helm) and for *gratiosa* ("beloved" – e.g. Helm, Pagliano – "influential" – e.g. Butler, Vallette). We have chosen "conduct" and "influential" since they seemed to fit the subsequent success of her prayers slightly better, but there is little to choose between the possibilities. See Moussy 1966, 397.

precibus ... porrectis: cf. Liv. 24, 30, 14 *ramos oleae ac uelamenta alia supplicum porrigentes orare* (see also *ibid.* 29, 16, 6; 30, 36, 5); *Met.* 3, 7 (57, 3 f.) *porrectisque in preces manibus*. The present expression doubtlessly originates in the praying gesture *manus porrigere*. Similarly Alcimus Avitus p. 125, 32 Peiper *angeli uota nostra in coelum porrigunt*; Cassiod. *Var.* 11, 13, 6 *preces nostras credidimus porrigendas*. At the same time it must be noted that *preces* is a technical term used for petitions received by an emperor (by means of *libelli*) see Millar 1977, 473, who quotes Plin. *Ep.* 10, 106; 107.

ad Caesaris numen: Millar *ibid.* 468 deals with the numinous aspect that imperial responses often had in the minds of the people receiving or hoping to receive them. He quotes Ov. *Pont.* 3, 1, 131-138 as the earliest instance of a specific analogy drawn between the divine oracles and the imperial divinity.

et marito reditum celerem: intercession with the emperor on behalf of others was common: during the 1st cent. A.D. the appeal was made orally, later also in writing. Whether *preces* here implies Plotina's return to Rome as Millar *ibid.* 540 appears to think is not clear, but the interpretation may find some support in *bonis artibus gratiosa* (then to be rendered "influential through her excellent address").

et adgressurae plenam uindictam impetrauit: the word *adgressura* is not common; it occurs in a similar context of brigandage e.g. in Ulp. *dig.* 10, 2, 4, 2 (cf. 29, 5, 3, 4), and in Zeno of Verona when he is dealing with the good Samaritan (*Tract.* I 37, 3, 10 ed. Löfstedt: ... *qui a latronibus adgressuram passus fuerat*). See also Weyman 1893, 357.

plenam uindictam is paralleled at 4, 31 (99, 5), where Venus says to her son: *uindictam tuae parenti, sed plenam tribue*. Summers 1967, 250 thinks that the regime at Rome, here too, cf. on 158, 22 above, is subtly disparaged, since the emperor reacts to an appeal on the part of one exiled through political intrigue. However, it must be noted that faith in Caesar's power, even on the part of robbers, is presented as unlimited.

159, 21-22 Denique noluit esse Caesar Haemi latronis col‹l›egium, et confestim interiuit: tantum potest nutus etiam magni principis: "In short, Caesar did not wish the existence of Robber Haemus' fraternity and forthwith it ceased to exist: so much power has even the nod of a great prince."

Denique: see vdPaardt 1971, 42 f. and the literature mentioned there for the various senses of *denique* in the *Met*. Here "in short" or "indeed, yes" would seem to fit best.

noluit esse: a curious phrase for a specific command on the part of Caesar. For *nolle* as a positive expression of refusal, however, there are parallels, see e.g. Cic. *Clu.* 149.

collegium: F has *coligium*. In fact the spelling of the word varies; there is epigraphical evidence for *conlegium, colligium* and *colegium* as well as a number of other forms. See *ThLL s.v.* 1591, 30 f. The word was also used by a robber at 4, 15 (86, 7); see *GCA* 1977, 119. Here, too, there is an element of humour in the use of an extremely respectable term for a robbers' band.

noluit ... interiuit: Bernhard 1927, 48 discusses the use of parataxis and notes several instances in which the second clause in a parataxis describes the result of the first: e.g. 1, 9 (8, 23-9, 2): *cauponem ... deformauit in ranam et nunc senex ille dolio innatans uini sui aduentores ... officiosis roncis raucus appellat.*

interiuit: F has *interibit*; the slight correction of ς is, of course, right. Callebat 1968, 127 thinks it likely that the choice of *interiuit* rather than *interiit* was dictated by metrical considerations; the form is very rare: see *ThLL s.v.* 2186, 34.

tantum potest nutus etiam magni principis: Callebat 1968, 329 'Cet emploi pléonastique de *etiam* auprès de *tantum* peut être rapproché d'un exemple analogue attesté... chez Tertullien'. See *An*. 56, 2, Waszink 1947, 568. It is equally possible and perhaps better to take *etiam* with *nutus*: cf. Helm-Krenkel "so viel vermag sogar ein Wink nur des groszen Kaisers". MacMullen 1966 App. B deals with the emperor's power to check the problem of brigandage. See also above on 158, 9f.

Tota denique factione militarium uexillationum indagatu confecta 159, 23-26 atque concisa ipse me furatus aegre solus mediis Orci faucibus ad hunc euasi modum: "When finally the entire band had been tracked down and cut up and slaughtered by military detachments, I myself barely managed to steal away alone from between the gaping jaws of Orcus, and I escaped in the following manner:"

factione: on the usually unfavourable connotation of the word see van der Paardt 1971, 75 and *GCA* 1977, 120 on 4, 15 (86, 8), where the word is also used of a robbers' band, and where its use is humorous. Here a similar humour may be intended, but one may also reason that Haemus is using the language in which the operation was reported to Caesar – equally humorous but more subtly so. It must be admitted, however, that *factio* does not always have an unfavourable connotation: in comedy in particular it is often a neutral word for a group.

militarium uexillationum: in the *Onos* the Haemus episode does not occur, but the band of robbers that has kidnapped the girl is caught by the military: 26, 3 ὄρθρος δὲ ἦν ἔτι καὶ ἐξαίφνης ἐφίσταται πλῆθος στρατιωτῶν ἐπὶ τοὺς μιαροὺς τούτους ἀφιγμένον κτλ. They are bound and taken to τὸν τῆς χώρας ἡγεμόνα. Apuleius gives Haemus/Tlepolemus a major part in catching those robbers but uses the military motif in the inserted tale.

indagatu: hapax, synonymous with the more common *indagatio* which does not occur in the *Met*. See also comm. on 162, 5.

ipse me furatus: cf. e.g. Sil. 14, 561 *exigua sese furatus Himilco carina*. Haemus carefully notes that he is a succesful *fur*.

mediis Orci faucibus: the addition of *e* (Vulcanius) is unnecessary. See Médan 1925, 47 f. on the abl. with *euadere*. The phrase is placed ἀπὸ κοινοῦ with *furatus* and *euasi*. See also 6, 14 (138, 20) *mediis e faucibus lapidis*. For *Orcus* see above on 151, 19 and below on 172, 3.

Bernhard 1927, 213 regards the various mythical expressions for death as euphemisms, including the present one; cf. 4, 20 (89, 16 f.) *faucibus ipsis hiantis Cerberi reluctabat*. In our view the poetic flavour imparts a strong and picturesque enhancement of the horrors of death; cf. e.g. Verg. *G*. 4, 467.

ad hunc ... modum: Callebat 1968, 214 discusses expressions with *ad* denoting conformity and the relative frequency of *ad hunc modum* and *ad istum modum*, the latter being either a conscious archaism or an expression taken from daily language.

CHAPTER VIII

Haemus relates how he escaped from danger. The pieces of gold he has stolen are donated to the robbers

sumpta ueste muliebri florida, in sinus flaccidos [h]abundante, mitel- 159, 26-160, 3
laque textili contecto capite, calceis femininis albis illis et tenuibus
indutus et in sequiorem sexum insertus atque absconditus, asello
spicas ordeacias gerenti residens per medias acies infesti militis
transabiui: "I donned a flowery woman's dress which flowed down in wide
folds, covered my head with a woven turban, slipped into those white, dainty
shoes and thus intruded and concealed myself among the weaker sex; then,
sitting on an ass carrying barley-ears, I made good my escape right through the
lines of the enemy soldiers".

sumpta ... florida: Haemus' disguise reflects that of Plotina (158, 27 f): both are examples of a pseudo-metamorphosis; see Tatum 1972, 309 (and n. 19). Junghanns 1932, 151 points out that Haemus' very 'Verstellungskunst' becomes fatal to the robbers; cf. Tatum 1969b, 507: 'Even Haemus himself used a disguise to escape his enemies, but his story of earlier disguises does not put them on their guard'.

florida can be both literal ("flowered") and figurative ("colourful"); cf. 2, 8 (31, 19) *floridae uestis hilaris color*; see also *GCA* 1977, 107.

in sinus flaccidos abundante: F and φ read *habundante*; the correction is by ς. The construction with *in* is unique and is explained by Callebat 1968, 235 as follows: the meaning of *abundare* is close to that of *undare, in* is used in consecutive sense. For *flaccidus* see Callebat 1968, 164; to the passages mentioned by him one might add *Soc*. pr. 105 (2, 9) *pendula et flaccida*, but it must be said that this prologue is generally regarded as spurious (see Beaujeu 1975, 7).

mitella ... textili: formally *mitella* is a diminutive of *mitra*, semantically – both here and in 8, 27 (198, 13) – its synonym; see Callebat 1968, 32. A man wearing a *mitra* (as in 8, 27) was considered effeminate, which is exactly the impression Haemus wants to create! See *R.E. s.v. mitra* (Schuppe); Heine 1962, 311, n. 1. *Textilis* – here as at 11, 8 (272, 17) – can refer both to the fabric ("woven") and to the construction of the turban ("wound").

calceis femineis albis illis et tenuibus: the disguise is described from head to foot. The shoes are called *Sicyonii*, as we know from e.g. Cic. *De Or*. 1, 231, where Socrates declines Lysias' help and makes the following comparison: *si mihi calceos Sicyonios attulisses, non uterer, quamuis essent habiles atque apti ad pedem, quia non essent uiriles*; cf. Lucr. 4, 1125; Lucil. 1161 M. (= 1181 K.). See Wilkins on Cic. *De Or*. 1, 231; Marquardt ʳ1964, 594; *R.E. s.v.* Schuh.

illis: *ille* refers here to something generally known (Wolterstorff 1917, 212; Callebat 1968, 277), both within the novel's world and outside it (both the robbers and the reader are familiar with this kind of shoe). For the position of *illis* see Callebat 1968, 279.

indutus: cf. 8, 27 (198, 16) *pedes luteis induti calceis* and *Flor*. 9 (12, 7); see vGeisau 1916, 78. *Inductus* (ς, cf. 48, 9), adopted by Oudendorp and favoured by Robertson ('fort. recte'), is unnecessary.

in sequiorem sexum insertus atque absconditus: F and φ's reading *incert*; is, quite in accordance with its meaning, not distinguished for clarity. It should mean *incertatus* which is in fact proposed by Hey and accepted by Robertson and Brandt-Ehlers. The archaic verb *incertare* occurs twice in the *Met*.: 5, 13 (113, 15) and 11, 16 (279, 10) and in both instances means "to render uncertain". With either *incertus* or *incertatus*, two difficulties remain. First, *incert(at)us* must mean here "unrecognisable", but for that there are no good parallels (the passages quoted by Augello 1977, 166, where *incertus* supposedly has that meaning, are not convincing). Secondly, if with Médan 1925, 70 and Callebat 1968, 230 *in* is taken as consecutive, Haemus would be saying that he has *become* the *sexus sequior* (cf. *fixus in lapidem* etc.) – a difficult thing for even Haemus to do. Helm mentions *intectus* (not his own conjecture; the reading is already found in ς), but this is not probable either and cannot be defended with 216, 19 f. *fide tenebrarum contectus atque absconditus*. For these reasons we prefer the reading *insertus* (found in ς; not a conjecture by Beroaldus, as e.g. Helm and Scazzoso indicate), which is palaeographically a very probable correction even if the expression *inserere in* is rare (see further Médan 1925, 72).

The expression *sexus sequior* occurs also in 10, 23 (254, 26); cf. 8, 11 (185, 23) *nec sequius aliquid suspicatus*. For the adjective see Médan 1925, 241; LHSz 2, 248. Norden 1912, 137, n. 3 explains the expression juridically: the women are 'schutzbedürftig'. A different explanation is given by e.g. Hildebrand: 'sequiorem nominavit Apuleius sexum femininum, quia deterior, peior masculino est'. In our passage both interpretations seem to be applicable, but in 254, 26 the latter certainly predominates.

asello: again an attractive 'woman' on an ass – for Charite and Lucius a piquant story. For the diminutive (a big woman on a little ass) see Callebat 1968, 373.

infesti militis: *miles* is naturally a collective word here. The meaning of *infestus* is here not "threatening" (Vallette, Schwartz) but more generally "hostile", as becomes clear from the following sentence.

transabiui: φ has *transiui*, but the reading of F is certainly correct; cf. 8, 4 (179, 14) and 8, 15 (189, 12). Médan 1925, 192 and Bernhard 1927, 121 point out the poetic aspect of the verb; Callebat 1968, 127 discusses the perfect forms in -*iui* of the compounds of *ire*.

160, 4-6 Nam mulierem putantes asinariam concedebant liberos abitus, quippe cum mihi etiam tunc depiles genae leui pueritia splendicarent: "For believing that they were dealing with a female ass-driver, they granted me a free passage; for my cheeks, which were still hairless then, shone with the smoothness of youth".

mulierem putantes asinariam: Callebat 1968, 451 assumes ellipsis of *me*. If one does not assume ellipsis, *asinaria* may be a noun; but the *ThLL* does not give any examples of that (neither does the combination with *mulier* occur elsewhere; cf. Médan 1925, 241).

According to Helm-Krenkel 1970, 412 ('Die Schilderung, die Kap. 4, 5 gegeben ist, passt nicht recht zu der hier von dem angeblichen Haemus selbst gegebenen') and Walsh 1970, 161, n. 2 ('an impossibly singular woman') the story is implausible. This is certainly true: one may wonder, for example, whether there were *Sicyonii* available in Haemus' size and whether it was customary for an ass-driver to wear such expensive clothes (especially shoes). Nevertheless, the reader's suspicion is not shared by the *milites*: their deception foreshadows that of the robbers.

concedebant liberos abitus: now the subject is plural. *Abitus* is ç's correction of *aditus*[1], which is convincingly rejected by Hildebrand: 'Latro ... iis (sc. militibus) non adpropinquavit nec sese immiscuit, sed libere et inoffensus acies eorum penetravit'. Robertson's conjecture *aditus et abitus* (*app. crit.*, cf. Pl. *Cist.* 33; Lucr. 1, 677) is superfluous, for *abitus* is a military term (*ThLL* s.vv. *abitus* and *abeo*), which fits the context very well; cf. Sil. 7, 136, where the codices have *aditus*, too! Bernhard 1927, 101 f. shows that Apul. has a preference for plural abstract nouns in *-us*.

quippe cum: see comm. on 155, 4-6.

etiam tunc: "even then", "still"; cf. 3, 10 (59, 22); 9, 20 (218, 8); 10, 3 (238, 15); the form *etiam tum* in 9, 5 (206, 6) and 10, 14 (247, 4). For the relation between *tum* and *tunc* see vdPaardt 1971, 65 f.

depiles: the *ThLL* gives two other instances: Varro frg. Non. 530; Mart. Cap. 8, 804. Médan 1925, 202 classes it under 'mots de la langue postérieure'.

leui pueritia: cf. Hor. *Carm.* 2, 11, 5 f. *fugit retro / leuis iuuentas et decor*, and Kiessling-Heinze *ad loc.*: '*levis* nicht = *imberbis* ... sondern von der glatten Haut der frischen Jugend'.

Nec ab illa tamen paterna gloria uel mea uirtute desciui, quanquam semitrepidus iuxta mucrones Martios constitutus, sed habitus alieni fallacia tectus, uilla⟨s⟩ seu castella solus adgrediens, uiaticulum mihi conrasi': "But I did not betray my father's glory or my own courage even though I was trembling a bit, so close to those martial swords; but protected by the deceptive disguise I forced my way single-handed into country-houses and castles and scraped together some travelling-money'".

illa ... paterna gloria: *illa* may be used as a general term of praise (Callebat 1968, 276) or it may refer back to 158, 12. For the position of *tamen* see Médan 1925, 228.

semitrepidus: a *hapax legomenon*, mentioned by Médan 1925, 132 (who emphasizes Apul.'s addiction to the prefix *semi-*); Bernhard 1927, 139. A brave man like Haemus never trembles all over, as vdVliet (who in his *app. crit.* proposed *saepe trepidus*) slanderously assumes.

iuxta mucrones Martios constitutus: compare the situation during the attack

---

[1] For *ab-* / *ad-* see Helm, Praef. *Flor.* xlvii.

on Charite's house 4, 26 (95, 8 f.). *Constitutus* is a substitute for the (non-existent) present participle of *esse*; see *GCA* 1977, 86; Waszink 1947, 259.

habitus alieni fallacia: inverse genitive; see Médan 1925, 317; Bernhard 1927, 96 f. At the moment of narration Haemus uses the same *fallacia*.

uilla⟨s⟩ seu castella: a self-evident emendation by ς for *uilla seu* in F and φ (see Helm, Praef. *Flor.* XLVII); it is adopted by practically all modern editors and defended by Augello 1977, 166. Helm-Krenkel take *uillas et* from Helm [1-2], but only vThiel follows them in this. Yet *seu* can be used as a synonym for *et*, as Hildebrand already argues; see Löfstedt 1911, 198; LHSz 2, 504. The conjecture by Mueller 1871, 25 *uillas, sed et* fits in well contextually, but is not very probable palaeographically. Callebat 1968, 56 and *AAGA* 1978, 172 assumes that *uilla* already has the meaning "village" here; but if so Haemus' enterprises would lose much of their credibility.

uiaticulum: an extremely rare word; according to the material from the *ThLL* Institute it only occurs in *Dig.* 5, 1, 18, 1 and Ulp. 167, 1. The use of the diminutive is ironical in view of the amount of money that Haemus offers; the irony is both the speaker's and the author's.

conrasi: Médan 1925, 180 considers *conradere* as belonging to the 'langue familière'; Callebat 1968, 514 goes even further in not excluding the possibility of influence from Plautus (*Poen.* 1363) or Terence (*Ad.* 242 etc.).

160, 10-11 et diloricatis statim pannulis in medium duo milia profudit aureorum: "and at once he tore his rags apart and poured out two thousand pieces of gold in their midst".

diloricatis: only in Cic. *De Or.* 2, 124 and Apul. Met. 6, 10 (135, 6).

pannuli: see comm. on 158, 8.

The mention of the number of the pieces of gold (worth 200,000 sesterces) is noteworthy. One can, of course, assume that the amount is mentioned by Haemus, but the text does not say so; and it is out of the question that Lucius the ass takes in their number at a glance. Perhaps we should see it as a remark of Lucius the narrator, but then he (or Apuleius) has deemed it unnecessary to insert a remark like *ut postea comperi*. It is perhaps wisest not to take these numbers too seriously; see comm. on 156, 22 f.

160, 11-15 et: 'En', inquit, 'istam sportulam, immo uero dotem collegio uestro libens meque uobis ducem fidissimum, si tamen non recusatis, offero breui temporis spatio lapideam istam domum uestram facturus auream': "and 'Look', he said, 'this is the entrance-fee or rather the dowry which I would like to offer to your company along with myself as a most trustworthy chief, if indeed you do not object: in a short time I shall make that stone house of yours a gold one'".

En: used only in direct discourse; see Heine 1962, 176; Callebat 1968, 90 with further literature.

istam sportulam: a *sportula* was originally a little basket with contents, especially meant as a gift for the *cliens*; see Marquardt [r]1964, 207 f. (At 1, 24: 22, 22 it is just a shopping-basket). Later it means "sum of money", such as one had to pay when entering *collegia*; cf. Lucius' initiation into the cult of Osiris, especially 11, 28 (289, 20) *sufficientem conrasi summulam*. Besides being deictic *istam* is perhaps also somewhat ironic and depreciative.

dotem: cf. Norden 1912, 100: 'Als Antrittsgeld schüttet der mutige Jüngling vor den erstaunten Augen der Briganten zweitausend Goldstücke aus, indem er dabei sagt *en istam sportulam, immo vero dotem collegio vestro libens offero* – gleich als ob das Band, das ihn von nun ab mit der Rotte verbinden soll, wie die Ehe "eine gesetzmässig volle Verbindung zu gegenseitiger Lebensgemeinschaft" sei'.

collegio uestro: naturally this is an illegal *collegium*; cf. Gaius as quoted in *Dig.* 3, 4, 1 pr. 1 (see Scharr 1960, 332 f.): *'Neque societatem neque collegium neque huiusmodi corpus passim omnibus habere conceditur: nam et legibus et senatusconsultis et principalibus constitutionibus ea res coercetur. Paucis admodum in causis concessa sunt huiusmodi corpora'*.

ducem fidissimum: evidently the robbers have forgotten that only *mortui* are trustworthy (91, 2 f.). Thrasyleon, the only one who lived up to his oath, very quickly joined the *manes*.

si tamen = *si quidem*; see LHSz 2, 496. For the weakened meaning of *tamen* see Löfstedt 1911, 27 f.

lapideam ... auream: Elmenhorst points out a similar promise of Augustus (Suet. *Aug.* 28), here perhaps ironically alluded to by Apuleius. Another possibility is a reference to Nero's famous *domus aurea*.

Here Haemus' lies reach their climax: his real intentions are to carry off the gold and load it on the ass (164, 8), who thus becomes an *asinus aureus* in a very special sense.

CHAPTER IX

Haemus becomes chief of the robbers and offers them counsel.

160, 16-18 Nec mora nec cunctatio, sed calculis omnibus ducatum latrones unanimes ei deferunt uestemque lautiusculam proferunt, sumeret abiecto centunculo diuite: "Without delay or hesitation the robbers unanimously and with one accord conferred the command upon him and offered him a somewhat smarter outfit; he should put that on and discard his rich rags".

nec mora nec cunctatio: a variation of the well-known turn of speech *nec mora cum*, for which see Callebat 1968, 445 f. and vdPaardt 1971, 29. vGeisau 1916, 286 compares Verg. *G*. 3, 110 *nec mora nec requies, at*; Callebat 1968, 435 does not exclude the possibility of a reminiscence, but the similarity is too vague to be given serious consideration.

calculis omnibus: cf. *calculo cunctorum* (152, 24) and comm. *ad loc*.

ducatum: this military term also at 10, 1 (236, 25 f.) *mille armatorum ducatum sustinebat*. See Médan 1925, 256; Callebat 1968, 131; for military terms in general *GCA* 1977, App. I.

unanimes: most editors read with F *unianimes*, a typically medieval variant of *unanimes* (φ), an adjective which regularly occurs in later Latin; see Callebat 1968, 125. With Robertson, Brandt-Ehlers and Augello 1977, 166 we prefer *unanimes* and take it that the *i* in *unianimes* has slipped in during transcription.

The unanimity 'seems to be underscored by the length of the colon' (Hijmans, *AAGA* 1978, 195).

deferunt ... proferunt: paronomasia with two compounds of the same simple verb; cf. 158, 6 f. *excipientem ... suscipientem*. See LHSz 2, 710.

uestem ... lautiusculam: the 'Nasalstrich' on *ueste* (F) has been added by a different hand; it is necessary, of course. *Lautiusculus* is a *hapax legomenon* (Médan 1925, 135, confirmed by the *ThLL*).

proferunt, sumeret: for parataxis instead of hypotaxis, see Bernhard 1927, 52 and Callebat 1968, 358 f. LHSz 2, 529 f. speaks of a 'Sog. Konjunktiv ohne *ut*'. The insertion ‹*quam rogant*› by vdVliet is not necessary.

abiecto centunculo diuite: the noun *centunculus* "tatters", "rags" occurs several times in the *Met.* (see Callebat 1968, 34) but is quite rare otherwise (for the places see Lopez 1970, 86, n. 2).

The history of the textual criticism concerning the remarkable *diuite* is given by Lopez 1970, 86 f. (To the conjectures mentioned by him the following may be added: *detrito* by Cornelissen 1888, 66; *sutili* by Helm in his *app. crit*.; *digne* by Castiglioni, who hesitantly offers still another possibility, namely *illo* inserted before *diuite*.) Lopez 1970, 87 f. rightly pleads for maintaining *diuite*: with Beroaldus, Giarratano, and Robertson he is of the opinion that the adjective refers to the *duo milia aureorum* sewn into the *centunculus*. Interpreted in this way, the expression *centunculus diues* is a typically Apuleian oxymoron[1] comparable with 1, 3 (3, 9 f.) *mendacium ... uerum*; 1, 8 (8, 7) *regina caupona*; 3, 10 (59, 20) *clementi uiolentia*; etc. See Bernhard 1927, 238 f.; Lopez 1970, 88; vdPaardt 1971, 165.

Sic reformatus, singulos exosculatus et in summo puluinari locatus cena poculisque magnis inauguratur: "Thus transformed, he kissed the men one by one; he was set in the place of honour and inaugurated with a banquet and with great goblets of wine". 160, 18-20

For *reformare* in the sense of *transformare*, see Callebat 1968, 153; this 'transformation' of Haemus is a metamorphosis within a metamorphosis!

exosculatus: the prefix *ex-* has the same intensive value as *de-*; see De Jonge 1941, 62; Callebat 1968, 515. Haemus' admission into the robbers' community is sealed with this kiss, which will prove to be a Judas kiss. See Kroll in *R.E.* Suppl. 5 (1931), 511 f. (especially 515).

summo puluinari: used here in the sense of "high seat", "seat of honour"; cf. *summus lectus*, the most important of the three couches standing around the table at a banquet. *Puluinar* is employed in its usual sense of "cushioned seat of the gods" in 4, 29 (97, 17) and 9, 9 (209, 18). *Puluinaria* means "sanctuary" in 6, 1 (129, 10) *puluinaribus sese proximam intulit*; see Grimal 1963, 98.

cena poculisque: F has *cenę* and originally also *puculisq;*. It is evident that *cenae* does not make sense; Oudendorp prefers *c(o)enaque et poculis*, and Hildebrand uses this reading to explain the process of corruption as follows *coenaque et poculis — coena et poculisque — coenae poculisque*; but in his own text Hildebrand writes *coena et poculis*. The most plausible reading, however, is *cena* in *ç*, further the old correction *poculis* seems preferable to *epulis*, which was proposed by Wiman 1927, 52.

inauguratur: here used ironically. The verb is usually employed of priests or consuls who are installed with the proper ritual (especially by consulting the omens).

Tunc sermonibus mutuis de uirginis fuga deque mea uectura et utrique destinata monstruosa morte cognoscit et, ubi locorum esset illa, percontatus deductusque, uisa ea, ut erat uinculis onusta, contorta et uituperanti nare discessit: "Then in his conversations with them, he learned about the girl's flight and my carrying her, and the monstrous death intended for us both. He asked where she was and was taken to her; when he had seen her, loaded with chains as she was, he came back with his nose turned up in disapproval". 160, 20-24

sermonibus mutuis: among the several possibilities for translating this phrase, "from conversations they held with each other" and "in his conversations with them" seem to fit the context best; perhaps in view of *percontatus* a slight

---

[1] Helm (*app. crit.*), Bernhard 1930, 209, and Augello 1977, 167 detect Apuleian irony in this passage, as in 148, 3; 152, 27; 152, 11 etc.

preference may be felt for the second.

de uirginis fuga... cognoscit: Médan 1925, 252 thinks that *cognoscere de* is a legal term here and translates it as follows: 'il fait une enquête sur la fuite de la jeune fille'. This is incorrect, since Haemus does not know yet of this flight; this is the first time he has heard about it.

monstruosa morte: cf. 153, 12 f. Lucius the narrator is responsible for the epithet, of course. For the shortened form of the adjective (*monstrosus*) see Ernout 1949, 44.

ubi locorum: Callebat 1968, 488 compares Pl. *Capt.* 958 and assumes that this expression is due to the influence of the comic poets (cf. Médan 1925, 40: 'constructions imitées du latin archaïque'). According to LHSz 2, 53 the expression belongs to colloquial language; this theory is more plausible.

onusta: the adjective comes naturally to someone with professional experience as a beast of burden.

contorta... nare: cf. 8, 26 (197, 22) *nare detorta*; Hor. *Sat.* 1, 6, 5 *naso suspendis adunco*; id. *Sat.* 2, 8, 64 *suspendens omnia naso*; Pers. 1, 40 f. *rides... et nimis uncis / naribus indulges*. See Otto 1890, 238 with the addition in Häussler 1968, 112 (Sonny); Callebat 1968, 73.

Later we will appreciate this attitude as another example of Haemus / Tlepolemus' histrionic talents.

160, 24-161, 3 et 'Non sum quidem tam brutus uel certe temerarius', inquit, 'ut scitum uestrum inhibeam, sed malae conscientiae reatum intra me sustinebo, si quod bonum mihi uidetur dissimulauero: "and he said, 'I am not so rude or certainly so reckless as to cross your decision, but I am going to be bothered by a guilty conscience if I keep to myself what seems good to me'".

brutus uel certe temerarius: the first adjective refers to his attitude towards the robbers, the second to his evaluation of his own situation.

uel certe: it is practically impossible to decide whether *uel certe* has a sense here of "at least" (not)" or "certainly (not)". The combination occurs in the *Met.* in both meanings; see Helm in his *app. crit.* at 104, 1; Giarratano *app. crit. ibid.*; Fernhout 1949, 19; Callebat 1968, 329.

reatum intra me sustinebo: a variation of 3, 6 (56, 22) *reatum sustineam*, where *sustinere* + object is a paraphrase of the passive; see vdPaardt 1971, 62, who also discusses the development of the meaning of *reatus* ("condition of an accused person" — "accusation", "charge").

si... dissimulauero: Haemus' own conduct is a classic example of *dissimulatio*!

161, 3-5 Sed prius fiduciam uestri causa sollicito mihi tribuite, cum praesertim uobis, si sententia haec mea displicuerit, liceat rursus ad asinum redire: "But first you must put your trust in me – for I am concerned about you – the more so as you can return again to the ass if this proposal of mine does not suit you".

fiduciam... tribuite: cf. 3, 4 (55, 10) *audientiam... tribuerit*; 4, 31 (99, 5) *uindictam... tribue*; see vdPaardt 1971, 50. Tactfully Haemus emphasises the priority of *fiducia*: he needs it for the success of his enterprise.

uestri causa sollicito: Classical Latin is *uestrā causā*; see Callebat 1968, 263; further literature in vdPaardt 1971, 106. The expression is ambiguous: not only Haemus but also Tlepolemus (who hides behind Haemus) is *latronum causa sollicitus*, i.e. *pro sponsa*.

sententia haec mea: on *hic meus* see Callebat 1968, 268.

rursus ad asinum redire: *asinum* used brachylogically for "plan, in which the ass plays a role". It is not impossible that Apul. lets Haemus make a pun on the proverbial expression ἀφ' ἵππων ἐπ' ὄνους —, which means ἀπὸ τῶν σεμνῶν ἐπὶ τὰ ἄσεμνα. Cf. Pl. *Aul.* 235 *ab asinis ad boues transcendere*; see Otto 1890, 42 (*s.v. asinus*) and 233 (*s.v. mulus*). For the redundant *rursus* see Callebat 1968, 542 f.; vdPaardt 1971, 98 f.

Nam ego arbitror latrones, quique eorum recte sapiunt, nihil anteferre lucro suo debere ac ne ipsam quidem saepe et aliis damnosam ultionem: "For it is my opinion that robbers who know their job should not put anything before their profit, not even revenge, which is often harmful even to others". 161, 5-8

quique: there are a few conjectures on this passage: *quiqui* by Colvius; *qui quidem* by Blümner, adopted by vdVliet (Robertson: 'fort. recte'); Rohde 1885, 103 suggests a lacuna before *quique*; Robertson hesitantly proposes to insert *bonae frugi* before *latrones*. The reading is correct, however: *quisque* is a quite common variant of *quisquis* or *quicumque*. See Petschenig 1882, 148; Callebat 1968, 285; LHSz 2, 201 f. with further literature. Helm's objection that this is the only occurrence in the *Met.* of *quisque* in this sense (in his *app. crit.* he mentions *quicumque* as an alternative reading) does not carry much weight and is probably even incorrect: Helm himself, with Hildebrand, interprets *quaeque* in 11, 17 (279, 22) as *quaecumque* (as do Giarratano-Frassinetti; but Robertson reads with Oudendorp *nauibusque quae*).

et aliis damnosam ultionem: Hildebrand and Eyssenhardt omit *et*; Brandt-Ehlers read *alias* instead of *aliis*, following Blümner and Damsté 1928, 21; Robertson prefers *ultis*, pointing out the frequent confusion of *a/u* and *i/t* in F (Augello 1977, 167 agrees; Frassinetti: 'fort. recte'). But the reading *et aliis* has been rightly defended by Hildebrand (though he himself reads *saepe aliis*) as follows: 'Ultio... quum etiam aliis hominibus, qui non lucri caussa agunt, perniciosa saepius sit, quo magis latronibus, qui hoc tantummodo considerant. Si igitur integram esse voluisset Apuleius sententiam, sine dubio scripsisset, *cum aliis, tum latronibus* vel *aliis* et *eoque magis latronibus. Et* particula hic *etiam, vel* significat'. For this meaning of *et alius* see LHSz 2, 483. For *damnosus* see Ernout 1949, 38; Callebat 1968, 82.

Note that the robbers are won over by theoretical reflections on banditry.

Ergo igitur si perdideritis in asino uirginem, nihil amplius quam sine ullo compendio indignationem uestram exercueritis: "So therefore, if you cause the girl to die in the ass, you will only give vent to your annoyance, 161, 8-10 without any profit".

ergo igitur: this pleonasm is common in the *Met.*; see vdPaardt 1971, 144 with further literature.

nihil amplius quam . . . exercueritis: Médan 1925, 343 points out the conciseness of the expression; compare 154, 3 *quid aliud quam meum crastinum deflebam cadauer*; see comm. *ad loc*. Haemus' remark fits well into the logic of his argument; moreover, it gives the reader, who has already recognised the absurdity of the robbers' proposals, the pleasant feeling that his opinion is now shared by someone else.

161, 10-12 Quin ego censeo deducendam eam ad quampiam ciuitatem ibique uenundandam: "In fact, I have a better proposal: take her to some town or other and sell her there".

For *quin* in the sense of "nay rather" cf. 3, 27 (72, 14 f.) *quin iam ego istum sacrilegum debilem claudumque reddam*; see Callebat 1968, 93; LHSz 2, 676.

deducendam: *deducere* is also the technical term for accompanying the bride to the groom's house; it really is this kind of *deducere* that Haemus has in mind!

quampiam: for the archaic *quispiam*, which occurs 27 times in the *Met.* but is quite rare generally, see Redfors 1960, 29; LHSz 2, 196.

uenundandam: the verb is used especially with regard to captured slaves (cf. 4, 24: 93, 14 *mancipium effecta*); it does not occur elsewhere in Apuleius.

Note the homoeoteleuton (-*am* 4 times) and the heavy clausula, which underscore the gravity of the proposal.

161, 12 Nec enim leui pretio distrahi poterit talis aetatula: "Such a young girl can't possibly sell for a low price".

nec . . . leui: for litotes with *nec* in the *Met.*, see Strilciw 1925, 109 (who does not include this passage).

distrahi: this verb still means "to sell separately", "to sell in small parcels" in Tac. *Ann.* 6, 17, but in the *Met.* the prefix *dis-* has lost its meaning and *distrahere* has become synonymous with *uendere*. See Marg. Molt 1938, 51; Callebat 1968, 56.

talis aetatula = *uirgo tali iuuentute*, as Marg. Molt 1938, 75 rightly observes. For *abstractum pro concreto* see Médan 1925, 315 f.

161, 12-17 Nam et ipse quosdam lenones pridem cognitos habeo, quorum poterit unus magnis equidem talentis, ut arbitror, puellam istam praestinare condigne natalibus suis fornicem processuram nec in similem fugam discur ⟨su⟩ ram, non nihil etiam, cum lupanari seruierit, uindictae uobis depensuram: "For I myself have known several brothel-keepers for some time, and one of them, I think, will be able to buy that girl for quite a few talents: she will go to a brothel in a manner that suits her rank and she won't be able to escape as she did before; besides, when she serves in a bawdy-house, you will get your revenge on her in no small measure".

nam et = *nam*; see vdPaardt 1971, 87 f. with a bibliography. Brandt-Ehlers take *et* with *ipse*: 'Ich kenne nämlich auch selber von früher her...', which, although not impossible, is not very probable.

lenones... cognitos habeo: for *habere* + participle as periphrastic perfect, see Callebat 1968, 304; Ernout-Thomas 1953, 223; LHSz 2, 319. Charite has to laugh at these words of Haemus (161, 26/27) – no wonder, since her cousin has only had eyes for her since childhood (94, 23 f.).

magnis... talentis: if the Attic talent, sometimes described as *talentum magnum* (e.g. Verg. *A*. 5, 248; see Williams *ad loc*.), is meant here, one would expect the addition of a number. Oudendorp and Hildebrand point out that *magnus* is often used for *multus*. Although *ThLL s.v*. 128, 37 f. gives only two examples of this (neither of which is our passage), that explanation seems to be the best; cf. Pagliano "per molti talenti". In the *Met*. mention may be made of 5, 15 (115, 12 f.) *magnis pecuniis*; in Tib. 1, 1, 2 the mss. have *iugera magna*, where most editors read, with the *excerpta, iugera multa*; but see Lee 1974, 111, who convincingly defends *magna*. *Paruus* for *paucus* we find in e.g. Prop. 1, 5, 25; 1, 18, 17; 4, 1, 23. See Svennung 1935, 323; Camps 1961, 55 f. (for a different opinion, see Enk on Prop. 1, 5, 25). Interchange of quality and quantity in general is a phenomenon typical of colloquial Latin; see especially Löfstedt 1911, 147 f.; also *GCA* 1977, 65.

As to the price Charite will fetch: Callirhoe, the heroine in Chariton's novel, is sold for one talent in silver (1, 14); the seller is called Theron, of all names – like Haemus' father! A subtle allusion by Apuleius?[1] For prices in general, see comm. on 156, 22 f.

equidem: cf. 3, 27 (72, 5) *roseis equidem recentibus* with the comm. by vdPaardt 1971, 192 f. (with literature).

praestinare: "to purchase"; Desertine 1898, 20 and Callebat 1968, 484 maintain that Apul. borrows this word from Plautus; see further *GCA* 1977, 123.

condigne natalibus suis: Vallette (14, n. 1) rightly points out the ambiguity of this combination of words, which can be taken both with *praestinare* and with the following future participle (see below). *Natales* is a word from the *sermo cotidianus*; see Callebat 1968, 152.

fornicem processuram: a formidable textual problem. The older editors try to solve the problem by inserting ‹in› (ς) before *fornicem* or by reading the participal form *perpessuram* which, as Oudendorp and Hildebrand remark, does not fit here at all. Other conjectures are:

1. *professuram* by Rohde 1875, 275 f. and Cornelissen 1888, 66 f., accepted by vdVliet. In that case *fornix* has to stand for *meretrix*, as in Suet. *Jul*. 49, 1.

2. *possessuram* by Haupt, who evidently takes *condigne... suis* with this participle. This reading is palaeographically less strong and somewhat improbable in the context.

3. *fornice prosessuram* by Purser 1906, 44 f. This is a most attractive conjecture because *meretrices* were also called *prosedae*; cf. Pl. *Poen*. 266 and Festus'

---

[1] At present Chariton's novel is universally dated to the first or second century A.D.; see e.g. Reardon 1971, 334, n. 55. For an even earlier date (first century B.C.) see Hägg 1971, 15, n. 1.

explanation (Paul. Fest. 252, 14 L) *prosedas meretrices Plautus appellat, quae ante stabula sedeant*. The verb *prosedere*, however, occurs in this meaning only in Isid. *Or.* 10, 229, who, like Festus, explains the noun.

Therefore it seems safest to maintain the transmitted *processuram* in spite of the fact that the accusative of direction (without preposition) with a non-topographical noun is an exception (Helm's references in his *app. crit.* are not decisive).

The sentence as a whole is extremely ironical: this is suggested especially by the ambiguous phrase *condigne natalibus suis* . Some translators take it with *fornicem*, e.g. Graves: "one of whom, I know, will pay you a really large sum for her and settle her in a suitably high-class establishment" – amusing, by all means, but grammatically not quite correct. More acceptable is Helm's view that *condigne* refers to *processuram* (*app. crit.*: 'quasi illa procedat dignitate'), by which an antithesis *processuram – discursuram* is created.

The selling of kidnapped girls to brothel-keepers regularly occurred both in daily life (Norden 1912, 81 f.) and in literature – in our case the classical novel (Junghanns 1932, 143, n. 44); perhaps also in the *Vorlage* of Apul.'s novel (*GCA* 1977, 178). Therefore it is ironical that the proposal is made by Haemus, rather than by the robbers themselves.

discur ‹su› ram: F and φ have *discurram*, which Hildebrand considers possible. But the correction by ς seems to be right; the strongest argument in its favour is the triple homoeoteleuton *-suram*.

161, 18-19 Hanc ex animo quidem meo sententiam conducibilem protuli; sed uos uestrorum estis consiliorum rerumque domini': "What I have put forward here is, in my opinion, a profitable proposal; but you are lords and master of your own decisions and affairs' ".

ex animo ... meo: according to Fulvius to be taken with *protuli*, and meaning "sincerely". Scioppius translates it with "in my opinion", to be taken with *conducibilem*; this interpretation, defended by Oudendorp, seems preferable: it is suggested by the antithesis *quidem ... sed*.

conducibilem: this adjective ("useful") occurs a few times in Plautus (*Bacch.* 52, *Cist.* 78, *Epid.* 256, etc.), then once in Rhet. Her. 2, 14, 21, and then again here in Apuleius. Therefore it may be a borrowing from Plautus, but of course we cannot be certain (as was Desertine 1898, 15).

sed uos ... domini: with these words Haemus has returned to his starting-point: he does not wish to influence their decision – an announcement which traditionally signals the opposite. Haemus' argumentation belongs to the *genus deliberativum* (as is also indicated by *in diutina deliberatione*, 161, 21), in which *utilitas* holds a pivotal position (cf. *sententia conducibilis*); see Leeman 1963, 1, 23 f. The numerous figures of speech and sound have been emphasized above.

CHAPTER X

Haemus' proposal is accepted; Lucius proves himself a moral ass.

Sic ille latronum fisci aduocatus nostram causam pertulerat, uirginis et asini sospitator egregius: "Thus that treasurer of the robbers' club had supported our cause – an excellent saviour of girl and ass". 161, 20-21

Helm (Praef. *Flor.* XIII) emphasizes the witticism of the expression *latronum fisci aduocatus*. Grimal 1958, 1449 elucidates: 'Le fisc est le trésor particulier de l'Empereur; il désigne ici toute "caisse collective"'; but this does not entirely explain the witticism. Apul. has Lucius allude to an office which was instituted by the emperor Hadrian, as Médan 1925, 253 observes. Cf. *SHA*, Ael. Spart., *Hadr.* 20, 6: *fisci aduocatum primus instituit*; R.E. I., 438 (Kubitschek): 'Zweck derselben war, die bis dahin den Verwaltungsbeamten zukommende Vertretung der Interessen des Fiscus in Streitigkeiten mit den Unterthanen vom eigentlichen Verwaltungswesen zu trennen'. See also Hirschfeld 1905, 48 f.

pertulerat: causam perferre is elsewhere found only in Quint. *Decl.* 249 (Ritter 20, 4 f.) *Qualem causam pertulerim, sic aestimare potestis.*

sospitator egregius: whereas Lucius was the (unsuccessful) *sospitator* of Charite (150, 16), Haemus/Tlepolemus is the *sospitator* of both. For nouns in *-tor* in the *Met.* see Luisa Gargantini 1963, 40.

Sed in diutina deliberatione ceteri cruciantes mora consilii mea praecordia, immo miserum spiritum, libentes tandem nouicii latronis accedunt sententiae et protinus uinculis exsoluunt uirginem: "But the deliberation of the others took a long time; by their delay in reaching a decision they tortured my heart, or rather my unhappy spirit. Finally they gladly acceded to the proposal of the newly arrived robber and released the girl from her fetters at once". 161, 21-25

in ... deliberatione: 'valeur causale et expression du moyen interfèrent' (Callebat 1968, 225); see also comm. on 161, 18 f.

cruciantes mora consilii mea praecordia: the torture is illustrated by the alliteration of *c* and *r*; one may imagine Lucius moaning: *immo miserum spiritum*. Médan 1925, 328 includes *praecordia* and *spiritum* among the 'unexpected expressions' – unexpected, of course, only by those who do not know that Lucius is an ass with a human mind.

libentes: Robertson, followed by Brandt-Ehlers and Scazzoso, reads *elidentes*; in that case the comma follows the participle instead of preceding it. In favour of Robertson's conjecture is the argument that *immo* marks a climax not only from *praecordia* to *spiritum*, but also from *cruciantes* to *elidentes* (with chiastic position). Robertson points out that *elidere* occurs in 8, 14 (188, 6) *statuit*

145

elidere... spiritum; 9, 38 (232, 11) *elidit... animam*; 10, 26 (258, 6) *sic elisum... effundit spiritum* (where *elisum* is a conjecture by vdVliet for *elisus* (F and φ), which most editors retain). Robertson's argument is considerably less strong palaeographically: it is difficult to explain the omission of *e-*, and the interchange of *b* and *d* is not mentioned in Helm's list of permutations (Praef. *Flor.* XLIII f.). Why, then, does Robertson object to *libentes*? *Libens* occurs three times in the singular in the *Met.* (105, 7; 160, 12; 260, 17); in the plural it is not found, except in our passage (the adverb *libenter* occurs eight times). It is true that the adverbially used form *libentes* is, on the whole, quite rare, but there are parallels; cf. Cic. *Ver.* 2, 3, 118 *libentes an inuiti dabant?*; Liv. 22, 32, 8 *animo ac uoluntate eorum qui libentes darent*. See also Löfstedt 1933, 2, 368 f.; LHSz 2, 172. We therefore agreee with Augello 1977, 168 that *libentes* should be retained.

tandem: cf. Junghanns 1932, 52, n. 74: 'Pausen werden von Apul. oft beseitigt (wenn es nicht retardierende, d.h. Spannungspausen sind!)'. This 'Spannungspause', however, occurs only in the narrated time, hardly in the narrative time: the narrator keeps up a swift pace here. The combination *libentes tandem* gives an almost antithetical juxtaposition; cf. also *tandem... protinus*.

nouicii latronis accedunt sententiae: again emphasis on Haemus' status, and accordingly on his marvellous persuasive powers. To the robbers – and to the experiencing Lucius, who supersedes the narrating Lucius here ('attraction of the narrating "I"'; see Romberg 1962, 96) – Haemus is *nouicius*, i.e. "newly acquired" (cf. 9, 15; 213, 25 f. *nouicium... asinum*); but actually he is a *latro nouus*.

accedunt sententiae: cf. Plin. *Ep.* 4, 10, 3 *confido accessurum te sententiae meae*; ibid. 10, 40, 1 (Trajan) *mihi sufficiet indicari cui sententiae accesseris*. Petschenig's (1882, 151) conjecture *accredis* (accepted by vdVliet and Gaselee) in *Met.* 1, 20 (18, 20 f.) *accedis huic fabulae* is certainly unnecessary.

161, 25-162, 1 Quae quidem simul uiderat illum iuuenem fornicisque et le‹n›onis audierat mentionem, coepit risu laetissimo gestire, ut mihi merito subiret uituperatio totius sexus, cum uiderem puellam, proci iuuenis amore nuptiarumque castarum desiderio simulato, lupanaris spurci sordidique subito delectari nomine: "As soon as she saw that young man and heard mention of a brothel and a brothel-keeper, she started to laugh very happily and could not keep still, so that I considered myself justified in criticising her whole sex, at the sight of a girl, who had feigned love for a young suitor and enthusiasm for a decent marriage, now delighting in the unexpected mention of a foul and filthy whorehouse".

For *simul* as a conjunction see Callebat 1968, 432 f.; LHSz 2, 638.

fornicis... lenonis... mentionem: ὕστερον πρότερον; cf. 161, 13 and 15.

coepit... gestire: for the initial position of *coepit*, see Bernhard 1927, 14. Callebat 1968, 304 regards *coepit... gestire* as a periphrasis of *gesti(u)it*. But this passage is hardly comparable to a paradigm of the phenomenon mentioned by Callebat, e.g. Petr. 29, 9 *interrogare ergo atriensem coepi, quas in medio picturas haberent*. There *interrogare coepi* is identical to *interrogaui* (see Perrochat and Smith *ad loc.*), but in our passage there is no question of 'Mechanisierung... und somit auch... semantische Entwertung' (LHSz 2, 319). *Gestire* means here *gestus facere*, as in e.g. 3, 24 (70, 9) *in auem similem gestiebam*; see vdPaardt 1971, 178.

merito: later it will turn out that this *uituperatio* is not deserved at all – the narrating Lucius knows this, but allows himself to be carried away by the indignation he felt in the past (see above on the 'attraction of the experiencing "I"'). Feldbrugge 1938, 62 finds this change of vision comical: 'He is indignant about her attitude, but though his feelings are sincere this indignation has a comical aspect: the author, Apuleius, knows it is only a disguise, so that there should not be any reason for anger'. (Instead of 'the author Apuleius' it would be more accurate to say 'the narrator Lucius'.)

proci iuuenis: the conjecture by Cornelissen 1888, 67 *probi* is unnecessary. For the adjectival use of *iuuenis* see *GCA* 1977, 68 with the literature mentioned; Ernout-Thomas 1964, 165 f.

amore ... desiderio simulato: Rohde 1885, 103 objects to *simulato* and proposes *dissimulato* (= *neglecto*); vdVliet admits this conjecture into his text. Rohde formulates his objection as follows: 'Dies (sc. *simulato*) könnte nur dann richtig sein wenn die *geheuchelte* Liebe zum Bräutigam und die Lust am lupanar gleichzeitig wären: natürlich versteht man gewöhnlich: da sie doch *früher* Liebe zum Br. geheuchelt hatte (cf. Helm *app. crit.*: *sed antea simulare uidebatur uirgo*); aber dann müsste dieses 'früher' durch *paulo ante, modo* oder dergl. ausgedrückt sein'. *Dissimulato* may be defended palaeographically by assuming haplography: *desiderio **di**ssimulato*. It seems better however to retain the manuscript reading: the antecedence can be sufficiently expressed by the absolute ablative; another possibility is to take *amore ... simulato* as an ablative of quality.

lupanaris .. nomine: *nomen* means here "the mention of"; see Williams (1960) on Verg. *A*. 5, 768 *non tolerabile nomen* (Williams reads *numen* in his text, but apparently prefers *nomen* in his commentary; so also Conington).

The sigmatism in the last part of the sentence is very expressive.

Et tunc quidem totarum mulierum secta moresque de asini pendebant iudicio: "And so the whole race of women and their morals then depended on the judgement of an ass". 162, 1-2

Et tunc quidem: distance of the narrator (perhaps also to be inferred from the length of the colon): it was an asinine judgment! This 'Erzählerdistanz' (see Lämmert 1955, 86 f.) is strikingly expressed in Rode's rendition of this passage: "'Ach, sie haben alle weder Sitten noch Charakter!' brach ich bei mir selbst voller Unwillen aus. Das schöne Geschlecht verzeih' es! Ich sprach's als – Esel". (Rüdiger 1960, 291, n. 1 notes: 'Hier zeigt Rodes Übersetzung (!) die Stilisierung ins rokokohaft Galante besonders deutlich'.)

totarum = *omnium*. See Médan 1925, 154; Callebat 1968, 287; vdPaardt 1971, 121.

secta: F and φ *recta*; em. ς. For the interchange of *s* and *r* see Helm, Praef. *Flor*. XLV. The meaning is "group", with the connotation of "lifestyle" (cf. Rode); see further *GCA* 1977, 136 f. Here the aspect 'lifestyle' is added by *moresque* which may be read as a hendiadys with *secta*.

de asini pendebant iudicio: a double hyperbaton, by which *asini* is emphasized.

Callebat 1968, 204 points out that authors of the classical period employ only the ablative without preposition after *pendere* used figuratively.

In *Met.* 10, 33, too, the ass gives vent to his moral indignation – and there too he criticises *libido* (this time men's). Cf. Schlam 1968a, 145: 'Such moralising is presented ironically, but the irony seems double edged. For moral judgment is indeed a sign of the human mind within an animal body'. See also id., *AAGA* 1978, 103.

In reference to this utterance of Lucius Heine 1962, 218 remarks that he 'neigt zo vorschnellen Urteilen, die er später mehrfach revidieren muss'. Lucius' judgment of the female sex may indeed seem somewhat rash, but one must remember his experiences with women have been far from satisfactory: Fotis, Pamphile, the gardener's wife, the *anus*. It is, therefore, hard to agree with Perry 1923, 201: 'In the *Metamorphoses*... women are often described for their own sentimental or picturesque value'; we cannot agree at all with id., 202: (of) 'the tale of the robber Haemus (VII. 6-8) *an unduly large proportion*... relates to the virtues of one Plotina'. Thus, seen from the limited perspective of Lucius-the-ass, the *sententia* is far from absurd – in contrast with vThiel 1971, 16 (on Apuleius): 'seine Eitelkeit verrät sich dort, wo er den Helden mit seinen eigenen Zügen und Urteilen ausstattet, auch wo sie gar nicht passen'; vThiel elucidates this by n. 47a: 'Entrüstung des "Philosophen" über die Verdorbenheit der Frauen VII 10 f.'. That Apuleius was vain is an interesting biographical side-light, but this passage is too narrow a base for such libel; we have a painfully obvious example of circular reasoning here.

162, 2-5 Sed ille iuuenis sermone repetito: 'Quin igitur', inquit, 'supplicatum Marti Comiti pergimus et puellam simul uendituri et socios indagaturi?: "But that young man spoke again, saying: 'So why don't we proceed to a prayer to Mars the Comrade, and after that both sell the girl and at the same time track down companions".

quin... supplicatum... pergimus: according to Médan 1925, 83 this is an example of the extension of the use of the supine, i.e. after verbs other than those indicating motion; cf. 159, 15 *suppetiatum conuocans*; but it is not quite clear why *pergere* is not a *verbum movendi*. Damsté 1928, 21 wants to read *supplicato* rather than *supplicatum*, referring to 10, 16 (248, 23) *cognito quod res erat.* In spite of Robertson's cautiously formulated approval ('fort. recte'), the conjecture is unnecessary, the future participles have a final meaning, as has *comparaturus* below; see vGeisau 1916, 278 f.

Marti Comiti: cf. 162, 14 f. *Marti Secutori Comitique.* Vallette (15, n. 2) remarks: 'Il ne semble pas que Mars (à la ressemblance, par exemple, de Mars *Vltor*) fut alors l'objet d'un culte officiel sous le vocable de Mars *Secutor*... ou *Comes*. Ce sont vraisemblablement des vocables imaginés pour la circonstance'. Mention is made of Mars as *Comes Augusti* (Wissowa 1912, 153; *RE* 14, 2, 1927), but it would be going rather far to suppose that a reference to that is intended here. For Mars as patron of robbers see *GCA* 1977, 166 f.

simul: for its position cf. 1, 25 (23, 20) *et nummis simul priuatus et cena.* See Bernhard 1927, 26.

indagaturi: *indagare* "to hunt for" is used of hounds mainly; in its literal sense it occurs 8, 4 (178, 22) *indagaturus feras* (referring to Tlepolemus/Haemus who, as a hunter, follows in his father's footsteps). Here it is used in its derived sense of "to trace (people)"; Cf. Pl. *Merc.* 623 *eo si pacto posset indagarier / mulier?* and the noun *indagatus* in 159, 24.

Sed, ut uideo, nullum uspiam pecus sacrificatui ac ne uinum quidem 162, 5-7 potatui adfatim uel sufficiens habemus: "But, as I see, we have no cattle anywhere to sacrifice and not even plenty of wine – or rather enough – to drink".

Sed: the conditions for a properly performed *supplicatio* cannot be met.

sacrificatui: according to the material of the ThLL Institute this noun is found only here.

potatui: before Apul. this noun is found in Sen. *Con.* 2, 1, 6. If, however, Médan is right in supposing that the reading there should be *nec nepotatus*, rather than *neque potatus*, this would be another 'neologism' of Apul. (but *potatus* in Seneca seems to be correct; see the edition of H. J. Müller 1888).

adfatim: see *GCA* 1977, 26.

uel sufficiens: Helm (not Robertson, as mentioned by Frassinetti in his *app. crit.*) wants to delete these words, obviously regarding them as a gloss. Armini 1928, 305 finds this irresponsible: 'Nam *adfatim uel sufficiens* nonne pulchrum est exemplum abundantiae Apuleianae?' Much more plausible is his second explanation: 'An *adfatim* 'abundanter' significat, *sufficiens* 'id ipsum quod opus est', ut sententia fiat: 'uinum non satis, nedum abundanter habemus'?' Thus, *uel* is used here correctiuely (see LS *s.v.* A2b).

Decem mihi itaque legate comites, quis contentus proximum 162, 7-9 castellum petam, inde uobis epulas ‹s›aliares comparaturus': "Let me, therefore, have ten men to accompany me – that will do. With them I will attack the nearest village and from there provide you with a sumptuous meal'".

legate: the technical meaning "to send along as a *legatus*" is no longer present here; cf. 9, 11 (211, 13) *rebar ... me ad alium ... laborem legatu‹m› iri*.

quis = *quibus*. See vdPaardt 1971, 159 f. with further references given there.

proximum castellum petam: Haemus now wants ten men to attack a *castellum*, whereas earlier he used to do so single-handed, according to his own words (160, 9) – an indication of the credibility of these feats. It appears from the context that *castellum* here means "village", rather than "stronghold"; this is also very clearly the case in 8, 15 (188, 23).

epulas ‹s›aliares: the correction by a more recent hand in F (which had *alia res* at first) is undoubtedly right; see *GCA* 1977, 168. For Mars-worshippers like the robbers, *epulae saliares* are 'gefundenes Fressen'.

Sic eo profecto ceteri copiosum instruunt ignem aramque cespite 162, 10-11 uirenti Marti deo faciunt: "After he had thus left, the others made a huge fire and built an altar with green sods for the god Mars".

149

Sic: "with these words" and/or "accompanied by ten *comites*".

aram...faciunt: there is a contrast between the fresh colour of the altar and the old age of the victim selected for Mars (*hircum annosum*). The main victims, in fact, will be the robbers themselves: they are made drunk with the captured wine, and (some of them) killed with their own swords.

For the different meanings of *facere* (here synonymous with *instruere*) in the *Met.*, see Callebat 1968, 172 f.

CHAPTER XI

Initial activities of the new leader.

Nec multo post adueniunt illi uinarios utres ferentes et gregatim pecua comminantes: "Not much later the foraging party got back carrying wineskins and herding a flock of farm animals". 162, 12-13

adueniunt: the word implies more than a simple arrival: Donatus notes on Ter. *Eun.* 259 *aduentus proprie exspectatorum necessariorumque dicitur*.

uinarios utres: the combination *uinarius uter* is also used in Plin. *Nat.* 28, 240. See Daremberg et Saglio *s.v. uter*.

gregatim: for adverbs ending in *-im* see vdPaardt 1971, 33 f.; Callebat 1968, 475 f.; *GCA* 1977, 26; 71; 169.

comminantes: for this verb *ThLL* cites the present passage only; Bernhard 1927, 120 says the word is coined by Apuleius. The compound *prominare*, too, occurs only once, also in Apuleius and also combined with *gregatim*: 9, 27 (223, 8 f.) *nam senex claudus... uniuersa nos iumenta... ad lacum proximum bibendi causa gregatim prominabat*. On the simplex *minare* see vdPaardt 1971, 200 f.; we intend to add a further note in *GCA* on 8, 30 (201, 18).

Vnde praelectum grandem hircum annosum et horricomem Marti Secutori Comitique uictimant: "From the flock they selected a large he-goat, old and shaggy, and sacrificed him to Mars the Helper and Companion". 162, 13-14

Vnde = ex quibus: see Callebat 1968, 293; LHSz 2, 208 f.

praelectum: the information placed at our disposal by the Thesaurus Institute at Munich shows that in the meaning "select" *praelegere* is found for the first time in Quint. *Inst.* 1, 8, 8 *pueris quae maxime ingenium alant atque animum augeant praelegenda*; elsewhere in Quintilian the word means "to read aloud", e.g. *Inst.* 1, 5, 11.

grandem: cf. below 162, 21; on the question whether *grandis* takes over the function(s) of *magnus*, see *GCA* 1977, 38.

hircum: Roscher *s.v. Mars* lists as this god's sacrificial animals oxen, rams, swine, the *equus october* and makes the hardly illuminating remark 'vereinzelt wird ein *hircus annosus et horricomis* dem Mars Secutor Comesque geopfert von den Latrones bei *Appul. Met.*'; *ThLL s.v. hircus* 2821, 25 f. indeed has no further instances of a *hircus* sacrificed to Mars. Possibly it is relevant in this context to note that *hircus* (as against *aries, caper*) is used primarily when objectionable qualities of the he-goat are intended: Hor. *Ars* 220 *carmine qui tragico uilem certauit ob hircum*; in particular the *hircinus foetor* (Firm. *Mat.* 8, 20, 4 *erit corpus eius foedis odoribus possessum ut hircini foetoris semper uirus exudet*); Hor. *S.* 1, 2,

27 *pastillos Rufillus olet, Gorgonius hircum.* For *hircus* denoting "lecher" see Pl. *Cas.* 550; *Mos.* 39.

annosum: a dubious qualification if one thinks of Col. 7, 6, 3 *ante sex annos celeriter consenescit, quod inmatura ueneris cupidine primis pueritiae temporibus exhaustus est*; thus the sacrifice may be a highly ironic compliment to the god if Servius' remark on Verg. *A.* 3, 118 applies: *ratio uictimarum fit pro qualitate numinum*: see in contrast the young animal at Hor. *Carm.* 3, 13, 3 f.

horricomem: cf. 4, 19 (89, 10) *canes etiam uenaticos auritos illos et horricomes*. *ThLL* offers no other instances than the two from Apuleius. On *-comis / -comus* see *GCA* 1977, 148.

Marti Secutori Comitique uictimant: the robbers' worship of Mars is dealt with in *GCA* 1977, 166 f. Here we may add that the specific titles and sacrifices are made to measure and designed to enhance the ironic tone pervading the episode of the robbers. The two epithets (not mentioned in Carter 1902) mark Mars as a subaltern officer.

Secutori: cf. 4, 12 (84, 12) (*Alcimum mortuum*) *bonum secutorem Lamacho dedimus*; 9, 17 (215, 30) *Myrmecem acerrimum relinquens uxori secutorem*.

Comitique: see above on 162, 4. Later Mars will be seen not to have responded even to the modest request for assistance implied in these epithets; Tlepolemus on the other hand shows himself an excellent *secutor comesque* to Charite – as does the ass.

uictimant: according to Médan 1925, 122 a neologism: cf. 170, 22 f. *quin... communem omnium adulterum illis... uictimamus hostiam*; Vulg. *Eccli.* 34, 24 *qui offert sacrificium ex substantia pauperum, quasi qui uictimant filium in conspectu patris sui.* A *uictima* refers to a sizable animal, see vdPaardt 1971, 37.

162, 15 Et ilico prandium fabricatur opipare: "Immediately afterwards a copious lunch was prepared".

Callebat 1968, 443 treats this brief sentence as an instance of 'brièveté narrative (phrase courte imprimant un mouvement vif à l'énoncé et dégageant avec clarté les éléments de la narration)'. Cf. Bernhard 1927, 39 f. The entire passage works towards an impression of speed – the robbers are hungry! Editors have punctuated accordingly.

prandium: see above on 160, 20 *cena*.

fabricatur: transitive, as everywhere in the *Met.*, cf. Callebat 1968, 295. See also above on 153, 27.

opipare: Apuleius is the first author in whose work both 2nd and 3rd declension forms of this adjective occur: in choosing he appears to look for euphonic variation in the endings of adjective and noun: 1, 24 (22, 8) *piscatum opiparem*; 2, 19 (40, 13) *mensae opipares*; 6, 19 (143, 2) *prandium opipare*; 9, 33 (228, 4) *opipari prandio* as against 5, 15 (115, 15) *opiparis muneribus*; *Soc.* 22 (33, 1) *opiparam supellectilem*; the only exception is 10, 13 (246, 16) *opiparas cenas. Ind. Apul.* (as well as Adlington-Gaselee, unlike the other translators and *ThLL*) treats *opipare* here as an adverb, probably incorrectly in view of the frequent combination of the adj. with a noun meaning "meal". The adverb occurs 5, 8 (109, 6) and *Soc.* 22

(32, 14). However lavish the lunch, one item on the menu may have been rather stringy and tough.

Tunc hospes ille: 'Non modo', inquit, 'expositionum prae-   162, 16-18
darumque, uerum etiam uoluptatum uestrarum ducem me
strenu‹u›m sentire debetis' et adgressus insigni facilitate
nauiter cuncta praeministrat:"Then the stranger said: 'You must look
on me as an energetic leader not only in selling and plunder, but also of your
jollifications'. And tackling the job with remarkable dexterity he efficiently
looked after everything".

Tunc = deinde, see Svennung 1935, 413 f.; Callebat 1968, 327.

expositionum: *ThLL* gives no other instances of the noun in this meaning, but the corresponding verb is often used in the meaning "to put up for sale" (e.g. 1, 24; 22, 8; cf. *OLD s.v.* 4a). The advantage of retaining the reading of F is that Haemus' claims may all be interpreted as grandiloquent references to items in our text: *expositiones* to the proposed sale of the girl (161, 12 f.); *praedae* to his own 'gift' of 2000 pieces of gold (160, 11); *uoluptates* to the robbers' last lunch. Perhaps *expositio* also carries with it the notion of "description", "explanation" (see *OLD s.v. exponere* 6a); in view of the long speech he has just made, Haemus might call himself a *dux expositionum* in that sense. See also Robertson 1924, 23. Robertson himself, however, prints Oudendorps's *exspoliationum* (spelling *exp-*), and gives a high mark to *expeditionum*, the ç reading adopted by all other modern editors.

uoluptatum ... ducem: cf. Hor. *Carm.* 2, 7, 25 f. *quem Venus arbitrum / dicet bibendi?* Tac. *Ann.* 16, 18 *elegantiae arbiter. ThLL* gives no parallel instances with *dux*. If the author had the function of *arbiter uoluptatum* in mind, replacing *arbiter* by *dux* would be suggested by the military character of the robbers' life and by the fact that it is hard to combine an arbiter's elegance with the strenuous activities of a cook.

ducem me ... sentire debetis: the construction of *sentire* with two accusatives is 'very rare' (LS); they cite Cic. *Off.* 1, 125; Val. Flac. 6, 501; see also Cic. *Phil.* 13, 24; *Fin.* 5, 24; Sen. *Helv.* 12, 1; KSt. 2, 1, 292 d. See also our note on 161, 19.

nauiter: adverb with *nauus*; LHSz 1, 499 note that 'Adjektivadverbien' in *-ter* in classical Latin are formed only with third declension adjectives, and in later periods occasionally with adjectives of the second declencion; but they also note *humaniter, inhumaniter, perhumaniter* in Cicero's Letters. Callebat 1968, 175 mentions several instances in Apuleius: *crebriter* (five times), *firmiter* (seven times), *ignaviter* (once), *largiter* (six times), *nauiter* (eleven times); see also vdPaardt 1971, 46 (*seueriter*) and 119 (*crebriter*); *GCA* 1977, 66 (*auiditer*); Callebat in *AAGA* 1978, 170.

Verrit, sternit, coquit, tuc‹c›eta concinnat, adponit scitule, sed prae-   162, 19-21
cipue poculis crebris grandibusque singulos ingurgitat: "He swept, laid
the table, cooked, stuffed sausages, served deftly, but above all he plied them
with many a large cup of wine".

The description of Haemus' activity as *dux uoluptatum* is marked by asyndeton (cf. 4, 33: 101, 7 f. *Maeretur, fletur, lamentatur*; see Callebat in *AAGA* 1978, 176); the first three items are disyllabic, two items of six syllables each follow, but the single activity that most advances the story has, with 21 syllables, more than all the previous ones together. Note the progressive chiastic placement of the verbs -*concinnat, adponit* –, – *ingurgitat*; also alliteration of *c* and *p*.

tucceta: André 1961, 146 remarks: 'Il n'est pas possible de savoir toujours s'ils (*sc.* les saucisses et saucissons) étaient consommés frais ou conservés, mais il est vraisemblable qu'ils étaient aussi mis en réserve dans le *carnarium*. On est sûr du fait pour... les *tucceta*, qui paraissent être des rillettes faites de boeuf hâchée et cuite dans la graisse'; in note 128 he points out that at 9, 22 (219, 24) *pulmenta recentia tuccetis temperat* they are contrasted with fresh meat. *Tucceta* were evidently a delicacy not meant for weight-watchers; cf. Pers. 2, 41 f. *poscis opem neruis corpusque fidele senectae./Esto age. Sed grandes patinae tuccetaque crassa/adnuere his superos uetuere Iouemque morantur.* See van Wageningen *ad loc.* and Purser 1910, 43 f. Elsewhere in the *Met. tucceta* are mentioned at 2, 7 (30, 17); 5, 15 (115, 2); 9, 22 (219, 24).

concinnat = *parat, componit*. See Callebat 1968, 171 f.; cf. 10, 13 (246, 8) (*pistor*) *qui panes et mellita concinnabat edulia.* Vallette's translation "dispose les viandes" implies an unlikely tautology with *adponit*.

scitule: on *scitulus* see Marg. Molt 1938, 60; on diminutive adjectives in Apul. see comm. 156, 22.

ingurgitat: cf. Gel. 15, 2, 3, where a *nebulo* tries to convince his audience that Plato was in favour of ebriety and *ingentibus poculis omne ingenium ingurgitabat*. A different construction is used with the verb *Met.* 4, 7 (79, 21) *quae... merum saeuienti uentri tuo soles... ingurgitare,* see *GCA* 1977, 66.

Perry 1923, 225 judges that 'the manner in which the robbers are captured through the help of the girl's fiancé may have been told (*sc.* in the original *Metamorphoseis*) more fully than in ch. 26 (of the *Onos*), and must have differed from the account given in Apuleius.' He thinks (n. 26) 'it is probable that in the original version this young man entered the robbers' service in the capacity of a cook, for that position had become vacant shortly before by the death of the old woman'. vThiel 1971, 1, 115 agrees. We think the hypothesis attractive but not compelling.

162, 21-24 Interdum tamen [in] simulatione promendi, quae poscebat usus, ad puellam commeabat adsidue, partisque subreptas clanculo et praegustatas a se potiones offerebat hilaris: "Meanwhile, however, pretending to fetch something he needed, he continually went up to the girl and cheerfully offered her titbits he had surreptitiously taken and drinks he had had a taste of".

Interdum = interim, see Callebat 1968, 323 f.: vdPaardt 1971, 28.

simulatione: F has *insimulatione*; *ThLL s.v. insimulatio* 1911, 14 f. points out that in the manuscripts the word appears instead of *simulatio* on more than one occasion, e.g. Symm. *Ep.* 7, 100; Oros. *Hist.* 2, 15, 1. Oudendorp tries *in simulatione*; Armini 1932, 87 defends the reading of F by taking *insimulatio* as an alternative form for *simulatio* ('låtsad förevändning'). The emendation, which is accepted by all modern editors, first occurs in ς (and therefore should not be attributed to Helm, who adduces in support 6, 28: 149, 27 and 9, 9: 209, 17).

commeabat: the narrator relinquishes the historic present. The transition to the imperfect is made smoother by *poscebat* in the relative clause.

clanculo: on this adverb, which does not occur before Apuleius, see Callebat 1968, 79 and vdPaardt 1971, 74 f.

praegustatas: the fact that the girl drinks willingly gives the reader a hint concerning the true relation between Charite and Haemus. Ov. *A.* 1, 4, 33 f. *si tibi forte dabit quod praegustauerit ipse (sc. maritus) / reice libatos illius ore cibos* advises the married woman who is in love with an outsider to reject the food and drink pre-tasted by her husband, but on the contrary to accept those pre-tasted by her lover; cf. Rohde ³1914, 175 n. 3, who refers *i.a.* to a similar situation in Ach. Tat. 2, 9. Charite does not reject the wine pre-tasted by her lover either. The Ovid and Apuleius passages mentioned, however, are the only ones in which the verb *praegustare* has an erotic connotation. Since it is also used in a context of precautionary measures against poisoning (Sen. *Con.* 9, 6, 19; Plin. *Nat.* 21, 12; Juv. 6, 633; see also Friedländer 1, 1910, 194 on *praegustatores* at the Imperial Court) it may contain a preliminary hint concerning the wine offered to the robbers.

offerebat: ellipsis of a pronoun in the dative; Callebat 1968, 452 omits this instance, though he notes one at line 26 below with *adlubescebat*.

hilaris: on *hilarus / hilaris* see *GCA* 1977, 32.

At illa sumebat adpetenter et non nunquam basiare uolenti promptis sauiolis adlubescebat. Quae res oppido mihi displicebat: "But she? She ate and drank eagerly and more than once when he tried to kiss her she gladly obliged with responsive kisses. This annoyed me very much". 162, 24-26

adpetenter: once again the adverb is preferred to the participle / adjective; before Apuleius the adverb is found only once: Cic. *Off.* 1, 33 *ne cupide quid agerent, ne adpetenter*. After Apuleius only in Amm. 29, 1, 16; Alc. Avit. *c. Eutr.* 1 p. 16, 9. For the sense compare Catul. 2, 3.

The participle *adpetens* is usually followed by an objective genitive. It is taken absolutely (as is the adverb here) in Cic. *Agr.* 2, 20; *de Orat.* 2, 182; *Tusc.* 3, 17.

non nunquam basiare uolenti: the same ἔρως takes possession of the ass at 149, 27-150, 1 *non numquam ... pedes decoros puellae basiabam*, where it is left to the reader to decide whether the imperfect is to be taken in iterative or conative sense (see above comm. *ad loc*).

basiare ... sauiolis: on *sauium*, see also 2, 10 (33, 11); vdPaardt 1971, 111. The diminutive is used effectively in Catul. 99, 2 and 14. The cluster of Catullan reminiscences in these phrases is striking. For other reminiscences of Catullus in Apuleius see Gatscha 1898, 149 and Butler-Owen 1914, LXII.

adlubescebat: the iterative imperfect appears to cancel out the ingressive force of *-sc*, see Bernhard 1927, 134. Before Apuleius the verb occurs in Pl. *Mil.* 1004 (impersonally in the meaning *libido me mouet*). It does not reappear until Apul. *Met.* 2, 10 (33, 16) *adlibescenti* (a restoration for F *adliuescente*; see also 9, 3 (205, 3-4) *ac si ... aquis adlibescerem*) and disappears again to return later in Mart.

Cap., e.g. 1, 25; 1, 31; 2, 181.

quae res: possibly Lucius' expressed indignation hides his remembered jealousy, cf. 149, 27 f. We intend to include a note on his moralising tendencies in our comm. on 8, 29 (200, 22-26).

oppido: see vdPaardt 1971, 77 on the history of this word, which is a favourite with Apuleius: in the *Met.* it occurs thirteen, in the other works a total of sixteen times.

162, 27-30 'Hem oblita es nuptiarum tuique mutui cupitoris, puella uirgo, et illi nescio cui recenti marito, quem tibi parentes iunxerunt, hunc aduenam cruentumque percussorem praeponis?': "Hey! Have you forgotten your wedding and your beloved lover, you a virgin girl, and do you prefer this newly arrived, blood-stained killer, to the man – I don't know his name – you have just married and whom your parents have joined to you?"

Hem: an exclamation denoting surprise, indignation or grief. It occurs frequently in comedy, but afterward does not surface until Apuleius; cf. 1, 6 (5, 18); 5, 23 (121, 13); 9, 23 (220, 22); see Bernhard 1927, 129; Hofmann ³1951, 21 f.; Luck 1964, 33; Callebat 1968, 87. The transition to a direct expression of the ass's thoughts is not preceded by *mecum cogitabam* or a similar expression (as e.g. at 151, 17 f.); cf. Ter. *Hau.* 128 *ubi uideo haec coepi cogitare 'hem...'*; Sulp. Rufus *Fam.* 4, 5, 4 *coepi egomet mecum sic cogitare: 'hem...'*; however, see the first phrase of the next chapter.

mutui cupitoris: a *mutuus cupitor* is someone who *cupiens cupitur*; cf. 4, 26 (94, 25 f.) *sanctae caritatis adfectione mutuo mihi pigneratus*. Médan 1925, 343 notes the 'concision et resserrement du style'. Cornelissen's conjecture (1888, (49) 67) *miselli cupitoris* is unnecessary.

puella uirgo: *uirgo* denotes the bride's virginity, which is not contradicted by *nuptiarum*, for *nuptias non concubitus sed consensus facit* (Ulp. *Dig.* 50, 17, 30); see *GCA* 1977, 194. (On the other hand, the wedding ceremonies are repeated or completed, see below on 164, 14 f.) On the combination of *uirgo* with a noun see vdPaardt 1971, 205 f.; the combination *puella uirgo* occurs in Ps. Apul. *Herb.* 103 L 7 *puer aut puella uirgo semen coriandri ad femur sinistrum feminae parientis teneat*.

nescio cui: here in view of *illi* not in the sense of *alicui*, but used for *quem qui sit nescio*. The identity of the newcomer is as yet not known to the ass: narrating Lucius makes the experiencing ass underscore this fact, since reproaches to the girl would be groundless if the noble animal were aware of the facts. See Romberg 1962, 95 f.

recenti: accentuation of the reproach: married such a short time, already adulterous.

quem tibi parentes iunxerunt: Pricaeus recalls Catul. 62, 62 f. *uirginitas non tota tua est, ex parte parentum est / tertia pars patrist, pars est data tertia matri, / tertia sola tua est: noli pugnare duobus, / qui genero sua iura simul cum dote dederunt*. Instead of *quem tibi* one might have expected *cui te* (indeed this is how Vallette and the Italian translators interpret the text). The usual formula is *(ad-, con-) iungere puellam uiro*: cf. 5, 20 (119, 2 f.) *hominem te (sc. Psychen) iungemus homini. ThLL s. vv.* has many instances. Perhaps the variant employed here is due to perspective: the absent partner is married to the one present. The girl is placed in the center also at 163, 7 f. *sponsum puellae ipsius*, where *ipsum* might have been expected.

aduenam: in view of 8, 31 (202, 14) *aduenam istum asinum . . . iugula* and the fact that *percussorem* has a qualifier (*cruentumque*), we think that *aduenam* here is used as an adjective ("just arrived").

cruentumque percussorem: cruentus gives further emphasis. Apuleius seems to like the combination (perhaps partly because of the sound effect): 174, 11 f. *abactorem indubitatum cruentumque percussorem*; 8, 8 (183, 16) *percussoris cruentam dexteram*; 9, 37 (231, 15) *at ille cruentus . . . percussor*; without *cruentus* in the vicinity *percussor* occurs only once: 8, 9 (184, 7 f.) *nequissimum percussorem*. On 'Bloody Haemus' see Hijmans 1978, 407 f.

Nec te conscientia stimulat, sed adfectione calcata inter lanceas et 162, 30-31
gladios istos scortari tibi libet? "Does your conscience not prick you? Does it please you to trample love underfoot and to behave like a whore among these spears and swords?"

conscientia stimulat: the sigmatism is sharpened by the following *tenues*.

adfectione: Charite herself spoke 4, 26 (94, 25) of *sanctae caritatis affectione* between her and Tlepolemus.

calcata: cf. 5, 29 (126, 15) *ut . . . tuae parentis . . . praecepta calcares*; Ov. *Am.* 3, 11, 5 *uicimus et domitum pedibus calcamus Amorem.*

inter lanceas et gladios: Oudendorp notes: 'Nusquam auctor lanceas dat latronibus. Sed formularis videtur locutio.' *ThLL s.v. gladius* 2015, 44 f. has no instances of this or similar combinations. It is likely that the narrator, who is inclined to emphasize, exaggerates here. Blümner 1905, 32 proposes *lances*: clever but unnecessary.

scortari: the use of this verb (in Apuleius only here; the noun *scortatus* occurs 5, 28: 125, 15) according to Callebat 1968, 516 shows 'une recherche d'expressivité et d'intensité autorisée par les modèles comiques'. He refers to Pl. *As.* 270; Ter. *Hau.* 206, but in comedy the word is used only of men: Pl. *As.* 270 *quando mecum pariter potant, pariter scortari solent (sc. Libanius et familiaris filius)*; *Merc.* 985 *nam si istuc ius est, senecta aetate scortari senes, ubi locist res summa nostra publica*. It is striking that the word occurs usually in combination with *potiones*: Ps. 1134 *edunt, bibunt, scortantur*; Ter. *Ad.* 102 and elsewhere. It is in our passage that the word is first used of women (cf. Non. 193 L *lupari, ut scortari uel prostitui*), and the *potiones* are still present. Met. 8, 1 (177, 7) presents a similar combination in the description of Thrasyllus: *luxuriae popinalis scortisque et diurnis potationibus exercitatus.*

In addition there is a pun in *scortari . . . corio* (below) since *scortum = corium*, see also comm. on 165, 17-20.

Quid, si quo modo latrones ceteri persenserint? Non rursum recurres 163, 1-3
ad asinum et rursum exitium mihi parabis? Re uera ludis de alieno

corio': "Suppose the other robbers notice somehow! Won't you once again come running back to the ass and won't you once again contrive death for me? You are truly playing around – with someone else's skin'".

Quid: &etschenig's conjecture (1882, 158) *quod* tried to give *persenserint* an object. This is not necessary; moreover, the complex sentence would be less emotionally charged than the two simple ones.

persenserint: Hildebrand paraphrases 'persenserint quis esset ille latro et quomodo puella ei se praeberet', but the robbers are no more able to guess at Haemus' true identity through the girl's behaviour than the ass is. (The latter will draw the right conclusions later from the conversations he has overheard.) Therefore it is better to supply for the suppressed object '... that you are willing to be a *scortum*', '*gratum tibi esse scortari*'. The implication would then be that the intoxicated robbers would assault her en masse and that she would try to escape.

Non = *nonne* occurs not only in Plautus (e.g. *Men.* 505 *tuom parasitum non nouisti?*), but also in Caesar and Cicero. The question suggests an affirmative answer; see Callebat 1968, 112; LHSz 2, 462.

rursum recurres: redundant use of *rursum* (facilitated by the alliteration) also above 161, 5 *rursus ad asinum redire*; see Marg. Molt 1938, 24; vdPaardt 1971, 98. Kronenberg's conjecture *recurrent* ('fortasse recte' Robertson) is quite undesirable, because *rursum recurres ad asinum et rursum exitium mihi parabis* is a witty allusion to the original plan of the robbers mentioned in 153, 12.

If the robbers find out their new leader is a traitor, they will force the girl to seek her (= their) refuge with the ass, her helper as always cf. 153, 11 *uirginalis fugae sequestro ministroque* (and as a result they will perhaps once again flee together). This means death for the ass, whereafter the girl will be playing around, not for long, with his skin, cf. 153, 13 *totisque uacuefacto praecordiis per mediam aluum nudam uirginem, ..., insuere*.

ludis de alieno corio: for this proverbial expression see Otto 1890, 92, who notes Mart. 3, 16, 3 *ebrius es: neque enim faceres hoc sobrius umquam / ut uelles corio ludere, Cerdo, tuo*. Tertullian's note *Pall.* 3, 3 *hoc soli chamaeleonti datum quod uulgo dictum est, de corio suo ludere* seems comparable. But Oehler *ad loc.* remarks 'ludere de suo corio esset secure agere suo periculo, quod nihil ad rem. Infracta igitur proverbi vi ludit solummodo ipsis vocabulis eius "ludere" et "corio"'; see also Gerlo 1940, 80.

CHAPTER XII

Tlepolemus captures the robbers and takes his Charite home.

Dum ista sycophanta ego mecum maxima cum indignatione disputo, 163, 4-8
de uerbis eorum quibusdam dubiis, sed non obscuris prudenti asino
cognosco non Haemum illum praedonem famosum, sed Tlepolemum
sponsum puellae ipsius: "While I, like the slanderer I was, debated these
things within me with the greatest indignation, I learnt from some of their
utterances – which, though ambiguous, were not obscure to a sensible ass – that he
was not the famous robber Haemus, but Tlepolemus, the fiancé of the girl
herself".

sycophanta: Bernhard 1927, 144 lists the word under the 'grecisms' occurring
'schon in Altlatein'. Apuleius uses it here only. The narrating I judges the
experiencing I with unnecessary severity: he is not really an accuser since
(perforce) he keeps his thoughts to himself, and his accusation is not deliberately
false, but merely unfounded.

de ... cognosco: the preposition has an 'instrumental' sense here: see Callebat
1968, 203; vdPaardt 1971, 154; in the instances mentioned by *ThLL s.v. cognoscere (de)* 1512, 8-14 *de* always means 'concerning', but *ibid.* 1511, 52-57 (*s.v. cognoscere ex*) our passage is mentioned as well as Vulg. *Psalm.* 118 (119), 152
initio cognoui de testimoniis tuis (ἔργων ἐκ) *quia* e.q.s.; Cassiod. *Var.* 4, 45
quatenus prouinciam se deseruisse ieiunam de copiae inuentione cognoscant
(Mommsen notes in the *app. crit.* on the latter passage: *de* om. EF). See also 8, 31
(202, 18) *de mea morte*.

dubiis: Lucius apologetically explains why he took so long to see through
Tlepolemus' disguise.

non obscuris: in view of the contrast with *dubiis* and the addition *prudenti asino*,
not a litotes as Strilciw 1925, 109 thinks.

prudenti asino: according to Junghanns 1932, 63 n. 91 an 'Anspielung auf die
gewöhnliche Eselsdummheit'; see also 4, 6 (78, 21 f.) and *GCA* 1977, 57. It should
be noted, however, that the ass is not usually symbolic of stupidity in Antiquity;
see e.g. Heine 1962, 302 n. 1; Scobie 1975, 26 f.; Tatum 1979, 47.

Haemum illum praedonem famosum, sed Tlepolemum: the ass quotes Haemus'
words (158, 11) though in a different order. Hijmans in *AAGA* 1978, 116
discusses the question how far Tlepolemus lives up to his adopted name; see also
Hijmans 1978, 407-414. The narrator gives a clear indication in the next few lines
how he knows Charite's name, but leaves it to the reader to conclude that he must
have learnt the real name of 'Haemus' in a similar way.

sponsum puellae ipsius: since the wedding ceremonies were not completed,
because of the robbers' intrusion, Tlepolemus is correctly named *sponsus*; that
Charite calls him *maritum meum* at 4, 27 (96, 2) is an understandable prolepsis on

her part; the legally not entirely correct label *recenti marito* at 162, 28 is due to the ass's indignation.

For the enallage of *ipsius* (adopted in our translation) see the note on 162, 28 f. *in fine*; see also Rothstein on Prop. 1, 12, 14 and LHSz 2, 159; Bernhard 1927, 243 still notes hiatus in the clausula, see however e.g. Fraenkel 1968, 29.

163, 8-11 Nam procedente sermone paulo iam c‹l›arius contempta mea praesentia quasi uere mortui: 'Bono animo es', inquit. 'Charite dulcissima; nam totos istos hostes tuos statim captiuos habebis': "For in the course of the conversation he said, quite loudly now, ignoring my presence as though I were really dead: 'Courage, dearest Charite; all those enemies of yours will soon be your captives'".

clarius: F has *carius*, but Beroaldus' conjecture is generally adopted. It may seem attractive to take *carius* with *inquit* (*contempta ... praesentia* would thus be tinged with irony,), but *ThLL* seems to offer no parallel for the combination.

As a curiosity, we mention Stewech's conjecture *hilarius* which he combines with the reading *quieuere mortui* of S (Audomarensis siue Bertianus s. XV) and a few 15th and 16th c. editions. The proposed sense is 'already a little more cheerfully they cuddled each other to death'; Stewech himself paraphrases 'tandem audentius se mutuo amplexos'; Hildebrand rightly remarks 'Quam parum hoc loco sufficiat, bene quisque intelligit'.

quasi uere mortui: this is the correction in ς for *quę siuere* (F) and *q̄siere* (φ). Conjectures such as *bruti* (Bursian 1881, 133) or *mori* (Plasberg coll. 10, 13: 246. 23 *nec enim tam stultus eram tamque uere asinus*) for *mortui*, and *quasi e re surdi* (Blümner 1896, 250 meaning 'wie von einem der der Natur der Sache nach nichts hört') are not very attractive for palaeographical reasons.

The ς reading is defended by Hildebrand, who remarks: 'Asinus autem *quasi vere mortuum* se nominat, quod nunc vere se mortuum esse putavit, quod Tlepolemus et Charite tam aperte agerent, et facile suspicionem latronibus ferre possent'. This explanation refers to a decision still to be taken by the robbers; most translators smuggle *iam* into their translations (e.g. Helm-Krenkel "als ob ich schon wirklich tot wäre") – apparently taking the phrase as a reference to the proposals of 6, 31 f. – or neglect *uere*. None of these solutions is entirely satisfactory.

It is however quite possible to take *quasi uere mortui* as a reference on the part of Lucius to his situation as an ass. The lovers do not even treat him as an exceptional case among asses and as a human he might as well be dead. Lucius knows that he is 'dead' as a human, but he is alive as a rational being. See the narrator's proud remark at 4, 6 (78, 21) *faxo uos quoque an mente etiam sensuque fuerim asinus, sedulo sentiatis*. Note the syntactic variation *mea* (abl.) – *mortui* (gen.): a similar construction is found at 8, 23 (195, 11) *ab emptione mea utpote ferocissimi*, see Callebat 1968, 337 and our comm. *ad loc*.

Finally we should note that the entire situation is narrated from the point of view of the ass as the narrator remembers it. Objectively speaking Tlepolemus and Charite would quite naturally ignore the presence of the ass. The humour of the situation lies precisely in the implicit tension the author evokes between the points of view of the ego-narrative and the critical reader.

bono animo es: the *anus* (4, 27: 96, 5 f.) used almost the same words to Charite; Lucius has twice been so addressed by Fotis (2, 10: 33, 18; 3, 23: 69, 21). This form of encouragement occurs in Pl.*Cist.* 73, *Mil.* 1342 (cf. 1206), *Rud.* 680. Merkelbach 1962, 75 n. 5 sees in these words a reference to the mysteries; see Gwyn Griffiths in *AAGA* 1978, 149 f.

Charite: the girl's name occurs here for the first time in the *Met.* It is a curious name occurring neither in Pape-Benseler 2, 1884, 1673, which has the women's names Χαρίτιν (*i.e.* Χαρίτιον), Χαριτώ, Χαριτῶσα and the men's names Χαρίτης, Χαρίτιος, Χαρίτων, nor in Bechtel 1917 (1964). Cf. Valpy *ad loc.*: 'A Graeco Χάρις, Gratia'; thus also vFranz 1970, IV 14. This Gratia is fetched from the cave not by Hermes but by Haemus. For the significance of the name see also Hijmans in *AAGA* 1978, 116.

totos istos hostes tuos statim: emphatic *t/s* repetition: *t* and *s* seven times each uninterrupted by other consonants over ten syllables.

et instanti‹a› ualidiore uinum iam inmixtum, sed modico tepefactum 163, 11-14
uapore sauciis illis et crapula uinulentiaque madidis ipse abstemius non cessat inpingere: "and, with increasing insistence, he never stopped forcing wine, now unmixed but slightly warmed, upon those fuddled men, sodden with booziness and wine-bibbing – but he himself stayed sober".

instantia: F and φ read *instanti*, the correction is made in ς.

ualidiore: the comparative refers to the activity described in 162, 21 (*ingurgitat*).

inmixtum: *ThLL* gives only four instances of the use of this word: this passage, Auson. *Epigr.*, 12 (p. 304 Prete) and Boeth. (*in Porph. comm. pr.* 2, 25; *sec.* 3, 3). The usual expression for "unmixed wine" is *merum*, see Médan 1925, 150. It is remarkable that *inmixtus* in this sense and *immiscere* (next sentence) are found so close together. The robbers offer a libation of unmixed wine at 4, 22 (91, 10), see *GCA* 1977, 166.

modico tepefactum uapore: since wine was usually mixed with tepid or warm water, the unmixed wine has to be warmed so as to avoid suspicion; see Vallette *ad loc.* n. 1. Representations of *caldaria* and *crateres* may be found in Paoli 1948, plates XLIII and XLIV; cf. also Charleston 1955, pl. 4a, 5a.

sausiis: the same transferred use of *saucius* "befuddled" is found in 9, 5 (206, 18 f.) *quanto me felicior Daphne uicina, quae mero et prandio matutino saucia cum suis adulteris uolutatur*; cf. Mart. 3, 68, 5 f. *hinc iam deposito post uina rosasque pudore / quid dicat nescit saucia Terpsichore*; Iust. 1, 8, 8 *Cyrus... saucios per noctem opprimit... Scythas*; id. 24, 8, 1 *Galli... hesterno mero saucii*. See Callebat 1968, 81.

crapula uinulentiaque: *ThLL s.v. crapula 1098, 42* lists *uinolentia* among the synonyms of *crapula*.

uinulentiaque is the reading in F; φ changes the spelling to *uinolentia*; see also 1, 11 (10, 15) *uinolentia*; but *Apol.* 59 (67, 16) *uinulentum*.

madidis: the transferred use of *madidus* occurs from Plautus onwards: *Am.* 1001 *faciam ut sit madidus sobrius*; cf. *Met.* 2, 31 (50, 21) *conpotores uino madidi*.

abstemius: Quint. *Inst.* 1, 7, 9 *abstemius ... ex abstinentia temeti composita uox est*; cf. Ernout-Meillet 1951, 1200 *s.v. temetum* (from **temum* 'boisson énivrante et stupéfiante, ou plutôt une plante'), who argue that *abstemius* is archaic and post-classical.

inpingere: cf. Cic. *Tusc.* 3, 44 *huic calix mulsi impingendus est*; Sen. *Ep.* 119, 6: *propter illas (diuitias) nulli uenenum filius ... impegit?*; for the combination *sauciis ... impingere* cf. Aug. *Serm.* coll. Morin p. 309, 6.

163, 14-16 Et hercules suspicionem mihi fecit, quasi soporiferum quoddam uenenum cantharis immisceret illis: "And bless me if he didn't make me suspect that he was mixing a soporific into their cups".

hercules: see vdPaardt 1971, 48 f. on the *sermo cotidianus* character of the interjection.

quasi: without comparative force; cf. Suet. *Tit.* 5, 3 *unde nata suspicio est quasi ... temptasset*; see Mooney *ad loc.*; KSt 2, 456; Callebat 1968, 337.

soporiferum: a poetic word that is found for the first time in Verg. *A.* 4, 486 *soporiferumque papauer*; see Pease *ad loc.* on the appropriateness of the word in that context.

cantharis: the word is borrowed from the Greek and occurs frequently in Plautus; see Callebat 1968, 61 for parallels. A representation of an earthenware *cantharus* (or *scyphus*) may be found in e.g. Charleston, 1955, plate C facing p. 24.

illis: we take the word as a dative of disadvantage; to take it with *cantharis* is barely possible.

163, 16-17 Cuncti denique, sed prorsus omnes uino sepulti iacebant, omnes parati morti: "Finally they were all, but absolutely all lying there buried in wine, all of them ready for death".

Cuncti denique, sed prorsus omnes: for the reinforcing use of *sed* cf. 10, 22 (254, 3) *totum me, sed prorsus totum recepit* (F has *prorsus sed*, Frassinetti adopts Scriverius' transposition, Robertson notes 'fortasse recte'); Plin. *Ep.* 1, 5, 8 *rogo mane uideas Plinium domi, sed plane mane*. See Bernhard 1927, 125; LHSz 2, 487; Callebat 1968, 91.

uino sepulti iacebant: with a slight variation the robbers share the fate of their late leader Lamachus, who *nunc iacet ... elemento toto sepultus* (4, 11: 83, 7). *uino sepulti* is a poetic expression which is first found in Verg. *A.* 2, 265 *urbem somno uinoque sepultam*. Austin *ad loc.* refers to Bowra *CQ* 23 (1929) 71 for the history of the expression; cf. 8, 11 (186, 4) *sepeliuit ad somnum* and our forthcoming comm. *ad loc.* Cf. Enn. *Ann.* 292 *nunc hostes uino domiti somnoque sepulti*, imitated by Lucr. 1, 133 and 5, 975.

omnes parati morti: for a full discussion of the textual and interpretative problem presented by this phrase see Appendix II.

163, 17-20 Tunc nullo negotio artissimis uinculis impeditis ac pro arbitrio suo constrictis illis, imposita dorso meo puella, dirigit gressum ad suam patriam: "Next, without any trouble he fettered them with the tightest possible bonds and thus constrained them as he pleased, put the girl on my back and turned his steps to his paternal city".

nullo negotio: "without any trouble"; cf. Nep. *Ag.* 5, 4 *sine negotio, cum uoluerint, nos oppriment*; Sen. *Ben.* 5, 12, 2 *(solutio) quae illi qui implicuit sine ullo negotio paret*.

dirigit gressum: Gatscha 1898, 147 cites Verg. *A.* 5, 162 and 11, 855 *huc dirige gressum* and 6, 194 *cursum... dirigite*. Vallette's translation "dirigea *nos* pas" ignores the formulaic character of the phrase. The combination with *ad patriam suam* (not e.g. *domum suam*) makes for a solemnity all the more striking after the humdrum *imposita dorso meo puella*.

CHAPTER XIII

Triumphal return of Charite and her liberators. Death of the robbers.

163, 21-22 **Quam simul accessimus, tota ciuitas ad uotiuum conspectum effunditur**: "As soon as we reached it, the entire population came rushing out to see the sight they had prayed for".

simul: on *simul* as a conjunction see Callebat 1968, 432 f.

tota ciuitas... effunditur: Pricaeus recalls among other instances how the entire Roman population came rushing out to welcome Vespasian after the capture of Jerusalem, Jos. *B.J.* 7, 69 – *si parua licet componere magnis*! Cf. also 3, 2 (53, 1 f.) *statim ciuitas omnis in publicum effusa mira densitate nos insequitur*. Walsh 1970, 58 n. 3 notes Liv. 31, 14, 12 *ciuitas omnis (sc. Atheniensis) obuiam effusa cum coniugibus ac liberis, sacerdotibus cum ignibus intrantem (sc. Attalum regem) urbem ac di prope ipsi exciti sedibus suis acceperunt*.

uotiuum: Apuleius appears to be the first author to use this word in the sense of *quod erat in uotis*, cf. 8, 30 (201, 22) *uotiuo hospitio* (see comm. *ad loc.*). The usual meaning before Apul. is "dedicated". See Médan 1925, 155; Callebat 1968, 154.

163, 22-23 **Procurrunt parentes, affines, clientes, alumni, famuli laeti faciem, gaudio delibuti**: "Parents, kinsmen, clients, protegees, slaves, with glad faces and glowing with joy, came running out".

Procurrunt: both the historic present and the position of the verb increase the dramatic character of the narrative; see Bernhard 1927, 12; Chausserie Laprée 1969, 347 f.

parentes, affines, clientes, alumni, famuli laeti: twice a triple homoeoteleuton, in *-es* and in *-i*: assonance of *a, i, u*.

parentes: in view of 164, 2 it seems more plausible to take the word as "parents" than as "kinsmen" in general.

alumni: 'vernae qui domi aluntur' (Valpy *ad loc.*)

Those who come running out are apparently listed in decreasing order of intimacy.

gaudio delibuti: the same expression is found at 11, 17 (280, 2 f.); cf. 10, 17 (249, 23) *delibutus gaudio*; 3, 10 (59, 14) *laetitia delibuti*; see vdPaardt 1971, 83.

163, 23-26 **Pompam cerneres omnis sexus et omnis aetatis nouumque et hercules memorandum spectamen, uirginem asino triumphantem**: "You might have seen a procession of both sexes and all ages and a new and, by heaven, memorable spectacle: a maiden riding in triumph on an ass".

pompam cerneres: for this rhetorical turn of phrase see Lausberg ²1963 para.

813 f.; Curtius ³1961, 441. The latter notes Macrobius, *Sat.* 5, 14, 9 f. on the epic mode of address, as at e.g. Verg. *A.* 4, 401 *migrantis cernas totaque ex urbe ruentis.* Cf. Pease *ad loc.*; also 4, 14 (85, 13) and in particular 8, 17 (190, 19) *cerneres non tam hercules memorandum quam miserandum etiam spectaculum.* The effectiveness of the 'tableau' technique used by Apuleius consists in the way it involves the actual reader in the narrated events through the appeal to the explicit or addressed reader. (On implicit and explicit reader see the literature mentioned by vdPaardt, *AAGA* 1978, 89 n. 31; add Iser 1972.) Cf. H. and K. Vretska on Cic. *Pro Arch.* 8 (1979, 103): 'Gesehenes galt, weil der Mensch dabei gewesen sein muss, als wahrheitssicherer als Gehörtes'. On this type of scenic presentation see also e.g. Junghanns 1932, 52 n. 75.

pompam: note the striking parallel with Psyche's marriage; Psyche, too, is the center of a *pompa populi prosequentis sese* (4, 35: 102, 16) when on her way to 'real marriage' (coming together with her husband: 5, 4: 106, 1). Because of her husband's absence only the legally required wedding ceremonies can be performed (4, 34: 101, 18-19).

omnis sexus et omnis aetatis: cf. Tac. *Ann.* 4, 62 *affluxere auidi talium ... uirile ac muliebre secus, omnis aetas*; the repetition of *omnis* gives the word a strong rhetorical emphasis; the combination of the two nouns is also found Sen. *Oed.* 53 *sed omnis aetas pariter et sexus ruit.*

hercules: on the use of the interjection see Heine 1962, 176 and *GCA* 1977, 175 f. See also above on 163, 14.

nouumque et ... memorandum spectamen: virgin riding an ass, the symbol of unbridled sexuality; see our note on 151, 4-8. If one interprets the novel as a unity of which the subjection to Isis is the climax, this striking image may be seen as an anticipation of Isis subjugating the *uoluptates.*

uirginem asino triumphantem: the *pompa* accompanying Charite vaguely evokes a *paruus triumphus* or *ouatio*; see Serv. on Verg. *A.* 4, 543: ... *proprie ouatio est minor triumphus, qui enim ouationem meretur, et uno equo utitur et a plebeis, uel ab equitibus Romanis deducitur ad Capitolium et de ouibus sacrificat* (objections to this etymology in Ernout-Meillet 1951, *s.v. ouo*); *qui autem triumphat, albis equis utitur quattuor et senatu praeeunte in Capitolio de tauris sacrificat.* Cf. Versnel 1970, 165 f. Massé 1934 detects an allusion to the flight of the Holy Virgin to Egypt (*Matth.* 2, 13 f.). Herrmann 1953, 189 objects that the words *nouum ... spectamen* make it clear that 'l'auteur n'a nullement l'intention de rappeler un précédent, quel qu'il soit' (confusing author and narrator); Ferguson 1961, 7 thinks that we have here a parody of the story of Palm Sunday in *Matth.* 21, 6-9; *John* 12, 12-15; see also Gaselee 1935, 319 n. 1. Concerning Apuleius and Christianity see Walsh 1970, 186 f., Griffiths 1975, 359, *AAGA* 1978, 153. For the symbolic meaning of the ass in the New Testament see Vogel 1973, 292.

Denique ipse etiam hilarior pro uirili parte, ne praesenti negotio ut 163, 26-164, 2
alienus discreparem, porrectis auribus proflatisque naribus rudiui
fortiter, immo tonanti clamore personui: "Finally, I myself was even
more pleased and, so as not to seem uninvolved and out of tune with the present
business, I pricked up my ears, flared my nostrils and manfully brayed with all

my strength – nay, rather sounded forth with the noise of thunder".

hilarior: the comparative may indicate that the ass's joy is but relative to the occasion. At 165, 9 the more positive expression *gaudens laetusque* is used in a situation in which the ass is looking forward to certain immediate pleasures (including perhaps, some roses); true and unalloyed joy is reserved for the last book, cf. 11, 14 (276, 18).

pro uirili parte: Vallette 1956, 17 n. 2 draws the attention to the humour of this expression in this situation, where we have an *asinus* rather than a *uir*. The connection with the verbs *rudiui* and *personui* produces an ἀπροσδόκητον that is the more striking after the strong hyperbaton, see also Callebat 1968, 470. Summers 1967, 252 on the present passage is irrelevant, since no inheritance is involved.

discreparem: literal and figurative meanings are combined in an ironic mixture: the noise of a braying ass is hardly melodious (see also above on 156, 11).

proflatisque naribus: the ordinary meaning of *proflare* is "to blow out", "to emit air", here "to puff out, blow up". The Thesaurus material at Munich appears to offer no precise parallels.

164, 2-5 Et illam thalamo receptam commode parentes sui fouebant, me uero cum ingenti iumentorum ciuiumque multitudine confestim retro Tlepolemus agebat non inuitum: "As for the girl, she was taken to her room and surrounded with care by her parents; as for me, Tlepolemus took me back immediately together with a large multitude of beasts of burden and townsfolk – by no means against my inclination".

commode: Don. *ad* Ter. *Hec.* 95: *commode pro blande et bene*.

parentes sui: the possessive pronoun is added to indicate intimacy; cf. 174, 15 *puerum illum parentes sui ... querebantur*; see LHSz 2, 175; Callebat 1968, 257.

ciuiumque is the reading of φ, F has *ouiumque*, though the ms. seems earlier to have had *ciuiumque*: the beginning of the word has been tampered with. We have here one of the instances in which φ rather than F preserves the correct reading, see Helm. Praef. *Fl.* xxxi.

retro: back to the robbers' den; there is an erasure after *o*: probably *p* (according to Helm *p* or *t*) has been erased after having been crossed out; for Lütjohann (1873, 466) this was sufficient reason for the conjecture *retrorsus* (cf. 4, 3: 76, 24 and 9, 10: 210, 9) or *retrorsum* (cf. 6, 3: 130, 26 and 6, 30: 152, 4); but since only one letter has been erased and Apuleius uses *retro* several times (3, 6: 56, 11; 4, 33: 101, 6; 6, 8: 133, 20; 9, 39: 232, 27) no change is necessary.

me ... non inuitum: hyperbaton and litotes, see Strilciw 1925, 110. One may be inclined to take *non inuitum* functionally, since it is reasonable that the ass should still be troubled by the injuries to his right leg and left hoof – they have been sustained this same day; see 147, 19 and 152, 6, but an explicit reason is given in the following sentence.

164, 5-6 Nam et alias curiosus et tunc latronum captiuitatis spectator optabam fieri: "For being inquisitive even at other times, on this occasion, too, I longed to be a witness of the capture of the robbers".

nam et alias curiosus et tunc ...: Rohde 1885, 103 f. wishes to read *[et] tunc* or, preferably, *curiosus ‹eram›* on the grounds that *et alias curiosus* demands a second adjective or participle. Médan 1925, 23 supposes that there is an ellipsis of an indicative form of *esse*. It is better to assume 'ellipsis' of a participle; in that case *et ... et* is not to be taken in the sense of "both ... and", but serves to give particular emphasis (in the meaning "also") to *alias* and *tunc*.

curiosus: the large literature on *curiositas* and the importance of this motif in the *Met.* is mentioned in Scobie 1975, 81 f. See also the extensive discussion in Gwyn Griffiths 1975, 248 f.

latronum captiuitatis spectator ... fieri: more picturesque than *latrones captiuos* (cf. Médan 1925, 317) *spectare*. In fact the expectations of the ass will be surpassed: the robbers will soon be executed.

Quos quidem colligatos adhuc uino magis quam uinculis deprehendimus: "We found them still shackled more by the wine than by their bonds". 164, 6-7

adhuc: translators appear to be divided on the question whether to take *adhuc* with *colligatos* or with *magis*. Since Apuleius nowhere else in the *Met.* combines *adhuc* with a comparative, it is preferable to take it with *colligatos*.

Totis ergo prolatis erutisque rebus et nobis auro argentoque et ceteris onustis ipsos partim constrictos, uti fuerant, prouolutosque in proximas rupinas praecipites dedere, alios uero suis sibi gladiis obtruncatos reli[n]quere: "So they unearthed everything and brought it out and loaded us with the gold and silver and the rest of the stuff. As for the men, part they rolled along, shackled as they were, and threw headlong into the nearby gorges, others they left slaughtered with their own swords". 164, 7-11

totis = omnibus, see comm. on 153, 12-16.

prolatis erutisque: hysteron proteron.

auro argentoque et ceteris: Bernhard 1927, 82 f. offers numerous instances of *-que et*.

partim ... alios: Bernhard 1927, 95 classifies the *variatio* in these words under the heading anantapodoton.

uti fuerant: it is possible that we have an instance of pluperfect for imperfect, see vdPaardt 1971, 54 (who does not cite our passage). This seems the more likely interpretation, but it is also possible to take the pluperfect in its basic sense to indicate the situation as it had been when the robbers were left to themselves (163, 18 f.); if so, the translation must be "shackled as before".

rupinas: F has *rapinas*, the emendation occurs in ς. In 148, 14 the same combination is found but in reverse order: *rupinas proximas*.

praecipites dedere: cf. 4, 5 (78, 7 f.) (*latrones alterum asinum*) *per altissimum praeceps in uallem proximam etiam nunc spirantem praecipitant*, where the same effective use of sounds (in particular *p* and *r*) is found. Apuleius carefully distinguishes between those activities in which the ass shares, and those in which he cannot share: *deprehendimus* (7), *praecipites dedere* (10), *reliquere* (11), *reueni-*

mus (12), *commisere* (13), *tradidere* (14). Strilciw 1925, 112 notes the 'homoioteleuton quattuor membrorum' (*-ēre*) and compares 5, 6 (107, 18 f.) *adnuat, uideat, mulceat, conferat.*

praecipites dedere ... obtruncatos reliquere: on the legal aspects of this instance of self-help justice see Summers 1967, 252 f. The robbers are treated exactly as the ass thought they would treat him (148, 14), cf. the way they dispose of the *anus* after she has hanged herself (152, 15 f.); see *GCA* 1977, 138.

suis sibi gladios obtruncatos: cf. 8, 14 (187, 22) (*Charite*) *in suo sibi sanguine peruoluta*; on *suus sibi* see Marg. Molt 1938, 55; Callebat 1968, 158; LHSz 2, 94; Scobie 1975, 93, who notes another eight instances in the *Met.*

164, 12 Tali uindicta laeti et gaudentes ciuitatem reuenimus: "Delighted by and rejoicing in such a fine revenge, we returned to the city".

laeti et gaudentes: for the combination of two synonymous notions see Médan 1925, 363; Bernhard 1927, 166; LHSz 2, 789; vdPaardt 1971, 70.

ciuitatem: for the accusative of direction without *in* see Armini 1928, 287; Marg. Molt 1938, 49; LHSz 2, 49.

164, 13-14 Et illas quidem diuitias publicae custodelae commisere, Tlepolemo puellam repetitam lege tradidere: "The treasure they handed into public custody; to Tlepolemus they gave legal possession of the bride he had regained".

publicae custodelae: F reads *publica custodela*, ς offers and Oudendorp proposes *publicae custodelae*; modern editors agree, and indeed that reading is preferable to conjectures like *in publicam custodelam* (Bursian) or *publica custodela custodiendas* (Castiglioni).

custodela: abstract "custody", see Gaius *Inst.* 2, 104 *pecuniamque tuam endo ... custodela mea esse aio.*

Tlepolemo: Plasberg thought it necessary to add «uero», but the asyndetic construction is typical of Apuleius; see vdPaardt 1971, 44.

lege tradidere: after the rude interruption of the wedding ceremony earlier (4, 26: 95, 8 f.), now all the formal requirements for the marriage can be fulfilled, e.g. the *deductio in domum mariti*; see Summers 1967, 254; *GCA* 1977, 200.

CHAPTER XIV

Praise for the ass; a meeting of an Awards Committee.

Exin me ‹su› um sospitatorem nuncupatum matrona prolixe curita- 164, 14-18
bat ipsoque nuptiarum die praesepium meum ordeo passim repleri
iubet fae[mi]numque camelo Bactrinae sufficiens apponi: "From then
onwards the lady, who called me her saviour, looked after me lavishly and on the
actual wedding day ordered my manger to be filled from end to end with barley
and enough hay to be served up for a Bactrian camel".

me ‹su›um sospitatorem nuncupatum: a persuasive and generally accepted emendation by Beroaldus of *meum sospitatorem e.q.s.* (F). Helm deals with Hildebrand's *memet sospitatorem* by showing that in the *Met. memet* is always used as a reflexive. Before we accept Beroaldus' conjecture, however, the ms. reading must be shown to be impossible. Could the *matrona* have been quoted directly: *Exin 'meum sospitatorem' nuncupatum e.q.s.*? The absence of *me* cannot count as an objection (for ellipsis of the personal pronoun in the acc. see Bernhard 1927, 160) and it would be a direct quotation of 150, 16 f. *te meum sospitatorem cotidie saginabo*. However, no instances of just this type of direct quotation come to mind; Beroaldus' proposal presupposes a simple corruption (a type of haplography) and it is to be preferred to such emendations as *me[um]* or *[me]‹su›um*, both of which imply a slightly more complex process of corruption.

matrona: we may hesitate between "the newly-wed matron", cf. Luc. 2, 358 *matrona ... translata uitat contingere limina planta*, and "the lady-of-rank", cf. 2, 2 (25, 15) and *GCA* 1977, 175. See also Liv. 10, 23, 10 *nec matronis solum, sed omnis ordinis feminis*. The latter sense is insufficiently represented in *OLD*, which gives only Fro. *Aur.* 1, 232 and 1, 244 (= 83, 19 vdH.): in both passages the word refers to a little princess. In our case the second sense may seem preferable, since the wedding is mentioned after the word *matrona* has been used. However, *ipsoque ... die ... iubet* is explicative with *curitabat* rather than a chronological element of the process.

prolixe: see for the spatial element of the etymology vdPaardt 1971, 179. Cf. e.g. 4, 2 (75, 24) where *OLD* interprets "wide-spread". Here the sense is a more abstract "lavishly", "generously", cf. e.g. 9, 11 (211, 1) *nouus dominus loca lautia prolixe praebuit*.

curitabat: Oudendorp *ad loc.* notes that he prefers this reading 'cum Schikerado, Lipsio etc.'; *qritatabat* F (the second *ta* redone by a later hand). Helm reports *qrutatabat*; see however Robertson and Frassinetti. The emendation is supported by *curuta* in the margin (first hand) and *curutabat* φ; it produces a hapax not just for Apuleius but for all authors in *ThLL*, but all editors accept the word. The formation of iterative forms in *-itare* (type *clamitare, rogitare*) is discussed in

169

LHSz 1, 548. For the spelling *qurare* for *curare* see *ThLL s.v. curo* 1496, 47 f.

curitabat... iubet: Bernhard 1927, 153 lists the change of tense under *variatio*, which is not very helpful: the imperfect denotes the continuing activity, the present the single command on a particular day; see Callebat 1968, 428. Of course the effect of the juxtaposition of these tenses is also one of liveliness. See below 164, 19 on *inprecer*.

ipso... die: the ass graciously appreciates the attention he receives, but which he doubtless feels is his due. The description of this second wedding day (cf. 4, 26, where the kidnapped girl gives an account of her disrupted wedding) differs from that of the first in accordance with the differing points of view of the narrators. See also below on 164, 22 *recens nupta*.

praesepium: *OLD* does not admit the meaning "manger". Yet at e.g. 175, 6 "manger" is more likely than "stall" (cf. Xen. *Eq.* 5, 1 where a horse is tied to a φάτνη; cf. Vulg. *Luc.* 2, 12 *inuenietis infantem pannis inuolutum et positum in praesepio*. For the sense of "stall" see e.g. Col. 6, 2, 3). The word is not a neologism as Médan 1925, 137 thinks; see e.g. Var. *R.* 1, 13, 6; Plin. *Nat.* 8, 29; Callebat 1968, 49 speaks of 'réalisme familier'. The precise shape of a *praesepe* (the more common form of the word) is hard to establish. See Daremberg et Saglio *s.v. stabulum* 1448; possibly an elongated structure along the wall of a courtyard would fit *passim*.

passim: Blümner 1905, 32 tried to solve the difficulty of reconciling *passim* with the usual shape of a manger by proposing *fartim*; cf. his solution for 3, 28 (72, 29) proposed 1896, 346. See vdPaardt 1971, 198 f. *ad loc*.

faenumque: *feminumque* F is corrected in ç. Did the mistake originate in a misread grammatical comment on *camelo*? (Cf. e.g. *De dub. nom. gramm.* 5, 576, 6: *cameli genere feminino dicendum*.) *ThLL* s.v. *camelus* 201, 63 f. lists the passages in which the word is feminine.

camelo Bactrinae sufficiens: the expression is apt, since camels were known in antiquity for their ability to go without water (e.g. Plin. *Nat.* 8, 68) or food (e.g. Hil. *in Matth.* 19, 11 *ieiunii inpatiens est*), and the ass, little though he knows it, will soon be on a meager diet; see below 165, 24 f. A similar hyperbolic qualification occurs 167, 17. For the κάμηλος Βακτριανός see Arist. *HA* 498 b 4 f.; 499 a 14 f.; Plin. *Nat.* 8, 67. The Bactrian camel has two humps, the Arabian camel has one. See also *RE* 10, 1824, 28 f. Junghanns 1932, 16 n. 15 notes Apuleius' tendency to precision. Cf. *Onos* 27, 1 ὄνος καὶ καμήλῳ ἱκανός. Junghanns' explanation is preferable to Bétolaud's who sees in the expression a mere display of irrelevant erudition (1, 465). See also above on 152, 13 and below on 172, 11.

164, 18-21 Sed quas ego condignas Fotidi diras deuotiones inprecer, quae me formauit non canem sed asinum, quippe cum uiderem largissimae cenae reliquiis rapinisque canes omnes inescatos atque distentos: "But what dire imprecations am I to utter to fit Fotis, who shaped me into not a dog but an ass, particularly since I saw all the dogs gorged and distended with the left-overs and stolen scraps from the enormous banquet".

condignas: one of the many words that occur in Plautus (*Amph.* 537-538; *Mil.*

505, cf. Desertine 1898, 13) and do not reappear until the second cent. A.D. The construction with *Fotidi* is supported by *Met.* 10, 12 (245, 27) *prouidentiae diuinae condignum accepit exitum*. ThLL s.v. 141, 38 cites several instances, e.g. Tert. *Cult. fem.* 2, 9. For the usual construction with abl. see LHSz 2, 128. Here *Fotidi* has to be taken ἀπὸ κοινοῦ with *condignas* and *inprecer*.

Fotidi: similar reminiscences of Fotis occur in 9, 15 (214, 15 f.) and 11, 20 (282, 4 f.); they seem to constitute little more than a reminder of the metamorphosis, but it is remarkable that the author keeps this character before us, whereas so many minor characters are dropped the moment their role has been played. See Vallette 1940, xxv f.; Heine 1962, 159. For Fotis' role and the importance of 3, 24 in the structure of the *Met.* see Heine in *AAGA* 1978, 28.

diras deuotiones: Leo deletes *deuotiones* (his reasons remained unpublished). *Dirae* by itself can have the sense of curses (as in the *Dirae* of the Vergilian Appendix), but it may also refer to ominous signs as e.g. in Cic. *Div.* 1, 29 *Etenim dirae, sicut cetera auspicia ut omina ut signa, non causas adferunt cur quid eueniat, sed nuntiant euentura nisi prouideris*. The passage in Cicero refers to the *dirarum obnuntiatio* by Ateius against Crassus, when the latter set out on his campaign against the Parthians. For a full discussion of the episode and its magic implication see Pease *ad loc.* and Flacelière-Chambry on Plut. *Crass.* 16, 6.

However, there is no reason to suspect *deuotiones*: Apuleius uses it on more than one occasion in the sense of "imprecations". See Marg. Molt on 1, 10 (9, 17): 'carminibus, quibus quis dis inferis vovetur'. See also 9, 23 (220, 12) *tunc uxor egregia diras deuotiones in eum deprecata. In bonam partem*: 11, 16 (279, 7) *deuotionibus faustis*. Also comparable is 2, 22 (43, 18) *diris cantaminibus*; Aug. *c. Faust.* 14, 1 *Christum ... diro deuotionis conuicio lacessiuit*. On the magic see Scobie 1975, 101 f. (on 1, 10: 9, 17). Somewhat different the passage in 2, 29 (49, 6) *an non putas deuotionibus meis posse Diras inuocari* (Zatchlas is threatening the reluctant corpse).

inprecer: Robertson prefers an imperfect subj. but, with the exception of Augello 1977, 169 (who compares the ind. imperf. κατηρώμην in *Onos* 27, 3: it is not clear how this is relevant to the argument), critics see no reason to change the text: a deliberative question in the past seems weaker than the conflation of narrating and experiencing I, which neatly picks up the vivid quality of *iubet*. See also 171, 7 *doleo* and comm. *ad loc.*

me formauit non canem: *formare* with double acc. also [Quint.] *Decl.* 8, 11: *indeprehensibile est quicquid nos elementorum uaria compago formauit*.

non canem sed asinum: Bernhard 1927, 61 lists the phrase among antithetic expressions that enliven the narrative. Here we may add that the reader has learnt earlier that the ass prefers human food (4, 1: 75, 1 f. raw vegetables; 4, 22: 92, 1 f. bread); later on an entire scene is based on this aspect of the ass (10, 13: 246, 15 f.). All these scenes occur also in the *Onos* (17, 4 f; 21, 3; the present one at 27, 3; the last at 46, 7). The tension between Lucius' human and animal aspects – he prefers human food, but the quantities are to be adapted to a bestial belly – is therefore part and parcel of the Vorlage.

reliquiis rapinisque: the sound effects may be illustrative of the sense. Cf. E. Fraenkel's impressionistic utterance on Catul. 42, 8 *mimice ac moleste* (1961, 48): 'If we press our lips together to produce the threefold m-sound, we shall not remain deaf to the contempt in this half-line.' Here we may in a similar way hear the dogs growling over their food; cf. the famous *canina littera* in Lucil. 2 and 377 f. Marx (= 5 and 307 f. Krenkel); Persius 1, 109 (with Conington-Nettleship and van Wageningen *ad loc.*).

inescatos atque distentos: the second is (of course) the result of the first (cf. Bernhard 1927, 168). The *Onos* (27, 3) ἑώρων γὰρ τοὺς κύνας εἰς τοὐπτανεῖον παρεισιόντας καὶ λαφύσσοντας πολλὰ κτλ. presents the process, Apuleius shows a picture of the results. *Inescare* is not used by Apuleius in its basic sense of "to entice with bait", but in the sense of "gorge", "stuff" (*esca* is both "food" and "bait"); cf. 10, 15 (248, 7 *liberalibus cenis inescatus* and (though not of food) 9, 24 (221, 15) *grauique odore sulpuris iuuenis inescatus*. For this sense *ThLL* quotes only *Vet. Lat. (Wirc.) Ier.* 23, 15 (where other versions read *cibare*) and Auspic. *ad Arbog.* 98. See also Callebat 1968, 57.

The sentence as a whole may be listed among the many passages in which the narrating I treats the experiencing I in an ironic manner; see e.g. Heine in *AAGA* 1978, 30.

164, 22-165, 1 Post noctem unicam et rudimenta Veneris recens nupta gratias summas apud suos parentes ac maritum mihi meminisse non destitit, quoad summos illi promitterent honores habituri mihi: "After a single night and a first lesson in the school of Venus the young bride never stopped mentioning to her parents and husband her intense gratitude towards me, until they promised to grant me the greatest honours".

Post noctem unicam et rudimenta Veneris: Heine 1962, 239 n. 2 discusses the narrator's wink at the reader and discovers a similar twinkle in 8, 4, where Charite has apparently told her husband not to hunt big game. The *rudimenta Veneris* are surely not witnessed by the ass. The chapter shows three pieces of information that imply the presence of the ass in situations in which his presence is not mentioned; the other two are Charite's pleading with her parents and husband in this same sentence and the meeting with friends in the next few lines. Lucius' presence is less unlikely in the second and third situation than in the first, nevertheless the entire passage constitutes a narrative problem for which see vdPaardt in *AAGA* 1978, 76 f.

unicam: see comm. on 148, 23.

rudimenta: in much the same sense in 6, 6 (132, 18) *thalami rudimentum*; in 8, 3 (178, 15) *furatrinae coniugalis ... rudimentum* (if the text is right) it seems to have the rare sense "lack of experience"; in 5, 12 (112, 20) it refers to Psyche's unborn child. The word is restored at 9, 11 (210, 21) *rudimentum seruitii*. *Rudis* is a term often applied to the inexperienced, in love or otherwise (Prop. 3, 15, 5; 4, 3, 12 *cum rudis urgenti bracchia uicta dedi*; 4, 16, 131; Ov. *Am.* 2, 1, 6; *Ars* 3, 559). *Rudimentum* occurs in the sense of "first attempt", "first schooling" e.g. Liv. 1, 3, 4; Verg. *A.* 11, 157; *Ciris* 44 f. (Lyne *ad loc.* emphasizes the many times it occurs in military contexts). Cl. Donatus' remark on Verg. *A.* 9, 203 is interesting as to the supposed origin of the image: *erudire est nouitatem indoctam hoc est rudem facere docendo meliorem. Tractum est hoc a uestibus, quae cum rudes sunt, nullam retinent gratiam et posita rudimentorum inluuie arte suscipiunt speciosissimam formam, quam inter initia non habebant.* (Cf. Ov. *Met.* 8, 640 *textum rude; Fast.* 4, 659 *ueste rudi tectus* and expressions like *rudimenta ponere* Liv. 31, 11, 15; Just. 7, 5, 3; 9, 1, 8; Suet. *Ner.* 22; cf. Stat. *Ach.* 1, 478 and Dilke *ad loc.*) If Donatus is right, there is no need to explain the *rudimenta Veneris* by means of the military metaphor so well known in the language of love, though, of course, *rudimenta militiae* is a common enough phrase.

recens nupta ... non destitit: there is a contrast, not so much between *recens* and the implication of time in *non destitit*, as between the expected preoccupation of the young bride and the fact that she spares a thought for the ass. The colon is a very long one (30 syllables). The length may illustrate the process described, see Hijmans in *AAGA* 1978, 194.

recens nupta: see above on 164, 16 *ipso nuptiarum die.* Here the narrator refers to the second, at 162, 28 *nescio cui recenti marito* he had in mind the first wedding day.

gratias ... meminisse: see vdPaardt 1971, 91, who thinks the expression is perhaps a grecism. To his instances we may add Tert. *Nat.* 2, 5, 10 *non lanis nec antidotis aut malagmatibus ipsis gratiam meministis, sed medicis.*

gratias: for the play on the name Charite see *GCA* 1977, 102 and Hijmans in *AAGA* 1978, 116.

promitterent honores habituri mihi: Petschenig proposes a change (*habitum iri*, Plasberg *habitu iri*; Helm *in app. crit. ad loc.* refers to four papers mentioned in *ALL*, Index I-X, 596, of which the most important is Brandt 1885, 349-354, on the fut. pass. inf. in *-uiri*; see KSt 1, 690; curiously enough the form is not mentioned in LHSz 1, 619), but the construction, which is Greek in origin, occurs with some frequency in Latin literature, e.g. Pl. *As.* 633 f. *argenti uiginti minae ... / quas hodie adulescens Diabolus ipsi daturus dixit*; Prop. 2, 9, 7 *uisura ... quamuis numquam speraret Ulixen*; Stat. *Theb.* 1, 347 f. *uenturaque rauco / ore minatur hiemps* (cf. Heuvel *ad loc.*); it is more frequent with perf. partic., e.g. 1, 14 (13, 10) but see Marg. Molt. *ad loc.*; 4, 34 (102, 5) *inuidiae nefariae letali plaga percussi sero sentitis*; *Apol.* 3 (3, 13 f.); 48 (55, 14); 51 (57, 25). Löfstedt 1933, 428 n. 3; LHSz 2, 363 f.

Conuocatis denique grauioribus amicis consilium datur, quo potissi- 165, 1-2
mum facto digne remunerarer: "Finally the weightier ones among their friends were called together for consultation on the question by what action I would best be given my due reward".

The committee meeting may be counted among the subtle bits of humour in the *Met.* Apuleius clearly uses it to give his readers a sense of the overblown self-importance of his narrator: in Latin literature the consultation of friends on important subjects occurs with some frequency; see e.g. Pl. *Poen.* 794 and Maurach *ad loc.*; *St.* 143 and Petersmann *ad loc.*; Catul. 41 and Kroll *ad loc.*; Cic. *Diu.* 1, 55; *Lael.* 44; *Fin.* 2, 55; Hor. *Epod.* 11, 25; Sen. *Ep.* 77, 5. See also I Hadot 1969, 166. More instances are collected in *ThLL s.v. amicus* 1907, 60 f. – and, of course, we remember Job and his friends.

denique: Marg. Helbers-Molt 1943, 131 takes *denique* here in the sense of *ergo, igitur*; see also vdPaardt 1971, 43. No doubt this is possible, but in view of *non destitit* above the sense "at last" is no less so.

consilium datur: presumably in the sense of *consulitur*, though this instance of *dare* + subst. as a periphrastic is marginal and does not occur in *ThLL s.v. do* 1686, 35 f. See also Bernhard 1927, 184 f. and Svennung 1935, 540. The phrase should not be explained with Médan 1925, 207 as an equivalent of *consilium aduocatur*.

quo . . . facto: thus F. Editors since Oudendorp read *pacto* which produces a considerably smoother text. Apart from the fact that smoothness is not necessarily a recommendation, there is a similar abl. (abs.?) at 3, 23 (69, 19) *sed quo . . . dicto factoue rursum exutis pinnulis illis ad meum redibo Lucium?*, which may lend just enough support to the ms. reading here.

remunerarer: Callebat 1968, 298 lists a number of instances in which the normally deponent verb is used actively or as a true passive; cf. Flobert 1975, 112; 644; also Moussy 1966, 278.

165, 3-4 Placuerat uni domi me conclusum et otiosum hordeo lecto fabaque et uicia saginari: "One speaker voiced his opinion that, stabled at home and free from work, I should be fattened with first quality barley, beans and vetch".

Placuerat: on the placement see Callebat in *AAGA* 1978, 179. The tense may be explained as a *plusquamperfectum pro imperfecto*. See LHSz 2, 321 and vdPaardt 1971, 54; however, most instances of the 'verschobenes Plusquamperfectum' occur in relative clauses and the author may have intended a real pluperfect in the sense that the proposal was withdrawn as the other proposal (*optinuit alius*) gained the upper hand.

uni: F has *uti* (also *ni* in mg.); cf. Helm Praef. *Fl.* xxxvi on this and other clarifications of F in the margins. See also above on 164, 15 *curitabat*, below on 175, 21. Though we hear of only two proposals, the circle of friends is not confined to two; cf. *alius* in the next line. For the dissolution of the collectivity into its component parts – a regular Apuleian technique – see Junghanns 1932, 70 n. 106 (cf. *Onos* 27, 4); Heinze [3]1915, 355 f.

hordeo: above (164, 15) *ordeo*; see *GCA* 1977, 167. Together with *faba* and *uicia*, it was apparently regular fodder for various animals. Cato *Agr. 27: sementim facito, ocinum, uiciam, faenum graecum, fabam, eruum, pabulum bubus*; see also *ibid*. 54; Var. *R.* 1, 31, 4-5. Col. 6, 3, 3 recommends vetches and *hordeum* for oxen; at 6, 27, 8 stallions are to be fattened *hordeo eruoque*. (On the order in which the various crops should be sown see e.g. Col. 2, 10, 29 and Richter on Verg. *G.* 1, 75.)

165, 4-7 sed optinuit alius, qui meae libertati prospexerat, suadens, ut rurestribus potius campis in greges equinos lasciuiens discurrerem daturus dominis equarum inscensu generoso multas mulas alumnas: "but someone else's proposal carried the day; he had looked ahead to my freedom and urged that I should be allowed to run free in the fields of the countryside and direct my lascivious sports towards the herds of horses – certain to give my masters many a mule-foal by generously mounting the mares".

sed optinuit: Bernhard 1927, 17 speaks of 'gedeckte Anfangsstellung'; for the sense of *optinuit* (equals *obtinuit causam*) see Callebat 1968, 302, who notes that it is particularly frequent in later Latin. Its use in a legal context occurs as early as Cic. *Q. fr.* 3, 3, 2. Callebat suggests that Apuleius may have borrowed from the legal usage, but Liv. 33, 25, 6 (a consul obtaining a province) is but one of several passages that cannot be classified under that heading. See *ThLL s.v.* 289, 31 f.

rurestribus: Médan 1925, 120 cites this adj. among neologisms. See *GCA* 1977, 36 with a ref. to Neue-Wagener 2³, 20.

in greges: vdVliet proposed *inter*, but Callebat 1968, 236, after discussing the possibility of taking *in* in the sense of *inter*, decides that direction of movement is the best interpretation. He compares Tert. *Apol.* 48, 3 (*ad hanc partem lasciuire*). A closer parallel is found in Macr. *Sat.* 2, 2, 5 *lasciuiente dictatore tam in matrem quam in puellam*.

greges equinos: Bernhard 1927, 111 discusses the increasing frequency with which adjectives replace descriptive genitives, for which he sees two sources: the *sermo cotidianus* and Augustan poetry. The problem appears to be less simple than Bernhard's treatment intimates. Löfstedt 1911, 76-81 defends the thesis that the phenomenon is more or less confined to 'Personen und persönlichen Begriffen' and later in his *Syntactica* (1, ²1956, 107-124) attacks Wackernagel's theory that the type *grex equinus* is older than the type *grex equorum* and notes a particular frequency in poetic texts and prose texts showing poetic traits. See also Christine Mohrmann 1961, 36 f. and 169-175.

daturus: Bernhard 1927, 43 f. collects numerous instances in which a participle following a main verb expresses an afterthought. For the future participle he refers to vGeisau 1916, 278, who collects the Apuleian instances, e.g. 162, 4-5 *pergimus et puellam simul uendituri et socios indagaturi*; see comm. *ad loc.* and LHSz 2, 390 (first instance in Gracchus *apud* Gel. 11, 10, 4, frequent from Tac. onwards).

inscensu generoso: Luisa Gargantini 1963, 40 collects the abstract verbal nouns with suffix *-tu(-su)* in Apuleius and characterizes them in general as elegant substitutes for abstracts in *-(t)io*. Most are hapax legomena and are used in the dative or ablative case. For *inscendere* as a technical term for the sexual act see comm. on 170, 13 f.

The precise sense of *generosus* seems to be in some doubt: it may mean "noble", in which case it fits the ass' self-importance (thus Norden 1912, 116, who notes that 166, 9 *concubinas* refers to a difference of class). *ThLL s.v.* 1801, 64 lists our passage with *de bestiis* (*laudat uirtutes earum uel proprias uel utilitatem.*) It may also be taken in the sense of πολύγονος ("philoprogenitively"); cf. Serv. on Verg. *A.* 10, 174. This would refer to a different sense of pride. Cf. Fernhout on *Met.* 5, 29 (126, 20), who is followed by Grimal.

multas mulas alumnas: a marked sound effect, which, curiously enough, returns in 165, 18 f.

The advice obviously is not without its economic aspect.

CHAPTER XV

The ass goes to his reward and is disappointed in his expectations.

165, 7-9 Ergo igitur euocato statim armentario equisone magna cum praefatione deducendus adsignor: "Therefore the groom in charge of the horseherd is summoned immediately and, with a long preamble, I am given into his care to be taken away".

Ergo igitur: the duplication occurs on several occasions in the *Met.*, e.g. 168, 16. See also 3, 19 (66, 5) and vdPaardt 144 *ad loc.*; 4, 2 (75, 9) and *GCA* 1977, 28 *ad loc.*

armentario equisone: cf. *equinis armentis* 166, 5 (in inverse order).

armentarius: the substantive is first attested in Varro *R.* 2 praef. 4; the adjective occurs from Apuleius onwards. See e.g. Sol. 5, 22; Ambr. *C. et Ab.* 2, 1, 4; Callebat 1968, 50; forms in *-arius* as indications of profession (often manual labour and specializations of slaves, e.g. *balnearius, cellarius, carbonarius*; also *retiarius, argentarius* and *asinarius, caprarius*) are discussed in LHSz 1, 298.

equisone: vdVliet reads *equisoni*, (presumably to be taken with *euocato armentario* and dependent on *adsignor*), but in view of Apuleius' loose handling of participle constructions (see Callebat 1968, 321) it is unnecessary. In Apul. *Apol.* 87 (96, 24) *equisones* are found side by side with *uillicones* and *upiliones* (respectively bailiffs and shepherds); cf. 8, 1 (176, 21) *Equisones opilionesque, etiam busequae, fuit Charite* . . .

That the ass is reasonably well off at the hands of the well-to-do but has trouble with the lower strata of society is hardly unexpected. This trait is one in which he differs essentially from the picaros of the 16th and 17th centuries: Lazarillo finds more sympathy in the lower than in the higher classes. See van Gorp 1978, 31.

magna cum praefatione: *praefatio* is an introductory statement e.g. in religious rites (Liv. 45, 5, 4) but by no means confined to that usage: Cic. *Ver.* 3, 187 uses it for the citation accompanying an award. In both cases the word has a certain solemnity, which seems to apply in our passage as well. For the concrete sense cf. Sen. *Con.* 2, 4, 6 *mulier, quae sine praefatione honeste nominari non potes* (a preceding statement), Val. Max. 6, 3, 1a *iustae ultionis . . . haec praefatio fuit*. For the ritual *praefatio* see Wissowa 1912, 412. The addition of *magna* (an *abusio* according to the standards of *Rhet. Her.* 4, 45) is unparalleled, but see Cic. *Att.* 5, 4, 1 *maxumo mandato*; Plin. *Nat.* 21, 2 *magna . . . admonitione*; *ThLL s.v. magnus* 130, 56 ff.; the expression does not represent anything in the *Onos*.

deducendus adsignor: the predicative use of gerundives after *dare* and similar verbs is not frequent in the passive, but occurs from Afran. *com.* 111 (*datur mihi custodiendus*) onwards; see LHSz 2, 372. The expression has the flavour of official language (*ThLL s.v. adsigno* 890, 91), and so has *euocato* ('rarius de uocatione qualis fit ex priuatis quibuslibet causis *ThLL s.v.* 1055, 78): the solemn tone of the final part of the previous chapter is continued.

Et sane gaudens laetusque praecurrebam sarcinis et ceteris oneribus 165, 9-12 iam nunc renuntiaturus nanctaque libertate ueris initio pratis herbantibus rosas utique reperturus aliquas: "And in fact, joyful and pleased, I was already running ahead, about to renounce luggage and other burdens on the spot and hoping that, after gaining my liberty, I would surely find at least some roses, since the meadows were in bloom at the beginning of spring".

The period gives a somewhat lush characterization of the ass's mood in the two sets of near synonyms (*gaudens laetusque* and *sarcinis et ceteris oneribus*; see Médan 1925, 363; Bernhard 1927, 166) coupled with the contrasting future participles. In addition the three main parts (*et... praecurrebam* 12, *sarcinis... renuntiaturus* 19, *nanctaque... aliquas* 31) show an increasing number of syllables dealing with respectively present mood, immediate future and more distant expectation. The *Onos* 27, 6 mentions the second item only.

gaudens laetusque: cf. 164, 12 *laeti et gaudentes*, also 163, 23 *famuli laeti faciem, gaudio delibuti*.

praecurrebam: whether the imperfect is to be taken *de conatu* or in a descriptive sense, the activity described is part and parcel of the characterization of an eager ass.

sarcinis et ceteris oneribus: cf. Petr. 117 *affirmabatque se aut proiecturum sarcinas aut cum onere fugiturum*.

renuntiaturus: as if carrying burdens were a favourite activity; the reader remembers the fate of the ass who gave up in 4, 5.

nanctaque libertate: for the passive sense of the participle cf. Hygin. *Fab*. 1, 2 and 8, 4 (*occasione nacta*, but see also 120, 5 *occasionem Iphigenia nacta*); Aurel. Victor *De Caes*. 33, 3 *nactisque in tempore nauigiis*. See Médan 1925, 11; Flobert 1975, 366.

ueris initio: we are still not many weeks away from the time of metamorphosis. See also below 166, 11 on *admissura*, and Introduction ....

herbantibus: Bernhard 1927, 139 speaks of a neologism, an unhelpful term for the hapax.

rosas utique reperturus aliquas: *utique* strengthening *reperturus* has the sense "doubtless", "certainly" (LHSz 2, 492 f.; Callebat 1968, 322-323); *aliquas* in the emphatic final position has the sense "at least some".

This is the only time during the ass's wanderings, apart from the beginning and the end, that the possibility of release is mentioned. Junghanns 1932, 61 and Heine 1962, 301 note that by and large the expectation of 'remetamorphosis' is thrust into the background; Heine *ibid*. n. 1 speaks of 'einer unbestimmten Zukunftshoffnung, die die Handlung nicht mehr bestimmt', and even so the thought of release is further qualified by a somewhat mercenary second thought.

Subibat me tamen illa etiam sequens cogitatio, quod tantis actis 165, 12-15 gratiis honoribusque plurimis asino meo tributis humana facie recepta multo tanta pluribus beneficiis honestarer: "But this further thought also occurred to me that, whereas so many thanks had been given and a great many honours granted to me as an ass, I should be honoured with all the more benefits once I regained my human shape".

The period appears to be designed to cause the reader to reflect on the ass's vanity. Charite was indeed grateful to him, but her own and her parents' gratitude was directed to an ass: a human's lack of success (see 151, 12 f.) might prove hard to forgive; but Apuleius is too subtle to include an explicit debunking scene such as the re-anthropomorphized Loukios has to undergo in *Onos* 56, where he confronts the onophiliac woman who expects bigger things from him. On this kind of 'implicit rhetoric' (the reader though formally confronted with an ego-narrative senses the critical presence of the author) see Anbeek 1978, 77 f.; 165 f.

subibat me ... sequens cogitatio: Rohde 1875, 276 comparing 9, 21 (218, 29) *consequenter*, argues that *sequens cogitatio* must refer to a thought that follows from the previous one and fits the situation, but that Apuleius would have expressed this by the word *consequens*. There seems to be insufficient reason to change the text in our passage. See Callebat 1968, 292; cf. e.g. 6, 20 (143, 23) where *offulae sequentis* refers back to *offulae cibo* in line 18. Helm-Krenkel translate "der nachfolgende Gedanke". It is not very likely that the sense of *sequens* should be restricted to the mere statement that this thought now follows in the account.

Bernhard 1927, 185 takes *subibat ... cogitatio* as periphrastic and notes that such periphrastic expressions are more common in Apuleius than in what he calls classical literature; he gives several instances. It should be noted, however, that with the descriptive imperfect *subibat* and the adjective *sequens* the present phrase conveys more than *cogitabam* does: we see the process of formation of a subsequent – and secondary – thought. Morelli 1913, 186 detects an echo in Sulp. Sev. *Ep.* 2, 1 *subieratque me illa quae saepius occupat cogitatio* (cf. also Sulp. Sev. *Dial.* 1, 22), but the expression occurs with some frequency from Livy onwards (e.g. Liv. 10, 45, 3; 42, 49, 4; Sen. *Ben.* 1, 11, 3; Plin. *Nat.* 36, 112). For *subibat me* see also above on 155, 19.

tamen: for the placement see Médan 1925, 217. Hildebrand prefers *tum* with ς to Oudendorp's *cum*. *Tamen*, however, need not have a strictly adversative force: see LHSz 2, 496 f., where parallels are presented for *tamen = autem*, δέ.

asino meo: see Médan 1925, 217, who contents himself with saying that we have an 'emploi très particulier de *meus* au lieu de *mihi* ou de *ego*'. The expression is unparalleled outside the *Met.* since the situation (the narrating I speaking with a certain fondness about the experiencing I as 'my ass' cf. 9, 13 (213, 4); 11, 16 (278, 16) or remembering how that ass 'spoke' of 'my Lucius' 10, 29 (260, 12); 11, 2 (267, 23)) does not occur elsewhere in the Latinity of the ancient world. It may be regarded as a clever device to remind the reader of the distance and tension between narrating and experiencing I. Cf. vdPaardt in *AAGA* 1978, 76 f.; Waszink on Tert. *An.* 35, 6 seems to interpret "my ass-shape" cf. *GCA* 1977, 27.

multo tanta: cf. 10, 21 (252, 19) *multo tanta impensius cura etiam nares perfundit meas*, where Leo deletes *cura* as a gloss; *Apol.* 3 (4, 20) *multo tanta ex animo laborat* (without comparative notion); *Fl.* 18 (37, 8) *multo tanta praestat illa*; *Soc.*

11 (18, 18 f.) *concretio multo tanta subtilior*. The textual situation in these passages (with the exception of 10, 21: 252, 19) is secure enough to accept the curious expression *multo tanta* + comparative notion for Apuleius, whether based on a confusion on his part as Marx argues (on Pl. *Rud.* 521; cf. Pl. *Bacch.* 1034 *sescenta tanta reddam*; Fro. *ad M. Caes.* 85, 18 vdH *decem tanta te amo*), or on such fairly well attested expressions as Pl. *Rud.* 521 *multo tanta miserior quam tu*; *Stich.* 339 *multo tanta plus quam speras*; *Men.* 800 *multo tanta illum accusabo, quam te accusaui, amplius*. Havet 1900, 579 in addition quotes the palimpsest reading at Cic. *Ver.* 3, 225 *quinquiens tanta... amplius*. He thinks the expression originates in an ellipsis of abl. *pecunia* (cf. also Pl. *Men.* 680 *bis tanta pluris*). Leo 1902, 99 thinks of an asyndeton ("for much... for so much"), also assuming an ellipsis of *pecunia*. Löfstedt 1956, 288 f. proposes to take *tanta* as neuter plural and the expression as a contamination of e.g. *multo miserior* and *multa tanta miser*. But, whatever the explanation, the evidence for the idiom is too strong to judge with LHSz 2, 136 'kaum zu halten'.

Sed ubi me procul a ciuitate gregarius ille perduxerat, nullae deliciae 165, 15-17 ac ne ulla quidem libertas excipit: "But when that herdsman had taken me a long way from the city, no delights nor even any liberty awaited me".

ubi... perduxerat: Médan 1925, 94 notes that the pluperfect after temporal *ubi* is not classical. Callebat 1968, 347 retorts that the pluperfect occurs in archaic authors as well as in Vergil, Livy, Tacitus. Cf. 5, 25 (122, 16) *sed ubi remigio plumae raptum maritum proceritas spatii fecerat alienum*... and Marg. Molt on 1, 19 (17, 16); see also LHSz 2, 651-2.

procul a ciuitate: there is no doubt that the distance is a long one. The word *procul* in the *Met.* is always used to indicate a considerable distance (given the circumstances) and where the distance is small the author requires *non procul* (above 147, 4). At 174, 12 the *uiator* cannot be taken to the magistrate until the next day; at 8, 1 (176, 15) the situation implies an almost complete lack of communication between the masters in the city and the slaves in the country; the ass's own subsequent adventures also presuppose a lack of supervision of the farm-slaves.

gregarius: Callebat 1968, 250 notes that adjectives with substantive force such as the present one occur regularly in Apuleius and more frequently than in authors of the 'classical' period. *Gregarius* in this sense (cf. 169, 16) is a first which is also attested for Ps. Matth. *evang.* 3, 4. Helm translates "Oberaufseher der Herden", in view of 169, 16 much honour for this simple herdsman. See also above on *armentarius* (165, 7).

nulla... excipit: there is a significant difference from the tale presented in *Onos* 27, 7-28, 1: ἐπεὶ δὲ ἥκομεν εἰς τὸν ἀγρόν, ταῖς ἵπποις μὲν ὁ νομεὺς συνέμιξεν καὶ ἦγεν ἡμᾶς τὴν ἀγέλην εἰς νομόν, ἐχρῆν δὲ ἄρα κἀνταῦθα ὥσπερ Κανδαύλῃ κἀμοὶ γενέσθαι. Concerning the different sequence of events Junghanns 1932, 80 n. 121 remarks: 'Man erkennt an dieser sachlichen Unwahrscheinlichkeit die nachträgliche Änderung; der Ὄνος-text bietet offensichtlich die ursprüngliche Fassung'. It may be that the original version is preserved in the *Onos*, but Apuleius' tale does not contain any intrinsic unlikelihood; indeed the reader is conditioned to expect nasty behaviour on the part of most of the characters that appear in the *Met*. See also below on 166, 5-7. The reference to Κανδαύλης, which in the Onos functions as a purely verbal reminiscence of Hdt. 1, 8, 2 χρῆν γὰρ Κανδαύλῃ γενέσθαι κακῶς, is left out by Apuleius, who prefers a closer tie between his mythical references and his narrative; see e.g. on 149, 18; 176, 14.

deliciae: the word is also used in an erotic sence at 9, 16 (215, 4) *dignus hercules solus omnium matronarum deliciis perfrui*, cf. 5, 31 (128, 15). Elsewhere (4, 24: 93, 15; 7, 6: 158, 26; 9, 32: 227, 6; 10, 15: 248, 17) the word refers to food or luxury in general. The various senses of the word are discussed by Quinn on Catul. 2, 1.

excipit: "awaited"; cf. e.g. Liv. 3, 47, 6 *cum... eum mulierum comploratio excepisset*; more instances in *ThLL s.v.* 1251, 50 f.

165, 17-20 Nam protinus uxor eius, auara equidem nequissimaque illa mulier, molae machinariae subiugum me dedit frondosoque baculo subinde castigans panem sibi suisque de meo parabat corio: "For his wife – indeed how avaricious and thoroughly evil-minded a woman she was! – forthwith put me under the yoke of a grinding machine and, by giving me a hiding every now and again with a leafy stick, tried to earn her daily bread for herself and her family at the expense of my hide".

The motif of a nasty woman who demands hard labour of the ass is repeated at 9, 14; see Riefstahl 1938, 73.

protinus: after l. 8 *statim*, l. 10 *iam nunc*, once again speed is suggested by the narrator.

uxor... mulier: for nasty women in the *Met*. and Apuleius' interest in characterization see Junghanns 1932, 59 n. 89. In *Onos* 28, 1-3 she is called Μεγαπόλη (the situation is described in more detail there than in Apuleius who adds the stick but omits the cakes Megapole bakes and eats herself) and characterized ironically: ἡ δὲ βελτίστη.

auara equidem: *auarę quidem* F. The emendation by Seyffert is easy and obvious. For *equidem* in this sense see 161, 14 and comm. *ad loc*. (The reading *quidem* in ς, cf. *auarā quidem* φ, finds insufficient support in 167, 7 and 188, 11 quoted by Helm: in both cases the phrase is *ille quidem*.)

auara... nequissimaque: juxtaposition of positive and superlative adjectives: see Médan 1925, 214; Callebat 1968, 401 f. lists a series of instances in which, as here, the positive adj. precedes. Cf. below 169, 25 *pigrum tardissimumque*; 6, 17 (141, 10); 9, 37 (231, 2). Further instances in Plautus (e.g. *Capt*. 278) and Arnob. (e.g. 1, 3). In a second series the superlative precedes: see on 169, 14 *ille deterrimus ac temerarius puer*.

illa: cf. 4, 12 (83, 18), see *GCA* 1977, 96 *ad loc*.; further discussions of pejorative *ille* in Callebat 1968, 277; vdPaardt 1971, 186.

mulier, molae machinariae: note that the sound effect of 165, 7 (*multas mulas alumnas*) is repeated here.

molae machinariae: see White 1975, 15 on *molae asinariae* and his Plate 2 b for an illustration from a relief in Ostia. Vallette describes the mill in a footnote on the present passage: *machinaria* refers not to a particular type of mill but to the fact that since it rotates it is a type of *machina*. Rode-Burck 237 emphasize the conical shape. See also 9, 11 (210, 18 f.). Médan 1925, 116 mistakenly notes that the word *machinarius* is a neologism. See Callebat 1968, 40. As early as Alf. *dig.* 32, 60, 3 (ca. 40 B.C.) the adjective qualifies an ass who supplies the power to a mill; cf. Ulp. *dig.* 33, 7, 12, 10. Solinus 5, 13 uses the word for Archimedes as an inventor of engines.

dedit ... parabat: the tense change is functional: actuality versus attempt.

subiugum me dedit: for the adj. *subiugus* cf. Prud. *Cath.* 3, 170 *subiuga tigridis ora premens*. At Gel. 17, 21, 36, where Hosius still read *consules ... subiugi missi*. Marshall prints *sub iugum* with a consensus of several manuscripts.

frondosoque baculo: cf. 3, 27 (72, 17) *frondosum fustem* and vdPaardt 1971, 195 *ad loc*. Callebat 1968, 384 speaks of 'caractérisation pittoresque', but Blümner 1896, 350 proposes *nodosoque*, Purser 1906, 46 *ponderosoque*. No change is necessary: the stick has just been cut. Cf. Ov. *Met.*2, 681 *baculum siluestre*; 15, 655 *baculum agreste*. See also comm. on 167, 10.

subinde = "souvent"; see Callebat 1968, 149; vdPaardt 1971, 127 with literature.

de meo parabat corio: see above on 163, 3 and vdPaardt 1971, 179, who notes the proverbial quality of the expression. If there is a proverbial expression involved it is a playful variant on *ludere de corio (alicuius)* cf. Otto 1890, 92 (our passage is the only one quoted in Nachträge 54).

Nec tantum sui cibi gratia me fatigare contenta, uicinorum etiam frumenta mercenariis discursibus meis conterebat, nec mihi misero statuta saltem cibaria pro tantis praestabantur laboribus: "And not content to wear me out just for her own food, she also used to grind the neighbours' wheat by hiring out my perambulations – but for such heavy labour I, poor wretch, was not given even the prescribed nutriments". 165, 21-24

me fatigare contenta: *contentus* with infinitive occurs also at 8, 22 (194, 8); cf. *Fl.* 18 (36, 12) *contentus scire*. *ThLL s.v. contentus* 680, 16 f. collects the instances, among which *Apol.* 28 is mentioned erroneously. See also LHSz 2, 350; Callebat 1968, 316; vdPaardt 1971, 68; vGeisau 1916, 267 regards these infinitives as grecisms (against Kretschmann).

mercenariis: *ThLL s.v.* 791, 82: 'scribitur saepe per unam n'. There is no reason to add a second *n* with F's corrector. *Onos* 28, 3 specifies: ἄλευρα τὸν μισθὸν αἰτοῦσα ἐξεμίσθου τὸν ἐμὸν ἄθλιον τράχηλον. The self-pity in the last few words is picked up in Apuleius' *misero ... pro tantis ... laboribus*.

statuta: the reference is to *magna cum praefatione* above line 8.

cibaria: the technical term for the allotment of food to slaves and cattle. See Callebat 1968, 39 f.

Namque hordeum meum frictum et sub eadem mola meis quassatum ambagibus colonis proximis uenditabat, mihi uero per diem laboriosae machinae adtento sub ipsa uespera furfures apponebat incretos ac sordidos multoque lapide salebrosos: "For my barley, roasted and crushed in that self-same mill by my own labours, she regularly sold to the 165, 24-166, 2 neighbouring peasants, but, though I had been riveted to the laborious machine all day long, only at nightfall did she give me unsieved husks, dirty and rough with gravel".

Namque: Bernhard 1927, 28 lists the passages in which the word occurs in first, second and third place.

frictum: Vallette derives the word from *frigo* "roast"; cf. *OLD s.v.* According to Callebat 1968, 38 it is to be connected with *fricare*, 'évoquant ici l'extraction du grain hors de la balle'. The latter interpretation seems unlikely in view of Plin. *Nat.* 18, 72-73: *Graeci perfusum aqua hordeum siccant nocte una ac postero die frigunt, dein molis frangunt. Sunt qui uehementius tostum rursus exigua aqua adspergant et siccent, priusquam molant e.q.s.*

laboriosae machinae: in the sense of *laboris plenus* the word *laboriosus* occurs frequently with activities etc. from Pl. *Merc.* 507 onwards; more rarely with concrete nouns (Rut. Lup. 2, 2 *uia*; Vell. 2, 113, 3 *iter*); with *machina* here only.

furfures: Callebat 1968, 48 treats the word under the heading 'réalisme familier, vocabulaire rural'. It may mean both the husks and the chaff of various types of grain. Pl. *Capt.* 807 implies that *furfures* are used as food for swine; cf. the gloss in Vat. 5141: *furfur crusca uel remula, unde uersus: fur simplex latro, fur duplex fit cibus apro.* Var. *R.* 2, 2, 19; 2, 7, 12 etc. gives *furfures* to sheep. They also have a medical application: Cels. 2, 33, 2; in Veg. *Mulomed.* 2, 36, 10 *furfures* are used together with *hordeum frixum* in a diet for a *uenter solutus*.

incretos... salebrosos: Bernhard 1927, 22 provides parallels for the position (after *furfures*) of the three adjectives, and *ibid.* 71 notes the tricolon (with crescendo).

incretos: from *cernere* = "sift" with privative *in* (against Hor. *S.* 2, 4, 75, where the form *incretum* derives from *incernere* = "to sprinkle on"). The only other instance of this usage occurs in *Vitae patr. Jur.* 1, 13 (138, 30) *ut nobis... hordeaceas incretasque solummodo parare iubeas in merendula pultes.*

salebrosos: usually not in this literal sense according to Médan 1925, 164. See also 8. 16 (190, 1) *saxa, quae salebrosa semita largiter subministrabat.* In a literal sense also in Ov. *Her.* 4, 103 (*latebrosa var. lect.*); Paul. Nol. *C.* 21, 120; Sid. Apol. *ep.* 3, 2, 3. The word is often used in a literary context, e.g. Sen. *Ep.* 100, 7 (*compositio*) *salebrosa et exiliens*; Quint. *Inst.* 11, 2, 46; cf. Jul. Victor 26 (447, 6 Halm) *nec praepropere loquaris... multo enim turpius, si offendas saepius quasi salebrosa festinatione.* See Ernout 1949, 26.

CHAPTER XVI

Misadventure among the horses.

Talibus aerumnis edomitum nouis Fortuna saeua tradidit cruciati- 166, 3-5
bus, scilicet ut, quod aiunt, domi forisque fortibus factis adoriae
plenae gloriarer: "When I had been utterly overcome by miseries of this sort,
cruel Fortune handed me over to new tortures, doubtless so as to enable me to
glory in a complete triumph on account of my courageous behaviour (as the
saying goes) both at home and abroad".

In this section of the *Met.* hope and despair, apparent good fortune and dire
misfortune, follow one another in a regular pattern; see Schlam 1968, 133.
Junghanns 1932, 58 n. 87; 80 notes that the changes of fortune are often
introduced by a general sentence. See also *GCA* 1977, 110. Here the announcement of the next trial precedes the description of the expected 'better things'.

aerumnis: for the archaic expression see above on 155, 18, where it is used of the
more general situation in which Lucius finds himself.

edomitum: the ellipsis of the pronoun is hardly remarkable; see Bernhard 1927,
160, who notes that an ellipsis occurs as often as the pronoun, when there is a
participle to pick up the syntactic function. See also Callebat 1968, 452. In
Apuleius *edomare* is used here only.

nouis . . . cruciatibus: the elegant hyperbaton emphasizes *nouis*.

Fortuna saeua: see comm. on 155, 21; Heine 1962, 170 n. 1; used in contradis-
tinction to *Fatum, fata*: see Riefstahl 1938, 30; Heine in *AAGA* 1978, 29 n. 45.

tradidit cruciatibus: *tradere* with the dative of an abstract noun is also found in
Suet. *Vit.* 14, 2 *quendam . . . supplicio traditum*.

scilicet: vdPaardt in *AAGA* 1978, 77 notes that *scilicet* is often employed to
safeguard the limited point of view of the narrator, who, of course, has no
knowledge of the mental activities of the dread Goddess. However, what is
involved here is not so much this aspect of narrative technique as the use of a
well-known philosophical topos: true glory is gained by a struggle with fortune;
see e.g. Sen. *Prou.* 2, 7; 3, 9.

domi forisque fortibus factis: the words *quod aiunt* mark the expression as a
fixed one and the alliteration strengthens the impression; however, if such a fixed
expression existed, *ThLL s.v. foris* 1042, 57f. presents little evidence, except
perhaps Sen. *Ep.* 95, 72 *Catonis domi forisque egregia facta*. It seems more likely
that Apuleius has combined two formulas. Instances of *domi forisque* are
collected in *ThLL s.v. foris* 1040, 47 f.; see also *s.v. domus* 1957, 79 f.; 1975, 11 f.;
for *fortia facta* see e.g. Sal. *Cat.* 59, 6 and Vretska *ad loc.*; Tac. *Germ.* 14, 1 and
Galli *ad loc.*; Verg. *A.* 1, 641; Liv. 26, 39, 3.

adoriae plenae: Groslot proposes *plenus*, which Robertson awards a *fortasse
recte*; Knoche in *ThLL s.v. glorior* 2095, 13 (indicating that *plenis* may be

183

preferable) agrees with Hildebrand in taking the phrase with *factis*. They are followed by vGeisau 1916, 252. Oudendorp takes the gen. *adoriae plenae* together with *gloriarer* as a grecism. There is no need for surgery and Oudendorp's interpretation finds support in 174, 8 *serae uindictae gratulabar*; see comm. *ad loc*. For the uncertain derivation of *adoria* (sometimes approached to *ador* = a kind of wheat, sometimes to *adoro*) see Butler on Apul. *Apol*. 17 (21, 2) *Manio Curio tot adoreis longe incluto* and vdPaardt 1971, 144. (*ThLL*, Walde-Hofmann, Ernout-Meillet, *OLD* reject the link with *ador*.)

166, 5-7 Equinis armentis nanque me congregem pastor egregius mandati dominici serius auscultator aliquando permisit: "For the egregious herdsman, obeying his master's orders rather late in the day, at last allowed me access to the herds of horses".

The order of events differs from that of the *Onos* (27,7-28, 1) in that there the ass is placed among the herds first, under the mill second. Junghanns 1932, 80 f. provides an excellent analysis of this passage, but to regard Apuleius' sequence as a 'sachliche Unwahrscheinlichkeit' (*ibidem* n. 121) and thus an unfortunate 'nachträgliche Änderung' on Apuleius' part seems unacceptable. On the contrary, Apuleius has been able to include two elements that are less prominent in the *Onos*: characterization of another nasty female, and the appropriate breeding time; see below on *permisit* and *admissuram* (166, 11). For Apuleius' working method see Mason in *AAGA* 1978, 6 f.

equinis armentis: see above 165, 6 *greges equinos* and comm. *ad loc*. For *armenta* (used 3, 18; 65, 23 of unspecified cattle) of horses see e.g. Verg. *A*. 3, 540; Col. 1 *praef*. 26. The distinction made by Isodorus (Orig. 12, 1, 8 *armenta equorum et boum sunt, greges caprarum et ouium*) is not observed by Apuleius.

nanque: this is the spelling of F; cf. 155, 9; 159, 12; also *quenque* 157, 3; 170, 1; 9, 2 (203, 28) and *quenquam* 155, 23. LHSz 2, 506 note that the position in third place occurs in Apuleius here only, but that the word is placed second from Livy onwards; see also Bernhard 1927, 28.

congregem: the present passage is the first in which the word occurs. See Callebat 1968, 138, who notes that after Apuleius it also qualifies humans and even inanimate objects.

pastor egregius: the word-play with *congregem* is unmistakable and serves once more to underline Apuleius' etymological interests. For a similar paronomasia see 4, 5 (78, 6-8) and *GCA* 1977, 52 *ad loc*. See also Westermann 1939, 126; Callebat 1968, 470 f. The expression may be ironic: 168, 5 *egregius agaso* certainly is.

mandati dominici: another instance of an adjective instead of a genitive of the noun, see above on 165, 6 *greges equinos*; Callebat, 1968, 138; cf. Petr. 28, 7 *sine dominico iussu*.

serius: thus F; φ in mg. has *serus* and is followed by some of the later manuscripts, as well as most of the older editions. Colvius has *serius* (interpretation not specified), which Hildebrand thinks must mean "serious". Helm 1955, 299 explains *qui nimis sero paruit*. For the combination adv. + noun see below on 169, 25; K. St. 2, 218 have numerous instances, e.g. Liv. 25, 9, 2... *ne quis agrestium procul spectator agminis falleret.*

auscultator: in Cic. *Part*. 10 *aut auscultator modo est qui audit aut disceptator* the word is confined to its objective literal sense; here it has the further notion of "he who obeys". Apart from these two passages it occurs in *Gloss*. 2, 305, 27; 341, 28.

aliquando: denotes an expected or longed-for moment. In this sense it is quite common with or without *tandem*, from Plautus onwards (e.g. *St*. 387; see also Petersmann *ad loc.*).

permisit: Hildebrand cites Col. 6, 24, 1 *mense Iulio feminae maribus plerumque permittendae*; a more relevant passage is Col. 6, 37, 1, where ass-stallions are described that are fit for producing mules: *Est et alterum genus admissarii furentis in libidinem, quod nisi astu inhibeatur, affert gregi perniciem. Nam et saepe uinculis abruptis grauidas inquietat et, cum admittitur ceruicibus dorsisque feminarum imprimit morsus. Quod ne faciat, paulisper ad molam uinctus amoris saeuitiam labore temperat, et sic ueneri modestior admittitur.* Seen against this background the sequence of events is rather less improbable than Junghanns thought (see above). The passage also provides an interesting side-light on the asinine point of view.

At ego tandem liber asinus laetus et tripudians graduque molli gestiens equas opportunissimas iam mihi concubinas futuras deligebam: "But I, a free ass at last, happy and capering and dancing with delicate step, was quite ready to choose the most likely mares to be my concubines". 166, 7-10

For the ass's optimism when things appear to go right see Junghanns 1932, 80 n. 20.

At ego: Bernhard 1927, 112 notes that the combination is typical for Apuleius and cites 23 instances; *ego* is used emphatically (in contrast with the *auscultator*). See 1, 1 (1, 1); vdPaardt 1971, 48 agrees with Feldbrugge 1938, 105 that in view of the ego-narrative the frequency is not remarkable.

tandem liber asinus: Gatscha 1898, 147 compares Verg. *A*. 11, 493. The context there is comparable as well: Turnus' eagerness for battle is illustrated as follows:

> *qualis ubi abruptis fugit praesepia uinclis*
> *tandem liber equus, campoque potitus aperto*
> *aut ille in pastus armentaque tendit equarum*
> *aut adsuetus aquae perfundi flumine noto*
> *emicat, arrectisque fremit ceruicibus alte*
> *luxurians luduntque iubae per colla, per armos.*

The simile has a long history as was noted by Macrobius. He cites Ennius *Ann*. 514-18 (*Sat*. 6, 3, 7) and Hom. *Il*. 6, 506 f., where the comparison is used for Paris (cf. *ibid*. 15, 263-269: Hector). A similar comparison occurs in Apoll. Rh. 3, 1259 f. (Jason).

laetus ... gestiens: Bernhard 1927, 71 notes an anisocolic tricolon = a tricolon crescendo, see Fraenkel 1957, 351 n. 1. For *et ... que* see *ibid*. 82.

tripudians – gestiens: according to Bernhard 1927, 168 the verbs show a relationship of cause and effect, as above in 164, 21 *inescatos atque distentos*, but *gestiens* especially with *gradu molli* seems to express a different type of movement rather than the result of *tripudiare*; Callebat 1968, 79 deals with *tripudiare* under the heading 'rélisme familier': a humorous kind of realism... For *gestiens* cf. vdPaardt 1971, 178, and comm. on 161, 26.

equas opportunissimas: Columella (6, 36, 1 f.) expatiates on the care with which the parents of a mule should be selected and combined. We are dealing, however, with a lascivious ass, as Heine 1962, 212 f. emphasizes against Hammer 1926, 242. On the importance of the ass's sexuality as a theme in the *Met.* see also Schlam in *AAGA* 1978, 100 f.

concubinas: the term refers to a human relationship. Norden 1912, 116 remarks: 'Eine treffendere Ausdrucksweise hätte der Autor sicher nicht wählen können, um den weiten Standesunterschied, der nach des "edlen" Mensch-esels Dafürhalten zwischen diesem und den vulgären Stuten angeblich klafft, gebührend zu kennzeichnen'. Of course the ass is thinking in terms of more than one mare – *uxores*, then, would hardly be the appropriate term. We have here another item in the continuing interplay between the human and animal worlds with the ass Lucius at the focal point; this interplay of course is present in the *Onos*, but Apuleius adds his own particular refinements. In this particular scene *Onos* 28 presents a counterpart for *adulterium* (see below on 14) but not for *concubinas*. The interplay shows as many aspects as there are permutations possible between a human ass and real humans and/or real animals. The range of situations varies from the scene in which the just metamorphosed Lucius turns up in the stable and is treated with hostility by his horse and the other ass (3, 26: 71, 17 f.) to the one in which he refuses publicly to exhibit his sexual prowess with a condemned (human) female (10, 34: 265, 13 f.), and includes e.g. the accusation by the *puer* of sexual advances towards humans (7, 21 – one of several scenes in which the theme ass = sexual symbol is elaborated, see above on *equas opportunissimas*), the scene in which the mother of the *puer* addresses the ass as if he can understand (which, of course, he can: 175, 5 f.), his enjoyment of food and the use his then owners make of him (10, 13 f.), but also such smaller items as the miscalculation above (165, 12) and the human qualification *capitale* with *exitium* below. See also *GCA* 1977, 2 and 30.

deligebam: the process is obviously not completed; on the imperf. *de conatu* see K St 2, 1, 120 f.; LHSz 2, 316.

166, 10-11 Sed haec etiam spes hilarior in capitale processit exitium: "But this more cheerful expectation, too, developed into a deadly disaster."

For the change of mood see above on 166, 3-5, for the length of this colon Hijmans in *AAGA* 1978, 208 n. 19.

capitale... exitium: the expression occurs in later periods: see Cod. Theod. 8, 5, 47 (385 A.D.) *sub capitalis exitii minis*; Ennod. *dict.* 14, 4 p. 468, 14 Hartel: *capitale mereretur exitium*; cf. Amm. 26, 10, 10 *capitalis... pernicies*. (The context of 174, 20 *caput... demere* indicates that that expression is not to be compared with the present one.) For the use of a human term see above on *concubinas*. Later on (170, 18) the *puer* will accuse the ass of causing a *poenale... exitium* with a very similar hyperbaton.

Mares enim ob admissuram ueterem pasti satianter ac diu saginati, 166, 11-15 terribiles [alios] alioquin et utique quouis asino fortiores, de me metuentes sibi et adulterio degeneri praecauentes nec hospitalis Iouis seruato foedere riualem summo furentes persecuntur [h]odio: "For the stallions, which as usual at breeding time had been fed to bursting and fattened over a long period, and were in any case frightening and of course stronger than any ass, were afraid of competition from me and kept an eye out for degenerative adultery. Flouting the pact of hospitality sanctioned by Jupiter they persecuted me as a rival in a rage of unsurpassed hatred".

ob admissuram ueterem: the reading of F and φ is defended by Wiman 1927, 52 f., who argues that *uetus* is used here in the sense of "ordinary", "usual" ("vanlig") just as *nouus* often means "unusual".[1] In support he cites Verg. *G.* 1, 378 *et ueterem in limo ranae cecinere querellam* and compares *pristina fortuna* ("his usual luck") at Caes. *Gal.* 4, 4, 26, 5. This defense did not convince Robertson ('sed uix sanum'). Though indeed the *uetus querella* of frogs seems to have little in common with a *uetus admissura* of stallions, *uetus* in the sense of "regular" also occurs in Cic. *De or.* 1, 168 *uetus atque usitata exceptio*, and perhaps even in an expression denoting regular sexual contact in Sal. *Cat.* 23: *erat ei cum Fuluia ... stupri uetus consuetudo*. *Admissura* is a regular service performed at a specific time of year (Col. 6, 27, 3 *circa uernum equinoctium*). For this reason we accept the ms. reading, though with consderable hesitation, and not without appreciation of several good attempts among the following conjectures: Wover, followed by Scioppius, Eyssenhardt, tries *ob admissuram ueneream*. Pricaeus reads *uenerem* with a late ms., but brackets the word as a gloss. *Venerem* is accepted by Béouard and Clouard (with *admissuram* possibly to be taken as an *asyndeton bimembre*?). Lipsius attempts an attractive *uberem*. Oudendorp sees possibilities in bracketing *admissuram* as a gloss with *uenerem* (this solution was adopted by Helm in his first and second editions), as well a reading *admissariam* (or *admissurae*) *uenerem*. vdVliet and Gaselee prefer *admissariam uenerem*. Haupt proposes *admissuram ueterinam*, Kempf *admissuram uenturam*, whereas Petschenig 1888, 765 guesses *in Venerem*, which may be taken with *pasti satianter*; cf. Col. 6, 24, 2 *satietate uerni pabuli pecudes exhilaratae lasciuiunt in uenerem* (concerning cattle) and *ibidem* 27, 8 *appropinquante uere hordeo eruoque saginandus ut ueneri supersit*, said of stallions. See also below comm. on 171, 12 *in uenerem surgere*.

pasti satianter: Oudendorp defends the expression against *passim satiati* (Wover). *Satianter* occurs also in the 5th cent.: Ps. Vigil. Thaps. *c. Mariuadum* 2, 18, but appears to have had no further currency.

The fattening of domestic animals before mating is also discussed (apart from the references in Columella mentioned above) by Varro *R.* 2, 1, 17 and 2, 8, 4 (with special reference to ass-stallions).

---

[1] Wiman takes "usual" as referring to the copulation of horse with horse as against the "unusual" copulation of ass with horse. The latter may be unusual in nature, but is not so when human breeders are controlling matters. Hence Wiman's explanation cannot be correct.

terribiles alioquin: there can be little doubt that *alios* of F is to be deleted with ς, Lütjohann 1873, 492 and all modern editors. See Helm, *Praef. Fl.* LI (neither Eyssenhardt's *terribiles riuales et alioquin [et]* nor Lindenbrogius' *alias [alioquin]* need discussion). Heine 1962, 149 n. 1 notes that fierce animals are a common feature in the bleak landscape of the *Met.* We may compare the dogs at 4, 3 (76, 20-23) and *GCA* 1977, 42 *ad loc.* See also 8, 17 (190, 12 f.). The particle *alioquin* is in regular use in the *Met.* especially in the sense of "in any case" or "as it is". See also Bernhard 1927, 127; Feldbrugge 1938, 109; Callebat 1968, 459 f. Cf., however, 171, 12, where it means "otherwise".

de me metuentes sibi: *de* denotes the source of expected evil. The construction occurs 6, 23 (146, 6) *nec prosapiae tantae tuae statuque de matrimonio mortali metuas*; 9, 27 *(223,22)*; *cf. Pl. Merc.* 520. The *Onos* (28) describes the emotion as follows: ἀεὶ γάρ με μοιχὸν ὑποπτεύοντες [τῶν ἵππων] τῶν αὐτῶν γυναικῶν... A similar use of *de* occurs 163, 5: see comm. *ad loc.*

adulterio degeneri praecauentes: Callebat 1968, 491 f. discusses this passage under the heading 'ablatifs complétant un verbe', but at 10, 9 (243, 25) we read *futurae quaestioni praecauens.* Liv. 3, 53, 1 construes with *ab.* For the human term *adulterium* see above on *concubinas.* The present situation allows the author to cause his narrator to have an ass ascribe human thoughts and emotions to a group of horses. See also comm. on 171, 23 *amatorem.*

mares... saginati: for the colometry see Hijmans in *AAGA* 1978, 207, n. 8.

hospitalis Iouis: see also 3, 26 (71, 21). The assumption that the laws of religion apply in the animal world accentuates the comic effect (see Junghanns 1932, 81) and belongs to the same interplay of human/animal worlds as discussed above on *concubinas.* Note the emphatic word order.

foedere: the word refers to an agreement between men, rather than to a law given by Jupiter, and therefore receives its content from *hospitalis* by enallage. In the sense of a pact between the divinity and mankind or men it occurs only in Christian authors, e.g. Hil. *Trin.* 2, 33 *intercessionis foedere*; Vulg. *Gen.* 6, 18.

summo... persecuntur odio: Bernhard 1927, 18 collects numerous instances in which the verb takes second last place. The strong hyperbaton *summo... odio* adds emphasis.

166, 16-21 Hic elatis in altum uastis pectoribus arduus capite et sublimis uertice primoribus in me pugillatur ungulis, ille terga pulposis torulis obesa conuertens postremis uelitatur calcibus, alius hinnitu maligno comminatus remulsis auribus dentiumque candentium renudatis asceis totum me commorsicat: "One lifted his vast chest, with his head high and his crest aloft, rained blows on me with his fore hooves; a second turned his thick, muscle-padded back and volleyed with his hind hooves; another menaced me with a malevolent whinny, laid his ears back, bared the adzes of his shining teeth and bit me all over".

The three stallions are not merely different in their methods of fighting (on the Apuleian trick of dissolving a multitude into its individual parts see Junghanns 1932, 70 n. 106, Feldbrugge 1938, 64, vThiel 1971, 13 n. 34) but their activities are sketched with differing sound mixtures (see Hijmans in *AAGA* 1978, 205 f.) and colon lengths. There are three main pauses, after *ungulis, calcibus, commorsicat* and six secondary pauses, after *pectoribus, uertice, conuertens, comminatus, auribus* and *asceis*. The first horse gets three cola, the second two, the last four.

pectoribus: for the poetic plural see *GCA* 1977, 42 and 58.

primoribus in me pugillatur ungulis: the word *pugillatur* turns the otherwise quite natural picture into a caricature of a human boxer. For *primoribus* see vdPaardt 1971, 193. *Pugillatur* occurs in the *Met.* here only; *Soc.* 21 (31, 15) has the inf. *pugillare* and passive *pugillatur*. Flobert 1975, 367 n. 2 mistakenly thinks that *pugillari* should be read in the latter passage. See also Charis. 439, 31 *pugillauit*.[1]

terga: for the poetic plural see above on *pectoribus*.

pulposis: the word occurs here for the first time (cf. Bernhard 1927, 139; Luisa Gargantini 1963, 38). See also Donatus on Ter. *Hec.* 441 *cadauerosa facie: Potest et pulposa intellegi et crassa quasi cadauerosa* ("bloated"). In the 5th/6th cent. Soranus 14 uses it in a technical medical sense: *apud uirgines ... quae deuirginatae non sunt (orificium matricis) pulposum et molle est*; cf. ibid. 9.

torulis: *corulis* F is corrected in ς. Médan 1925, 168 notes that the meaning of the word has been changed slightly. Cf. Pl. *Am.* 144 "tuft of hair"; Var. *L.* 5, 167; Amm. 16, 12, 24; 29, 1, 31. Vitr. 2, 9, 3 employs the word in the sense "sapwood". However, *torus* can mean "muscle", e.g. Claudius Hermerius, *Mulomedicina Chiron*. 780 *lato et ... musculorum toris ... neruoso pectore* (of horses), cf. *feminibus torosis (ibidem)*, and it seems possible therefore that Apuleius uses the diminutive in that sense, without reference to Plautus or Varro. For the development of this diminutive see Hakamies 1951, 18 and 111 f.

postremis ... calcibus: see *GCA* 1977, 40.

uelitatur: Bernhard 1927, 133 regards the word as a vulgarism and ibid. 196 as a military term; Callebat 1968, 517 notes that it conveys an archaic and picturesque image; *GCA* 1977, 39 translates "a swift-running skirmish". Apuleius always uses it in a military sense, whether literally as here (cf. 9, 1: 202, 5 and 9, 37: 231, 14) or metaphorically (see 5, 11: 112, 3; 5, 21: 119, 17; 8, 25: 197, 1; 9, 15: 214, 12; 9, 29: 225, 2; *Apol.* 2 (2, 15). The etymology of the word *ueles* is not entirely certain (cf. Walde-Hofmann and Ernout-Meillet *s.v.* who suggest a possible link with *uelox*) but Is. *Orig.* 9, 3, 43 and 18, 57 connects it with *uolitare*. F's corrector produced *uolitatur* – it seems far-fetched to think that he may have done that under the influence of Isidorus' etymology. There is only one (doubtful) instance of a deponent *uolitari* "fly" in Fortun. *Germ.* 70, 187; see Flobert 1975, 241.

remulsis auribus: the expression has given trouble, since *remulcere aures* means "to stroke in order to quieten down" in 1, 2 (2, 13) and *remulceo* elsewhere also can have a recreative flavour (e.g. Stat. *Theb.* 7, 93; Apul. *Met.* 5, 15: 115, 5). Hence *Ed. Rom.* and Hildebrand, citing ς, print *remissis auribus*. Oudendorp prefers the ms. reading. A good parallel is found in Cass. *Var.* 7, 15, 3 (of a

---

[1] The Thesaurus Institute at Munich has provided us with the following instances apart from the ones mentioned: *V.L.* 1. *Cor.* 9, 26 *non sic pugilor* ap. Aug. *in Psalm.* 57, 7 who adds *pugilari enim est pancratium facere*; ibidem 75, 18; SHA *Gall.* 8, 3 (? *pugillantes*), Aug. *Vtil. Ieiun.* 4, 5 (= 1 *Cor.* 9, 26), Boeth. *In categ. Ar.* 253c (Migne) *potentia pugillandi*. Certainly active: *Gramm.* suppl. 68, 9; Aug. *Serm.* 216, 6, 6; *Acta Concil. Oec.* 1, 5 (285, 11 Schwartz); *Gloss.* 2, 426, 7.

statue): *Mirabitur formis equinis signa etiam inesse feruoris. Crispatis enim naribus ac rotundis, constrictis membris, auribus remulsis credet forsitan cursus appetere, cum se metalla nouerit non mouere.*

dentium candentium: cf. Nemes. *Cyneg.* 164 *tunc etiam niueis armantur dentibus ora.* Though white teeth occur frequently in Latin literature (e.g. Pl. *Epid.* 429; Verg. *A.* 7, 667) the present combination does not seem to occur elsewhere. The shining white quality implies fearsome danger; it is underscored by the inflectional rhyme. See for rhyme Callebat in *AAGA* 1978, 187, who refers to Westermann 1939, 137 f.

asceis: the mss. are reported differently in Helm, Robertson, Giarratano-Frassinetti. Helm notes that the original reading of F was *asteis*, changed by a later hand into *costis*, Robertson and Giarratano-Frassinetti cannot read the latter word and report *'astis* uel *costis'*. Helm implies that φ is a witness to F's *asteis* (cf. Praef. *Fl.* xxxi); Robertson does not report φ and Frassinetti gives *'hastis* φ'.

Oudendorp, faced with an unsatisfactory *hastis*, tries *saxis*. Lütjohann 1873, 467 emends to read *asceis*, comparing Plin. *Nat.* 18, 2: *Atque cum arbore exacuant limentque cornua elephanti et uri, saxo rhinocerotes, utroque apri dentium sicas...* This emendation is generally accepted. *Ascea* (or *ascia* is a carpenter's or joiner's instrument; cf. Cic. *Leg.* 2, 59. The activity for which the *ascea* is used is termed *dolare* (Don. on Ter. *Eun.* 515). *OLD* translates "axe", but "adze" seems more appropriate both to the shape of teeth and to the activity mentioned.

totum me commorsicant: Feldbrugge 1938, 64 notes the ironic self-pity (both *totum* and the strengthening *com-*) as well as the exaggeration. The verb occurs also 10, 22 (253, 22) *commorsicantibus oculis* (cf. 2, 19: 33, 7 *morsicantibus oculis*) but nowhere else in Latin. See also below on 170, 8.

166, 21-23 Sic apud historiam de rege Thracio legeram, qui miseros hospites ferinis equis suis lacerandos deuorandosque porrigebat: "I had read just the same thing in history about a Thracian king, who used to thrust his wretched guests at his wild horses to tear apart and devour".

The episode of the stallions is concluded by a reference to the horses of Diomede. For this type of conclusion see comm. on 176, 13; Junghanns 1932, 19 n. 22.

apud historiam: Callebat 1968, 216 places this use of *apud* in the larger context of *apud* as a *sermo cotidianus* substitute for *in*, which was introduced into literary prose as early as Sallust. Parallels for the specific expression here occur in Pomp. *gramm.* 5, 187 *apud antiquos libros*; Tert. *Nat.* 2, 12 *apud litteras uestras*; Aug. *C.D.* 14, 7 *apud sacras litteras*. For further instances see *ThLL s.v. apud* 338, 20 f. Concerning the question *historia* or *fabula* see comm. on 151, 4-6.

de rege Thracio legeram: it is not necessary to take *de rege* with *historiam* as Callebat 1968, 204 appears to do. The narrator implies that the ass Lucius remembered his mythology and thereby reminds the reader once more of his human aspect.

qui... porrigebat: the length of the colon and its function is discussed by Hijmans in *AAGA* 1978, 196. For the story of Diomede, to whose cruel practice

Hercules put an end, see e.g. Apollod. *Bibl.* 2, 5, 8; Diod. Sic. 4, 15, 3 f.; Hyg. *Fab.* 30; 250. Cf. also references in e.g. Lucr. 5, 30; Ov. *Ep.* 9, 67.

ferinis: Helm proposed *feris*, but did not print it in view of 2, 4 (28, 9) *iam in ceruum ferimus* (said of Actaeon). The parallel is not exact since in our passage the brute bestiality of Diomede's horses is meant; cf. e.g. Sen. *Cl.* 1, 25, 1 *ferina ista rabies est sanguine gaudere ac uolneribus*. Nevertheless it is not necessary to change the text.

miseros hospites ... lacerandos deuorandosque porrigebat: vdVliet proposed *proiciebat* which produces good sense, but so does *porrigebat*, which is construed with object + gerundive on several occasions, e.g. Sen. *Ben.* 2, 12, 1 *porrexit osculandum sinistrum pedem*; Suet. *Tit.* 9, 3; Juv. 6,597; Auson. 13, 2, 37 (p. 263 Peiper); Mart. Cap. 2, 140; Apon. 12 *hunc esse librum qui prophetae Ezechieli intus et foris scriptus deuorandus porrigitur*; Cod. Theod. 8, 5, 23, 7. If anything, the more controlled action of *porrigere* helps to convey the deliberate cruelty of Diomede, whose twisted psyche is further developed in the next phrase.

adeo ille praepotens tyrannus sic parcus hordei fuit, ut edacium iumentorum famem corporum humanorum largitione sedaret: "in fact that mighty tyrant was so tight-fisted with his barley, that he satisfied the hunger of his famished animals by lavishing human bodies upon them". 166, 23-167, 2

adeo: in this sense ("actually", "indeed") the word does not commonly occur in first place. Cf. Pl. *Most.* 629; Apul. *Apol.* 15, 7 *adeo uir omnium sapientissimus speculo etiam ad disciplinam morum utebatur*. See *ThLL s.v. adeo* 612, 41 f. for further instances.

sic parcus hordei fuit: the incongruity of this parsimony produces a lovely bit of satire. See Junghanns 1932, 19 n. 22; 63 n. 91; 81; Heine 1962, 192 n. 6.

famem: F has *fam̄* (but the original writing was redone), which acc. to editors should be read as *famen*; *fam̄* φ (= *famem*) in that case is to be seen as a correction. We are not convinced that the abbreviation is unambiguous.

largitione: Apuleius' penchant for abstracts is well known; see Médan 1925, 318, who gives a large number of instances in which an abstract noun is substituted for a verbal phrase or subordinate clause.

Note the carefully arranged order in which the interlocking arrangement of *famem* and *largitione*, both with preceding genitives, is varied by the chiastic placement of the adjectives and nouns of those genitives, three of which produce flectional rhyme as did the gerundives of the first part of the period.

CHAPTER XVII

The ass falls into the clutches of a sadist.

167, 2-4 Ad eundem modum distractus et ipse uariis equorum incursibus rursus molares illos circuitus requirebam: "In the same way I, too, was torn in pieces by the repeated attacks of the horses, and I yearned for those perambulations of mine in the tread-mill again".

Ad eundem modum: i.e. like the aforementioned guests of the *rex Thracius* (Diomedes). Callebat 1968, 214 regards *ad... modum* as a possible archaism (coll. Enn. *var.* 76; Cato *Agr.* 42). In the case of a related expression (*ad istum modum*) he hesitates between archaism and borrowing from the contemporary colloquial language; *ad eundem modum* may well also be colloquial.

equorum: the reading of φ. In F *equorum* has been changed to *equarum*; the part played by the mares in this incident has obviously escaped the scribe.

incursibus: the noun occurs in the plural in 168, 17, too; before Apul. in Verg. *G.* 3, 407; Suet. *Vesp.* 8, 4; Quint. *Inst.* 10, 7, 3. See Bernhard 1927, 101 f. on Apul.'s preference for plural abstracts.

rursus: used pleonastically; cf. 8, 24 (196, 7). See also Callebat 1968, 542 f.; *GCA* 1977, 139.

molares illos circuitus: *molaris* in its sense of "pertaining to the mill" occurs for the first time in this passage, according to the *ThLL s.v.*; otherwise the adjective pertains to the millstone. See further our comm. on 165, 6.

167, 4-5 Verum Fortuna meis cruciatibus insatiabilis aliam mihi denuo pestem instruxit: "But Fortune, insatiable of my torments, had devised yet another plague for me".

Fortuna meis cruciatibus insatiabilis: this description of Fortuna as a monster with an *insatiabilis profundusque uenter* is applied to Lucius himself in 175, 7 by the mother of the sadistic boy. For Fortuna's role see further our comm. on 155, 21 and the literature mentioned there, notably Tatum 1969a, 94, n. 184. The construction of *insatiabilis* with the ablative is less frequent than that with the genitive; with the ablative also Liv. 4, 13, 4 *ut est humanus animus insatiabilis eo quod fortuna spondet*.

Observe the repetition of *i* and *a* sounds; Médan 1925, 270 points out the sequence of dactyls in this unit.

pestem instruxit: the heavy clausula (dispondeus) accentuates the threatening danger; see Hijmans, *AAGA* 1978, 198 f.

167, 6-8 Delegor enim ligno monte deuehundo, puerque mihi praefectus imponitur omnibus ille quidem puer deterrimus: "For I was charged with carrying wood down from the mountains. A slave was appointed to be in charge of me, and that boy was the very worst in all the world".

puer: this boy is a slave, employed by the *equiso*, who belongs to the staff of Tlepolemus and Charite (Vallette *ad loc.*; Heine in *AAGA* 1978, 40, n. 58). So Lucius has fallen very low; cf. Heine, *ibid.*, 30: 'Lucius, who before his transformation had been bent on being a member of the high society (...), now becomes a beast of burden of the lowest strata and thereby gains access to new things and matters, which before his transformation he could never have witnessed and experienced from his socially secure standpoint'.

omnibus: many have taken offense at this reading. To mention a few conjectures: ς has *omnibus modis*; Guilielmus *omnimodis*; vdVliet ‹prae› *omnibus*; Helm in his Teubner edition (1-3²) ‹ex› *omnibus* (also Pagliano); Robertson, reverting to *omnium* of the editio Vincentina (1488), reads *omnium unus*. But most modern editors (among them Helm-Krenkel) retain *omnibus*, as did Oudendorp (who regarded *omnibus ... deterrimus* as a contamination of *deterior omnibus* and *deterrimus omnium*). *Omnibus* is defended as an ablative of respect (= *omnino*) by Kroll 1914, 361, who mentioned our passage as an amplification to Löfstedt's (1911, 49) discourse on *totum, ex toto, in totum* meaning "durchaus". Löfstedt writes: 'Hier werden zum Schluss auch *per omnia* und *in omnia* berührt; seltener ist *omnibus*, z.B. Dict. II 16 *agri ... depraedati omnibusque uastati (...)* oder noch härter Paulin. Nolan. *Epist*. XII 6 *deus omnibus* ("durchaus") *ueritas* (von Hartel Patrist. Stud. V 7 mit noch einem zweiten Beispiel desselben Schriftstellers verteidigt).' Thus already Dederich on Dict. 2, 16 (see Hildebrand 1842, 588a).

ille: used in a pejorative sense, as in 168, 20 *puer ille nequissimus*; 169, 14 *ille deterrimus ac temerarius puer*. See Callebat 1968, 277; *GCA* 1977, 96.

puer: this (second) *puer* is lacking in ς; Hildebrand, Eyssenhardt, vdVliet, and Gaselee omit it, too. But this repetition within a short space can be functional: it may be used to express the rage of the narrating I, who identifies with the experiencing I. Helm 1904, 519 f. mentions a number of similar repetitions in the *Apol.* and the *Fl.*; Bernhard 1927, 153 f. (who does not mention our passage) sees only the 'stylistic error', but observes generously: 'selbst die besten Stilisten wie Cicero sind diesem Fehler nicht immer entgangen.' See further LHSz 2, 820 f.

Nec me montis excelsi tantum arduum fatigabat iugum, nec saxeas tantum sudes incursando contribam ungulas, uerum fustium quoque crebris ictibus perdite dedolabar, ut usque plagarum mihi medullaris insideret dolor: "Not only did the steep height of the lofty mountain tire me out, not only did I wear away my hooves by stubbing them against stony peaks, but I was also whacked unrestrainedly by numerous blows with cudgels, so that I felt the pain of the strokes in my very marrow". 167, 8-12

Neither Lucius nor the reader of this sentence is given a moment's rest: four long cola illustrate the ass's efforts. See Hijmans, *AAGA* 1978, 198 and n. 20.

Nec ... tantum, nec ... tantum, uerum ... quoque: in Apul. this combination occurs only here. See Redfors 1960, 38 for a survey of all variants, the most frequent of which is *non modo ... uerum etiam*.

In the parallel passage in *Onos* 29, 1 f. the cumulation of Lucius' predicaments is rendered as follows: πρῶτον μὲν ὑψηλὸν ὄρος ἀναβαίνειν ἔδει, ὀρθὴν δεινῶς ὁδόν, εἶτα καὶ ἀνυπόδητος ὄρει ἐν λιθίνῳ. καὶ μοι συνεξέπεμπον ὀνηλάτην, παιδάριον ἀκάθαρτον. τοῦτό με καινῶς ἑκάστοτε ἀπώλλυεν. πρῶτον μὲν ἔπαιέν με καὶ τρέχοντα λίαν οὐ ξύλῳ ἁπλῷ, ἀλλὰ τῷ ὄζους πυκνοὺς ἔχοντι καὶ ὀξεῖς, καὶ ἀεὶ ἔπαιεν εἰς τὸ αὐτὸ τοῦ μηροῦ, ὥστε ἀνέῳκτό μοι κατ' ἐκεῖνο ὁ μηρὸς τῇ ῥάβδῳ· ὁ δὲ ἀεὶ τὸ τραῦμα ἔπαιεν.

montis excelsi ... arduum fatigabat iugum renders the part ὑψηλὸν through ὁδόν. Whereas the *Onos* mentions the elements 'high' and 'steep' in two separate sentences, Apuleius has combined them into one.

saxeas ... sudes incursando contribam ungulas: renders and explains ἀνυπόδητος ... λιθίνῳ. In view of this parallelism Beroaldus and Hildebrand must be right in explaining *saxeae sudes* as *saxa acuta* (cf. LS *s.v. sudis*: "rocky peaks, crags"); at any rate their explanation is preferable to Oudendorp's *saxeae sudes = radices in saxis iacentes*.

incursare: "to knock (against obstacles) when moving" (*OLD*) occurs as an intransitive a few times in Ovid (e.g. *Met.* 14, 189 *luminis orbus / rupibus incursat*; as a transitive verb it is also found in Tert. *Cult. Fem.* 2, 13 *in tenebris derelicta a multis incurseris* and Hil. *Trin.* 2, 22.

contribam: there is no need for conjectures like *conturbabam* (ς), *contundebam* (Oudendorp), *contribulabam* (id.), *contriueram* (vdVliet) or its abbreviated form *contriram* (Hildebrand *dubit.*), and *conterebam* (Beroaldus and – obviously independently – Damsté 1928, 21). We have here the imperfect of the verb *contrire*, which has developed from the perfect *contriui* (of *contero*) as *prostrare* from *prostraui*, and *irari* from *iratus sum*. See Thielmann 1886, 542; *ThLL s.v. contero*.

fustium ... crebris ictibus perdite dedolabar: a comparison with the parallel passage in the *Onos* is quite instructive here. First our attention is attracted by a difference in composition: Apul. has moved the παιδάριον ἀκάθαρτον – the *puer deterrimus* – to the beginning of the sentence, so that all misery for Lucius the ass literally begins with this *puer*. Next, a description of the stick with which the ass is beaten has disappeared, probably because a similar *frondosum baculum* has been mentioned just before (165, 19), in the hand of the *nequissima mulier* (anonymous in Apul.). Apuleius underscores the malice of the action by the use of *dedolare* (cf. Hor. *Sat.* 1, 5, 23 *fuste dolat*), actually a technical term for hewing or chiselling a block of wood or stone into the right shape (cf. 6, 13: 138, 13 *crustallo dedolatum uasculum*); thus Lucius is implicitly seen as an inanimate object; see Callebat 1968, 70. We cannot regard this verb as a euphemism (Bernhard 1927, 193).

For *perdite* (a conjecture by Hildebrand, see below F and φ have *pcliue*, which Oudendorp wants to read as *procliue = procliuiter* = 'prono ad verberandum animo manuque'; thus also Eyssenhardt, Clouard, and Kronenberg 1928, 51 (coll. Pl. *Capt.* 336). Other conjectures are *persaepe* (ς); *prolixe* (Luetjohann, followed by vdVliet, Gaselee, and Robertson); *prodige* (Bursian); *per diem* (Purser); *perdius* (Plasberg); *praeclare* (Castiglioni 1931, 489). Armini (1928, 306) stays quite close to the transmission with his conjecture *per ‹pro›cliue*, which he explains as follows: 'etiam in descensu ... ligni mole molestus adsidue vapulabat'. Armini sees the passage *uerum . . . quoque* as an indication that not only the ascent but also the descent was a *uia dolorosa*; he supports this view in a deuterology (1932, 82 f.), by pointing out a passage in the *Onos* subsequent to the one quoted above: καὶ ἄνωθεν ἡ κατάβασις ὀξεῖα ἦν· ὁ δὲ καὶ ἐνταῦθα ἔπαιεν.

Although Armini's conjecture is admirable, it must be observed that the sentence *nec me montis . . . dedolabar* is first and foremost a counterpart of the *Onos*-passage (the earlier *Onos*-passage), which emphasizes the terror of the climb in general. Hildebrand's conjecture *perdite* – generally accepted by modern editors – is palaeographically as minor a change as Armini's; in the meaning "in a recklessly violent or unrestrained way" (*OLD s.v.*) it can easily be defended with a reference to με καινῶς ἑκάστοτε ἀπώλλυεν.

ut usque plagarum mihi medullaris insideret dolor: according to Beroaldus, Pricaeus and Floridus this is a sort of hypallage for *usque medullas insideret mihi plagarum dolor*; thus also Médan, who translates (1925, 344): "de sorte que je ressentais jusque dans mes moelles la douleur des coups". Oudendorp gave two other explanations of *usque*: 'significat vel *continuo semper perpetuo* vel *tantum non, adeo vehementer*, et *eo usque* ut medullas penetraret dolor'. The first explanation is preferred by Hildebrand and Forcellini *s.v.* – rightly, we think. Hildebrand points out Hor. *Sat.* 1, 2. 65 *poenas dedit usque*, where the adverb means "immer wieder" (see Kiessling-Heinze *ad loc.*). Verg. *Ecl.* 9, 64 *cantantes licet usque – minus via laedit – eamus* could also be an example of this use if one follows Page in taking *usque* with *cantantes*, translating "we can go singing all the way" (but see Coleman *ad loc.* for a different opinion).

medullaris: found in Apul. for the first time here. *ThLL s.v.* mentions also Antidot. Brux. 156 *ad febrem medullarem*.

plagarum dolor: observe the hyperbaton and the alliteration of *r*.

coxaeque dexterae semper ictus incutiens et unum feriendo locum 167, 12-15
dissipato corio et ulceris latissimi facto foramine, immo fouea uel
etiam fenestra nullus tamen desinebat identidem uulnus sanguine
delibutum obtundere: "because he struck the blows all the time on my right hip and kept hitting one place, the skin had broken and a very wide open sore – or rather a hole or a window – had formed; yet he did not stop pounding over and over again on that wound which was steeped in blood".

The sadism of the young ass-driver is given full force by a sonorous sentence; see Heine 1962, 150 (with note 1). For some reminiscences of these cruelties in the short story *Psyche* by the Dutch author Louis Couperus (strangely enough not in his *De verliefde ezel*), see Elisabeth Visser, *AAGA* 1978, 242.

coxae: only here in the *Met.*, possibly because of its cacophony: the usual word, in Apul. as elsewhere, is *femur*. See Callebat 1968, 51.

dexterae: typically Apuleian specificity; cf. *Onos* 29, 2 καὶ ἀεὶ ἔπαιεν εἰς τὸ αὐτὸ τοῦ μηροῦ.

incutiens . . . fereindo: *variatio*. For the ablative of the gerund in the sense of a present participle, see Callebat 1968, 319.

ulceris latissimi facto foramine, immo fouea uel etiam fenestra: cf. *Onos* 29, 2 ὥστε ἀνέῳκτό μοι κατ' ἐκεῖνο ὁ μηρὸς τῇ ῥάβδῳ. Apuleius' phrase is an anisocolic tricolon with crescendo (Bernhard 1927, 71) and quadruple iteration of the expressive *f*-sound (Médan 1925, 306). Feldbrugge 1938, 64 rightly calls it a comical hyperbole (see also Junghanns 1932, 52, n. 76): the (implied) author here ridicules the narrator's pity for his former self.

nullus = non; cf. 8, 19 (192, 4) *an nulli scitis, quo loco consederetis*? See Médan 1925, 222 and Callebat 1968, 416 for more passages in the *Met*. This intensifying *nullus* is very rare in post-classical prose: Apul. is one of the few who use it (Hofmann ³1951, 80).

uulnus sanguine delibutum obtundere: a pathetic final effect is gained by the assonance of *u* and (possibly) by the clausula; see Hijmans, *AAGA* 1978, 199.

sanguine delibutum: also in 3, 1 (52, 15); see vdPaardt 1971, 26.

For *obtundere*, see *GCA* 1977, 39 and comm. on 176, 5. The verb refers to a very painful and humiliating kind of beating. Not all blows received by Lucius are of this kind: Charite's slaps (149, 23) do not hurt him; those of the *uiator* (173, 2) do not impress him much.

167, 16-17 Lignorum uero tanto me premebat pondere, ut fascium molem elefanto, non asino paratam putares: "Moreover, he loaded me with such a great weight of wood that you would think that the mass of fagots was intended for an elephant, not for an ass".

The comical exaggeration is also found in the *Onos* (29, 3) εἶτα μοι ἐπετίθει φορτίον ὅσον χαλεπὸν εἶναι καὶ ἐλέφαντι ἐνεγκεῖν. Repetition of the motif of the heavy burden, cf. 3, 28 (73, 4); 4, 4 (77, 8); 147, 14.

lignorum: *linorum* F, 'sed emend. eadem (fort.) manus'; Apuleius specifies here the more general φορτίον.

uero: renders εἶτα, so it has a cumulative rather than an adversative sense. See LHSz 2, 494.

fascium: F originally has *farcium*; φ even *sarcinum*, which may be an anticipation of *sarcina* in 19. The correction is, of course, necessary.

elefanto: with ς one may emend to *elephanto* (thus e.g. Frassinetti). Helm follows F, also in 1, 9 (9, 9), which has *elephantum*. Since it cannot be determined whether Apul. followed a uniform orthographical system, we prefer to follow the principal manuscript. See *GCA* 1977, 210 f.

167, 17-21 Ille uero etiam quotiens in alterum latus praeponderans declinarat sarcina, cum deberet potius grauantis ruinae fustes demere et leuata paulisper pressura sanare me uel certe in alterum latus translatis peraequare, contra lapidibus additis insuper sic iniquitati ponderis medebatur: "But that was not all: whenever the overweight burden had slipped down to one side, whereas he should have taken away sticks from the side where the burden was too heavy and threatened to fall and eased me by relieving the pressure for a while, or at least have restored the balance by shifting them to the other side, on the contrary he added extra stones and tried in that way to remedy the unevenness in weight.

There is a striking parallelism with *Onos* 29, 4: εἰ δέ μοι περιπῖπτον ἴδοι τὸ φορτίον καὶ εἰς τὸ ἕτερον ἐπικλῖνον, τῶν ξύλων ἀφαιρεῖν καὶ τῷ κουφοτέρῳ προσβαλεῖν καὶ τὸ ἴσον ποιεῖν, τοῦτο μὲν οὐδέποτε εἰργάσατο, λίθους δὲ μεγάλους ἐκ τοῦ ὄρους ἀναιρούμενος εἰς τὸ κουφότερον καὶ ἄνω νεῦον τοῦ φορτίου προσετίθει.

If the *Onos* is a faithful reflection of the *Vorlage,* Apuleius has omitted elements from it rather than added to it: he regarded as superfluous information the fact that the stones were big and that they were taken from the mountain. The metaphor of *sanare* and *mederi* is new, however.

uero etiam: a continuous cumulation of Lucius' misery; see Junghanns 1932, 82.

quotiens: renders εἰ in the *Onos* passage (translated by *si* in 168, 4). See Ruiz de Elvira 1954, 128 for the indicative in iterative clauses.

grauantis ruinae fustes demere: the syntax is complicated. Médan 1925, 319 regards this as one of the cases where an abstract noun is preferred to a 'proposition complétive', but this says more about the French language than about the Latin. When we leave aside the theoretical possibility that *grauantis* is a plural accusative (and *ruinae* a dative), there are two possibilities for the genitive *grauantis ruinae*: a possessive genitive or a genitive dependent on *demere*. The latter type suggests to Löfstedt ²1965, 2, 417 an influence from the Greek, and to demonstrate such influence in this passage is very easy (τῶν ξύλων ἀφαιρεῖν in the *Onos, c.q. Vorlage*). On such separative genitives see further *GCA* 1977, 162 f. and the literature mentioned there, to which should be added LHSz 2, 83.

A *grauans ruina*, then, would be "a burden falling on account of being heavy", with *ruina* abstr. pro concreto (= *sarcina ruens*) and *grauare* in the sense "be heavy" (thus *ThLL s.v.*)

leuata paulisper pressura: many translators take *paulisper* with *sanare*, but its position indicates that it modifies *leuata*. For this verb, which here has its usual meaning "lighten" but in the *Met.* often means "lift" as well, see Callebat 1968, 157.

pressura: F and φ have *presura*; the correction is by ς. Médan 1925, 164 and Callebat 1968, 75 translate it in a concrete sense "burden", "weight", but the usual abstract meaning "pressure" seems much more attractive here in view of the context (thus also *OLD s.v.*).

sanare me: Helm mentions in his *app. crit.* the possibility of *iuuare*, but retains *sanare*, which is frequently found in its transitive sense; cf. e.g. Cic. *Fam.* 5, 16, 1 *consolationem, quae leuare dolorem tuum posset, si minus sanare potuisset.* Blümner 1894, 307 takes offense at the object *me* and wants to replace it by *eam*, sc. *sarcinam*: '*sarcina* ist sowohl zu *peraequare* als zu *sanare* ein ganz passendes Objekt, und speziell *sanare* dann im selben Bilde gesagt, wie nachher *mederi*'. It is incorrect to say that *peraequare* would require an object; cf. in the *Onos* καὶ τὸ ἴσον ποιεῖν.

lapidibus additis insuper: for the adverbial *insuper* ("in addition"), see comm. on 167, 22 f.; for the pleonasm in combination with *addere* see Callebat 1968, 543, who suggests influence by Plautus.

sic = οὕτως; see vdPaardt 1971, 25 with literature.

iniquitati... medebatur: F has *iniquitate*; another hand changed the second *i* into an *e*. In ς an emendation has been made to *iniquitati* or *iniquitatem*. The accusative is defended by Oudendorp and Hildebrand *ad loc.*, Desertine 1898, 86, and Médan 1925, 32; it is adopted by Eyssenhardt and vdVliet, too. Certainly many parallels can be adduced for *mederi* with the accusative (beginning with Ter. *Phor.* 822; see Dziatzko-Hauler *ad loc.* and further KSt 2, 1, 311 and LHSz 2, 32); but Apul., who uses the verb *mederi* seven times in all (in the *Met.* only here), always constructs it with a dative (thus Helm – rightly – in his *app. crit.*). Since *-ti* and *-tem* are palaeographically equally defensible, Apuleius' usual practice should turn the scale in favour of the dative.

CHAPTER XVIII

Lucius has a hard time.

Nec tamen post tantas meas clades inmodico sarcinae pondere con- 167, 22-168, 3
tentus, cum fluuium transcenderemus, qui forte praeter uiam defluebat, peronibus suis ab aquae madore consulens ipse quoque insuper lumbos meos insiliens residebat, exiguum scilicet et illud tantae molis superpondium: "And yet, after all this misery of mine, he was not satisfied with the excessive weight of the burden: whenever we crossed a stream (which happened to flow along the road), to crown everything he would even jump up on to my hind-quarters himself, to save his boots from getting wet in the water, and remain sitting there – that in itself only a small addition, of course, to the weight of such a large bulk".

post ... clades: for Apul.'s preference for plural abstracts, see Médan 1925, 324. *Clades* refers here to the torments described in the previous chapter. See further our comm. on 174, 23.

cum fluuium transcenderemus: unlike Helm-Krenkel we regard the subjunctive as iterative (cf. 168, 3 f.). This subjunctive is rare in Cicero and Caesar (according to Wilkins on *De or.* 1, 232 it is even 'doubtful whether any of the instances quoted from Cicero really require us to admit this deviation from his ordinary practice'). In Livy and Nepos this subjunctive occurs more often; in Silver Latin it is gaining ground. See KSt 2, 2, 206; LHSz 2, 624.

praeter uiam: Kronenberg proposed *per uiam*, reasoning (presumably) that a river which flows along the road does not need to be crossed. The parallel passage *Onos* 29, 5 ποταμὸς ἦν ἀέννᾳος ἐν τῇ ὁδῷ, does not solve the problem. Yet *praeter* seems preferable in view of the prefix in *defluebat*; with *per* the simple verb would suffice.

peronibus: this is the original reading in F (⨍oīb;) and the marginal reading in φ. In F *peronibus* has been changed into *pedibus*, which is also found in α; φ has *per omnibus*, which makes no sense. The reading *peronibus* can easily be defended with Luetjohann 1873, 467 by a reference to the parallel passage in the *Onos*: ὁ δὲ τῶν ὑποδημάτων φειδόμενος. Here again is a typically Apuleian specification (cf. 152, 13 with comm.). The *pero* is a farmer's boot of rough leather; cf. Verg. *A.* 7, 690 *crudus tegit altera* (sc. *uestigia*) *pero*; Sid. Apoll. *Epist.* 4, 20 *setosus pero*. See Lau 1967, 117 with n. 2.

peronibus suis ab aquae madore consulens: cf. 8, 16 (189, 18) *clunibus meis ⟨ab⟩ adg⟨r⟩essionibus ferinis consulebam*, where ⟨ab⟩ is a generally accepted addition by ς (haplography). *ThLL s.v. consulo* gives the impression that this remarkable use of *consulere* is found in Apul. only; *OLD*, however, rightly adds Fro. Aur. 2, 72 (= 142, 18/19 vdH.) *a labore graui digitis consului*.

aquae madore: cf. 1, 13 (13, 1) *quoad me urinae spurcissimae madore perluerunt*.

199

Scobie *ad loc.* views *mador* as a possible archaism because this (quite rare) noun occurs in Sall. *Hist.* 4, 16 only, before it is found in Apul. (afterwards in Amm. Marc. 20, 6, 6 and 30, 1, 10; Mart. Cap. 2, 165) – but this evidence is an insufficient basis for this supposition.

insuper: preposition or adverb? It is generally regarded as a preposition here. See Médan 1925, 224; *Index Apul. s.v.*; Callebat 1968, 238; Marg. Molt and Scobie on 1, 25 (23, 13) *et profusa in medium sportula iubet officialem suum insuper pisces inscendere ac pedibus suis totos obterere*; Gwyn Griffiths on 11, (279, 6) *et insuper fluctus libant intritum lacte confectum.* In the last-mentioned passage *insuper* must be a preposition; also in 8, 5 (180, 3) *iaculum, quod gerebat, insuper dorsum bestiae contorsit. ThLL* mentions for the preposition *insuper* in Apul. only the last two passages and regards *insuper* in our passage as an adverb (= *praeterea*) – probably rightly: we can offer the following passage as a parallel (3, 7: 57, 14): *at ille non contentus, quod mihi nec adsistendi solacium perhibuit, insuper exitium meum cachinnat. Insuper* may well be an adverb in 23, 13, too. *Lumbos meos* is therefore the direct object of *insiliens*; cf. 3, 18 (65, 19) *fores insiliunt*; 8, 5 (179, 25) *protinus insiliunt equos.*

exiguum ... superpondium: irony on Lucius' part. Petschenig 1882, 158 adds ‹haut› (mark the incorrect mentioning of *haud* in Helm's *app. crit.*), thus taking away the irony which he thinks too flat to be authentic. *De gustibus ...* The noun *superpondium* is not a 'neologism' (Bernhard 1927, 139) but in fact a *hapax legomenon* (according to the material of the Thesaurus Institute).

168, 3-11 Ac si quo casu limo caenoso ripae supercilio lubricante [h]oneris inpatientia prolapsus deruissem, cum deberet egregius agaso manum porrigere, capistro suspendere, cauda subleuare, certe partem tanti oneris, quoad resurgerem saltem, detrahere, nullum quidem defesso mihi ferebat auxilium, sed occipiens a capite, immo uero et ipsis auribus totum me compilabat [cidit] fusti grandissimo, donec fomenti uice ipsae me plagae suscitarent: "And whenever I accidentally slipped and fell in the miry mud on the slippery edge of the bank, because I could not cope with the load, that first-rate ass-driver ought to have held out his hand, pulled me up by my halter, lifted me by the tail, at any rate removed part of so heavy a burden, at least until I got up again – but he did not come to my aid at all, worn out though I was. Starting at my head, yes at my very ears, he beat me up all over with a huge stick until the very blows – as if they were a salve for my wounds – brought me to my feet again".

This passage closely resembles the parallel passage in *Onos* 30, 1-2 (for the differences see below): εἰ δέ ποτε καὶ οἷα κάμνων καὶ ἀχθοφορῶν καταπέσοιμι, τότε δὴ τὸ δεινὸν ἀφόρητον ἦ. οὐ γὰρ ἦν καταβάντος χεῖρά μοι ἐπιδοῦναι κἀμὲ χαμόθεν ἐπεγείρειν καὶ τὸ φορτίον ἀφελεῖν ἄν ποτε, οὔτε χεῖρα ἐπέδωκεν, ἀλλὰ ἄνωθεν ἀπὸ τῆς κεφαλῆς καὶ τῶν ὤτων ἀρξάμενος συνέκοπτέ με τῷ ξύλῳ, ἕως ἐπεγείρωσίν με αἱ πληγαί.

si ... prolapsus deruissem: for *si* with an iterative subjunctive cf. 168, 18 and 9, 8 (208, 12). That there is an influence from the Greek *Vorlage* here (as well as in 168, 18) is possible, but not necessary: 208, 12 has no parallel in the *Onos* and probably not in the *Vorlage* either (vThiel 1971, 132). For the development of temporal *si*, see Callebat 1968, 353 f.; LHSz 2, 353 f.

quo casu: Callebat 1968, 472 points out the ambiguity of *casus*, which can mean both "fall" and "accident". A similar pun is found in Verg. *A.* 5, 350 *me liceat casus miserari insontis amici*: see Williams *ad loc.*; Quinn 1968, 398.

limo caenoso ripae supercilio lubricante: this detail is not mentioned in the *Onos*. Feldbrugge 1938, 65 rightly remarks: 'The cause of his falling is sought in the circumstances' (indeed the *Onos* has here κάμνων only). This indicates an intentional change by Apuleius, who more than once has Lucius emphasize the steepness and slipperiness of the roads; see Heine 1962, 149 with n. 2. For an allegorical interpretation of Lucius' progress there is an obvious relation with 11, 15 (277, 7): *Nec tibi natales ac ne dignitas quidem, uel ipsa, qua flores, usquam doctrina profuit, sed lubrico uirentis aetatulae ad seruiles delapsus uoluptates curiositatis inprosperae sinistrum praemium reportasti*. See Gwyn Griffiths *ad loc.*; id. in *AAGA* 1978, 156 f.; Sandy, *ibid.* 130.

caenoso: a pleonasm, according to Bernhard 1927, 175; Callebat 1968, 384 is more likely to be right in emphasizing the 'caractérisation pittoresque'; see also Ernout 1949, 35.

ripae supercilio lubricante: among modern editors Robertson, Brandt-Ehlers, Frassinetti, and vThiel follow Oudendorp in reading *supercilia* (so that *lubricante* modifies *limo*); before Oudendorp, Floridus had suggested *supercilium*. Oudendorp's arguments are: 'ablativorum nimius hac in periodo concursus' and 'verbum *lubricare* numquam non est activum, sive lubricum facere'. The last argument deserves attention. *ThLL s.v.* mentions three instances in which *lubrico* is used intransitively: besides our passage Vulg. *Thren.* 4, 18 *lubricauerunt uestigia nostra in itinere platearum nostrarum* (but it is by no means certain that *uestigia* is the subject) and Ven. Fort. *Carm.* 1, 21, 3 *lubricat hic quoniam tenuato Egireius haustu* (where *lubricat* is similar to *serpit*). The latter instance is quite late; *ThLL* does not preclude the possibility of Oudendorp's conjecture being right ('haud inepte'), in which case *lubricare* would be taken transitive. But taking into consideration analogous verbs like *albicare*, which plainly can be used in both a transitive and an intransitive sense (cf. Hor. *Carm.* 1, 4, 4), it seems quite possible that *lubricans* means here "slippery" (thus *OLD*). As to Oudendorp's conjecture, one might argue with Hildebrand that *supercilia* does not fit well with the singular *ripae*: one would expect *riparum* instead.

oneris inpatientia: cf. in the *Onos* ἀχθοφορῶν. *Oneris* is φ's correction of *honeris* in F; see further our comm. on 171, 18.

egregius agaso: cf. Feldbrugge 1938, 65: 'The ass-driver is sarcastically called *"egregius agaso"*. He should have helped him, not only by holding out his hand to him as in the O., but also by *"capistro suspendere, cauda sublevare"*. The latter is typically realistic'. See Bernhard 1927, 239 for the ironical use of *egregius*.

capistro suspendere: Oudendorp expresses a preference in his comm. for inserting *os* between *capistro* and *suspendere* (Ruhnken accepted it into the text). Although palaeographically this is a fine conjecture, it is not defensible in the context: the object is *me*, which does not need to be mentioned explicitly (see Callebat 1968, 451). Moreover, the combination *capistro suspendere, cauda subleuare* is a more precise rendition of χαμόθεν ἐπεγείρειν (thus rightly Hildebrand; cf. Feldbrugge's remark quoted in the preceding note). For *capistrum*, see comm. on 173, 8.

cauda subleuare: see 4, 5 (78, 1).

certe: the reading in φ. It seems that in F the *Nasalstrich* over the final *e* has been deleted: α has *certam*, but the adverb is certainly correct.

quoad resurgerem saltem: evidently an addition by Apuleius, with which 'Ap. accentuates the victim's modesty and makes him even more pathetic' (Feldbrugge 1938, 65). For the frequency and the different meanings of *quoad* in the *Met.*, see Callebat 1968, 346 f.

occipiens: for *occipere* see comm. on 149, 13.

compilabat [cidit]: in F and φ there is a lacuna of four letters after *compilabat*, but according to Helm, Robertson, and Giarratano nothing has been erased here. The reading *compilabat* is generally accepted as the correct one, and Lipsius' conjecture *concipilabat* regarded as unnecessary (see vdVliet 1896, 461). The verb is found in the *Met.* also at 9, 2 (204, 8). In both cases its meaning must be "give a thrashing", "beat up", although normally the verb means "rob", "plunder". According to Walde-Hofmann *s.v.* we have here an etymological pun: whereas *compilare* meaning "plunder" is derived from the adjective *pilatus* ("close-pressed", "dense"), it is used here meaning "thrash", as if it were derived from *pilum ("pounder", "pestle")* – a typically Apuleian procedure (see our comm. on 170, 4-7).

It is improbable that in Petr. 62, 12 *domum fugi tamquam copo compilatus* the participle has the meaning found in Apul., as Georges *s.v.*; Ciaffi 1960, 132; Callebat 1968, 77 suppose. Friedländer and Perrochat *ad loc.* hesitate between "robbed" and "beaten up"; but see e.g. Smith 1975, 174, who gives some good arguments for the former meaning. Thus also *ThLL* and *OLD*.

[cidit]: in all probability a gloss (= *concidit*) to explain the exceptional *compilabat*. On the proposal of Beyte 1888, 58 f. it is deleted by vdVliet, Giarratano-Frassinetti, Robertson, Terzaghi, Helm (-Krenkel), Brandt-Ehlers, and vThiel; see also Wiman 1927, 53 and Augello 1977, 170. The latter adds two more conjectures to the already impressive list, namely *scitule* and *concidens*[1], but eventually agrees with those who are for deletion.

fusti grandissimo: cf. 4, 3 (76, 8 f.) *cum grandi baculo furens decurrit adreptumque me totum plagis obtundit*; see *GCA* 1977, 38.

fomenti uice: ironical addition by Lucius (or Apuleius). For *uice* with preceding genitive, see Callebat 1968, 232.

168, 11-16 Idem mihi talem etiam excogitauit perniciem. Spinas acerrumas et punctu uenenato uiriosas in fascem tortili nodo constrictas caudae meae pensilem deligauit cruciatum, ut incessu meo commotae incitataeque funestis aculeis infeste me conuulnerarent: "He invented the

---

[1] Cf. Luetjohann's *concidendo*, suggested by συνέκοπτε. In addition to the conjectures mentioned by Augello – Helm[3] *ad incitas* (coll. 3, 28: 73, 3; see vdPaardt 1971, 200), Damsté *ad exitium* and Brakman *identidem* – the following should be mentioned: *scilicet* (Castiglioni, followed by Scazzoso), *ceciditque* (Gaselee), and *cotidie* (Armini 1928, 306 f.). Helm[1,2] and Pagliano obelize.

following torment for me, too. He tied together very sharp thorns – effective on account of their venomous sting – into a bundle with a twisted knot, and fastened it to my tail as a hanging implement of torture: as I walked they were set going with increasing speed, and cruelly wounded me with their deadly spikes".

Idem . . . excogitauit perniciem: cf. *Onos* 30, 3 καὶ μὴν καὶ ἄλλο κακὸν εἰς ἐμὲ ἀφόρητον ἔπαιζεν.

Spinas acerrumas et punctu uenenato uiriosas: *Onos* 30, 3 confines itself to ἀκανθῶν ὀξυτάτων φορτίον (Feldbrugge 1938, 65). Elis. Visser in *AAGA* 1978, 242 points out Couperus' story *Psyche*, which contains an obvious allusion to this passage.

punctu uenenato: Oudendorp prefers *puncto*, which is found in 5, 23 (121, 2) – although Helm reads with Floridus *punctu* there as well, ingeniously defended by Blümner 1905, 31 and Fernhout *ad loc.* – but it is a question here not of "poisonous points" but rather of "evil stings". Hildebrand rightly observes: 'Spinae . . . venenatae sunt, quae veneni instar carnem penetrant et intolerabiliter mordent, exitiumque parant'. For a slightly different figurative meaning of *uenenatus*, cf. e.g. Cic. *Phil.* 13, 35 *quamquam uos eos adsentationibus et uenenatis muneribus uenistis deprauatum*; Ov. *Tr.* 2, 566 *nulla uenenato littera mixta ioco est*.

uiriosas: this is the reading of F and φ; α has *uirosas* ("poisonous"), which has been adopted by many editors. *Viriosas*, defended by Armini 1928, 307, is retained by Helm[3], Robertson, Terzaghi, Brandt-Ehlers, Helm-Krenkel, and vThiel. Augello 1977, 170 f. is also convinced by Armini's arguments; moreover, he finds it significant that Helm has abandoned his former preference for *uirosa(s?)*. It is questionable whether Armini's reference to 9, 14 (213, 16) – where the baker's wife is described as: *saeua scaeua, uiriosa ebriosa, peruicax pertinax* (F. em.), is relevant: the meaning in that passage has to be "nymphomaniac", which leads to the obvious emendation *uirosa* (see Ernout 1949, 52 and Callebat 1968, 83). Armini's argument that the parallelism of the number of syllables requires the reading *uiriosa* is not so strong as it seems (*pace* Augello): with *uirosa* one ends up with 4+6+6 syllables (elision!); see further Bernhard 1927, 86. More important is Armini's reference to *Mul. Chir.* 735 *uiriosa enim res est*. The material from the ThLL Institute gives further Plac. *Med.* 5, 32 (rec. β) *uiriosius hoc fit (sc. medicamen) cum in cornu caprae suspendatur diebus uiginti*. Cf. Tert. *adv. Val.* 16; *Anim.* 19, 4 with Waszink *ad loc*. The adjective obviously belongs in the medical sphere ("potent", "effective") and is therefore quite appropriate here. Cf. Hildebrand's translation: 'die schärfsten Dornen, die durch ihren wie Gift schmerzenden Stich wirkten'.

in fascem: for consecutive *in* see Callebat 1968, 228.

tortili nodo: the adjective ("twisted") occurs before Apul. almost exclusively in poetry (Verg. *A.* 7, 351; Ov. *Ep.* 15, 252; id., *Met.* 1, 336 and 13, 915; Luc. 6, 198; but also Plin. *Nat.* 9, 163); afterwards it is found in prose more regularly. It fits excellently into the somewhat affected style of this sentence.

pensilem . . . cruciatum: a daring combination, with *cruciatus* used in a concrete sense: "instrument of torture".

commotae incitataeque: the increasingly rapid motion (*incitatae*) is illustrated by the *t*-iteration.

funestis aculeis infeste me conuulnerarent: an illustrative clausula (dispondaeus + ditrochaeus). Oudendorp proposes to read *infestae* instead of the adverb (see Callebat 1968, 414 for the predicative use of *infestus*) but we agree with Hildebrand that this is not an improvement; the same applies to Leo's suggestion to delete *infeste* and to read *infestis aculeis*. The somewhat pleonastic combination is intended to accentuate the narrator's indignation as he recounts the torments inflicted upon his former self.

CHAPTER XIX

The *puer* plays with fire.

Ergo igitur ancipiti malo laborabam. Nam cum me cursu proripueram fugiens acerbissimos incursus, uehementiore nisu spinarum feriebar: si dolori parcens paululum restitissem, plagis compellebar ad cursum: "So I was up against a two-headed evil. For when I dashed off in an attempt to escape the harsh onslaughts, I was hit the more vehemently by the impact of the thorns; if I stood still for a little while, to avoid the pain, I was forced by blows into a trot". 168, 16-20

Ergo igitur: see comm. on 165, 6.

ancipiti malo: cf. 4, 11 (82, 15) *in ancipiti periculo*. The translation explicates the implied metaphor of a two-headed monster. The assonance of *i* and *a* possibly underscores the threat.

Ergo ... laborabam: has no parallel in the *Onos*. Since the texts generally correspond here very closely (and therefore approximate the 'Vorlage' with some precision), it is likely that this sentence is an addition by Apuleius. Feldbrugge 1938, 65 is of the opinion that additions like this give 'a more personal touch' to the story. The next sentence, again, does have a parallel in the *Onos* (30, 4): εἰ μὲν γὰρ ἀτρέμα προίοιμι φυλαττόμενος τῶν ἀκανθῶν τὴν προσβολήν, ὑπὸ τῶν ξύλων ἀπωλλύμην, εἰ δὲ φεύγοιμι τὸ ξύλον, τότ' ἤδη τὸ δεινὸν ὄπισθεν ὀξὺ προσέπιπτεν. Observe the inverted order.

me cursu proripueram: Bernhard 1927, 178 lists this among the instances in which a substantival adverbial expression is added pleonastically to the verb, cf. 169, 12 *memet ... saltu totum abicio* (see comm. *ad loc.*). Médan 1925, 241 regards the combination as a new expression for *(se) proripere* and points out 9, 1 (202, 26) *abrupto cursu me proripio totis pedibus*, where *cursu* has a modifier: accordingly, it is not pleonastic. The function of *cursus* in our passage is mainly to mark the parallelism in the sentence, which yields a *polyptoton* (*cursum*) and *adnominatio* (*incursus*).

fugiens acerbissimos incursus: here the blows of the *puer* are meant; for the term *incursus* cf. 167, 3 and comm. *ad loc*. The horses' attacks as well as the *puer*'s blows are a concretization of the *instabiles incursiones* (1, 6: 6, 6) of Fortuna; see Schlam 1968a, 134.

acerbissimos: the correction occurs in φ; F has *aceruisssimos*. For the interchange *b/u* see Helm, Praef. *Fl.* XLVI.

nisu: *OLD* translates "pressure", but "thrust", "impact" seems more appropriate.

si ... restitissem: as in 168, 4 *si* is constructed with an iterative subjunctive; *variatio* with *cum* with the pluperfect indicative.

dolori parcens: this combination is not found elsewhere (*ThLL s.v. dolor*);

205

Médan 1925, 247 compares *parcens famae*.

168, 20-22 Nec quicquam uidebatur aliud excogitare puer ille nequissimus quam ut me quoquo modo perditum iret, idque iurans non numquam comminabatur: "That wicked boy seemed to have nothing else in mind but to bring about my death by whatever means he could, and more than once he threatened, with oaths, to do just that".

puer ille nequissimus: strongly coloured, in contrast to the *Onos* which only has: καὶ ὅλως ἔργον ἦν τῷ ὀνηλάτῃ τῷ ἐμῷ ἀποκτείνειν με. For the pejorative *ille*, see Callebat 1968, 277. For *nequissimus*, see *ibid.*, 399 f.; this is one of the most frequent superlatives in the *Met.*, which tells us more about the narrator than about anyone else.

perditum iret: perhaps more expressive than *perderet*; cf. 151, 20 and comm. *ad loc.*

id ... comminabatur: *id* refers to *ut ... iret* and is the direct object of *comminabatur*, not of *iurans*; Colvius' (later withdrawn) conjecture *deos* (sc. *iurans*) is therefore unnecessary. For the ellipsis of *mihi*, see Callebat 1968, 451.

168, 23-26 Et plane fuit, quod eius detestabilem malitiam ad peiores conatus stimularet; nam quadam die nimia eius insolentia expugnata patientia mea calces in eum ualidas extuleram: "And there certainly was something to goad his detestable malice to more evil attempts. For one day, when my patience was overcome by his excessive insolence, I had vigorously lashed out at him with my hooves".

The narrator's prospective comment has shifted with respect to *Onos* 31, 1: ἐπεὶ δέ ποτε ἅπαξ κακὰ πάσχων πολλὰ οὐκέτι φέρων πρὸς αὐτὸν λὰξ ἐκίνησα, εἶχεν ἀεὶ τοῦτο τὸ λὰξ ἐν μνήμῃ. See Junghanns 1932, 85. Lucius' violent behaviour is mentioned in 175, 18 by the *puer*'s mother.

plane: cf. 1, 24 (22, 2) *plane quod est mihi summe praecipuum, equo ... faenum atque ordeum ... tu, Photis, emito*. Marg. Molt *ad loc.* rightly explains *plane* as *si licet plane dicere*.

fuit, quod: Médan 1925, 90 thinks that *quod* stands for *cum* here, i.e. *fuit, quod*: "it happened that". If so, the subject would be the *puer* himself, which is improbable. It seems more plausible that we have a consecutive relative clause of the type *est, quod gaudeas* (Pl. *Tri.* 310); see LHSz 2, 559.

quadam die: cf. ποτε ἅπαξ in the *Onos*: for the gender of *dies* in the *Met.* see GCA 1977, 22. Hijmans, *AAGA* 1978, 207 (n. 9) points out the uncertainty of the length of the colon: if *quadam die* defines *expugnata* only, there would be a (functionally) long colon, namely *nam ... mea*; in all likelihood, however, *quadam die* qualifies both *expugnata* and *extuleram* (thus also Oudendorp and Hildebrand, judging from their punctuation).

nimia eius insolentia expugnata patientia mea: a striking assonance of *i* and *a*: the cup of *insolentia* is overflowing (*nimia* has its full, still unweakened meaning here). For the use of the military metaphor *expugnare*, see Neuenschwander 1913, 71.

ualidas: the adjective is strongly emphasised by the hyperbaton; see Callebat 1968, 412.

Denique tale facinus in me comminiscitur. Stuppae sarcina me satis onustum probeque funiculis constrictum producit in uiam deque proxima uillula spirantem carbunculum furatus oneris in ipso meditullio reponit: "Therefore he devised the following outrage against me. He loaded me well with a burden of hemp, tied it securely with ropes, and brought me out on the road. From the nearest farm-house he stole a live coal and put it exactly in the middle of the load". 168, 26-169, 3

Instead of an expression similar to *Denique ... comminiscitur*, *Onos* 31, 2 gives an explanation for the hemp's presence: the ass-driver had to transport it ἐξ ἑτέρου χωρίου εἰς ἕτερον χωρίον. Because this element is absent in Apul., it seems that the *puer* loads the ass with the hemp solely to provide fuel for the torture – verily a *facinus*, which once again accentuates the cruelty of this (fictitious) world. This leads Apul. to devise an unusual source for the coal: whereas in the *Onos* the coal is obviously found in the fireplace of the farm from which the hemp is carried, Apul. has the *puer* steal it from a house where he has no business at all. How the *puer* managed all this without being noticed, Lucius does not tell us, of course. In 169, 17 the *puer* gives his own version of the incident.

Denique: used here in the sense of *ergo, igitur*. See Marg. Molt 1943, 129 f.; Callebat 1968, 325 f.

satis = ualde; see Callebat 1968, 541.

probeque: a generally accepted conjecture by Stewech for *propeque* in F, which does not make sense here – no more does *propere*, found in some more recent mss. For *probe = bene*, see vdPaardt 1971, 62.

funiculis: the diminutive does not seem to have its proper meaning here, any more than in *uillula* (Callebat 1968, 56).[1] In the *Onos* mention is made of 'a very uncomfortable rope': δεσμῷ ἀργαλέῳ εὖ μάλα (= *probe*) προσέδησε με τῷ φορτίῳ (cf. *constrictum*, which also goes with *me*).

de ... uillula: Callebat 1968, 201 takes *de proxima uillula* with *carbunculum*: *de* is to indicate 'l'origine d'un objet'. But it seems better to take *de ... uillula* with *furatus*; cf. *Onos* 31, 2: ἐκ τῆς ἑστίας κλέψας δαλὸν ἔτι θερμόν.

spirantem carbunculum: the meaning of *spirantem* becomes clear from the Greek counterpart ἔτι θερμόν. Médan 1925, 146 lists *spirans* among the participles which have acquired an entirely new meaning. An exact parallel was hard to obtain, but a comparable use is found in Isid. *nat.* 47, 4 (Becker) *cuius (sc. gehennae) ignis perpetua incendia spirabunt ad puniendos peccatores. Nam sicut hi montes (i.e. Aetna) tanta temporis diurnitate usque nunc flammis aestuantibus perseuerant, ita ut numquam extingui possint, sic ignis ille gehennae ad crucianda corpora dampnatorum finem numquam est habiturus*. It is also possible to inter-

---

[1] Callebat's remark that *uillula* has lost its diminutive value in *all* cases in the *Met.* seems incorrect. Cf. 3, 29 (73, 19) *Nam cum multas uillulas et casas amplas praeterimus*, where the antithesis strongly suggests the meaning "small houses".

pret *spirans* as "alive", e.g. in Verg. *A.* 4, 64 *pectoribus inhians spirantia consulit exta* (see Pease *ad loc.*); cf. 3, 18 (65, 12) *capillos... dat* (sc. Pamphile) *uiuis carbonibus adolendos.* Callebat 1968, 44 points out that *carbunculum* (Helm: '*b* ex *u* al. m. corr.') is practically synonymous with *carbonem* here; its more common meaning is "ulcer", "tumor".

oneris in ipso meditullio: cf. 3, 27 (72, 3) *pilae mediae... in ipso fere meditullio.* For the etymology of *meditullium,* see vdPaardt 1971, 191.

169, 3-8 Iamque fomento tenui calescens et enutritus ignis surgebat in flammas et totum me funestus ardor inuaserat, nec ullum pestis extremae suffugium nec salutis aliquod apparet solacium et ustrina talis moras non sustinet et meliora consilia praeuertitur: "The fire, growing and nourished by the light fuel, rose up in flames, and a deadly heat had already completely pervaded me. No escape from utter disaster, no hope of salvation presented itself: such a burning admits of no delay and forestalls any well-considered plan".

Onos 31, 3 has no counterpart of these pyrological reflections, but only mentions the fire itself: τὸ δὲ (sc. τὸ στυππεῖον)... εὐθὺς ἀνάπτεται, καὶ λοιπὸν οὐδὲν ἔφερον ἄλλο ἢ πῦρ ἄπλετον.

fomento tenui: fomentum occurs 168, 11 in the more usual meaning of "remedy"; here it is a synonym of *fomes* "fuel" (used especially of wood; in this context the hemp and the ropes). Cf. Hildebrand *ad loc.*: 'Equidem puto, verba *calescens et enutritus* indicare *tenue fomentum* esse stuppae sarcinam, ut *tenue* hic sit gracile et subtile, quod eo magis in flammas surgere potest. Crassa enim si fuisset et firma materies, carbo eam inflammare non potuisset'.

surgebat... inuaserat... apparet: on the general subject of change of tenses, see Bernhard 1927, 152 f., who thinks that the only possible reason – in most cases – is the author's preference for *variatio.* Callebat 1968, 428 gives a correct analysis of our passage: 'alternance ici d'imparfait (développement de l'action et tableau) de plus-que-parfait (évocation dans son cours du résultat de l'action et donc suggestion de rapidité) et d'un présent (brusque actualisation dramatique)'.

in flammas: for consecutive *in*, see Callebat 1968, 230.

totum me funestus ardor inuaserat: cf. Petr. 120, 70 *funesto aestu*; this *ardor* is to be extinguished by water and mud only; another, more intimate form of *ardor* could only be quenched by Fotis. Cf. 2, 7 (31, 7) *Nam... si ego* and the sub-narrator's reflection in 8, 2 (178, 6-8).

pestis extremae: cf. 4, 31 (99, 8) *hominis extremi*; 3, 5 (56, 2) *extremos latrones*; see vdPaardt *ad loc.* In a literal sense, too, this *pestis* is *extrema.*

nec... aliquod apparet solacium: for the ellipsis of *mihi* see Callebat 1968, 451. For *aliquod* instead of *ullum,* see LHSz 2, 195.

ustrina: the usual meaning is "place for burning"; cf. Serv. *ad* Verg. *A.* 3, 22 *apparatus mortuorum 'funus' dici solet, extructio lignorum 'rogus', subiectio ignis 'pyra', crematio cadaueris 'bustum', locus 'ustrina'.* The meaning here seems to be abstract: "fire", "burning" (see Luisa Gargantini 1963, 37), for which there is a good parallel in Sol. *Coll. Rer. Mem.* 19, 13 *si fugare angues gestias (cornu cerui) ures, quae ustrina... nidore uitium aperit... si cui inest morbus comitialis.*

moras non sustinet et meliora consilia praeuertitur: the reading in F is disputed. Helm reads *non sustinens*, but according to Robertson the copyist never intended to write *-ns*, but a final *t* (which turned out somewhat odd). Elmenhorst was the first to mark *non sustinet* as the correct reading, which is adopted by Brandt-Ehlers, Frassinetti, and vThiel. Helm's reading (followed by Gaselee, Giarratano, Terzaghi, Pagliano, and Scazzoso) can be interpreted in two ways. Helm himself translates: 'und ein solcher Brand, der kein Zögern verträgt, macht auch bessere Entschliessungen unmöglich'; apparently he regards *et* as an adverb. Completely different is the view taken by Adlington-Gaselee: 'in such a burning it was not possible for me to stand still, and there was no time to advise better' (from which it appears that the sentence can be read not only as a general *sententia*, but also as a description of Lucius' specific situation; we opt for the former alternative). Adlington-Gaselee apparently regard *sustinens* as a *participium pro uerbo finito*; for this term see Pfister 1912, 207 and Löfstedt 1911, 249. Both solutions are somewhat far-fetched; more acceptable is Hildebrand's proposal to read *non sustinens ‹est› et*. For this periphrastic conjugation cf. 175, 12 *est enim congruens*; see Leky 1908, 35 and Callebat 1968, 320. For the phenomenon in general see Löfstedt 1911, 245 f.; Svennung 1935, 432 f.; KSt 2, 1, 159; LHSz 2, 388. Perhaps too facile is the deletion of *et* (ς, Eyssenhardt, vdVliet, Clouard); definitely objectionable is the old 'correction' *non sustinens sed* (α). We prefer, therefore, the reading of F (teste Rob.).

meliora: there is no reason for conjectures like *maturiora* (Oudendorp, followed by vdVliet), *diutiora* (Blümner 1894, 307/8), *pleniora* (Kronenberg) or *timidiora* (Helm, app. crit.). The comparative has approximately the meaning of the positive here; cf. 5, 5 (106, 16) *Fortuna saeuior*; see Fernhout *ad loc.* and LHSz 2, 168 f.

praeuertitur: cf. 4, 5 (77, 22) *Sed tam bellum consilium meum praeuertit sors deterrima*. As a deponent the verb occurs in 173, 4 *Sed illa Fortuna... tam opportunum latibulum misera celeritate praeuersa nouas instruxit insidias*. This time Sors or Fortuna does not put a spoke in Lucius' wheel: on the contrary, she extends a helping hand – albeit for a single moment only.

CHAPTER XX

Fortuna seems to smile on Lucius – but her favourable disposition will not last long.

169, 8-10   Sed in rebus scaeuis adfulsit Fortunae nutus hilarior nescio an futuris periculis me reseruans, certe praesente statutaque morte liberans: "But in my precarious situation Fortuna's glance shone more amiably on me; even though she perhaps reserved me for future dangers, at any rate she saved me from the instant death that had been decided upon".

Sed: marks – as so often – a turning-point, especially in the changes of fate; cf. GCA 1977, 38.

in rebus scaeuis: cf. 156, 15 *scaeuitas Fortunae* and see comm. *ad loc.*

adfulsit: cf. Liv. 30, 30, 15 *mihi talis... fortuna adfulsit*; Amm. 27, 10, 3 *inopina... spes laetiorum adfulsit*. Here *Fortuna* has been particularized to *nutus Fortunae*.

nutus: "eye", "glance"; cf. 4, 12 (83, 10) *saeuum Fortunae nutum* and comm. on 150, 2, where we retain *nutu* with the mss. Fortuna's intervention introduces here – as in 7, 16; 17; 25 – a new pericope, in which a new action is about to take place. See Junghanns 1932, 58, n. 87 and 163, n. 76; Riefstahl 1938, 30.

nescio an: a phrase which is already a fixed adverbial expression in the classical period (LHSz 2, 543); like *forsitan, quippe, utpote* it is then constructed with a participle (see Médan 1925, 80). The formula is also found in 157, 22. Fortuna appears to show herself in a more benevolent aspect now (Heine 1962, 169), but at the same time it occurs to Lucius that the benevolence of this moment may only result for him in a confrontation with new dangers. Fortuna remains unpredictable; see the extensive note on 155, 21. The reader, on the other hand, knows that Lucius' ordeals are by no means over yet; see vdPaardt, *AAGA* 1978, 76 f.

futuris periculis me reseruans: what these dangers are will soon become clear from 170, 22 f.

reseruans... liberans: rhyme of the participles, both at the end of a pericope. This rhyme is often connected with other devices (Bernhard 1927, 225): for example, *nescio... reseruans* has 14 syllables if we read *nescio an* with synaloephe, and so has *certe... liberans*.

statuta morte: cf. 156, 20 *statuto consilio*.

169, 10-14   Nam forte pluuiae pridianae recens conceptaculum aquae lutulentae proximum conspicatus ibi memet inprouido saltu totum abicio flammaque prorsus extincta tandem et pondere leuatus et exitio liberatus euado: "For I happened to see a pool close by, recently formed by yesterday's rain, full of muddy water; with a bound I threw myself right into it, head over heels; when the flames were wholly extinguished I finally came out, delivered from my burden and freed from disaster".

pridianae: a rather rare adjective, also used by Apul. in *Apol.* 6 (7, 21) (in a quotation from an unknown author about a kind of toothpaste) *conuerritorem pridianae reliquiae* and in *Met.* 11, 7 (271, 20) *pruinam pridianam*. *OLD* adds Plin. *Nat.* 28, 248 *pridiana balnea*; Suet. *Tib.* 34, 3 and *Cal.* 58, 1.

conceptaculum: attested from Plin. *Nat.* 2, 115 on. Apul. uses it also in 6, 13 (138, 9) *undae proxumaeque conceptaculo uallis inclusae*, where it probably means *conceptus* = "basin", "tank". For the formation with the suffix *-culum*, see LHSz 1, 313 (where *conceptaculum* is not mentioned, however).

aquae: Médan 1925, 363 (cf. also 335) points out that two nouns are used synonymously, the latter (*aquae*) being the complement of the former (*pluuiae*) and used in the genitive. We do not agree with Médan that Apul. does this 'par amour de variété'. The word-order is quite mannered: noun ... adjective (*pluuiae pridianae*); adjective ... noun; noun ... adjective plus another adjective (*proximum*) which modifies *conceptaculum* (mentioned three words earlier). vdVliet's addition *plenum* after *luculentum* is not necessary, although the accumulation of genitives is certainly striking.

conspicatus: for the intensity of this verb, see vdPaardt 1971, 129.

ibi = eo; see *GCA* 1977, 62. Strictly taken, *ibi* is redundant, but our author has a liking for such redundancies: he strives for the greatest possible exactness and for copiousness as well (Bernhard 1927, 181).

memet inprouido saltu totum abicio: Bernhard 1927, 178 lists this with the instances in which a nominal adverbial expression pleonastically modifies a verb. One may have a different opinion on the term 'pleonastically'.

inprouido: "blindly", "headlong". Comparable is Liv. 10, 28, 10 *improuida fuga* (which is preceded by *lymphaticus pauor*) and 22, 39, 21 *festinatio inprouida est et caeca*. The word has always an active meaning in Apul., e.g. 3, 18 (65, 20) *improuidae noctis deceptus caligine*; see vdPaardt 1971, 139.

Hijmans (*AAGA* 1978, 169) points out that 10-12 (*nam forte ... conspicatus*) is one long colon, preceded by two shorter ones (*sed ... hilarior* and *nescio ... reseruans*), which creates 'a certain amount of suspense' in the auditor. The possibility of rescue – on seeing the mud-pool – is expressed by one quite long colon (*nam forte ... conspicatus* has 29 syllables), whereas the following jump into the water (*ibi ... abicio*) is described by a shorter colon.

pondere leuatus ... exitio liberatus: alliteration, rhyme, and 'wachsende Glieder'.

tandem ... euado: the translators connect *tandem* either with *liberatus* (Brandt-Ehlers, Scazzoso) or with *euado* (Rode, Vallette, Helm, Schwartz). The latter translation is more probable, for the combination *tandem euado* occurs in Apul. also 1, 7 (7, 8) *latronibus obsessus atque omnibus priuatus tandem euado* – admittedly without hyperbaton of *tandem*, but with rhyme of the preceding participles. Elsewhere *tandem* does occur in a strong hyperbaton: 2, 32 (51, 23) *quod tandem ... spiritus efflauerit*, where a similar dramatic effect seems to have been intended as in our passage. Another argument for the connection of *tandem* with *euado* is the repetition of *et* (*et pondere leuatus et exitio liberatus*).

169, 14-18 Sed ille deterrimus ac temerarius puer hoc quoque suum nequissimum factum in me retorsit gregariisque omnibus adfirmauit me sponte uicinorum foculos transeuntem titubanti gradu prolapsum ignem ultroneum accersisse mihi: "But that evil, insolent boy shifted the blame for this rotten trick of his, too, on to me, and declared to all the shepherds that I had deliberately passed the neighbours' coal-pans with staggering step, had allowed myself to fall, and had intentionally brought the fire upon myself".

ille: used in a pejorative sense, see *GCA* 1977, 47.

deterrimus ac temerarius: the superlative if followed by a positive (Callebat 1968, 403; cf. Bernhard 1927, 168). The reverse order is found in 169, 25 *pigrum tardissimumque*.

retorsit: Médan 1925, 252 regards *retorquere crimen in aliquem* as a general expression, borrowed from juridical language. LS mentions Just. 34, 4, 2 *ut in auctorem retorqueat scelus* and *Dig.* 38, 2, 14, 6.

gregariis: Callebat 1968, 250 f. regards the nominal use of an adjective as a characteristic of colloquial language. According to him, *gregarius* is used in this way for the first time by Apul. (here and 165, 16 in the sense of *armentarius, equiso*). ThLL mentions after Apul. only Ps. Matth. *Evang.* 3, 4. But the word does occur as a noun before Apul., although in the meaning "private soldier": Tac. *Hist.* 2, 75 *Volaginium e gregario ad summa militiae prouectum*.

foculos: "brazier", but not like the one next to an altar, to receive the gifts of wine and incense, preliminary to sacrifice (see Wissowa [2]1912, 417): it is not clear how the ass would come upon such a cult utensil on his journey. For the same reason it would hardly be a brazier for cooking purposes, as e.g. in Juv. 3, 262 *bucca foculum excitat*; cf. also Fotis' *foculus* (*Met.* 2, 7: 31, 7), although this is not necessarily a brazier but rather a fire in the hearth. In this passage it probably is a simple pan of coals – ceramic, portable (see e.g. Burr Thompson 1971, pl. 14). Cato mentions *foculos* in his chapter '*quomodo uineae iugera C instruere oporteat* (*Agr.* 11, 5): ... *falculas* (*faculas codd.*) *rustarias X, foculos II, forpices II*, etc.; they are pans in which live coals are kept for the purpose of making a fire quickly whenever the activities in the vineyard call for it, e.g. to burn cut vine-tendrils.

transeuntem ... prolapsum: the asyndeton between participles is characteristic of Apul.'s style; see vdPaardt 1971, 44.

titubanti gradu: cf. 2, 31 (51, 8) *titubante uestigio*, see deJonge ad loc. ('*titubare saepe de ebriis dicitur*'). Another example is 1, 18 (17, 1) *gradu titubo*. See also *GCA* 1977, 71 f. Observe the alliteration with *transeuntem*.

ultroneum: the adjective is used predicatively (Bernhard 1927, 110; Callebat 1968, 415). *Onos* 31, 6 has the same: παριὼν ἑκὼν ἑαυτὸν ἐνσείσαιμι τῇ ἑστίᾳ. It is a relatively rare word, which – except for five times in Apul. (e.g. 1, 19: 18, 14; see Marg. Molt *ad loc.*) – only occurs Vulg. *Exod.* 25, 2 *ab omni homine qui offeret ultroneus, accipietis illas* (sc. *primitias*); thus LS.

accersisse mihi, et: this is the correct reading and punctuation, proposed by Petschenig 1881, 149. F has *accessisse, mihi et*; Lipsius *arcessisse, mihi et*. The confusion of *accedere* and *accersere* is not uncommon in the mss. (see *ThLL s.v. accedere* 253, 78), but *accedere* is impossible here: the context requires a transitive verb. For the problem of the correct spelling (*accersisse* instead of *arcessisse*) see comm. on 153, 7. It appears from *ThLL s.v.* 452, 78 that the phrase *ignem accersere* is not found elsewhere. Closest to our passage are Col. 2, 16 *arcessitam et aduectam humum* and Sen. *Nat.* 4a, 2, 29 *aqua illo incumbit quo uis caloris... arcessit*. These passages deal with 'res naturales'.

et arridens addidit: 'Quo usque ergo frustra pascemus inigninum istum?': "and grinning he added: 'So how long shall we feed that fire-animal in vain?'"   169, 18-19

quo usque: the same question had been asked 3, 27 (72, 12); see vdPaardt 1971, 194, who sees this as a parody on Cic. *Cat.* 1, 1 rather than on Sall. *Cat.* 20, 9. The use of the quotation from Cicero (or Sallust) – referring to the villain Catilina – throws a bright light upon the (reputed) villainy of the ass. The same question was asked in 147, 20 f. (see our comm. *ad loc.*): *quo usque... ruptum istum asellum... frustra pascemus*? In all instances the question is how much longer this useless (in the eyes of the questioner) ass should be allowed to live. There are no other occurrences of *quo usque* in the *Met*. See also Westerbrink, *AAGA* 1978, 66, who compares 8, 23 (195, 14) *quem ad finem cantherium istum uenui frustra subiciemus*? Here, too, the question is asked in a comparable context.

ergo: the considerations in 14-18 lead up to a conclusion, which is formulated as a direct question introduced by *ergo*. Cf. Norden on Verg. *A.* 6, 456 f.; LHSz 2, 511. The boy asks the question *arridens*. Why? The answer is connected with the solution to another problem, namely which reading we accept in 19: F and φ have *inigninum*, but a more recent hand wrote in φ in the margin ^e_c *igninum*. Most scholars do not know what to do with this, hence *ignigenum* ς; *ignigerum* uir doctus quidam; *igniarium* Oudendorp; *inquilinum* Leo; *ignigenam* Damsté 1928, 20, n. 2; *hinnum igninum* (palaeographically attractive) Helm-Krenkel, Frassinetti, vThiel; *Inuum* Verdière 1963, 187. All these conjectures are too complicated to be acceptable, as Armini 1928, 307 rightly argues. This also applies to Helm's conjecture in his text (1931) ‹as›in‹um› *igninum*. Besides, the *puer*'s grin is not accounted for by these conjectures. It is explained, however, by Armini in his defense of the transmitted *inigninum*. His reasoning is as follows: *igninus* is derived from *ignis* as *collinus* from *collis*, *marinus* from *mare*, *alpinus* from *Alpes*; accordingly there is no grammatical objection to the form *igninus*, though it is not attested elsewhere. From *igninus* is derived – *per iocum* – the form *inigninus* = *qui in igne uersatur*. See also LHSz 1, 326 f. who show the high frequency of the suffix *-inus*, denoting origin or place. Therefore the objections of Helm 1930, 511 and Heraeus (1932, 80: 'bedenkliche sprachliche Bildungen') are unfounded: "originating from fire", "living in fire" easily becomes "permanently living in fire", "always getting into the fire". As a description of Lucius' habits this epithet is, of course, exaggerated but it does fit in with 169, 5 *totum me funestus ardor inuaserat* (once again pointed out by Armini 1932, 84 f.). For one who accepts a contextually understandable conjecture like *ignigenum* or *asinum igninum* it is difficult to apprehend the 'corruption' into *inigninum* as a jocular neologism; but this jocularity explains the grin of the *puer* 'comme satisfait d'un trait d'esprit' (thus Vallette in his note).

Armini 1932, 85 f. points out further that the word *inigninus* may raise associations with the dreaded 'fire-animal', the salamander, which was believed to be invulnerable to fire; see Arist. *HA* 552 B 17 διὰ τοῦ πυρὸς βαδίζουσα κατασβέννυσι τὸ πῦρ and Plin. *Nat.* 10, 188 *huic tantus rigor ut ignem tactu restinguat non alio modo quam glacies*. We do not wish to exclude these possibilities; nor do Robertson, who includes *inigninum* ('dubitanter') in his text, and Giarratano and Scazzoso, who also retain *inigninum*.

Kronenberg 1928, 38 defends *igninum* (the reading of φ *in margine*, adopted by vdVliet and followed by Purser, Terzaghi, and Augello 1977, 171 f.): he writes it with a capital initial and compares it to names of deities like Argentinus, Iugatinus, Statilinus; cf. Aug. *C.D.* 4, 21. What interests us is the fact that Kronenberg recognizes the jocular character of the name, though we prefer *inigninum*.

Vallette points out in the note mentioned above that the situation in Apul. is different from that in the *Onos*. The proposal of the grinning *puer* – to stop feeding the fire-animal – is absent in the *Onos*, and so naturally, is the pun with *inigninum*; only after the ass's attempts at rape (ch. 21 in the *Met.*) does the *Onos* have the boy's master propose to butcher the ass.

Finally: it is difficult to determine how closely the 'fire-animal' and the role of fire in this chapter are related with the 'fieriness' of which the ass is accused in ch. 21; that such a relation is suggested does not seem impossible.

169, 20-24 Nec multis interiectis diebus longe peio‹ri›bus me dolis petiuit. Ligno enim, quod gerebam, in proximam casulam uendito uacuum me ducens iam se nequitiae meae proclamans imparem miserrimumque istud magisterium rennuens querelas huius modi concinnat: "A few days later he assaulted me with far meaner tricks. For when, having sold at a nearby cottage the wood which I was carrying, he was leading me along unladen, he shouted that he was no longer up to my depravity; in renouncing his miserable job as drover, he fabricated accusations of this kind:"

Nec multis interiectis diebus: litotes, formed with the negative *nec*. See Strilciw 1925, 109; vdPaardt 1971, 49.

ligno . . . ducens: *Onos* 32, 1 κομίσας γάρ με ἐς τὸ ὄρος . . . κομίσας οἴκαδε is more detailed in its description of how the boy drives the ass into the mountains to fetch wood for selling. Apul., on the other hand, gives a more dramatic description than the *Onos* of the *puer*'s slander and feigned indignation (direct discourse both in *Onos* and Apul.); see Junghanns 1932, 85.

casulam: the word is first found at *Mor.* 6; its next occurrence is in Apuleius (Luisa Gargantini 1963, 42).

ducens . . . proclamans . . . rennuens: a 'Partizipialkonglomerat', such as is often found in our author; see *GCA* 1977, 82.

querelas: "complaint", "accusation". In 2, 3 (26, 21) *absit . . . ut Milonem hospitem sine ulla querela deseram* it means "Grund zur Klage" (Helm); in the same meaning 10, 14 (247, 17). Here it has the post-classical meaning of "accusation", "allegation". Summers 1967, 99 discusses only *Met.* 2, 3.

concinnat: occurs frequently in Apul. (and Plautus). Usually it occurs in the sense of *facere, parare* (as e.g. 3, 13: 62, 4 and vdPaardt *ad loc.*; 6, 24: 146, 23; 162,

20). In this passage it means – as in 5, 27 (124, 12) *concinnato mendacio* and 8, 12 (186, 11) – *artificiose confingere*.

CHAPTER XXI

New accusations from the *puer*: the ass allegedly attempts to assault people!

169, 24-26 'Videtis istum pigrum tardissimumque et nimis asinum? Me prae⟨ter⟩ flagitia nunc nouis periculis etiam angit: " 'Do you see that creature – lazy as slow can be, all too much an ass? Apart from his other outrages, now he is also frightening me by putting me in new dangers".

Videtis: the interrogative clause lacks an interrogative particle (see Marg. Molt on 1, 8: 8, 15 and Callebat 1968, 112); this gives the question an emotional character (see KSt 2, 2, 501).

pigrum tardissimumque: the positive is followed by the superlative: the reverse of 169, 14. Cf. 165, 18 above.

nimis asinum: this combination of *nimis* with a noun does not seem to have a parallel. Oudendorp and Hildebrand mention only *Met. 9, 28* (224, 12) *admodum puer* and (for the idea) Luc. 1, 1 *plus quam ciuilia bella*. One may add Tac. *Dial.* 1 *iuuenis admodum* and *Met.* 10, 13 (246, 23) *uere asinus*. *OLD s.v.* mentions in addition Stat. *Ach.* 2, 37 *nimis o suspensa nimisque / mater*, but in spite of Dilke 1954 *ad loc.* it is difficult to decide whether *nimis* modifies *mater* or *suspensa*. For adverbs combined with nouns in general, see LHSz 2, 171. Blümner's addition of *asininum* before *asinum* is unnecessary. Médan 1925, 314 maintains that Apul. is playing here with the meanings "ass" and "stupid"; he illustrates this with examples from comedy. This word-play is indeed present here, but much more important are the associations of lecherousness and sexual potency connected with the ass; see Scobie 1975, 31 n. 18; Schlam in *AAGA* 1978, 100 f. with literature.

praeter: F and φ have p̄, which is read as *praeter* by vdVliet, Giarratano, Terzaghi, Helm, Scazzozo, and vThiel. Salmasius, Scriverius, Pricaeus, Robertson, and Frassinetti read *post*. Wassaeus conjectures *pro cetero flagitio,* Hildebrand *prae cetero flagitio,* Robertson (hesitantly) *post uetera*. *Post* followed by an accusative of *ceterus* is a combination which does not occur elsewhere in Apul., whereas a form of *ceterus* after *praeter* is found more than once (3, 29: 73, 23; 4, 13: 85, 2; 5, 2: 104, 18; 157, 23). F has p̄ in 4, 13 (85, 2) as well; *GCA* 1977, 108 *ad loc.* rightly calls the reading *praeter* 'an ancient and reasonable correction'. *Praeter* occurs 50 times in Apul., almost always in the figurative sense of "except"; see Parigger 1941, 86.

The boy does not mention which other outrages are at issue – he may refer to the kicks dealt out to him by the tormented ass (168, 15). The *Onos* does not speak of any outrages at all; Apul. mentions them to increase the dramatic force of the passage.

periculis etiam: vdVliet (following the codex Dorvillianus) *etiam periculis*. It is not necessary to deviate from the reading of the principal mss.: *etiam* may both precede and follow the word it modifies, or even be separated from it (see KSt 2. 2, 53). The reading in F presents a clausula (ditrochaeus) that is no less usual than that presented by *etiam periculis*.

Vt quemque enim uiatorem prospexerit, siue illa scitula mulier seu uirgo nubilis seu tener puellus est, ilico disturbato gestamine, non numquam etiam ipsis stramentis abiectis, furens incurrit et homines amator talis appetit: "For as soon as he spots any passer-by, whether it is a pretty woman or a marriageable girl or a boy of tender years, he immediately upsets his load, sometimes even throws off his packsaddle, rushes at them like a maniac, and hurls himself – this great lover – upon people!" 169, 26-170, 4

The *puer*'s present accusation of attempted assaults must be addressed to the *gregarii*, as was the accusation in ch. 20: one of the shepherds, at any rate, reacts to this accusation with a proposal to butcher the ass (170, 22). In the Onos, on the other hand, the παῖς accuses the ass of intentionally setting himself on fire without addressing anyone in particular: the accusation of attempted rape is uttered to the δεσπότης, who proposes (33) to butcher the animal. Vallette supposes in his note *ad loc.* that this δεσπότης is the slave who supervises the παῖς.

enim: comes third in the sentence, as is possible in classical prose, too; see LHSz 2, 508.

uiatorem: vdVliet proposes a partitive genitive *uiatorum* after *quemque*, quoting as example 10, 5 (240, 8) *quisque praesentium*. But this is not necessary: see KSt 2, 363, who quote Pl. *As.* 246 *supplicabo ... ut quemque amicum uidero*.

prospexerit: iterative subjunctive. See Löfstedt 1907, 8; vGeisau 1916, 284; deJonge on 2, 5 (29, 6); Callebat 1968, 354; LHSz 2, 636. Byrrhena warned Lucius 2, 5 (29, 5) to be on his guard against Pamphile: *Nam simul quemque conspexerit speciosae formae iuuenem, uenustate eius sumitur* etc.; if the young men in question do not pay attention to her advances, she changes them into stones, *pecua et quoduis animal* (29, 10). Lucius did not heed Byrrhena's warning, was changed (albeit by a mistake of Photis) into an animal, and is now accused of the same licentious behaviour as Pamphile.

siue illa scitula mulier seu uirgo nubilis seu tener puellus est: a continuous chiasmus in this syndetic tricolon; see Bernhard 1927, 33. The addition of *sit* after *illa* (thus ς) would disrupt the balanced structure of this tricolon.

scitula: see Marg. Molt on 1, 7 (7, 10); Callebat 1968, 511 f.; vdPaardt 1971, 119.

nubilis: "marriageable", as in Verg. *A.* 7, 53 *filia ... iam matura uiro, iam plenis nubilis annis*. Like *scitula* and *tener*, *nubilis* emphasizes sexual attractiveness; this appears from the *inuitatio ad nuptias*, with *nuptiae* in the sense of *coitus* (see below).

puellus: an archaic word, found in Lucilius (ap. Non. 158, 18L); Enn. *Ann.* 221; Varro; Lucr.; Suet. *Cal.*; Apul. (only here). The diminutive noun is modified by the adjective *tener* which also denotes smallness; this shows that the noun has lost some of its diminutive force (Bernhard 1927, 137); cf. Callebat, *AAGA* 1978, 169 on *parua casula* in 4, 6 (79, 10). Gatscha 1898, 153 regards *tener puellus* as an imitation of Lucilius.

puellus est: this is an emendation by vdVliet, adopted by many editors (Helm, Robertson, Terzaghi, Frassinetti, vThiel). F has *puellu sese*; another hand has added an *s* after the *u*. vdVliet's emendation – the simplest – is to be preferred to *puellus sese . . . inruit* (Oudendorp); *puellos, eos* (Eyssenhardt); *puellus, ecce* (Guilielmus, Giarratano, Scazzoso); *puellus, e re* (Luetjohann 1873, 467). Augello 1977, 102 prefers Robertson's tentative proposal *puellus e se*. Gwyn Griffiths 1975, 27 (in a discussion of Lucius' ability to 'do things like a man') points out that 'an interpretation of *asellus* as *cinaedus*, illustrated in the association of the ass with catamites (8.26, with the priest of Dea Syria . . .; cf. 7.21, his readiness to violate a *tener puellus*), is illuminated from Greek sources'. See also vThiel 1971, 1, 185 n. 56.

gestamen: according to Médan 1925, 190 this noun is mostly used by poets. The first examples are, indeed, found in Vergil and Ovid, but from Sen. (*Ben*. 3. 37, 1 *Vicit Aeneas patrem, ipse eius ‹in› infantia leue tutumque gestamen*), Plin. *Nat*. 32, 23, and Tac. onwards the word is found in prose as well.

stramentis: the usual meaning is "straw, litter, bundles of straw" (LS). Here it probably has the rare meaning "packsaddle" as in Caes. *Gal*. 7, 45 *stramenta mulorum*, where Kraner-Dittenberger-Meusel[21] 1967 *ad loc*. remark: '*stramenta* bedeutet . . . wahrscheinlich dasselbe, was Liv. teils mit *strata*, teils mit *clitellae* bezeichnet: "Packsättel", auf denen man nicht reiten konnte'. For an illustration of a *clitella* ("packsaddle"), see Daremberg-Saglio 1, 1260.

incurritur: for the meaning "to hurl oneself on someone in blind passion", "to rush toward", cf. Juv. 6, 331 *seruis incurritur* (sc. *a femina impudica*).

homines amator talis: the object comes before the subject, which is not the usual word-order (Bernhard 1927, 19). Its prominent position gives *homines* strong emphasis, which underlines the *puer*'s indignation.

170, 4-7 et humi prostratis illis inhians illicitas atque incognitas temptat libidines et ferinas uoluptates auersa Venere inuitat ad nuptias: "after he has thrown them on the ground, he eagerly tries to force his illicit and unheard-of lusts upon them and incites his bestial desires to a union which Venus is averse to".

illis inhians illicitas atque incognitas . . . libidines: there is strong assonance of *i* in the first part of the sentence (*illis . . . libidines*) and alliteration of *u* in the second (*uoluptates . . . inuitat*). This marks the two parts as independent elements, as does the (mild) chiasmus of *temptat libidines* and *uoluptates . . . inuitat* and the similarity of rhythm in *temptāt lībīdīnēs* and *īnuītāt ād nūptīās*.

Because of the difficulty of the combination *ferinas uoluptates inuitare ad nuptias* (in which the *Onos* offers no help – it has only γαμεῖν ἐβούλετο), most editors have thought it necessary either to add a participle after *ferinas* (*instruens* Kronenberg; *auens* Castiglioni; *parans* Helm; *uoluens* Giarratano, Scazzoso) or to write *-que* after *auersa* (Kaibel, followed by Robertson and Augello 1977, 172 f.). Other proposals: *feminas uolutatas* instead of *ferinas uoluptates* (a fantasy of Pricaeus'); a transposition of *uoluptates* after *illicitas* (vdVliet); *uoluptates ‹et›* (Bursian and Terzaghi). Hildebrand is one of the few who retain the reading of the ms.; with Oudendorp (who, however prints Pricaeus' conjecture in his text) he explains the expression as 'irritare et accendere voluptuosum impetum, et ferinum ardorem ad humanas nuptias'. *Inuitare aliquem ad nuptias* is a phrase which occurs more than once (*ThLL s.v. inuito* 229, 11 f.). An example of *inuitare* with an abstract object, quoted by Hildebrand, is Cic. *Fin.* 5, 6 *ut ipsum* (subject, i.e. *id in quo prudentia uersaretur*) *per se inuitaret et alliceret appetitum animi*; another instance is *Met.* 8, 2 (177, 14). A more relevant example (because of *ad* and the abstract object) is Tert. *Pud.* 18 p. 261, 24 *paenitentia ad se clementiam inuitat* (*ThLL s.v.* 232, 71). Although this is not directly comparable to *uoluptates inuitare ad nuptias*, we propose – albeit hesitantly – to retain the reading in F, for which we offer the following three arguments.

Firstly, any change or addition will cause the light chiasmus *temptat libidines – uoluptates ... inuitat* to become even less pronounced, and the links between the two parts of the sentence will be weakened. (By itself, this argument is not especially strong.) Secondly, it seems that for comic effect Apuleius is making the *puer* convey his pretended indignation by the use of ludicrously high-flown language, of which *uoluptates inuitare ad nuptias* is a striking example. Thirdly it is possible that a pun on *uita* is hidden in *inuitare* ("infuse life into", "arouse", "incite"); this would increase the comic effect of the pompous phrase and explain the absence of a parallel for *uoluptates inuitare*. Apul. certainly uses *euitare* in a paronomastic way: *Met.* 3, 8 (58, 6) *tres tam ualidos euitasse iuuenes*, see Löfstedt 1936, 95 and vdPaardt 1971, 73; one might use the evidence of this pun to restore the conjecture *euitabar* 9, 32 (227, 14; cf. Löfstedt *ibid.*); see *ThLL s.v.* for parallels in Ennius and Accius. We find another pun on *uita* in 8, 6 (181, 12) *inuita remansit in uita*. Apul. has no other obvious examples of *inuitare* with a pun on *uita*; nor does *ThLL s.v. inuitare* give any examples. But such a play on words seems natural; cf. Isid. *Orig.* 20, 2, 1 *uictus proprie uocatus quia uitam retinet; unde et ad cibum uocare inuitare dicitur*. Consequently, in view of Apul.'s obvious pun in *euitare*, a similar pun in *inuitare* is not inconceivable. The puer has already made one daring neologism (169, 19 *iniginum*) and our author has a marked preference for this type of 'Umdeutungen', puns, and neologisms (Löfstedt 1936, 100 with a discussion of a series of examples in the *Met.*). Interestingly enough, another 'Umdeutung' is promptly offered by *quidam de illo coetu rusticorum* (171, 18), this time in the sexual sphere: *detestatio* "castration" (see comm. *ad loc.*).

The only one, apart from Hildebrand, to defend the transmitted text is vGeisau 1912, 35: 'VII, 21 aut cum Helmio... emendandus est aut ita interpretandus: *et – ferinas voluptates – aversa Venere invitat ad nuptias* (acc. ad totam sententiam appositione adiunctus)'. The latter proposal should not be rejected out of hand: *eos/eas* can be supplied as the object, as in e.g. 8, 23 (195, 1) *annonae copiosae beata celebritas inuitabat*. However, we still prefer the three arguments we advanced above, especially the second and third.[1]

[1] Prof. Philippa Goold suggests a totally different explanation; according to her *ferinas uoluptates* 'means "the objects of his bestial desire", *uoluptates* being a synonym for *deliciae* or *amores*', and she thinks 'that the boy is accusing the ass of trying, however ineptly and grossly, to win the favours of the people he attacks.' However, we prefer to regard *ferinas uoluptates* as a further explanation of *incognitas libidines*, both phrases describing the ass's lusts, rather than their objects.

inhiare: *ThLL* s.v. 1957, 79 formulates this as *pressius de libidine*. The verb is found in this sense Lucr. 1, 36 *pascit amore auidos inhians in te ... uisus* (sc. Mars), *Ciris* 132, and Aug. *C.D.* 14, 16; in the *Met.* 5, 23 (121, 7) *in eum ... inhians* and 5, 27 (124, 16) *caeca spe ... inhians* (preceded by *uesanae libidinis*).

auersa Venere: the combination also occurs in SHA, Capit. *Alb.* 11 *mulierarius inter primos amatores, auersae Veneris semper ignarus et talium persecutor*. It is a term for 'unnatural lusts', called *illicitas atque incognitas ... libidines* by the *puer*; someone else will soon (24) refer to the ass's *monstruosae nuptiae*. Cf. Heine 1962, 211 and 211 n. 1, who argues that sodomy with animals generally was regarded as a *libido incognita* in antiquity; see also Schlam, *AAGA* 1978, 101.

nuptias = *coitus*, cf. *Rhet. Her.* 4, 45 *cuius mater cottidianis nuptiis delectetur* (mentioned as an example of *translatio, obscenitatis causa*) and *Met.* 10, 34 (265, 10). Cf. Pl. *Cist.* 43 f. *haec quidem ecastor cottidie uiro nubit, nupsitque hodie, nubet mox noctu*.

170, 7-8 Nam imaginem etiam sauii mentiendo ore improbo compulsat ac morsicat: "For, actually mimicking the appearance of kissing, he butts and bites them with his shameless snout".

Nam ... etiam: after the *inuitatio ad nuptias* this seems to be something of an anticlimax. The *Onos* mentions the attempt at kissing before the *inuitatio ad nuptias*.

sauium: for the use of this word, see vdPaardt 1971, 111. To the literature offered there, add Tränkle 1960, 126, who says that the word belongs to the 'ältere Umgangssprache' and that Propertius is the last one to use it; after him we find it in archaisers like Apuleius, Gellius, and Fronto.

mentiri: in Apul. the verb is often found constructed with an object (Médan 1925, 32; Callebat 1968, 180). The earliest example of this usage is Pl. *Mil.* 35 *adsentandumst quidquid hic mentibitur*. The combination *imaginem sauii mentiri* does not occur elsewhere. For the ablative of the gerund used as a present participle, see vdPaardt 1971, 145; Callebat 1968, 319.

improbo: "shameless", *speciatim in re amatoria*, with many examples in *ThLL* s.v. 691, 51.

compulsat: according to *ThLL* this verb is used in its proper sense only here; figuratively in Fulg. *Aet.* p. 162, 11 *deo compulsante* (= *impellente*) *succensa Iudith ... processerat*. It is used in the sense of *confligere* by Tert. *Apol.* 20 and Corip. *Ioh.* 8, 423 (Bernhard 1927, 121).

morsicat: this, too, is a rare word. *ThLL* mentions, besides *Met.* 2, 10 (33, 7), only Paul. *Fest.* 60, 12 L.

170, 8-10 Quae res nobis non mediocris lites atque iurgia, immo forsitan et crimina pariet: "This matter will cause us serious quarrels and disputes – yes, maybe even criminal charges".

lites atque iurgia: the same combination occurs in Juv. 6, 268 *Semper habet lites alternaque iurgia lectus, / in quo nupta iacet*. The absence of *lites atque iurgia* – explicitly mentioned – in a grave inscription is typical of a happy marriage: *CIL*

5, 7066 *sine litibus et iurgiis* (he lived with his wife); cf. *ThLL s.v. iurgium* 666, 31 which also mentions *CIL* 9, 1530 *sine iurgiis, sine querella*; Plin. *Ep.* 8, 5, 1 *sine iurgio, sine offensa*. The combination *lites atque iurgia* is therefore almost a hendiadys. It does not seem right to translate our passage in a strictly juridical way, as does Summers 1967, 256: 'civil suits (*lites*), controversies (*iurgia*) and criminal charges (*crimina*)'. Possible juridical implications of the ass's behaviour are saved for the last part of the sentence (*forsitan et crimina*); this is the sentence's climax, introduced by *immo* (cf. 155, 23).

pariet: the material from the ThLL Institute offers only one parallel for the combination *crimina parere*: Pub. *Sent.* N 45 *nocentem qui defendit, sibi crimen parit*. Apul. uses the verb with the object *contentiones* 10, 14 (247, 25). Cf. Apul. *Pl.* 2, 16 *uitia, quae contra naturam sunt, pariunt exsecrabilitatem* (viz. *quod malitia perfecta seditionem mentibus pariat – ibid.* above); observe in this example the combination of *parere* with *uitia contra naturam*; cf. 170, 6 *auersa Venus*. The point is obvious: unnatural *nuptiae* bring forth *crimina*.

Nunc etiam uisa quadam honesta iuuene, ligno quod deuehebat 170, 10-14
abiecto dispersoque, in eam furiosos direxit impetus et festiuus hic amasio humo sordida prostratam mulierem ibidem incoram omnium gestiebat inscendere: "Even just now, seeing a comely young lady, he threw down the wood he was carrying and scattered it, ran towards her at a furious speed, and – a pretty lover indeed – flung the woman on the dirty ground and desired to mount her right there before the eyes of everybody".

Nunc: for its meaning "just now" (referring to the immediate past) *OLD* mentions Pl. *Mer.* 884 (in dialogue) *Quo nunc ibas? Exulatum*; *Mos.* 477, Petr. 46, 7. In 9, 16 (215, 6) this meaning of *nunc* is emphasized by the combination *nunc nuper*. See Bernhard 1927, 172; LHSz 2, 799.

honesta: more than once Apul. uses this adjective in the sense of *pulchra, speciosa*: 10, 30 (261, 19) *puella uultu honesta*; *Apol.* 4 (6, 2) *philosophos ab ore honestissimos*.

iuuene: among the examples of its occurrence as a feminine are Gracch. (Plin. *Nat.* 7, 122); Ov. *Ars* 1, 63.

abiecto: cf. 170, 3 *stramentis abiectis*.

deuehebat: cf. 169, 21 *ligno ... quod gerebam*.

in eam: picks up the ablative *iuuene*. It is a loose expression, not uncommon in colloquial language; see Bernhard 1927, 45 n. 2; Callebat 1968, 321. According to LHSz 2, 139 f. it is used for the sake of clarity.

festiuus: ironical in the sense of "fine", "pretty"; cf. Cic. *Flac.* 91 *materculae suae festiuus filius*. The adjective has a sexual connotation in these passages, as it has 3, 23 (69, 14) and 2, 7 (31, 2) *festiue*. Without an ironical or sexual connotation 2, 18 (39, 16) *cenulae* and 11, 6 (270, 23) *spectacula*.

amasio: also found 3, 22 (69, 1); see vdPaardt 1971, 168. *Amasius*, too, is found, e.g. Pl. *Cas.* 590; *Truc.* 658. For the formation of this noun, see LHSz 1, 300.

humo: ablative of place (Callebat 1968, 194); cf. 170, 4 *humi*. The *Onos* does not tell us that the ground is *sordida*; the detail is typical of Apul.'s dramatization of the situation (see comm. on 169, 20-24): as the γυνή becomes a *iuuenis honesta* and the ground gets dirty a greater contrast is created (cf. Junghanns 1932, 86).

incoram: Callebat 1968, 240 says that this word originated from a desire to emphasize *coram*, in imitation of ἔναντι vs ἄντι (from which the construction with the genitive was borrowed as well). According to him, the word was not coined by Apuleius; it is a Graecism which entered into the 'parler commun'. *ThLL* mentions Apul. as the only author who uses this word: in addition to this passage 9, 10 (209, 23); 9, 15 (214, 1); 10, 5 (240, 25); as an adverb 9, 42 (235, 28) and 10, 23 (254, 20). As an adverb it is found in Symm. *Ep*. 9, 129 *quando... praeciperes, quod incoram positus* (i.e. *praesens*) *improbasti*. See also LHSz 2, 259. The *Onos* does not mention the fact that the alleged assault had taken place *incoram omnium*.

inscendere: in the sense "cover", "mount" it is only found here and 10, 22 (253, 14). The sole occurrence of the noun *inscensus* is 165, 7.

170, 14-18 Quod nisi ploratu questuque femineo conclamatum uiatorum praesidium accurrisset ac de mediis ungulis ipsius esset erepta liberataque, misera illa compauita atque dirupta ipsa quidem cruciabilem cladem sustinuisset, nobis uero poenale reliquisset exitium: "And had not some passers-by, summoned by the woman's weeping and wailing, run to the rescue and snatched her from between his hooves and thus freed her, that poor woman, trampled and torn to pieces, would herself have suffered an excruciating calamity and would have bequeathed death to us in retribution".

Quod nisi: used on the analogy of *quod si*; see Médan 1925, 90.

uiatorum praesidium: the abstract noun takes the place of an adverbial phrase ("to the rescue"); it is modified by the concrete noun (in the genitive), which is the logical subject of the verb. See Médan 1925, 319; Bernhard 1927, 96. Hijmans, *AAGA* 1978, 191 comments on the colometry of this passage.

ipsius: "his", referring to the aforementioned animal. For the anaphorical use of *ipse*, see Callebat 1968, 283 f. The next line has *ipsa quidem* in the meaning of "herself", contrasting with *nobis uero* (18).

erepta liberataque: *liberata* is the result of *erepta*; this relation is expressed by *-que*. See Bernhard 1927, 168.

compauita: this is the only occurrence in Latin of the verb *compauire*; see Bernhard 1927, 120. *Compauita* is explained by the following *dirupta*; here we have the reverse of *erepta liberataque* (Bernhard 1927, 168). The simple verb *pauire* is used almost exclusively in the technical term *pauire terram* (cf. *pauimentum*). *Pauire* has a rare compound *depuuere*: Paul. *Fest*. 61, 14 L; Lucil. 1245 *misellam depuuiit* (-*uit* al.); Naev. *Com*. 134 *depuuit me miseram*. The combination with *miser* in these cases, as in our text, is notable. Fest. 207, 13 L mentions a verb *obpuuiare*. A connection with παίω – suggested by Paul. *Fest*. 61, 16 L – is questioned by Walde-Hofmann ³1938 and Ernout-Meillet ³1951 (both *s.v. pauire*): 'en somme étymologie obscure'.

cruciabilem cladem: alliteration. The adjective *cruciabilis* appears in the second century A.D. not earlier than Gellius and Apul. (Luisa Gargantini 1963, 34; Callebat 1968, 134). This may be accidental, since the adverb *cruciabiliter* is already found in Pl. *Pseud*. 950. Apuleius has the adjective five times, always in the meaning of *qui cruciatuum est plenus, qui cruciatum affert*: *Met.* 1, 7 (6, 22); 2,2 (25, 8); *h.l.*; 9, 13 (212, 23); 10, 3 (238, 10). The adjective has, accordingly, an active meaning in Apul.; see LHSz 1, 349 (who do not mention *cruciabilis*; nor does Löfstedt 1936, 84 f.). It is found with passive meaning (*qui cruciatum admittit, cruciari potest*) in Lact. *Inst.* 7, 20, 9 *ut* (sc. *animae*) *si non extinguibiles in totum, tamen cruciabiles fiant per corporis maculam* and Ps. Prosp. *Carm. de prou.* 225.

clades: "calamity" in our translation implies bodily harm as Cic. *Carm.* frg. 32. 26 *luctifica clades nostro infixa est corpori* and Liv. 2, 13, 1 (*ThLL s.v.* 1241, 21 f.)

sustinuisset: for the meaning "endure" cf. Caes. *Gal.* 1, 31, 13 *imperia*; 8, 39, 3 *aestatem*.

poenale exitium: "death penalty". This rare combination also occurs Rut. Ruf. *Hist.* 5, 133 (cf. 3, 5, 6 *feralis poena exitium*). See also 166, 10 *capitale ... exitium* with our comm.

The narrator implies that the *puer*'s accusations are utterly unfounded; hence the emphasis on Lucius' indignation (169, 14 *deterrimus ... puer*; 169, 24 *concinnare*; 170, 19 *mendaciis*).

From a biological point of view these accusations are improbable. Psychopathological sources do mention examples of women copulating with animals (see e.g. R. Grassberger, *Die Unzucht mit Tieren*, Vienna 1968, 5 on zoophily in women; as a source from antiquity Juv. 6, 334 may be quoted; Scobie 1975, 31 n. 18 mentions additional passages), but it is most improbable for a male ass to take the initiative (thus Grassberger 16, who knows only a case of a dog playing an active part).

But the ass in our story is a metamorphosed man, which makes the situation different. Ironically enough, the ass recently suffered an amorous defeat when (ch. 14 and 16) he went looking for *concubinas futuras* in the pastures but was shamefully chased away by the stallions; this fact makes the boy's accusation hurt all the more. Another consideration is that the ass is not completely innocent where women are concerned: he told us 4, 23 (92, 19) that Charite was a girl 'to give ideas even to an ass like me' (*concupiscendam*); 150, 1 he tries to kiss the girl's feet. When it comes to copulating with the *matrona pollens et opulens* (10, 21) there are no indications that this takes place *asino inuito* – even if the initiative comes from the lady – and there is no question of moral scruple on the ass's part. Lucius-the ass shows indignation only when (10, 29 and 34) he hears of a condemned woman with whom he is to copulate *publice* (265, 14) – cf. *incoram omnium* 170, 13 which was added by Apuleius[1] – and with whom, most probably, he is to take the initiative. He appears to be quite selective in his indignation.

---

[1] See Heine 1962, 210 f.; Gwyn Griffiths, too (*AAGA* 1978, 153 f.), points out that the ass shows different attitudes toward copulation with the two ladies; cf. also Tatum 1969b, 522 f.

CHAPTER XXII

On account of the alleged assault the ass is to be butchered.

170, 19-21 Talibus mendaciis admiscendo sermones alios, qui meum uerecundum silentium uehementius premerent, animos pastorum in meam perniciem atrociter suscitauit: "By adding to such lies other stories which put even more of a burden on my modest silence, he cruelly incited the shepherds to ruin me".

Talibus: note how often in this book a new pericope starts with a form of the adjective *talis*: 156, 19; 157, 18; 164, 12; 166, 3; 170, 19 (book 4 only 76, 3; 87, 17; 94, 16; book 8 has none; book 9 only 224, 5; book 10 only 260, 1). *Talis* sums up the preceding events or utterances and introduces the new action which logically results from them.

admiscendo: Callebat 1968, 320 mentions *admiscendo* in this passage as one of the few examples in which the ablative of the gerund has preserved its instrumental force.

sermones alios: these stories are only alluded to, never actually told. This mere reference contributes to establishing a brisk tempo ('tempo' defined as the relation between narrative time and narrated time) – something which is characteristic of book 7 in general; see vdPaardt, *AAGA* 1978, 84 f.

uerecundum silentium: the modesty which was characteristic of Lucius as a human being – even a *uirginalis uerecundia* (1, 23: 21, 8) – is retained by him even as an ass (Heine 1962, 211; Scobie 1975, 124; *GCA* 1977, 173). The ass's *uerecundum silentium* makes the *mendacia* told about him all the more heinous. His natural modesty would have kept him from answering even if he had not already been rendered speechless by the nature of the lies; and physically, too, of course, he is speechless. Consequently, the adage 'silence implies consent' is applicable to him, which may be another reason for him to feel oppressed. Something similar has happened to him at 156, 8 f., where he complains that he is unable to defend himself against false accusations: his attempts to say '*non feci*' failed.

premerent: the subjunctive in the relative clause has some consecutive force. Callebat 1968, 342 f. points out that Apul. sometimes uses the subjunctive in such circumstances, sometimes the indicative.

atrociter: Apul. has the adverb in this passage only. The adjective, too, is rare: *atrocissimum* 173, 1 and *atrox* in *Apol.* 102 (113, 23).

170, 22-24 Denique unus ex illis: 'Quin igitur publicum istum maritum', inquit, 'immo communem omnium adulterum illis suis monstruosis nuptiis condignam uictimamus hostiam': "Finally one of them said: 'then why don't we slaughter this public spouse, or rather this indiscriminate adulterer of everyone – slaughter him as a victim, as his monstrous unions richly deserve?'"

In the first part of the spoken sentence (*quin . . . nuptiis*) *i*'s and *u*'s, varied by a few *o*'s, prevail, whereas from *condignam* on there is a predominance of *a*, varied with *i*. Cf. Hijmans, AAGA 1978, 201 f.

Quin: by itself or with *igitur* it often stands at the beginning of a sentence to give the question a greater intensity (Callebat 1968, 92). With *igitur* it occurs also 1, 13 (12, 6) and 162, 3.

publicum maritum: *ThLL* offers no other example of this oxymoron.

monstruosis nuptiis: the phrase expresses the same notion as *auersa Venere* (170, 6), and is an equally unusual combination, according to *ThLL*. The shepherds' indignation at the unusual situation is expressed by equally unusual word-combinations. The adjective *monstruosus* is used 160, 22 to describe the inhuman death devised by the robbers for Charite and the ass. 10. 15 (248, 17) *monstruosas asini delicias* describes something unnatural, too – the nice titbits which actually are meant for human beings. In 5, 16 (115, 18) *de tam monstruoso fatuae illius mendacio* the adjective indicates the absurdity of Psyche's supposed lie.

condignam: the word is found for the first time Pl. *Am.* 537 *ecastor condignum donum, qualest qui donum dedit*; next Quint. *Decl.*; it becomes more frequent after Apul., who uses it here and in 164, 18 and 10, 12 (245, 27).

nuptiis condignam . . . hostiam: 156, 20 *manibus uirginis decretam me uictimam*, too, has the theme of the ass being sacrificed as a punishment, in which the type of punishment has some connection with the crime: he wanted to escape with Charite and will be punished with her sewn within his belly. Simple slaughter does not have a similar link with the type of crime here. That link will be forged at 171, 12 f. when the peasants decide to castrate him. As to the practice of sacrificing asses, Olck in his article in *RE* (*s.v.* Esel 654, 23 f.) can mention only three examples from the Greco-Roman world (the other examples are from the Persians and Hyperboreans), namely in Tarentum to the winds, in Lampsacus to Priapus, and our passage. The sacrifice to Priapus is narrated by Ovid (*Fast.* 1, 391 *caeditur et rigido custodi ruris asellus*); it is performed as a punishment of the ass because by his braying he had frustrated Priapus' amorous advances toward Lotis.

uictimamus: also found 162, 15; see our comm. *ad. loc.*

et 'Heus tu, puer', ait, 'obtruncato protinus eo intestina quidem canibus nostris iacta, ceteram uero carnem omnem operariorum cenae reserua: "and he said: 'You there, boy! Butcher him at once and throw his intestines to the dogs, but save the rest – all the meat – for the labourers' meal'". 170, 25-171, 2

Heus: a word from colloquial language; see Bernhard 1927, 129 (who does not mention our passage); Marg. Molt on 1, 3 (3, 14); Callebat 1968, 88; vdPaardt 1971, 55. Morelli 1913, 181 goes rather far in assuming that our passage has influenced SHA Jul. Val. 8, 14 *interpellat puer et 'heus tu' inquit*.

iacta: Apuleius' usage is in accordance with the *sermo cotidianus*: *iactare* occurs nine times in the *Met.*, *iacere* only once. *Iactare* is sometimes modified by an intensifying adverb: 4, 3 (76, 12); 10, 2 (237, 27) *crebriter* and 8, 4 (179, 13) *hac illac*. See Callebat 1968, 391, who ascribes Apuleius' use of this verb to his inclination to *copia dicendi* as much as to his use of *sermo cotidianus*; Ernout 1954, 162; 4, 12 (83, 17) *uestem stragulam ... iactare* see *GCA* 1977, 95, where the verb has its original, intensive force; see comm. *ad loc*. Cf. also Petr. 64, 8 (*cani*) *iactans candidum panem*.

ceteram: for its somewhat pleonastic use, compare 3, 10 (59, 16) *una de ceteris statuis uel columnis* (said of Lucius, not without reason: it creates the impression that Lucius, too, is a statue or a column). Cf. vdPaardt 1971, 210 with a reference to Löfstedt 1950, 188, who quotes 8, 16 (189, 19) *me* (sc. *asinum*) *cursu celeri ceteros equos antecellentem*.

carnem: the meat of asses was eaten; there was a special marketplace in Athens, where it was sold. Sausages were made from mixed ass- and dog-meat. Xen. *Anab*. 2, 1, 6 mentions soldiers in the field butchering asses for their meal. It seems that it was mainly for the poor; Gal. *Vict. Atten*. 66 even maintains that only asses eat ass-meat because the meat is tough and induces biliousness. Rich Persians, on the other hand, regarded it as a birthday-treat (Hdt. 1, 133). The Romans preferred the meat of the wild ass, which was imported especially for that purpose; Maecenas introduced the delicacy of ass colt's meat (Plin. *Nat*. 8, 170). See *RE* VI *s.v.* Esel 642, 15 f.; Kathleen Freeman 1945, 39; André 1961, 143. The ass is again in imminent danger of being butchered at 8, 31 where he has to serve as a (partial) substitute for a *cerui pinguissimum femus*; the meat has to be heavily seasoned (202, 16) to disguise the change in meat.

operariorum: Apul. uses the word in this passage only. *OLD* mentions as its first occurrence Pl. *Vid.* 21 *operarium ... ru‹s condu›c‹ere›*; cf. 25 *est tibi in mercede seruus*. These are hired workers, often farm-hands (cf. *rus* and Col. 11, 2, 40 *Bonus operarius prati iugerum desecat*) who may or may not be *serui*. They are probably identical with the *rustici* mentioned 171, 9.

171, 2-4 Nam corium adfirmatum cineris inspersu dominis referemus eiusque mortem de lupo facile mentiemur: "But his hide we will toughen by sprinkling ashes on it, and then take it back to our masters: we will easily make them believe that he has been killed by a wolf'".

Nam: introduces a sentence which explains the motive for the proposal made in the previous sentence. The statement that the hide is needed to deceive their masters explains why the previous sentence does not include a proposal to use the hide, like the meat, to the advantage of the speaker and his friends. Apart from this casual function, *nam* has a somewhat adversative connotation as well (as appears from our translation); see LHSz 2, 506 on 'quasi-adversative' *nam* with its first example Suet. *Aug*. 83 *ludebat cum pueris minutis, quos facie et garrulitate amabiles undique conquirebat ...; nam pumilos atque distortos ... ut ludibria naturae ... abhorrebat*. See further Marg. Molt 1938, 84; Callebat 1968, 329 with literature.

adfirmatum: in the sense "harden", "strengthen", this verb is also used by Apul. 11, 2 (267, 20): *tu* (sc. *dea*) *fortunam conlapsam adfirma*. It is one of the words which Apul. uses in their literal meaning, whereas normally they are used in a figurative sense (cf. Médan 1925, 165). *ThLL* does not give any other example of this use of *affirmare*. It is safe to say that it is characteristic of Apuleius to use words in their etymologically literal meaning (more examples in Koziol 1872, 291); conjectures like *offirmatum* (Stewech) and *adsiccatum* (Rohde) are therefore unnecessary, despite the fact that the ms. is difficult to read at this point.

cineris inspersu: φ has *inspersum*; F *inspersu*, where the abbreviation symbol seems to have been erased. The noun *inspersus* (i.e. *actio inspergendi*) occurs only here and 9, 30 (225, 20) *comae... sordentes inspersu cineris*. Cf. Koziol 1872, 270 and Médan 1925, 113 under 'néologismes'.

Damsté 1928, 22 objects to *cineris*: the shepherds would hardly think (he argues) that sprinkling ashes on the hide would be sufficient to convince their masters that the animal had been killed by a wolf; consequently, he wants to read *cruoris*. But the shepherds wish to preserve the ass's hide (which they need as evidence) because they do not know when they will see their masters again. Sprinkling ashes on the hide is an approved method of preservation; cf. 4, 14 (85, 24) and *GCA* 1977, 115-6, where ashes are sprinkled on the bear-skin to make it supple and dry. The shepherds need this evidence because the ass was a favourite of the *domini*: he had been the first to try to help Charite escape (6, 27 f.); at her eventual rescue he had been her mount (7, 12 f.) and had been addressed by her as *sospitator* (164, 15); as a reward he had been sent to pasture with the mares (165, 7).

mortem... mentiemur: for the construction with a direct object, see 170, 7 above with our comm. *ad loc.*

mortem de lupo: *de* indicating the cause, used attributively after a noun, occurs more than once in the *Met.*; see Callebat 1968, 202; vdPaardt 1971, 154; LHSz 2, 264. Callebat *ibid.* considers the possibility of contamination of *mentiri de aliquo* and *mentiri rem*. One could also say that the existence of both phrases made it easier for Apul. to use this succinct expression. Médan 1925, 66 compares 8, 31 (202, 18) *salus de mea morte*.

In 4, 14 a she-bear is butchered and eaten; the skin is preserved and saved for Thrasyleon's disguise: he plans to use it to deceive Demochares. In this passage the preserved ass-hide is to be used to deceive the *domini*.

Sublata cunctatione accusator ille meus noxius, ipse etiam pastoralis 171, 4-8
exsecutor sententiae, laetus et meis insultans malis calcisque illius
admonitus, quam inefficacem fuisse mehercules doleo, protinus
gladium cotis adtritu parabat: "Without delay that criminal accuser of
mine – being also the executioner of the shepherds' sentence – began to sharpen
his sword at once on a whetstone, cheerful and jubilant about my misery and
mindful of that kick which – I am damned sorry to say – had not been effective".

accusator ille meus: the *puer*, who is ready to proceed to the execution of the sentence.

noxius: LS *s.v.* mention some examples of the meaning "criminal"; Suet. *Cal.* 27, 1 *ex noxiis laniandos adnotauit* (sc. Caligula); *Nero* 12, 1 *munere... neminem occidit, ne noxiorum quidem. Noxii* are kept as food for wild animals 4, 13 (84, 22).

pastoralis: "of the shepherds". See Bernhard 1927, 110 f. on the increasing use of the adjective instead of the genitive of the noun; cf. also 165, 6 *greges equinos* with our comm. The proposal to butcher the ass has apparently been accepted and the *puer* wants to get on with the execution without further delay; the shepherds have apparently reached a collective decision. A similarly joint decision is made at 8, 23 (194, 29) *Inibi larem sedesque perpetuas pastores illi statuere decernunt*.

exsecutor sententiae: nouns in *-tor* are frequently found in Apul.; see Bernhard 1927, 105 and *GCA* 1977, 68 with further literature. This noun is used with an objective genitive also Vell. 2, 45, 1 *malorum propositorum executor acerrimus*; Macer *Dig.* 49, 1, 4 pr. *ab exsecutore sententiae appellare non licet*; Hier. *Ep.* 153, 5; often in *Cod. Theod.* (see *ThLL s.v.* 1844, 57 f.). Norden 1912 and Summers 1967 do not discuss the word.

laetus et meis insultans malis calcisque illius admonitus: the impression that this is a tricolon is weakened by the change from *et* to *-que* (Bernhard 1927, 82). On the other hand, it is possible to observe 'wachsende Glieder' in the tricolon.

calcis: Bernhard 1927, 163 points out that *calx* ("hoof") is brachylogically used for "kick with a hoof" here; it also has that meaning 3, 26 (71, 10). The kick referred to was given in ch. 19 (168, 25).

mehercules: according to Bernhard 1927, 129 this is an 'Einschlag des volkssprachlichen Elements'. Callebat 1968, 177 has a slightly different opinion; he points out that *mehercules* also occurs in e.g. Cicero's letters, which makes it more probable that *mehercules* belongs to the *sermo familiaris*. Cf. also *GCA* 1977, 175 f.

doleo: Callebat 1968, 428 believes that the use of the present tense in this narrative in the past has a 'valeur intensive qui prolonge dans l'état actuel un sentiment éprouvé à un moment déterminé antérieur'. Another possibility is that the narrator (the re-transformed ass) deplores even now – i.e. at the time he tells the story – that his kick did not hit the mark; this illustrates well the intensity of his hate (at the time) toward the *puer*. A comparison with 147, 4 is instructive: *sed astans ego non procul dolebam mehercules, quod pugillares et stilum non habebam*. It is also a means to remind the reader of the 'in persona-Identität von erzählendem Ich und erlebendem Ich' Stanzel, [8]1976, 35).

protinus: as in 170, 25, it emphasizes the 'immediate'; this underlines the *puer*'s vindictiveness and the great danger in which the ass finds himself.

gladium: Helm-Krenkel 1970 translates "das Schlachtmesser", Schwartz "the knife". The lexica do not offer a parallel for this meaning of *gladius*; therefore it is better to translate with "sword" as most translators do: Adlington, Butler, Vallette ("fe ler"), Brandt-Ehlers ("einem Säbel"), Scazzoso, and Augello. By using this word, the narrator draws a parallel with the execution of a human being and draws attention to the ever-present tension between Lucius the man and Lucius the ass.

adtritu: first attested in Sen. *Nat.* 1, 14, 5 *Attritu aeris (et saepius)* and Plin. *Nat.* 2, 113. It occurs in the *Met.* 8, 4 (179, 9) *(dentibus) attritu* and 10, 28 (259, 16). The mss. read *adt-* in our passage only, elsewhere *att-*.

parabat: the conative imperfect renders με αὐτίκα ἤθελεν ἀποσφάττειν of

Onos 33, 2. The ass will be in danger of being butchered on another occasion: 8, 31 the cook is making preparations. That chapter (and book 8) ends with the same image as does our chapter: *destinatae iam lanienae cultros acuebat* – observe the use of *cultros* in that episode.

CHAPTER XXIII

On second thoughts it seems preferable to emasculate the ass.

171, 9-12 Sed quidam de coetu illo rusticorum: 'Nefas', ait 'tam bellum asinum sic enecare et propter luxuriem lasciuiamque amatoriam criminatos opera seruitioque tam necessario carere: "But someone from that group of peasants said: 'What a shame to kill such a fine ass in that way and, through accusing him of self-indulgence and amorous lasciviousness, forgo his labour and services that we need so much'".

de: for the partitive use of *de*, see *GCA* 1977, 140.

illo: according to Bernhard 1927, 215 this is a rare example of hypallage of a pronoun, of which he gives one other example in the *Met.*, namely 8, 12 (186, 24) *tuo luminum cruore libabo*; he calls it 'ein ausgesprochener Poetismus'. In our opinion, however, it is not necessary to speak of hypallage: true, the preceding text does not mention a *coetus rusticorum* in so many words, but the word *rustici* must refer to the shepherds who have gathered to pronounce the *pastoralis sententia* (171, 5).

Nefas: Callebat 1968, 114 points out that a nominal sentence with ellipsis of the verb is quite frequent in colloquial language and in rapid dialogue where gestures and tone will clarify an abbreviated sentence; cf. LHSz 2, 419 f. A comparable case is 2, 8 (31, 24) *quod nefas dicere, nec quod sit ullum huius rei tam dirum exemplum*, although there we can still sense some of the religious meaning of *nefas* (Helm translates: "es ist schon ein Frevel, es nur zu sagen"); possibly there is also a semantic connection between *nefas* (‹ *fari*) and *dicere* as in Cic. *Sen.* 5, 13 *uidetis nefas esse dictu miseram fuisse talem senectutem*.

bellum: because of the context, one could argue that this diminutive has retained its ironical value here (Hofmann ³1951, 143 f. and Callebat 1968, 379); on the other hand one should bear in mind that a realistic herdsman is speaking, who is sorry to see such a handsome animal destroyed.

enecare: thus F, where a different hand has written *necare* over the line. φ has *enicare*, but with an *e* written over the *i*. The recentiores (ς) have *enecare*. No objections can be raised to *enecare* (*ThLL s.v.* has many examples). As to the variant spelling *enicare*, *ThLL s.v.* 561, 66 f. points out that this weakened form is recommended by the mss. of Plautus, Terence, and Varro, but that the form *enecare* has been re-established from Laberius onward. Thus it seems preferabhe to opt for this form, along with the editors.

luxuriem: "self-indulgence" is the general term, more strictly defined by *lasciuiam amatoriam*; see Bernhard 1927, 165 (less correct Médan 1925, 362 who regards this as a superfluous synonym).

criminatos: the whole passage from *sed* (171, 9) to *alioquin* (171, 12) is barely legible in F; a more recent hand has written *criminatus* over the illegible line, φ has *criminatum,* A *crimina tamen.* Since *criminatus* is impossible to retain, we have a choice: either to read *criminatos* based on *criminatus* (F *al. m.*) (so Helm, Frassinetti, Augello 1977, 173), or to read *criminatum* with φ, which had probably been copied already before F became illegible, as do Oudendorp, Hildebrand, Brandt-Ehlers, Robertson, Terzaghi, Scazzoso. If *criminatos* is read, *nos* must be supplied as subject for the infinitives; if one refers *criminatum* with *te* or *eum* supplied, the killing becomes the private enterprise of the *accusator.* We prefer *criminatos* because of the *pastoralis sententia* (171, 5): the shepherds have reached their verdict by collective agreement.

Conjectures like *et crimina [tum]* (Novák), *inanem reatum* (Brakman), *amatoria crimina, tam ‹utili› opera* (vdVliet), *criminatum ‹et‹* (Giarratano, who deletes *et* before *propter luxuriem*) are unnecessary because the readings of the main mss. yield a perfectly acceptable sentence.

The verb *criminari,* 'verbe juridique entré dans la langue générale, mais resté technique', is not found in poetry except in Phaedrus and Prudentius (Flobert 1975, 78). Flobert's statement deserves some specification as far as the *Met.* is concerned: in two passages, namely 8, 28 (199, 10) *Infit uaticinatione clamosa conficto mendacio semet ipsum incessere atque criminari* (about the priest of Dea Syria) and 11, 6 (270, 24) *figuram tuam repente mutatam sequius interpretatus aliquis maligne criminabitur* (Isis speaking to the ass just before his retransformation into a man), it is made clear by an explicit phrase (*conficto mendacio* and *maligne* respectively) that the accusation is false. In the three other occurrences, namely our passage, secondly 174, 10 *meum ... Bellerofontem, abactorem indubitatum cruentumque percussorem criminantes* a man is falsely accused of killing the *puer* – a bear had killed him), and finally 10, 14 (247, 6) *Illi uero postremo etiam mutuo sese rapinae turpissimae criminabantur* (the two baker-bothers are falsely accused of eating the titbits – the ass had eaten them), *criminari* occurs in a context where the *reader* knows that the accusation is false. Cf. the description given at the beginning of the lemma in *ThLL*: "i.q. calumniari, falso uel maligne arguere".

The verb *accusare,* which is notably frequent in the *Apology* (37 times vs *criminari* twice), does not occur in the *Met.,* but its derivatives *accusatio* and *accusator* do. No other example of *criminari propter* seems to exist. The noun *criminatio* (3, 29: 74, 5; see vdPaardt 1971, 206) has this subjective element as well, so that it is identical with *calumnia, maligna accusatio.*

opera seruitioque: again the latter noun specifies the former.

cum alioquin exsectis genitalibus possit neque in uenerem nullo modo surgere uosque omni metu periculi liberare, insuper etiam longe crassior atque corpulentor effici: "whereas otherwise, if his genitals were cut off, he could by no means rise to the occasion, and could free you from all fear of danger, and furthermore he might even become much fatter and stouter".

171, 12-15

alioquin: "otherwise", see also *GCA* 1977, 25 and 79; our comm. on 166, 11-15.

exsectis: *exsecare* is the technical term for this operation, cf. e.g. Petr. 119, 21 *surripuere uiros, exsectaque uiscera ferro / in uenerem fregere*; Suet. *Nero* 28, 1

Puerum... exectis testibus.

genitalibus: the plural is used here as in 1,9 (8, 22) and *Apol.* 33 (39, 17). The singular is found 10, 22 (253, 19) and *P.* 1, 16, 22.; see Callebat 1968, 53 who gives examples of plural and singular in other authors as well. It seems that Apul. does not use the singular and plural indiscriminately: 10, 22 refers to the *mentula* whereas 1, 9 and our passage refer primarily to the *testiculi*. In *Apol. 33 (39, 17)* the distinction is not clear, while *P.* 1, 16, 22 is wrongly quoted by Callebat: *genitale* is used as an adjective there (*genitale seminium*).

nullo modo: can be read with some difficulty in F; φ and ς have *ullo modo*. Practically all editors adopt F's reading, and rightly: cases of a double negation are not uncommon, especially in colloquial language; see Callebat 1968, 99, who remarks that in Apul. such cases regularly occur in direct discourse; Hofmann ³1951, 97 f.; vdPaardt 1971, 62 f.; LHSz 2, 804 f. (Leky 1908 and Bernhard 1927 do not mention this passage).

in uenerem: see Callebat 1968, 227 for this '*in* finale': although rare in early and classical Latin, its use greatly expands in Tacitus and Seneca; it is frequent in the *Met.* (see also LHSz 2, 274). Cf. *Met.* 3, 20 (67, 14) *bacchamur in Venerem* and 9, 24 (221, 8) *miscebatur in uenerem*. The metonymous use of *Venus* in the context of animals occurs in Verg. *G.* 2, 329 *et Venerem certis repetunt armenta diebus* and 3, 267; also in authors on animal husbandry like Columella, e.g. 6, 27, 10 *si admissarius iners in uenerem est*.

in uenerem surgere: other examples of this combination do not exist, apparently. Cf. 169, 4 *ignis surgebat in flammas*.

Thus the type of punishment is linked with the nature of the indictment, see our note on *nuptiis condignam... hostiam* (170, 24).

longe crassior: for *longe* with the comparative, see our comm. on 169, 20.

crassior atque corpulentior: one may agree with Bernhard 1927, 167 that it is hard to distinguish the two adjectives in meaning, except for the fact that *crassus* – unlike *corpulentus* – is not used of living beings exclusively. *Corpulentus* is found for the first time Pl. *Epid.* 10 *corpulentior uidere atque habitior*: afterward not until Col. 6, 3, 5 *nitidumque et hilare et corpulentum pecus*. From Tertullian on it becomes a philosophical notion used in the sense of *corporalis*. Apul. may have chosen the adjective (which he also uses 8, 26: 198, 1) for the sake of its archaizing, Plautine colour: cf. Callebat 1968, 509.

171, 15-19 Multos ego scio non modo asinos inertes, uerum etiam ferocissimos equos nimio libidinis laborantes atque ob id truces uesanosque adhibita tali detestatione mansuetos ac mansues exinde factos et [h]oneri ferundo non inhabiles et cetero ministerio patientes: "Many that I know of – not only slow asses but also the fiercest horses, suffering from an excess of rut and for that reason wild and mad – have after similar surgery become tame and gentle, suitable for carrying a load and for rendering other services".

Multos: this is the first word of the sentence and therefore has the emphasis; *ego*, which is often used unemphatically in the *Met.* (see Bernhard 1927, 111 f.) or at most serves to call attention back to the speaker (see Callebat 1968, 94), has no special emphasis. The fact that the castrator knows many cases naturally adds cogency to his arguments. *Multos* is chiastically divided into two groups: *asinos inertes* and *ferocissimos equos*.

The ass must have been pleased to hear the castrator put asses on a par with horses. He regarded himself as equal to a horse when in ch. 16 *laetus et tripudians* he frolicked into the pasture looking for *equae*; at 152, 10 he is said – albeit maliciously – to surpass Pegasus in speed; at 8, 16 (189, 19) it pleases him that everyone is surprised at the speed with which he outruns the horses. Cf. also *GCA* 1977, 31 on 75, 15-18.

inertes: cf. Psysiogn. 119 *asinus animal est iners, frigidum, indocile, insolens.* The ass gets the same epithet 9, 39 (233, 18). The adjective is not unamusing here: the accusations against the ass do not suggest any *inertia in rebus ueneriis*.

nimio libidinis: for the nominalized adjective *nimium*, followed by a partitive genitive, cf. e.g. Cic. *Ver.* 3, 78 *noluit . . . nimium lucri dare.* See vGeisau 1916, 262; vdPaardt 1971, 199; *GCA* 1977, 32.

laborantes: *laborare*, with the adjective of the disease one suffers from, is the usual medical term; cf. e.g. Larg. 16 *nec . . . quisquam stultus non horum morborum aliquo laborat.* The castrator is described as a quite different personality from the *puer* and the shepherd, who is speaking from 170, 22 onward: he is characterized as a calm, professional man (this is illustrated by his use of medical terminology – to him, the ass is a 'case' like any other) but at the same time he shows himself as somewhat pedantic in mentioning his successes in the treatment of other cases.

truces uesanosque: another characteristic of the castrator's language seems to be the use of two adjectives which are either synonymous or in which the latter specifies the former; cf. 171, 11; 18; and 23.

detestatione: Apul. is the only author who uses *detestatio* in the sense of castration – apparently associating it with *testes* "testicles"; see Löfstedt 1936, 101, who also points out that this pun turns the operation into something atrocious – interestingly enough not perceived as such by the professional castrator but by the narrator. It is therefore hard to determine on which level this play on words takes place – the level of the castrator or that of the narrator.

The pun on *testes* ("witnesses" and "testicles") is a favourite in comedy; see Pl. *Cur.* 32 *quod amas ama ‹to› testibus praesentibus* with the note of Ernout 1935 and Monaco 1969, who for a similar pun (on *intestatus* and *testes*) adduces Pl. *Cur.* 621 *licet te antestari? Non licet. / Iuppiter te, miles, perdat, intestatus uiuito* (although some editors delete this verse) and *Mil.* 1416 *si intestatus non abeo hinc, bene agitur pro noxia*. Luisa Gargantini 1963, 39 refers to *detestatio* in the sense "castration" as a neologism. This does not seem right: the sense "castration" never became fashionable through Apuleius – it remained a *hapax*; it is rather a play on words, similar to those we have observed on the previous pages (always in the conversation of *shepherds!*): *inuitat* 170, 7; to a somewhat less degree *adfirmatum* 171, 2.

adhibita: *adhibere*, too, is used in a medical sense; cf. Dict. 2, 10 *adhibentes curam uulneri* (see 171, 22 below).

mansuetos ac mansues: this reading of F and φ is retained only by Hildebrand, vdVliet, and Gaselee. The old conjecture *mites* instead of *mansues* – by Pricaeus, who refers to Gel. 5, 14, 21 *mitis et mansues* (sc. *leo*) – is adopted by Robertson,

Terzaghi, Frassinetti, Helm, and vThiel; Oudendorp, referring to *Onos* 33, 5 ἥμερός τε... καὶ πίων, proposes *pingues*, in which he is followed by Giarratano and Scazzoso.

Is it necessary to replace *mansues*, which is unquestionable in the mss., by a conjecture? *Mansues* occurs, in addition to Gellius, Varro *Men.* 364 *leonem*; Pl. *As.* 145 and (of people) 504; Acc. *Trag.* 454 *mansues misericordia*; Apul. *Met.* 11, 8 (272, 16). The word evidently belongs to the category of words which are attested in early Latin but which do not re-appear until the second century A.D., particularly in Apuleius (cf. Bernhard 1927, 131). Consequently no objections can be raised against the word as such. Another question is whether *mansuetos* – the regular word used of animals (see *ThLL s.v.* 330, 39 f.; *Met.* 9, 8: 208, 18 and 10, 35: 265, 27 *asinum*) – is to be regarded as a gloss on *mansues* which has crept into the text (cf. Paul. Fest. 141 L *mansues pro mansuetus*). On this assumption Vossius deleted *mansuetos ac*. Castiglioni 1931, 488, using the same argument, conjects that the original reading was *mites ac mansues*, in which *mites* was subsequently eliminated through the intrusion of the gloss *mansuetos* for *mansues*. Castiglioni's emendation (which has the same word order as the Gellius passage quoted above) is quite ingenious, but not strong enough for us to question the reading of the mss. Sets of two synonymous or almost-synonymous adjectives occur remarkably often in our chapter: 171, 14 *crassior atque corpulentior*; 171, 17 *truces uesanosque*; 171, 23 *trucemque... insuauem*. For that reason one cannot raise any objections against *mansuetos ac mansues* (Castiglioni's conjecture, too, has two closely synonymous adjectives). More serious is Helm's argument that one would expect the reverse word-order *mansues ac mansuetos* as in 4, 9 (81, 19) *solus ac solitarius*; 4, 31 (99, 6) *unum et... unicum*; *Apol.* 7 (8, 22) *libero et liberali* – with the longer word following the shorter. These adjectives are not only synonymous but also derived from the same stem (Augello 1977, 173 f.). It is questionable whether a reverse order should be excluded on the ground of these examples. Lindholm 1931, 83 shows that in Plautus the longer synonym comes second much more often with adjectives than with nouns, but there are exceptions – and even more in Terence; e.g. Pl. *Men.* 1004 *indignum et malum*; Ter. *Ph.* 94 *miserum et graue*, 1008 *miserandum et malum*. There are also examples where the longer of two cognate words comes second: e.g. the usual order is *pudor... pudicitia*; but on the other hand Pl. *Am.* 840 *per pudicitiam et pudorem et sedatum cupidinem*; Ter. *An.* 326 *per amicitiam et per amorem obsecro*. Especially when the fine distinction between the various meanings has faded, there are many examples of combinations that have the shorter word at the end, e.g. Pl. *Mil.* 837 *bono supromo et promo*; Ter. *Hau.* 297 *sordidatam et sordidam*. On these grounds Lindholm 86 n. 1 defends *mansuetos ac mansues* in our passage. In short: the reading in F is not impossible and can therefore be retained.

exinde: as in 147, 23 (see our comm. *ad loc.*), the temporal meaning preponderates although there is a slight admixture of its causal connotation ("for that reason"). *Exinde* is added somewhat pleonastically to the preceding absolute ablative *adhibita... detestatione*.

oneri: *honeri* in F has been emended in φ as in 168, 4 above. Because in the other five instances 1, 9 (9, 9); 4, 21 (91, 6); 165, 10; 168, 7; 169, 3 – all the mss.

have the unaspirated reading, it seems right to be consistent. Gel. 2, 3, 1 says that *ueteres nostri* said *honera* and *honustum*; 2, 3, 4 he remarks: *in his... uerbis omnibus litterae seu spiritus istius nulla ratio uisa est, nisi ut firmitas et uigor uocis quasi quibusdam neruis additis intenderetur.*

ferundo: traces of the gerundive in *-undus* are still apparent in Cicero, e.g. *Agr.* 2, 93 *ferundum* and *Ver.* 5, 25 *gerunda*. Even during the Empire this form is found – beside that in *-endus* – both in inscriptions and literature. Sommer 1914, 617 observes that *-undus* is frequent in words with a radical syllable containing an *e*, like *ferundo* in this passage and *deuehundo* 167, 6 above. Since the mss. unanimously offer the form in *-undus*, there seems to be no reason to deviate from that reading.

oneri ferundo: most probably the ass would not have found consolation in the words of Sen. *Ep.* 71, 26 *uires suas nouit* (sc. *homo sapiens*): *scit se esse oneri ferendo.*

non inhabiles: a litotes, quite frequent from Col. onward: e.g. 6, 1, 1 *boues... laboris... et culturae patrii soli non inhabiles* (*labori* γ). It is not mentioned by Koziol 1872 and Strilciw 1925.

cetero ministerio patientes: this is the reading in F, which is retained against the reading *ceteri ministerii* in ς. The dative with *patientes* (in the sense "capable of enduring") is unusual; no other example of this usage can be found. LHSz 2, 88 does mention a dative with *pati*, but there the verb is equivalent to *concedere*, e.g. Vitr. 2, 1, 9 *neque aliter natura rerum praeceptis physicorum ueras patitur habere explicationes*. The dative in our passage may be explained as expressing purpose; its use is supported by the parallelism with *oneri ferundo*.

Denique nisi uobis suadeo nolentibus, possum spatio modico interiecto, quo mercatum proxumum obire statui, petitis e domo ferramentis huic curae praeparatis ad uos actutum redire trucemque amatorem istum atque insuauem dissitis femoribus emasculare et quouis ueruece mitiorem efficere': "In short – unless you do not want to take my advice – I can, after a short time in which I intend to go to the near-by market, go home and get my instruments that are ready for use in this treatment; then return to you immediately; and after spreading the thighs of this rough and savage lover, emasculate him and make him gentler than any wether'". 171, 20-172, 2

nolentibus: in the sense of *inuitus* it is found from Celsus onward; see LHSz 2, 386.

possum: Bernhard 1927, 14 points out that, in a main clause directly following a dependent clause, the verb frequently comes first.

mercatum: *ThLL* s.v. 790, 45 f. gives the following definition: "commercium hominum statis temporibus habitum", i.e. a market held on a restricted and fixed number of days, often in connection with *ludi*, as in Pl. *Men.* 27 and Liv. 33, 32, 2 *concilium Asiae Graeciaeque is mercatus erat* (sc. *ludi Isthmii*). It is important for the castrator not to miss this market, as the emphatic *statui* indicates.

obire: "to go to". Cf. for this neutral meaning Cic. *Fam.* 7, 1, 5 *facis ut nostras uillas obire... possis*; *Fin.* 5, 29, 87 *cur tantas regiones barbarorum pedibus obiit, tot maria transmisit? Met.* 8, 29 (200, 15) *balneas obeunt.*

ferramentum: *ThLL* s.v. 570, 74 mentions numerous examples of *ferramentum* as a medical instrument, e.g. Cels. 3, 21, 10 *ferramentisque candentibus . . . uenter exulcerandus*.

curae: *cura*, too, is widely used as a medical term in the meaning "treatment", "medical care" (*ThLL* s.v. 1465, 11 f. *de curatione aegroti*); e.g. Plin. *Nat*. 7, 58 *si quando medicina et cura uicere*; Dict. 2, 10 *adhibentes curam uulneri*; Ser. Samm. 807-8 *tam multae innumeri species mihi uulneris adsint, / ut nequeam proprias cunctis adscribere curas*. The connotation of *cura* "worry" seems ironical here – not to the shepherds but to the reader.

actutum: Callebat 1968, 521 points out that the word is frequent in Plautus but then becomes isolated and occurs in contexts whose language does not especially belong to the *sermo cotidianus*; it is rather archaizing. The word occurs five times in Apul.

trucem . . . insuauem: the latter adjective expresses in a negative way what is expressed positively by the former adjective; see Bernhard 1927, 167. It is the fourth example in this chapter of the use of two adjectives with synonymous or near-synonymous meanings.

amatorem: *ThLL* s.v. 1828, 49 f. mentions only three other passages where this word is used of animals: Gel. 6, 8 *tit. amatore delphino et puero amato*; Apul. *Met*. 3, 23 (69, 14) *quam pulchro . . . matronae perfruentur amatore bubone*; Vulg. *Ier*. 5, 8 *equi amatores et emissarii facti sunt* (ἵπποι θηλυμανεῖς). These passages are slightly different from ours because they have *amator* as a qualifier of the animal in question. Cf. 170, 22 *maritum* qualifying the ass.

insuauem: occurs also 5, 28 (125, 20) *insuaue fastidium*; 9, 16 (214, 24) *insuauis et odiosi mariti*; and 9, 32 (227, 16) *lactucae . . . insuaues*. The only other passages mentioned by *ThLL* are Hor. *S*. 1, 3, 85 *nisi concedas, habeare insuauis* and V.L. *Sap*. 2, 12.

dissitis: *ThLL* s.v. 1458 f. lists our passage under the meaning *"discernere, seiugare"* (with *Met*. 6, 10: 136, 3 *separatimque distributis dissitisque generibus* and Aus. *Epit. Mer*. 35, 1) and remarks that others derive it from 'dis-situs i.q. situ disiunctus' 1493, 18 f., where it quotes *Met*. 9, 15 (214, 19); 10, 4 (239, 15); *Fl*. 2, 7; Arn. 1, 55, and a few later occurrences. Bernhard 1927, 139 calls *dissitus* an Apuleian neologism and quotes, besides this passage, *Met*. 9, 15; 10, 4; and *Fl*. 2, 7; he does not distinguish them as *ThLL* does. Médan 1925, 183 classifies our passage under 'langue archaïque' because it is already found in Lucr. 3, 143 *cetera pars animae per totum dissita corpus*. Although opinions vary, we may point out that our passage demands a transitive meaning of the verb – *dissitus*, therefore, must be the past participle of *disserere*.

emasculare: attested for the first time in Apuleius; *ThLL* mentions in addition Serv. *A*. 6, 661 and Pall. *Hist. Mon*. 1, 17. These passages refer to human beings. The usual term is *castrare*, which is often used of people, but it is the regular technical term in the case of animals: Col.; Varro; Plin. *Nat*.; Veg. *Mul*. (see *ThLL* s.v. 546, 81 f.). It cannot be accidental that the narrator uses here the less common, 'human' term in the case of a metamorphosed ass; cf. the use of *amator* in the previous line.

ueruece: the sheep or wether as a symbol of gentleness is already found in Ter. *Ad*. 534 *tam placidum quasi ouem reddo*; the expression has become proverbial, see Otto 1890, 261; Bernhard 1927, 219. Cf. *Met.* 8, 25 (196, 16), where someone who wants to sell the ass recommends his merchandise with the words: *ueruecem, ... non asinum uides.*

CHAPTER XXIV

Before the castration is put into effect, a she-bear appears. Panic-stricken, Lucius manages to escape both the bear and the *puer*.

172, 3-5 Tali sententia mediis Orci manibus extractus, set extremae poenae reseruatus maerebam et in nouissima parte corporis totum me periturum deflebam: "By this proposal I was snatched from the very clutches of Orcus but, because I was reserved for the severest punishment, I grieved, and I wept bitterly at the thought that in the hindermost part of my body the whole of me would perish".

Tali: see 170, 19 with our comm.

mediis Orci manibus: see Callebat 1968, 405 f.; vdPaardt 1971, 80 f. with comm. on 151, 19 for the occurrences of *Orcus* in the *Met.* – 6, 8 (134, 7) has *Orci cancros* in which Psyche finds herself. A better comparison with this passage is 159, 25 *Orci fauces*, which the ass has escaped as he has escaped the *manus Orci* here. No parallels can be found for the combination of *manus* and Orcus; comparable to some degree is Ov. *Am.* 2, 6, 39 *optima prima fere manibus rapiuntur auaris* (sc. *mortis*). Cf. also Liv. 9, 6, 3 *uelut ab inferis extracti* and see Otto 1890, 258. The possibility of a pun on *Manes* should not be excluded: the ass has already escaped from an ordeal described at 156, 20 *manibus uirginis decretam me uictimam*.

mediis: the addition of *mediis* increases the drama of the situation; cf. 159, 25 *mediis Orci faucibus euasi*; 170, 15 *de mediis ungulis . . . erepta*; 9, 1 (203, 10) *mediis lanii manibus ereptus*.

extractus: this is the reading in ς, with *retractus* added by another hand in a lacuna; F has *extracto*, apparently changed from *extractus* by a second hand. Leky 1908, 35 defends *extracto* as an example of careless use of the ablative absolute which is found a few times in Apul., e.g. 3, 12 (61, 8) with the note of vdPaardt 1971, 97. The editors, however, generally print *extractus*: the first hand in F is hardly legible in this passage so that the evidence of the second hand in F is not conclusive.

extremae poenae: refers to capital punishment in 10, 11 (245, 3) *desperatissimum istum latronum certum extremae poenae*. To Lucius the ass, however, the worst punishment is castration: his genital preoccupation is pointed out by vdPaardt 1971, 181. Cf. also Heine 1962, 212; Schlam in *AAGA* 1978, 100 f. If the world of this novel corresponds to the reality of the first two centuries A.D., Lucius' fear of castration as a theme is topical in view of more or less contemporary legislation: castration of people – including slaves – had been prohibited from Domitian on: Suet. *Dom.* 7, 1 *castrari mares uetuit*. Hadrian extended the law to forbid the castration even of consenting persons; see *Dig.* 48, 8, 4, 2 *nemo liberum seruumue, inuitum sinentemue, castrare debet neue quis se sponte castrandum praebere debet* (*RE s.v. castratio*). Consequently, if Lucius the ass were to be castrated, he would definitely have been expelled from the society he belonged to as Lucius the man. Cf. also *Onos* 33 ὡς ἀπολέσων αὐτίκα τὸν ἐν τῷ ὄνῳ ἄνδρα.

reseruatus: a recurrence of the notion that the ass has escaped death, only to be plunged even deeper into misery (cf. our comm. on 169, 9). His temporary salvation has been nothing but a trick of Fortuna – it only makes his castration possible.

in nouissima parte corporis: viz. the genitals. Usually an animal's *nouissima pars corporis* refers to the tail (*cauda*). *Cauda* can also be used of people, meaning *mentula*; cf. Hor. *S.* 1, 2, 45 *accidit ut cuidam testis caudamque salacem / demeterent ferro* (observe that this passage, too, refers to castration) and *S.* 2, 7, 49. *Pars* can be used in the same sense but always with a modifier, like *nouissima* in this passage: e.g. Ov. *Ars* 2, 584 *partibus obscenis opposuisse manus*; *Am.* 3, 7, 69 *pars pessima nostri*; Cels. 7, 18, 1 *ea quae in naturalibus partibus circa testiculos oriri solent*. The pun in our passage on the special meaning of *pars* and *cauda* (the latter used of people) makes it unnecessary to deviate from the unanimous reading in the mss. with conjectures like *nobilissima* (Barth, recommended by Oudendorp and Hildebrand) or the charming *nauissima* (Purser 1906, 47). For *nouissima* in its local or geographical sense, see Ov. *Tr.* 3, 13, 27 *dum me terratum pars paene nouissima, Pontus ... habet*.

deflebam: cf. 154, 3 *meum crastinum deflebam cadauer*, where the ass's reaction to his impending doom is the same.

periturum deflebam: has the same number of syllables as the preceding *reseruatus maerebam*.

Inedia denique continua uel praecipiti ruina memet ipse quaerebam   172, 5-8
extinguere moriturus quidem nihilo minus, sed moriturus integer: "So I wanted to destroy myself by a continuous fast or by throwing myself from a great height – I would die none the less, but at least I would die intact".

inedia ... continua uel praecipiti ruina: a chiasmus in which the two adjectives *continua* and *praecipiti* are antonyms; cf. Bernhard 1927, 32. The robbers (153, 26 see comm. *ad loc.*) decide to put Charite in the belly of the butchered ass and let her die of *inedia* (see our comm. *ad loc.*), against Charite's will, naturally. In the next book Charite would willingly kill herself by *inedia* 8, 7 (181, 28) from grief over Tlepolemus' death. In fiction, death by fasting is not uncommon in comparable circumstances, cf. the widow of Ephesus in Petr. 111, 3 (*mortem inedia persequentem*). The blind Thrasyllus, in his turn, will decide to seek death in the same way 8, 14 (188, 6).

denique: in the sense of *ergo, igitur*; cf. vdPaardt 1971, 43.

ruina: the initiative presumably comes from the ass; cf. *Onos* 33 ῥῖψαι ἑαυτόν. At 148, 13 he fears that the robbers will throw him down a precipice (148, 2 one of them says: *eum ... praecipitabo*) – naturally against his will (like Charite). Now, however, the ass is prepared to throw himself down a precipice willingly; obviously he fears castration more than anything. Thus it appears from the context that *ruina* denotes here a "deliberate fall".

There is a similar, equally pathetic, reflection by Charite on alternative methods of suicide at 4, 25 (94, 7): *Laqueus aut gladius aut certe praecipitium procul dubiis capessendum est* (see *GCA* 1977, 187 f.); note that there *praecipitium* has an 'active' meaning, like *ruina* in our passage. (For certain similarities in Charite's and the ass's fate, see Merkelbach 1962, 2 f. and Schlam 1968, 40 f.) A supporting argument for the 'active' meaning of *praecipiti ruina* may be found in Luc. 8, 654 (where the noble Cornelia ponders on different ways to take her life after the murder of Pompey) *Aut mihi praecipitem, nautae, permittite saltum, / aut laqueum collo tortosque aptare rudentes: / aut aliquis Magno dignus comes exigat ensem.*

Actually, the ass has no choice – the speedy return of the castrator (*spatio modico interiecto* 171, 20) leaves no time for a hunger-strike. This adds a touch of irony to his pathetic reflection on methods of suicide: the narrator ridicules his former self.

quaerebam: for *quaerere* in the sense of *uelle*, see vdPaardt 1971, 166 and the bibliography given there.

memet ... extinguere: cf. 6, 17 (141, 12), where Psyche says to herself *quid te ... praecipitio, misella, quaeris extinguere?* Observe that *praecipitio* is (again) synonymous with *ruina* in our passage.

moriturus ... moriturus: the rhetorical repetition of the same word emphasizes the pathos of this passage; a modifier is added to the second participle. See Bernhard 1927, 234.

integer: this word is found seven times in the *Met.*, always in its original meaning "whole", "intact"; e.g. 2, 22 (43, 24) *integrum corpus*; 2, 24 (44, 20) *nasus integer*. Once before (3, 9: 58, 13 at the impending rack) Lucius the man expressed his fear of dying mutilated; see vdPaardt 1971, 77 who points out that people in antiquity wished to be buried with their body intact. The panic-stricken ass forgets that jumping into a ravine will not be conducive to preserving the *integritas* of his body!

172. 8-10 Dumque in ista necis meae decunctor electione, matutino me rursum puer ille peremptor meus contra montis suetum ducit uestigium: "And while I was still in doubt as to the choice of my death that boy, my executioner, led me again early in the morning to the usual mountain-path".

decunctor: the verb is surrounded by a noun (*electione*) and a qualifying pronoun (*meae*), as is *ducit* by a noun (*uestigium*) and a qualifying adjective (*suetum*). The compound *decunctari* is used by Apul. also 10, 3 (238, 14); since the word does not occur anywhere else, it is possible that Apul. coined the word; cf. Bernhard 1927, 120.

matutino ... peremptor: a complete hexameter; cf. Médan 1925, 267 and our comm. on 156, 11-15.

peremptor: nouns in *-tor* occur frequently in Apuleius; see Bernhard 1927, 105. It is found also 3, 9 (58, 16) (see vdPaardt 1971, 78) and 8, 13 (187, 16). The word occurs first Sen. *Oed.* 221 *et quis peremptor incluti regis fuit?*; then in Apuleius; next Hil. *Myst.* 9, 4 *uulnus non ad peremptum, sed ad peremptorem refertur*; then Amm., Prud., Aug., and others. Médan's remark (1925, 188) that the noun belongs to the 'mots poétiques rares' seems therefore incorrect. The feminine *peremptrix* is found from Tertullian onward.

contra: the only other occurrence of *contra* after a verb of moving, indicating the direction, is 174, 1. LHSz 2, 228 calls this usage 'später und selten'; cf. Vitr. 2 *praef.* 1 *Incessit contra tribunal regis*; *Pass. Eust.* p. 470. Callebat 1968, 218 supposes that this usage is derived from the 'langue familière'.

montis uestigium: Oudendorp and Hildebrand explain this expression as 'uia in qua inerant uestigia asini, quamque assidue consueuerat ire'; but the text explicitly says *montis uestigium*. Hildebrand offers as a comparison Lucr. 1, 406 (*canes ut... naribus inueniunt intectas fronde quietes*) *cum semel institerunt uestigia certa uiai* but that does not have the required image, either: that the hounds smell the 'certain track of the road' (i.e. the path) may indeed be due to the fact that they smell the game that has gone over that path – but the text does not say that explicitly. It seems better to start from Sen. *Oed.* 768 *Redit memoria tenue per uestigium, / cecidisse nostri stipitis pulsu obuium* and Man. 1, 676 *recta... deuexo fallit uestigia cliuo* (sc. *zodiacus*) ("conceals by its downward slope the straightness of its path", transl. Goold 1977). These two examples show the possibility of *uestigium* meaning "road", "path"; the combination *uestigium montis* is possible on the analogy of e.g. Caes. *Civ.* 1, 4, 5 *ab itinere Asiae Syriaeque* and Curt. 3, 7, 6 *iter saltus*. Wasse's proposal *uestigium montis = pes montis* is rejected by Hildebrand, though it is supported by Avien. *Orb. Terr.* 480 *indeque Cemsi / gens agit, in rupis uestigia Pyrenaeae / protendens populos* with the Greek parallel in Dionys. *Periheg.* 338 ὑπαὶ πόδα: Wasse's proposal is possible even if the material from the ThLL Institute offers no other parallels for *uestigium montis* "foot of the mountain". We prefer the meaning "mountain-path" because "foot of the mountain" suggests a setting in the plain, whereas the previous descriptions of the scenery – albeit vague – suggest mountains (e.g. 167, 6 and 8 and the possibility of throwing the ass down a precipice). Brandt's conjecture *fastigium* – against the unanimous evidence of the mss. – is therefore unnecessary (even though in Apul. *Pl.* 1, 7 the reading *uestigiis* was emended into *fastigiis* by Goldbacher, followed by Thomas and Beaujeu).

Iamque me de cuiusdam uastissimae ilicis ramo pendulo destinato paululum uiam supergressus ipse securi lignum, quod deueheret, recidebat: "And now, having tied me to a hanging branch of a giant oak, he had gone a little way off the road and was cutting wood with his axe to carry down the mountain". 172, 10-12

Iamque: see our comm. on *ecce* 172, 13 below.

cuiusdam: has the meaning of an indefinite article. See e.g. *GCA* 1977, 38 and our comm. on 172, 22 below.

ilicis: another instance of an Apuleian specification. True, this part of the story is absent in the *Onos*, but Junghanns 1930, 16 n. 15 points out that at 8, 30 (201, 11) the ass is tied to an oak where *Onos* 38, 7 merely mentions a δένδρον μέγα. In other passages, too, Apul. always specifies trees: cypresses (cf. 152, 13 with our comm. *ad loc*), fig trees, etc. Cf. also 167, 12 *coxae... dexterae* with our comm. *ad loc*.

pendulo: this word is often found in Augustan poetry, e.g. *Culex* 52 *pendula proiectis carpuntur et arbuta ramis*; Ov. *Met.* 7, 117 *pendula... palearia*. Only from Columella onward is it found in prose; cf. Médan 1925, 191.

destinato de: cf. 8, 30 (201, 11) *de quadam quercu destinatum*.

supergressus: the boy crosses the road and goes a little way off the road to do his work. *Supergredi* is attested from Columella (7, 9, 13) and Seneca onward.

securi: 8, 30 (201, 14) has the ablative *secure*; cf. Callebat 1968, 123. Neue-Wagener 1, 334 offer more material: *securi* is the most frequent form by far, beginning with Pl. *Ps.* 158, Cic. *Ver.* 1, 3, 7, etc. The only other occurrence of *secure* is Tert. *Pud.* 16, 12. See also LHSz 1, 439.

deueheret: vdVliet wants to read *deueherem*, basing his conjecture on 167, 6 *delegor... ligno monte deuehendo*. This is unnecessary: it is perfectly normal to say that a man is taking a load somewhere, even if a beast of burden is actually carrying the load; see 174, 2 *nemora unde lignum puer solebat gerere*.

172, 13-14 Et ecce de proximo specu uastum attollens caput funesta proserpit ursa: "But lo and behold, out of a nearby cave there crept, raising her huge head, a deadly she-bear".

Et ecce: introduces the sudden reversal of the situation. See e.g. Heine 1962, 174; vdPaardt 1971, 87; *GCA* 1977, 157 and 170. Chausserie Laprée 1969, 546 points out that this function of *ecce* (interrupting one scene to introduce another) increases in later Latin, particularly in Apuleius. The sudden reversal has already been prepared for by *iamque* 172, 10 above (so-called 'iam de préparation', Chausserie Laprée 1969, 497 f.), which in combination with an imperfect (*recidebat*) almost always results in *cum inversum*. The function of *cum* is performed here by *ecce*.

uastum attollens caput: this combination is reminiscent of epic poetry: Ov. *Hal.* 70 *uictor* (sc. *equus*)... *altum attollat caput*; Stat. *Theb.* 9, 414 *surgit/spumosum attollens apicem*; Sil. 2, 157 *leonis/terribilem attollunt... rictum*; 6, 225 *immensum attollit corpus* (sc. *draco*). Apul. borrows the sequence adjective-verb-noun here and in the following *funesta proserpit ursa*; cf. Bernhard 1927, 25.

proserpit: F has *sēpit* with r written over the *e* by the same hand. The first occurrence of the verb is Pl. *As.* 695 *bestia* (referring to a snake as in *Poen.* 1034 and *St.* 724); then Var. *L.* 5, 68 (also of a snake); not again until Apuleius: at 6, 14 (139, 1) it refers to *dracones* (*Apol.* 85: 94, 10 *uipera*); at 4, 19 (89, 1) it refers to a *seruulus* sneaking closer. The use of *proserpere* suggests the stealthy approach of a snake (observe the many *s*-sounds in the last part of the sentence), which during the day has taken refuge in a cave, cf. Aug. *Gen. litt.* 3, 9, 13 *dracones in speluncis requiescere perhibentur*. Our author has used numerous means to increase the suspense: the 'peripetic' *ecce*; the emphasis on the huge (*uastum*) head even before we know what kind of monster this will turn out to be; the suggestion (by the epic tone and the use of *proserpere*) that it is a *draco* – with the sudden disclosure in the last word of the sentence (after *funesta*) that it is an *ursa*. The conjecture *prorepit* (Blümner 1894, 308) is not necessary, even though *prorepere* is used 4, 18 (88, 8) of a disguised bear (Thrasyleon). But there the reader knows the situation; here *proserpere* is used to enhance the ἀπροσδόκητον.

ursa: curiously enough all non-Italian translators render this word "bear"; Carlesi, Augello, and Scazzoso are the only ones who rightly translate "orsa". GCA 1977, 109 points out that the bear's gender is, indeed, important: the *ursa* is larger, and therefore more dangerous (*funesta*) and frightening (*uastum attollens caput*) than the male.

Quam simul conspexi, pauidus et repentina facie conterritus totum corporis pondus in postremos poplites recello arduaque ceruice sublimiter eleuata lorum, quo tenebar, rumpo: "As soon as I saw her, frightened and terrified by the sudden sight I put the weight of my whole body on the knee-joints of my hindlegs and by raising my head high I broke the thong with which I was tied".

For the colometry of this sentence, see Hijmans, *AAGA* 1978, 208 n. 21.

Quam: Bernhard 1927, 54 calls this a case of 'Verschränkung der Relativsätze'; modern editors, however, place before *quam* a period, not a comma. LHSz 2, 569 note that the choice between 'relative Verschränkung' and 'relativischer Anschluss' is often a question only of punctuation. See our comm. on 154, 2 above.

facie: this noun is found combined with *repentinus* also in Sen. *Nat.* 1, 6, 4 *repentina eius* (sc. *arcus*) *facies et repentinus interitus*.

pauidus ... conterritus: another two-word combination where the first, more general word is specified by the second; see Bernhard 1927, 166.

poplites: not merely "knees", but more specifically "knee-joints".

recello: for the meaning of this rare verb see Paul. Fest. 343 L *recellere reclinare*. The verb is found Lucr. 6, 573 *inclinatur enim retroque recellit* (sc. *terra*); Liv. 24, 34, 10 *cum ... ferrea manus ... recelleret ad solum* (apparently intransitive in these two passages); Prud. *Cath.* 9, 74 *obice extrorsum reculso* (but there are variant readings). The only other occurrences are in Apuleius, here and 10, 22 (254, 5). According to Callebat 1968, 182 the construction with the accusative is on the analogy of verbs like *reclinere* (read: *-are*). See also Médan 1925, 9.

sublimiter eleuata: Callebat 1968, 544 regards this combination as a case of 'renforcement pléonastique d'une forme verbale par un adverbe', so common in our author; for a similar situation cf. 4, 3 (76, 11) *lumbis eleuatis in altum*. The notion 'high' is also expressed by *ardua* (see Bernhard 1927, 179); observe how the same notion is expressed by different parts of speech: adjective, adverb, participle.

meque protinus pernici fugae committo perque prona non tantum pedibus, uerum etiam toto proiecto corpore propere deuolutus immitto me campis subpatentibus, ex summo studio fugiens immanem ursam ursaque peiorem illum puerum: "at once I took to headlong flight and let myself quickly roll down, not only with my feet but with my whole body stretched forward, and dashed down to the fields below, fleeing for all I was worth from the frightful bear and the boy that was even worse than she".

The whole sentence shows strong alliteration, especially of *p: protinus pernici; perque prona ... pedibus; proiecto corpore propere;* 15 above *corporis pondus in postremos poplites.*

committo is the reading in φ and a*; F has *cōcitato* (*citato* seems to have developed from *mitto*). *Concitato* can only be regarded as an absolute ablative: *meque protinus pernici fugae concitato* "and after I had incited myself to a speedy flight". However, the shift from ablative absolute to attributive participle (*deuolutus*) would be most unusual if not impossible. Moreover, *se concitare* is generally constructed with *in* – only once with *ad* (*Met.* 4, 18: 88, 24); see *ThLL s.v.* 64, 78 f. For these reasons we prefer the reading *committo*. This is one of the places where φ, rather than F, has retained the correct reading; see Helm, *Praef. Flor.* XXXI.

me fugae committo: this combination occurs also Vell. 2, 72, 3 *fugae fortunaeque se commisit.* Cf. *Met.* 2, 18 (40, 11) *cenae me committo.*

prona: for the nominal use of *pronus*, cf. 4, 6 (79, 1) *perque prona delapsus* and *GCA* 1977, 59 *ad loc.*

deuolutus: usually an ass will let himself roll down sideways; that he now does so with his whole body stretched forward is another indication of his terror. The description given here (hard though it is to visualise the movement) is actually that of the *ruina* considered earlier (172, 6); but whereas it was then intended to be a method of suicide, it is now a life-saving device. Added to the ass's fear of castration there is now an imminent danger (the bear) which leads him to undertake an actual *ruina*.

immitto me campis: the usual construction is *se immittere in*, but cf. 2, 29 (48, 24) *Immitto me turbae* and deJonge *ad loc.* Bernhard 1927, 181 discusses the phenomenon that, when the sentence falls apart into two coordinate halves, the object (here *me*) is repeated in the second part: he ascribes this to the author's wish to be as precise as possible. Our passage differs from the others mentioned by Bernhard in that the same personal pronoun is used twice; in the other passages the first object is a noun, which is repeated in the second half by a personal pronoun (cf. 3, 17: 64, 24 and vdPaardt 1971, 130 *ad loc.*). This leads us to think that the construction in our passage was chosen because of chiasmus and paronomasia (*me ... committo ... immitto ... me*).

subpatentibus: this compound may have been coined by Apul. (cf. Bernhard 1927, 120); it also occurs 8, 20 (192, 19) *quae* (sc. *fouea*) *fruticibus imis subpatet.* The material from the ThLL Institute mentions no other occurrences of this verb.

ex summo studio: φ has *et summo*; F has a small lacuna before *summo*. Colvius' emendation *ex* is adopted by all editors except vdVliet. Cf. 8, 5 (179, 25) and 9, 15 (214, 7) *ex summo studio* but 6, 10 (136, 2) *summo studio*; Apul. apparently varies, but since *et* is impossible and F shows a lacuna before *summo*, Colvius' proposal seems right. Callebat 1968, 207 speaks of '*ex* instrumental'.

fugiens: the main verb is followed by a participle, as often in Apul.; see Bernhard 1927, 44.

immanem: Heine 1962, 149 points out that the animals in the *Met.* are often of exaggerated fierceness. The stallions (166, 12) are *terribiles* and *furentes* (166, 15), the bear is *funesta* and *immanis*, etc. This is true, but the bear is also in a literal sense *funesta* and therefore *immanis*: she will in fact kill the boy.

illum: the demonstrative is clearly used both to 'emphasize and to call attention to the most important person in an episode'; thus Callebat 1968, 278.

ursaque peiorem illum puerum: these words are another proof of the ass's fear of castration: the worst the *ursa* can do is kill him, but a fate worse than death – castration – awaits him on account of the *puer*'s allegations (cf. 172, 3 *extremae poenae*). Yet these words reveal an absurdity: if the boy really is so much worse than the bear, why has the ass not broken away sooner? Now that the bear appears, he proves that he can.

The end of the sentence (*immanem* ... *puerum*) has been composed with care: *ursam ursaque* is called an example of *iteratio* by Strilciw 1925, 114; we prefer to regard it as a polyptoton (see for this figure of speech Bernhard 1927, 236 f. and vdPaardt 1971, 56 and further literature given there); further the use of the 'wachsende Glieder' procedure emphasizes the greater danger represented by the *puer*. These stylistic procedures enhance the conclusive effect of this sentence.

In Apul. the castration plan is thwarted by the sudden appearance of a bear, in the *Onos* by the arrival of a messenger announcing the death of the young couple, which causes the shepherds to flee. The passage in the *Met.* starting 172, 8 (in which the *puer* takes the ass to the mountains again to fetch wood) is not found in the *Onos*; Apul. has inserted an additional death here (at least if we assume that the Vorlage, too, lacked an episode of this kind) at a pause in the narrative. vThiel 1971, I 118 f. maintains that this addition is due to Apuleius' 'moralische Betrachtungsweise': the *puer* has to be punished for his slander. We cannot disprove this thesis; at any rate, the addition gives Apul. the opportunity for a theatrical story – moreover, this passage is the first in a series of violent deaths which extend far into Book 8: Tlepolemus, Charite, Thrasyllus, shepherd (see vThiel 1971, I 154).

CHAPTER XXV

The ass has escaped both the bear and his tormentor, but alas! he is caught by a passer-by and together they run into the sinister shepherds again.

172, 22-24 Tunc quidam uiator solitarium uagumque me respiciens inuadit et properiter inscensum baculo, quod gerebat, obuerberans per obliquam ignaramque me ducebat uiam: "Then some passer-by spotted me, wandering about by myself; he got hold of me, climbed quickly on my back and, thrashing me with the stick he carried, led me along a secondary road I was unfamiliar with".

quidam: the use of this pronoun in this passage fits exactly the definition in LHSz 2, 196: 'ein gewisser, den man nicht näher bestimmen kann oder will'. Graur 1969, 378 f. argues that *quidam* in Apul. often is used as an indefinite article; see *GCA* 1977, 38 and 166; our comm. on 172, 10.

solitarium: Apuleius uses this adjective quite often (seven times in the *Met.*), sometimes with a clearly stylistic purpose, e.g. 4, 9 (81, 19) *solus ac solitarius* (see *GCA* 1977, 78 f.) and 173, 17 *solutum et solitarium* with sound-effect and variation of syllables (cf. 171, 18 *mansuetos ac mansues*). Elsewhere rhythmical reasons may account for Apul.'s choice of *solitarius* rather than *solus*. For the suffix *-arius*, see LHSz 1, 299.

uagumque: Vallette 27 n. 1 suggests that this adjective means more than just "wandering about": it implies that what wanders is no one's property. He quotes [Quint.] *Decl.* 13, 7 p. 253 Lehnert, where a rich man poisons a poor man's bees and defends himself by saying that the bee is an *animal liberum et uolucre et uagum et extra imperia positum*, i.e. no one's property by nature; our ass is no one's property by accident. This interpretation seems attractive but is somewhat dubious: in legal sources (e.g. *codices Theod.* and *Justin.*) *uagus* only means "wandering" and is used especially of runaway slaves and tax-evaders; in the *Institutiones* of Gaius and Justinian the word does not occur at all; whether it does in the *Digest* is hard to ascertain.[1] Vallette too easily assumes (presumably on the basis of the passage in ps.-Quint. quoted above) that *uagum* and *extra imperia positum* are synonyms; but they are not. We therefore prefer to keep the usual translation "wandering" without special connotations. Still, the fact remains that the *uiator*'s greed is aroused by the straying ass; that he is interested only in the finder's reward (173, 17) seems dubious.

respiciens: as to its meaning, Non. 711, 31 L rightly remarks: *prospicere et respicere distant, ut aduorsum uidere prospicere recte dicatur; respicere quasi retro aspicere*. Apul. generally uses the compound in the same way, but here the prefix is evidently weakened: the verb means no more than "to see", "to spot".

---

[1] We owe this information to Prof. H. J. Scheltema.

inuadit: usually this verb has a connotation of hostility and violence: cf. 159, 10 *inuadimus et diripimus omnia*; Cic. *S. Rosc.* 23 *in praedia huius inuadit*. See also Schmidt, 1979, 174. Callebat 1968, 427 remarks on the variation in tense *inuadit ... ducebat*: 'cet emploi ... relève d'abord et surtout du style narratif, où il constitue un élément artiste de variété et souvent également de pittoresque'. Bernhard 1927, 152 f. is of the same opinion and concludes: 'In den meisten der genannten Beispiele für den Gebrauch der variatio ist es unmöglich, irgend einen anderen Grund hiefür anzugeben, als eben des Autors Streben nach Mannigfaltigkeit'. We, however, think that the use of tenses is functional at least in our passage: 172, 23 *inuadit* shows sudden action; 172, 24 *ducebat*, 173, 1 *commodabam* and 173, 2 *commouebar* show a duration; 173, 5 *instruxit* indicates a sudden new whim of Fortune.

properiter: on the suffix in general, see *GCA* 1977, 66 *auditer*. *Properiter* is archaic and extremely rare; *OLD* quotes Pac. *Trag.* 332 and Acc. *Trag.* 629, and then nothing until Apuleius – this passage and 6, 26 (148, 5) – and Sept. *Poet.* 16. This Septimius Serenus was a contemporary of Apul.; see Schanz 3, 1905, 23 f., who appreciates the last-mentioned fragment *animula miserula properiter abiit* 'durch seine Zierlichkeit'. The adverb evidently suits the style of *nouelli poetae* like Septimius.

inscensum: F has restored the ending *sû* after an initial change; the passive participle is also found in ς; φ, on the other hand, has *inscendens*, in which the same hand wrote a *d* instead of an original *s*.

obuerberans: this verb is not found anywhere before Apul., who uses it only in its literal meaning: 9, 9 (209, 11) *Philebum ... pugnis obuerberant*; 9, 28 (224, 11) *ferula nates eius obuerberans*. After Apul. it remains rare: *ThLL s.v.* mentions only Ps.-Ambr. *Paenit.* 17, p. 990[c] and Iulian. *Aug. C. Iul. Op. Imperf.* 2, 1, where it has a figurative meaning: "be envious of", "insult".

abliquam ... uiam: *obliquus* often qualifies words meaning "road"; cf. Liv. 5, 16, 5 *obliquis tramitibus*; 41, 2, 1 *obliquis itineribus* with Weissenborn-Müller's note: "schräg laufenden, d.i. seitwärts, zur Seite". It often has the connotation "zig-zag", as in Sen. *Marc.* 18, 3 *obliqua fulmina*.

ignaram: here in the passive sense ("unknown", "unfamiliar") which is less common than the active sense, but is found in Latin of all periods; e.g. Sall. *Iug.* 18, 6 *ignara lingua*; 52, 4 *regio hostibus ignara*; Tac. *Ann.* 2, 13 *per occulta et uigilibus ignara* (cf. Furneaux *ad loc.*); Gel. 9, 12, 20 tells us *'Ignarus' aeque utroqueuersum dicitur, non tantum qui ignorat, sed et qui ignoratur*.

me dūcēbāt uĭãm: it seems to us that this sequence was preferred to *uĭãm mē dūcēbāt*, firstly because of euphonic reasons (three times *-am* in close proximity is not pleasant to the ear), and secondly because Apul. prefers the clausula of spondee + cretic to the heavier dispondaeus. See also Bernhard 1927, 250 f.

Nec inuitus ego cursui me commodabam relinquens atrocissimam uirilitatis lanienam: "Eagerly I lent myself to a gallop leaving behind an atrocious and bloody assault on my virility". 172, 24-173, 2

Nec inuitus: a quite common litotes which is functional here (see our translation); cf. 164, 4 and vdPaardt 1971, 49.

me commodabam: for the meaning "accommodate oneself to", "lend oneself to", cf. 3, 17 (65, 3) *his artibus suis commodatum* (= *aptum*). The metaphorical use with *se* as an object is not very common; cf. Sen. *Nat.* 6, 3, 4 (sc. *inquirendo causas*) ... *se non tantum commodet* (sc. *animus*), *sed impendat*; Quint. *Inst.* 2, 8, 4 *se commodaturum singulis*.

relinquens: in the sense "leave behind by removing oneself" this verb is quite common. Cf. 8, 15 (188, 19) *detestabilem illum exectorem uirilitatis meae relinquentem*; 9, 17 (215, 30) *Myrmecem ... relinquens uxori secutorem securam dirigit profectionem*; 10, 23 (254, 25) *sarcina praegnationis oneratam eam relinquebat*; Sil. 16, 502 *iamque hos, iamque illos populo mirante relinquit*.

atrocissimam: see our comm. on 170, 21.

lanienam: F has *laniẽ nã*. The ˜ over the *e* seems to have been added by a different hand; a second hand in φ has emended to the correct reading *lanienam*. For this word see *GCA* 1977, 183; it seems to be used in an abstract sense here as everywhere else in Apul., e.g. 2, 30 (50, 6) and 9, 1 (202, 24). It is understandable that this bloody vision has haunted the ass throughout the last episode. That the narrator uses the term *uirilitas* with regard to the ass (cf. 171, 13 *uenerem* and 172, 1 *emasculare*) is not surprising. In fact, Col. 6, 26, 3 uses it of animals, too.

173, 2-3 Ceterum plagis non magnopere commouebar quippe consuetus ex forma concidi fustibus: "For the rest I was not much bothered by the blows because I was used to being beaten up with clubs in the approved manner".

Ceterum: Helm 1957, 142 classifies it under the heading 'der einfach anreihende (*sc.* Gebrauch), durch den etwas Neues hinzugefügt wird: "im Übrigen".'

plagis non ... commouebar: the ass's feelings and reactions are mostly determined by the circumstances. Here he is not bothered by the blows, but elsewhere (e.g. ch. 28, when he is belaboured with the *pertica* and the burning *titio*) he finds them unbearable; at 4, 3 he believes he will die from the blows of a *grande baculum*.

quippe: it is found combined with a participle in poetry from Lucr. 3, 190 onward (according to LHSz 2, 385 perhaps under the influence of ἅτε), in prose from Sal. *Or. Phil.* 5 onward; later in Livy, Tacitus, etc.

ex forma: this seems to be a juridical idiom: in official language the expression means "in due legal form"; see e.g. *CIL* 3, 411, 14 *edite ex forma sententiam*; Fro. Aur. *Ep.* 5, 52 (81 vdH) *Petit nunc procurationem ex forma suo loco ac iusto tempore*; Gel. 13, 15, 1 *In edicto consulum ... scribitur ex uetere forma perpetua*: many other examples in *ThLL s.v.* 1080, 61 f. Apparently Apul. uses the term for humorous effect.

concīdi: a strong term, as appears from e.g. Cic. *Ver.* 1, 122 *solitus uirgis plebem Romanam concidere*; 3, 56 *cum pugnis et calcibus concisus esset, ... mille promisit* (compare the treatment administered to the *uiator* 173, 15); Juv. 3, 300 *pulsatus rogat et pugnis concisis adorat*. Cf. further 168, 10 where *cidit* may be a corrupted form of *concidit* (see our comm. *ad loc.*).

173, 4-6 Sed illa Fortuna meis casibus peruicax tam opportunum latibulum misera celeritate praeuersa nouas instruxit insidias: "But Lady Fortune, persistently intent on my misfortune, again with deplorable speed forestalled this timely means of escape and set a new trap".

Sed: see our comm. on 167, 4; 169, 8; etc. Apuleius' method of introducing a new débâcle is characteristic.

illa: almost "we know her by now": 'pour déterminer avec plus d'insistance un thème important' (Callebat 1968, 278).

meis casibus peruicax: we do not know whether *casibus* is a *dativus incommodi* or an ablative (as most lexica assume). Its meaning must be "persistently intent on". Tacitus constructs it with a genitive twice (*Ann.* 4, 53 *Agrippina peruicax irae* and *H.* 4, 5 *recti peruicax*); this innovation on his part can be explained on the analogy of *tenax*, which is found with the genitive from Verg. *A.* 4, 188 onward. See KSt 1, 451 and LHSz 2, 80. Apul. uses the adjective of Venus 5, 31 (128, 7) *animo peruicaci*; of the baker's wife 9, 14 (213, 17); of Thrasyllus 8, 7 (182, 1) *instantia peruicaci*; of the ass himself 9, 2 (204, 13) *peruicaci rabie possessus*.

Etymologically the word consists of *per*, the root of *uincere*, (see Ernout and Walde-Hofmann *s.v.*), and the suffix *-ac-*. The suffix indicates a passionate inclination towards something (usually objectionable): *edax, bibax, fallax, rapax*, etc.; see LHSz 1, 376. Apul. uses adjectives of this type quite often, e.g. *capax* 2, 5 (29, 13); 10, 3 (238, 27); 11, 11 (275, 1); *Pl.* 1, 5 (87, 5). He usually constructs *tenax* with a genitive: *Pl.* 2, 8 (111, 2) *tenax iusti*. See vGeisau 1916, 246 (who does not mention our passage).

latibulum: the usual meaning in classical authors is "hiding-place"; Apul., too, has it in this sense, e.g. 8, 29 (200, 29) *praedam absconditam latibulis aedium rati*; cf. 8, 6 (180, 18). He is, however, the first to use it in a figurative sense ("a means of concealment") in this passage; 5, 19 (118, 6) *omissis tectae machinae latibulis* ("sans ... recourir aux engins camouflés", Vallette); and *Apol. 1* (1, 20) *quaerere occepit ex diffidentia latibulum aliquod temeritati*. *ThLL s.v.* 1005, 14 f. gives further examples of the abstract use in later Latin. Classical authors use *latebrae* for the abstract meaning; see Callebat 1968, 169.

Another example of this shift in meaning – from concrete to abstract – is *laniena* (173, 2); elsewhere it means "butcher shop"; here it is used in the sense of "carnage", "bloody assault"; see *GCA* 1977, 183 f.

misera celeritate: vdVliet objects to the reading *misera* of the principal mss.; he proposes *mira* (see 3, 2: 53, 16 *mira celeritate*; vdPaardt 1971, 35), referring to a similar corruption in 2, 6 (29, 24), where Wower is right in changing *miseris* to *miris*. Robertson supports this idea; Helm, on the other hand, prefers to retain *misera*, convinced by Armini 1928, 308, who interprets *misera* as "miserabilis", "flebilis", "fatalis" and refers to 5, 12 (113, 1) *festinantes impia celeritate nauigabant* and 9, 20 (218, 2) *misera trepidatione*. This seems correct: Lucius the narrator is distressed at the new ordeals awaiting Lucius the ass – the adjective *misera* is quite appropriate.

praeuersa: in the sense "prevent", "anticipate", both the active is found (e.g. 5, 13: 114, 6 *praeuertit statim lumen nascentis diei*) and the deponent (as in our passage). See also our comm. on 169, 8.

instruxit insidias: the usual expression is *struere insidias*. However, Catul. 21, 7

249

also has the compound: *insidias mihi instruentem / tangam te*, which leads Kroll to conclude that this must be an archaism.

173, 6-9 Pastores enim mei perditam sibi requirentes uacculam uariasque regiones peragrantes occurrunt nobis fortuito statimque me cognitum capistro prehensum attrahere gestiunt: "For my shepherds, who were ranging the area in all directions in their search for a lost heifer, happened to run into us; they recognized me at once, took me by my halter and tried to pull me along with them".

perditam: on its meaning "perdre", "égarer" (as in 9, 41: 235, 3), see Callebat, *AAGA* 1978, 172.

sibi: it is hard to decide whether this is *datiuus auctoris* with *perditam*, or *datiuus commodi* with *requirentes*. The author probably chose its position in order to combine both meanings.

uariasque regiones: this accounts for their presence on this secondary road.

capistro: in its usual meaning "halter" it also occurs 151, 14; 168, 6; 9, 4 (205, 14); 10, 21 (253, 6). According to the lexica its derivation is not quite certain, although an etymological connection with *capere* seems obvious (thus LHSz 1, 313).

gestiunt: the historical present, on a level with *occurrunt*, again indicates action; the imperfect *testabatur* below indicates duration. See our comm. on 172, 23.

173, 9-11 Sed audacia ualida resistens ille fidem hominum deumque testabatur: 'Quid me raptatis uiolenter? Quid inuaditis?': "But the other resisted bravely and vigorously and called upon gods and men: 'Why are you pulling at me in this violent way? Why are you attacking me?'"

audacia ualida: observe the striking sound effect.

resistens: this is the reading in F; *st* is the result of a corrected *d*; for the sake of clarity the same hand rewrote *resistens* in the margin.

Quid me raptatis: the frequentative is somewhat poetic and usually means "seize and carry off", "snatch", etc. Cf. Pl. *Aul.* 632 *quid me raptas*? Perhaps this parallel was vdVliet's reason for punctuating as follows: *Quid me raptatis? Violenter quid inuaditis?* But the position of the adverb is less pleasing; moreover, it interrupts the symmetry of *Quid... Quid*.

inuaditis: see our comm. on 172, 23 above.

173, 12-14 'Ain, te nos tractamus inciuiliter, qui nostrum asinum furatus abducis? Quin potius effaris, ubi puerum eiusdem agasonem, ne[c]catum scilicet, occultaris?': '"What? We, we are treating you rudely, is it? Didn't you steal our ass and aren't you leading him away? Rather, why don't you tell us where you hid the boy who was his driver – killed him no doubt'".

Ain: apart from being the reading of F and φ, it is also much more lively than

An which, according to Frassinetti, is found in ς, and is recommended by Eyssenhardt. From Plautus onward *ain* is a regular element in colloquial language, expressing surprise; cf. Hofmann ³1951, 43 f. It occurs a few more times in Apul.: 1, 8 (8, 7) *'Ain tandem?'*; 3, 22 (69, 1) *'Ain', inquit, 'uulpinaris, amasio...'* (see vdPaardt *ad loc.*); 6, 2 (129, 20) *'Ain, Psyche miseranda?'*

inciuiliter: this adverb – in Apul. found in this passage only – which originally means "in a manner inappropriate to a citizen" in time acquires the somewhat broader meaning "unreasonable", "impolite". It becomes a technical term in juridical language, e.g. Ulp. *Dig.* 3, 3, 15 *inscium... procuratorem teneri satis inciuile est*; 4, 2, 23, 3 *iudex inciuiliter extorta restitui... iubeat.*

Quin... occultaris?: the accusation becomes much more serious; a climax is gradually building up.

effaris: F had *efferatis* at first, but the mistake was corrected by the same hand.

agasonem: in the sense of "ass-driver", also e.g. 6, 18 (142, 1) *claudum asinum... cum agasone simili*. It is in particular the stable-boy who takes care of horses and asses, and as such he is on a par with the *equiso* 165, 8. LHSz 1, 362 lists *agaso* with the nouns in *-o* which are 'nicht sicher herleitbar', like e.g. *caupo, leno, calo, tiro.*

et ilico detractus ad terram pugnisque pulsatus et calcibus contusus   173, 14-18
infit deierans nullum semet uidisse ductorem, sed plane continatum solutum et solitarium ob indiciuae praemium occupasse, domino tamen suo restituturum: "at once he was pulled down to the ground, pummelled with punches and bruised with kicks, while he started to swear that he had seen no driver but had come upon the ass untethered and unattended, and had appropriated him because of the reward, but would restore him to his owner".

ilico: "on the spot" or "at once"? See *GCA* 1977, 40 f. We have a slight preference for "at once" here because it enlivens the narration and quickens the pace.

The alliteration of *t... t... t..., p... p..., c... c... c...* is extremely functional in emphasizing the shepherds' violence.

infit: in practice this verb occurs in the third person only, mostly in the sense "began to speak"; cf. 2, 13 (36, 5) *infit ad eum*. It may be followed by direct discourse or accusative and infinitive (as in this passage; cf. also e.g. Liv. 3, 71, 6 *Ibi infit se tertium et octogensimum agere*). Bernhard's view (1927, 133), that it is a vulgarism, is incorrect; see *GCA* 1977, 186.

continatum: this rather rare deponent (with the same meaning as *occurrere*) is quite frequent in Apul.: 1, 24 (22, 11, cf. Marg. Molt *ad loc.*); 5, 31 (127, 26); 6, 18 (142, 1); 11, 6 (270, 14) (?); 11, 22 (284, 4). *ThLL s.v.* 720, 64 considers the etymology uncertain. The mss. show many corruptions because the scribes confuse it with *continuus, continuare* etc.; an example of this confusion may be observed in e.g. Helm's *app. crit.* on 1, 24 (22, 11).

solutum et solitarium: alliteration and assonance; see Bernhard 1927, 220 with numerous examples; on *solitarius* see our comm. on 172, 22.

Apul.'s omission of the noun of the direct object, as in this passage *asinum*, is not very common, but it is more frequent than the omission of the dative noun of the indirect obj., for instance.

ob indiciuae praemium: Vallette 28, n. 1 rightly remarks that an *index* is not only a person who informs against a criminal, but also one who retrieves – or assists in retrieving – a lost person or object, often a runaway slave. His reward is the *indiciua*. Cf. *indicivae nomine* 6, 8 (133, 21) where a very special reward is offered for the recovery of the fugitive Psyche. A good illustration of this notion is offered by Iul. Vict. *Rhet.* 4, 4 p. 390, 8: *is, cuius filius non comparebat, edixit se certam pecuniam daturum ei, qui filium sibi exhibuisset; quidam mortuum ostendit: petit indiciuam*.

occupasse: again a technical term from civil law: "to take possession of" (*sc*. of a *res nullius*, as in this case the ass without a legitimate owner). Cf. *Dig.* 41, 1, 3 pr. *Quod enim nullius est, id ratione naturali occupanti conceditur; Dig.* 41, 7, 1 *res pro derelicto habita ... occupantis fit*. See Norden 1912, 160; Summers 1967, 259. It is not clear whether our *uiator* knew the rule *res nullius occupanti cedit*: if Apul. makes him use the verb in a legal sense, he does so to characterize him, no doubt. But the *uiator* makes it clear that he has appropriated the stray ass only temporarily and plans to give it back to its owner: thus he hopes to escape unscathed.

tamen: indicates a notion in contrast to *occupasse*, following which one might have expected *quidem*.

173, 18-22 'Atque utinam ipse asinus', inquit, 'quem numquam profecto uidissem, uocem quiret humanam dare meaeque testimonium innocentiae perhibere posset: profecto uos huius iniuriae pigeret': "'And if only the ass himself – I surely wish I had never seen him – could speak with a human voice and bear witness to my innocence: you would surely be ashamed of this injustice'".

utinam: this word (along with the three preceding words) has become blurred in F, but φ and ς give sufficient certainty.

profecto: vdVliet wants to delete this word as a dittography (see 173, 21 below) but Helm rightly points out that the combination *numquam profecto* is found also in *Apol.* 2 (3, 2) and 40 (47, 17). The emphatic force of this expression is completely understandable in this situation.

uidissem: this seems to be an optative subjunctive, with *utinam* to be supplied. vdVliet, however, proposed to replace *utinam* (18) by *si* and to insert *utinam* after *quem* (19). Although his reasons are understandable, this seems too drastic. The same objection applies to Haupt's *uidisse uellem*. In defense of the transmitted construction Leo refers to Tib. 1, 10, 11 where the poet complains, after singing the praises of the peaceful days of yore, *Tunc mihi uita foret, uulgi nec tristia nossem / arma nec audissem corde micante tubam* ("would that I had lived then: and that I had never known..."). A similar construction is found Ov. *Am.* 2, 16, 15-18 (cursing those who made long journeys): (*solliciti iaceant*) *aut iuuenum comites iussissent ire puellas* "they should at least have ordered that girls should go along as companions to young men". But these parallels are not completely convincing; moreover, they do no occur in a relative clause. Perhaps Apul.'s construction is a Graecism: cf. Hom. *Od.* 4, 699 ὃ μὴ τελέσειε Κρονίων; *Od.* 13, 41-42 τά μοι θεοὶ οὐρανιῶες / ὄλβια ποιήσειαν. See Schwyzer, *Griechische Grammatik* 2, 323. We have not been able to find a clear example of a similar wish in a relative clause in Latin. One might argue that we have here a case of attraction: i.e. that the subjunctive *uidissem* has been used under the influence of *quiret* (see KSt, 2, 201 f.). But the strong *profecto* makes this less plausible.

uocem... dare: a somewhat curious combination, which must mean "produce a (human) voice"; but cf. similar combinations like *dare dicta, sermonem, sonum, uerba*.

uocem... humanam: no one would welcome this more than the ass himself, for quite selfish reasons, of course. Other tragicomic episodes which play with the idea of the ass regaining his human voice, are e.g. 156, 10 (see our comm. *ad loc.*) and 8, 29 (200, 23).

Amusingly enough, the ass has often wished in the past that he could regain his voice to prove his own innocence; here an outsider utters the same wish, to prove his own innocence. The opinion of the mother of the deceased *puer* is completely the reverse; she maintains (175, 14) that the ass never would be able to prove his innocence, even if he had a voice.

quiret: Apul. likes this verb (nineteen occurrences); moreover, he must have wished for some variation from *posset* (21). vdVliet wants to delete *posset* as a gloss on *quiret*; Leo, on the other hand, is sure that *posset* was added because of the clausula.

testimonium... perhibere: this is a technical term in juridical language for "bear witness". Varro *R.* 2, 5, 1 makes a senator say: *ueni mi aduocatus... ut testimonium perhibere possis*; Gai. *Inst.* 2, 104 *ita testor itaque uos, Quirites, testimonium mihi perhibetote*. In the same solemn tone Apul. 2, 24 (44, 22) *Vos in hanc rem, boni Quirites, testimonium perhibetote*. See Summers 1967, 113 f.

Sic adseuerans nihil quicquam promouebat. Nam collo constrictum 173, 23-174, 2 reducunt eum pastores molesti contra montis illius siluosa nemora, unde lignum puer solebat egerere: "These assurances, however, got him no further; for the aggresive shepherds led him with a rope round his neck back towards the wooded slope of the mountain where the boy used to fetch wood".

nihil quicquam: the pleonastic use of the pronouns is somewhat archaic (comic poets, Cato; but also Livy), but makes its re-entry in the second century A.D. (Suet., Gel., Apul.); the combination *nihil quicquam* is most frequent of all. See LHSz 2, 801 f.; *GCA* 1977, 66; Callebat 1968, 97 ('pléonasme de renforcement').

collo constrictum: like Philebus and his comrades 9, 9 (209, 12), the innocent *uiator* is led away to his punishment like a criminal.

molesti: "troublesome", because they are so aggressive. We think that conjectures like *maesti* (Helm) or *confestim* (Leo) are unnecessary; we would rather mention Oudendorp's suggestion *modesti* which is characterized by the same irony as e.g. 6, 26 (148, 3) *mitissimi homines* (who had recently discussed the different ways of killing the ass as cruelly as possible) or 6, 30 (152, 11) *benignus iocatur comes* (the narrator's description of the sadist who tormented him); many other examples in Bernhard 1927, 238 f.

253

contra: as a preposition after a verb of moving only here and 172, 9; see our comm. *ad loc.*

siluosa: the objections raised against this form (as a pleonasm with *nemora*) are unjustified; not all forests are equally dense, and the boy naturally chose the most suitable forest for his wood-trade. Kronenberg's suggestion *siluosi* (based on 8, 15: 188, 21 *Siluosi montis asperum... iugum*) is therefore unneccessary; even more so *cliuosa* (Cornelissen). The combination *cauae... cauernae* in Verg. *A.* 2, 52 is not pleonastic either; see Austin *ad loc.*

CHAPTER XXVI

The death of the *puer* brings grief to his parents, danger to a traveller, respite for the ass.

Nec uspiam ruris aperitur ille, sed plane corpus eius membratim laceratum multisque dispersum locis conspicitur: "He himself could not be found anywhere in the neighbourhood, but his dead body was discovered, entirely dismembered and spread over a wide area". 174, 3-5

Nec uspiam ruris aperitur: no other instances of *uspiam* with genitive are found in the *Met.*, but see *Fl.* 14 (19, 5) *uspiam gentium*; Aug. *Ep.* 164, 7 *uspiam scripturarum*; the synonym *usquam*+genitive is found 2, 20 (41, 9) *usquam gentium*. The combination of *uspiam* with a form of *reperire* occurs at 9, 30 (226, 5) *nec uspiam reperta illa muliere*.

ruris is regarded as suspect by Blümner (1905, 33) and Damsté (1928, 22 f.). Blümner not only regards the addition of *ruris* to *uspiam* as superfluous, since the entire scene is set in the country, but also as somewhat odd since the *puer*'s corpse is found somewhere on the forested mountain-side. Therefore he proposes *uiuus* for *ruris* ('fortasse recte', Robertson). Damsté thinks this 'nimis frigide dictum' and conjectures *Osiris*; in that case, the narrator, by mentioning this famous victim of dismemberment, is making anticipatory reference to the *puer*'s fate, which is about to be disclosed. The reading *ruris*, however, may be retained: the word may have been added for mere emphasis; moreover *rus* is generally used in contrast not with forest, but with city; finally, the notion *uiuus* is present in *ille*, contrasted as it is with *corpus eius* ("his lifeless body").

aperitur: most modern editors read *reperitur* with ς and Oudendorp, but the original reading of F *aperitur* (changed by a second hand in rasura to *operitur*), which also occurs in φ and A, is retained by Hildebrand (though he admits it is 'non usitatum de hominibus'), Eyssenhardt and *ThLL s.v. aperio* 216, 60. Conjecture (the status of the reading in ς is no more than that) is not really necessary, in view of Cic. *Sul.* 88 *aperientur maiorum imagines* (which may provide a parallel) and, in particular, Germ. *Arat.* 672 *claris aperitur flexibus Anguis*. The verb may possibly be a technical term borrowed from the language of mystery-cults. See also Verg. *A.* 6, 406: *aperit ramum qui ueste latebat*.

plane: to be taken with *laceratum*; one might even consider taking it with *conspicitur*, an even stronger hyperbaton, comparing 4, 20 (89, 12) *sed plane ... prospicio*, but in the latter passage 'the hyperbaton is made possible by the fact that the two intervening phrases are distinct cola' (*GCA ad loc.*), whereas here *plane ... laceratum* produces a better contrast with the preceding phrase.

membratim: see the note on 148, 15-16.

174, 5-7 Quam rem procul dubio sentiebam ego illius ursae dentibus esse perfectam et hercules dicerem quod sciebam, si loquendi copia suppeditaret: "To me it was beyond doubt that this had been performed by the she-bear's teeth, and I would certainly have said what I knew, had I had the power of speech".

ego: unlike 171, 15 added with emphasis: *I* (the ass!) was the only one who suspected the truth; the others only saw the dead body.

esse perfectam: ironic; as if a major feat had been performed. From the point of view of the ass however a major feat has indeed been performed: he is rid of at least this plague.

hercules: see the note on 163, 14.

sciebam: the phrase *procul dubio sentiebam* is now replaced by *sciebam*: what the ass truly knew is limited to the event he has observed himself: the arrival of the she-bear. On the use of the indicative see Callebat 1968, 358.

dicerem..., si... suppeditaret: the use of the unreal condition springs from the thoughts of the experiencing I; the narrating I of course does have *loquendi copia*. For imperf. subj. in unreal conditions of the past see LHSz 2, 662. Médan 1925, 272 notes the heroic clausula (with preceding dactyl).

si loquendi copia suppeditaret: cf. Cic. *de Orat.* 3, 124 *facile suppeditat omnis apparatus ornatusque dicendi*; there, as here, a dative of advantage is lacking; see Bernhard 1927, 160; Callebat 1968, 451 gives further instances.

174, 7-8 Sed quod solum poteram, tacitus licet serae uindictae gratulabar: "But I did the one thing I could do: I silently congratulated myself on my revenge, late though it was".

quod solum poteram: on the parenthesis as an intervention of the narrator, here in the shape of a relative clause, see Callebat 1968, 463.

licet serae: on *licet* with adjective or adverb see vdPaardt 1971, 80 for instances and literature. The phrase serves to underline once more the intense suffering of the ass and the narrowness of his escape.

uindictae gratulabar: see the note on 166, 5; at *Ep. Trai.* 10, 14 *Victoriae tuae... gratulor*, OLD takes *uictoriae* as a dative expressing cause of congratulation, but see LHSz 2, 83 who cite our passage as a 'Gen. des Sachbetreffs'. *ThLL* take the verb in the sense of *gaudere* (*s.v. gratulor* 2253, 14), see also comm. on 174, 26.

174, 8-10 Et cadauer quidem disiectis partibus tandem totum repertum aegreque concinnatum ibidem terrae dedere: "The body, when, despite the dispersal of its parts, they had found it all and had with difficulty pieced it together, they entrusted to the earth on the spot".

cadauer... aegre concinnatum: cf. Sen. *Phaed.* 1256 f. (*Chorus ad Theseum*) *disiecta genitor membra laceri corporis / in ordinem dispone et errantes loco restitue partes*; see also comm. on 172, 5 concerning the desire of the ancients to be buried *integri*.

disiectis partibus: vdVliet thinks that *collectis* should be added after these words: there is no need for this conjecture if the abl. abs. is taken in a concessive sense.

terrae dedere: the circumlocution (for *sepeliuerunt*) makes a stately impression: cf. Acc. *trag.* 112 *qui ... terraest datus*; the use of *-ere* for *-erunt* may add to the effect (see LHSz 1, 607 f.). Apuleius uses the ending twice elsewhere in similar contexts: 6, 30 (152, 15) *suo sibi funiculo deuinctam dedere praecipitem* (sc. the old woman); 8, 14 (187, 26 f.) *(Chariten) marito perpetuam coniugem reddidere*. For the ending *-ere* see Austin on Verg. *A.* 2, 53; Löfstedt 1911, 36 ff; *Synt.* 2, (1933), 295 f.

meum uero Bellerofontem, abactorem indubitatum cruentumque 174, 10-14 percussorem criminantes, ad casas interim suas uinctum perducunt, quoad renascenti die sequenti deductus ad magistratus, ut aiebant, poenae redderetur: "my Bellerophon, however, whom they incriminated as an undoubted cattle robber and bloody slayer, they took in fetters to their huts for the time being. At daybreak the next day, they said, he would be taken to the magistrates for punishment".

Bellerofontem: just as the *puer* was lifted above his level by the solemn expression employed for his interment, so now the traveller is given a higher status when Lucius/the ass calls him "my Bellerophon"; thereby Lucius also associates himself with Pegasus, a comparison already made by one of the robbers at 152, 10 (see comm. *ad loc.*). The traveller has in common with Bellerophon the fact that he is not guilty – at least of the second crime he is accused of, though he appears to be guilty of the first. Heine 1962, 190 f. notes that on several occasions Apuleius emphasizes the difference in level between the mythological figure and the human person (often socially or morally inferior) who is compared to that figure. But he adds 'Aber es wirkt nicht mehr rein komisch, wenn Lucius, der bei etwa der Hälfte der mythologischen Anspielungen das Vergleichssubjekt abgibt, meistens gerade in einer kläglichen, lächerlichen oder abstossenden Situation einen Vergleich herausfordert'.

abactorem ... percussorem: note the chiastic placement and the rhyme.

abactorem: cf. Isid. *Orig.* 10, 14 *abactor est fur iumentorum et pecorum quem uulgo abigeum uocant*. On the juridical implications see Summers 1968, 260; see also 8, 29 (200, 27).

cruentumque percussorem criminantes: *c(r)*-alliteration and *u*-assonance with illustrative function. For the predicative acc. with *criminari* cf. Porph. on *Hor. Carm.* 3, 7 13 *quae Bellerofonten (!) hospitem ... adulterum criminata est*; Auson. *Ep.* 26, 21 *terram infidelem nec feracem criminans*.

interim: Apuleius uses the adverb not only in the sense "in the meantime", (e.g. 10, 6: 241, 15 f. *Magistratus interim ... deprecari*; 10, 16: 249, 8 f. *Interim conuiuium summo risu personabat*), but also in the sense "for the time being" cf. 5, 16 (116, 5) *Ergo interim ad parentes nostros redeamus*; 6, 21 (144, 20) *Sed interim quidem tu prouinciam ... exsequere nauiter*; 11, 9 (273, 12) *quod argumentum referebat interim maiorum antecantamenta uotorum*. In our passage both meanings are acceptable: cf. Médan 1925, 157.

quoad: here with final connotation as is possible also with *dum* + subj. Apul.

prefers *quoad* to *dum* and *donec*; see LHSz 2, 654 f.; Callebat 1968, 346 f.

renascenti die sequenti: the poetic flavour of the description of dawn (see note on 154, 5 f.), this time voiced by shepherds, is strengthened by the rhyming and slightly redundant *sequenti*; the redundancy is insufficient reason to delete the word with Leo; for the rhyme see Bernhard 1927, 224 f.; cf. Sen. *Her. O.* 862 f. *haec renatum prima quae poscit diem / Oeta eligatur*.

poenae redderetur: there is no hint as to the man's further fate, cf. 8, 23, where the *pagani* are forgotten as soon as Lucius loses sight of them.

174, 15-18 Interim, dum puerum illum parentes sui plangoribus fletibusque querebantur, et adueniens ecce rusticus nequaquam promissum suum frustratus destinatam sectionem meam flagitat: "While in the meantime the parents of the *puer* bewailed him with lamentations and tears, lo and behold, the peasant arrived and – by no means failing his promise – insisted on my being operated on as planned".

Interim, dum: Helm III² reads *interimdum*, cf. 5,28 (125, 6); his argument that Apuleius has *dum* with imperfect indicative in these two passages only, however, is insufficient reason for the combination. For *dum... et* Callebat 1968, 496 compares Pl. *Ba.* 279 *dum circumspecto, atque ego lembum conspicor*. He notes that the construction recalls Plautine usage and adds a vivid element; and on page 533 he rightly suggests, that in view of the sentence structure, *dum* is here a simple particle of time without true subordinating force. On *dum* with imperfect or present in the main clause see LHSz 2, 613.

plangoribus fletibusque: Callebat in *AAGA* 1978, 176 notes the pathos of the 'expression abondante'.

querebantur: only after the *puer* has been laid in his grave do the parents start their mourning: apparently they have been spared the horrible sight. That they have been notified of their son's death is not mentioned: the details are left to the readers' imagination, and the action is continued quickly.

et: thus F: the word is lacking in φ and ς, whose scribae apparently and understandably gave *dum* subordinating force; however, the word should be retained; see the note on line 15 above (*interim, dum*).

et adueniens ecce: cf. 4, 8 (80, 6 f.) *et ecce... adueniunt* with *GCA* 1977 ad loc. *et... ecce*: see our note on 172, 13.

adueniens: apparently the shepherds have been awaiting the return of the peasant who went to the market. See our note on 162, 12.

nequaquam promissum suum frustratus: cf. Cassiod. *In psalm.* 131, 11 *frustrare est... in irritum promissa deducere*.

sectionem meam: the usual meaning of *sectio* is "operation": Plin. *Nat.* 25, 150 (*sucus mandragorae*) *bibitur... ante sectiones punctionesque ne sentiantur*; Ambr. *De Paen.* 18 *cum admoverit tuo uulneri ferramentum, celerior cura sectionis efficitur*; Aug. *C.D.* 7, 27 speaks of *sectione membrorum* as well as *abscisione genitalium*. In view of these passages it is likely that *sectionem meam* is a technical medical expression (rather than 'signification restreinte' Médan 1925, 159) to denote castration (cf. above on 171, 17 *laborantes*).

'Non est', in his inquit unus, 'indidem praesens iactura nostra, sed 174, 18-22
plane crastino libet non tantum naturam, uerum etiam caput quoque
ipsum pessimo isto asino demere. Nec tibi ministerium deerit istorum': "'No', one of them said, 'our loss today has nothing to do with that.
Tomorrow, however, as far as we are concerned, you may certainly take away
from that rotten ass not only his private parts but his very head. And these people
here will be only too pleased to help you'."

Non est: following Luetjohann 1873, 483. Helm III read ⟨At⟩ *'non est in his'*, presuming an instance of haplography; asyndeton, however, is not uncommon in Apuleius and Helm III² recanted.

'Non est', in his inquit unus: Helm III took *in his* with the preceding words (curiously enough referring to 4, 8: 80, 16); Helm III² and Helm-Krenkel punctuate *'non est', in his inquit unus* referring — correctly now — to the same passage (*inter eos unus*) as well as to 153, 1 *unus omnium*.

indidem: the ass's supposed sexual misbehaviour is meant; see 171, 10.

praesens iactura nostra: sc. the death of the *puer*; the lost cow that the shepherds had been looking for (173, 6) is no longer remembered.

plane: notwithstanding its position this adverb appears to emphasize *libet* rather than *crastino*.

crastino: cf. 2, 11 (34, 15) *imber aderit crastino*; but 1, 24 (22, 17) *crastino die scies*.

naturam: "the private parts"; Callebat 1968, 53 notes Varro *R*. 2, 7, 8; 3, 12, 4 for this usage; see vdPaardt 1971, 180.

etiam ... quoque: for the redundancy, which derives from the language of comedy and returns as an archaism in the 2nd cent. A.D., see Callebat 1968, 531.

pessimo isto asino demere: for the dative *isto* (only in Apuleius) Neue-Wagener 2, 398 also quote 5, 31 (127, 29) *isto meo pectori*; 6, 17 (141, 14) *laborique isto temere succumbis?*; 11, 15 (277, 21) *uultum laetiorem candido isto habitu tuo congruentem*; see Médan 1925, 5. Nic. Heinsius' conjecture *demetit* (*ad* Ov. *Met.* 5, 104) was accepted by Oudendorp and commended by Robertson with 'fortasse recte', but is unnecessary.

nec tibi ministerium deerit istorum: most translators take *istorum* to refer to the shepherds of the group. There can be little doubt that the *pastores* have been operating as a group since 174, 1; cf. 174, 12 *perducunt*; 14 *aiebant*; the group acquires a spokesman in line 18 (*unus*), who points at his colleagues as future assistants in the intended surgery.

CHAPTER XXVII

The ass hears a sermon on a juridical text concerning his alleged misbehaviour.

174, 23-25 Sic effectum est, ut in alterum diem clades differretur mea. At ego gratias agebam bono puero, quod saltem mortu⟨u⟩s unam carnificinae meae dieculam donasset: "Thus it came about that my disaster was postponed till the next day. I on my part gave thanks to that fine *puer* for giving me at least by his death one little day's grace before my execution".

clades: the disaster meant is the castration and/or decapitation of the ass; at 170, 17 the word was used of injury to a young woman (see comm. *ad loc*).

At ego: on the frequency of *at ego* see vdPaardt 1971, 48; on the colometry of this and the next sentence see Hijmans in *AAGA* 1978, 198.

gratias agebam: the ass is giving thanks mentally (note the iterative imperfect), but because of his physiological structure he is unable to utter the words (cf. 156, 12 *nullo pacto disserere potui*); the translation "I felt grateful" (thus Butler, cf. Brandt-Ehlers, Schwartz) is too weak a rendering of the Latin.

bono puero: not during his life, but only by dying has the *puer* unintentionally shown any signs of *bonitas*, at least with respect to the ass. For the ironic use of *bonus* see Bernhard 1927, 239; vdPaardt 1971, 53 (with literature); our note on 152, 11-12 and 174, 1.

saltem: we take the word with *mortuus* (notwithstanding 6, 16; 140, 20 *ad unam saltem dieculam*; but note the word order there) since this ensures that the preceding *bono puero* gets the proper ironic flavour.

mortuus: F has *mort*; (i.e. *mortus*) with a correction (?) by a second hand. The correction in φ is obviously correct.

carnificinae: at 173, 2 *laniena* was used to refer to his castration only. *Carnificina* here presumably refers to an even more terrible, composite fate, since decapitation has been mentioned at 174, 20. For *carnificina* see also *GCA* 1977, 183.

dieculam: according to Callebat 1968, 377 the diminutive, precisely by limiting the notion *dies*, produces an expressive suggestion of subjective time.

174, 26-175, 1 Nec tamen tantillum saltem gratulationi meae quietiue spatium datum: "But no, not that little time was given me to be pleased or rest".

tantillum: one imagines a deictic gesture emphasizing this word. See Friedrich on Catul. 99, 6; Callebat 1968, 520; vdPaardt 1971, 61.

gratulationi: the word refers back to 174, 8 *tacitus licet serae uindictae gratulabar*. As often *gratulatio* is here used in the sense of *gaudium*; see *ThLL s.v.* 2250 'generatim de quavis laetitia cum privata tum publica'.

saltem: used twice in two lines, but even a poet like Vergil does not avoid similar repetitions. See Austin on Verg. *A.* 2, 505 and the literature mentioned there.

nam mater pueri, mortem deplorans acerbam filii, fleta et lacrimosa 175, 1-5 fuscaque ueste contecta, ambabus manibus trahens cinerosam canitiem, heiulans et exinde proclamans stabulum inrumpit meum tunsisque ac diuerberatis uehementer uberibus incipit: "for the mother of the *puer* mourning her son's bitter death, weeping floods of tears and dressed all in black, with both hands tearing loose her ashstrewn grey hair, wailing and crying out incessantly, rushed into my stable and, violently beating and striking her breasts, began to speak:"

mater pueri: in a typical manner Apuleius seems to have added this character; vThiel 1971, 11 n. 22; Mason in *AAGA* 1978, 4 ff. See also the final remark on 172, 21.

mortem deplorans acerbam: *acerbus* has here the double meaning of "cruel", "harsh" (the *puer* having been devoured by a bear) and "untimely", "premature", see Austin on Verg. *A.* 6, 429. In inscriptions a person's *mors* occurring before that of his parents is often termed *acerba,* see Hoogma 1959, 212; ter Vrugt-Lentz 1960, 69.

fleta et lacrimosa: cf. 3, 8 (57, 18) *lacrimosa et flebilis,* see vdPaardt 1971, 70 *ad loc. ThLL* give the present passage only for the active meaning of the passive participle *fletus*; KSt 2, 1, 97 f. and LHSz 2, 290 f. discuss the phenomenon without mentioning *fletus* as an instance. On *lacrimosus* see Ernout 1949, 21 and 82; Callebat 1968, 383.

fuscaque ueste contecta: cf. 2, 23 (44, 7 f.) *matronam flebilem fusca ueste contectam.*

trahens: the usual expression for this gesture of mourning is *scindere*: Accius in Cic. *Tusc.* 3, 62 *scindens dolore identidem intonsam comam*; Verg. *A.* 12, 870 *infelix crinis scindit Iuturna solutos*; Ov. *Met.* 11, 683. Forcellini points out that it was customary in the Jewish world to tear out one's hair as an expression of grief, cf. Vulg. *Esdr.* 1, 9, 3 *euelli capillos capitis mei,* but that in the Greek and Roman world the hair was loosened. In addition *trahere lanam* means "spin wool", so that it is preferable not to take *trahens* as *simplex pro composito* (= *extrahere*) but to translate "tearing loose". Pricaeus notes 10, 6 (241, 3 f.) *trahensque cinere sordentem canitiem.* For mourning gestures see also Toynbee 1971, 47; Kenner 1960, 57; for the Greeks, Vermeule 1979, 262 f.

cinerosam: *ThLL s.v.* 1062, 44 indicates that the word is not found before Apuleius, who uses it with a different shade of meaning at 4, 18 (88, 1 f.); see *GCA* 1977, 136 and Ernout 1949, 57. It occurs again only in the 6th cent. (in the sense of *cineri similis*) in Dioscorides 4, 105 *capnos ... herba est ... alba et cinerosa.*

canitiem: *abstractum pro concreto*; cf. Catul. 64, 224 *canitiem terra atque infuso puluere foedans*; Verg. *A.* 12, 611 *canitiem immundo perfusam puluere foedans.* In Apuleius the word is always used in this concrete sense, except at 10, 34 (265, 4), where it denotes the grey-white colour of goat's hair. It is the usual hair-colour attributed to mourning mothers: the word provides no information concerning the woman's age (or that of her son).

The custom of putting ashes on one's hair as a sign of mourning is found as early as Homer *Il.* 18, 23 f. ἀμφοτέρῃσι δὲ χερσὶν ἑλὼν κόνιν αἰθαλόεσσαν/ χεύατο κὰκ κεφαλῆς. Similarly, outside the area of Greco-Roman culture, e.g. Vulg. *2 Sam.* 13, 19 *aspergens cinerem capiti suo.*

exinde: Wiman 1927, 57 defends the meaning "incessantly" ("oupphörligt", "ideligen") referring to 147, 12 *fustibus exinde tundentes*; he also compares 165, 19 *frondosoque baculo subinde castigans* and 6, 14 (139, 5 f.). Callebat 1968, 159 f. cites our passage and 8, 24 (196, 14) *sed exinde odiosus emptor aliud de alio non desinit quaerere*; Helm's reference to 5, 29 (126, 13) is not relevant here.

proclamans: cf. Quint. *Inst.* 11, 3 170 *nam etiam orbos uiduasque uideas in ipsis funeribus canoro quodam modo proclamantis.*

stabulum inrumpit meum: though the intransitive use of *inrumpere* is more frequent, the transitive use is not uncommon, see *ThLL s.v. irrumpo* 444, 78-445, 18.

tunsisque ac diuerberatis uehementer uberibus: in mourning the mother behaves as many *gnatorum in funere matres / cum incultum cano soluent a uertice crinem / putridaque infirmis uariabunt pectora palmis* (Catul. 64, 349 f.).

diuerberatis: the expression, forceful in itself, is further strengthened by *uehementer.*

uberibus: Apuleius uses *ubera* only when describing mourning women: 4, 34 (102, 3) *u. tundere*; 5, 7 (108, 10) *u. plangere*; 8, 7 (181, 19) *u. pulsare*; in all other cases he uses *papillae*; *mamma* does not occur in Apuleius.

The sentence introducing the words of the mourning mother shows a great deal of emotional colouring: several duplications (*fleta et lacrimosa*; *heiulans et proclamans*; *tunsis ac diuerberatis*), sound effect through preponderance of *a* (almost a third of all vowels), and alliterations: *cinerosam canitiem.*

175, 5-9 'Et nunc iste securus incumbens praesepio uoracitati suae deseruit et insatiabilem profundumque uentrem semper esitando distendit nec aerumnae meae miserae uel detestabilem casum defuncti magistri recordatur: "'And now this creature here is leaning over his manger without a care in the world and gives himself up to his voracity and stretches his insatiable and bottomless belly by eating continually without a thought for my miserable grief or the gruesome fate of his dead master".

Et nunc: it is possible that the woman had started her lamentations even before entering the *stabulum* and is now continuing her complaints in a manner audible to the ass. It is also possible, however, that the lamentation starts with *Et nunc* as an expression suggestive of the many emotions whirling inside her, before she can find words to express them. Pricaeus compares Verg. *A.* 4, 215 *Et nunc ille Paris cum semiuiro comitatu.* (Pease notes 'in scorn' and cites Prop. 2, 21, 7 *et nunc inter eos tu sermo es.*) In the two other passages of the *Met.* where a sentence starts with *Et nunc* (2, 30: 50, 9 and 4, 11: 83, 6) the sentence closes a tale.

securus incumbens praesepio: Pricaeus notes Varro, *Men.* 260 *habens antepositam alimoniam ... neque post respiciens neque ante prospiciens.* Cf. also 9, 13 (212, 13) *circa praesepium capita demersi.*

praesepio: see comm. on 164, 16.

uoracitati suae deseruit: while the robbers themselves *auida uoracitate cuncta contruncant* (152, 19) one of them inveighs against the *asino semper pigro quidem, sed manducone summo* (153, 10). The ass himself is quite aware of his healthy appetite: 10, 15 (248, 7 f.) *Interea liberalibus cenis inescatus et humanis adfatim cibis saginatus corpus obesa pinguitie compleueram*; 10, 16 (249, 3) *iam bellule suffarcinatus... esurienter exhibitas escas adpetebam*. Junghanns 1932, 154, n. 57 refers to 4, 22 (92, 6-10); see *GCA* 1977, 171 *ad loc.*

semper esitando: Callebat 1968, 484 thinks that the addition of adverbs such as *semper* or *auide* (1, 19: 17, 7 f.) shows that the iterative-intensive character of *es(s)itare* is no longer felt; see also Ernout-Meillet and LHSz 1, 529 and 548.

aerumnae meae miserae: assonance (*ae... ae... ae... ae*) and alliteration (*m... m*) enhance the effect of these words.

miserae: F has *misereĩ* (i.e. *miseretur*); *ĩ* has been added by another hand (with an unusual shape to the compendium). That reading is accepted by all modern editors; it produces a neat correspondence: *miseretur ~ recordatur* after the previous *deseruit ~ distendit*. φ and a* however, have *misere* (i.e. *miserae*). Oudendorp, who himself adopted *miseretur*, noted that *miserae* may be defended: it is true that *recordatur* with that reading first has a genitive (*aerumnae*), then an accusative (*casum*), but such a change of case constitutes no objection in Apuleius; cf. 3, 2 (52, 22) *magistratibus eorumque ministris* (abl.) *et turbae miscellaneae* (gen.) *cuncta completa* (with vdPaardt's note, 1971, 30); 8, 1 (177, 7) *luxuriae popinalis* (gen.) *scortisque et diuturnis potationibus* (abl.) *exercitatus*; see also Bernhard 1927, 150 f. Since the architecture of the cola is more even if *miserae* is read (24-22-27 instead of 24-22-10-18), and since the tetracolon in Apuleius usually consists of fairly small elements (see Bernhard 1927, 77 f.), there is much to be said for the original reading of the manuscripts.

sed scilicet senectam infirmitatemque meam contemnit ac despicit et impune se laturum tantum scelus credit: "but of course he despises and looks down on my old age and infirmity and thinks that he will get away without punishment after such a crime". 175, 9-11

sed scilicet: the woman herself gives an explantion for the (in her eyes) callous behaviour of the ass: *scilicet* functions as a sign that the woman herself imputes these thoughts to the ass; thus the established perspective (cf. vdPaardt in *AAGA* 1978, 79) is preserved. See also *GCA* 1977, 50).

senectam infirmitatemque meam contemnit ac despicit: two more or less synonymous nouns are combined with two synonymous verbs, as often in Apuleius: see Strilciw 1925, 116; Bernhard 1927, 166 and 169. Here too we find the duplication noted above at 175, 2 f.

impune se laturum tantum scelus: originally the expected object with *impune ferre* was something like *praedam*: cf. Cic. *Fam*. 13, 77, 3 *cum multos libros surripuisset nec se impune laturum putaret*; see also Butler-Barber and Enk on Prop. 1, 4, 17. Afterwards it becomes a colloquial expression in the sense "remain unpunished"; cf. Kroll on Catul. 78a,.3 *uerum id non impune feres*. A further step in the development is the addition of an object like *scelus*: cf. 1, 2 (11, 20 f.) *impune se laturum meas contumelias putat*.

tantum scelus: the fact that the ass has not tried, at least not successfully, to protect the *puer* from the murderer, is not something the woman knows from her own observation: having accepted the account of the shepherds she regards the ass's passive attitude as criminal; see further on 175, 24.

credit. At: Rohde reads *creditat*; however ingenious the proposal must be rejected since *utcumque* in the *Met.* is nowhere used in initial position.

175, 11-13 At utcumque se praesumit innocentem; est enim congruens pessimis conatibus contra noxiam conscientiam sperare securitatem: "No doubt he takes his innocence for granted; for that is always something that accompanies evil attempts: to hope for freedom from danger despite one's guilty conscience".

At: F has *an*, but the same hand has added *t* over the *n*; in itself *an...innocentem?* produces an acceptable phrase, but *at* is to be preferred: the woman is very definite in her conviction as is repeatedly made clear (9 *scilicet*; 13 f. *pro deum fidem*; 19 *certe*). *At* fits in with the firm tone, see Callebat 1968, 422: 'Notre auteur a... très souvent recours à cette conjonction pour assurer... un enchaînement ferme et vif du récit'; see also *GCA* 1977, 67. On the other hand her questions employ the second person singular and are phrased so as to taunt the ass. For the confusion of *an* and *at* see *GCA* 1977, 185.

utcumque: Pricaeus prefers *utique*: cf. 5, 29 (126, 19 f.) *Sed utique praesumis... te solum generosum*. The conjecture is unnecessary: the woman's firmness has been expressed by *at* (see above); *utcumque* suggests utter amazement ('how in the world is it possible?'). See Callebat 1968, 322; *GCA* 1977, 144.

est enim congruens: the sequence of thoughts is not exactly logical: *noxia conscientia* contradicts the presumption of *innocentia*; but logic is hardly to be expected in the emotional state in which the woman finds herself; perhaps we may assume an element of ἠθοποιία.

Callebat notes (1968, 320) that the construction of a participle with *est* such as *congruens est* with infinitive is very common from Augustan Latin onwards; several instances of *congruens est* (from Pliny the Younger onwards) are collected in *ThLL s.v.* 302, 67-70; in Apuleius however the construction is avoided; the only other instance cited by Callebat is 169, 7 *sustinens est*, but there, as Callebat himself admits, the text is uncertain; see our note *ad loc.*

praesumit: cf. 11, 29 (290, 20 f.) *teque de isto numero merito praesume semper beatum*. Callebat 1968, 167 lists the word with those items of the *sermo cotidianus* that gained currency in imperial and later Latin, see also vdPaardt 1971, 114.

contra noxiam conscientiam: *contra* is used here in the sense "contrary to", "not in conformity with". Because he assumes the phrase to mean "in order to still a guilty conscience", Purser 1906, 47 f. arrives at the entirely unnecessary conjecture *superare securitatem* ("that there should be plenty of freedom from anxiety").

sperare: vdVliet reads *parare*, but his reference Tac. *Agr.* 16, 5 *innocens Bolanus et nullis delictis inuisus caritatem parauerat loco auctoritatis* offers insufficient support for a conjecture which is in itself unnecessary.

Nam pro deum fidem, quadrupes nequissime, licet precariam uocis 175, 13-17
usuram sumeres, cui tandem uel ineptissimo persuadere possis
atrocitate‹m› istam culpa carere, cum propugnare pedibus et arcere
morsibus misello puero potueris?: "For by the gods, wicked quadruped,
even if you were to borrow for a moment the use of language, who in the world –
however naive – could you persuade that such an atrocity is blameless, when you
could have protected the poor boy with your feet and defended him with your
teeth?"

pro deum fidem: see Hofmann 1926, 27 f. who discusses the original full
expression and its elliptical successors.

quadrupes nequissime: *nequissimus* (Apul. does not use the positive) in the
sense "vile", "worthless" occurs very frequently in the *Met.*, e.g. 8, 31 (202, 18)
nequissimo uerberoni; 9, 1 (202, 22) *nequissimus carnifex* etc. It was, of course, a
common term of abuse in comedy, cf. Ilona Opelt 1965, *passim*.

Norden 1912, 69 n. 4 thinks that this speech of the woman to the ass is no more
humorous than that of a peasant to his chicken (9, 33: 228, 8 f.): domestic animal
and slave belong to the same level in the Roman (legal) eye. The humour of the
passage lies in the fact that the woman, rather than give the ass a beating,
addresses him. It is the same type of humour as Cervantes uses when he makes (1,
25) Don Quixote address his Rosinante. Sandy in *AAGA* 1978, 140 n. 63 notes:
'One need only read Cervantes' "Dogs' Colloquy" in *Exemplary Novels* to
discover how a better writer could exploit the notion of cognitive animals for
satire and social commentary'.

licet ... sumeres: cf. Varro, *L.* 7, 2 *multum licet legeret*; for *licet* with (paratac-
tic) imperf. subj. see Callebat 1968, 349 f.; LHSz 2, 605.

precariam: *precarius* denotes that which one receives upon asking (*prex*) a
favour from another: possession and use of it therefore depend on another's
benevolence and therefore may be uncertain or temporary; cf. 11, 21 (283, 7)
ipsamque traditionem ad instar uoluntariae mortis et precariae salutis celebrari.
Sen. *De Tr. An.* 11, 1 (*sapiens*) *non mancipia tantum possessionesque et dignitatem,
sed corpus quoque suum ... seque ipsum inter precaria numerat*.

The playful thought 'if the ass could speak', here an unrealistic utterance, is
used humorously by Apuleius on several occasions, e.g. 173, 20 *utinam...
asinus... uocem quiret humanam dare*. The situation is different at e.g. 8, 29 (200,
23), where the ass himself wishes (and fully expects) to produce a human sound.

possis: after the unreal condition expressed by *sumeres*, the present subjunctive
expresses 'une possibilité à envisager' (Callebat 1968, 350 n. 898).

atrocitatem istam: F and φ read *atrocitate*, but the emendation in ς is obviously
right; *atrocitas* refers to the gruesome way in which the *puer* has died, *istam* to the
fact that the ass was involved.

carere: F shows an erasure above this word; according to Helm initial *u* and
final *re* may still be recognized; Robertson assumes that *uacare* (written in the
first hand) was erased; φ and a* have *uacare*. There is no reason to deviate from
F's reading, for *culpa carere* occurs at Ter. *Hec.* 662 *Censen te posse reperire ullam
mulierem / quae careat culpa?*: Cic. *Tusc.* 5, 4 *culpaque omni carens*. The addition
‹*tua*›, proposed by Bursian and accepted by Robertson, is unnecessary.

cum propugnare pedibus et arcere morsibus misello puero potueris: Médan 1925,

265

306 notes that the interlaced alliterations *p p p m m p p* illustrate the *pedum pugni* and the *maxillae motus*.

arcere ... misello puero: for the dative of advantage with *arcere* cf. Verg. *G.* 3, 154 *hunc* (sc. *asilum*) *quoque ... arcebis grauido pecori*; a comparable construction is found with *defendere*, Verg. *Ecl.* 7, 47 *solstitium pecori defendite*; Hor. *Carm.* 1, 17, 3 *defendit aestatem capellis* (but see 175, 18 *moriturum ... defendere*) and with *depellere*, Cic. *Red. Sen.* 8, 19 *seruitutem depulit ciuitati*; Verg. *A.* 5, 726 f. *qui classibus ignem / depulit*. Many further instances are given in KSt. 2, 1, 314.

misello: a word with strong emotional connotations that is used frequently by Apuleius (e.g. 156, 22 *misellam puellam parturibam*). It is used in particular for dear ones who are dead: Petr. 65, 10 *Scissa lautum nouemdiale seruo suo misello faciebat*; also in funeral inscriptions, e.g. *CIL* 1: 2525. In Catul. 3, 16 it is applied to Lesbia's *passer*.

175, 17-19 **An ipsum quidem saepius incursare calcibus potuisti, moriturum uero defendere alacritate simili nequisti?** "Or were you actually able, when he was alive, to attack him again and again with your hooves, but could not, when he was dying, defend him with the same alacrity?"

For the rhetorical parataxis, see KSt 2, 2, 168; note the parallelism in the word order: object – adverb – infinitive – ablative – finite verb (though *saepius* has no correspondent in the second colon, *simili* none in the first). Hijmans in *AAGA* 1978, 208 n. 18 notes the cluster of long cola. For the variation of *posse* with *(ne)quire* or *nescire* cf. 152, 8 *putres isti tui pedes fugere possunt, ambulare nesciunt* (where, as here, rhyme is to be noted: see Bernhard 1927, 148); 173, 18 f. *Atque utinam ipse asinus ... uocem quiret humanam dare meaeque testimonium innocentiae perhibere posset*.

ipsum: in view of the contrast *ipsum quidem* versus *moriturum uero* the word *ipsum* here has the force of *ipsum uiuum*; cf. also 174, 3 *ille* versus *corpus eius*.

incursare calcibus: another instance of illustrative alliteration combined with assonance (*i u a a i u*). The *puer* apparently told his mother about the event of 168, 25.

moriturum: F has *morituram*, φ emends to *moriturum*.

175, 19-22 **Certe dorso receptum auferres protinus et infesti latronis cruentis manibus eriperes, postremum deserto derelictoque illo conseruo magistro comite pastore non solus aufugeres:** "Surely you should have taken him on your back to carry him away at once and rescue him from the bloody hands of the wicked robber and finally you should not have deserted and let down your fellow slave, your master, your comrade, your herdsman to escape all by yourself".

The mother, being, unlike the reader, unaware of the rôle of the she-bear, has apparently accepted the account of the shepherds (cf. 173, 12-14).

auferres ... eriperes: for the jussive of the past cf. Verg. *A.* 8, 643 *at tu dictis, Albane, maneres*; see KSt. 2, 1, 187; LHSz 2, 336.

deserto derelictoque: *derelictoque* is a marginal reading in F, apparently written by the same hand as the main body of the text, which shows *deiectoque* (as does φ). Helm and Robertson both think the marginal readings valuable (see also above 165, 3-4; Helm Praef. *Fl.* xxxiv; Robertson 1924, 27 f.) and Robertson accepts *derelictoque* here; so did Oudendorp since (1) *derelictoque* avoids the hysteron proteron which results if *deiectoque* is read, (2) in view of *dorso receptum* the mother does not think that the *puer* was riding the ass (cf. also *ductorem* 173, 16) and (3) Apuleius likes to use synonyms; cf. above 175, 2 *fleta et lacrimosa*; for the combination here cf. Verg. *A.* 2, 18 *desertosque uidere locos litusque relictum*.

conseruo magistro comite pastore: the asyndetic combination of four independent notions does not occur elsewhere in Apuleius, see Bernhard 1927, 77. Note that in the a b a b arrangement the b elements contrast with the a elements.

An ignoras eos etiam, qui morituris auxilium salutare denegarint, quod contra bonos mores id ipsum fecerint, solere puniri?: "Or don't you know that those wo have refused to give saving help to people in danger of their lives are commonly punished, if only because they have acted against the dictates of morality?" 175, 25-26

An ignoras: the rhetorical question is humorous in presupposing a certain amount of legal knowledge on the part of the addressee, the ass. Furthermore, unlike the reader the woman is quite unaware that this ass has a human intellect and in that respect is by no means her inferior.

eos etiam ... solere puniri: Norden 1912, 68 f. sees in these words an allusion to the S.C. Silanianum (see *RE s.v.* Silanus), which laid down that a slave who was in a position to help his master when in danger, but did not do so, was punished along with the murderer; Norden regards the allusion as all the more interesting, since Apuleius bases the threatened punishment not on strictly legal grounds, but on popular ethics (*boni mores*). The appeal to *boni mores* (however ancient a principle) appears in Roman Law only in the first cent. *A.D.*, as Norden himself says (*ibid.* 67). The woman's remark therefore may in Apuleius' time have been read as a reference to the law of the land.

solere puniri: possibly because of the clausula (cret. + troch.) Apuleius has chosen this order rather than *puniri solere*.

Sed non diutius meis cladibus laetaberis, homicida: "But you will no longer rejoice in my calamities, you murderer". 175, 22-25

meis cladibus: on the plur. of abstracts in Apul. see Médan 1925, 324; Bernhard 1927, 101 f.

laetaberis: deponent, as usually in Apuleius; forms of the active (with causative meaning) are found in 3, 11 (60, 13) and 5, 14 (114, 20); see vdPaardt 1971, 90; Flobert 1975, 73. The woman's notion that the ass is pleased by the death of her son and her announcement that his joy will not last long are in full agreement with the memory of the narrator: *nec tamen tantillum saltem gratulationi meae quietiue spatium datum* (174, 26 f.).

267

175, 26-176, 1 Senties, efficiam, misero dolori naturales uires adesse': "You will feel – I'll see to that – that bitter grief has its own natural powers"'.

Senties, efficiam: for the parataxis see Callebat 1968, 106 f. Oudendorp prefers to read *sentias*, but fut. ind. after *faxo* is often found in Plautus, see *ThLL s.v.* 104, 60 f.

CHAPTER XXVIII

The dreaded punishment takes place; the ass, however, does not succumb, thanks to his very last resource.

et cum dicto subsertis manibus exsoluit suam sibi fasciam pedesque   176, 1-7
meos singillatim inligans indidem constringit artissime, scilicet ne
quod uindictae meae superesset praesidium, et pertica, qua stabuli
fores offirmari solebant, adrepta non prius me desiit obtundere,
quam uictis fessisque uiribus suopte pondere degrauatus manibus
eius fustis esset elapsus: "no sooner said than done: putting her hands under
her clothes she loosened her breast-band; with it she tied my hindlegs one by one
and lashed them tightly together with the intention, of course, that no means of
revenge be left to me; then, grabbing a stick with which they used to prop the
stable-door, she did not stop whacking me until her strength gave out and she
was so tired that the club, borne down by its own weight, slipped out of her
hands".

et cum dicto: 'dient dazu, nach einer Rede den Faden der Erzählung wieder aufzunehmen'; thus Bernhard 1927, 50 with a series of examples of this expression in the *Met*. In our passage, however, we cannot speak of an actual interruption: the woman is going to carry out her recently expressed resolution at once and with great energy.

subsertis: in its literal meaning this compound is quite rare and restricted to late Latin; much more common is *insero*, e.g. Ter. *Hau*. 563 *Vidin ego te modo manum in sinum huic meretrici / inserere?* In a figurative sense *subsero* can mean "subjoin" or "give to understand", e.g. Amm. 16, 7, 4 (see deJonge *ad loc*.).

suam sibi: both here and at 5, 1 (104, 8) the two reflexive pronouns seem to be functional. Apuleius likes to use these combinations also when they are pleonastic, e.g. 164, 11 *suis sibi gladiis* (see our comm. *ad loc.*).

fasciam: Robertson prefers here the spelling *fasceam* because he discerns the vague contours of an *e* in F; he finds another argument in *fasceola* 2, 7 (30, 19). *ThLL s.v.* 296, 26 prefers the spelling *fascia* because it is found in the best mss. Consequently the problem remains unresolved.

The *fascia* in this passage is a *pectorale strophium* or a *fascia pectoralis feminarum ad sustinendas uel cohibendas papillas, mamillare* (*ThLL*). From the description of Fotis 2, 7 (30, 19) *russea fasceola praenitente altiuscule sub ipsas papillas succinctula* it appears that the *fascia* is sometimes coloured. Women wear this long, wide band wound around the breasts. Daremberg-Saglio 2, 980 shows a statuette of a female form (Venus?), which indicates how the rolled-up *fascia* will be wrapped around (fig. 2879); another picture (2880) shows the *fascia* held up by shoulder-straps. Naturally, the garment occurs often in elegiac poetry, e.g. Prop. 4, 9, 49; Ov. *Ars* 3, 274, 622; *Rem*. 338; see also Mart. 11, 104, 7. Tac. *Ann*.

15, 57 describes how Epicharis hangs herself with her *fascia: uinclo fasciae, quam pectori detraxerat, in modum laquei ad arcum sellae restricto indidit ceruicem*.

pedesque meos: the word *pedes* can be used both of people and of animals; used by the narrator, this produces a comical effect. Here it must refer to the ass's hindlegs, which are tied together to prevent kicking (the perverted woman does not foresee that the ass will score a direct hit in a different way). The same method of hobbling is practised in Italy even at this day: Sardinian peasants, for example, tie their asses' hindlegs with a rope which is tightened crosswise. That this happened exactly the same way in Antiquity, appears indirectly from Veg. *Mulomed*. 1, 38, 10 *posteriora crura quasi inligata habebit* (sc. *mulus*). The situation is tragic in SHA Capit. *Alb*. 5, 9 *purpurea matris illigatus est fascea* (*sc*. Albinus); here, too, the *fascia* is an easily available substitute for a rope.

singillatim: a widely used adverb. For Apuleius' preferance for adverbs in *-tim*, see *GCA* 1977, 39 and our comm. on 162, 13 *gregatim*.

indidem: used instrumentally here in the sense of "with the same means", "with that". Cf. 8, 28 (199, 16) *indidem* (= *eo flagro*) *sese . . . comulcat*; 10, 21 (252, 18) *meque indidem* (= *eodem oleo*) *. . . perfricat*. Cf. also Iul. Val. 1, 37 p. 48, 5 *auri . . . ea copia . . ., ut humum . . . consternere indidem possim*. See also our comm. on 174, 18.

constringit artissime: cf. 163, 18 *artissimis uinculis impeditus ac . . . constrictis illis*.

scilicet: by the didactic tone (cf. *GCA* 1977, 94; 140; etc.) the narrative perspective is preserved.

uindictae: according to Vallette it means here "revenge" ("ma vengeance"), according to others (e.g. Helm-Krenkel) "deliverance". In the seventeen passages listed in *Ind. Apul.* where *uindicta* occurs, the meaning is always "revenge"; for a different interpretation one needs strong arguments. We think that "revenge" fits in very well: this virago expects the hated animal – whom she thinks capable of anything – to react to her punishment: he has been known to kick (4, 3: 76, 11-14).

pertica: this is a long stick, frequently mentioned in agricultural works. It can be used as a support for a frame in viticulture (Cato *Agr*. 33, 4; Var. *R*. 1, 8, 2; Col. 4, 12, 1; etc.); to knock olives off the tree (Var. *R*. 1, 55, 2; Plin. *Nat*. 15, 3, 11) or nuts (*Nux* 68, 69); as a perch for chickens (Var. *R*. 3, 9, 7; Col. 8, 3, 7; Pall. 1, 26); as a fowler's lime-twig (Fest. 19 L), and for threshing (Plin. *Nat*. 18, 72, 298). Apparently it is used for a variety of things on a farm; here it is propped at a slant against the stable-door to keep it shut. Understandably enough the woman seizes this stick in her hurry. Another passage where the *pertica* is used to bring an unwilling ass to heel is Pl. *As*. 589. Nowhere in literature is it a fixed element with a door; therefore we are of the opinion that Helm-Krenkel's translation "die Stange, mit welcher die Stalltür fest zugemacht zu werden pflegte" is hard to defend.

The surveyor's *pertica* (an official measuring-rod with a fixed length of 10 ft.) is, of course, not relevant to this passage.

offirmari: according to *OLD* this is the only passage where *offirmare* has its literal meaning. However, the given translation ("to make firm against attack, secure") seems not quite right; more correct is "to prop". Its figurative meanings ("to make obdurate or inflexible" and "to make up one's mind on") are much more common; Apul. has it 10, 10 (244, 22) *offirmatus mira praesumptione nullis uerberibus... succumbit....*

adrepta: φ has *arrepta*; F wrongly *abrepta*. If our interpretation of *pertica* is right, *adrepta* fits the context better: the woman grabs the first piece of wood she sees. This very common corruption (an ever-recurring problem for the scribe) has its origin in the archetype, which was written in majuscles; cf. Koestermann, *Praef.* Tac. *Ann.* 1960, X; Helm, *Praef. Flor.* XLVII. The other passages confusing *adripio* and *abripio* are 1, 23 (21, 4); 1, 25 (23, 3); 4, 3 (76, 9); 4, 27 (96, 2); 5, 24 (121, 20); 9, 38 (232, 18). The correction is sometimes made by φ, sometimes by the recentiores, occasionally by the same hand in F (e.g. 1, 25: 23, 3). See vdPaardt 1971, 59; *GCA* 1977, 39 and 203.

obtundere: a person can do this with his fists, as Sosia finds out in Pl. *Am.* 606 *sum optusus pugnis pessume*. Against an ass harder instruments are needed: 4, 3 (76, 9) *grandi baculo... me totum plagis obtundit* (see *GCA* 1977, 39); 167, 15 it is done with a *fustis*; here a *pertica* is used.

quam... esset elapsus: Helm compares this to 5, 22 (120, 11), but the situation is actually quite different there: panic-stricken, Psyche drops the weapon with which she wanted to punish herself.

suopte: Apul. uses this suffix only once elsewhere in the *Met.*: 9, 25 (221, 28) *adseuerans breui absque noxa nostri suapte inimicum eius uiolentia sulpuris periturum*. This is surprising because it is a favourite 'Identitätspartikel' from Plautus onward, especially after possessive pronouns and connected with an ablative; e.g. *Capt.* 371 *tuopte ingenio*; *Mil.* 605 *tuopte... consilio*; *Mer.* 970 *suapte culpa*. The combination with a personal pronoun (e.g. *mepte*) is rare. For its etymology (*-pte* related to **poti(s)*?) and usage, see Sommer 1914, 448 f. and LHSz 1, 466.

esset elapsus: a similar expression is used by Pliny *Ep.* 2, 1, 5 of an elderly man: *liber, quem forte acceperat grandiorem, et seni et stanti ipso pondere elapsus est*.

Tunc de brachiorum suorum cita fatigatione conquesta procurrit ad focum ardentemque titionem gerens mediis inguinibus abtrudit usque, donec solo, quod restabat, nisus praesidio liquida fimo strictim eg[r]esta faciem atque oculos eius confoedassem: "Then she complained at her arms tiring so quickly; she ran to the fireplace, fetched a burning piece of wood and thrust that between my buttocks again and again until, resorting to the only means that remained to me, I befouled her face and eyes with a squirt of dung, ejected at close quarters". 176, 7-11

procurrit: the verb is well-chosen: it shows with what haste and impetuosity she is carrying on her cruel work.

titionem: not so much a "live coal" (Jack Lindsay) as a "glowing firebrand" (Adlington-Gaselee) or "ein brennendes Scheit" (Helm-Krenkel); this is evident from the definition in Lact. *Inst.* 4, 14 *titionem uulgus appellat extractum foco torrem semiustum et extinctum* (*extinctum* does not apply to our passage, of course). Non. 268 L explains *titionem* as *fustem ardentem*. Hyginus uses exactly the same term in describing the myth of Althaea (*Fab.* 171: *Atropos titionem*

271

ardentem aspexit in foco) and that of Meleager (*Fab*. 174: *Althaea ... titionem ex arca prolatum in ignem coniecit. ita ... filium interfecit*). It must be the regular term in this myth; for metrical reasons Ovid cannot use it in *Met*. 8, 451-526 (see 176, 13 below on *delirantis Althaeae*). Surprisingly, *titio* is a term of abuse in Vulg. *Is*. 7, 4 *noli timere, et cor tuum ne formidet a duabus caudis titionum fumigantium istorum, in ira furoris Rasin, regis Syriae et filii Romeliae*. See LHSz 1, 365.

mediis inguinibus obtrudit: ThLL s.v. *inguen* 1580, 10, quoting our passage, defines it as *genitalia*; if so, *obtrudere* should be rendered by "strike against". But presumably her action is different; most lexica and translations give an equivalent to "thrust into", e.g. Vallette "me l'enfonce entre les cuisses"; Helm-Krenkel 'mitten in den Unterleib ... stossen". This woman is just as sadistic as her son (169, 2 f.), so both interpretations are conceivable

usque: φ has merely *obtrudit*, A has *obtruditurque*, F has *obtrudit; q*; in which *q*; is hardly legible. Thus Saumaise's proposal *usque* must be correct. The combination *usque donec* does not occur elsewhere in the *Met*., but *usque dum* does (2, 17: 39, 8); the latter also occurs *Apol*. 80 (89, 10) and *Fl*. 18 (36, 15).

liquida fimo ... egesta: the principal mss. F and φ have the feminine ending -*a* for both the adjective and the participle (the latter is spelled *egresta*, but φ has deleted the *r* by means of a dot). Apul. uses *fimus* once more 4, 3 (77, 4) – where the ass repels an adversary in a similar way – but there none of the mss. takes it as a feminine: *fimo fistulatim excusso*. The form *fimo* is consistent with classical usage, whether it is taken as neuter (according to *ThLL* 765, 76 *s.v. fimum* this is the usual form in the pre-Christian period) or masculine (as the grammarians emphatically prescribe, e.g. Char. *GLK* 1, 32, 1 *masculina semper singularia ... (ut) fimus*; in almost identical terms Diom. *GLK* 1, 327, 18.[1] Usually Apul. adheres to classical usage as far as gender is concerned (cf. Callebat 1968, 242: 'Apulée fait preuve dans l'emploi des genres d'une fidélité assez remarquable à l'usage classique'); a few deviations occur, derived from colloquial language, e.g. 10, 30 (261, 20) *diadema candida*; 3, 13 (61, 26) *lorum quempiam* (see vdPaardt 1971, 104); 1, 13 (12, 11) *paruo humo* (see Marg. Molt 1938, 73). That Apul. varies the gender (*fimus* masculine or neuter in bk. 4, feminine in this passage) is unusual but not unique; another example is *humus*, which is feminine 1, 19 (18, 10) (but here the mss. offer different readings). Oudendorp emended our passage – presumably for the reasons mentioned above – to *liquido ... egesto*; we prefer, somewhat hesitantly, to adhere to the reading of the principal mss.

strictim: probably this means "closely" (LS); cf. Pl. *Capt*. 268 *strictim ... attonsurum* ("close to the skin") and Apul. *Fl*. 15 (20, 17) *cithara balteo caelato apta strictim sustinetur*. Helm's translation "im Strahl" and Vallette's "d'un jet de ..." are attractive in this context because of the etymological relation with *stringere*, but there are no convincing parallels. For adverbs in *-im*, see above on 176, 2 *singillatim*.

egesta: the description is hardly less vivid than that in 4, 3 (77, 4); cf. *GCA* 1977, 45.

---

[1] Presumably this is one of the reasons why in modern editions of Pliny the masculine form is preferred whenever the mss. leave a choice, e.g. *Nat*. 18, 145 *fimo addito* (ed. H. Le Bonniec 1972) and 19, 120 *fimo ingesto* (ed. J. André 1964).

confoedassem: in classical Latin the usual mood after *donec* "until" is the indicative; a subjunctive (always indicating purpose) is quite rare, e.g. Pl. *Rud.* 812 *nei istunc istis inuitassitis / usque adeo donec qua domum abeat nesciat*. In later authors (like Tacitus) such a final subjunctive is occasionally found (e.g. *Ann.* 1, 32, 4 *Septimius, cum perfugisset ad tribunal... eo usque flagitatus est, donec ad exitium dederetur*) but it gives rise to a much freer usage, so that Chausserie-Laprée 1969, 627 concludes 'En résumé, *donec*, dans sa fonction de rupture et de mise en scène, n'est suivi du subjonctif, concurremment avec l'indicatif, que chez Tacite, et cette dualité de mode n'a aucune signification particulière'. We find the same in Apul., who uses this conjunction relatively often (eleven times): sometimes it has a final connotation, expressed by a subjunctive (e.g. 9, 7: 207, 22 *otiosus adsiste, donec... istud tibi repraesentem* or 10, 9: 243, 29 (*sc. aureos*) *anulo tuo praenota, donec altera die... comprobentur*); five times we find an indicative as in classical Latin (e.g. 9, 7: 208, 1 *demonstrat..., donec... faber... coactus est*); often he uses the subjunctive for no obvious reason, as in this passage and 10, 34 (265, 3) *perpluit imbre, donec... mutarent*. LHSz 2, 629 rightly concludes: 'mehr noch im Spätlatein tritt der Konj. ohne ersichtlichen Grund ein'.

Qua caecitate atque faetore tandem fugata est a me pernicies: ceterum titione delirantis Althaeae Meleager asinus interisset: "By this blinding and stench, ruination was finally averted from me: otherwise the ass Meleager would have perished by the glowing firebrand of a raving Althaea". 176, 11-13

a me pernicies: this is the reading in F, although the *s* has been added (probably by a different hand). Robertson therefore changed the text to *a mea pernicie*, which also makes good sense with a change of subject; but we do not think that there is enough reason for this change. The position of the subject at the end of the sentence makes for emphasis, even theatricality; cf. Bernhard 1927, 19.

ceterum = ceteroquin "otherwise", "sonst". It appears from *ThLL* 972, 52 f. that this meaning is found in Latin of all periods, e.g. Ter. *Eun.* 452 *ceterum / idem hoc tute melius quanto inuenisses, Thraso!*; Liv. 3, 40, 11 *ceterum... sibi placere de eo... senatu disceptante agi*; but in Apul. it is quite rare. Helm 1957, 131 f. discusses all passages where Apul. uses *ceterum* in its different gradations: firstly, identical to *ceteroquin* "otherwise"; secondly, causal "for" (see Redfors 1960, 39 f.); thirdly, adversative "on the contrary"; fourthly, "for the rest", "besides". Helm finds only four clear-cut cases of the meaning *ceteroquin*, three of which occur in the *Met.* (this passage; 5, 5: 106, 21; 5, 19: 118, 3), one in *Apol.* 41 (48, 13), and in addition one in the treatise περὶ ἑρμηνείας 7 (185, 23). Remarkably enough, *ceterum* occurs 24 times in the *Apol.* but only 10 times in the *Met.*, where it is never used causally or adversatively — twice it occurs in the sense of "besides", introducing a new element into the expressed thought (173, 2; 11, 29: 290, 21). On *ceterum* in general, see KSt2, 2, 79 *Anm.* 2; LHSz 2, 492; *ThLL* 972, 52 f.

delirantis Althaeae: according to the myth (told in detail by Ovid and briefly by Hyginus; see above on 176, 9 *titionem*), the Parcae determined at Meleager's birth that his life would end when a particular piece of fire-wood was burnt. When Meleager killed his uncles (the brother of his mother Althaea) his mother flew into a passion and burnt the wood to avenge her brothers, thus causing the death of her son. See Roscher *s.v.* Meleagros 2591 f. and our note on 176, 9 *titionem*. In Greek tragedy the theme was treated by Sophocles (*Tr. G. F.* 4, ed. Radt 345 f.) and Euripides (*Tr. G. F.* ed. Nauck 525 f.). The ass actually has the same experience as Meleager in Ov. *Met.* 8, 516 *uritur et caecis torreri uiscera sentit / ignibus*. In Ovid this leads to the victim's death, in Apuleius to his salvation (after his violent reaction); this adds to the humour of our passage. Thus Vallette 31 n. 3 is not quite right in remarking that there are but few similarities in subject matter between the myth and this scene.

The many allusions to mythology in the *Met.* have been collected by Bernhard 1927, 207 f. They often occur at the end of a pericope or scene, e.g. 151, 7-9; 152, 9-10. These short, pointed comparisons are reminiscent of Plautus; cf. Fraenkel 1922, 169 f. See further our comm. on 149, 18-19; vdPaardt 1971, 140 with a bibliography.

It is impossible to trace whether the mythological allusion in our passage occurred in the Vorlage or not, since it is absent in the *Onos*. Usually these mythological digressions are regarded as typically Apuleian.

interisset: this is the reading of the mss.; Floridus prefers *interissem* which is approved by Robertson and Helm ('fort. recte') and Frassinetti ('non male'). Oudendorp, on the other hand, thinks this emendation unnecessary because Apuleius more than once writes *meus asinus* in the sense of *ego asinus* or *meus Lucius* meaning *ego Lucius*. We agree with Oudendorp: Lucius often speaks of the ass he used to be in a somewhat detached way, which creates a humorous effect: e.g. 155, 17 *illius beati Lucii... facta comparatione*; 9, 13 (212, 21) *ueterisque Lucii fortunam recordatus... maerebam*; 10, 29 (260, 12) *quae me priori meo Lucio redderent*.

Thus the book ends with a dramatic episode – actually a stylistic device of the epic: cf. the end of Verg. *A.* 2 with Creusa's disappearance, 5 with Palinurus' death, 6 Marcellus' death, 11 Camilla's, 12 Turnus'. A similar dramatic climax can be found at the end of each book of the *Georgics*. Horace, too, often ends an ode with an allusion to death, funeral, or underworld; see Schrijvers 1973, 139 f. Another example is Mart. 10, 47, 13 *summum nec metuas diem nec optes*. Apuleius, too, has found a fine conclusion with the verb *interisset*.

After this dramatic climax the book – and with it the day – has come to a reassuring end; the next day, after the interlude of the night, the author will again increase the suspense both for Lucius and the reader.

For Apuleius' way of concluding a book, see e.g. Junghanns 1932, 126 n. 13; each book is a unit and its end indicates a pause.

APPENDIX I

6, 26 (147, 22) *Pessumo pede domum nostram accessit*

Our comm. *ad loc.* mentions a combination of three associations. For each of these some further information is collected below.[1]

a. There can be no doubt that from the early empire onwards Romans felt safer in approaching their objective with the right foot forward. Vitruvius 3, 4, 4 may take account of this attitude when prescribing an uneven number of steps leading to a temple: *gradus in fronte constituendi ita sunt, ut sint semper impares; namque cum dextro pede primus gradus ascendatur, item in summo templo primus erit ponendus.* Unhappily he does not elaborate on the reasons why this is desirable.[2]

The association *dexter = propitius* is well-known (e.g. Ov. *Fast.* 1, 67; see also Stemplinger 1948, 99) and Vergil combines *dexter* and *pede secundo* in *A.* 8, 302.[3] There are a few parallels. Petronius' Trimalchio (*Sat.* 30) stations a slave at the entrance to his *triclinium* to shout *dextro pede!* whenever anyone enters and Juv. 10, 5 uses the same expression in the sense "auspiciously": *quid tam dextro pede concipis* (Mayor *ad loc.* has collected several parallels). Compare, too, Sil. It. 7, 171 f. *Attulit hospitio . . . pes dexter et hora Lyaeum.* The expression returns later in Prud. *Contra Sym.* 2, (2), 78 *cessisse parentibus omne / idolium semper feliciter et pede dextro.* Since Prudentius is quoting (or paraphrasing) Symmachus, his use of the expression does not entitle us to conclude that it has become a fixed idiom without a living superstition behind it. Indeed, there is a curious scholion on [Ov.] *Ibis* 101 (*ominibusque malis pedibusque occurrite laeuis*) saying: '*In gaudio occurritur dextro pede, in funere laeuo*', and it is likely that *dexter* and *laeuus* are intended both in a literal and a metaphorical sense.

Apuleius' *sinistro pede* finds a parallel in the passage on superstitions in Johannes Chrysostomus (*Comm. on Paul. ad Eph.* IV 12 t. XI 94 B-C Montef., also quoted by Haupt, *Opusc.* II 255 f.), in which we read among several other instances: ἐγὼ αὐτὸς τῷ ἀριστερῷ προὔβην ποδί· καὶ τοῦτο συμφορῶν σημεῖ-

---

[1] The present note is confined to a few items concerning *foot* and *entrance* and the beliefs surrounding those. For literature see e.g. *RAC* 8, 726; Riess in *RE* XVIII, 1 (1942) *s.v. omen* 350-378; Händel in *RE* XXXIII, 2 (1959) *s.v. prodigium* 2283-2296.

[2] Compare the precept in Iambl. *V.P.* 156: εἰσιέναι δὲ εἰς τὰ ἱερὰ κατὰ τοὺς δεξιοὺς τόπους παραγγέλλει, ἐξιέναι κατὰ τοὺς ἀριστερούς, τὸ μὲν δεξιὸν ἀρχὴν τοῦ περιττοῦ λεγομένου τῶν ἀριθμῶν καὶ θεῖον τιθέμενος, τὸ δὲ ἀριστερὸν τοῦ ἀρτίου καὶ διαλυομέ-'νου σύμβολον τιθέμενος. The remark looks very much like a neo-pythagorean canonization of an existing practice. See on the other hand Ov. *Pont.* 3, 2, 50 *templa manent hodie uastis innixa columnis, / perque quater denos itur in illa gradus.*

[3] Cf. *A.* 10, 255 *Phrygibusque adsis pede, diua, secundo.*

ov.[4] There are some passages that support the notion of a superstitious fear of the left foot. Augustus was superstitious: Suet. *Aug.* 92: *auspicia et omina quaedam pro certissimis obseruabat: si mane sibi calceus perperam ac sinister pro dextro induceretur, ut dirum.*[5] A different version of what may be the same story occurs in Plin. *Nat.* 2, 7, 24: *Diuus Augustus prodidit laeuum sibi calceum praepostere inductum quo die seditione militari prope adflictus est.*[6] The superstition is also mentioned by John Chrysostom (*ibid.*): νῦν ὁ οἰκέτης ὁ μιαρὸς τὰ ὑποδήματα ἐπιδιδοὺς πρῶτον ὤρεξε τὸ ἀριστερόν· συμφοραὶ δειναὶ καὶ ὕβρεις. In this context several further passages may be mentioned. Horace *Ep.* 2, 37 has: *i, bone, quo uirtus tua re uocat, i pede fausto*. Here *pede fausto* is at once a statement and a wish. A wish is found also in Ov. *Fast.* 1, 514 *ripaque felici tacta sit ista pede*. Bömer notes that the expression *felici . . . pede*, but not the notion, is unique. (Curiously enough Frazer does not comment on this passage.) St. Augustine has an interesting remark in *Ep.* 17 (44) *ad Max. Gram.*: *Nam Phanio quid aliud significat quam boni pedis hominem, id est cuius aduentus adferat aliquid felicitatis? sicut solemus dicere secundo pede introisse cuius introitum prosperitas aliqua consecuta sit*. In the same category is to be listed the Suda expression (2977) πρώτῳ ποδί: ὁ οἰωνιζόμενοι λέγειν εἰώθασι. It is not surprising, then, that Chiron drops the poisoned arrow on his left foot (Ov. *Fast.* 5, 398).

One might expect that the reverse of *bonus pes* is *malus pes*, yet Kroll denies that this is the sense of that combination at Catul. 1, 22 *uos hinc interea ualete abite | illuc, unde malum pedem attulistis*. Yet the suggestion that we have to do both with *pes* = "metre" and *pes malus* = "ill-omened foot" (cf. below on Prop. 3, 1, 5) is most attractive.[7] See also Ov. *Tr.* 2, 15 f. *at nunc . . . | saxa malum refero rursus ad icta pedem*,[8] a line which combines the ominous toe-stubbing (see below) with the unlucky foot.

Finally there are a few passages in which *pes* has an ominous sense but in interrogative (and therefore uncertain) form. Thus Ov. *Her.* 21, 71 f. *Quo pede processi? Quo me pede limine moui? Picta citae tetigi quo pede texta ratis?*[9] In the Loeb edition (1914) Grant Showerman explains his translation of *quo pede* ("with what step"), as meaning "(with) eager and spirited (step)", but the context clearly demands an underlying "how inauspiciously". Prop. 3, 1, 5 f. addresses the *manes* of Callimachus and Philetas: *dicite quo pariter carmen tenuastis in*

---

[4] The left foot is exceptional in indicating untoward things: usually in Rome the left, in Greece the right is the favourable side. See Cic. *Div.* 1, 12 and 2, 82 with Pease *ad loc.*; Fordyce on Catul. 45, 8 f. and Austin on Verg. *A.* 2, 693 note that Roman poets are inconsistent in their preferences for left or right.
[5] Cf. Friedländer 3, ³1920, 158; Gardthausen 1891, 496 f.; Stemplinger 1922, 27.
[6] Cf. the Pythagorean precept in Iambl. *Protr.* 21 D 58 C 6 = de Vogel *Gr. Ph.* 1, 29): εἰς μὲν ὑπόδησιν τὸν δεξιὸν πόδα προπάρεχε, εἰς δὲ ποδόνιπτρον τὸν εὐώνυμον.
[7] There is no need for the punctuation *malum!* (occurring for the first time, as far as we know, in the commentary of François Noel, Paris 1803). The same ambiguity occurs in the Dutch poet Bertus Aafjes, *Gedichten* 1947 'O vers, wat zijn uw voetjes zwaar'.
[8] For parallels see Luck *ad loc*. In the Dutch proverb 'Een ezel stoot zich in 't gemeen geen tweemaal aan dezelfde steen' the ominous quality has disappeared. Cf. the idiom 'met het verkeerde been uit bed stappen'.
[9] Cf. e.g. Houwaert, *Lusth. d.M.* 1, 338 (1582): 'Och wat voet mocht ick doen ierst voorsetten?'

antro, / quoue pede ingressi, quamue bibistis aquam. Brouckhusius notes 'referebat enim quem pedem cui praeponerent; dextrum an sinistrum' citing a number of the passages mentioned above. See also Butler-Barber and Camps *ad loc.*, who cite Ov. *Fast.* 1, 514 (quoted above) and note the triple function of *quo pede*: (a) the manner of entry; (b) its ominous quality and (c) a reference to *pes* as a metrical foot (see also Quadlbauer 1968, 92).

b. The *pedis offensio* also has a widely acknowledged ominous connotation. An implied reference to this belief is found as early as Eur. *Heraclidae 730* ὄρνιθος οὕνεκ' ἀσφαλῶς πορευτέον. Most of the parallels have been noted by Ogle 1911, 251 ff. and Pease on Cic. *Div.* 2, 84 *quae si suscipiamus, pedis offensio nobis et abruptio corrigiae et sternumenta erunt obseruanda*. Perhaps the most famous literary use of the omen occurs in Vergil *A*. 2, 242 f. *quater ipso in limine portae / substitit atque utero sonitum quater arma dedere*.[10] See also Austin *ad loc.*, who refers to *Catul*. 61, 166 f. *transfer omine cum bono/limen aureolos pedes*, a passage which fits better in the context of c below. Cf. Pl. *Cas*. 815.

There are several instances in Ovid: *Met*. 10, 452 *ter pedis offensi signo est reuocata, ter omen / funereus bubo letali carmine fecit*; cf. *Her*. 13, 88; *Am*. 1, 6, 8; 1, 12, 3 f.; *Tr*. 1, 3, 55 f.; 2, 15 f. (quoted above under a); 3,4, 33 f. We cite Tibullus 1,3, 19 f.: *O quotiens ingressus iter mihi tristia dixi / offensum in porta signa dedisse pedem* (cf. 1, 7, 62). Kirby Flower Smith rightly notes *ad loc.* that the bad omen is particularly relevant at the start of an undertaking and at a threshold (see below under c).[11] Hence the anecdote concerning Tiberius Gracchus in Iul. Obsequens 27 (86), Val. Max. 1, 4, 2 and Plut. *Ti. Gr*. 17: leaving his house on the last morning of his life he stubbed his toe so violently that he wounded himself.[12]

Pliny lists *offensiones pedum* with other *omina* (*Nat*. 2, 24) but regards them as minor ones.[13] August. *De doctr. christ*. 2, 20, 31 lists a number of superstitions, *redire domum si procedens offenderit* amongst them. (For several Dutch examples see *WNT s.v.* voet (1975) 331: the early Dutch expression 'den voet tegen den dorpel stooten' signifies arriving without being welcome / arriving in a bad mood.) Biblical parallels may be found e.g. in Ps. 90, 12 *in manibus portabunt te ne*

---

[10] Cf. Sen. *Ag*. 628 f., where we find the much vaguer *tremuitque saepe / limine in primo*. See Tarrant 1976 *ad loc*. The story of the arrival of the Magna Mater in Rome provides an instance of a similarly ominous incident upon entrance: her ship was drawn up river, but got stuck. No one was able to move it until Claudia Quinta refuted the rumours that had maligned her chastity by pulling it free singlehanded. The accounts (collected by Frazer on Ov. *F*. 4, 291-348) usually concentrate on Claudia's chastity, but Ovid has time to note the horrifying impact of the evil omen on the bystanders (303 f.): *illa uelut medio stabilis sedet insula ponto / attoniti monstro stantque pauentque uiri*.

[11] Cf. also such expressions as *inoffensum ... pedem* Tib. 1, 7, 62; Ov. *Am*. 1, 6, 8; *Tr*. 3, 4, 33 f.; Ambr. *hex*. 1, 4, 14 p. 12, 21: *qui ... bonis operibus dextra laeuaque munitus inoffenso saeculi huius freta studet uestigio transire*.

[12] Add Plut. *Demetr*. 29, 2; *Cras*. 17, 6.

[13] Stubbing one's toe is not always ominous: Chrysippus could use it in a comparison: τῷ δ' ἀγαθῷ τὸ τὴν οὐσίαν ἀποβαλεῖν οἱονεὶ δραχμὴν ἀποβαλεῖν καὶ τὸ νοσῆσαι οἷον προσκόψαι (Plut. *Stoic. Repugn*. 30, 1048b = *SVF* 3, 153). Petronius 132 *et qui offenderunt saepe digitos, quidquid doloris habent; in pedes deferunt* does not necessarily refer to the ominous *pedis offensio*. Ogle 1911, 253 also quotes the doubtful instances in Novius, *Macc. Ex*. fr. 2 (Ribb. 2, 262) and Petr. 138.

forte offendat ad lapidem pes tuus (cf. Matth. 4, 6; Luc. 4, 11) and Ps. 114, 8 *quia eripuit animam meam de morte, oculos meos a lacrimis, pedes meos ab offensa.*[14]

The point of several anecdotes is precisely how such a bad impression is averted by the quick wit of the main actor. Thus much the same story is told of Scipio and Caesar by respectively Frontinus *Strat.* 1, 12, 1[15] and Suet. *Jul.* 59.[16] Frontinus adds another but similar story about Ceasar.[17] Augustus, too, turns the bad omen of a stumble into a good one in Dio Cassius 42, 58, 2-3 (cf. 62, 2).

Not every fall can be interpreted in the same manner,[18] but Dion. Hal. (exc.) 12, 16 (23) expresses his amazement that Camillus, who slips and falls while sacrificing, a portent that is easy to interpret, should have omitted to ward off impending evil.[19] Julian on the contrary, when the man who helps him into the saddle slips, *exclamauit ilico audientibus multis cecidisse qui eum ad culmen extulerat celsum*: it later turns out that Constantius died at that very moment (Amm. 2,1, 1, 2).[20]

c. It is not possible here to discuss all the beliefs surrounding the crossing of a threshold or boundary.[21] Yet these beliefs are relevant here since the robber at 6, 26 (147, 21 f.) says that the ass *pessumo pede domum nostram accessit* and the evil omen therefore applies to his entering, or at least approaching the house or abode of the robbers. One might even think of the possibility that the ass has actually entered the house left foot first.[22] On the other hand the context also insists on the fact that the ass is lame and there is an obscure reference to a Pythagorean saying that one should not pass the place where an ass had collapsed. The source of this reference is Hermippus (*ap.* Jos. *c. Ap.* 1, 164 = *FHG* 3, 41), who regards this as a precept borrowed from the Jews. But if this indication has any relevance to the *Met.* it probably should be quoted at 4, 5 (77, 24 f.) where the other ass has collapsed. (B. L. H.)

---

[14] Cf. also Appian *Syriaca* 56; see the expressions *lapis offensionis, petra scandali* at Jes. 8, 14; 1 Petr. 2, 7.
[15] *Scipio ex Italia in Africam transportato exercitu cum egrediens naue prolapsus esset et ob hoc attonitos milites cerneret, id quod trepidationem adferebat constantia et magnitudine animi in hortationem conuertit et 'plaudite' inquit 'milites, Africam oppressi'.*
[16] *Prolapsus etiam in egressu nauis uerso ad melius omine: teneo te, inquit, Africa.*
[17] *C. Caeasar, cum forte conscendens nauem lapsus esset 'teneo te, terra mater' inquit. Qua interpretatione effecit ut repetiturus illas a quibus proficiscebatur terras uideretur.*
[18] Different, though also with religious connotation, Liv. 8, 6, 2; Tac. *Germ.* 39.
[19] Cf. also 23, 1, 1, 6.
[20] Cf. Val. Max. 1, 5, 2; 1, 6, 6.
[21] E.g. Frazer on Ov. *F.* 2, 537. For rites at the threshold Bömer on Ov. *F.* 3, 137. Very full details in Ogle 1911, 253-271; see also *Handwörterbuch des deutschen Aberglaubens* (ed. Bächtold-Stäubli 1927-1942) vol. 7, 1520; R. Cavendish, *The Powers of Evil in Western Religion, Magic and Folk Belief,* London 1975, 231 ff. Verg. *A.* 2, 242 f. is, of course, relevant here too.
[22] It is hard to decide whether the fact that the Vampire Empousa has an ass's foot (and she is connected with Hecate) has anything to do with the robbers' revulsion. Cf. Ar. *Ran.* 293 f. and the Scholia *ad loc.*; also Lucian *V.H.* 2, 46. On the other hand, Stemplinger 1948, 122 indicates (without source) that an ass's left forehoof, when buried under the threshold, wards off evil.

APPENDIX II

7, 12 (163, 17) *Cuncti denique, sed prorsus omnes uino sepulti iacebant, omnes parati morti.*

φ: omnes parati morti; F: ōs *partī mortui* (with an erasure of ca. 6 spaces in the margin); AU: *omnes partim parati mortui*; E: *omnes partim parati morti*; S: *omnes partim mortui.*

Stewech: *iacebant humi, partim parati morti*; Colvius, Wover, Stewech: *iacebant latrones, partim parati morti*; Wower, Pricaeus: *iacebant, omnes passim parati morti*; Oudendorp, Valpy, Bétolaud, Clouard: *iacebant parati morti*; Groslotius: *iacebant, omnes pransi parati morti*; Hildebrand (1): *iacebant, omnes parati morti*; Hildebrand (2): *iacebant, partim mortui*; Novàk: *iacebant.*; Rohde 1875, 276: *iacebant ad somnos, partim mortui*; Purser: *iacebant, omnes partes mortui*; Eyssenhardt: *iacebant, omnem partim mortui*; vdVliet: *iacebant, omni parati morti*; Helm, Giarratano, Robertson, Terzaghi, Brandt-Ehlers, Pagliano, Scazzoso, vThiel: *iacebant, omnes pariter mortui*; Frassinetti, Augello: *iacebant, omnes partim mortui*; Gaselee: *iacebant, omnes pares mortuis*; Armini 1928, 305: *iacebant, omnes partitim* (or *raptim*) *mortui*; Armini 1932, 83: *iacebant, sparsim* (or *fartim*) *mortui.*

The uncorrected reading of F, *omnes partim mortui*, is defended by Frassinetti 1960, 128 and Augello 1977, 168. The latter sees an oxymoron in the *omnes partim* with the result that the sentence ends with an anti-climax: 'non erano tutti morti'. Augello himself rightly calls this interpretation bizarre. If retained, *partim* is better taken with the subsequent *mortui*. Thus Stewech, Colvius, Rohde and Eyssenhardt, all of whom locate the corruption in *omnes*, where, however, it should definitely not be sought. Frassinetti on the other hand takes *partim* in the meaning *magna ex parte*, referring to Tac. *Ann.* 1, 32 *tum conuulsos laniatosque et partim exanimos ante uallum aut in amnem Rhenum proiciunt*, but in that passage the desired 'senso maggiorativo' is not beyond doubt. See now *GCA* 1977, 170 for better instances. Frassinetti supports *partim mortui* by referring to 2, 25 (46, 4) *quis esset magis mortuus*. This parallel is not a very happy one, since in our passage there is no question of a comparison between two dead people; but though gradations in death are denoted by several expressions in Latin (e.g. *intermortuus, semimortuus, permortuus*), *partim mortuus* appears not to be among them.

We are not alone in rejecting *partim*: Wower *omnes passim parati morti*, Groslotius *omnes pransi parati morti*, Purser *omnes partes mortui*, Armini *omnes partitim (raptim, sparsim, fartim) mortui*, Helm *omnes pariter mortui*. The proposals by Wower and Groslotius may be objected to on the grounds that they both offer two conjectural words in place of the single word *partim*.

The conjectures of Armini and Helm — apart from the palaeographical unlikelihood of some, e.g. *sparsim* — may be objected to on the grounds that retaining *mortui* creates difficulties of interpretation. None of the robbers is dead; their death will be described in detail at 164, 9. The reader is forced to add *quasi*, cf. He-Kr. 'lagen alle... wie tot da'. Gaselee's conjecture *omnes pares mortuis* deals with this problem, but brings us no closer to the original reading. The reading in φ, a close and accurate copy of F, and the readings in the younger mss. show that F had in the marginal erasure (which is later in date than φ) *parati*. In the small erasure above *p* F must have shown a reference or correction sign. The scribe of φ in any case took it too be a correction sign. Augello objects to the reading of φ, because it is, in his opinion, the *lectio facilior*, but he is demonstrably wrong: some insight, not shown by the scribes of AUE, is needed to emend *mortui* after the adoption of the correction *parati*. The absence of expunction of the *u* in F has led to strange readings in the younger manuscripts.

If we adopt *parati morti* of φ as a good emendation for *partim mortui* of F, there is no need for other conjectures for *partim*, nor for corrections of *omnes* (i.e. Oudendorp's *iacebant parati morti* and vdVliet's *iacebant omni parati morti* are superfluous).

The emendation in φ is preferable also from the point of view of content: Tlepolemus' recapture of Charite corresponds in outline with Vergil's description of the capture of Troy by the Greeks. (1) The Greeks build a horse as high as a mountain: *A.* 2, 15 *instar montis equum... aedificant*. Tlepolemus tells the robbers that his name is *Haemus*, a doubly significant name (not only meaning "bloody", but also the name of a well-known mountain: see Hijmans in *AAGA* 1978, 115. (2) The Trojans, after bringing the horse within the walls, have started drinking: *A.* 2, 265 *urbem somno uinoque sepultam*. The robbers allow themselves to be made drunk after taking in Haemus. (3) The Trojans will die at the hands of the Greeks who come into the city later: *A.* 2, 333 *stat ferri acies mucrone corusco / stricta, parata neci*. The robbers, *parati morti*, die at the hands of Tlepolemus and his helpers. It is not impossible, therefore, that Charite's recapture constitutes an *imitatio cum uariatione* of Vergil's description of the capture of Troy.[1]

---

[1] This appendix has for the most part been written by Miss A. van Kempen, whose contribution we hereby gratefully acknowledge.

GENERAL INDEX

A

abitus 160, 4-6
abl. absolutus 154, 8-10; 157, 2-11
abl. instr. 147, 4-6; 156, 19-22; 157, 2-11; 170, 19-21
abl. instr + genit. obj. 149, 10-13
abl. loci 151, 1-4; 178, 10-14
abl. qual. 161, 25-162, 1
abl. resp. 167, 6-8
abl. sep. 159, 7-11
abl. temp. 154, 21-155, 4
abl. "complétant un verbe" 166, 11-15
abstemius 163, 11-14
abstractum pro concreto 151, 6-9; 157, 2-11; 159, 11-17; 161, 12; 167, 17-21; 175, 1-5
abundare 159, 26-160, 3
accedere + acc. 147, 22-24
accersere 169, 14-18
Acc. *trag.* 112 174, 8-10; 454 171, 15-19; 629 172, 22-24
accusare 171, 9-12
acc. adv. 151, 18-20
acc. reg. 152, 11-12; 161, 12-17
acc. of direction with *in* 164, 12
acerbus 175, 1-5
ad 159, 23-26
adeo 166, 23-167, 2
adfatim 162, 5-7
adgressura 159, 17-21
adhibere 171, 15-19
adhinnire 149, 22-26
(ad)ìnstar. + gen. 157, 2-11
Adjektiva (Häufung der -) 157, 11-18
adj. in -arius 172, 22-24
adj. instead of descriptive genitives 165, 4-7
adj. instead of the genit. of a noun 153, 8-12; 166, 5-7
adj. in -ilis 153, 16-18
adj. in -osus 153, 16-18
adjective (nominalized) 171, 15-19
adj. pleonastic 150, 13-17; 150, 17-151, 1
adlubescere 162, 24-26
ad modum 167, 2-4
adnominatio 168, 16-20
adoria 166, 3-5
adornare 150, 9-11
adpetenter 162, 24-26
adplodere 149, 8-10
adripere 176, 1-7
adscisci 157, 18-20
adsensi 157, 18-20
adulterium 166, 11-15
aduena (adj.) 162, 27-30

281

adv.+noun   166, 5-7
adv. in -tim   148, 13-16;   159, 11-17;   176, 1-7
adverbs in -im   162, 12-13;   176, 7-11
adv. in -iter   148, 5-9;   172, 22-24
adv. in (i)ter   150, 11-13;   162, 16-18
Ael. Spart. *Hadr.* 20, 6   161, 20-21
aeque   147, 18-20
aerumna   153, 23-27;   155, 17-156, 1
Aesch. *Agam.* 1604   157, 21-158, 2
Aesch. *Prom.* 17   158, 3-7;   192   158, 3-7;   218   158, 3-7
(adfirmare) affirmare   171, 2-4
Afran. *com.* 111   165, 7-9
Africanism   155, 17-156, 1
agaso   173, 12-14
ain   173, 12-14
Alc. Avit. *c. Eutr.* 1 p. 16, 9   162, 24-26
alacer   149, 3-4
Alf. *dig.* 32, 60, 3   165, 17-20
alioquin   166, 11-15;   171, 12-15
aliquando   166, 5-7
aliquantisper   149, 10-13
aliquis   165, 9-12
allegorical interpretation   151, 12-15;   155, 8-10
allegory   168, 3-11
alliteration   148, 13-16;   150, 1-3;   150, 5-9;   152, 7-10;   152, 24;   153, 16-18;   154, 5-8;   154, 13-18;   154, 18-21;   155, 4-6;   156, 19-22;   156, 22-157, 2;   157, 2-11;   157, 21-158, 2;   158, 3-7;   158, 19-21;   159, 11-17;   161, 21-25;   162, 19-21;   163, 1-3;   166, 3-5;   167, 8-12;   167, 12-15;   169, 10-14;   169, 14-18;   170, 4-7;   170, 14-18;   172, 17-21;   173, 14-18;   174, 10-14;   175, 1-5;   175, 5-9;   175, 13-17;   175, 17-19;
alumnus   163, 22-23
amasio   170, 10-14
amator   171, 20-172, 2
ambiguity   148, 21-23;   150, 3-5;   150, 11-13;   155, 8-10;   161, 3-5;   161, 12-17;   168, 3-11
ambiguity (Apuleian -)   152, 1-3
Ambr. *C. et Ab.* 2, 1, 4   165, 7-9
Ambr. *Hex.*   1, 4, 14 p. 12, 21   appendix I, n. 11
Ambr. *de Paen.* 18   174, 15-18
Ambr.   *Parad.* 3, 15   158, 25-28
Ambr. *Serm.*   49   156, 8-11
ambulare   152, 7-10
amicus   165, 1-2
Amm. 14, 2, 2   149, 3-4;   14, 5, 6   157, 21-158, 2;   14, 9, 2   157, 21-158, 2;   14, 15, 2   155, 17-156, 1;   16, 7, 4   176, 1-7;   16, 8, 4   157, 21-158, 2;   16, 12, 24   166, 16-21;   17, 13, 34   154, 13-18;   19, 8, 8   158, 8-9;   20, 6, 6   167, 22-168, 3;   21, 6, 6,   157, 2-11;   21, 8, 1   148, 5-9;   22, 1, 1, 2   appendix I *sub* b;   22, 7, 5   158, 21-22;   22, 9, 11   158, 8-9;   23, 1, 1, 6   appendix I, n. 19;   25, 5, 8   148, 5-9;   26, 6, 15   158, 8-9;   26, 10, 10   166, 10-11;   27, 10, 3   169, 8-10;   28, 1, 55   155, 10-16;   28, 1, 55   155, 10-16;   29, 1, 16   162, 24-26;   29, 1, 31   166, 16-21;   30, 1, 10   167, 22-168, 3;   30, 8   155, 17-156, 1;   30, 10, 6   154, 11-13;   31, 2, 5   158, 8-9;   31, 10, 8   157, 21-158, 2
an   154, 13-18
anagnorisis   158, 3-160, 15
anantapodeton   164, 7-11
anaphora   150, 5-9;   170, 14-18
"Anfangsstellung" (gedeckte)   165, 4-7

anfractus   147, 12-14
anicula   147, 3; 152, 14-18
antepollere + acc.   157, 21-158, 2
Anthol. Pal   3, 7   149, 14-20
anticipation   163, 23-26
anticlimax   170, 7-8
Antidot. Brux. 156   167, 8-12
antithesis;   151, 4-6;   152, 1-3;   154, 18-21;   155, 17-156, 1;   161, 12-17;   161, 18-19;   164, 18-21;   168, 26-169, 3
anus   147, 3
aperire   174, 3-5
Apic.   2, 42   153, 16-18
ἀπὸ-κοινοῦ construction   159, 23-26;   164, 18-21
Apollod. *Bibl.*   2, 5, 8   166, 21-23;   3, 5, 5   149, 14-20
Apoll. Rh.   3, 1259 f.   166, 7-10
Apon.   12   166, 21-23
aposiopesis   158, 17-19
App. *Syr.* 56   appendix I, n. 14
ἀπροσδόκητον   153, 18-23;   163, 26-164, 2;   172, 13-14
Apul. *Apol.*   *1 (1, 20)*   173, 4-6;   *2 (2, 15)*   166, 16-21;   *2 (3, 2)*   173, 18-22; *3(3, 13f.)*   164, 22-165, 1;   *3 (4, 20)*   165, 12-15;   *4 (6, 2)*   170, 10-14;   *4 (6, 11f.)*   150, 11-13;   *4 (6, 12)*   150, 11-13;   *6 (7, 21)*   169, 10-14;   *7 (8, 22)* 171, 15-19;   *8 (9, 22)*   148, 16-19;   *13 (15, 21)*   157, 21-158, 2;   *15, 7*   166, 23-167, 2;   *15 (17, 29)*   158, 28-159, 4;   *16 (18, 18)*   157, 18-20;   *17 (21, 2)* 166, 3-5;   *17 (21, 11)*   147, 4-6;   *25 (29, 15)*   149, 10-13;   *25 (29, 15)*   155, 6-8;   *27 (31, 21)*   157, 18-20;   *28*   165, 21-24;   *33 (39, 17)*   171, 12-15;   *37 (43, 8)*   156, 15-18;   *40 (47, 17)*   173, 18-22;   *41 (48, 13)*   176, 11-13;   *41 (48, 16)*   157, 18-20;   *48 (55, 14)*   164, 22-165, 1;   *51 (57, 25)*   164, 22-165, 1;   *51 (58, 5)*   149, 13-14;   *59 (67, 16)*   163, 11-14;   *62 (70, 24)*   156, 15-18;   *63 (71, 22)*   157, 21-158, 2;   *80 (89, 10)*   176, 7-11;   *85 (94, 10)*   172, 13-14;   *87 (96, 6)*   159, 7-11;   *87 (96, 24)*   165, 7-9;   *98 (108, 23)*   155, 17-156;   *102 (113, 23)*   170, 19-21
Apul. *As.*   *23 (59, 19f.)*   157, 18-20
Apul. *Flor.*   *1, 1 (1, 1)*   128, 24-149, 2;   *2 (2, 6-7)*   149, 4-5;   *2 (2, 7)*   171, 20-172, 2;   *9 (12, 7)*   159, 26-160, 3;   *11 (16, 3)*   153, 16-18;   *11, 2 (16, 12)*   148, 3-16; *13 (18, 4-5)*   149, 13-14;   *14 (19, 5)*   174, 3-5;   *17 (32, 4)*   156, 11-15; *18 (37, 8)*   165, 12-15;   *18, (37, 10)*   158, 17-19;   *18 (39, 3)*   155, 17-156, 1; *18 (36, 12)*   165, 21-24;   *18 (36, 15)*   176, 7-11;   *19 (40, 15f)*   149, 20-22
Apul. *Met.*   *1, 1 (1, 1)*   166, 7-10;   *1, 1 (1, 7)*   155, 10-16;   *1, 1 (1, 10)*   158, 22-25; *1, 1 (1, 11)*   155, 17-156, 1;   *1, 2 (2, 13)*   166, 16-21;   *1, 2 (11, 20f)*   175, 9-11;   *1, 3 (3, 9)*   149, 14-20;   *1, 3 (3, 9f)*   160, 16-18;   *1, 3 (3, 14)*   170, 25-171, 2;   *1, 5 (4, 20)*   152, 11-12;   *1, 5 (5, 6)*   157, 21-158, 2;   *1, 5 (5, 9)*   147, 22-24; *1, 6 (5, 15)*   157, 11-18;   *1, 6 (5, 18)*   162, 27-30;   *1, 6 (6, 6)*   168, 16-20;   *1, 6 (6, 7)*   157, 21-158, 2;   *1, 7 (6, 18)*   155, 10-16;   *1, 7 (6, 22)*   170, 418;   *1, 7 (7, 1)*   149, 22-26;   *1, 7 (7, 8)*   169, 10-14;   *1, 7 (7, 10)*   169, 26-170, 4;   *1, 8* 155, 17-156, 1;   *1, 8 (8, 1)*   155, 17-156, 1;   *1, 8 (8, 7)*   160, 16-18;   *1, 8 (8, 7)* 173, 12-14;   *1, 8 (8, 15)*   169, 24-26;   *1, 9 (8, 22)*   171, 12-15;   *1, 9 (8, 22-9, 2)* 159, 21-22;   *1, 9 (9, 6f)*   158, 28-159, 4;   *1, 9 (9, 9)*   167, 16-17;   *1, 9 (9, 9)* 171, 15-19;   *1, 10 (9, 17)*   164, 18-21;   *1, 10 (9, 18)*   147, 3;   *1, 10 (10, 1)* 151, 25-27;   *1, 11 (10, 15)*   163, 11-14;   *1, 11 (10, 20)*   149, 10-13;   *1, 11 (10, 24)*   147, 14-18;   *1, 12 (11, 9)*   158, 28-159, 4;   *1, 12 (11, 21-12, 1)*   155, 17-156, 1;   *1, 13 (12, 6)*   170, 22-24;   *1, 13 (12, 11)*   176, 7-11;   *1, 13 (12, 23)*   154, 1-2;   *1, 13 (13, 1)*   167, 22-168, 3;   *1, 14 (13, 8)*   148, 21-23;   *1, 14 (13, 10)*   164, 22-165, 1;   *1, 14 (13, 18)*   151, 12-15;   *1, 14 (13, 20)*   151, 25-27;   *1, 16 (14, 19)* 159, 4-7;   *1, 16 (15, 4)*   152, 1-14;   *1, 17 (15, 18)*   149, 3-4;   *1, 17 (15, 24)* 156, 1-5;   *1, 18 (16, 8)*   154, 5-8;   *1, 18 (17, 1)*   169, 14-18;   *1, 19 (17, 7f)* 175, 5-9;   *1, 19 (17, 16)*   165, 15-17;   *1, 19 (18, 10)*   176, 7-11;   *1, 19 (18, 14)*

283

169, 14-18; *1, 20 (18, 20)* 161, 21-25; *1, 20 (19, 3)* 149, 10-13; *1, 21 (19, 17)* 148, 5-9; *1, 21 (19, 18)* 156, 1-5; *1, 22 (20, 4)* 147, 22-24; *1, 22 (20, 12)* 154, 21-155, 4; *1, 22 (20, 12)* 155, 10-16; *1, 22 (21, 1)* 148, 5-9; *1, 23 (21, 4)* 176, 1-7; *1, 23 (21, 7)* 156, 7-8; *1, 23 (21, 8)* 170, 19-21; *1, 23 (21, 9)* 156, 1-5; *1, 23 (21, 16)* 159, 7-11; *1, 23 (21, 21f.)* 147, 10-12; *1, 23 (21, 21)* 147, 14-18; *1, 24 (22, 2)* 168, 23-26; *1, 24 (22, 8)* 162, 15; *1, 24 (22, 8)* 162, 16-18; *1, 24 (22, 11)* 173, 14-18; *1, 24 (22, 11)* 173, 14-18; *1, 24 (22, 14)* 151, 27-152, 1; *1, 24 (22, 17)* 153, 12-16; *1, 24 (22, 17)* 174, 18-22; *1, 24 (22, 22)* 160, 11-15; *1, 25 (23, 3)* 176, 1-7; *1, 25 (23, 20)*; 162, 2-5; *1, 26 (24, 1)* 152, 3-5.

Apul. Met. *2, 2 (25, 8)* 170, 14-18); *2, 2 (25, 15)* 164, 14-18; *2, 2 (25, 20)* 147, 22-24; *2, 2 (26, 8)* 149, 4-5; *2, 3 (16, 21)* 169, 20-24; *2, 3 (26, 17f)* 147, 22-24; *2, 4 (27, 7)* 147, 4-6; *2, 4 (28, 9)* 166, 21-23; *2, 5 (29, 6)* 169, 26-170, 4; *2, 5 (29, 10)* 169, 26-170, 4; *2, 5 (29, 13)* 173, 4-6; *2, 6* 148 10-11; *2, 6 (29, 24)* 173, 4-6; *2, 6 (30, 2)* 149, 20-22; *2, 7 (30, 13)* 154, 1-2; *2, 7 (30, 17)* 162, 19-21; *2, 7 (30, 19)* 176, 1-7; *2, 7 (31, 1f)* 154, 21-155, 4; *2, 7 (31, 2)* 170, 10-14; *2, 7 (31, 7)* 169, 3-8; *2, 7 (31, 7)* 169, 14-18; *2, 8 (31, 19)* 159, 26-160, 3; *2, 8 (31, 24)* 171, 9-21; *2, 10 (33, 11)* 162, 24-26; *2, 10 (33, 16)* 162, 24-26; *2, 10 (33, 18)* 163, 8-11; *2, 10 (33, 7)* 166, 16-21; 2, 10 (33, 7) 170, 7-8; *2, 11 (34, 4)* 149, 3-4; *2, 11 (34, 15)* 153, 12-16; *2, 11 (34, 15)* 174, 18-22; *2, 11 (34, 17)* 152, 3-5; *2, 12 (35, 1)* 155, 10-16; *2, 12 (35, 9)* 151, 4-6; *2, 13 (35, 18)* 156, 15-18; *2, 13 (35, 21)* 158, 22-25; *2, 13 (36, 5)* 173, 14-18; *2, 15 (37, 11)* 155, 10-16; *2, 17 (39, 3)* 149, 20-22; *2, 17 (39, 3)* 159, 7-11; *2, 17 (39, 8)* 176, 7-11; *2, 18 (39, 16)* 170, 10-14; *2, 18 (40, 11)* 172, 17-21; *2, 19 (40, 13)* 162, 15; *2, 20 (41, 9)* 174, 3-5; *2, 20 (42, 2)* 147, 4-6; *2, 21 (42, 11)* 157, 2-11; *2, 22 (43, 18)* 164, 18-21; *2, 22 (43, 24)* 172, 5-8; *2, 23 (43, 30)* 156, 22-157; *2, 23 (44, 7f)* 175, 1-5; *2, 24 (44, 20)* 147, 4-6; *2, 24 (44, 20)* 172, 5-8; *2, 24 (44, 22)* 173, 18-22; *2, 25 (45, 16)* 151, 25-27; *2, 25 (46, 4)* Appendix II; *2, 26 (46, 10)* 147, 4-6; *2, 26 (46, 17)* 154, 21-155, 4; *2, 28 (48, 17)* 158, 15-16; *2, 29 (48, 24)* 172, 17-21; *2, 29 (49, 13)* 148, 3-4; *2, 29 (49, 6)* 164, 18-21; *2, 30 (50, 6)* 172, 24-173, 2; *2, 30 (50, 9)* 175, 5-9; *2, 30 (50, 13)* 150, 1-3; *2, 31 (50, 21)* 163, 11-14; *2, 31 (51, 6)* 155, 10-16; *2, 31 (51, 8)* 152, 7-10; *2, 31 (51, 8)* 169, 14-18; *2, 32 (51, 15)* 154, 13-18; *2, 32 (51, 23)* 169, 10-14; *2, 33 (44, 1)* 148, 13-16.

Apul. Met. *3, 1 (52, 15)* 167, 12-15; *3, 1 (52, 19)* 151, 12-15; *3, 2 (53, 4)* 149, 22-26; *3, 2 (53, 16)* 173, 4-6; *3, 2 (52, 22)* 175, 5-9; *3, 3 (53, 24)* 156, 1-5; *3, 3* 158, 3-160, 15; *3, 3 (54, 11)* 150, 11-13; *3, 4 (55, 10)* 161, 3-5; *3, 5 (55, 24)* 149, 3-4; *3, 5 (55, 24)* 154, 13-18; *3, 5 (56, 2)* 169, 3-8; *3, 6 (56, 10)* 154, 13-18; *3, 6 (56, 11)* 164, 2-5; *3, 6 (56, 18)* 154, 18-21; *3, 6 (56, 19)* 158, 19-21; *3, 6 (56, 22)* 160, 24-161, 3; *3, 7 (57, 3f)* 159, 17-21; *3, 7 (57, 10)* 159, 7-11; *3, 7 (57, 14)* 167, 22-168, 3; *3, 7 (57, 15f)* 147, 4-6; *3, 7 (57, 11)* 156, 5-7; *3, 8 (57, 18)* 175, 1-5; *3, 8 (58, 6)* 170, 4-7; *3, 9 (58, 13)* 172, 5-8; *3, 9 (58, 16)* 172, 8-10; *3, 9 (58, 19)* 153, 3-7; *3, 9 (58, 20)* 149, 8-10; *3, 10 (59, 14)* 163, 22-23; *3, 10 (59, 16)* 170, 25-171, 2; *3, 10 (59, 20)* 160, 16-18; *3, 10 (59, 22)* 160, 4-6; *3, 11 (60, 1)* 147, 4-6; *3, 11 (60, 13)* 175, 25-26; *3, 11 (60, 18)* 159, 17-21; *3, 12 (60, 23f)* 158, 22-25; *3, 12 (61, 8)* 172, 3-5; *3, 13 (61, 26)* 152, 3-5; *3, 13 (61, 26)* 176, 7-11; *3, 13 (62, 4)* 169, 20-24; *3, 14 (62, 11)* 152, 3-5; *3, 14 (62, 15)* 156, 15-18; *3, 16 (64, 10)* 152, 3-5; *3, 17 (64, 24)* 172, 17-21; *3, 17 (65, 3)* 172, 24-173, 2; *3, 18 (65, 12)* 168, 26-169, 3; *3, 18 (65, 14f)* 159, 17-21; *3, 18 (65, 19)* 167, 22-168, 3; *3, 18 (65, 20)* 169, 10-14; *3, 18 (65, 23)* 166, 5-7; *3, 19 (66, 5)* 165, 7-9; *3, 20 (67, 11)* 155, 10-16; *3, 20 (67, 13)* 154, 5-8; *3, 20 (67, 14)* 171, 12-15; *3, 21 (68, 2)* 151, 25-27; *3, 22 (68, 27)* 159, 7-11; *3, 22 (69, 1)* 170, 10-14; *3, 22 (69, 1)* 173, 12-14; *3, 23 (69, 14)* 170, 10-14; *3, 23 (69, 14)* 171, 20-172, 2; *3, 23 (69, 19)* 165, 1-2; *3, 23 (69, 21)* 154, 11-13; *3, 23 (69, 21)* 163, 8-11; *3, 24* 164, 18-21; *3, 24 (70, 4)* 154, 21-155,

284

4;   *3, 24 (70, 9)*   161, 25-162, 1;   *3, 24 (70, 11)*   148, 11-19;   *3, 24 (70, 15)* 156, 11-15;   *3, 24 (70, 17)*   159, 11-17;   *3, 24 (70, 22)*   151, 16-18;   *3, 26 (71, 8f)*   148, 16-19;   *3, 26 (71, 10)*   171, 4-8;   *3, 26 (71, 15)*   156, 15-18;   *3, 26 (71, 17f)*   166, 7-10;   *3, 26 (71, 21)*   147, 10-12;   *3, 26 (71, 21)*   166, 11-15   *3, 27* intr. p. 1;   *3, 27 (72, 3)*   168, 26-169, 3;   *3, 27 (72, 5)*   intr. p. 3;   *3, 27 (72, 5)*   161, 12-17;   *3, 27 (72, 10)*   155, 10-16;   *3, 27 (72, 12)*   147, 20-22;   *3, 27 (72, 12)*   169, 18-19;   *3, 27 (72, 14f)*   161, 10-12;   *3, 27 (72, 17)*   165, 17-20; *3, 27 (72, 20-21)*   155, 10-16;   159, 11-17;   *3, 28*   155, 10-16;   *3, 28 (72, 21f)* 159, 7-11;   *3, 28 (72, 29)*   164, 14-18;   *3, 28 (73, 3)*   168, 11-16;   *3, 28 (73, 3-8)*   155, 6-8;   *3, 28 (73, 4)*   147, 10-12;   *3, 28 (73, 4)*   167, 16-17;   *3, 28 (73, 5)* 159, 7-11;   *3, 28 (73, 6)*   154, 5-8;   *3, 29 (73, 16-18)*   156, 8-11;   *3, 28 (72, 21 f)*   154, 11-13;   *3, 29 (73, 19)*   168, 26-169, 3;   *3, 29 (73, 23)*   169, 24-26;   *3, 29 (74, 5)*   171, 9-12.

Apul. *Met.*   *4, 1 (74, 1f)*   154, 5-8;   *4, 1 (74, 15f)*   148, 5-9;   *4, 1 (75, 1f)*   152, 19-20;   *4, 1 (75, 1)*   164, 18-21;   *4, 2 (75, 9)*   156, 19-22;   *4, 2 (75, 9)*   165, 7-9;   *4, 2 (75, 15)*   151, 4-6;   *4, 2 (75, 15-18)*   171, 15-19;   *4, 2 (75, 16)*   149, 3-4; *4, 2 (75, 17-18)*   149, 22-26;   *4, 2 (75, 19)*   156, 15-18;   *4, 2 (75, 24)*   164, 14-18;   *4, 3*   173, 2-3;   *4, 3 (76, 3)*   170, 19-21;   *4, 3 (76, 8)*   168, 3-11;   *4, 3 (76, 9)*   147, 14-18;   *4, 3 (76, 9)*   176, 1-7;   *4, 3 (76, 9)*   176, 1-7;   *4, 3 (76, 11-12)* 149, 8-10;   *4, 3 (76, 11)*   172, 14-17;   *4, 3 (76, 11-14)*   176, 1-7;   *4, 3 (76, 12)* 170, 25-171, 2;   *4, 3 (76, 14)*   147, 12-14;   *4, 3 (76, 20-23)*   166, 11-15;   *4, 3 (76, 24)*   164, 2-5;   *4, 3 (77, 1)*   149, 3-4;   *4, 3 (77, 4)*   176, 7-11;   *4, 3 (77, 4)* 176, 7-11;   *4, 4 (77, 8)*   167, 16-17;   *4, 5*   165, 9-12;   *4, 5 (77, 22)*   169, 3-8; *4, 5 (77, 23)*   147, 4-6;   *4, 5 (77, 24 f)*   appendix I sub c;   *4, 5 (77, 24-26)* 147, 24-148, 2;   *4, 5 (78, 1)*   168, 3-11;   *4, 5 (78, 6-8)*   166, 5-7;   *4, 5 (78, 7f)* 164, 7-11;   *4, 5 (78, 8)*   148, 12-13;   *4, 5 (78, 8)*   148, 12-13;   *4, 5 (78, 10)* 157, 11-18;   *4, 6*   152, 11-12;   *4, 6 (78, 21)*   163, 4-8;   *4, 6 (78, 21)*   163, 8-11;   *4, 6 (78, 24)*   148, 13-16;   *4, 6 (79, 1)*   172, 17-21;   *4, 6 (79, 10)*   169, 26-170, 4;   *4, 7*   148, 21-23;   *4, 7 (79, 13f)*   147, 4-6;   *4, 7 (79, 19)* 154, 2-3;   *4, 7 (79, 21)*   162, 19-21;   *4, 7 (79, 23)*   149, 22-26;   *4, 7 (79, 24)*   158, 3-7;   *4, 7 (80, 5f)*   152, 19-20;   *4, 8*   158, 3-160, 15;   *4, 8*   158, 3-160, 15;   *4, 8 (80, 6f)* 174, 15-18;   *4, 8 (80, 15f)*   152, 7-10;   *4, 8 (80, 16)*   174, 18-22;   *4, 8 (80, 17)* 154, 11-13;   *4, 8 (80, 21)*   147, 10-12;   *4, 8 (80, 22)*   intr. p. 3, n. 9;   *4, 8 (80, 24)*   156, 22-157, 2;   *4, 9-21*   158, 3-160, 15;   *4, 9 (81, 9)*   159, 11-17;   *4, 9 (81, 16f)*   158, 22-25;   *4, 9 (81, 19)*   171, 15-19;   *4, 9 (81, 19)*   172, 22-24;   *4, 10 (82, 2)*   intr. p. 3, n. 9;   *4, 10 (82, 12)*   159, 11-17;   *4, 11*   157, 2-11;   *4, 11 (82, 15)*   168, 16-20;   *4, 11 (82, 18)*   159, 7-11;   *4, 11 (82, 18)*   159, 7-11;   *4, 11 (82, 21f)*   153, 12-16;   *4, 11 (82, 23)*   149, 14-20;   *4, 11 (82, 25)*   158, 3-7;   *4, 11 (83, 4)*   intr. p. 3, n. 9;   *4, 11 (83, 6)*   175, 5-9;   *4, 11 (83, 7)*   163, 16-17;   *4, 12*   152, 21-24;   *4, 12*   157, 2-11;   *4, 12 (83, 10)*   169, 8-10;   *4, 12 (83, 14)* 149, 20-22;   *4, 12 (83, 17)*   170, 25-171, 2;   *4, 12 (83, 18)*   165, 17-20;   *4, 12 (83, 21-22)*   158, 21-22;   *4, 12 (83, 22)*   159, 17-21;   *4, 12 (84, 12)*   162, 13-14; *4, 13 (84, 22)*   171, 4-8;   *4, 13 (85, 2)*   169, 24-26;   *4, 14*   171, 2-4;   *4, 14 (85, 13)*   163, 23-26;   *4, 14 (85, 25)*   171, 2-4;   *4, 15 (86, 7)*   159, 21-22;   *4, 15 (86, 8)*   159, 23-26;   *4, 15 (86, 18-19)*   147, 10-12;   *4, 15 (86, 18)*   154, 21-155, 4;   *4, 16 f*   158, 3-160, 15;   *4, 16 (86, 21)*   154, 21-155, 4;   *4, 16 (86, 25)*   154, 21-155, 4;   *4, 16 (86, 27f)*   159, 17-21;   *4, 17 (87, 13)*   156, 1-5;   *4, 17 (87, 14-16)*   159, 7-11;   *4, 17 (87, 17)*   170, 19-21;   *4, 17 (87, 18)*   157, 18-20;   *4, 18 (88, 1f)*   175, 1-5;   4, 18 (88, 7 f)   159, 11-17;   *4, 18 (88, 8)*   172, 13-14;   *4, 19 (89, 1)*   172, 13-14;   *4, 19 (89, 10)*   162, 13-14;   *4, 20 (89, 12)*   174, 3-5;   *4, 20 (89, 16f)*   159, 7-11;   *4, 20 (89, 16 f)*   159, 23-26;   *4, 20 (90, 4)*   154, 13-18; *4, 21*   157, 2-11;   *4, 21 (90, 11)*   154, 11-13;   *4, 21 (90, 17f)*   158, 3-7;   *4, 21 (91, 2f)*   160, 11-15;   *4, 21 (91, 6)*   171, 15-19;   *4, 21 (91, 8)*   156, 22-157, 2; *4, 22 (91, 12f)*   152, 19-20;   *4, 22 (92, 1)*   164, 18-21;   *4, 22 (92, 3)*   159, 7-11;   *4, 22 (92, 6-10)*   175, 5-9;   *4, 22 (92, 8)*   148, 21-23;   *4, 22 (91, 10)*   163, 11-14;   *4, 22 (91, 11)*   158, 3-7;   *4, 23 (92, 12 f)*   147, 4-6;   *4, 22 (91, 12 f)* 148, 5-9;   *4, 23 (92, 19)*   170, 14-18;   *4, 23 (93, 2)*   intr. p. 3;   *4, 23 (92, 24f)* intr. p. 3, n. 10;   *4, 24 (93, 4)*   147, 24-148, 2;   *4, 24 (93, 9)*   147, 3;   *4, 24 (93, 13)*   151, 18-20;   *4, 24 (93, 14)*   152, 21;   *4, 24 (93, 14)*   161, 10-12;   *4, 24 (93, 15)*   165, 15-17;   *4, 24 (93, 20)*   158, 3-7;   *4, 25 (94, 4)*   147, 3;   *4, 25 (94, 5)*   158, 3-7;   *4, 25 (94, 7)*   172, 5-8;   *4, 26*   157, 11-18;   *4, 26*   164, 14-18;   *4, 26 (94, 16)*   170, 19-21;   *4, 26 (94, 18)*   149, 8-10;   *4, 26 (94, 23 f)*   161, 12-17;   *4, 26 (94, 25)*   162, 27-30;   *4, 26 (94, 25)*   162, 30-31;   *4, 26 (95, 8 f)*   160, 6-10;   *4, 26 (95, 1)*   intr. p. 3;   *4, 26 (95, 8)*   164, 13-14;   *4, 26 (95, 15)*   157, 2-11;   *4, 27 (95, 21)*   150, 5-9;   *4, 27 (96, 2)*   156, 19-22;   *4, 27 (96, 2)*   163, 4-8;   *4, 27 (96, 2)*   176, 1-7;   *4, 27 (96, 5)*   163, 8-11;   *4, 27 (96, 14)*   intr. p. 1;   *4, 27 (96, 15)*   intr. p. 1;   *4, 28 (96, 16)*   158, 19-21;   *4, 28-6, 24*   intr. p. 1;   *4, 29 (97, 17)*   160, 18-20;   *4, 30*   148, 10-11;   *4, 30*   148, 10-11;   *4, 31 (99, 5)*   159, 17-21;   *4, 31 (99, 5)*   161, 3-5;   *4, 31 (99, 6)*   171, 15-19;   *4, 31 (99, 8)*   169, 3-8;   *4, 33 (100, 21)*   153, 16-18;   *4, 33 (101, 2)*   147, 18-20;   *4, 33 (101, 6)*   164, 2-5;   *4, 33 (101, 7)*   162, 19-21;   *4, 34 (101, 17)*   156, 19-22;   *4, 34 (101, 18-19)*   163, 23-26;   *4, 34 (102, 3)*   175, 1-5;   *4, 34 (102, 5)*   164, 22-165, 1;   *4, 35 (102, 16)*   163, 23-26.

Apul. *Met.*   *5, 1 (104, 8)*   176, 1-7;   *5, 2 (104, 18)*   169, 24-26;   *5, 3 (105, 3)*   150, 17-151, 1;   *5, 3 (105, 5)*   149, 10-13;   *5, 3 (105, 7)*   161, 21-25;   *5, 4 (106, 1)*   163, 23-26;   *5, 5 (106, 16)*   156, 15-18, 169, 3-8;   *5, 5 (106, 21)*   176, 11-13;   *5, 5 (107, 2)*   156, 19-22;   *5, 6 (107, 18)*   147, 18-20;   *5, 6 (107, 18 f)*   164, 7-11;   *5, 6 (107, 28)*   158, 10-15;   *5, 7 (108, 10)*   175, 1-5;   *5, 8 (109, 6)*   162, 15;   *5, 8 (109, 13)*   157, 21-158, 2;   *5, 9 (109, 23)*   155, 17-156;   *5, 9 (109, 24)*   147, 18-20;   *5, 9 (110, 1)*   158, 21-22;   *5, 10 (110, 18 f)*   158, 28-159, 4;   *5, 10 (110, 25 f)*   159, 17-21;   *5, 11 (112, 3)*   166, 16-21;   *5, 12 (112, 20)*   164, 22-165, 1;   *5, 12 (113, 1)*   173, 4-6;   *5, 13 (113, 15)*   159, 26-160, 3;   *5, 13 (113, 16-17)*   158, 3-7;   *5, 13 (114, 6)*   173, 4-6;   *5, 14 (114, 20)*   175, 25-26;   *5, 15 (115, 2)*   162, 19-21;   *5, 15 (115, 5)*   166, 16-21;   *5, 15 (115, 9)*   149, 13-14;   *5, 15 (115, 12 f)*   161, 12-17;   *5, 15 (115, 15)*   162, 15;   *5, 16 (115, 18)*   170, 22-24;   *5, 16 (115, 20)*   157, 21-158, 2;   *5, 16 (116, 5)*   174, 10-14;   *5, 18 (117, 11)*   156, 19-22;   *5, 19 (118, 3)*   176, 11-13;   *5, 19 (118, 6)*   173, 4-6;   *5, 20 (118, 20)*   159, 7-11;   *5, 20 (119, 1)*   154, 13-18;   *5, 20 (119, 2)*   158, 3-7;   *5, 20 (119, 2)*   162, 27-30;   *5, 21 (119, 9)*   159, 11-17;   *5, 21 (119, 11)*   156, 19-22;   *5, 21 (119, 17)*   166, 16-21;   *5, 22*   158, 28-159, 4;   *5, 22 (119, 20)*   156, 15-18;   *5, 22 (120, 2)*   149, 5-8;   *5, 22 (120, 7)*   159, 11-17;   *5, 22 (120, 11)*   176, 1-7;   *5, 22 (120, 16)*   150, 11-13;   *5, 23 (121, 2)*   168, 11-16;   *5, 23 (121, 7)*   170, 4-7;   *5, 23 (121, 13)*   162, 27-30;   *5, 24 (121, 20)*   176, 1-7;   *5, 25 (122, 16)*   165, 15-17;   *5, 25 (123, 5)*   153, 7-8;   *5, 26 (123, 12)*   151, 25-27;   *5, 26 (123, 14)*   152, 3-5;   *5, 26 (123, 21)*   156, 19-22;   *5, 26 (123, 23)*   147, 18-20;   *5, 27 (124, 12)*   169, 20-24;   *5, 27 (124, 16)*   170, 4-7;   *5, 27 (124, 18 f)*   148, 13-16;   *5, 28 (125, 6)*   174, 15-18;   *5, 28 (125, 9)*   151, 6-9;   *5, 28 (125, 15)*   162, 30-31;   *5, 28 (125, 20)*   171, 20-172, 2;   *5, 29 (126, 11)*   148, 5-9;   *5, 29 (126, 13)*   156, 11-15;   *5, 29 (126, 13)*   156, 11-15;   *5, 29 (126, 13)*   175, 1-5;   *5, 29 (126, 15)*   162, 30-31;   *5, 29 (126, 19 f)*   175, 11-13;   *5, 29 (126, 20)*   165, 4-7;   *5, 30 (127, 7-8)*   158, 3-7;   *5, 31 (127, 26)*   173, 14-18;   *5, 31 (127, 29)*   174, 18-22;   *5, 31 (128, 5)*   151, 16-18;   *5, 31 (128, 7)*   173, 4-6;   *5, 31 (128, 15)*   165, 15-17.

Apul. *Met.*   *6, 1 (129, 9)*   149, 20-22;   *6, 1 (129, 10)*   160, 18-20;   *6, 2 (129, 20)*   173, 12-14;   *6, 3 (130, 26)*   164, 2-5;   *6, 4 (131, 14)*   159, 4-7;   *6, 5*   148, 10-11;   *6, 5 (132, 8)*   148, 19-20;   *6, 5 (132, 8-9)*   148, 19-20;   *6, 6 (132, 18)*   164, 22-165, 1;   *6, 7 (133, 11)*   147, 4-6;   *6, 8 (133, 20)*   164, 2-5;   *6, 8 (133, 21)*   173, 14-18;   *6, 8   (134, 7)* 172, 3-5;   *6, 9 (134, 14)*   151, 27-152, 1;   *6, 9 (134, 19)*   156, 19-22;   *6, 9 (136, 14 f)*   152, 14-18;   *6, 10 (135, 6)*   160, 10-11;   *6, 10 (136, 2)*   172, 17-21;   *6, 10 (136, 3)*   171, 20-172, 2;   *6, 13 (138, 9)*   169, 10-14;   *6, 13 (138, 13)*   167, 8-12;   *6, 14 (139, 1)*   172, 13-14;   *6, 14 (139, 5 f)*   175, 1-5;   *6, 16 (140, 15)*   149, 20-22;   *6, 16 (140, 17 f)*   159, 17-21;   *6, 16 (140, 20)*   174, 23-25;   *6, 17 (141, 10)*   165, 17-20;   *6, 17 (141, 13)*   156, 19-22;   *6, 17 (141, 12)*   172, 5-8;   *6, 17 (141, 14)*   174, 18-22;   *6, 18 (141, 17)*   153, 7-8;   *6,*

18 (142,1f) 147,20-22; *6, 18 (142,1)* 173,12-14; *6, 18 (142,1)* 173,14-18; *6, 18 (142, 16)* 149, 8-10; *6, 19 (143, 2)* 162, 15; *6, 20 (143, 23)* 165, 12-15; *6, 21 (144, 20)* 156, 19-22; *6, 21 (144, 20)* 174, 10-14; *6, 21 (144, 22)* 149, 20-22; *6, 21 (144, 23)* 154, 1-2; *6, 22 (145, 6)* 159, 7-11; *6, 23 (146, 6)* 166, 11-15; *6, 24 (146, 23)* 169, 20-24; *6, 25-32* intr. p. 1; *6, 25-7, 28* 148, 9-10; *6, 25 (147, 3)* 148, 21-23; *6, 25 (147, 3-6)* intr. p. 1; *6, 25 (147, 4)* 171, 4-8; *6, 25 (147, 19)* 164, 2-5; *6, 26 (147, 20)* intr. p. 2; *6, 26 (147, 21 f)* appendix I sub c; *6, 26 (147, 22)* appendix I; *6, 26 (148, 3)* 173, 23-174, 2; *6, 26 (148, 5)* 172, 22-24; *6, 26 (148, 20)* 156, 7-8; *6, 27 f* 171, 2-4; *6, 27 (149, 19)* 147, 3; *6, 28 (150, 1)* 170, 14-18; *6, 29* 151, 12-15; *6, 29 (151, 4-8)* 163, 23-26; *6, 30 (152, 4)* 164, 2-5; *6, 30 (152, 6)* 164, 2-5; *6, 30 (152, 11)* 173, 23-174, 2; *6, 30 (152, 15)* 174, 8-10; *6, 30 (152, 17)* 147, 3; *6, 31* 156, 19-22; *6, 31* 163, 8-11; *6, 31-32* intr. p. 2.

Apul. *Met.* 6, 25-32 + Bk 7 *147, 4* 165, 15-17; *147, 7* 147, 14-18; *147, 8* 147, 22-24; *147, 9* 147, 12-14; *147, 10* 148, 5-9; *147, 10* 152, 19-20; *147, 10* 158, 17-19; *147, 12* 155, 4-6; *147, 12* 175, 1-5; *147, 14* 167, 16-17; *147, 14-15* 148, 5-9; *147, 16* 147, 12; *147, 17* 147, 18-20; *147, 17* 153, 16-18; *147, 18* 152, 5-7; *147, 19* 148, 21-23; *147, 20 f* 152, 21-24; *147, 20* 169, 18-19; *147, 21 f* 147, 6-10; *147, 22 f* 152, 11-12; *147, 23* 171, 15-19; *148, 2* 148, 12-13; *148, 2* 148, 12-13; *148, 2* 172, 5-8; *148, 3 f* 152, 11-12; *148, 3* 152, 19-20; *148, 3* 160, 18-20; *148, 4* 147, 22-24; *148, 4* 152, 5-7; *148, 4-5* 148, 16-19; *148, 4-5* 148, 21-23; *148, 9* 155, 4-6; *148, 9* 159, 11; *148, 12* 156, 1-5; *148, 13* 148, 9-10; *148, 13* 172, 5-8; *148, 14* 164, 7-11; *148, 14* 164, 7-11; *148, 15-16* 174, 3-5; *148, 19-20* 149, 5-8; *148, 21-22* 149, 4-5; *148, 23* 164, 22-165, 1; *149, 3* 152, 3-5; *149, 3* 157, 21-158, 2; *149, 4* 148, 21-23; *149, 4* 149, 22-26; *149, 5-6* 149, 14-20; *149, 6-7* 158, 28-159, 4; *149, 7* 149, 20-22; *149, 7* 152, 3-5; *149, 13* 152, 5-7; *149, 13* 168, 3-11; *149, 18* 165, 15-17; *149, 18-19* 176, 11-13; *149, 19* 147, 3; *149, 19* 158, 28-159, 4; *149, 20* 152, 3-5; *149, 20-21* 149, 22-26; *149, 23* 167, 12-15; *149, 25* 148, 21-23; *149, 25* 150, 17-151; *149, 27 f* 153, 12-16; *149, 27* 162, 24-26; *149, 27-150, 1* 162, 24-26; *150, 2* 169, 8-10; *150, 10* 150, 13-17; *150, 13-15* 150, 9-11; *150, 14* 149, 13-14; *150, 16* 150, 17-151; *150, 16* 161, 20-21; *150, 16 f* 164, 14-18; *150, 17* 152, 19-20; *150, 22* 159, 17-21; *151, 1* 149, 14-20; *151, 4-6* 166, 21-23; *151, 7-9* 176, 11-13; *151, 12* 165, 12-15; *151, 14* 173, 6-9; *151, 17* 162, 27-30; *151, 19* 159, 23-26; *151, 19* 172, 3-5; *151, 20* 168, 20-22; *151, 24* intr. p. 2; *151, 24* 148, 20-21; *151, 24* 150, 13-17; *152, 3* 148, 21-23; *152, 4* 148, 9-10; *152, 5-7* 147, 20-22; *152, 6* 147, 18-20; *152, 7 f* 152, 13-14; *152, 6-7* 149, 13-14; *152, 7-10* 148, 4-5; *152, 8* 175, 17-19; *152, 9-10* 176, 11-13; *152, 10* 171, 15-19; *152, 10* 174, 10-14; *152, 11* 160, 18-20; *152, 11-12* 174, 23-25; *152, 13* 164, 14-18; *152, 13* 172, 10-12; *152, 15 f* 164, 7-11; *152, 17* 147, 3; *152, 19* 153, 8-12; *152, 19* 175, 5-9; *152, 21 f* intr. p. 3; *152, 22* 153, 18-23; *152, 23* 153, 18-23; *152, 24;* 153, 18-23; *152, 24* 155, 10-16; *152, 24* 160, 16-18; *152, 27* 160, 18-20; *153, 1* 174, 18-22; *153, 3* 151, 25-27; *153, 4* 153, 18-23; *153, 6* 153, 12-16; *153, 7* 169, 14-18; *153, 8* 153, 18-23; *153, 10 f.* 160, 20-24; *153, 10* 175, 5-9; *153, 11* 163, 1-3; *153, 12* 154, 2-3; *153, 12* 163, 1-3; *153, 13* 163, 1-3; *153, 13* 167, 22-168, 3; *153, 16-18* 148, 9-10; *153, 26* 172, 5-8; *153, 27* 162, 15; *7, 1-3 (154 f)* intr. p. 1; *7, 1-2 (154 f)* intr. p. 2; *154, 2* 172, 14-17; *154, 3* 161, 8-10; *154, 3* 172, 3-5; *154, 5* 156, 11-15; *154, 5 f* 174, 10-14; *154, 6* 154, 18-21; *154, 6* 155, 17-156; *154, 10* 154, 18-21; *154, 13* 154, 18-21; *154, 12* 154, 18-21; *154, 15* 155, 4-6; *154, 16* 154, 18-21; *154, 16* 155, 4-6; *154, 17-18* 147, 10-12; *154, 17-18* 147, 10-12; *154, 18-19* 155, 4-6; *154, 21* 156, 1-5; *154, 21-22* 155, 4-6; *154, 22* 154, 18-21; *154, 23* 154, 18-21; *154, 24* 154, 18-21; *154, 24* 155, 4-6; *155, 3* 154, 18-21; *155, 4-6* 149, 14-20; *155, 4-6* 160, 4-6; *155, 9* 147, 10-12; *155, 9* 156, 15-18; *155, 9* 166, 5-7; *155, 10* 156, 15-18; *155, 10-16*

155, 4-6; *155, 11* 155, 8-10; *155, 13* 155, 4-6; *155, 17* 176, 11-13; *155, 18* 153, 23-27; *155, 18* 155, 10-16; *155, 18* 166, 3-5; *155, 19* 156, 19-22; *155, 19* 165, 12-15; *155, 21* 158, 17-19; *155, 21* 166, 3-5; *155, 21* 167, 4-5; *155, 21* 169, 8-10; *155, 23* 166, 5-7; *155, 23* 170, 8-10; *156, 2* 149, 3-4; *156, 2* 148, 12-13; *7, 4-13 (156 f)* intr. p. 1; *156, 4* 154, 18-21; *156, 7-8* 148, 21-23; *156, 8* 170, 19-21; *156, 10* 173, 18-22; *156, 11* 163, 26-164, 2; *156, 11-15* 172, 8-10; *156, 12* 174, 23-25; *156, 12* 174, 23-25; *156, 15* 169, 8-10; *156, 17* 147, 10-12; *156, 19* 155, 17-156, 1; *156, 19* 170, 19-21; *156, 20* 153, 18-23; *156, 20* 169, 8-10; *156, 20* 170, 22-24; *156, 20* 172, 3-5; *156, 21* 153, 12-16; *156, 22 f* 160, 10-11; *156, 22 f* 161, 12-17; *156, 22* 162, 19-21; *156, 22* 175, 13-17; *156, 25* 148, 5-9; *7, 5 (157 f)* intr. p. 3; *157, 3* intr. p. 3, n. 9; *157, 3* 166, 5-7; *7, 5-8 (157 f)* intr. p. 3; *7, 5-8 (157 f)* intr. p. 3; *157, 16* 158, 3-160, 15; *157, 18* 170, 19-21; *157, 21 f* 157, 11-18; *157, 21-22* 158, 3-7; *157, 22* 169, 8-10; *157, 23* 169, 24-26; *157, 24* 158, 10-15; *158, 6* 160, 16-18; *158, 8* 160, 10-11; *158, 12* 160, 6-10; *7, 6-8 (158, 15-160, 15)* 162, 1-2; *158, 10-15* 157, 21-158, 8; *158, 11* 163, 4-8; *158, 12* 147, 18-20; *158, 20* 159, 4-7; *158, 22* 158, 17-19; *158, 26* 165, 15-17; *158, 27 f* 159, 26-160, 3; *159, 3-4* 148, 19-20; *159, 6* 158, 25-28; *159, 6* 159, 11-17; *159, 7 f* 158, 17-19; *159, 7-11* 159, 17-21; *159, 8* 158, 25-28; *159, 8* 159, 11-17; *159, 10* 172, 22-24; *159, 12* 166, 5-7; *159, 15* 162, 2-5; *159, 22 f* 158, 9-10; *159, 24* 162, 2-5; *159, 25* 172, 3-5; *159, 25* 172, 3-5; *159, 26 f* 158, 25-28; *7, 9 (160 f)* intr. p. 2; *160, 9* 162, 7-9; *160, 10* 156, 22-157; *160, 10* 157, 11-18; *160, 10* 158, 8-9; *160, 11 f* 157, 18-20; *160, 11* 162, 16-18; *160, 12* 161, 21-25; *160, 16* 152, 24; *160, 16 f* 157, 18-20; *160, 18* 157, 21-158, 2; *160, 20* 162, 15; *160, 21* 148, 5-9; *160, 22* 170, 22-24; *160, 23* intr. p. 4, n. 12; *161, 2-3* 158, 3-160, 15; *161, 5* 163, 1-3; *161, 8* 153, 7-8; *161, 9* 152, 1-3; *161, 12* 148, 9-10; *161, 12* 162, 16-18; *161, 13* 161, 25-162, 1; *161, 14* 165, 17-20; *161, 15* 161, 25-162, 1; *161, 18* 161, 21-25; *161, 19* 162, 16-18; *161, 21 f* intr. p. 3; *161, 21* 161, 18-19; *161, 25* intr. p. 4, n. 12; *161, 25* 159, 11-17; *161, 26* 166, 7-10; *161, 26/27* 161, 12-17; *161, 27* 155, 17-156; *162, 3* 170, 22-24; *162, 4* 162, 13-14; *162, 4-5* 165, 4-7; *162, 5* 159, 23-26; *162, 12* 174, 15-18; *162, 13* 159, 7-11; *162, 13* 176, 1-7; *162, 15* 152, 19-20; *162, 15* 170, 22-24; *162, 16* intr. p. 2; *162, 19* 149, 20-22; *162, 20* 169, 20-24; *162, 21* 162, 13-14; *162, 21* 163, 11-14; *162, 28* 163, 4-8; *162, 28* 163, 4-8; *162, 28* 164, 22-165, 1; *163, 3* 165, 17-20; *163, 5 f* intr. p. 1; *163, 5* intr. p. 5; *163, 5* 166, 11-15; *163, 6* intr. p. 5; *163, 6-8* 157, 21-158, 2; *7, 12 (163, 7)* 158, 10-15; *163, 7* 162, 27-30; *163, 10* 147, 3; *7, 12 (163, 10)* intr. p. 1; *7, 12 f (163)* 171, 2-4; *163, 14* 163, 23-26; *163, 14* 174, 5-7; *163, 17* Appendix II; *163, 18* 164, 7-11; *163, 18* 176, 1-7; *163, 23* 165, 9-12; *163, 24* 151, 4-6; *163, 25* 150, 13-17; *164, 1-2* 156, 8-11; *164, 2* 163, 22-23; *164, 7-8* 157, 11-18; *164, 8* 160, 11-15; *164, 9* appendix II; *164, 10* 148, 13-16; *164, 10* 148, 13-16; *164, 10* 152, 14-18; *164, 11* 176, 1-7; *164, 12* 165, 9-12; *164, 12* 170, 19-21; *7, 14-16 (164 f)* intr. p. 1; *164, 15* 165, 3-4; *164, 15* 165, 3-4; *164, 15* 171, 2-4; *164, 16* intr. p. 3; *164, 16 f* 152, 19-20; *164, 16* 164, 22-165, 1; *164, 16* 175, 5-9; *164, 18* 170, 22-24; *164, 19* 164, 14-18; *164, 21* 166, 7-10; *164, 22 f* intr. p. 3; *164, 22* 164, 14-18; *164, 24 f* 150, 5-9; *7, 15 (165)* intr. p. 3; *165, 3 f* 152, 19-20; *165, 6* 155, 8-10; *165, 6* 166, 5-7; *165, 6* 166, 5-7; *165, 6* 167, 2-4; *165, 6* 168, 16-20; *165, 6* 171, 4-8; *165, 7* 165, 15-17; *165, 7* 165, 17-20; *165, 7* 170, 10-14; *165, 7* 171, 2-4; *165, 8* 173, 12-14; *165, 9* 163, 26-164, 2; *165, 10* 171, 15-19; *165, 11* intr. p. 3; *165, 12* intr. p. 2; *165, 12* 166, 7-10; *7, 14 (165, 1)* intr. p. 2; *165, 16* 169, 14-18; *165, 17-20* 162, 30-31; *165, 18* 165, 4-7; *165, 18* 169, 24-26; *165, 19* 167, 8-12; *165, 24 f* 164, 14-18; *165, 26* intr. p. 3; *166, 1* intr. p. 3; *166, 3-5* 166, 10-11; *166, 3* 170, 19-21; *166, 5* 165, 7-9; *166, 5-7* 165, 15-17; *166, 5* 174, 7-8; *166, 7* intr. p. 3; *166, 8* 171, 15-

19;   *166,9*   165,4-7;   *166,10*   170,14-18;   *166,11*   165,9-12;   *166,11*   165, 9-12;   *166,11*   166,5-7;   *166,11-15*   171,12-15;   *166,12*   172,17-21;   *166, 14*   166,7-10;   *166,15*   172,17-21;   *7,16 (166,23)*   157,2-11;   *7,17-28 (166 f)*   intr. p. 1;   *167,3*   168,16-20;   *167,4*   173,4-6;   *167,6*   172,8-10;   *167,6* 171, 15-19;   *167,7*   165, 17-20;   *167,8*   172, 8-10;   *167,10*   165, 17-20; *167,12*   172,10-12;   *167,15*   176,1-7;   *167,17*   164,14-18;   *167,22*   167, 17-21;   *168,3*   167,22-168,3;   *168,4*   167,17-21;   *168,4*   168,16-20;   *168,4* 171, 15-19;   *168,5*   166,5-7;   *168,6*   173,6-9;   *168,7*   171,15-19;   *7,18 (168,9)*   149,13-14;   *168,10*   173,2-3;   *168,11*   169,3-8;   *168,15*   169,24- 26;   *168,16*   165,7-9;   *168,17*   167,2-4;   *168,18*   168,3-11;   *168,20*   167, 6-8;   *168,23*   169, 20-24;   *168,24*   intr. p. 3;   *168,25*   171, 4-8;   *168,25* 175, 17-19;   *7,21 (169 f)*   166,7-10;   *7,21 (169 f)*   169,26-170,4;   *169,1* 147, 10-12;   *169,2 f*   176,1-7;   *169,3*   171, 15-19;   *169,4*   171, 12-15; *169,5*   169,18-19;   *169,7*   175,11-13;   *169,8*   173,4-6;   *169,8*   173,4-6; *169,9*   172, 3-5;   *169,9*   158,25-28;   *169,12*   168,16-20;   *169,14*   165, 17-20;   *169,14*   167,6-8;   *169,14*   169,24-26;   *169,14*   170,14-18;   *169,16* 165, 15-17;   *169,17*   168,26-169,3;   *169,18*   153, 3-7;   *169,18*   153, 3-7; *7,20 (169,16)*   intr. p. 2;   *169,19*   170, 4-7;   *169,18*   147, 20-22;   *169,20* intr. p. 3;   *169,20*   171,12-15;   *169,20-24*   170,10-14;   *7,21 (169,20)*   intr. p. 2;   *169,21*   170,10-14;   *169,24-170,18*   169,18-19;   *169,24*   170, 14-18;   *169,25*   165,17-20;   *169,25*   166,5-7;   *169,25*   169,14-18;   *170,1* 166,5-7;   *170,3*   170,10-14;   *170,4-7*   168,3-11;   *170,4*   170,10-14;   *170, 6*   170,8-10;   *170,6*   170,22-24;   *170,7*   171,2-4;   *170,7*   171,15-19;   *170, 8*   166, 16-21;   *170,9*   148, 9-10;   *170,13*   158, 17-19;   *170,13 f*   165, 4-7; *170,13*   170,14-18;   *170,15*   172,3-5;   *170,17*   174,23-25;   *170,18*   166, 10-11;   *170,19*   170,14-18;   *170,19*   170,19-21;   *170,19*   172,3-5;   *170,21* 172, 24-173, 2;   *7,22-23 (170 f)*   intr. p. 2;   *170,22*   162,13-14;   *170,22* 169, 8-10;   *170,22*   169,26-170,4;   *170,22*   171,20-172,2;   *170,22*   171, 15-19;   *170,24*   171,12-15;   *170,25*   171,4-8;   *171,1*   172,8-10;   *171,2* 171, 15-19;   *171,5*   171, 9-12;   *171,5*   171, 9-12;   *171,7*   147, 4-6;   *171,7* 164, 18-21;   *171,9*   170,25-171,2;   *171,10*   147,4-6;   *171,10*   174,18-22; *171,11*   171,15-19;   *171,12*   166,10-11;   *171,12*   170,22-24;   *171,13* 172, 24-173, 2;   *171,14*   171,15-19;   *171,15*   174,5-7;   *171,17*   171,15-19; *171,17*   174,15-18;   *171,18*   168, 3-11;   *171,18*   170, 4-7;   *171,18*   171, 15-19;   *171,19*   148,9-10;   *171,20*   intr. p. 3;   *171,20*   172,5-8;   *171,22* 171, 15-19;   *171,23*   166,11-15;   *171,23*   171,15-19;   *171,23*   171,15-19; *172,1*   172,24-173,2;   *172,3*   159,23-26;   *172,3*   172,17-21;   *172,5*   153, 23-27;   *172,5*   174,7-8;   *172,6*   172,17-21;   *172,8*   172,17-21;   *172,9* intr. p. 3;   *172,9*   173, 23-174, 2;   *172,10*   152, 3-5;   *172,10*   172, 13-14; *172,11*   164,14-18;   *172,13*   172,10-12;   *172,13*   174,15-18;   *172,21* 175, 1-5;   *172,22 f*   148, 24-149, 2;   *172,22*   172,10-12;   *172,22*   173, 14- 18;   *172,23*   148,5-9;   *172,23*   173,6-9;   *172,23*   172,22-24;   *172,24*   148, 9-10;   *7,24 (172,17 f)*   152,7-10;   *172,24*   172,22-24;   *173,1*   170,19-21; *173,1*   172,22-24;   *173,2*   167,12-15;   *173,2*   172,22-24;   *173,2*   173,4- 6;   *173,2*   174,23-25;   *173,2*   176,11-13;   *173,4*   169,3-8;   *173,5*   172,22- 24;   *173,6*   174,18-22;   *173,8*   168, 3-11;   *173,12-14*   175,19-22;   *173,15* 173, 2-3;   *173,16*   175, 19-22;   *173,17*   172, 22-24;   *173,17*   172, 22-24; *173,18*   intr. p. 2;   *173,18 f*   173,17-19;   *173,20*   175,13-17;   *174,1*   174, 18-22;   *174,1*   174, 23-25;   *174,2*   172,10-12;   *174,3*   175, 17-19;   *174,8* 166, 3-5;   *174,8*   174, 26-175, 1;   *174,10*   171,9-12;   *174,11*   162,27-30; *174,12*   165, 15-17;   *174,12*   174, 18-22;   *174,14*   174, 18-22;   *174,15* intr. p. 3;   *174,15*   164,2-5;   *174,18*   174,18-22;   *174,18*   176,1-7;   *174, 19*   153,12-16;   *174,20*   166,10-11;   *174,20*   174,23-25;   *174,23*   intr. p. 3; *174,23*   167,22-168,3;   *7,25 (174,16)*   intr. p. 2;   *7,26 (174,10)*   152,7-10; *174,26*   174, 7-8;   *174,26 f*   175, 25-26;   *175,2 f*   175, 9-11;   *175,2*   175, 19-22;   *175,3-4*   147,10-12;   *175,5*   152,19-20;   *175,5 f*   166,7-10;   *175,6* 164, 14-18;   *175,7*   167, 4-5;   *175,9*   175, 11-13;   *175,12*   169, 3-8;   *175,*

289

13 f 175, 11-13; *175, 14* intr. p. 2; *175, 14* 149, 3-4; *175, 14* 149, 3-4; *175, 14* 173, 18-22; *7, 27 (175, 17)* 156, 19-22; *175, 18* 168, 23-26; *175, 18* 175, 13-17; *175, 19* 175, 11-13; *175, 19* 175, 11-13; *175, 21* 165, 3-4; *175, 24* 175, 9-11; *176, 2* 176, 7-11; *176, 5* 167, 12-15; *176, 9* 176, 11-13; *176, 13* 166, 21-23; *176, 13* 176, 7-11; *176, 14* 165, 15-17.

Apul. *Met.* *8, 1 (176, 15)* 165, 15-17; *8, 1 (176, 21)* 165, 7-9; *8, 1 (176, 22)* 156, 19-22; *8, 1 (177, 5)* 158, 19-21; *8, 1 (177, 7)* 162, 30-31; *8, 1 (177, 7)* 175, 5-9; *8, 1 (177, 8)* intr. p. 3; *8, 2 (177, 10 f)* 159, 7-11; *8, 2 (177, 10 f)* 159, 7-11; *8, 2 (177, 11)* intr. p. 3; *8, 2 (177, 14)* 170, 4-7; *8, 2 (177, 21)* 158, 10-15; *8, 2 (178, 6-8)* 169, 3-8; *8, 3 (178, 15)* 164, 22-165, 1; *8, 4* 164, 22-165, 1; *8, 4 (178, 22)* 162, 2-5; *8, 4 (179, 5)* 159, 11-17; *8, 4 (179, 9)* 171, 4-8; *8, 4 (179, 10)* 156, 1-5; *8, 4 (179, 13)* 170, 25-171, 2; *8, 4 (179, 14)* 159, 26-160, 3; *8, 5 (179, 25)* 167, 22-168, 3; *8, 5 (179, 25)* 172, 17-21; *8, 5 (180, 3)* 167, 22-168, 3; *8, 5 (180, 6)* 149, 3-4; *8, 6 (181, 2)* 151, 18-20; *8, 6 (181, 3 f)* 154, 8-10; *8, 6 (181, 12)* 170, 4-7; *8, 6 (180, 18)* 173, 4-6; *8, 7 (181, 19)* 175, 1-5; *8, 7 (181, 28)* 153, 23-27; *8, 7 (181, 28)* 172, 5-8; *8, 7 (182, 1)* 173, 4-6; *8, 7 (182, 10)* 148, 9-10; *8, 8 (183, 13)* 158, 17-19; *8, 8 (183, 16)* 162, 27-30; *8, 9 (184, 7)* 162, 27-30; *8, 11 (185, 23)* 159, 26-160, 3; *8, 11 (185, 27)* 154, 21-155, 4; *8, 11 (186, 4)* 163, 16-17; *8, 11 (186, 6)* 148, 19-20; *8, 12)186, 24)* 171, 9-12; *8, 12 (186, 11)* 169, 20-24; *8, 13 (187, 5)* 155, 17-156, 1; *8, 13 (187, 6)* 158, 28-159, 4; *8, 13 (187, 7)* 158, 25-28; *8, 13 (187, 16)* 172, 8-10; *8, 14 (187, 22)* 164, 7-11; *8, 14 (187, 26 f)* 174, 8-10; *8, 14 (188, 1)* 165, 17-20; *8, 14 (188, 6)* 153, 23-27; *8, 14 (188, 6)* 161, 21-25; *8, 14 (188, 6)* 172, 5-8; *8, 15 (188, 7)* 150, 1-3; *8, 15 (189, 12)* 159, 26-160, 3; *8, 15 (188, 9)* intr. p. 3, n. 10; *8, 15 (188, 19)* 172, 24-173, 2; *8, 15 (188, 21)* 173, 23-174, 2; *8, 15 (188, 23)* 162, 7-9; *8, 15 (189, 4)* 147, 14-18; *8, 16 (189, 18)* 167, 22-168, 3; *8, 16 (189, 19)* 170, 25-171, 2; *8, 16 (189, 19)* 171, 15-19; *8, 16 (189, 22 f)* 152, 7-10; *8, 16 (190, 1)* 165, 24-166, 2; *8, 17 (190, 12 f)* 166, 11-15; *8, 17 (190, 19)* 159, 7-11; *8, 17 (190, 19)* 163, 23-26; *8, 17 (190, 24)* 147, 4-6; *8, 18 (191, 11)* 152, 13-14; *8, 18 (191, 22)* 147, 6-10; *8, 19 (192, 4)* 167, 12-15; *8, 20 (192, 19)* 172, 17-21; *8, 20 (192, 25)* 159, 11-17; *8, 22 (194, 8)* 165, 21-24; *8, 22 (194, 10)* 157, 11-18; *8, 22 (194, 12 f)* 153, 18-23; *8, 23* 174, 10-14; *8, 23-25* intr. p. 2, n. 5; *8, 23 (194, 29)* 171, 4-8; *8, 23 (195, 1)* 170, 4-7; *8, 23 (195, 14)* 169, 18-19; *8, 24 (195, 21)* 155, 17-156, 1; *8, 24 (196, 7)* 167, 2-4; *8, 24 (196, 14)* 175, 1-5; *8, 24 (196, 15)* 153, 3-7; *8, 25 (196, 16)* 171, 20-172, 2; *8, 25 (196, 18 f)* 151, 9-11; *8, 25 (196, 23)* 154, 13-18; *8, 25 (196, 24)* 147, 3; *8, 25 (197, 1)* 166, 16-21; *8, 26* 169, 26-170, 4; *8, 26 (197, 22)* 160, 20-24; *8, 26 (197, 25)* 147, 4-6; *8, 26 (197, 25)* 147, 4-6; *8, 26 (198, 1)* 158, 19-21; *8, 26 (198, 1)* 171, 12-15; *8, 27 (198, 13)* 159, 26-160, 3; *8, 27 (198, 16)* 159, 26-160, 3; *8, 28 (199, 10)* 149, 13-14; *8, 28 (199, 10)* 171, 9-12; *8, 28 (199, 16)* 176, 1-7; *8, 29 (200, 15)* 171, 20-172, 2; *8, 29 (200, 22-26)* 162, 24-26; *8, 28 (199, 23)* 148, 24-149, 2; *8, 29 (200, 23)* 175, 13-17; *8, 29 (200, 23)* 173, 18-22; *8, 29 (200, 25)* 156, 8-11; *8, 29 (200, 27)* 174, 10-14; *8, 29 (200, 29)* 173, 4-6; *8, 30 (201, 11)* 172, 10-12; *8, 30 (201, 12-13)* 155, 10-16; *8, 30 (201, 14)* 172, 10-12; *8, 30 (201, 22)* 163, 21-22; *8, 31* 171, 4-8; *8. 31 (202, 11 f)* 150, 3-5; *8, 31 (202, 14)* 153, 7-8; *8, 31 (202, 14 f)* 153, 12-16; *8, 31 (202, 14)* 162, 27-30; *8, 31 (202, 16)* 170, 25-171, 2; *8, 30 (201, 18)* 162, 12-13; *8, 31 (202, 18)* 163, 4-8; *8, 31 (202, 18)* 171, 2-4; *8, 31 (202, 18)* 175, 13-17.

Apul. *Met.* *9, 1 (202, 5)* 166, 16-21; *9, 1 (202, 22)* 175, 13-17; *9, 1 (202, 24)* 172, 24-173, 2; *9, 1 (202, 26)* 168, 16-20; *9, 1 (203, 9)* 149, 4-5; *9, 1 (203, 10)* 172, 3-5; *9, 2 (203, 28)* 166, 5-7; *9, 2 (204, 8)* 168, 3-11; *9, 2 (204, 13)* 173, 4-6; *9, 3 (205, 3-4)* 162, 24-26; *9, 4 (205, 14)* 173, 6-9; *9-5 (206, 6)* 160, 4-6; *9, 5 (206, 10)* 149, 3-4; *9, 5 (206, 18)* 163, 11-14; *9, 7 (207, 22)* 176, 7-11; *9, 7 (207, 25)* 147, 4-6; *9, 7 (208, 1)* 176, 7-11; *9, 8 (208, 12)* 168, 3-11; *9, 8 (208, 18)* 171, 15-19; *9, 9 (209, 11)* 172, 22-24; *9, 9 (209,*

12) 173, 23-174, 2; *9, 9 (209, 18)* 160, 18-20; *9, 10 (209, 22)* 158, 17-19; *9, 19 (209, 23)* 170, 10-14; *9, 10 (210, 9)* 164, 2-5; *9, 11 (210, 18 f)* 165, 17-20; *9, 11 (211, 1)* 164, 14-18; *9, 11 (211, 3)* 162, 7-9; *9, 11 (211, 4)* 150, 17-151, 1; *9, 11 (211, 20)* 147, 18-20; *9, 11 (210, 21)* 158, 28-159, 4; *9, 11 (210, 21)* 164, 22-165, 1; *9, 11 (211, 22)* 149, 3-4; *9, 12 (212, 3)* 157, 21-158, 2; *9, 12 (212, 3)* 157, 21-158, 2; *9, 12 (212, 6)* 158, 8-9; *9, 13 (212, 13)* 175, 5-9; *9, 13 (212, 21)* 155, 10-16; *9, 13 (212, 21-23)* 155, 17-156, 1; *9, 13 (212, 21)* 176, 11-13; *9, 13 (212, 23)* 159, 11-17; *9, 13 (212, 23)* 170, 14-18; *9, 13 (213, 4)* 165, 12-15; *9, 14* 165, 17-20; *9, 14 (213, 6 f)* 150, 11-13; *9, 14 (213, 8)* 149, 13-14; *9, 14 (213, 16)* 168, 11-16; *9, 14 (213, 17)* 173, 4-6; *9, 15 (213, 25)* 161, 21-25; *9, 15 (214, 1)* 158, 17-19; *9, 15 (214, 1)* 170, 10-14; *9, 15 (214, 7)* 172, 17-21; *9, 15 (214, 12)* 166, 16-21; *9, 15 (214, 11)* 153, 8-12; *9, 15 (214, 15 f)* 164, 18-21; *9, 15 (214, 17 f)* 147, 4-6; *9, 15 (214, 17)* 155, 17-156, 1; *9, 15 (214, 19)* 171, 20-172, 2; *9, 16 (214, 24)* 171, 20-172, 2; *9, 16 (215, 4)* 165, 15-17; *9, 16 (215, 6)* 170, 10-14; *9, 17 (215, 24)* 149, 22-26; *9, 17 (215, 30)* 162, 13-14; *9, 17 (215, 30)* 172, 24-173, 2; *9, 18 (216, 20)* 159, 26-160, 3; *9, 19 (217, 4)* 156, 19-22; *9, 20 (217, 20)* 159, 7-11; *9, 20 (217, 22)* 158, 22-25; *9, 20 (218, 2)* 173, 4-6; *9, 20 (218, 6)* 152, 13-14; *9, 20 (218, 8)* 160, 4-6; *9, 20 (218, 9)* 156, 11-15; *9, 21 (218, 29)* 165, 12-15; *9, 22 (219, 24)* 162, 19-21; *9, 22 (219, 24)* 162, 19-21; *9, 23 (220, 9)* 154, 5-8; *9, 23 (220, 12)* 164, 18-21; *9, 23 (220, 19 f)* 150, 1-3; *9, 23 (220, 22)* 162, 27-30; *9, 24 (221, 8)* 171, 12-15; *9, 24 (221, 11 f)* 154, 5-8; *9, 24 (221, 15)* 164, 18-21; *9, 25 (221, 28)* 176, 1-7; *9, 25 (222, 4)* 157, 11-18; *9, 27 (223, 8 f)* 162, 12-13; *9, 27 (223, 22)* 166, 11-15; *9, 27 (223, 28)* 151, 21-25; *9, 28 (224, 5)* 170, 19-21; *9, 28 (224, 9)* 154, 5-8; *9, 28 (224, 11)* 172, 22-24; *9, 28 (224, 12)* 169, 24-26; *9, 28 (224, 20)* 154, 8-10; *9, 29 (225, 2)* 166, 16-21; *9, 30 (225, 11)* 149, 4-5; *9, 30 (225, 11)* 149, 4-5; *9, 30 (225, 19)* •157, 21-158, 2; *9, 30 (225, 19)* 157, 21-158, 2; *9, 30 (225, 20)* 171, 2-4; *9, 30 (226, 5)* 174, 3-5; *9, 32 (227, 6)* 165, 15-17; *9, 32 (227, 14)* 170, 4-7; *9, 32 (227, 16)* 171, 20-172, 2; *9, 33 (228, 4)* 162, 15; *9, 33 (228, 8 f)* 175, 13-17; *9, 36 (230, 9)* 158, 21-22; *9, 36 (230, 13)* 157, 2-11; *9, 37 (231, 2)* 165, 17-20; *9, 37 (231, 6)* 149, 14-20; *9, 37 (231, 14)* 166, 16-21; *9, 37 (231, 15)* 162, 27-30; *9, 38 (232, 11)* 161, 21-25; *9, 38 (232, 18)* 176, 1-7; *9, 39 (233, 18)* 171, 15-19; *9, 39 (232, 27)* 164, 2-5; *9, 39 (233, 9 f)* intr. 2 n. 5; *9, 40 (233, 38)* 149, 8-10; *9, 41 (234, 24)* 155, 17-156, 1 *9, 41 (235, 3)* 173, 6-9; *9, 42 (235, 23)* 149, 13-14; *9, 42 (235, 28)* 170, 10-14.

Apul. Met. *10, 1 (236, 13)* 149, 5-8; *10, 1 (236, 25 f)* 160, 16-18; *10, 2 (237, 9)* 159, 7-11; *10, 2 (237, 24)* 159, 11-17; *10, 2 (237, 27)* 170, 25-171, 2; *10, 3 (238, 10)* 170, 14-18; *10, 3 (238, 14)* 172, 8-10; *10, 3 (238, 15)* 160, 4-6; *10, 3 (238, 27)* 173, 4-6; *10, 4 (239, 5-6)* 157, 2-11; *10, 4 (239, 15)* 171, 20-172, 2; *10, 5 (239, 27)* 152, 19-20; *10, 5 (240, 8)* 169, 26-170, 4; *10, 5 (240, 10)* 159, 17-21; *10, 5 (240, 14)* 148, 24-149, 2; *10, 5 (240, 25)* 158, 17-19; *10, 5 (240, 25)* 170, 10-14; *10, 6 (241, 3 f)* 175, 1-5; *10, 6 (241, 9)* 148, 9-10; *10, 6 (241, 15 f)* 174, 10-14; *10, 6 (241, 21)* 157, 2-11; *10, 8 (243, 5)* 152, 24; *10, 8 (243, 6)* 156, 7-8; *10, 9 (243, 19)* 156, 22-157, 2; *10, 9 (243, 25)* 166, 11-15; *10, 9 (243, 29)* 176, 7-11; *10, 10 (244, 22)* 176, 1-7; *10, 11 (245, 3)* 172, 3-5; *10, 12 (245, 15)* 147, 4-6; *10, 12 (245, 27)* 164, 18-21; *10, 12 (245, 27)* 170, 22-24; *10, 12 (246, 23)* 169, 24-26; *10, 13 f* 166, 7-10; *10, 13 (246, 8)* 162, 19-21; *10, 13 (246, 15 f)* 164, 18-21; *10, 13 (146, 16)* 162, 15; *10, 13 (246, 23)* 163, 8-11; *10, 14 (247, 4)* 160, 4-6; *10, 14 (247, 5)* 157, 18-20; *10, 14 (247, 6)* 171, 9-12; *10, 14 (247, 17)* 169, 20-24; *10, 14 (247, 25)* 170, 8-10; *10, 15 (248, 7)* 164, 18-21; *10, 15 (248, 7 f)* 175, 5-9; *10, 15 (248, 17)* 165, 15-17; *10, 15 (248, 17)* 170, 22-24; *10, 16 (248, 23)* 162, 2-5; *10, 16 (249, 3)* 175, 5-9; *10, 16 (249, 7)* 153, 3-7; *10, 16 (249, 8 f)* 174, 10-14; *10, 17 (249, 23)* 163, 22-23; *10, 19 (251, 11-12)* 155, 10-16; *10, 19 (251, 20)* 158, 19-21; *10, 20 (252, 44 f)* 154, 5-8; *10, 21* 170, 14-18; *10, 21 (252, 15)* 158, 9-10; *10, 21 (252, 18)* 176, 1-7; *10, 21 (252, 19)* 165,

291

12-15; *10, 21 (252, 19)* 165, 12-15; *10, 21 (253, 6)* 173, 6-9; *10, 22 (253, 14)* 170, 10-14; *10, 22 (253, 19)* 171, 12-15; *10, 22 (253, 22)* 166, 16-21; *10, 22 (254, 4)* 163, 16-17; *10, 22 (254, 5)* 172, 14-17; *10, 23 (254, 20)* 170, 10-14; *10, 23 (254, 25)* 172, 24-173, 2; *10, 23 (254, 26)* 159, 26-160, 3; *10, 24 (255, 17f)* 150, 1-3; *10, 24 (256, 6)* 149, 20-22; *10, 26 (257, 23)* 154, 13-18; *10, 26 (258, 6)* 161, 21-25; *10, 27 (258, 20)* 148, 5-9; *10, 27 (258, 20)* 158, 9-10; *10, 28 (259, 11)* 149, 14-20; *10, 28 (259, 16)* 171, 4-8; *10, 29* 170, 14-8; *10, 29* 165, 12-15; *10, 29 (260, 1)* 170, 19-21; *10, 29 (260, 12)* 176, 11-13; *10, 29 (260, 17)* 161, 21-25; *10, 30 (261, 10)* 159, 11-17; *10, 30 (261, 18)* 159, 11-17; *10, 30 (261, 19)* 170, 10-14; *10, 30 (261, 20)* 176, 7-11; *10, 31 (262, 16)* 158, 28-159, 4; *10, 32 (263, 24)* 152, 24; *10, 33* 162, 1-2; *10, 33 (264, 20)* 150, 17-151, 1; *10, 34* 170, 14-18; *10, 34 (265, 3)* 176, 7-11; *10, 34 (265, 4)* 175, 1-5; *10, 34 (265, 7)* 147, 4-6; *10, 34 (265, 10)* 170, 4-7; *10, 34 (265, 13f)* 166, 7-10; *10, 35 (265, 27)* 171, 15-19; *10, 35 (266, 8)* 154, 5-8.

Apul. *Met.* *11, 2 (267, 16)* 154, 5-8; *11, 2 (267, 17)*; *11, 2 (267, 19)* 150, 3-5; *11, 2 (267, 20)* 171, 2-4; *11, 2 (267, 22)* 149, 3-4; *11, 2 (267, 23)* 165, 12-15; *11, 4 (268, 22)* 150, 11-13; *11, 5 (269, 13f)* 159, 17-21; *11, 6 (270, 14)* 173, 14-18; *11, 6 (270, 23)* 170, 10-14; *11, 6 (270, 24)* 171, 9-12; *11, 7 (271, 20)* 169, 10-14; *11, 8 (272, 4)* 147, 4-6; *11, 8 (272, 5f)* 158, 25-28; *11, 8 (272, 16)* 171, 15-19; *11, 8 (272, 17)* 159, 20-160, 3; *11, 8 (272, 18)* 152, 7-10; *11, 9 (272, 22)* 154, 13-18; *11, 9 (273, 12)* 174, 10-14; *11, 11 (275, 1)* 173, 4-6; *11, 14 (276, 18)* 163, 26-164, 2; *11, 14 (276, 25)* 159, 7-11; *11, 14 (276, 28)* 156, 7-8; *11, 14 (277, 1)* 152, 13-14; *11, 15 (277, 7)* 168, 3-11; *11, 15 (277, 12)* 150, 17-151, 1; *11, 15 (277, 18)* 155, 17-156, 1; *11, 15 (277, 21)* 174, 18-22; *11, 16 (278, 6 f)* 158, 19-21; *11, 16 (278, 7)* 150, 1-3; *11, 16 (278, 16)* 165, 12-15; *11, 16 (279, 7)* 164, 18-21; *11, 16 (279, 6)* 167, 22-168, 3; *11, 16 (279, 10)* 159, 26-160, 3; *11, 17 (279, 22)* 161, 5-8; *11, 17 (280, 2f)* 163, 22-23; *11, 20* 155, 8-10; *11, 20 (281, 17)* 154, 5-8; *11, 20 (281, 18)* 155, 6-8; *11, 20 (282, 3)* 154, 5-8; *11, 20 (282, 3-4)* 155, 10-16; *11, 20 (282, 4f)* 154, 21-155, 4; *11, 20 (282, 4f)* 164, 18-21; *11, 20 (282, 6 f)* 147, 10-12; *11, 21 (283, 7)* 175, 13-17; *11, 22 (284, 4)* 173, 14-18; *11, 22 (284, 17f)* 152, 1-3; *11, 23 (284, 22)* 149, 20-22; *11, 23 (284, 26)* 152, 3-5; *11, 26 (288, 1)* 147, 4-6; *11, 27 (288, 19 f)* 152, 5-7; *11, 28 (289, 13)* 158, 25-28; *11, 28 (289, 20)* 160, 11-15; *11, 29 (290, 20 f)* 175, 11-13; *11, 29 (290, 21)* 176, 11-13; *11, 30 (291, 6)* 158, 22-25.

Apul. *Mun.* *10 (145, 20)* 149, 10-13; *36, 12* 152, 13-14.

Apul. *Pl.* *1, 5 (87, 5)* 173, 4-6; *1, 7* 172, 8-10; *1, 12 (96, 10)* 149, 20-22; *1, 16, 22* 171, 12-15; *2, 8 (111, 2)* 173, 4-6; *2, 16* 170, 8-10; *2, 17 (244)* 159, 7-11; *2, 230* 158, 19-21.

Apul. *Soc.* *1 (6, 9)* 157, 18-20; *3 (10, 12)* 155, 17-156, 1; *5* 159, 7-11; *6, 133 (14, 2)* 149, 14-20; *11 (18, 18f)* 165, 12-15; *21* 159, 7-11; *21 (31, 15)* 166, 16-21; *22 (32, 14)* 162, 15; *22 (33, 1)* 162, 15; *2 (33, 11)* 150, 9-11; pr. *105 (2, 9)* 159, 26-160, 3.

Apul. περὶ ἑρμηνείας *7 (185, 23)* 176, 11-13

apud 166, 21-23

arbiter 151, 21-25

arbitrari 154, 13-18

arcere+dat. of advantage 175, 13-17

archaic words 155, 16-156, 1

archaism (pseudo-) 156, 1-5

archaism 149, 14-20; 166, 3-5; 166, 16-21; 167, 2-4; 167, 22-168, 3; 169, 26-170, 4; 171, 20-172, 2; 173, 4-6; 174, 18-22

Arion 151, 6-9

Ar. *Aves* 719 f 147, 22-24

Ar. *Ran.* 293 f appendix I, n. 22

Arist. *HA* 499 a 14 f 164, 14-18; 498 b. 4f 164, 14-18; 552 B 17 169, 18-19

armenta   166, 5-7
Arn.   1, 3   165, 17-20;   1, 55   171, 20-172, 2;   5, 16   149, 8-10
Arnob. Maior   V 32   158, 3-7
ars   159, 17-21
ascea   166, 16-21
asellus   159, 26-160, 3
asininus   148, 24-149, 2
Asinius Marcellus   152, 5-7
asinus   161, 3-5;   169, 24-26
assonance   156, 11-15;   156, 19-22;   156, 22-157, 2;   163, 22-23;   167, 4-5;   167, 12-15;   168, 16-20;   168, 23-26;   170, 4-7;   174, 10-14;   173, 14-18;   175, 5-9;   175, 17-19
astutulus   149, 4-5
asyndeton   150, 13-17;   162, 19-21;   169, 13-14;   169, 14-18;   174, 18-22;   175, 19-22
asyndeton (adversative -)   152, 7-10
at   175, 11-13
at ego   166, 7-10;   174, 23-25
atrocitas   175, 13-17
atrociter   170, 19-21
Aug. *Acta Concil. Oec.*   1, 5   166, 16-21
Aug. *C.D.*   4, 21   169, 18-19;   14, 7   166, 21-23;   15, 27   151, 6-9;   14, 16   170, 4-7;   7, 27   174, 15-18
Aug. *de Doctr. Christ.*   2, 20, 31   appendix I sub b.
Aug. *Ep.*   17 (44)   147, 22-24,   appendix I sub a;   129, 1   156, 22-157, 2;   129, 7   156, 22-157, 2;   133, 1   156, 22-157, 2;   164, 7   174, 3-5;   187, 24   148, 24-149, 2
Aug. *c. Faust.*   14, 1   164, 18-21;   19, 7   147, 6-10
Aug. *Gen. Litt.*   3, 9, 13   172, 13-14;   15, 496, 24 f   153, 18-23
Aug. *de Vtil. Ieiun.*   4, 5 (= 1 Cor. 9, 26)   166, 16-21
Aug. *in Psalm.* 57,7   166, 16-21;   75, 18   166, 16-21
Aug. *Serm.*   178, 9, 10   153, 12-16;   216, 6, 6   166, 16-21
Aug. *Serm.* coll. Morin,   p. 309, 6   163, 11-14
Aug. *c. Jul. op. imp.*   4, 56   148, 24-149, 2;   14, 24   148, 24-149, 2
aula   158, 19-21
Aurel. Vict. *de Caes.*   33, 3   165, 9-12
Aurel. Vict. *Epit.*   20, 9   152, 14-18
auscultare   153, 7-8
auscultator   166, 5-7
Aus. *Ecl.*   8, 32   153, 3-7
Aus. *Ep.*   13, 2, 37   166, 21-23;   26, 21   174, 10-14
Aus. *Epigr.*   41, 12   163, 11-14
Aus. *Epit. Her.*   32, 1   171, 20-172, 2
Aus. *Parent.* 27   148, 5-9
Auspic. *ad Arbog.* 98   164, 18-21
auersa Venus   170, 4-7
Avien. *Orb. Terr.* 480   172, 8-10
Avit. Brac. *Lucian. epist. rec. B3*   148, 21-23

B

beatitudo   150, 17-151
Bellerophon   152, 7-10
Bell. Afr.   5   149, 14-20;   25, 5   149, 14-20;   39, 4   149, 14-20;   41, 2   14-20;   42, 1   147, 12-14;   66, 2   149, 14-20;   68, 3   149, 14-20;   75, 4   149, 14-20
bellus   147, 4-6

benignus   152, 11-12
boare   156, 11-18
Boeth. *In categ. Ar.* 253 c (Migne)   166, 16-21
Boeth. *in Porph. comm. pr.*   2, 25   163, 11-14
Boeth. *in Porph. comm. sec.*   3, 3   163, 11-14
bono animo esse   163, 8-11
bonus   152, 11-12;   174, 23-25
brachylogy   161, 3-5;   171, 4-8
breuiculus   147, 14-18
"brièveté narrative"   162, 15
bulla   150, 13-17

C

cadauer   154, 2-3
Caecil. *com.*   196   153, 7-8
Cael. Aur. *Chron.*   5, 10, 123   157, 21-158, 2
Caes. *Ciu.*   1, 4, 5   172, 8-10
Caes. *Gal.*   1, 31, 13   170, 14-18;   4, 4, 26, 5   166, 11-15;   5, 13, 3   155, 4-6;   6, 31   155, 17-156, 1;   7, 45   169, 26-170, 4;   8, 39, 3   170, 14-18
calceus   159, 26-160, 3
calculus   152, 24;   160, 16-18
Callimachus *Hymn. in Del.*   63 f.   158, 10-15
Candidus   155, 8-10
calx   171, 4-8
camelus   164, 14-18
canities   175, 1-5
cantharus   163, 14-16
capistrum   173, 6-9
capitale exitium   166, 10-11
carbunculus   168, 26-169, 3
carnificina   174, 23-25
carpere   148, 9-10;   158, 17-19
Cassiod. *in Psalm.*   131, 11   174, 15-18
Cassiod. *Var.*   4, 45   163, 4-8;   7, 15, 3   166, 16-21;   11, 13, 6   159, 17-21
Cass. Dio   42, 58, 2-3   appendix I sub b.;   68, 5, 5   158, 22-25
castellum   162, 7-9
castratio   172, 3-5
castration (fear of)   172, 17-21
castrator   171, 15 f
casus   168, 3-11
Cat. *Agr.*   11, 5   169, 14-18;   27   165, 3-4;   33, 4   176, 1-7;   42   167, 2-4;   54   165, 3-4
Cato *Dict.*   78   150, 11-13
Catul.   2, 1   165, 15-17;   2, 3   162, 24-26;   3, 16   175, 13-17;   14, 22   appendix I sub a;   17, 14-15   156, 1-5;   21, 7   173, 4-6;   23, 26-27   150, 3-5;   36   150, 3-5;   41   165, 1-2;   42, 8   164, 18-21;   44   150, 3-5;   44, 15   147, 6-10;   45, 8 f.   appendix I n. 4;   50, 3   149, 22-26;   50, 15   148, 21-23;   61, 166 f.   appendix I sub b;   62, 62   162, 27-30;   63, 40   154, 5-8;   63, 75   154, 8-10;   64   151, 4-6;   64, 177 f.   148, 23-24;   64, 224   175, 1-5;   64, 258   158, 25-28;   64, 308   158, 25-28;   64, 349 f   175, 1-5;   76, 17   150, 5-9;   78 a, 3   175, 9-11;   99, 2   162, 24-26;   99, 6   174, 26-175, 1;   99, 14   162, 24-26;   108, 4 f.   153, 18-23
cauda   172, 3-5
causa finalis   151, 21-25
Cels.   2, 33, 2   165, 24-166, 2;   3, 21, 10   171, 20-172, 2;   7, 81, 1   172, 3-5
cenam inuadere   152, 14-18

censere + inf. pass.   152, 21-24
Cens.   6, 6   154, 18-21
centunculus   157, 21-158, 2;   160, 16-18
Cervantes *Don Quixote*   1, 25   175, 13-17
ceterum   173, 2-3;   176, 11-13
ceterus   170, 25-171, 2
change of case   175, 5-9
change of tenses   169, 3-8
Char. *GLK*   1, 32, 1   176, 7-11
Charite   147, 3
Charite (play on the name)   163, 8-11;   164, 22-165, 1
Chariton   161, 12-17;   1, 14   161, 12-17
chiasmus   153, 18-23;   153, 23-27;   158, 28-159, 4;   162, 19-21;   166, 23-167, 2;   169, 26-170, 4;   170, 4-7;   171, 15-19;   172, 5-8;   172, 17-21;   174, 10-14
cibaria   165, 21-24
Cic. *Ac.*   2, 108   159, 4-7
Cic. *Agr.*   2, 20   162, 24-26;   2, 93   171, 15-19
Cic. *Arch.*   8   163, 23-26;   31   157, 18-20
Cic. *Att.*   5, 4, 1   165, 7-9;   5, 11   159, 7-11;   5, 12   159, 7-11;   9, 13, 4   149, 22-26
Cic. *Brut.*   245   155, 6-8
Cic. *Cael.*   28   157, 11-18;   40   157, 2-11;   55   159, 11
Cic. *Carm. frg.*   7, 5   153, 18-23;   22, 16   153, 18-23;   32, 26   170, 14-18
Cic. *Cat.*   1, 1   169, 18-19;   1, 2   155, 17-156, 1;   1, 16   153, 12-16;   2, 1   148, 12-13;   2, 1, 2   158, 21-22;   3, 21   148, 12-13
Cic. *Clu.*   21   155, 10-16;   149   159, 21-22
Cic. *Diu.*   1, 12   appendix I n. 4;   1, 30   164, 18-21;   1, 55   165, 1-2;   2, 82   appendix I n. 4;   2, 84   147, 22-24;   2, 84   appendix I sub b;   2, 141   147, 3
Cic. *Fam.*   4, 13, 3   147, 4-6;   5, 1, 2   147, 4-6;   5, 2, 9   147, 4-6;   5, 5   154, 21-155, 4;   5, 12, 2   147, 4-6;   5, 12, 3   149, 20-22;   5, 16, 1   167, 17-21;   7, 1, 5   171, 20-172, 2;   8, 13, 1   158, 17-19;   12, 7, 2   156, 11-15;   13, 77, 3   175, 9-11
Cic. *Fat.*   1   156, 11-15
Cic. *Fin.*   2, 55   165, 1-2;   5, 4   155, 4-6;   5, 6   170, 4-7;   5, 24   162, 16-18;   5, 29, 87   171, 20-172, 2
Cic. *Flac.*   91   170, 10-14
Cic. *Font.*   45   158, 17-19
Cic. *Inu.*   1, 2-4   intr. p. 2 n. 6;   1, 37   147, 22-24;   2, 14   147, 22-24;   2, 49, 145   156, 19-22
Cic. *Lael.*   44   165, 1-2
Cic. *Leg.*   2, 28   155, 17-156, 1;   2, 59   166, 16-21;   3, 46   155, 17-156,1
Cic. *Lig.*   24   156, 1-5;   30   156, 8-11
Cic. *Mil.*   17   156, 5-7;   30   158, 17-19
Cic. *Mur.*   8   149, 4-5;   60   155, 17-156, 1
Cic. *N.D.*   1, 4   148, 12-13;   1, 95   150, 17-151;   3, 18   149, 4-5;   3, 63   155, 17-156, 1;   3, 68   150, 3-5;   3, 82   155, 10-16;   3, 89   151, 1-4
Cic. *Off.*   1, 33   162, 24-26;   1, 125   162, 16-18;   3, 90   155, 17-156
Cic. *de Orat.*   1, 32-33   intr. p. 2 n. 6;   1, 68   156, 11-15;   1, 168   166, 11-15;   1, 231   159, 26-160, 3;   1, 232   167, 22-168, 3;   2, 124   160, 10-11;   2, 182   162, 24-26;   3, 124   174, 5-7
Cic. *Part.*   10   166, 5-7
Cic. *Phil.*   3, 6   157, 2-11;   3, 18   156, 5-7;   4, 5   157, 2-11;   5, 28   157, 18-20;   8, 27   157, 18-20;   10, 14   158, 17-19;   13, 24   162, 16-18;   13, 35   168, 11-16;   14, 22   156, 11-15
Cic. *Pis.*   69   149, 22-26
Cic. *Q. fr.*   1, 1, 5   156, 1-5;   3, 3, 2   165, 4-7
Cic. *Red. Sen.*   8, 19   175, 13-17
Cic. *S. Rosc.*   23   172, 22-24;   70   156, 5-7;   89   150, 3-5

295

Cic. Sen. 5, 13   171, 9-12;   15, 51   153, 16-18
Cic. Sest. 93   157, 11-18;   96   150, 17-151
Cic. Sul. 33   148, 12-13;   48   152, 19-20;   77   155, 6-8;   88   174, 3-5
Cic. Tul. 54   155, 4-6
Cic. Tusc. 1, 48   147, 3;   1, 118   159, 4-7;   2, 2   155, 6-8;   3, 17   162, 24-26;   3, 62   175, 1-5;   3, 44   163, 11-14;   4, 2   155, 17-156, 1;   5, 4   175, 13-17
Cic. Ver. 1, 3, 7   172, 10-12;   1, 122   173, 2-3;   2, 3, 65   156, 1-5;   2, 3, 118   161, 21-25;   3, 67   147, 22-24;   3, 56   173, 2-3;   3, 187   165, 7-9;   3, 225   165, 12-15;   5, 14   156, 8-11;   5, 25   171, 15-19
CIL 1, 2525   175, 13-17;   3, 411, 14   173, 2-3;   5, 7066   170, 8-10;   9, 1530   170, 8-10
cinerosus   175, 1-5
cinis   171, 2-4
circumlocutio   158, 3-7
Ciris   132   170, 4-7;   44 f.   164, 22-165, 1
clades   170, 14-18;   174, 23-25
clanculo   162, 21-24
claudicare   152, 5-7
Claudius Hermerius *Mulomedicina Chiron*.   780   166, 16-21
clausula   149, 20-22;   150, 17-151, 1;   151, 18-20;   155, 17-156, 1;   156, 11-15;   158, 22-25;   161, 10-12;   167, 4-5;   167, 12-15;   168, 11-16;   169, 24-26;   172, 22-24;   173, 18-22;   174, 5-7;   175, 22-25
clausula (hiatus in the –)   162, 4-8
clausula heroica   158, 3-7
Clem. Al. *Strom*.   5, 6, 3   intr. p. 2 n. 6
climax   148, 3-4;   152, 21-24;   155, 10-16;   155, 17-156, 1;   173, 12-14
clitella   169, 26-170, 4
cluster of long cola   175, 17-19
Cod. Just.   9, 20, 7   155, 17-156, 1;   10, 15, 1, 1   158, 3-7
Cod. Theod.   8, 5, 23, 7   166, 21-23;   8, 5, 47   166, 10-11;   12, 1, 74   147, 22-24;   16, 5, 31   158, 21-22
cognoscere de   160, 20-24
coins   156, 22-157, 2
Col. 1 praef. 26   166, 5-7;   2, 10, 29   165, 3-4;   2, 16   169, 14-18;   4, 12, 1   176, 1-7;   6, 1, 1   171, 15-19;   6, 2, 3   164, 14-18;   6, 3, 3   165, 3-4;   6, 3, 5   171, 12-15;   6, 24, 1   166, 5-7;   6, 26, 3   172, 24-173, 2;   6, 27, 3   166, 11-15;   6, 27, 8   165, 3-4;   6, 27, 8   166, 11-15;   6, 27, 10   171, 12-15;   6, 36, 1 f.   166, 7-10;   6, 37, 1   166, 5-7;   7, 6, 3   162, 13-14;   7, 9, 13   172, 10-12;   8, 3, 7   176, 1-7;   10, 165   156, 11-15;   11, 2, 40   170, 25-171, 2
collective words   159, 26-160, 3
collegium   159, 21-22;   160, 11-15
colloquial language   152, 1-3;   155, 6-8;   157, 2-11;   169, 14-18;   170, 10-14;   170, 25-171, 2;   171, 9-12;   171, 12-15;   173, 12-14;   176, 7-11
colloquial Latin   161, 12-17
colloquial style   167, 2-4
colometry   147, 6-10;   148, 10-11;   166, 11-15;   170, 14-18;   172, 14-17;   174, 23-25
colon   167, 8-12;   168, 23-26;   169, 10-14
colon, length of   160, 16-18;   164, 22-165, 1;   166, 10-11;   166, 16-21;   166, 21-23
comic influence   155, 17-156, 1
commendaticiae litterae   154, 21-155, 4
commilito   158, 3-7
comminare   162, 12-13
se commodare   172, 24-173, 2
commodum   156, 12-157
commonere   149, 22-26
commorsicare   166, 16-21

296

comparare   148, 12-13
comparative with the function of the positive   154, 21-155, 4
comparere   155, 4-6
compauire   170, 14-18
compendiosus   152, 1-3
compilare   168, 3-11
compound with e–   155, 17-156, 1
comprobatus   157, 18-20
compta   150, 11-13
compulsare   170, 7-8
conceptaculum   169, 10-14
conceptus   169, 10-14
concinnare   162, 19-21;   169, 20-24
concubina   166, 7-10
condignus   164, 18-21
conducibilis   161, 18-19
congestare   150, 11-13
congrex   166, 5-7
congruus   154, 18-21
coniunx   156, 15-18
conjugatio periphrastica   169, 3-8
conlustrare   154, 5-8
conradere   160, 6-10
consarcinare   157, 21-158, 2
conspicari   169, 10-14
constitutus   160, 6-10
consulere   167, 22-168, 3
contamination   156, 5-7
contentus + inf.   165, 21-24
continari   173, 14-18
contra (after a verb of moving)   172, 8-10
contra   173, 23-174, 2;   175, 11-13
contrast   148, 16-19;   149, 20-22;   154, 13-18;   164, 22-165, 1;   175, 17-19
contruncare   152, 19-20
Corip. *Ioh.*   8, 423   170, 7-8
corium   165, 17-20
corpulentus   171, 12-15
coxa   167, 12-15
Couperus   167, 12-15;   168, 11-16
crapula   163, 11-14
crassities   157, 21-158, 2
crastino = cras   153, 12-16
criminari   171, 9-12
cruciabilis   170, 14-18
cruciatus   168, 11-16
cruentus   162, 27-30
crustatus   157, 21-158, 2
Culex 52   172, 10-12
cum primum + plu. perf. subj.   159, 7-11
cum   172, 13-14
cupressus   152, 13-14
cura   171, 20-172, 2
curiositas-motif   164, 5-6
curitare   164, 14-18
Curt.   3, 7, 6   172, 8-10;   4, 5, 11   159, 4-7;   4, 14, 25   158, 3-7;   6, 11, 16   147, 18-20
custodela   164, 13-14
Cypr. *Epist.*   22, 1   158, 3-7

297

D

damnosus   161, 3-8
dare + predicative gerundive   165, 7-9
dare + subst.   165, 1-2
dative (sympathetic)   158, 3-7
dat. auct.   158, 19-21;   173, 6-9
dat. commodi   173, 6-9
dat. of disadvantage   163, 14-16
dat. pro genit.   158, 3-8
de   166, 11-15;   171, 2-4;   171, 9-12
de instrumentale   163, 4-8
decoriter   150, 11-13
decunctor   172, 8-10
decutere   158, 17-19
dedere praecipitem   152, 14-18
dedolare   167, 8-12
De dub. nom. gramm.   5, 576, 6   164, 14-18
deducere   156, 1-5;   161, 10-12
delibutus   163, 22-23;   167, 12-15
delicatus   149, 22-26
deliciae   165, 15-17
denique   156, 1-5;   159, 21-22;   165, 1-2;   168, 26-169, 3;   172, 5-8
dentes candentes   166, 16-21
deponent with passive meaning   148, 9-10;   155, 6-8
detestatio   170, 4-7;   171, 15-19
deuersari   155, 17-156, 1
deuotio   164, 18-21
dexter = propitius   appendix I sub a
dicolon   154, 5-8
Dict.   2, 10   171, 15-19;   2, 10   171, 20-172, 2;   2, 16   167, 6-8
Dido   151, 18-20
diecula   174, 23-25
dies   155, 10-16;   168, 23-26
Dig.   2, 30, 2   147, 20-22;   3, 4, 1 pr. 1   160, 11-15;   5, 1, 18, 1   160, 6-10;   10, 1, 10   151, 21-25;   17, 2, 82   156, 22-157, 2;   31, 1, 89   152, 21-24;   38, 2, 14, 6   169, 14-18;   41, 1, 3   173, 14-18;   41, 7, 1   173, 14-18;   48, 8, 2   172, 3-5;   48, 16, 6, 3   156, 22-157, 2
diminutive   147, 14-18;   149, 4-5;   156, 19-22;   159, 26-160, 3;   160, 6-10;   166, 16-21;   168, 26-169, 3;   169, 26-170, 4;   171, 9-12;   174, 23-25
diminutive adjectives   162, 19-21
Diod. Sic.   4, 15, 3 f.   166, 21-23
Diom. *GLK*   1, 327, 18   176, 7-11
Dion. Hal.   12, 16 (23)   appendix I sub b
Dionys. Perihcg.   388   172, 8-10
Dioscorides   4, 105   175, 1-5
Dirce   149, 14-20
dirus   164, 18-21
dispar   157, 21-158, 2
disserere   156, 11-15
dissimulatio   158, 3-160, 15;   160, 24-161, 3
dissitus   171, 20-172, 2
dissolution of collectivity   165, 3-4
distinere   152, 14-18
distrahere   161, 12
dittography   156, 15-18
domi forisque   166, 3-5

domus   147, 22-24;   152, 11-12
donec+subj.   176, 7-11
Claud. Donat   II 46, 13   158, 3-7;   157, 16   158, 3-7   520, 7   158, 3-7;   11, 690 f.
     158, 3-7
Don. on Ter. *Ad.*   413   154, 21-155, 4
Don. on Ter. *Eun.*   259   162, 12-13;   515   166, 16-21
Don. on Ter. *Hec.*   95   164, 2-5;   441   166, 16-21
Don. on Verg. *A.*   9, 203   164, 22-165, 1
dos   160, 11-15
dramatic climax   176, 11-13
ducenarius 158, 17-19
dudum 157, 11-18
dum+imperf. ind.   174, 15-18
dum...iam   152, 19-20
"Du-Stil"   150, 3-5
dux   162, 16-18

E

ecce   147, 4-6;   147, 6-10;   152, 7-10;   152, 13-14;   174, 15-18
"echolalic responsions"   159, 17-21
edissere   156, 11-15
edomare   166, 3-5
edulia   150, 13-17
egenus   158, 8-9
ego   171, 15-19
ego-narrative   166, 7-10
egregius   168, 3-11
ellipsis   152, 21;   159, 11-17;   160, 4-6;   162, 21-24;   164, 5-6;   165, 12-15;   168,
     20-22;   169, 3-8;   171, 9-12;   175, 13-17
ellipsis   (of the pronoun) 166, 3-5
emasculare   171, 20-172, 2
emphasis   176, 11-13
en   160, 11-15
enallage   152, 7-10;   163, 4-8;   166, 11-15
enarrare   155, 17-156, 1
enim   169, 26-170, 4
Enn. *Ann.*   212V 154, 5-8;   221 169, 26-170, 4;   257 158, 3-7;   292 f 163, 16-17;
     514-18 166, 7-10
Enn. *Sat.*   3, 7   155, 17-156, 1;   6, 3, 7   166, 7-10
Enn. *scen.*   30   158, 25-28;   102   159, 4-7;   117 f.   148, 13-16
Enn. *uar.*   76   167, 2-4
Ennod. *dict.*   14, 4, p. 468, 14   166, 10-11
epic poetry   172, 13-14
epic style   163, 23-26
epiklesis   150, 5-9
Ep. Trai.   10, 14   174, 7-8
epiphora (polyptotic–)   158, 28-159, 4
epitheton   160, 20-24;   171, 15-19
epulae saliares   162, 7-9
equester   149, 22-26
equidem   161, 12-17
ergo   169, 18-19
ergo igitur   161, 8-10;   165, 7-9
"Erzählerdistanz"   162, 1-2
esse   158, 19-21

et   156, 1-5
et alius   161, 5-8
et cum dicto   176, 1-7
et ecce   172, 13-14
et...et   164, 5-6
etiam   159, 21-22
etiam tum   160, 4-6
etiam tunc   160, 4-6
euphemism   159, 23-26
Eur. *Alc.*   158, 3-7
Eur. *Antiop.*   fr. 48, 62   149, 14-20
Eur. *Bacch.*   298 f.   147, 3
Eur. *Heracl.*   730   appendix I sub b
Eur. *Ion*   1150   154, 5-8
Eur. *Med.*   401-409   148, 10-11;   502 f.   148, 23-24
Eur. *T.F.F.* Nauck   525 f.   176, 11-13
Europa   151, 6-9
Eutr.   6, 12, 3   158, 25-28
euadere + abl.   159, 23-26
"éventualité"   156, 1-5
ex instrumental   172, 17-21
exanclare   159, 4-7
ex animo meo   161, 18-19
excarnificare   155, 10-16
excipere   165, 15-17
excitus   149, 14-20
ex forma   173, 2-3
exinde   147, 10-12;   147, 22-24;   155, 4-6;   171, 15-19;   175, 1-5
exoculare   155, 17-156, 1
explicit reader   163, 23-26
exponere   162, 16-18
expositio   162, 16-18
expostulare   151; 16-18
expugnare   168, 23-26
exsecare   171, 12-15
extremus   155, 17-156, 1;   169, 3-8

F

fabricare   153, 23-27
fabula   147, 4-6;   151, 4-6
facere   150, 3-5
facere = instruere   162, 10-11
facies   157, 2-11
factio   159, 23-26
"fait réel"   156, 1-5
famosus   158, 10-15
fartilis   153, 16-18
fascia   176, 1-7
fera   153, 18-23
ferramentum   171, 20-172, 2
festinus   153, 3-7
festiuus   170, 10-14
Fest.   19L   176, 1-7;   115L   153, 8-12;   207L   148, 20-21;   207, 13L   170, 14-18;   314L   154, 1-2
fictional narrative   151, 4-6

300

fimus/-um   176, 7-11
finire   148, 21-23
Firm. *Math.*   4, 12, 8   147, 22-24;   6, 12, 1   150, 17-151, 1;   8, 20, 4   162, 13-14
firmiter   151, 16-18
flaccidus   159, 26-160, 3
fletus   175, 1-5
floridus   159, 26-160, 3
Flor.*Epit.*   2, 17, 7   147, 24-148, 2
fluctuare   156, 19-22
foculus   169, 14-18
foedus   166, 11-15
fomentum   169, 3-8
formare + double acc.   164, 18-21
formonsus   150, 5-9
forms in –arius   165, 7-9
formulaic diction   150, 5-9
fornix   161, 12-17
Fortuna   150, 3-5;   155, 17-156, 1;   156, 15-18;   166, 3-5;   167, 4-5;   169, 8-10
fortuna   158, 17-19
Fortun. *Germ.*   70, 187   166, 16-21
Fotis   164, 18-21
frigere   165, 24-166, 2
Frixum   151, 6-9
Fro. *Aur.*   1, 122   149, 3-4;   1, 232   164, 14-18;   1, 244   164, 14-18;   2, 72 (= 142, 18/19 vdH)   167, 22-168, 3;   5, 52 (81 vdH)   173, 2-3;
Fro. *ad M. Caes.*   85, 18 vdH   165, 12-15
Fron. *Str.*   1, 12, 1   appendix I sub b
fugere   158, 25-28
fuit quod   168, 23-26
Fulg. *Aet.*   p. 162, 11   170, 7-8
furfur   165, 24-166, 2
future simple   148, 21-23

G

Gal. *Vict. Atten.*   66   170, 25-171, 2
Gaius *Inst.*   2, 104   164, 13-14;   173, 18-22
gannitus   149, 20-22
Gel.   2, 3, 1   171, 15-19;   2, 3, 4   171, 15-19;   5, 13   156, 5-7;   5, 14, 21   171, 15-19;   3, 19, 4   154, 21-155, 4;   6, 8   171, 20-172, 2;   6, 16, 4   157, 18-20;   7, 10   149, 20-22;   9, 12, 20   172, 22-24;   11, 10, 4   165, 4-7;   12, 1, 3   158, 3-7;   13, 15, 1   173, 2-3;   14, 15   158, 15-16;   15, 1, 3   158, 25-28;   15, 2, 3   162, 19-21;   15, 4, 3   149, 20-22;   15, 10   152, 14-18;   19, 12, 1   157, 18-20;   20, 1, 39   157, 2-11;   15, 12   158, 25-28;   15, 12, 3   155, 17-156, 1;   17, 5, 3   149, 4-5;   17, 21, 36   165, 17-20
geminatio   155, 6-8
generosus   65, 4-7
genit. expl.   157, 2-11
genit. (inverse –)   160, 6-10
genit. in –um   156, 22-157
genit. obj.   149, 10-13;   150, 11-13;   152, 19-20;   155, 4-6;   155, 0-8;   171, 4-8
genit. part.   148, 24-149, 2;   169, 26-170, 4;   171, 15-19
genit. qual.   151, 6-9
genit. relat.   153, 8-12
genit. subj.   152, 19-20

301

genus deliberatiuum   161, 18-19
Germ. *Arat.*   672   174, 3-5
gerund   170, 7-8
gerundive in —undus   171, 15-19
"Gesetz der wachsenden Glieder"   152, 21-24;   169, 10-14;   171, 4-8;   172, 17-21
gestamen   169, 26-170, 4
gestire   147, 6-10;   151, 12-15;   161, 25-162, 1;   166, 7-10
gladius   162, 30-31;   171, 4-8
gladius nudus   158, 28-159, 4
gloria   150, 17-151, 1
Gloss.   2, 426, 7   166, 16-21;   2, 305, 27   166, 5-7;   2, 341, 28   166, 5-7
gnarus + acc. c. inf.   151, 16-18
graecism   163, 4-8;   164, 22-165, 1;   166, 3-5;   170, 10-14;   173, 18-22
Gramm. suppl.   68, 9   166, 16-21
grandis   162, 13-14
grassare   159, 7-11
gratias agere   174, 23-25
gratias meminisse   164, 22-165, 1
gratiosus   159, 17-21
gratulari   174, 7-8
gratulatio   174, 26-175, 1
grauans ruina   167, 17-21
grauare   167, 17-21
gregarius   165, 15-17;   169, 14-18
grex equinus   165, 4-7

H

habere + part. perf. pas.   161, 12-17
Haemus   intr. p. 3-4-5-6;   158, 10-15;   Appendix II
Haemus (significance of the name)   163, 4-8
hair-styling   150, 11-13
hapax   149, 14-20;   150, 13-17;   154, 5-8;   156, 22-157, 2;   159, 23-26;   160, 6-10;
    160, 16-18;   162, 5-7;   164, 14-18;   165, 9-12;   167, 22-168, 3;   171, 15-19
Heges.   1, 44, 3   158, 17-19
hem   162, 27-30
hendiadys   155, 10-16;   170, 8-10
herbare   165, 9-12
hercules   163, 14-16;   163, 23-26;   174, 5-7
(h)eriscere   151, 21-25
Hermippos   *FHG* 3, 41   appendix I sub b
Herod.   1, 24   151, 6-9;   1, 133   170, 25-171, 2;   1, 8, 2   165, 15-17
heus   170, 25-171, 2
hexameter   154, 5-8;   158, 3-7;   172, 8-10
hic   148, 12-13
hic meus   161, 3-5
Hier. *Ep.*   107, 6   147, 20-22;   108, 3   158, 17-19;   153, 5   171, 4-8
Hier. *in Ezech.*   7   158, 8-9
Hier. *Orig. Ez.*   11, 283   153, 23-27
Hier. *Vita Caes. Arel.*   2, 15   158, 8-9
Hil. *Hymn. Christ.*   34   159, 7-11
Hil. *in Matth.*   19, 11   164, 14-18
Hil. *Myst.*   9, 4   172, 8-10
Hil. *Trin.*   2, 33   166, 11-15;   2, 22   167, 8-12
hilarus/hilaris   162, 21-24
Hippocr. *cib.*   23   166, 16-21

hircus   162, 13-15
Hirt. *Gal.*   8, 8, 2   158, 22-25
hirudo   148, 16-19
historia   151, 4-6;   166, 21-23
Hist. Apol.   1, 1   158, 19-21;   37   154, 8-10
Hom. *Il.* 1, 4 f.   153, 18-23;   3, 210   157, 21-158, 2;   3, 227   157, 21-158, 2;   6, 506 f.   166, 7-10;   15, 263-269   166, 7-10;   18, 23 f.   175, 1-5;   24, 348   157, 21-158, 2
Hom. *Od.*   4, 699   173, 18-22;   9, 19 f.   158, 10-15;   11, 320   157, 21-158, 2;   13, 41-42   173, 18-22;   20, 18   148, 10-11
homoeoteleuton   150, 5-9;   151, 6-9;   152, 1-3;   156, 19-22;   158, 3-7;   161, 10-12;   161, 12-17;   163, 22-23;   164, 7-11
honestus   170, 10-14
honores   150, 9-11
Hor. *Ars* 99   147, 4-6;   220   162, 13-14
Hor. *Carm.*   1, 4, 4   168, 3-11;   1, 4, 16   151, 25-27;   1, 5, 13 f.   151, 1-4;   1, 9, 6   152, 11-12;   1, 17, 3   175, 13-17;   1, 18, 16   147, 3;   2, 7, 25   162, 16-18;   2, 11, 5 f.   160, 4-6;   3, 1, 28   156, 1-5;   3, 7, 13   174, 10-14;   3, 13, 3   162, 13-14;   3, 21, 13-20   147, 3;   3, 29, 30   155, 17-156, 1;   4, 4, 11   157, 21-158, 2
Hor. *Ep.*   1, 1, 24   149, 20-22;   1, 5, 16 f   147, 3;   1, 6, 28   159, 11;   2, 1, 72   147, 4-6;   2, 1, 199 f   147, 4-6;   2, 2, 37   appendix I sub a;   2, 2, 126 f   147, 3
Hor. *Epod.*   7, 15   156, 8-11;   8, 7   152, 7-10;   11, 10   150, 1-3;   11, 13-14   147, 3;   11, 25   165, 1-2
Hor. *S.*   1, 2, 27   162, 13-14;   1, 2, 45   172, 3-5;   1, 2, 65   167, 8-12;   1, 3, 85   171, 20-172, 2;   1, 4, 89   147, 3;   1, 5, 23   167, 8-12;   1, 6, 5   160, 20-24;   1, 6, 13   158, 25-28;   1, 7, 13   155, 10-16;   1, 1, 6   147, 4-6;   1, 10, 66   151, 4-6;   2, 1, 32 f.   151, 1-4;   2, 4, 75   165, 24-166, 2;   2, 6, 78   147, 4-6;   2, 7, 49   172, 3-5
hordeum   165, 3-4
horricomis/–comus   162, 13-14
hospitium   155, 10-16
humour   158, 10-15;   159, 23-26;   163, 26-164, 2;   165, 1-2;   175, 13-17;   175, 22-25;   176, 11-13
Hyg. *Astr.*   2, 4 (35, 16) 148, 21-23
Hygin. *Fab.*   1, 2   165, 9-12;   7 and 8   149, 14-20;   8, 4   165, 9-12;   30   166, 21-23;   120, 5   165, 9-12;   171   176, 7-11;   174   176, 7-11;   250   166, 21-23
hypallage   167, 8-12
hypallage (of a pronoun)   171, 9-12
hyperbaton   153, 12-16;   153, 18-23;   158, 15-16;   162, 1-2;   164, 2-5;   166, 3-5;   166, 10-11;   166, 11-15;   167, 8-12;   168, 23-26;   169, 10-14;   174, 3-5
hyperbole   164, 14-18;   167, 12-15
hysteron proteron   164, 7-11

I

I: attraction of the experiencing "I"   161, 25-162, 1
I: experiencing I   163, 4-8;   165, 12-15;   167, 6-8;   171, 4-8;   174, 5-7
I: narrating I   intr. p. 5;   163, 4-8;   164, 18-21;   165, 12-15;   167, 6-8;   171, 4-8;   174, 5-7
I: attraction of the narrating "I"   161, 21-25
iactare   170, 25-171, 2
Iambl. *Protr.* 21 D 58 C 6   appendix I, n. 6
Iambl. *V.P.* 156   appendix I, n. 2
iam et   148, 3-4
iamque   159, 4-7;   172, 10-12

303

ibi=eo   169, 10-14
ibidem=ibi   154, 21-155, 4
idem   155, 4-6
idoneus   147, 22-24
ignarus   172, 22-24
ilex   172, 10-12
ilico   173, 14-18
illac   151, 16-18
ille   156, 22-157, 2;   158, 10-15;   159, 26-160, 3;   160, 6-10;   165, 17-20;   167, 7-8;   168, 20-22;   169, 14-18;   172, 17-21;   173, 4-6
immanis   172, 17-21
se immittere in   172, 17-21
immo marking a climax   161, 21-25
immo uero   155, 17-156, 2
imperf. de conatu   149, 14-20;   165, 9-12;   166, 7-10;   171, 4-8
imperf. (descriptive –)   165, 9-12;   165, 12-15
imperf. on –ibam   156, 19-22
imperf. iterative   174, 23-25
impersonal passive   157, 2-11
impetus fortunae   156, 1-5
impetus saeuus   156, 1-5
implicit reader   163, 23-26
"implicit rhetoric"   165, 12-15
implied author   intr. p. 5
improbus   170, 7-8
impune ferre   175, 9-11
in   158, 25-28;   159, 26-160,3
in + acc.   151, 9-11
in causale   161, 21-25
in (consecutive)   168, 11-16;   169, 3-8
in finale   171, 12-15
in =inter   165, 4-7
inalbare   154, 5-8
inalbere   154, 5-8
inaugurare   160, 18-20
incernere   165, 24-166, 2
incertare   159, 26-160, 3
incingere   158, 25-28
inciuiliter   173, 12-14
incoram + gen.   158, 17-19
incoram   170, 10-14
incretus   165, 24-166, 2
incubare   159, 7-11
incuria + genit. obj.   150, 11-13
incurrere   169, 26-170, 4
incursare   167, 8-12
incursus   167, 2-4
indagare   162, 2-5
indagatus   159, 23-26
index   155, 120-16;   173, 14-18
indicative in iterative clauses   167, 17-21
indicium + genit. obj.   155, 4-6
indiciua   173, 14-18
indidem   176, 1-7
iners   171, 15-19
inescare   164, 18-21
infelix   151, 18-20

infestus   159, 26-160, 3
inf. fut. pass.   164, 22-165, 1
infit   156, 22-157, 2;   173, 14-18
infortunium   158, 25-28
ingerere   147, 18-20
ingratis   152, 5-7
inguen   176, 7-11
ingurgitare   162, 19-21
inhiare   170, 4-7
inigninus   169, 18-19
inmixtus   163, 11-14
inoculare   150, 13-17
inoculatus   150, 13-17
inprouidus   169, 10-14
inquirere   154, 13-18
inrepere   154, 21-155, 4
inrumpere   175, 1-5
insatiabilis + abl.   167, 4-5
inscendere   165, 4-7;   170, 10-14
inserere in   159, 26-160, 3
insiciatus   153, 16-18
insistere + dat.   157, 2-11
inspersus   171, 2-4
instar   157, 2-11
insuper   167, 17-21;   167, 22-168, 3
integer   172, 5-8
intempestus   151, 25-27
inter – (praefix)   151, 27-152, 1
interdum = interim   162, 21-24
interim   174, 10-14
interire   176, 11-13
intermiscere + dat./ + abl.   151, 12-15
interuisere   151, 27-152, 1
inuadere   172, 22-24
inuidia   158, 21-22
inuitare   170, 4-7
ipse   170, 14-18
irony   147, 3;   148, 5-9;   148, 16-19;   151, 4-6;   152, 11-12;   152, 14-18;   155, 17-156, 2;   157, 11-18;   158, 28-159, 4;   160, 6-10;   161, 12-17;   162, 1-2;   162, 13-14;   163, 26-164, 2;   166, 5-7;   166, 16-21;   167, 22-168, 3;   168, 3-11;   170, 10-14;   171, 9-12;   171, 20-172, 2;   174, 23-25;   174, 5-7
irony (Apuleian –)   160, 18-20
irony (dramatical –)   151, 9-11
Isid. *Nat.*   47, 4   168, 26-169, 3
Isid. *Orig.*   7, 6, 4 c   148, 16-19;   9, 3, 43   166, 16-21;   9, 18, 57   166, 16-21;   10, 14   174, 10-14;   10, 189   154, 8-10;   10, 229   161, 12-17;   10, 244   154, 21-155, 4;   10, 247   154, 21-155, 4;   16, 3, 5   153, 16-18;   19, 22, 23   147, 6-10;   20, 2, 1   170, 4-7
iste   150, 3-5;   158, 8-9;   160, 11-15;   174, 18-22
iste tuus   152, 7-10
iterative forms on –itare   164, 14-18
Itin. Alex.   25, 26, 34, 52   159, 11-17
iubere + inf. pass.   152, 21-24
iudicium   155, 17-156, 2
(ad–, con–) iungere puellam uiro   162, 27-30
iuuenis   161, 25-162, 1
iuuenis (feminine)   170, 10-14

305

iuxtaposition   164, 14-18;   165, 17-20
iuxtaposition of synonyms   158, 25-28
iuxtaposition (antithetical)   161, 21-25

J

jealousy   162, 24-26
Ioh. Chrys. *Comm.* on *Paul. ad Eph.* IV 12 t. XI 94   appendix I sub a
Ioh. Chrys. (Haupt *Opusc.* II 255 f.)   appendix I sub a
John   12, 12-15   163, 23-26
joke   148, 24-149, 2;   156, 8-11
Ios. *Antiq.*   7, 7, p. 194, 13   158, 3-7
Jos. *B.J.*   7, 69   163, 21-22
Jul. Val.   1, 24   150, 11-13;   1, 37   176, 1-7;   1, 43   159, 11-17;   2, 5   157, 11-18;   2, 27   159, 11-17;   2, 29   150, 11-13
Jul. Victor   26 (447, 6)   165, 24-166, 2
Iul. Vict. *Rhet.*   4, 4, p. 390, 8   173, 14-18
Iulian. *Aug. c. Iul. Op. Imperf.*   2, 1   172, 22-24
juridical expression   159, 26-160, 3
juridical language   169, 14-18;   173, 12-14;   173, 18-22;   174, 10-14
juridical term   173, 2-3;   173, 14-18
jussive of the past   175, 19-22
justice   164, 7-11
Iust.   1, 8, 8   163, 11-14;   2, 12, 24   149, 5-8;   4, 4, 7   157, 2-11;   7, 5, 3   164, 22-165, 1;   9, 1, 8   164, 22-165, 1;   24, 8, 1   163, 11-14;   34, 4, 2   169, 14-18
Juv.   3, 40   155, 17-156, 1;   3, 99   158, 10-15;   3, 262   169, 14-18;   3, 300   173, 2-3;   6, 268   170, 8-10;   6, 331   169, 26-170, 4;   6, 334   170, 14-18;   6, 597   166, 21-23;   6, 605   155, 17-156, 1;   6, 633   162, 21-24;   6, 638   156, 8-11;   7, 197 f.   155, 17-156, 1;   10, 5   appendix I sub a;   12, 27   151, 1-4;   14, 201-3   158, 8-9

L

labia   156, 11-15
laborare   171, 15-19
lacinia   156, 22-157, 2
lacrimosus   175, 1-5
Lact. *Inst.*   4, 14 14   176, 7-11;   7, 20, 9   170, 14-18
"langue archaïque"   147, 6-10;   153, 16-18;   171, 20-172, 2
"langue familière"   147, 18-20;   149, 10-13;   149, 22-26;   150, 5-9;   160, 6-10;   172, 8-10
"langue postérieure"   148, 24-149, 2;   152, 19-20;   154, 13-18
laniena   173, 2-3
laqueum induere   152, 13-14
largiri   153, 7-8
largitio   166, 23-167, 2
Larg.   16   171, 15-19
Laruae   151, 25-27
latibulum   173, 4-6
latrocinium   156, 5-7
latrocinium + preposition instead of a genit. obj.   156, 1-5
lauacrum   150, 11-13
lautiusculus   160, 16-18
legal term   156, 22-157, 2;   165, 4-7
leuis   160, 4-6

libentes as adverb   161, 21-25
libertas   150, 5-9
licet   148, 21-23;   156, 7-8;   175, 13-17
licet + adj. (adv.)   174, 7-8
lites atque iurgia   170, 8-10
litotes   148, 9-10;   155, 4-6;   159, 11;   161,12;   164, 2-5;   169, 20-24;   171, 15-19;
   172, 24-173, 2
Liv.   1, 3, 4   164, 22-165, 1;   1, 7, 6   149, 13-14;   1, 9, 6   149, 22-26;   2, 13, 1
   170, 14-18;   3, 40, 11   176, 11-13;   3, 47, 6   165, 15-17;   3, 53, 1   166, 11-15;
   3, 71, 6   173, 14-18;   4, 13, 4   167, 4-5;   5, 16, 5   172, 22-24;   5, 22, 3   148,
   5-9;   8, 6, 2   appendix I n. 18;   8, 9, 9   158, 25-28;   9, 8, 13   154, 1-2;   9, 6, 3
   172, 3-5;   9, 34, 18   156, 1-5;   10, 23, 12   164, 14-18;   10, 28, 10   169, 10-14;
   10, 45, 3   165, 12-15;   22, 32, 8   161, 21-25;   22, 39, 21   169, 10-14;   24, 23, 9
   149, 20-22;   24, 30, 14   159, 17-21;   24, 34, 10   172, 14-17;   25, 9, 2   166, 5-
   7;   25, 36, 11   148, 5-9;   25, 38, 8   158, 3-7;   26, 39, 3   166, 3-5;   26, 39, 9
   155, 4-6;   27, 17, 16   147, 10-12;   28, 27, 3   155, 6-8;   29, 16, 6   159, 17-21;
   30, 30, 16   169, 8-10;   30, 36, 5   159, 17-21;   31, 11, 15   164, 22-165, 1;   31,
   14, 12   163, 21-22;   33, 25, 6   165, 4-7;   33, 32, 2   171, 20-172, 2;   33, 41, 5
   157, 2-11;   40, 31, 5   149, 22-26;   40, 35, 12   157, 2-11;   41, 2, 1   172, 22-24;
   41, 21, 7   153, 18-23;   42, 49, 4   165, 12-15;   45, 5, 4   165, 7-9;   45, 5, 11
   155, 16-17
longe + comparative   169, 20-24;   171, 12-15
lorica   152, 11-12
lorus   152, 3-5
lubricare   168, 3-11
Luc.   1, 1   169, 24-26;   2, 358   164, 14-18;   4, 6-7   158, 28-159, 4;   4, 11 appendix I sub b;   6, 198   168, 11-16;   6, 538 f.   152, 14-18;   8, 645   147,
   18-20;   8, 654   172, 5-8
Lucian V.H.   2, 46   appendix I n. 22
Lucil.   2   164, 18-21;   377   164, 18-21;   617   158, 19-21;   747   157, 21-158, 2;
   898   158, 17-19;   1161 M   159, 26-160, 3;   1245   170, 14-18
Lucr.   1, 36   170, 4-7;   1, 133   163, 16-17;   1, 406   172, 8-10;   1, 525   149,
   20-22;   1, 677   160, 4-6;   1, 1032   153, 16-18;   2, 8   155, 17-156, 1;   3, 143
   171, 20-172, 2;   3, 190   173, 2-3;   4, 543   155, 4-6;   4, 1125   159, 26-160, 3;
   5, 30   166, 21-23;   5, 461 f.   154, 5-8;   5, 889   157, 21-158, 2;   5, 975   163,
   16-17;   6, 573   172, 14-17;   6, 1231   155, 17-156, 1
lucrum capere   147, 22-24
lucubrare   151, 25-27
lusus verborum   *see* wordplay
luxuries   171, 9-12

M

Macer *Dig.*   49, 1, 4   171, 4-8
machinarius   165, 17-20
Macr. *Sat.*   2, 2, 5   165, 4-7;   3, 16, 11   147, 3;   5, 14, 9   163, 23-26;   7, 8, 1
   153, 16-18
Macr. *in Somn. Scip.*   1, 6, 23   149, 10-13
magnus   161, 12-17;   165, 7-9
mandare   158, 13-18
manducus   153, 8-12
Manes   151, 25-27;   156, 19-22
Man.   1, 676   172, 8-10;   5, 160   148, 4-5
mansuetudo   153, 3-7
mansuetus/mansues   171, 15-19
Mars Comes   162, 2-5

Mars 162, 13-14
Mart. 1, 41, 11 158, 25-28; 1, 53, 5 158, 25-28; 2, 26 150, 1-3; 3, 16, 3 163, 1-3; 3, 68, 6 163, 11-14; 9, 36, 11 158, 25-28; 10, 47, 13 176, 11-13; 10, 63 158, 22-25; 11, 104, 7 176, 1-7; 14, 3 f. 147, 4-6
Mart. *Sp.* 7 153, 18-23
Mart. Cap. 1, 25 162, 24-26; 1, 31 162, 24-26; 2, 140 166, 21-23; 2, 165 167, 22-168, 3; 2, 181 162, 24-26; 8, 804 160, 4-6
masculus 148, 19-20
matrona 164, 14-18
Matth. 2, 13 f 163, 23-26; 4, 6 appendix I sub b; 21, 6- 9 163, 23-26
meditullium 168, 26-169, 3
medullitus 155, 17-156, 1
mehercules 147, 4-6; 171, 4-8
Meleagros 176, 11-13
membranulum 148, 16-19
membratim 148, 13-16; 174, 3-5
membrum 154, 21-155, 4
Menander *Aspis* 97, 148 155, 17-156, 1
Menander *fragm.* 463 155, 17-156, 1
mentiri + obj. 170, 7-8; 171, 2-4
mercatus 171, 20-172, 2
merito 156 1-5
metaphor 148, 9-10; 150, 3-5; 154, 5-8; 156, 19-22; 157, 11-18; 158, 22-25; 166, 16-21; 167, 17-21; 168, 16-20; 168, 23-26
metonymy 150, 11-13; 171, 12-15
metre 149, 13-14
military terms 147, 6-10; 157, 2-11; 158, 3-7; 158, 10-15; 160, 4-6; 160, 16-18; 166, 16-21
miluus 149, 4-5
minare 162, 12-13
Minuc. 22, 2 157, 18-20
miscere 159, 11-17
misellus 156, 19-22; 175, 13-17
miser 173, 4-6
mitella 159, 26-160, 3
mitra 159, 26-160, 3
molaris 167, 2-4
molestus 173, 23-174, 2
monetalis 158, 25-28
monilia 150, 9-11
monstrare 152, 1-3
monstruosus 170, 22-24
Mor. 60 169, 20-24
mors extrema 155, 10-16
mors suprema 155, 10-16
mors ultima 155, 10-16
"mots de la langue postérieure" 160, 4-6
"mots poétiques rares" 172, 8-10
Mul. Chir. 735 168, 11-16
multi numero 155, 10-16
multo tanta + comp. 165, 12-15
mutuus cupitor 162, 27-30
mythology 176, 11-13
mythology in the *Met.* 151, 6-9

N

"Nachstellung der Partizipia"   159, 11-17
Naev. com.   70   158, 17-19;   134   170, 14-18
nam   171, 2-4
nam et   155, 6-8
nam et = nam   161, 12-17
nare   151, 6-9
narrare   155, 17-156, 1
narrative (dramatic –)   159, 4-7
narrative (ego–)   163, 8-11;   165, 12-15
narrative levels   intr. p. 4
narrative technique   164, 22-165, 1;   166, 3-5
narrator   intr. p. 3, 5
natales   161, 12-17
natare   151, 6-9
natura   174, 18-22
nauiter   149, 20-22;   162, 16-18
nec   169, 20-24
nec mediocris   148, 9-10
nec mora nec cunctatio   160, 16-18
nec - neue   158, 8-9
nec... tantum... uerum... quoque   167, 8-12
nec... utique = nec... omnino   153, 8-12
nefas   171, 9-12
negation   171, 12-15
Nemes. *Cyn.*   22   149, 14-20;   164   166, 16-21
neologism   151, 12-15;   162, 5-7;   162, 13-14;   165, 4-7;   170, 4-7;   170, 25-171, 2; 171, 20-172, 2
Nep. *Ag.*   5, 4   163, 17-20
Nep. *Att.*   15, 3   155, 17-156, 1
Nep. *Praef.*   4   155, 4-6
ne... quidem   153, 3-7
nequissimus   168, 20-22;   175, 13-17
nescio an + participle   169, 8-10
nescio qui   162, 27-30
nihil quicquam   173, 23-174, 2
nil quicquam   155, 10-16
nimis   153, 18-23
nimium   156, 11-15;   171, 15-19
nimius   156, 11-15
nisi quod   159, 11-17
nisus   168, 16-20
nodosus   152, 3-5
nolens   171, 20-172, 2
nolle   159, 21-22
nomen   161, 25-162, 1
nominalized participles   154, 13-18
nominatim   159, 11-17
non = nonne   163, 1-3
Non. 25 L   153, 8-12;   54 L   154, 21-155, 4;   79, 5 L   156, 11-15;   158, 18 L   169, 26-170, 4;   179, 21 L   147, 10-12;   193 L   162, 30-31;   202, 8 L   155, 17-156, 1; 227 L   148, 5-9;   268 L   176, 7-11;   703, 13 L   158, 19-21;   711, 31 L   172, 22-24
nos   152, 1-3
notoria   156, 22-157, 2
notorius   156, 22-157, 2

nouns in –o   173, 12-14
nouns in –tor   161, 20-21;   171, 4-8;   172, 8-10
nouicius   161, 21-25
nouissima pars corporis   172, 3-5
nouissimum   148, 10-11
Nouius, *Macc. Ex. fr.* 2   appendix I, n. 13
noxius   171, 4-8
nubilis   169, 26-170, 4
nucleus   150, 13-17
nudus   153, 12-16
nullo negotio   163, 17-20
nullus = non   167, 12-15
numerare   153, 23-27
nunc   170, 10-14
nuntium   154, 8-10
nuptias = coitus   170, 4-7
nutus   150, 1–3;   169, 8-10
Nux   68, 69   176, 1-7

O

obire   171, 20-172, 2
obliquus   172, 22-24
Iul. Obsequens   27 (86)   appendix I sub b
obtundere   147, 14-18;   167, 12-15;   176, 1-7
obuerberare   172, 22-24
occipere   149, 13-14;   152, 5-7;   168, 3-11
occisio   147, 22-24
occupare   173, 14-18
ociter   147, 14-18
offensio pedis   appendix I sub b
officium   158, 19-21
offirmare   176, 1-7
omen   147, 22-24
Onos   15   154, 2-3;   17, 4   164, 18-21;   21, 3   164, 18-21;   22, 5   147, 10-12;   22, 6   147, 10-12;   22, 7   147, 14-18;   22, 7   147, 18-20;   22, 8   147, 22-24;   22, 8   147, 22-24;   22, 8   147, 24-148, 2;   23   147, 10-12;   23   148, 5-9;   23   149, 22-26;   23, 4   149, 3-4;   23, 4   151, 21-25;   23, 7   149, 8-10;   23, 7   149, 13-14;   23, 8   149, 14-20;   23, 9   149, 20-22;   23, 10   150, 3-5;   23, 10   150, 5-9;   23, 10   151, 9-11;   24   151, 12-15;   24, 1   151, 21-25;   24, 1   151, 25-27;   24, 2   148, 20-21;   24, 3   152, 1-3;   24, 6   152, 13-14;   24, 6   152, 13-14;   24, 7   152, 14-18;   25   153, 12-16;   25   153, 12-16;   25   153, 12-16;   25, 8   153, 23-27;   26   162, 19-21;   26, 3   159, 23-26;   27; 1   164, 14-18;   27, 3   164, 18-21;   27, 3   164, 18-21;   27, 3   164, 18-21;   27, 4   165, 3-4;   27, 6   165, 9-12;   27, 7-28, 1   165, 15-17;   27, 7-28, 1   166, 5-7;   28   166, 7-10;   28   166, 11-15;   28, 1-3   165, 17-20;   28, 3   165, 21-24;   29, 1   167, 8-12;   29, 1   167, 8-12;   29, 2   167, 12-15;   29, 2   167, 12-15;   29, 3   167, 16-17;   29, 4   167, 17-21;   29, 5   167, 22-168, 3;   30, 1-2   168, 3-11;   30, 3   168, 11-16;   30, 3   168, 11-16;   30, 4   168, 16-20;   31   169, 14-18;   31, 1   168, 23-26;   31, 2   168, 26-169, 3;   31, 2   168, 26-169, 3;   31, 3   169, 3-8;   32, 1   169, 20-24;   33   169, 26-170, 4;   33   171, 4-8;   33   171, 15-19;   33   172, 3-5;   33   172, 5-8;   38, 7   172, 10-12;   46, 7   164, 18-21;   56   165, 12-15
onustus   147, 6-10
operarius   170, 25-171, 2
opinio   155, 17-156, 1
opiparis/–us   162, 15

310

oppetere   157, 2-11
oppido   162, 24-26
opportunus   148, 20-21
optinere   165, 4-7
Orcus   151, 18-20;   172, 3-5
Orib. *Syn.*   5, 43   157, 21-158, 2
Oros. *Hist.*   2, 15, 1   162, 21-24
Osiris-cult   152, 5-7
ostendere   152, 1-3
otium   150, 17-151
Ov. *Am.*   1, 2, 30   147, 3;   1, 4, 31   162, 21-24;   1, 6, 8   appendix I sub b;   1, 6, 8 appendix I, n. 11;   1, 12, 3 f.   appendix I sub b;   2, 1, 6   164, 22-165, 1;   2, 5, 6   156, 8-11;   2, 6, 39   172, 3-5;   2, 16, 15-18   173, 18-22;   3, 7, 69   172, 3-5;   3, 11, 5   162, 30-31;   3, 11, 47   157, 2-11
Ov. *Ars*   1, 63   170, 10-14;   2, 584   172, 3-5;   3, 274   176, 1-7;   3, 450   156, 11-15;   3, 559   164, 22-165, 1;   3, 622   176, 1-7
Ov. *Ep.*   3, 43   149, 10-13;   9, 21   149, 10-13;   9, 67   166, 21-23;   10, 84   153, 18-23;   13, 81   158, 28-159, 4;   15, 252   168, 11-16
Ov. *Fast.*   I 67   appendix I sub a;   1, 391   170, 22-24;   1, 514   appendix I sub a;   2, 537   appendix I, n. 21;   2, 782   158, 3-7;   3, 137   appendix I, n. 21;   4, 291-348   appendix I, n. 10;   4, 659   164, 22-165, 1;   5, 398   appendix I sub a
Ov. *Hal.*   70   172, 13-14
Ov. *Her.*   4, 103   165, 24-166, 2;   13, 88   appendix I sub b;   21, 71 f.   appendix I sub a
Ov. *Ib.*   169 f.   153, 18-23;   535 f   149, 14-20
Ov. *Met.*   1, 212   159, 7-11;   1, 336   168, 11-16;   1, 647   156, 11-15;   2, 485   156, 11-15;   2, 681   165, 17-20;   2, 833 f   151, 6-9;   3, 213   148, 5-9;   4, 56   153, 12-16;   4, 785 f   152, 7-10;   5, 104   174, 18-22;   5, 262 f   152, 7-10;   6, 87 f   158, 10-15;   7, 117   172, 10-12;   7, 432   147, 3;   8, 113   148, 23-24;   8, 451-526   176, 7-11;   8, 516   176, 11-13;   8, 640   164, 22-165, 1;   8, 709 f   158, 8-9;   8, 717-718   156, 11-15;   10, 112 f   150, 13-17;   10, 126 f   153, 16-18;   10, 452   appendix I sub b;   11, 683   175, 1-5;   13, 915   168, 11-16;   14, 129 f   151, 12-15;   14, 189   167, 8-12;   15, 655   165, 17-20
Ov. *Pont.*   2, 3, 30   158, 21-22;   ,3, 1, 131-138   159, 17-21;   3, 2, 50   appendix I, n. 2;   3, 7, 3   148, 5-9
Ov. *Rem.*   338   176, 1-7;   634   149, 22-26
Ov. *Tr.*   1, 3, 55 f   appendix I sub b;   2, 15 f   appendix I sub a;   2, 15 f   appendix I sub b;   2, 566   168, 11-16;   3, 4, 33 f   appendix I sub b;   3, 4, 33 f   appendix I, n. 11;   3, 9, 28   148, 13-16;   3, 13, 27   172, 3-5;   5, 1, 13   158, 21-22
oxymoron   147, 3;   160, 16-18;   170, 22-24

P

P. Mich.   214   158, 25-28
pabulum   147, 24-148, 2
pacare itinera   157, 2-11
Pac. *fr.*   366   155, 17-156, 1
Pac. *Trag.*   332   172, 22-24
paene   155, 10-16
Pall. *Hist. Mon.*   1, 17   171, 20-172, 2;   1, 26   176, 1-7
Paneg.   91, 7   159, 4-7
pannulus   158, 8-9;   160, 10-11
parallelism   149, 22-26;   151, 6-9;   157, 2-11,   157, 11-18;   158, 3-7;   168, 11-16;   168, 16-20;   171, 15-19;   175, 17-19
"Parallelismus der Gliederung"   155, 17-156, 1
parataxis   151, 1-4;   160, 16-18;   175, 26-176, 1

311

parataxis (rhetorical −)   175, 17-19
parentes   150, 5-9
parenthesis   157, 21-158, 2;   159, 7-11;   159, 17-21
parere   170, 8-10
parody   intr. p. 4, 5, 6;   147, 20-22;   148, 4-5;   150, 3-5;   150, 5-9;   154, 1-2; 158, 10-15;   163, 23-26;   169, 18-19
paronomasia   147, 12-14;   147, 18-20;   151, 21-25;   157, 11-18;   160, 16-18;   166, 5-7;   172, 17-21
parricidium   156, 5-7
part. fut.   147, 10-12;   154, 13-18;   165, 4-7
part. fut. with final meaning   162, 2-5
partim   Appendix II
"Partizipialkonglomerat"   158, 25-28;   169, 20-24
"Partizipialkonstruktion"   155, 10-16
parus   166, 23-167, 2
paruus   161, 12-17
passim   164, 14-18
pass. part. of a deponens   165, 9-12
Pass. Eust. p. 470   172, 8-10
pastoralis   171, 4-8
pathos   174, 15-18
Paul. *ad. Tit.*   1, 17   153, 8-12
Paul's *Acts*   27, 1 f   158, 28-159, 4
Paul. *Dig.*   50, 17, 142   156, 8-11
Paul. Fest.   60, 12L   170, 7-8;   61, 14L   170, 14-18;   61, 16L   170, 14-18;   103L   147, 18-20;   152L   171, 15-19;   252, 14L   161, 12-17;   343L   172, 14-17;   347, 10L   158, 25-28
Paul. Nol. *Carm.*   15, 333   148, 4-5;   21, 120   165, 24-166, 2
Paul. Nol. *Epist.*   XII 6   167, 6-8
Paul. *Sent.*   5, 24   156, 5-7
"Pechvogel" theme   149, 3-4
pectinare   150, 9-11
Pegasus   152, 7-10
pendere de   162, 1-2
pendulus   156, 11-15
pentameter   156, 11-15
per   153, 12-16;   155, 10-16
perdere   173, 6-9
perdite   167, 8-12
perducere   157, 21-158, 2
perfect forms in −iui   159, 26-160, 3
periphrasis   151, 18-20;   161, 25-162, 1;   165, 1-2
periphrastic expression   156, 12-15
periphrasis of the verb   160, 24-161, 3;   161, 3-5
periphrastic perfect   161, 12-17
permittere   166, 5-7
pero   167, 22-168, 3
perpolire   150, 11-13
Pers.   1, 40 f.   160, 20-24;   1, 109   164, 18-21;   2, 41   162, 19-21;   5, 144   148, 19-20
personification   158, 21-22
pertica   176, 1-7
peruenire + acc. (without preposition)   152, 11-12
peruicax   173, 4-6
peruigil   158, 28-159, 4
pes   147, 22-24;   176, 1-7;   appendix I passim
pes dexter   appendix I sub a

pes malus   appendix I sub a n. 7
pes sinister   appendix I sub a
Petrarch   151, 12-15
Petr. 13   156, 22-157, 1;   28, 7   166, 5-7;   29, 9   161, 25-162, 1;   30   appendix I sub a;   46, 7   170, 10-14;   62, 12   168, 3-11;   64, 8   170, 25-171, 2;   65, 10   175, 13-17;   111, 3   172, 5-8;   117   165, 9-12;   119, 21   171, 12-15;   120, 70   169, 3-8;   132   appendix I n. 13;   135, 4   158, 25-28;   138   appendix I n. 13
Phaed.   App. 14   149, 20-22;   App. 14   151, 4-6;   2, 6, 11   147, 14-18
Philo *Quod det*.   66 (204 M)   intr. p. 2 n. 6;   126 (215M)   intr. p. 2 n. 6
Physiogn.   4 (7, 4)   148, 19-20;   119   171, 15-19
pietas   149, 8-10
pilatus   168, 3-11
pilum   168, 3-11
Plac. *Med*.   5, 32   168, 11-16
plane   157, 21-158, 2;   168, 23-26;   174, 18-22
Plato *Phdr*. 246 ab   156, 15-18;   247 b   156, 15-18;   253 d-255 a   156, 15-18
Plato *Rep*.   377 cd   147, 4-6
Plato *Symp*.   217 e   147, 3
Pl. *Am*.   144   166, 16-21;   232   156, 11-15;   367   157, 21-158, 2;   491   157, 11-18;   525   155, 17-156, 1;   537   170, 22-24;   537-538   164, 18-21;   606   176, 1-7;   620   148, 5-9;   840   171, 15-19;   1001   163, 11-14;   1106   149, 14-20;   1118   153, 23-27
Pl. *As*.   145   171, 15-19;   246   169, 26-170, 4;   270   162, 30-31;   504   171, 15-19;   589   176, 1-7;   633   164, 22-165, 1;   695   172, 13-14;   855   153, 8-12
Pl. *Aul*.   2   158, 10-15;   235   161, 3-5;   363   151, 27-152;   528   152, 21-24;   632   173, 6-9;   704   158, 10-15
Pl. *Bac*.   52   161, 18-19;   279   174, 15-18;   573   158, 10-15;   831   148, 23-24;   975   152, 19-20;   1034   165, 12-15
Pl. *Capt*.   185   153, 16-18;   268   176, 7-11;   278   165, 17-20;   336   167, 8-12;   371   176, 1-7;   692   157, 21-158, 2;   807   165, 24-166, 2;   958   160, 20-24
Pl. *Cas*.   95   157, 21-158, 2;   550   162, 13-14;   590   170, 10-14;   703   149, 22-26;   815   appendix I sub b
Pl. *Cist*.   33   160, 4-6;   43 f.   170, 4-7;   73   163, 8-11;   78   161, 18-19;   307-8   149, 22-26
Pl. *Cur*.   32   171, 15-19;   90   150, 13-17;   621   171, 15-19
Pl. *Epid*.   10   171, 12-15;   256   161, 18-19;   407-408   157, 11-18;   429   166, 16-21;   455   157, 21-158, 2;   659   149, 14-20
Pl. *Men*.   27   171, 20-172, 2;   505   163, 1-3;   574 f.   158, 3-7;   680   165, 12-15;   800   165, 12-15;   1003   149, 14-20;   1004   171, 15-19;   1020   149, 14-20
Pl. *Mer*.   507   165, 24-166, 2;   520   166, 11-15;   623   162, 2-5;   639   147, 14-18;   884   170, 10-14;   900   148, 5-9;   925   158, 25-28;   970   176, 1-7;   985   162, 30-31
Pl. *Mil*.   35   170, 7-8;   505   164, 18-21;   605   176, 1-7;   837   171, 15-19;   1004   162, 24-26;   1053   149, 14-20;   1206   163, 8-11;   1342   163, 8-11;   1416   171, 15-19
Pl. *Mos*.   40   162, 13-14;   477   170, 10-14;   629   166, 23-167, 2
Pl. *Per*.   122   147, 10-12;   503   147, 22-24
Pl. *Poen*.   266   161, 12-17;   452   158, 17-19;   794   165, 1-2;   1034   172, 13-14;   1292   149, 4-5;   1363   160, 6-10
Pl. *Ps*.   158   172, 10-12;   199 f.   149, 14-20;   353   157, 21-158, 2;   540   157, 21-158, 2;   571   149, 10-13;   852   149, 4-5;   950   170, 14-18;   1134   162, 30-31;   1157   158, 17-19
Pl. *Rud*.   521   165, 12-15;   535   153, 8-12;   624   149, 14-20;   622   155, 17-156, 1;   680   163, 8-11;   731   155, 17-156, 1;   770   147, 24-148, 2;   812   176, 7-11;   824   148, 23-24;   1079   157, 11-18;   1083   149, 14-20
Pl. *St*.   143   165, 1-2;   339   165, 12-15;   380   149, 13-14;   387   166, 5-7;   456   151, 27-152, 1;   554   152, 19-20;   723   156, 11-15;   724   172, 13-14

313

Pl. *Trin.*   310   168, 23-26;   1046   157, 18-20
Pl. *Truc.*   111   156, 1-5;   658   170, 10-14;   954   158, 25-28
Pl. *Vid.*   21   170, 25-171, 2;   25   170, 25-171, 2
plecti   155, 17-156, 1
pleonasm   161, 8-10;   167, 2-4;   167, 17-21;   168, 3-11;   168, 11-16;   168, 16-20;   169, 10-14;   170, 25-171, 2;   171, 15-19;   172, 14-17;   173, 23-174, 2
Plin. *Nat.*   2, 7, 24   appendix I sub a;   2, 16   155, 17-156, 1;   2, 22   155, 17-156, 1;   2, 24   appendix I sub b;   2, 113   171, 4-8;   2, 115   169, 10-14;   2, 156   152, 14-18;   4, 54   159, 4-7;   7, 57-60   158, 22-25;   7, 58   171, 20-172, 2;   7, 122   170, 10-14;   7, 197 f   155, 17-156, 1;   8, 29   148, 16-19;   8, 29   164, 14-18;   8, 67;   164, 14-18;   8, 68   164, 14-18;   8, 170   170, 25-171, 2;   8, 183   147, 20-22;   9, 59, 122   156, 8-11;   9, 163   168, 11-16;   10, 17   169, 18-19;   10, 52   153, 16-18;   11, 223   159, 4-7;   13, 69   147, 4-6;   14, 141   147, 3;   15, 3, 1   176, 1-7;   16, 126   148, 16-19;   18, 2   166, 16-21;   18, 72, 298   176, 1-7;   18, 72-73   165, 24-166, 2;   18, 145   176, 7-11;   18, 249   159, 4-7;   19, 120   176, 7-11;   21, 2   165, 7-9;   21, 12   162, 21-24;   25, 150   174, 15-18;   28, 240   162, 12-13;   28, 248   169, 10-14;   32, 23   169, 26-170, 4;   36, 34   149, 14-20;   36, 51   149, 10-13;   36, 107   153, 18-23;   36, 112   165, 12-15
Plin. *Ep.*   1, 5, 8   163, 16-17;   1, 6, 1   147, 4-6;   1, 14, 9   148, 12-13;   2, 1, 5   176, 1-7;   4, 10, 3   161, 21-25;   4, 11   155, 17-156, 1;   4, 21, 3   158, 22-25;   6, 13, 3   159, 4-7;   7, 19, 4   158, 25-28;   8, 5, 1   170, 8-10;   8, 14, 19   154, 1-2;   10, 40, 1   161, 21-25;   10, 106;   107   159, 17-21
Plin. *Paneg.*   83, 84   158, 22-25
Plotina   intr. p. 4;   158, 28-159, 4
pluperfect.   157, 21-158, 2
"verschobenes Plusquamperfectum"   149, 3-4;   164, 7-11;   165, 3-4
plural   150, 13-17
plural (poetic)   166, 16-21
plural of abstract nouns   154, 21-155, 4;   167, 2-4;   167, 22-168, 3;   175, 25-26
plural (of abstract nouns in –us)   160, 4-6
plures   155, 10-16
plusculus   154, 21-155, 4
Plut. *Crass.*   16, 6   164, 18-21;   17, 6   appendix I, n. 12
Plut. *def. orac.*   432 E   147, 3
Plut. *Demetr.*   29, 2   appendix I, n. 12
Plut. *Pomp.*   32, 8   158, 25-28
Plut. *Sol. anim.*   973 A   intr. p. 2 n. 6
Plut. *Stoic. Repugn.*   30, 1048 b   appendix I n. 13
Plut. *Ti. Gr.*   1, 3 f   158, 22-25;   17   appendix I sub b
poenale exitium   170, 14-18
poeticism   149, 20-22;   150, 3-5;   154, 5-8;   158, 8-9;   158, 25-28;   159, 11-17;   159, 23-26;   159, 26-160, 3;   163, 14-16;   163, 16-17;   165, 4-7;   174, 10-14
point of view   166, 3-5;   175, 9-11;   176, 1-7
polyptoton   158, 3-7;   168, 16-20;   172, 17-21
polysyndeton   153, 3-7
pompa   163, 23-26
Pomp. gramm.   5, 187   166, 21-23
poples   172, 14-17
popularis   154, 13-18
porrigere + obj. + gerundive   166, 21-23
postulare = accusare   154, 18-21
postulari   156, 1-5
postuma diligentia   152, 14-18
potatus   162, 5-7
praeceps   172, 5-8
praecipere + inf. pass.   152, 21-24
praeda   162, 16-18

praedo   158, 10-15
praefatio   165, 7-9
praegustare   162, 21-24
praelegere   162, 13-14
praenotare   147, 4-6
praesens   151, 1-4;   156, 8-11
praesens historicum   156, 19-22
praesepium   164, 14-18;   175, 5-9
praesidium + gen. obj.   155, 6-8
praesidium   152, 1-3;   170, 14-18
praestare   152, 1-3
praestinare   161, 12-17
praesumere   175, 11-13
praeter   169, 24-26
praeuertere   173, 4-6
prandium   162, 15
precarius   175, 13-17
prefix (ex-)   160, 18-20
pressura   167, 17-21
probe   150, 9-11;   158, 19-21
probe = bene   168, 26-169, 3
probissima   151, 27-152
procul   165, 15-17
producere   156, 8-11
producere in conspectum   147, 10-12
proflare   163, 26-164, 2
progestans   150, 13-17
proicere   158, 21-22
prolepsis   163, 4-8
prolixus   164, 14-18
pron. poss.   164, 2-5
pronounciation   156, 8-11
pronus   172, 17-21
prope   147, 12-14
properare + inf.   151, 27-152
properiter   148, 5-9;   172, 22-24
Prop.   1, 4, 17   175, 9-11;   1, 5, 25   161, 12-17;   1, 8, 11   158, 8-9;   1, 12, 14   163, 4-8;   1, 16, 32   150, 1-3;   1, 18, 17   161, 12-17;   2, 9, 7   164, 22-165, 1;   2, 21, 7   175, 5-9;   2, 28, 35   155, 4-6;   3, 1, 5   appendix I sub a;   3, 15, 5   164, 22-165, 1;   3, 15, 11   149, 14-20;   4, 1, 23   161, 12-17;   4, 1, 131   164, 22-165, 1;   4, 3, 12   164, 22-165, 1;   4, 6, 76   147, 3;   4, 9, 49   176, 1-7
prorsus   158, 9-10
prosedere   161, 12-17
proserpere   172, 13-14
protinus   171, 4-8
proverbial expression   158, 3-7;   163, 1-3
prouidentia diuina   151, 1-4
Prud. *Cath.*   3, 170   165, 17-20;   9, 74   172, 14-17
Prud. *Contra Sym.*   2 (2)   78   appendix I sub a
Ps.   90, 12   appendix I sub b;   114, 8   appendix I sub b
Ps. Ambr. *Paenit.*   17, p. 990^c 172, 22-24
Ps. Apul. *Herb.*   103 L7   162, 27-30
Ps. Matth. *Euang.*   3, 4   165, 15-17;   3, 4   169, 14-18
pseudo-metamorphosis   159, 26   160, 3
Ps. Prosp. *Carm. de prou.*   225   170, 14-18
Ps. Quint. *Decl.*   10, 16   147, 14-18;   364, 5   148, 21-23
Ps. Verg. *Cat.*   9, 59-69   147, 3

315

Ps. Victor *epit. de Caes.*   42, 21   158, 22-25
Ps. Vigil. Thaps. *c. Mariuadum*   2, 18   166, 11-15
Pub. *Sent.*   N45   170, 8-10
puellus   169, 26-170, 4
puer   167, 6-8;   168, 26-169, 3;   169, 24 f
pugillare   166, 16-21
pugillares   147, 4-6
pulposus   166, 16-21
punctus uenenatus   168, 11-16
puluinar   160, 18-20
puluinaria   160, 18-20
puter   152, 7-10

Q

Quad. *Hist.* 12   157, 2-11
quadripedi cursu   149, 22-26
quadripes   149, 3-4
quaerere   172, 5-8
quam = qualem   153, 7-8
quampiam   161, 10-12
quamquam + subj.   156, 11-15
quatere   152, 11-12
-que   158, 3-7
querela   169, 20-24
qui   147, 4-6
quidam   147, 6-10;   152, 13-14;   172, 10-12;   172, 22-24
quin   161, 10-12
quin (igitur)   170, 22-24
Quint. *Decl.*   4, 8   158, 3-7;   8, 11   164, 18-21;   11, 10   156, 8-11;   13, 7   172, 22-24;   249   161, 20-21
Quint. *Inst.*   1, 5, 11   162, 13-14;   1, 6, 21   158, 3-7;   1, 6, 40   159, 4-7;   1, 7, 9   163, 11-14;   1, 8, 8   162, 13-14;   1, 8, 19   147, 4-6;   1, 9, 2   147, 4-6;   2, 8, 4   172, 24-173, 2;   2, 16, 15   intr. p. 2 n. 6;   3, 8, 38   157, 2-11;   5, 10, 11   154, 18-21;   8, 3, 24 f.   153, 23-27;   8, 3, 26   155, 7-156, 1;   8, 84   153, 12-16;   9, 2, 4   155, 4-6;   9, 3, 66 f.   147, 4-6;   9, 4, 83   147, 6-10;   10, 7, 1   157, 2-11;   10, 7, 3   167, 2-4;   11, 2, 46   165, 24-166, 2;   11, 3, 146   158, 25-28;   11, 3, 170   175, 1-5
Q. Cic. *poet. fr.*   1, 16   154, 5-8
quippe cum   155, 4-6;   160, 4-6
quippe + partic.   173, 2-3
quis = quibus   154, 21-155, 4;   162, 7-9
quisque   156, 5-7
quiuis   156, 1-5
quoad   168, 3-11;   174, 10-14
quod   147, 4-6
quod + subjunctive   151, 12-15
quo usque   147, 20-22;   169, 18-19

R

raptare   173, 9-11
"réalisme familier"   164, 14-18
recellere   172, 14-17
redundancy   147, 10-12;   148, 16-19;   149, 13-14;   149, 14-20;   156, 5-7;   156, 15-

18;   157, 18-20;   161, 3-5;   163, 1-3;   169, 10-14;   174, 10-14;   174, 15-18; 174, 18-22
reformare   158, 25-28;   160, 18-20
regius   151, 4-6
"relative Verschränkung"   154, 2-3
relegatio   158, 25-28
relegatio ad tempus   159, 4-7
relinquere   172, 23-173, 2
reluctare   157, 21-158, 2
remeare + acc. reg.   154, 13-18
remulcere aures   166, 16-21
remunerari   165, 1-2
renuntiare + dat.   157, 2-11
repetition (of motifs)   149, 3-4;   167, 16-17
repetition   150, 5-9;   158, 28-159, 4;   163, 23-26;   167, 6-8;   169, 10-14;   172, 5-8;   174, 26-175, 1;   175,9-11
repetition (of t/s)   163, 8-11
replaudere   149, 22-26
replicare   151, 12-15
respicere   172, 22-24
retorquere   169, 14-18
reuocare   149, 5-8
Rhet. Her.   1, 3, 5   156, 8-11;   2, 14, 21   161, 18-19;   2, 36   155, 17-156, 1;   4, 24   156 1-5;   4, 31   147, 22-24;   4, 34   170, 4-7;   4, 45   165, 7-9;   4, 47, 60   156, 8-11
rhetoric   163, 23-26
rhetorical question   175, 22-25
rhyme   149, 5-8;   149, 20-22;   166, 16-21;   166, 23-167, 2;   169, 8-10;   169, 10-14
rhythm   156, 11-15;   158, 3-7;   170, 4-7;   172, 22-24
rudimentum   164, 22-165, 1
rudis   151, 4-6;   164, 22-165, 1
ruina   167, 17-21;   172, 5-8   172, 17-21
Rut. Ruf. *Hist.*   5, 133;   170, 14-18
ruptus   147, 20-22
rurestris   165, 4-7
rursum   163, 1-3
rursus   161, 3-5;   167, 2-4
Rut. Lup.   2, 2   165, 24-166, 2

S

Sacr. Leon. 308 Petri apostoli   150, 17-151, 1
sacrificatus   162, 5-7
sacrifice of the ass   170, 22-24
sadism   167, 12-15
saepicule   149, 22-26
saginare   150, 13-17
Sal. *Cat.*   20, 9   147, 20-22;   20, 9   169, 18-19;   23   166, 11-15;   47, 1   157, 18-20;   58, 17   158, 3-7;   59, 6   166, 3-5;   61, 1   147, 6-10
Sal. *Hist. fr.*   2, 87   149, 13-14;   3, 98   151, 16-18;   4, 16   167, 22-168, 3
Sal. *Iug.*   12, 5   159, 11-17;   18, 6   172, 22-29;   52, 4   172, 22-24;   58, 6   147, 14-18;   78, 4   149, 10-13;   87, 2   158, 3-7;   107, 1   158, 3-7
Sal. *Or. Phil.*   5   173, 2 3
salus   150, 5-9
Salvianus *Gub.*   5, 9, 45   155, 17-156, 1

317

sanare   167, 17-21
sat   150, 3-5
satianter   166, 11-15
satis = ualde   168, 26-169, 3
saucius   163, 11-14
sauium   170, 7-8
scabere   149, 26-150, 1
scaena   149, 14-20
scaeuitas   156, 15-18
"Schadenfreude"   151, 21-25
Schol. on Apoll. Rhod.   1090   149, 14-20
Schol. Ov. *Ibis*   101   appendix I sub a
Schol. on Stat. *Theb.*   4, 570   149, 14-20
Schol. Veron. Verg. *A.*   7, 266   158, 17-19
scilicet   151, 12-15;   166, 3-5;   175, 9-11;   176, 1-7
scitulus   169, 26-170, 4;   162, 19-21
scortari   162, 30-31
scortum = corium   162, 30-31
scrupulus   148, 9-10
secta   163, 3-7;   157, 2-11;   162, 1-2
sectio   174, 15-18
secum   148, 3-4;   152, 19-20
secum considerare   152, 19-20
securis   172, 10-12
sed   150, 17-151, 1;   153, 7-8;   163, 16-17;   169, 8-10;   173, 4-6
sed et   159, 11-17
sedulus   154, 21-155, 4
self-contradiction   155, 10-16
semel ac saepius   156, 11-15
semimortuus   148, 21-23
semitrepidus   160, 6-10
Sen. *Con.*   1, 7, 9   148, 21-23;   2, 1, 6   162, 5-7;   2, 4, 6   165, 7-9;   9, 6, 19   162, 21-24;   10, 1, 2   154, 13-18;   10, 2, 6   156, 8-11
Sen. *Ag.* 628 f.   appendix I, n. 10
Sen. *Ben.*   2, 12, 1   166, 21-23;   1, 11, 3   165, 12-15;   3, 37   169, 26-170, 4;   5, 12, 2   163, 17-20
Sen. *Cl.*   1, 25, 1   16, 21-23
Sen. *Ep.*   9, 10   158, 25-28;   24, 24   148, 21-23;   26, 4   148, 9-10;   29, 5   158, 19-21;   71, 26   171, 15-19;   74, 4   158, 21-22;   77, 5   165, 1-2;   85, 6   153, 7-8;   90, 17   153, 18-23;   95, 72   166, 3-5;   100, 7   165, 24-166, 2;   114, 22   15, 7-10;   119, 6   163, 11-14;   120, 18   148, 9-10;   122, 11 f.   154, 5-8
Sen. *Helu.*   12, 1   162, 16-18;   16, 7   158, 25-28
Sen. *Helu.*   12, 1   162, 16-18;   16, 7   158, 25-28
Sen. *Her. O.*   862 f.   174, 10-14
Sen. *Marc.*   16, 3   158, 22-25;   18, 3   172, 22-24
Sen. *Med.*   451   148, 23-24;   461   147, 18-20
Sen. *Nat.*   1, 6, 4   172, 14-17;   1, 14, 5   171, 4-8;   4, 2, 29   169, 14-18;   6, 3, 4   172, 24-173, 2
Sen. *Oct.*   532   158, 22-25
Sen. *Oed.*   53   163, 23-26;   221   172, 8-10;   768   172, 8-10
Sen. *Phaed.*   1256 f.   174, 8-10
Sen. *Phoen.*   19 f.   149, 14-20
Sen. *Prou.*   2, 7   166, 3-5;   2, 10   148, 10-11;   3, 2   158, 21-22;   3, 9   166, 3-5;   6, 6   148, 21-23;   6, 7-10   148, 13-16
Sen. *De Tr. An.*   11, 1   175, 13-17
sententia   154, 2-3
sentire + two acc.   162, 16-18

318

Sept. *Poet.* 16   172, 22-24
Sept. Ser.   16   148, 5-9
sequester   153, 8-12
sequius   159, 26-160, 3
Ser. Samm.   807-8   171, 20-172, 2
Serg. *Gramm.*   4, 477, 11   159, 4-7
serius   166, 5-7
sermo cotidianus   148, 5-9;   149, 13-14;   149, 14-20;   159, 4-7;   160, 20-24;   161, 12-17;   163, 14-16;   165, 4-7;   166, 21-23;   170, 25-171, 2;   175, 11-13
sermo familiaris   149, 20-22;   171, 4-8
sermo uulgaris   153, 7-8
Serv. on Verg. *A.*   2, 374   154, 21-155, 4;   3, 22   169, 3-8;   3, 18   162, 13-14;   4, 593   163, 23-26;   6, 456   154, 8-10;   6, 661   171, 20-172, 2;   10, 174   165, 4-7;   11, 571   153, 18-23;   11, 896   154, 8-10
Serv. on Verg. *G*   1, 437   154, 8-10
seruus   155, 10-16
seta   150, 11-13
seu   160, 6-10
sexuality   166, 7-10
SHA, Capit. *Alb.*   5, 9   176, 1-7;   11   170, 4-7
SHA, Gall.   8, 3   166, 16-21
SHA, Jul. Cap. *Albin.*   12, 12   153, 12-16
SHA, Jul. Val.   8, 14   170, 25-171, 2
SHA, Capit. *M. Ant. Phil.*   17, 7   158, 3-7
si   150, 5-9
si + iterative subjunctive   168, 3-11
sic   158, 3-7;   162, 10-11
sic = οὕτως   167, 17-21
si tamen   160, 11-15
Sid. Apol. *Ep.*   3, 2, 3   165, 24-166, 2;   4, 20   167, 22-168, 3
sigmatism   150, 3-5;   161, 25-162, 1;   162, 30-31
sigmatism plus t-iteration   150, 3-5
Silanus   175, 22-25
Sil.   2, 157   172, 13-14;   2, 247   155, 6-8;   5, 416   155, 10-16;   6, 225   172, 13-14;   7, 171   appendix I sub a;   7, 136   160, 4-6;   14, 561   159, 23-26;   16, 351   148, 4-5;   16, 502   172, 24-173, 2;   16, 506   148, 4-5
simplex pro composito   150, 1-3;   152, 3-5
simul   159, 11-17;   161, 25-162, 1;   162, 2-5;   163, 21-22
singillatim   176, 1-7
Sis. *Mil.* 4   149, 20-22
socius + gen. / + dat.   158, 25-28
sodomy with animals   170, 4-7
Sol. *Coll. Rer. Mem.*   5, 13   165, 17-20;   5, 22   165, 7-9;   19, 13   169, 3-8
soliloquy   148, 10-11;   148, 19-20
solitarius   172, 22-24;   173, 14-18
Soph. *Tr.* 6 F. 4 ed. Radt 345 f.   176, 11-13
Soph. *Tr.* 555   155, 17-156, 1
soporifer   163, 14-16
Soranus   9   166, 16-21;   14   166, 16-21
sors fatalis   159, 4-7
sound   158, 3-7
sound effect   165, 4-7
"Spannungspause"   157, 21-158, 2;   161, 21-25
speaker   intr. p. 5
spirans   168, 26-169, 3
spirare   150, 1-3
sportula   160, 11-15

Stat. *Ach.* 1, 478   164, 22-165, 1;   2, 37   169, 24-26
Stat. *Silu.* 2, 4   intr. p. 2 n. 6;   3, 2, 47   151, 6-9;   3, 5, 2   158, 28-159, 4;   3, 5, 12   154, 13-18;   4, 7, 30   158, 22-25
Stat. *Theb.* 1, 347 f.   164, 22-165, 1;   3, 345   158, 3-7;   3, 583   147, 6-10;   5, 105   149, 5-8;   7, 93   166, 16-21;   9, 414   172, 13-14;   9, 689   150, 9-11;   12, 495   158, 8-9
statuere   156, 19-22
stipendium   158, 22-25
stramenta   169, 26-170, 4
strictim   176, 7-11
stupidity of the ass   163, 4-8
suasus   149, 22-26
sub   155, 4-6
subinde   165, 17-20
subire   155, 17-156, 1
subjunctive   154, 13-18;   157, 2-11;   157, 18-20;   170, 19-21;   173, 18-22;   174, 5-7;   175, 13-17
subjunctive (iterative)   167, 22-168, 3;   169, 26-170, 4
subpatere   172, 17-21
subserere   176, 1-7
Suda 2977   appendix I sub a
sudis   167, 8-12
Suet. *Aug.*   18, 1   158, 25-28;   28   160, 11-15;   83   171, 2-4;   92   appendix I sub a
Suet. *Cal.*   27, 1   171, 4-8;   58, 1   169, 10-14
Suet. *Cl.*   44   147, 12-14
Suet. *Dom.*   7, 1   172, 3-5;   8, 2   158, 25-28;   23, 1   154, 21-155, 4
Suet. *Gal.*   16   157, 18-20
Suet. *Jul.*   1, 2   154, 13-18;   49   161, 12-17;   49, 2   158, 25-28;   59   appendix I sub b;   82, 1   154, 5-8
Suet. *Nero*   12, 1   171, 4-8;   22   164, 22-165, 1;   23, 1   158, 25-28;   28, 1   171, 12-15
Suet. *Tib.*   34, 3   169, 10-14;   65   157, 21-158, 2;   5, 3   163, 14-16;   9, 3   166, 21-23
Suet. *Ves.*   4, 10   149, 14-20;   8, 4   167, 2-4;   16, 2   158, 19-21;   21   158, 19-21
Suet. *Vit.*   14, 2   166, 3-5;   16   158, 25-28
suetus   152, 3-5
suffix in –inus   169, 18-19
suffix -pte   176, 1-7
suicide-motif   152, 13-14;   152, 14-18
Sulp. Rufus *Fam.*   4, 5, 4   162, 27-30
Sulp. Sev. *Dial.*   1, 22   165, 12-15
Sulp. Sev. *Ep.*   2, 1   165, 12-15
super + acc.   147, 14-18
super   154, 13-18
supergredi   172, 10-12
superlatives   155, 17-156, 1
supernatare   151, 6-9
superpondium   167, 22-168, 3
suppedito   155, 6-8
suppetias ferre   149, 14-20
suppetiatum   159, 11-17
supplere   157, 18-20
supplicatory style   150, 13-17;   150, 3-5
suspicere   156, 19-22
suspirare   150, 1-3
sustinere   153, 18-23;   160, 24-161, 3;   170, 14-18

320

suus sibi 152, 14-18; 164, 7-11
syllables 149, 22-26
syllables (number of –) 158, 28-159, 4
symbolic meaning of the ass 163, 23-26
Symm. *Ep.* 3, 31 149, 10-13; 4, 31 158, 3-7; 7, 100 162, 21-24; 9, 125 (10, 4) 156, 22-157; 9, 129 170, 10-14
synaloephe 149, 20-22; 169, 8-10
"Synonymik koordinierter Begriffe" 155, 17-156, 1
synonym(s) 150, 9-11; 152, 24; 154, 18-21; 154, 21-155, 4; 163, 11-14; 164, 12; 169, 10-14; 171, 20-172, 2; 171, 12-15; 171, 15-19; 172, 5-8; 175, 9-11; 175, 17-19; 175, 19-22

T

tabernula 159, 7-11
"tableau" technique 163, 23-26
tabula 151, 1-4
Tac. *Ag.* 16 175, 11-13
Tac. *Ann.* 1, 32 Appendix II; 1, 32, 4 176, 7-11; 1, 46, 1 157, 2-11; 1, 50, 3 148, 5-9; 1, 64 152, 3-5; 2, 13 172, 22-24; 2, 21 157, 2-11; 3, 2 149, 13-14; 4, 2 154, 21-155, 4; 4, 53 173, 4-6; 4, 62 163, 23-26; 4, 71 158, 21-22; 6, 17 161, 12; 6, 50, 5 148, 10-11; 14, 16 154, 21-155, 4; 14, 49 156, 19-22; 15, 37 149, 10-13; 15, 57 176, 1-7; 15, 63, 3 156, 8-11; 15, 71, 3 158, 25-28; 16, 28 162, 16-18
Tac. *Dial.* 1 169, 24-26; 29 147, 4-6
Tac. *Germ.* 14, 1 166, 3-5; 39 appendix I, n. 18
Tac. *Hist.* 1, 3, 1 158, 25-28; 1, 25, 3 157, 21-158, 2; 2, 75 169, 14-18; 2, 80 152, 3-5; 3, 85 147, 18-20; 4, 5 173, 4-6; 4, 19 157, 18-20
talis 170, 19-21; 172, 3-5
tam 154, 2-3
tamen 160, 11-15
tamen = autem 165, 12-15
tam magnus = tantus 154, 2-3
tantillus 174, 26-175, 1
tautology 156, 1-5
temetum 163, 11-14
tempo intr. p. 3 b.; 170, 19-21
temptare periculum 159, 11
temporarius 159, 4-7
temulentus 147, 3
Ter. *Ad.* 242 160, 6-10; 534 171, 20-172, 2; 560 f. 147, 10-12; 639 149, 10-13
Ter. *An.* 79 149, 13-14; 229 147, 3; 248 158, 25-28; 326 171, 15-19 653 148, 5-9
Ter. *Eu.* 51 149, 20-22; 452 176, 11-13
Ter. *Hau.* 128 162, 27-30; 206 162, 30-31; 222 147, 4-6; 297 171, 15-19; 385 152, 19-20; 563 176, 1-7; 565 147, 4-6; 813 152, 21-24; 1011 147, 4-6
Ter. *Hec.* 662 175, 13-17
Ter. *Ph.* 74 158, 17-19; 94 171, 15-19; 199 156, 1-5; 822 167, 17-21; 988 147, 18-20; 1008 171, 15-19
Tert. *An.* 19, 4 168, 11-16; 33, 10 155, 17-156, 1; 35, 6 165, 12 15; 56, 2 159, 21-22; 101 162, 30-31
Tert. *Apol.* 19 155, 17-156, 1; 20 170, 7-8; 48, 3 165, 4-7
Tert. *Cult. fem.* 2, 9 164, 18-21; 2, 13 167, 8-12

Tert. *Fug.* 2   155, 17-156, 1
Tert. *Herm.*   3 (129, 11)   149, 20-22
Tert. *Ieiun.*   10, 3 p. 286, 17   158, 3-7
Tert. *Nat.*   1, 10, 25   158, 8-9;   1, 11, 1   148, 24-149, 2;   2, 5, 10   164, 22-165, 1;   2, 12   166, 21-23
Tert. *Pall.*   3, 3   163, 1-3
Tert. *Pud.*   16, 12   172, 10-12;   18 p. 261, 26   170, 4-7
Tert. *Scorp.*   10 (168, 24)   148, 21-23
Tert. *Val.*   16   168, 11-16;   27   153, 16-18
testes   171, 15-19
testimonium perhibere   173, 18-22
tetracolon   175, 5-9
textilis   159, 26-160, 3
Theocr.   29, 1   147, 3
Theophilus *Ad Autol.*   2, 10   intr. p. 2 n. 6;   2, 22   intr. p. 2 n. 6
Tib.   1, 1, 2   161, 12-17;   1, 1, 67   156, 19-22;   1, 3, 19 f.   appendix I sub b;   1, 3   27 f.   151, 1-4;   1, 3, 85   147, 4-6;   1, 7, 37   147, 3;   1, 7, 62   appendix I sub b;   1, 7, 62   appendix I, n. 11;   1, 10, 11   173, 18-22;   3, 7, 155   157, 2-11
time (narrated)   intr. p. 2 b;   147, 6-10
time (narrative—)   147, 6-10
tirocinium   157, 2-11
Titin. *Com.*   83   147, 10-12
titio   176, 7-11
titubare   152, 7-10;   169, 14-18
Tlepolemus   intr. p. 3 f.
topos   154, 5-8;   172, 3-5
tortilis   168, 11-16
torulus   166, 16-21
totus   158, 10-15
totus = omnis   153, 12-16;   162, 1-2;   164, 7-11
tractus   149, 10-13
tradere + dat. of an abstract noun   166, 3-5
trahere   175, 1-5
Treb. Pollio *Claud.*   17   156, 22-157, 2
trepidatio   147, 14-18
tricolon   165, 24-166, 2;   167, 12-15;   169, 26-170, 4;   171, 4-8
tricolon (anaphoric)   151, 6-9
tricolon (anisocolic)   166, 7-10
tricolon crescendo   166, 7-10
tripartition   150, 3-5
tripudiare   166, 7-10
tuburcinari   147, 10-12
tucceta   162, 19-21
tum   160, 4-6
tumultus   149, 14-20
tunc   150, 1-3;   160, 4-6
tunc = deinde   162, 16-18
turbela = turba   154, 13-18
Turp. *Com.* 2   147, 10-12
tyrannica potestas   157, 2-11

U

uber   175, 1-5
ubi + pluperfect   165, 15-17
ubi locorum   160, 20-24

Ulp.   167, 1   160, 6-10
Ulp. *Dig.*   1, 18, 6, 5   158, 18-21;   3, 3, 15   173, 12-14;   4, 2, 23, 3   173, 12-14;
     10, 2, 4, 2   159, 17-21;   29, 5, 3, 4   159, 17-21;   33, 7, 12, 10   165, 17-20;   50,
     17, 30   162, 27-30
ultroneus   169, 14-18
"Umdeutung"   170, 4-7
unde = ex quibus   162, 13-14
unicus   148, 21-23;   159, 17-21;   164, 22-165, 1
unus   152, 3-5
urbicus   158, 25-28
ursa   172, 13-14
uspiam + gen.   174, 3-5
usque   167, 8-12
ὕστερον πρότερον   161, 25-162, 1
ustrina   169, 3-8
ut   152, 21-24
uter   162, 12-13
uti   154, 13-18
utique   165, 9-12
utpote   152, 21
ut primum + imperf. ind.   154, 5-8
utrumque   175, 11-13

V

uacillare   152, 7-10
uacuefacere   153, 12-16
uadere   154, 1-2
uagus   172, 22-24
V. Fl.   4, 469   153, 3-7;   5, 141   158, 28-159, 4;   5, 382 (381)   147, 10-12;   6, 501
     162, 16-18;   7, 546   148, 4-5
Val. Max.   1, 4, 2   appendix I sub b;   1, 5, 2   appendix I, n. 20;   1, 6, 6   appendix
     I, n. 20;   3, 1, 1   158, 25-28;   4, 6   158, 25-28;   4, 6   158, 25-28;   6, 3, 1a
     165, 7-9
uapor   153, 16-18
Var. *L.*   5, 68   172, 13-14;   5, 110   153, 16-18;   5, 167   166, 16-21;   6, 7   151,
     25-27;   6, 86   154, 8-10;   7, 2   175, 13-17;   7, 104   156, 11-18;   9, 25   157,
     18-20;   10, 2, 168   156, 11-15;   10, 10   157, 18-20
Var. *Men.*   260   175, 5-9;   364   171, 15-19;   386   156, 11-15;   509   149, 14-20
Var. *frg. Non.*   530   160, 4-6
Var. *R.*   1, 8, 2   176, 1-7;   1, 13, 6   164, 14-18;   1, 31, 4-5   165, 3-4;   1, 55, 2
     176, 1-7;   2 praef. 4   165, 7-9;   2, 1, 17   166, 11-15;   2, 2, 19   165, 24-166, 2;
     2, 5, 1   173, 18-22;   2, 7, 8   174, 18-22;   2, 7, 12   165, 24-166, 2;   2, 8, 2
     148, 24-149, 2;   3, 9, 7   176, 1-7;   3, 12, 4   174, 18-22
uariatio   148, 23-24;   149, 14-20;   151, 9-11;   152, 11-12;   158, 10-15;   164, 7-11;
     164, 14-18;   167, 12-15;   168, 16-20;   169, 3-8;   172, 22-24
Veg. *Mul.*   1, 11, 12   147, 20-22;   1, 38, 10   176, 1-7;   2, 36, 10   165, 24-166, 2;   4,
     1, 9   147, 20-22
uel certe   160, 24-161, 3
uelitari   166, 16-21
Vell.   1, 16, 3   155, 17-156, 1;   2, 22, 4   150, 11-13;   2, 45, 1   171, 4-8;   2, 72, 3
     172, 17-21;   2, 113, 3   165, 24-166, 2
ueluti   150, 13-17
Ven. Fort. *Carm*   1, 21, 3   168, 3-11
uenundare   161, 10-12
verbs in –ficare   152, 21-24;   155, 10-16

323

uerecundus 170, 19-21
Verg. A. 1, 95-96 157, 2-11; 1, 147-153 153, 1; 1, 171 156, 19-22; 1, 378 158, 10-15; 1, 521 153, 1; 1, 524 158, 3-7; 1, 641 166, 3-5; 2, 15 appendix II; 2, 28 175, 19-22; 2, 52 173, 23-174, 2; 2, 53 174, 8-10; 2, 242 f appendix I sub b; 2, 242 appendix I, n. 21; 2, 265 163, 16-17; 2, 265 appendix II; 2, 275 156, 19-22; 2, 333 appendix II; 2, 446-447 155, 10-16; 2, 505 174, 26-175, 1; 2, 693 appendix I, n. 4; 3, 270 159, 4-7; 3, 540 166, 5-7; 3, 587 151, 25-27; 3, 631 153, 12-16; 4, 2 148, 9-10; 4, 32 148, 9-10; 4, 64 168, 26-169, 3; 4, 68 151, 18-20; 4, 83 158, 3-7; 4, 188 173, 4-6; 4, 215 175, 5-9; 4, 328 158, 19-21; 4, 401 163, 23-26; 4, 427 156, 19-22; 4, 486 163, 14-16; 5, 162 163, 17-20; 5, 248 161, 12-17; 5, 350 168, 3-11; 5, 726 f. 175, 13-17; 5, 768 16 25-162, 1; 5, 813 147, 22-24; 5, 732 147, 22-24; 6, 194 163, 17-20; 6, 258 155, 6-8; 6, 406 174, 3-5; 6, 429 175, 1-5; 6, 456 f. 169, 18-19; 6, 685 157, 2-11; 6, 856 f. 151, 6-9; 7, 53 1, 26-170, 4; 7, 194 153, 1; 7, 278 150, 9-11; 7, 351 168, 11-16; 7, 620 159, 7-11; 7, 667 166, 16-21; 7, 690 167, 2-168, 3; 7, 784 157, 21-158, 2; 8, 160 157, 21-158, 2; 8, 162 157, 21-158, 2; 8, 224 148, 4-5; 8, 302 appendix I sub a; 8, 596 149, 22-26; 8, 643 175, 19-22; 8, 649 154, 13-18; 10, 149 156, 19-22; 10, 255 appendix I, n. 3; 10, 324 157, 21-158, 2; 10, 596 159, 7-11; 11, 157 164, 22-165, 1; 11, 251 153, 1; 11, 493 166, 7-10; 11, 505 159, 11; 11, 793 154, 13-18; 11, 855 163, 17-20; 11, 875 149, 22-26; 12, 306 158, 28-159, 4; 12, 475 147, 24-148, 2; 12, 611 175, 1-5; 12, 870 175, 1-5
Verg. Ecl. 6, 15 f. 147, 3; 6, 31 f. 147, 3; 7, 47 175, 13-17; 9, 64 167, 8-12; 10, 4 151, 12-15
Verg. G 1, 75 165, 3-4; 1, 378 166, 11-15; 1, 491 f 158, 10-15; 2, 329 171, 12-15; 2, 504 158, 19-21; 3, 110 160, 16-18; 3, 154 175, 13-17; 3, 183 149, 10-13; 3, 267 171, 12-15; 3, 407 167, 2-4; 3, 435 158, 8-9; 4, 301 157, 21-158, 2; 4, 467 159, 23-26
ueritas 151, 6-9
uero 167, 16-17
uero etiam 167, 17-21
"Verschränkung der Relativsätze", cf. "relativischer Anschluss" 172, 14-17
verse units 156, 11-15
ueruex 171, 20-172, 2
uestigium montis 172, 8-10
uestri causa = uestra causa 161, 3-5
uetus 166, 10-11
Vet. Lat. 1 Cor. 9, 26 166, 16-21
Vet. Lat. (Wirc.) Ier. 23, 15 164, 18-21
Vet. Lat. Luc. 15, 12 154, 18-21
Vet. Lat. Sap. 2, 12 171, 20-172, 2
uiam lucubrare 151, 25-27
uiaticulum 160, 6-10
uibrare 156, 11-15
uice + genit. 168, 3-11
uicinia 159, 11-17
uictimare 162, 13-14; 170, 22-24
Marius Victorinus 6, 34, 9 K 156, 8-11
uidere 148, 10-11
uilla 160, 6-10
uillula 168, 26-169, 3
uindicta 176, 1-7
uino sepelire 163, 16-17
uir 158, 22-25
uirgo (adj.) 162, 27-30

uiriosus 168, 11-16
uiscera 153, 18-23
Vitae patr. Jur. 1, 13 (138, 30) 165, 24-166, 2
Vitr. 2 praef. 1 172, 8-10; 2, 1, 9 171, 15-19; 2, 9, 3 166, 16-21; 3, 4, 4 appendix I sub a
uiuacitas 158, 3-7
uocem dare 173, 18-22
uocula 149, 22-26
uoluptas 170, 4-7
uoracitas 152, 19-20
uotivus 163, 21-22
vulgarism 166, 16-21
Vulg. 2 *Cor.* 3, 2 154, 21-155, 4
Vulg. *Deut.* 21, 22 155, 17-156
Vulg. *Eccli.* 34, 24 162, 13-14
Vulg. *Esdr.* 1, 9, 3 175, 1-5
Vulg. *Exod.* 25, 2 169, 14-18
Vulg. *Gen.* 6, 18 166, 11-15
Vulg. *Ier.* 5, 8 171, 20-172, 2
Vulg. *Is.* 7, 4 176, 7-11; 8, 14 appendix I, n. 14
Vulg. *Luc.* 2, 12 164, 14-18
Vulg. 1 *Petr.* 2, 7 appendix n.14
Vulg. *Prou.* 23, 18 148, 10-11
Vulg. *Psalm.* 118 (119), 152 163, 4-8
Vulg. 2 *Sam.* 13, 19 175, 1-5
Vulg. *Thren.* 4, 18 168, 3-11
uultus 151, 9-11

W

witticism 161, 20-21
wordorder 149, 20-22; 160, 6-10; 166, 11-15; 169, 10-14
wordplay 150, 5-9; 150, 11-13; 151, 21-25; 154, 21-155, 4; 155, 4-6; 155, 17-156, 1; 156, 15-18; 166, 5-7; 169, 24-26; 170, 4-7; 171, 15-19; 172, 3-5

X

Xen. *Anab.* 2, 1, 6 170, 25-171, 2
Xen. *Cyr.* 3, 3, 45 158, 3-7
Xen. *Eq.* 5, 1 164, 14-18
Xen. *Eph.* 1, 1 158, 19-21

Z

Zacynthus 159, 4-7
Zeno Veron. *Tract.* I 37, 3, 10 159, 17-21
Zenob. 5, 42 147, 4-6
zona 158, 25-28

Printed in the United States
By Bookmasters